D1715230

JEWISH SECTS,
RELIGIOUS MOVEMENTS,
and
POLITICAL PARTIES

Studies in Jewish Civilization—3

JEWISH SECTS, RELIGIOUS MOVEMENTS, and POLITICAL PARTIES

Proceedings of the Third Annual Symposium
of the Philip M. and Ethel Klutznick
Chair in Jewish Civilization
held on Sunday-Monday,
October 14-15, 1990

Menachem Mor, Editor

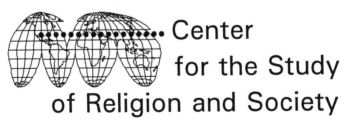 Center
for the Study
of Religion and Society

CREIGHTON UNIVERSITY
PRESS
Omaha, Nebraska

Creighton University Press
2500 California Plaza
Omaha Nebraska 68178 USA

Copyright **Creighton University** 1992

Library of Congress Cataloging-in-Publication Data

Jewish Sects, Religious Movements, and Political Parties
/Menachem Mor, editor.
p. cm.--(Studies in Jewish civilization; [3])
Papers delivered at the third annual Symposium of the
Philip M. and Ethel Klutznick Chair in Jewish Civilization
at Creighton University on October 14-15, 1990.
1. Jews--Jewish Sects--Congresses.
2. Jews--History--Congresses.
3. Judaism--History--Congresses.
4. Israel--Political Parties--Congresses.
5. Jews--Religious Movements--Congresses.
I. Mor, Menachem. II. Philip M. and Ethel Klutznick
Chair in Jewish Civilization. Symposium (3rd :
1990 : Creighton University) III. Series.
DS148.J47 1992
305.892'4073--dc20

Library of Congress Catalog Card Number: 92-073317
ISBN: 1-881871-04-5 cloth

CREIGHTON
UNIVERSITY

Robert Cohen

in Memoriam

Robert Cohen was born in Deventer, Holland (December 10, 1946), and died in Jerusalem (April 6, 1992). He earned his B.A. (1972) from the Hebrew University, his M.A. (1975) and his Ph.D. (1976) from Brandeis University. In 1976 he immigrated to Israel and taught at the University of Haifa. For many years during the good old days, Robert and I shared an office in the University's Department of History. We remained very close despite the subsequent moves and geographical distances between us. Devora, the children, and I always looked forward to his visits. We loved those stimulating discussions on history and other topics, especially the ongoing arguments about the Boston Celtics versus the Chicago Bulls, and the last week's Israeli or U.S. sporting events. He was my very dear friend and great partner. I shall miss him.

Menachem Mor

CONTENTS

PREFACE

The papers in this collection were delivered at the Third Annual Symposium of the Philip M. and Ethel Klutznick Chair in Jewish Civilization at Creighton University on October 14 and 15, 1990.

Many people have been involved in the preparation of the symposium. I would like to thank all of them for their support and commitment. I wish to especially acknowledge those who were directly involved in the hard work that made it possible: my colleagues from Creighton University, Charles Harper, Professor of Sociology, and Bryan Le Beau, Director of Creighton University's Center for the Study of Religion and Society, were enthusiastic members of the academic committee of the symposium. I would like to thank James Finnegan, Special Advisor to the Vice-President for University Public Relations, who has worked with me from the very beginning of the first symposium, and whose guidance has been consistently encouraging and helpful. Special thanks go to Betty Davis from the Creighton University Public Relations Department, and to Beth Seldin-Dotan, Director of the Jewish Cultural Arts Council, who were so instrumental in the success of the symposium. I also want to thank a group with a deep commitment to Jewish education--The College of Jewish Learning--especially Caryn Rifkin, Steve Riekes, Forest Krutter, and Darlene Golbitz. Maryellen Read did a remarkable job in editing the entire collection. I wish to thank the following for their financial contributions which made the symposium possible:

The Jewish Cultural Arts Council
The Ike and Roz Friedman Foundation
The Milton S. and Corinne N. Livingston Foundation
The Henry Monsky Lodge of B'nai B'rith
The Jewish Memorial Foundation in New York
A. A. and Ethel Yossem Endowment Fund

Menachem Mor, Chairholder
Klutznick Chair in Jewish Civilization
Creighton University, Omaha, Nebraska
June, 1992

Jewish Sects, Religious Movements, and Political Parties is the third volume in the series, **"Studies in Jewish Civilization,"** published by the Center for the Study of Religion and Society through Creighton University Press. For information about the collection, the series, the symposium, the Klutznick Chair in Jewish Civilization, or the Center for the Study of Religion and Society, please contact the Center.

EDITOR'S INTRODUCTION

On October 14-15, 1990, the Klutznick Chair in Jewish Civilization at Creighton University sponsored its Third Annual Symposium, *Jewish Sects, Religious Movements and Political Parties*. The symposium focused on the dualistic phenomena characterizing Judaism throughout the ages--pluralism versus sectarianism, religiosity versus secularity, universalism versus separatism--the issues challenging Jewish groups, religious movements and political parties today. These chapters, many expanded or revised for publication here, were presented as original papers during the symposium.

The opening section focuses on the Samaritans, considered by some to be the most ancient Jewish Sect. Three papers directly and indirectly deal with the essential question of whether Samaritanism should be considered Judaism or another religion.

Ernest Boyd Whaley analyzes the account of the founding of the Gerizim temple in Josephus' *Antiquities,* 11.297-347. Josephus' complex narrative is woven around a series of references to the military campaigns of Alexander the Great as he moved through the Levant to Egypt. We learn from it that the socio-political fabric of Samaria was complex and cannot be comprehended from any single perspective. The narrative indicates that the traditional Hebrew holy place at Mt. Gerizim emerged in the Persian period as a center of Hebrew worship, and not as one founded in opposition to the Jerusalem temple. While it is true that Gerizim became an alternative to Jerusalem, and the two sites came into conflict, the conflict itself does not adequately explain the origin of the Hebrew tradition surrounding Gerizim.

Louis H. Feldman examines the ambivalence of Josephus' attitude toward the Samaritans. On the one hand Josephus refers to the Samaritans as a nation (*ethnos*) with political aspirations of their own, parallel to and independent of the Jews. Josephus does not mention the Samaritans as a variety of Judaism or as a divergent group such as the Sadducees, or the Essenes. Indeed, in his account of their origin, Josephus clearly looks upon them as non-Jews who call themselves "kinsmen of the Jews," but who, historically, were brought to Samaria by the Assyrians. On the other hand, there is no reference in Josephus to the foreign origin of the Samaritans. According to Josephus, Samaritans, at least at the outset, were treated as Jews by Alexander the Great and by Antiochus Epiphanes. In his account of Alexander, Josephus refers to Samaritans as apostates from the Jewish nation. He claims that Jews who had violated the dietary laws or the Sabbath regarded Samaritans not as foreigners, but as heterodox Jews, and felt comfortable in taking refuge with them.

Benyamim Tsedaka, a modern Samaritan, asserts that Judaism and Samaritanism should not be considered separate religions, but two traditions that have evolved simultaneously from a single source tradition of the Second Temple era. This common source, and the fact that Samaritans and Jews lived side by side in Israel during the Second Temple era, resulted in the many similarities between the two traditions. According to Tsedaka, the evolution of the Jewish tradition was more complex and rapid than that of the Samaritan tradition because the historical development of the two segments of the Israelite people were different. Similarly, the ideological differences between the two traditions were the result of different geographical and historical backgrounds, and of the mutual isolation of Jews from Samaritans.

The next chapters deal with some historical issues about Jewish Christian sects, Jewish sects during the Islamic period, the Sabbatean Movement, the *Haskalah* and Jewish radicalism in Russia, the Lubavitch Hasidim, and the Jewish youth movements.

Richard A. Freund addresses Jewish Christian sects and the Jewish Christian debate in the early centuries of the common era. He investigates the existence of a number of Jewish-Christian sects which are mentioned extensively in Patristic literature in the second through the fourth centuries C.E. These groups are characterized by their insistence upon the importance of Jewish law and Jesus in the formulation of their ideologies. Significantly, these Jewish-Christian sects did not neatly fit into developing rabbinic Judaism, nor did they fit in the post-Pauline Church. Through their major role in the so-called "Jewish-Christian Debate," they influenced the self-definition process of Jews and Christians during these centuries.

Some minor Jewish sects during the first centuries of Islam are the subject of *Steven M. Wasserstrom's* paper. He examines the varied and scattered evidence for each of these sects with special emphasis on recent discoveries and on the significance of each group for the study of Jewish history. The survey deals with: *'Isawiyya,* known from dozens of works of medieval Muslim literature dealing with Judaism under early Islam; the *Jewish-Gnostics,* with reference to the report by the 8th-century by Theodor bar Khonai; *Jewish-Christians,* portrayed after the Arab conquest in an extremely complex and disparate literature; and a variety of little known *Jewish sects.* While the Rabbinates largely--though not entirely--ignored these groups, the Muslims wrote on them extensively.

Jacob Barnai looks at the social background of the Sabbatean Movement in Smyrna, Sabbatai Zevi's place of birth. He evaluates the social aspects of the phenomena, and presents some of the links between the Jewish society in Smyrna and the emergence of the Sabbatean movement and its extensive expansion. The chapter explores how the movement was influenced by Sabbatai Zevi's teachers, friends, and by the ideological, economic, and social issues of his time.

Erich E. Haberer elucidates the connection between *Haskalah* and the rise of Jewish radicalism in Russia. He demonstrates the vital connection between early pre-Zionist expressions of Jewish radical behavior and the penetration of enlightenment ideas into the communities of Russian Jewry. He shows that the formation of an enlightened, secularized Russian Jewish intelligentsia in conditions of conflict, both *vis-a-vis* traditional Jewish society and Russian autocratic regimentation, led to its radicalization and political involvement in Russian revolutionary affairs. The *Haskalah,* exemplified in the upbringing and eventual activism of well-known Jewish revolutionaries, engendered and nourished this complicated process.

Chaim Schatzker introduces the historical domains in which the Jewish Youth Movements played an important, and at times, a very central role. He defines the Jewish youth movement as an historical phenomenon. In each one of these areas--German Jewry from the beginning of the century; the history of Zionism in Western and Eastern Europe; the history of the Kibbutz movements; the Holocaust and resistance; and the surviving remnant--the Jewish youth movement was unique and distinct from other organizational operations.

The singular active religious response to the Holocaust during the war itself is the topic of *Gershon Greenberg's* chapter. *Mahane Israel* of Lubavitch, under the leadership of Joseph Isaac Schneersohn, established *"Goshen,"* an eschatological community of refuge. *Mahane Israel* sought to transform the cosmos through the ultimate, religious values inherent to the cosmos. This active religious response distinguished itself from theological interpretation, Zionist solutions, and from physical revolt. Schneersohn and *Mahane Israel* aimed for total *Teshuvah* to establish conditions which would enable the messiah to come. Each Jew faced a choice--either return in *Teshuvah* and "journey" to *Goshen*, or be lost forever.

The following section is devoted to issues about Jewish feminism and American Jewry. *Rela Geffen Monson* treats the role of women in rituals in Orthodox synagogues. Though segregation of the sexes remains the dominant mode in Orthodox synagogues, the women's movement and the Jewish women's movement have not been without influence. Several aspects of this influence are documented and analyzed: the study of Torah; birth ceremonies for baby girls; Bat Mitzvah; the study of Talmud; secular leadership roles e.g. boards of schools and congregations; women's prayer groups in the United States and in Israel; the development of the Women's *Tefila* network; literature produced by Orthodox women and men supporting these "innovations" (the development of rhetoric); and innovations in the synagogue service itself. Centrist or moderate Orthodoxy has been significantly influenced by the Jewish feminist movement. In lesser, but still important ways, even the more right wing of Orthodoxy has been touched by this phenomenon.

Stuart Schoenfeld touches the new phenomenon of adult Bat Mitzvahs, which have become frequent ritual events involving hundreds of women each year. Often reported as emotionally powerful events for the individuals who go through them, adult Bat Mitzvahs contribute to the vitality of many congregations. Though these rituals involve women, the adult Bat Mitzvah has not been high on the Jewish feminist agenda, and the extent to which it is a feminist ritual is not clear. Schoenfeld examines the relationship of this ritual to Jewish feminist issues through a study of the experience of a group of women who had a joint Bat Mitzvah at a large Reform temple. He studies some of the dilemmas faced by the women and their congregations in the encounter between an attractive ideological movement and the practical realities of conventional practice.

Developing the thesis that two patterns in thinking touch the core of Jewish existence, *G. Philip Points* analyzes Blu Greenberg's bridging *Halakhah* and the women's movement, and Marc Ellis' call for the transformation of Holocaust theology. Fears for the survival of the Jewish people and for survival of religious living for Jews are at hand in the thoughtful efforts to resolve issues presented by the women's movement. Fears for the survival of Israel cause authentic Jewish theological perspectives on justice and peace to be silenced or simply lost from sight. Both Greenberg and Ellis are concerned about pluralism in opposition to sectarianism in the Jewish experience. Greenberg and Ellis carefully consider the conflict between religiosity secularity. The third phenomenon characterizing historic Judaism is universalism facing separation. As Jews in America, Greenberg and Ellis provide patterns of thinking which have a special place in the midst of a dispersed people which for two thousand years has kept its faith intact.

Since the time of the formation of the American Reform movement, and especially after the establishment of a Commission on Social Justice in the early 1950s, Reform officials, both lay and rabbinic, have issued numerous statements pertaining to a variety of social issues. This corpus of remarks is particularly appropriate sample for investigating how these Jews seek to define the boundaries that separate and those that would not separate Jews from other Americans. *Joel D. Gereboff* explores the tension between particularism and universalism experienced by American Jews. The range of issues, the geographic scope, and the reasoning, rhetoric, and justifications of the resolutions reveal the authors' perspective of the relationship between universalism and particularism in Judaism. Changes in the thinking of Reform leaders on these matters are noted and explained within the broader context of the American Jewish experience.

In the minds of the traditionalists, Sabbath observance is central to religious life. *Morris S. Gorelik* traces the responses of traditionalist rabbis to the antinomian and compromising tendencies of their communities regarding the status of the non-Sabbath observer. Special emphasis is directed at the responsa literature of the modern period, specifically the latter years of the nineteenth and twentieth centuries. The collision between traditionalist Judaism and occidental culture led to explosive results and severe divisions within the community. The rabbis, perforce attempted to cope with the resistance to adherence to traditionalist beliefs and practices. This confrontation has intensified due to the existence of the State of Israel with its attendant political complexities, ethnic divisions and religious cultural struggle. Gorelik discusses the perceptions, motives and suppositions that serve as the philosophic foundation of the *Halakhic* dynamics. To traditionalists, Sabbath observance is the centrality of religious life, therefore he analysis the status of the non-Sabbath observer. How did the rabbis react to non-observance? What are their perceptions of social realities? How did theological views affect their decisions? The particular definition of this status will determine the relational stance of the traditionalist towards the non-conformist.

Mervin F. Verbit conducts a study of the ways in which students affiliated with the major American Jewish religious "movements" perceive their own and the other movements. Respondents rated descriptions of the Orthodox, Conservative, Reform and Chassidic approaches as to appropriateness and applicability. Verbit's study of the data suggests areas of strength and of concern as we try to encourage amity among Jews.

The last section of the collection is devoted to modern yIsraeli political parties. *Sondra M. Rubenstein* surveys the history of the Communist movement prior to and after the establishment of the State of Israel, focusing on the policies and activities of the reorganized and temporarily reunited Communist Party of Israel (MAKI). Often joining forces with MAPAM's communist-leaning fellow travelers, MAKI attempted to follow the Moscow line, which frequently caught them by surprise. Rubenstein examines events such as the internationalization of Jerusalem, the acceptance of United States aid, German reparations, the Korean war, and the two Chinas--central issues in the history of the party which created problems for the Israeli communist leadership.

Yaacov Goldstein deals with the 1977 Israeli political upheaval. The Likud bloc--the historical Rightist successors to the Revisionist Party along with the Liberals--were elected to govern, putting an end to the 50-year-long reign of the Labor Party, heirs of *Mapai*. Ruling authority passed from Center-Left to Right. Most of the ideological-political disputes in Israel today find their origins in the parties' ideological-political history. Goldstein surveys the ideological-political dispute between the "Right" and the "Left" in Israel, focusing on issues like: the socialist outlook; social and nationalistic goals; the nationalist centers of gravity and the importance of the city; the *Histadrut*-General Federation of Labor as an all-inclusive organization or just a trade union; the conflicting views of peace as a goal and territorial compromise ("territories for peace") versus the historic right of the Jewish people to the Land of Israel (integrity of the Land "Greater Israel").

The religious political parties of Israel are very different political creatures, as the next two papers demonstrate. *Gary S. Schiff* traces the origins of the phenomenon of religious political parties to their historical, ideological, organizational and sociological roots in Europe, and follows their development in the State of Israel. Their diverse attitudes and behaviors on such diverse contemporary issues as Sephardim and Ashkenazim, the peace process and the territories are explored and compared.

Alan Dowty presents the religious-secular accommodation in Israeli politics. Religious politics in Israel appears to be a classic expression of Jewish political traditions, and of what political scientists term a "consociational" method of maintaining democracy in deeply divided societies. Negotiated compromise and power-sharing between religious and non-religious political groups have been the rule in the pre-state Zionist movement as well as in Israel. In essence, the religious minority has a veto power over major changes that would injure its basic interests. Both sides are dissatisfied with basic aspects of the status quo, but neither is in a position to challenge it seriously. On the other hand, most parties have some stake in the status quo, since they could lose ground if it were set aside. Few, if any, of the specific religious-secular issues over recent years involve challenges to the basic status quo; they represent border skirmishes rather than full-scale warfare.

A panel discussion, "American Jewry—One or Many Judaisms?" presented by *Joseph R. Rosenbloom, Rela Geffen Monson, David A. Teutsch,* and *Morris S. Gorelik* concludes the proceedings. The panelists represent the different movements in American Jewry: Reform, Conservative, Reconstructionist, and Orthodox.

LIST OF CONTRIBUTORS

Jacob Barnai

Department of Jewish History,
University of Haifa
Haifa 31999 ISRAEL

Alan Dowty

Government and International Studies,
University of Notre Dame
Notre Dame, IN 46556

Louis H. Feldman

Department of Classics,
Yeshiva University
500 W. 185th St.
New York, NY 10033

Richard A. Freund

Department of Philosophy & Religion,
University of Nebraska at Omaha
Arts & Sciences 228
Omaha, NE 68182

Rela Geffen Monson

Dean for Academic Affairs,
Gratz College
Old York Road & Melrose Ave.
Melrose Park, PA 19126

Joel D. Gereboff

Department of Religious Studies,
Arizona State University
Tempe, AZ 85287-0402

Yaacov Goldstein

Eretz Israel Studies,
University of Haifa
Haifa 31999 ISRAEL

Morris S. Gorelik

Yeshiva University
500 W. 185th St.
New York, NY 10033

Gershon Greenberg

Department of Philosophy & Religion,
The American University
Washington, D.C. 20016-8056

CONTRIBUTORS

Erich E. Haberer

Centre for Russian & East European
Studies,
University of Toronto
100 St. George St.
Toronto, Ontario CANADA M6G 2A1

Menachem Mor

Klutznick Chair in Jewish Civilization,
Creighton University
2500 California Plaza
Omaha, NE 68178

G. Philip Points

Religion Program,
Transylvania University
Haupt Humanities Building, Room 208
Lexington, KY 40508

Joseph R. Rosenbloom

Department of Classics,
Washington University
St. Louis, MO 63130

Sondra M. Rubenstein

Communications Department,
Hofstra University
Dempster Hall; Hempstead Tpke.
Long Island, NY 11550

Chaim Schatzker

Department of Jewish History,
University of Haifa
Haifa 31999 ISRAEL

Gary S. Schiff

President, Gratz College
Old York Road & Melrose Ave.
Melrose Park, PA 19126

Stuart Schoenfeld

Department of Sociology,
Glendon College, York University
2275 Bayview Ave.
Toronto, Ontario CANADA M4N 3M6

David Teutsch

Executive Vice President,
Reconstructionist Rabbinical College
Church Road & Greenwood Ave.
Wyncote, PA 19095

Benyamim Tsedaka

"A.B."--"Institute of Samaritan Studies"
P.O. Box 1012
Holon 58110 ISRAEL

Mervin F. Verbit

Department of Sociology,
Brooklyn College, C.U.N.Y.
Brooklyn, NY 11210

Steven M. Wasserstrom

Department of Religion,
Reed College
Portland, OR 97202-8199

Ernest Boyd Whaley

Mt. Carmel United Methodist Church
5100 South Old Peach Tree Road
Norcross, GA 30092

JOSEPHUS' *ANTIQUITIES* 11.297-347: UNRAVELING THE EVIDENCE REGARDING THE FOUNDING OF THE GERIZIM TEMPLE AND THE BACKGROUND OF THE SAMARITAN RELIGIOUS COMMUNITY

Ernest Boyd Whaley

Introduction

Contemporaneous written references to a Samaritan temple on Gerizim are rare (cf. 2 Macc 6:2), and the *Antiquities* and *Jewish War* of Josephus provide the primary extant ancient narrative sources for reconstructing the history of such a cult place.[1] The evidence from Josephus is conflicted, however, and must be carefully weighed. As a result, a plethora of ideas has developed regarding the history of a Gerizim temple and its relationship to what became known as the Samaritan Religious Community (henceforth: SRC).

While Josephus speaks about the origin(s) of the SRC in several places,[2] the central story for unraveling the history of a Samaritan temple on Mt. Gerizim is the account of its founding in *Ant.* 11.297-347. The first step in the process of adequately weighing the Josephan material is a careful analysis of the narrative.

The Problem of Sources and the Narrative Structure

History of Source Criticism

The Josephan account is a complex narrative strung together around a series of references to the military campaigns of Alexander the Great through the Levant to Egypt. After reporting the death of Nehemiah (*Ant.* 11.183), and the story of Esther (*Ant.* 11.184-296), Josephus concludes *Antiquities* 11 with his first extended narrative in the *Antiquities* without explicit biblical parallel.[3] *Ant.* 11.297-347 is a lengthy section with no single identifiable extant source, but with many connections to known traditions and ideas, including connections to the canonical book of Nehemiah. Even if some relationship is assumed with the canonical book of Nehemiah, Josephus appears to have woven his story from other fabric as well.

At the close of the 19th century, Adolphe Büchler reached the conclusion that Josephus used multiple sources for this section.[4] Although Büchler was concerned with delimiting the sources used by Josephus rather than with a thorough analysis of the narrative structure,[5] his conclusion that there are three sources is a valuable beginning. He argued that the three had simply been placed beside one another, and not interwoven in any way. His first source concerned Sanballat, Manasseh, and Alexander's permission to build the Gerizim temple (*Ant.* 11.302-3; 306-17; 321-25; and 345). The second told of Alexander's visit to Jerusalem *(Ant.* 11.317-20 and 325-39), and the third contained a brief description of the Macedonian expedition against the Persians (*Ant.* 11.304-5; 313-14; 316,317; 320 and 325).[6] Büchler's recognition of this "Alexander itinerary" is perhaps his most important contribution to the study of the structure of *Ant.* 11.297-347.

S. Mowinckel argued for two sources behind Josephus's narrative.[7] In the first, the Sanballat-Manasseh narrative, he included §§302-3, 306-12, and 321-24. The other, the Jaddua-Alexander narrative, he delimited as §§313-20, 325b-45.[8]

Against Büchler, and consequently against Mowinckel as well, H.G. Kippenberg argues that the Sanballat-Manasseh story is not a unity,[9] but incorporates several different sources, including one essentially "anti-Josephan" source. Kippenberg's "anti-Josephan" source described the SRC as Jewish, made up of renegade and apostate Jews, and not as Persian or Cuthean, in origin. Kippenberg labels this so-called "anti-Josephan" source the "Shechemite" source, reflecting what he believes to be the characteristic name given to the community while the city of Shechem flourished (between ca. 330 and 97 B.C.E.).[10] Kippenberg concludes that Theodotus could have been the source of the Shechemite traditions which included the stories in *Ant.* 1.337 (parallel Genesis 34) and *Ant.* 5.233-53 (parallel Judges 9) as well as *Ant.* 11.302ff.[11]

The material Kippenberg links in his "Shechemite" source falls prey to his own criticism, however. It does not present a unified perspective. §§310 and 312 share features that Kippenberg identifies as from the Shechemite source, and yet they are clearly focused around Darius, demonstrating that in his time many priests and Israelites were located in Samaria by Sanballat. §§313-17 have none of the peculiar features of the so-called "Shechemite" source and function in the story to shift the focus away from Darius to Alexander the Great. There is a significant degree of detail regarding the conquests of Alexander in this section which set it apart from the other material in Kippenberg's "Shechemite" source. §§340 and 342 shift to the city of Shechem without explanation and without Sanballat, although he is mentioned in connection with soldiers committed to Alexander (§345).[12]

On the other hand, there are features in the Sanballat-Manasseh narrative which argue strongly for its unity. Throughout the narrative, Sanballat is described very consistently. In §303 he is depicted as a politically astute leader. In §310, when he is confronted with the impending failure of the political marriage of his daughter, he demonstrates these qualities. He again is shown with the same political awareness in §315a, in a sentence which intrudes into the detailed accounts of Alexander's progress. When Darius is defeated, Sanballat seizes the opportunity to express his submission and loyalty to Alexander, and continues to press his own agenda (§§321-24). He is presented as an old man in §311, then dies in §325--a detail which many see as thoroughly redactional, but which is nevertheless prepared for by the remark in §311. Throughout the Sanballat-Manasseh narrative, Sanballat is pictured as politically astute. He is not pictured as a military leader, contrary to the portrait we are given in the book of Nehemiah. The only mention of soldiers appears in the distinctly different material in §§340-45. The consistency of his character argues for the narrative unity of the material in what we have termed the "Sanballat-Manasseh" story. In short, the *traditionsgeschichtlich* analysis of Kippenberg must be corrected by a critical literary analysis of the narrative.

Features of the Narrative Unit

Ant. 11.297-301 can be considered as a narrative unit for several reasons. The section begins with the end of Esther, after which there is no explicit biblical parallel, and ends with the end of *Antiquities* 11. Three themes link the material. First, the Alexander itinerary of the conquest of Palestine forms the chronological framework for the unit, beginning in §302 and ending with the death of Alexander in §346. Second, three of the stories in this section deal with the tensions within the Jerusalem priesthood at the end of the Persian period. The murder in the temple during the high priesthood of Johanan (§§297-301) connects the high priesthood of Eliashib (*Ant.* 11.158 and resumed in §297), with that of Jaddua (§302). Josephus thus sets the entire narrative within the context of the priesthoods of two men, Johanan and Jaddua. Finally, the theme of the founding of the Samaritan temple on Gerizim is interwoven throughout from at least §302 until the last line of Book 11. For the first time in the *Antiquities* we can unambiguously speak of a religious community centered at Gerizim. In these ways the narrative section §§297-347 is affirmed as a unity.

Ant. 11.297-347 is best understood, however, as a narrative complex which breaks into the following substructures:

1) the Johanan-Jesus narrative §§297-301;
2) the Sanballat-Manasseh narrative §§302-3, 306-12, 315a, 321-24;
3) the Jaddua-Alexander narrative §§317b-20a, 326-339;

4) the Alexander itinerary §§304-5, 313-14, 315b-17a, 320, 325, 340a, 346a;
5) the Shechemite encounter with Alexander §§340b-45;
6) the concluding summary statement §§346-47.

There are three major narrative complexes:

1) the Johanan-Jesus narrative, *Ant.* 11.297-301;
2) the Sanballat-Manasseh narrative §§302-3, 306-12, 315a, 321-24;
3) the Alexander-Jaddua narrative §§317b-20a, 326-39).

The two minor narrative complexes: (the Shechemite encounter with Alexander *Ant.* 11.340b-45; and a concluding summary statement §§346-47), are woven together by an itinerary of Alexander the Great (*Ant.* 11.304-5, 313-14, 315b-16, 320, 325, 340a, and 346a.

The Johanan-Jesus narrative tells the story of the murder of Jesus by his brother, the High Priest Johanan (§§297-301), and is followed by, and akin to the story of the excommunication of Manasseh by the high priest Jaddua (§§302-3, 306-12, 315a, and 321-24). This second story will be called the "Sanballat-Manasseh" story. I agree with the analysis of Mowinckel, and exclude §§313-317 from this narrative complex. Only §315a, referring to the action of Darius, is part of the Sanballat-Manasseh complex.

§315b represents the editorial comment of Josephus. The material in §§313-20 is problematic in that §§313-16 are only superficially connected to the Sanballat-Manasseh narrative by §315a, and §§317-20 never mentions the name of the high priest, Jaddua, who is central to the narrative following §326. Throughout §§313-20 there are references to very specific military actions on the part of Alexander, which suggests the material is related to the other itinerary notices regarding Alexander. It would seem that Josephus used this section (§§313-20) to join together the Sanballat-Manasseh narrative and the third narrative complex, (the Jaddua-Alexander story), creating a fictional framework for the two stories out of the itinerary of Alexander. The itinerary of Alexander (§§304-5, 313-14, 316-317a, 320, 325, 340a, and 346a) is thus used as a framework within which to insert the other narrative pieces.

Both the story of the encounter of the high priest, Jaddua, with Alexander the Great (§§317b-20a, 326-39), and the story of the Shechemite encounter with the great king (§§340b-45) focuses attention on the privileges given and denied various Hebrew people under Hellenistic rule. The conclusion of *Antiquities* 11 (§§346b-47) is similar to the conclusion of *Antiquities* 9, and is the editorial comment of Josephus. Both §§346b-47 and *Ant.* 9.288-91 focus on the so-called "political expediency" by which Josephus characterized the Samaritans.[13]

There are inescapable connections between the Sanballat-Manasseh narrative and the Jaddua-Alexander story, as well. Jaddua is present in the Sanballat-Manasseh story (cf. §§302 and 321) whether or not he was originally integral to it. A contrast is drawn between the Jewish high priest's rejection of an alliance with Alexander (§§317-18), and the alliance freely offered by Sanballat (§321). The reactions of Alexander are anger in the first instance (§319), and gladness in the second (§322). When the Jaddua-Alexander narrative is again resumed in §326, Jaddua's agony of fear contrasts with Sanballat's recognition of the favorable time for his designs (§321).

The language of alliance and submission ties these two stories together on a conceptual level aside from the pattern noticed by Büchler.[14] If the reference to the Phoenicians and Chaldeans (§330) is taken as a reference to the surrounding nations, as throughout *Antiquities* 11, the theme of opposition to the restoration community is to be found in both stories as well (cf. §303 and §330). The stories are thus bound together by careful design, and the hand of Josephus in constructing the narrative is visible throughout.

It is likely that the various pieces of the narrative represent sources (written or otherwise) reworked by Josephus in the *Antiquities*. He was able to employ multiple written sources for a section of his narrative, as demonstrated by his telling of the monarchical period from both the books of Kings and Chronicles. In numerous cases throughout the first eleven books of the *Antiquities,* when Josephus departs from the MT or the LXX, he does so to incorporate an exegetical insight or tradition known from other contemporaneous Jewish literature. Josephus was probably heir to (an) exegetical tradition(s) which he represents in his narrative. It is likely, therefore, that Josephus does employ sources in constructing *Ant.* 11.297-347, but he has reworked them to reflect his own interests and narrative structure.

The Sanballat-Manasseh Narrative

There are several indications that the Sanballat-Manasseh narrative echoes authentic Samaritan traditions. The narrative (§§302-3) sets the story in the reign of a Persian king Darius, and gives the first indication that the setting of these events at the time of Alexander the Great is secondary. The material on the Cuthean origin of the Samaritans is found elsewhere in the

Antiquities and is probably part of Josephus' editorial framework.[15] As the narrative of §306 would naturally follow that of §303, the §304-5 report on the itinerary of Alexander intrudes. §§306-7 report the conflict initiated by the elders in Jerusalem regarding the marriage of Manasseh to a "foreign" wife and their demand that he divorce her. §312 repeats the theme. The issue of the extent of inclusiveness of the second temple community in Jerusalem was critical in the late Persian period. This issue, especially associated with the restoration of the temple and the work of Ezra and Nehemiah, indicates the Jewish perspective of the narrative as it stands.

Mowinckel viewed the Greek term translated "over which he ruled" (§310) as evidence that Josephus' source understood the nature of Samaria as a military colony in the Persian period.[16] He viewed the reference to the army of Samaria in Neh 3:34 as evidence that Samaria was a military colony under Sanballat and referred to Sanballat's bringing eight thousand people to Alexander (*Ant.* 11.321) as military support. However, at this point, Josephus uses the usual term for subjects of a ruler--not for soldiers--to refer to these eight thousand people. Furthermore, the promises of hegemony in §310, far from envisioning a military colony, present instead the basis for a theocratic government in Samaria. The high priest is promised the authority to rule the country from his position as head of the temple and state. This concept could be the echo of an actual Samaritan tradition by which the government was restored to its rightful place under the authority of the high priest.

Kippenberg argues that Josephus' picture of Sanballat, (especially in §310), portrays the establishment of the cult on Gerizim in a way that could not have been the basis of a Samaritan story, however. Sanballat attempts to secure the marriage of his daughter to the ambitious Jerusalemite priest, Manasseh, by offering him a temple of his own. In his opinion, the narrative thus disallows any valid religious motivation or tradition as the basis for the Gerizim temple.[17]

Kippenberg believes that the Samarian political community actually had nothing to do with the establishment of the cult on Gerizim,[18] which was begun by disenfranchised priests from the Jerusalem cult. In this regard, he follows the analysis of A. Alt[19] and before him of L. Haefeli,[20] arguing for the non-Israelite, foreign, and immigrant character of the Samarian population from the time of the Assyrian conquest. In this respect, Kippenberg opposes the scenario suggested by Wright and Cross, that Shechem, (and by consequence the Gerizim cult), was reestablished by disenfranchised Samarians following the Macedonian colonization of the city of Samaria. Instead he views the Gerizim cult as entirely derivative from the Jerusalem community.

While the picture of a group of Jerusalemite priests entering the SRC is a likely one (§310), the simplest reading gives the clear indication that the ruling group in Samaria did play a significant role in the development of the Gerizim cult. There is evidence from Josephus, as well as other sources, that Yahweh was worshiped in Samaria from the time of the Assyrian conquest and throughout the Persian period.[21] The Hebrew religion did not have to be imported from Jerusalem, even though association between the two territories must be assumed. Therefore, Gerizim could have been as deeply indebted to its Samarian ancestors as to its Judean ones. The vision of a Samarian theocracy centered in Gerizim is, in any case, one which would have been most clearly valued by the SRC itself.

Other characteristics of the Sanballat-Manasseh story would have been valued primarily from a Samaritan perspective as well. For example, the statement in §310 that the temple would be built in Gerizim, "which is the highest of the mountains near Samaria," at least reflects the awareness of the Samaritan tradition that Gerizim is the highest peak, even though Ebal is physically taller.[22]

There is also some possibility that the orthography of the name of the holy mountain in §312 reflects a Samaritan source. It is Kippenberg's contention that the Samaritans employed *"hargarizim"* as the name of the mountain, so that *"har"* is understood as part of the name rather than as a separate word. He argues that a Greek transliteration of the name as *"Argarizein"* (*War* 1.63) must reflect a Samaritan spelling as well; that even spellings which do not follow the normal Greek word order, (such as in *Ant.* 11.312), reflect the use of a Samaritan source, even though he believes it has been reworked from a Jewish perspective.[23]

In any case, the choice of Gerizim as the site of a Hebrew temple cannot be viewed as merely fortuitous. Rowley has demonstrated the extent to which Old Testament traditions themselves point to Gerizim as an important center of Israelite religion.[24] Kippenberg, as well, notes the important place of Gerizim in the traditions of blessing in Deuteronomy (Dt 11:29; 27:12; Josh 8:33; Judg 9:7, 37), in which Gerizim is associated with the first altar built after the people of Israel entered the promised land.[25] There was probably a strong tradition of its importance in any circle which valued the Pentateuchal stories. Gerizim on its own, aside from any schismatic Jerusalemite priestly group or from the political intrigues of Sanballat, could make a strong case for being a legitimate Hebrew cult site--perhaps the legitimate Hebrew cult site.

Ant. 11.311 begins with the notice that Sanballat "undertook these things with the consent of King Darius," creating the impression not only that Darius is central to the narrative, but that progress is already being made on the things promised by Sanballat to Manasseh. Mowinckel refers to the Sanballat-Manasseh story as *"ein Geschichtserzählung,"* which he defines as "a popular story of historical events."[26] He notes that as a rule, the popular *"Geschichtserzählung"* operated without unnecessary accessory characters. If the narrative had intended from the beginning to tell how Sanballat obtained permission from Alexander for building the temple, then it would not have been necessary to introduce Darius at first, unless the narrative wished to tell of the necessity for Sanballat to go over from Darius to Alexander in order to reach his goal. But of this it says nothing.[27]

Mowinckel concludes that the disloyalty of Sanballat is not the point of the narrative as it now stands. Instead, the illegal marriage of the high priest, Manasseh, is the central issue. Thus, the function of Darius is left unfocused by the narrative as it is presently shaped, and Mowinckel suggests that a former version of the story would have hinged on Darius in some way.

These considerations all lead to the conclusion that originally the narrative must have told of Sanballat and Darius, and that the introduction of Alexander and the defection of Sanballat are secondary additions.[28] According to Mowinckel, the narrative, as Josephus presents it, reflects Jewish polemic against the Samaritans, who saw, in the official Persian recognition of their cult place, a restoration of ancient Israelite tradition. The Jewish polemic, on the other hand, preserves Persian respect for the Jerusalem cult, and instead, places Gerizim under the authority of (the then unknown) Alexander. Mowinckel identifies the Persian king as Darius II Nothos (424-404 B.C.).

It is not necessary to accept all of Mowinckel's reconstruction[29] to see that there is a strong indication of an earlier form of the story which was focused around Sanballat and Darius. Perhaps the earlier form would have also included particularly Samaritan elements which are now only echoed.

The story continues in *Ant.* 11.312 with the notice that "many priests and Israelites were involved in such marriages," so that many followed Manasseh to the North. They were granted money and land by Sanballat, who in every way attempted to win favor for Manasseh. The intermarriage problem, addressed throughout the Persian period, apparently reflects one of the lines of demarcation among rival priestly circles.[30] The narrative depicts the SRC as including Jerusalemite priests and lay persons who either were expelled from, or left, the Jerusalem cult voluntarily over this issue of intermarriage. The Sanballat-Manasseh narrative describes the SRC as having been made up of a broad spectrum of priests and Israelites who, because of their marriages, now forsook the Jerusalem cult.

The SRC is not pictured as living only around Gerizim or Shechem, but throughout the territory under the hegemony of Sanballat. §§311-12 describe the establishment of a broad-based community, with a significant priestly population, which no longer held Jerusalem as its center. It is Kippenberg's opinion that the cult at Gerizim was founded, like Qumran, to be a community of priests,[31] but in §312, and later in the distinctive material in §§340, 344 and 346, the laity play a central role as well. In §§340, 344, and 346, where the Samaritan/Shechemites are depicted as renegades and accused persons from the Jerusalem community, they are given no priestly identity. In the Shechemites' meeting with Alexander (§340), their spokesperson is not identified at all. In fact, after the Sanballat-Manasseh narrative, Josephus does not refer to the Samaritan priesthood again. The different picture of the Samaritan community painted by §§340, 344, and 346 is not only one indication of the distinctiveness of that later material from the Sanballat-Manasseh narrative, but also it points to the basis of the SRC in the popular culture. The SRC and the Gerizim cult represented more than the defection of a few priests from Jerusalem.

After the intrusion of §§313-320, which function to join the Sanballat-Manasseh narrative and the Jaddua-Alexander narrative to the Alexander itinerary,[32] the Sanballat-Manasseh narrative resumes, although without the echoes of authentic Samaritan traditions which occurred in the early portions. Alexander is thoroughly integrated into this section of the narrative. §321 functions redactionally to tie the various pieces of the narrative to the framework of the Alexander itinerary.[33] §§322-23 tell of Sanballat's going over to Alexander and of his winning Alexander's approval for the temple project. §324 pictures Alexander giving direct approval for the building of the temple and Sanballat bringing his energy to bear on its completion.

It is the opinion of most that this must represent a Samaritan tradition, as it is hardly conceivable, given the anti-Samaritan sentiments among the Jews, that a Jew would have written of Alexander's approval for the Gerizim temple.[34] The fact is, however, that it is only from a Jewish source that we know of the tradition of Alexander's legitimation of the Samaritan temple.[35] Extant Samaritan tradition refers to a visit of Alexander to Shechem, but none reports the building of the temple under Alexander.

We must contrast the permission given by Alexander in §324, however, with the later ignorance of Alexander regarding the Samaritan cult. In §343 Alexander receives the Shechemites who invite him to their city and to honor their temple. In the conversation following their request for respite from tribute in the sabbath year, Alexander reveals that he does not know who these people are. There is no hint that he has given permission for the building of a temple.[36]

Although many scholars accept that a Samaritan temple was built on Gerizim at, or around, the time of Alexander, the Sanballat-Manasseh narrative is the only evidence for it. The association of this story with Alexander is highly questionable, not to mention the fact that it implies a very brief period in which the temple was constructed, perhaps as short as seven months.[37] That the necessary resources, manpower, and energy for such a project were available in a time of severe political upheaval and war is hardly conceivable. It is also true that §§321-25 have none of the echoes of Samaritan tradition which were found in the earlier portions of the Sanballat-Manasseh narrative.

A number of scholars thus place the building in the Persian period.[38] Tcherikover, for example, follows the analysis of Schalit[39] in concluding that the building of the temple was carried out round about the year 400, as a result of a prolonged struggle between two parties in Judea, that of Nehemiah and Ezra on the one hand, and the pro-Samaritan faction on the other.[40]

Marcus places the building in the period of Nehemiah as result of his policies,[41] as does Mowinckel.[42] Mowinckel argues that the building of the Gerizim temple is merely the natural consequence of Nehemiah's actions. He sets an early date for the construction of the Gerizim temple as part of Darius II's organization of the empire.[43] He believed that a military colony like Samaria would have been provided with a temple, and, with their exclusion from Jerusalem, another site would have been chosen.[44] Of the story related by Josephus (*Ant.* 11.297-347), Mowinckel would discard the Hellenistic chronology, polemical and biased as it is, but he would retain the so-called "historical nucleus" of the story, namely the request from Sanballat to Darius II for permission to build the temple.[45]

Others dismiss the story entirely. Vink contends that Mowinckel's thesis:

> . . . is irreconcilable with the Elephantine papyri. The petition
> for the rebuilding of the Yahu temple would certainly have

contained a reference to the temple on Mt. Gerizim, and would
have been addressed to the priesthood of Samaria as well.[46]

Vink argues that it is highly improbable that Josephus's story is based
on a historical nucleus and that it is more likely a legendary elaboration of
Nehemiah 13:28.[47]

As for archaeological data regarding the Samaritan temple on Gerizim,
most have followed the construction offered by G.E. Wright that the
foundation of the Samaritan temple on Gerizim was discovered under the
foundation of the Hadrianic temple there, and that it was built around 400
B.C..[48]   Grabbe thinks, in fact, that this is the only piece of Josephus'
narrative which has been corroborated.[49]

Bowman, along with Montgomery,[50] notes, however, that for the
Samaritans "a natural outcropping of rock 48'x 36' is the most holy place" on
the mountain, not the site identified by Robert Bull as the foundation of the
Gerizim temple under the Hadrianic temple building.[51]   And recent
excavations on Gerizim have cast a strong shadow of doubt on Wright's
interpretation of the Drew-McCormick findings. R. Pummer reports that in
April, 1984, excavations were begun on the main peak of Mt. Gerizim on the
southwest corner of the plateau:

> . . . Only remains of the Hellenistic period were present. Even
> though interpretations are still very tentative, the excavator (I.
> Magen, the staff officer for Archaeology in Judea and Samaria)
> believes there may have been a large temenos surrounded by a
> wall or walls within which stood a temple. . . . Josephus, in his
> report of the destruction of the Samaritan temple by John
> Hyrcanus, says that the latter defeated "the Cutheans, the race
> inhabiting the country surrounding the temple modelled on that
> in Jerusalem" (*Bell* 1:63; cf. also *Ant.* 13.255-56). And in fact
> further down the slope of the mountain can still be seen the
> remains of buildings which may have been the Samaritan town
> surrounding the temenos, possibly the Luza (Louza) of
> Eusebius' Onomasticon (120,11) and of Samaritan tradition.[52]

Magen has concluded that no Hellenistic remains are to be found on
Tell er-Ras, and no evidence of a temple has emerged from his investigation
of the Hellenistic town on the peak. The Samaritan literature does not mention
a temple on Gerizim, only an altar.[53] It does mention a sanctuary built in
Luza near the tabernacle.[54] While the Delos inscription #2 probably refers to

a temple on Gerizim,[55] we are left with the situation that even the most certain fact with which Josephus's narrative could be corroborated remains open to question.[56]

§§321-24, although somewhat distinct from the earlier portions of the Sanballat-Manasseh narrative, represent its continuation and climax. The narrative is concluded in §325a with the notice of the death of Sanballat. §325 states the he died within nine months of Alexander's appearance in Palestine. Sanballat's death is no surprise since he was called an old man in §311 and the fulfillment of his promises to Manasseh are basically completed §324, except that hegemony over the territory ruled by Sanballat was given to Alexander rather than to Manasseh (cf. §321).

The death of Sanballat as the conclusion to the story is a typical feature of Josephus's style. He rarely overlaps the lives of two significant figures. It is interesting, as well, that Manasseh and Nikaso also disappear from the story at this point. They are not mentioned in §§340-45, where we would expect them to appear if the later material was related, except artificially by Josephus himself, to the Sanballat-Manasseh narrative.

Conclusions

The evidence of Sanballat-Manasseh story for the founding of the Samaritan temple on Gerizim remains obscure. Josephus' thorough rewriting of his material--emphasizing themes which concerned him and avoiding verbatim recounting of his sources--results in a tightly woven narrative. The seams and most obvious differences are apparent, but precise identification of his sources and inherited material is not possible. Since we have considered only one piece of the narrative cloth (the Sanballat-Manasseh narrative), it must be accepted by assertion that the other pieces present equally complex pictures. Whether taken from the works of a previous historian, from Samaritan or Jewish sources in Alexandria, from some type of history of the high priesthood in Jerusalem, from Nehemiah, from a tradition of exegesis which had expanded the Nehemiah story, from some combination of the above, or from none of these, Josephus' story of the founding of the Gerizim temple is responsible for at least three plausible historical scenarios.

Mowinckel's analysis, which points to a Persian period founding of the temple, leads to the discovery of several echoes of undeniably authentic Samaritan tradition. Mowinckel demonstrates that there could have been a story behind Josephus' version, perhaps even behind the source of Josephus' story, which knew of the founding of a temple under Persian authority. The temple at Elephantine, and the correspondence from that Jewish/Hebrew community to both Jerusalem and Samaria, are certain indications that the presence of a temple outside Jerusalem was not in itself a schismatic phenomenon, and that authority for the Hebrew religion was located both in Judah and Samaria prior to the Hellenistic period. That Gerizim was chosen as the site of the Samaritan temple is clearly a theological, exegetical, or traditional decision. It is not merely a military or political one. The promise that political hegemony would be given to the priests reflects the interests of a priestly community, which could be Jewish, but which could also be the memory of an authentic Samaritan tradition.

The Sanballat-Manasseh story is also responsible for the view that the temple was built at the time of Alexander's conquest of Palestine. The ingenious reconstructions of the Wadi Dâliyeh papyri by F.M. Cross, the interpretations of the findings of the American excavations in Shechem, and the interpretations of the Samaritan Pentateuch offered by Purvis, have led to a scenario in which the ousted Persian/Cuthean ruling aristocracy moved from the city of Samaria after Alexander's conquest and reestablished themselves around the traditional holy place at Gerizim.

Josephus tells us that the priests who founded the temple on Gerizim were not foreign immigrants to the North, but were Jews from Jerusalem. The exclusivist policies of one strain of second temple Judaism defined the boundaries for appropriate marriages so as to make ineligible a significant portion of the population. Not all circles of priests defined the boundaries so exclusively, however. At least from the times of Ezra and Nehemiah, the relative strengths of the various groups can be measured in the seemingly continual ebb and flow surrounding the issue of "intermarriage." The Gerizim temple, a Hebrew enclave in the midst of non-Hebrew territory, was founded by a group of these Jerusalem priests at a time when they were forced out of Jerusalem. Their resources and energy account for the rebuilding of Shechem as well as for the establishment of a temple on Gerizim.

While it is true that the temple on Gerizim, (if indeed there was a temple there), must have been founded at only one time, each of these scenarios has much to commend it and requires that much be accepted without confirmation. From the literary analysis, it seems likely that there was a story of the founding of a temple on Gerizim during the Persian period. Without the corroborating physical evidence, even such a story would remain only one of the viable choices.

Endnotes

1. Gerizim occurs in *War* 1.63; 3.307; *Ant.* 4.305,306; 5.69,235; 11.310,340,346; 12.7,10,257,259; 13.74,74,78,255; 14.100; and 18.85.   The Gerizim temple is mentioned in *Ant.* 11.310,340,346; 12.10,257,259; and 13.74,78,255,256. In *Ant.* 12 and 13, the temple is the object of Jewish attack either by political or military means, presumably because it threatens the hegemony of Jerusalem. Only in 12.257,259 does Josephus attempt to present an inside look at the religious community loyal to Gerizim. In that case the Samaritan religious community (henceforth: SRC) is pictured as claiming Sidonian heritage and as rejecting any Jewish connection. From the time of its founding to its destruction by John Hyrcanus (the parallel text in *War* 1.63 does not report the destruction of the temple, only the defeat of the Cutheans), Josephus allows two hundred years for the existence of a Samaritan temple on Gerizim. From the incidental remark in *War* 1.63, we learn that the temple was modelled on that in Jerusalem. Cf. the similar statement regarding the temple at Leontopolis (*Ant.* 13.72).

2. *Ant.* 9.277-82, 288-91; 10.183-85.

3. Several details suggest some relationship to the final chapters of the canonical book of Nehemiah. For example, the name of the governor of Samaria is the same (Sanballat); all the names of the high priests could have come from Nehemiah 12:10 and 22 cf. Lester Grabbe, "Josephus and the Reconstruction of the Judean Restoration," *JBL* 106 (1987), 261; and a story of the intermarriage of a brother of the high priest with a daughter of Sanballat and the consequent excommunication of the transgressor is told in Neh. 13:28.   H.G. Kippenberg, *Garizim und Synagoge:* Traditionsgeschichtliche Untersuchungen zur samaritanischen Religion der aramäischen Periode (Berlin, 1971), 52; cf. also Kippenberg, and Gerd A. Wevers, *Textbuch zur neutestamentlichen Zeitgeschichte* (Göttingen, 1979), 89 and 91, contends that "the narrative of Manasseh stands much nearer Neh. 12f. and presents an wholly and entirely Jewish perspective of the report. The scant notice in Neh. 13:28 developed into the legend concerning the origin of the Samaritan community. That the imagined report already deviated very widely from the narrative of Nehemiah is demonstrated by the varying genealogies." Cf. also G. Hölscher *Palästina in der persischen und hellenistischen Zeit* (Berlin, 1903), 39, who contends that the Manasseh story is most simply taken "as a mistaken exegesis of the Nehemiah passage." A note in the French translation of Josephus by Chamonard states regarding *Ant.* 11.302ff that "the origin of this section could be Neh. 13:28. . . . Josephus, or rather the document he followed, reduced the age of this episode by a century, invented the name of the anonymous brother, and made him not the brother but the grandson of Joiada. He has also transformed Sanballat the Horonite, mentioned frequently in Nehemiah, into a Persian governor of Samaria and has given him, contrary to all probability, a daughter with a Greek name, Nicasô." H.H. Rowley "Sanballat and the Samaritan Temple," *Men of God: Studies in Old Testament History and Prophecy* (New York, 1963), 265, takes these same differences with caution, however, stating that "the report of Josephus should not simply be united with Neh. 13:28." He points out that "Nehemiah does not give us the name of the priest of his story, whereas in Josephus's story we are given the name of the priest and also his wife's. In Nehemiah's story the

priest is the brother of Johanan, whereas in Josephus's he is his son. In Nehemiah's story there is no mention of the Samaritan temple, whereas that is essential to Josephus's, and here the date of the erection of the temple is very precisely fixed," Rowley, 249). Lester Grabbe concludes that Josephus could not have used the canonical book of Nehemiah because the severe condensation of the material from Nehemiah early in *Antiquities* 11 (cf. *Ant.* 11.5.6-8 §§159-83) is in such contrast with the equally severe expansion which would be represented in the last sections of the book and would, in his judgement, represent a unique use of the source material. Therefore, he concludes that Josephus is working from a non-canonical, expanded version of the book of Nehemiah. Such a conclusion does not follow, however, after a full analysis of the biblical paraphrase of Josephus, where he is found to employ precisely these two techniques, compression and expansion, in the retelling of the stories of the Bible. H.G.M. Williamson, *Israel in the Books of Chronicles,* (Cambridge, 1977), 25, came to the same conclusion in response to the analysis of Karl-Friedrich Pohlman *Studien zum Dritten Ezra: Ein Beitrage zur Frage nach dem ürsprunglich Schluß des Chronistischen Geschichtwerks* (Göttingen, 1970). Williamson argues that Josephus could have used the canonical book of Nehemiah, even though he abbreviated it drastically.

4. Adolphe Büchler, "La relation de Josèphe concernant Alexandre le Grand," *REJ* 36 (1897): 1-26. Although Büchler's analysis excludes *Ant.* 11.297-301.

5. Büchler, "La relation de Josèphe concernant Alexandre le Grand," see n. 4 above, makes a clear statement of purpose that ". . . we propose only to demonstrate the diverse parts of which the account of Josephus is composed, to study this as much as possible from the perspective of his sources, and to determine the tendenz and the time (epoch) of composition."

6. Cf. Büchler, "La relation de Josèphe concernant Alexandre le Grand," see n. 4 above, 4. He viewed §§304-5 as intrusive into the first story, but §§313-14 as indispensable to the Sanballat-Manasseh narrative, in his opinion, thus inextricably linking the first source with Alexander the Great. Büchler regarded *Ant.* 11.325 as a redactional comment inserted by the one who combined the various sources, Büchler, "La relation de Josèphe concernant Alexandre le Grand," see n. 4 above, 6, but the information it contained he saw as part of the Alexander source. He regarded the repetition of the report of the siege of Tyre (*Ant.* 11.317, and 325) as evidence that Josephus has merely juxtaposed two sources.

7. S. Mowinckel, "Josephus und das Nehemiabuch," *Studien zu dem Buche Ezra-Nehemia,* vol. 2: *Die Nehemia-Denkschrift* (Oslo, 1964), 110.

8. It is his opinion that §325 is the redactor's attempt to tie the two stories together, §§346-47 form the conclusion to which §§304-05 serve as the introduction.

9. Ralph Marcus (*Josephus,* Loeb Classical Library 6:509) maintained the unity of the Sanballat-Manasseh story, in agreement with Büchler and Mowinckel, and refers to the assertion by Hölscher that its immediate source was Alexander Polyhistor. Hölscher suggested that Josephus followed Alexander Polyhistor; see his *Die Quellen des Josephus*

für die Zeit vom Exil bis zum jüdischen Kriege (Leipzig, 1904), 43ff. He was followed by E. Norden, "Josephus und Tacitus über Jesus Christus und eine messianische Prophetie," *Neue Jahrbücher für das klassische Altertum* 16 (Leipzig, 1913): 661. Hölscher later rejected Josephus's account as a late and worthless legend, however, and held that the section of Josephus with which we are concerned is an unhistorical legend of Jewish-Alexandrian origin, following Büchler. Cf. Hölscher, *REJ.* 9, 2 (1916) 1968; *HSAT* loc cit.; and *Geschichte der israelitischen und jüdischen Religion* (Geissen, 1922), 172. F.M. Cross "A Reconstruction of the Judean Restoration," *JBL* 94 (1975): 5 note 11 places §§302-3, 306-12, and 347 together as the historically accurate nucleus of the text.

10. Kippenberg's "Shechemite" source includes *Ant.* 11.312-17, 321-25, 340, 342, 346 and 12.10 (*Garizim und Synagoge,* 55-56). The use of name "Shechemite" is the basic clue to the period in which the source material was edited, according to Kippenberg. In his opinion, it must have been during the time when the city flourished. One of the weaknesses of Kippenberg's analysis, even though he admits to it (*Garizim und Synagoge,* 53 note 118), is that the references to "Shechemites" in the earlier books of the *Antiquities* are not considered (cf. *Ant* 1.337; 5.240-53). When these references are considered, the term designates nothing more than an inhabitant of the city of Shechem Cf. B. Whaley, *Samaria and the Samaritans in Josephus's Antiquities 1-11,* unpublished dissertation (Emory University, 1989). On the other hand, Josephus's use of the term *"Sikimitai"* to designate an inhabitant of the city is consistent with his use elsewhere of the term *"Samareian"* to designate the inhabitants of the city of Samaria. There is no reason to suppose a special source behind this section on the basis of the occurrence of the term *"Sikimitai."*

11. Kippenberg, *Garizim und Synagoge,* 56 note 123.

12. H.G.M. Williamson also criticizes, in particular, Kippenberg's attempt to see in this material a separate source. Williamson argues that its elements are too fragmentary to stand alone and therefore have to be drawn into association with other elements which are generally agreed to be historically quite unreliable, such as the connection of Alexander with the founding of the Samaritan temple. Williamson also remarks on the inconsistency of Kippenberg's critique of Büchler. Kippenberg accepted *Ant.* 11.312-37, 321-25, 340, 342, 344-47, and 12.10. as part of the Shechemite source, just as in Büchler's analysis, but he omitted 302f and 306-11 without explanation. For these reasons Williamson questions the source-critical analysis of Kippenberg, Williamson, *Israel in the Books of Chronicles,* see n. 3 above, 137 note 4. He accepts, on the other hand, the view that "a substantial number of priests who left Jerusalem for Shechem (*Ant.* 11.312, 322b, 340, and 346) were early adherents to its new cult community," Williamson, *Israel in the Books of Chronicles,* see n. 3 above, 137-38.

13. Grabbe's analysis, "Josephus and the Reconstruction of the Judean Restoration," see n. 3 above, tends to oversimplify the narrative structure. He recognizes three narrative portions which have no biblical parallel: *Ant.* 11.7.1 §§297-301, Joannes and Bagoses; *Ant.* 11.7.2 - 8.2 §§302-12 + 11.8.4 §§321-325 + 11.8.6-7 §§340-347, Manasseh, Sanballat and the Samaritan temple; and *Ant.* 11.8.4-5 §§326-39, Alexander and the

Jewish High Priest. §§313-21 are not discussed by Grabbe, but these are crucial sections for understanding the structure of §§297-347. He also does not note the intrusion of the Alexander itinerary into the text, for example at *Ant.* 11.304-5. Furthermore, association of §§340-47 with the Sanballat-Manasseh tradition is highly suspect. The concluding material §§346b-47 is more similar to other summary statements made by Josephus himself, while the problematic "Shechemite" material in §§340b-45 represents a shift in focus to the city of Shechem with no mention of Samaria. It certainly reflects a time later than the Persian period which is the basis of the Sanballat-Manasseh narrative.

14. Büchler, "La relation de Josèphe concernant Alexandre le Grand," see n. 4 above, 13, notes the contrast of Jaddua's loyalty (§318) with the expediency of Sanballat (§321); the brief political interest shown by Alexander to the Gerizim cult (§324) with the extensive interest shown by Alexander in his journey to Jerusalem and his sacrificing at the temple (§331 and §§336-39); and the fact that Sanballat sent troops to Alexander (§§321 and 345) as opposed to the choice offered to any who wished to join from among the Jews (§339). These facts led him to conclude "that the history of Jaddua is an imitation of the narrative concerning Sanballat. The imitation was motivated by the desire to replace the glorification of the Samaritan temple recounted to the Alexandrians with a description of the honors rendered by Alexander to the sanctuary of Jerusalem."

15. Cf. *Ant.* 11.21-22.

16. Mowinckel, *Studien* 2, see n. 7 above, 112.

17. Contra Büchler, according to whom, there is no negative word spoken about the Samaritans in §§304-39. Kippenberg, however, sees the description of Sanballat (§310) as anti-Samaritan.

18. Kippenberg, *Garizim und Synagoge,* see n. 3 above, 47.

19. A. Alt, "Zur Geschichte der Grenze zwischen Judäa und Samaria," *PJ* 31 (1935), reprinted in *Kleine Schriften zur Geschichte des Volkes Israels II* (München, 1953): 361; and "Der Stadtstaat Samaria," *Kleine Schriften III* (München, 1959): 301.

20. L. Haefeli, *Geschichte der Landschaft Samaria von 722 vor Chr. bis 67 nach Chr.* (Münster, 1922), 68.

21. Cf. for example, the number of Yahwistic names found in the Wadi Dâliyeh Papyri F.M. Cross,"The Papyri and their Historical Implications," *AASOR* 41 (Cambridge, 1974): 20. The Elephantine Papyri also address the officials in Samaria with a Yahwistic religious question. We must ask whether this would have been seen as appropriate had there been no affiliation with the Hebrew religion. Rowley has also pointed out that there is evidence for considering Sanballat a Yahwist since he gave his sons Yahwist names and his daughter married into the Jerusalem high priestly family. H.H. Rowley, "The Samaritan Schism in Legend and History," *Israel's Prophetic Heritage.* Essays in Honor of James Muilenburg (New York, 1962), 208; cf. also "Sanballat and the Samaritan Temple," 166. There is no reason to suppose that Yahwism was ever

supplanted as the primary religion of the region as we have seen from the discussion of the Assyrian conquest of the area.

22. R. Pummer, *The Samaritans* (Leiden, 1987), 8; and more recently "Samaritan Material Remains," *The Samaritans,* Alan Crown, ed. (Tübingen, 1989), 135-77, remarks that "the belief that Mt. Gerizim is the place which God has chosen is the cardinal tenet that separates Samaritans from Jews. Despite the greater height of Mt. Ebal, Mt. Gerizim is considered by the Samaritans to be the highest of all mountains."

23. H.G. Kippenberg, *Garizim und Synagoge,* see n.3 above, 54-56. Cf. also Rita Egger, *Josephus Flavius und die Samaritaner:* Eine terminologische Untersuchung zur Identitätsklärung der Samaritaner (Göttingen, 1986), 294-95.

24. Rowley, "Sanballat and the Samaritan Temple," see n. 21 above, 275, note 2, points to many who think Deuteronomy had Shechem in mind as the chosen place; cf. B. Luther, in Ed. Meyer, *Die Israeliten und ihre Nachberstämme* (Halle, 1906), 542ff.; G.A. Danell, *Studies in the Name Israel* (Upsala, 1946), 56; I. Engnell, "Israel and the Law," *Symbolae Biblicae Upsaliences* 7 (Upsala, 1946): 21f. He refers favorably to W.F. Albright, *From the Stone Age to Christianity* (Garden City, N.Y., 1957), 241, who argues that Deuteronomy had material from Shechem as its nucleus. Others have argued that Ezekiel too may have had Shechem in mind. Cf. C. Mackay, *Princeton Theological Review* 20 (1922): 399ff., 661ff.; 21 (1923): 372ff.; 22 (1924): 27ff.; *ET* 34 (1922-3): 475ff.; 55 (1943-4): 292ff.; and *CQR* 119 (1934-35): 173ff.; Gaster, *The Samaritans,* 15; J. Smith, *The Book of the Prophet Ezekiel* (London, 1931), 66ff.; L.E. Browne, *Ezekiel and Alexander* (London, 1952), 10,17ff.; W.L. Wardle, *Supplement to Peake's Commentary* (1936), 12f.. Rowley remarks that "so long ago as 1771, G.J.L. Vogel, in his annotations on the posthumously published work of G.L. Oeder, *Freye Untersuchung über einige Bücher des A.Ts.,* 386ff., maintained that Ezek. 40-48 were written in the Samaritan interest to persuade the Jews to abandon the Jerusalem Temple for a new shrine," Rowley, "Sanballat and the Samaritan Temple," see n. 21 above, 276 note 1.

25. Kippenberg, *Garizim und Synagoge,* see n. 3 above, 58 note 128.

26. Mowinckel, *Studien* 2, see n. 7 above, 111.

27. Mowinckel, *Studien* 2, 114.

28. Mowinckel, *Studien* 2, 115.

29. For example, it is difficult to accept that Alexander's stamp of approval on the Gerizim temple was somehow less appealing than the approval of the Persian King. Mowinckel's case rests on the assumption that the Jewish version of the story arose very early in the Hellenistic period.

30. Cf. Williamson, *Israel in the Book of Chronicles,* see n. 3 above, 138.

31. Kippenberg, *Garizim und Synagoge,* see n. 3 above, 57-58. Cf. also Leo Haefeli, *Geschichte der Landschaft Samaria von 722 vor chr. bis 67 nach chr.* (Münster, 1922), 58-59, who had argued many years earlier that especially *Ant.* 11.8.2 §306-12 reflected the historical origin of the SRC. He bases his argument on the fact that the Samaritans kept the same law as the Jews (the Torah), their temple was like that in Jerusalem, and it had a Jewish priesthood. And because Sanballat states to Alexander that many Jews wanted to build a temple in Samaria (§323), he sees the founding of the SRC as the work of the "AM HA'ARETZ" who were excluded from Jerusalem by the work of Nehemiah.

32. The exception is §315a, which is part of the Sanballat-Manasseh narrative.

33. Cf. Büchler, "La relation . . . ," see n. 4 above 6; and Mowinckel, *Studien* 2, see n. 7 above, 114.

34. Cf. M. Delcor, "Vom Sichem der Hellenistichen Epoche zum Sychar des Neuen Testaments," *ZDPV* 78 (1962): 36, who contends that ". . . it is hardly to be questioned that this report goes back to a Samaritan source which wished to trace back the origin of the holy place (Heiligtums) to Alexander the Great himself."

35. A thorough study of Josephus' remarks concerning Samaria and the Samaritans confirms that he was not as anti-Samaritan as is commonly assumed. Cf. Whaley, *Samaria and the Samaritans in Josephus's Antiquities 1-11,* see n. 10 above.

36. A further indication of the distinctiveness of §§340-45.

37. Cf. the notice of Sanballat's death in §325.

38. Eybers rejects Josephus' account of the building of the temple as unhistorical primarily because the implied time of construction (one year) is too short, but also because of the apparent chronological problems with the rest of the story. He also points to the broad evidence for not-so-cordial relations between the Samaritans and Alexander (for example in Curtius Rufus and now by interpretation from the Wadi Dâliyeh finds) which contrasts with the picture of Sanballat's acquiring approval from Alexander for building the temple "Relations between Jews and Samaritans in the Persian Period," *Biblical Essays* 9 (1966): 80. Rowley notes that a number of scholars basically accept the dating of the temple to the period of Alexander. Cf. A.E. Cowley, in *JE* 10 (1905): 671a; E. Kautsch, in *Herzog-Kautch, PRE* 7 (1906): 431 (3rd edition, English translation in *The New Schaff-Herzog Encyclopedia* 10 (1911): 188a; A.E. Cowley, *EBib* 4 (1907): col 4260; I. Spak, *Der Bericht der Josephus über Alexander der Grossen* 12; C. Steuernagel, *Einleitung* (1912), 42; J. Touzard, "Les Juifs au Temps de la Période Persiane," *RB* 24 (1915): 109f.n.; L.E. Browne, *Early Judaism* (1929 edition), 207; R. Kittel, *GVI* 3, 680; E. Sellin, *Geschichte* 2 (1932): 170; G. Ricciotti, *Histoire d'Israel* 2 (1948): 199 (new edition, French trans. by R. Auvray); R. Pfeiffer, *Introduction* (1941), 809; T.H. Gaster, *UJE* 9 (1943): 336a; I.G. Matthews, *The Religious Pilgrimage of Israel* (1947), 239n.; A. Médebielle, *Esdras-Néhémie* (in Clamer's *Sainte Bible,* 1949), 383. Rowley refers as well to Oesterley, *History of Israel* 2(Oxford, 1955):157, who assigns it to the middle of the fourth century. P. Antoine (*SDB* 3, col 546) notes that

Eusebius, cf. Migne, *P.G.* 19 (1857): col 488, says that this temple was built under Alexander, but observes that Eusebius here depends on Josephus, and has no independent value. M.H. Segal, "The Marriage of the High Priest to the Daughter of Sanballat and the Building of the Temple on Gerizim," in *Assaf Festschrift on his Sixtieth Birthday,* (Jerusalem, 1953), 410ff. (in Hebrew); maintains that the temple was built at the time Josephus states, but not in that manner. He holds that the Samaritans seized the opportunity afforded by the decline of the Persian power to erect the temple, but not with Alexander's permission, and thinks it might have been built by descendants of Sanballat, and the priests might have been descendants of Manasseh. Rowley, "Sanballat and the Samaritan Temple," see n. 21, 258-59 note 3, concludes that for this interesting suggestion there is nothing but unsupported conjecture and that ". . . if the building of the Temple is divorced from any relation with Alexander, as well as with Sanballat, it can only be said that Josephus does not offer any evidence whatever of such a building "Sanballat and the Samaritan Temple," 260. Rowley, 262, n.1, names the following scholars as holding a fifth century date for the construction of the temple: Wellhausen, Berthian Ryssel, Stade, Ryle, Cheyne, Wilson, Heidet, Cook, Kennett, Antoine, Kalt, van Dodewaard, Born, Metzinger, Davis-Gehman, Reicke, Mowinckel.

39. A. Schalit, "A Chapter in the History of the Party Conflict in Jerusalem at the end of the Fifth Century and at the Beginning of the Fourth Century B.C.," *Commentationes in memorium Johannis Lewy* (Jerusalem, 1949), 252-72, (in Hebrew).

40. Tcherikover, *Hellenistic Civilization and the Jews* (New York, 1979), 419-20 note 12. He contends that the data in *Ant.* 12.256 cannot be taken as independent information confirming the building of the temple in the time of Alexander. Instead in *Ant.12.256,* Josephus must be seen to be "repeating his former story of Alexander (*Ant.* 11.297-347), Yadoa and Sanballat in the self-same paragraph, and has made a simple calculation in 'round' figures of the years which intervened, in his view between Alexander and John Hyrcanus."

41. Marcus, *Josephus,* see n. 9 above, 6:504.

42. Mowinckel, *Studien* 2, see n. 7 above, 106.

43. Mowinckel, *Studien* 2, 118.

44. Mowinckel, *Studien* 2, 111, argues on the basis of Neh 3:34 that Samaria was a Persian military colony under Sanballat the Horonite.

45. Cf. Mowinckel, *Studien* 2, 118; cf. also 111 and 115.

46. J.G. Vink, "The Date and Origin of the Priestly Code in the Old Testament," *The Priestly Code and Seven Other Studies* (Leiden, 1969), 52.

47. Vink, "The Date and Origin of the Priestly Code in the Old Testament," 52-53.

48. E.F. Campbell *BA* 28 (1965): 21; *RB* 72 (1965): 419-20; R.J. Bull, *BASOR* 180 (1965): 39ff.; R.J. Bull, G.E. Wright, "Newly Discovered Temples on Mount Gerizim in Jordan," *HTR* 58 (1965): 234-37.

49. Grabbe, "Josephus and the Jewish Restoration," see n. 3 above, 262.

50. J.A. Montgomery, *The Samaritans* (NY, 1968), 36.

51. J. Bowman, "The History of the Samaritans," *AbrN* 18 (1978/79): 101-15.

52. Reinhard Pummer, *The Samaritans,* see n. 22 above, 36.

53. Neubauer, "Chronique samaritaine," *Journal Asiatique* 14 (1869): 410 (text), 438 (translation); and Kippenberg, *Garizim und Synagoge,* 49.

54. Neubauer, 399 (text), 434-35 (translation).

55. Philippe Bruneau, "'Les Israélites de Délos' et la Juiverie Délienne," *BCH* 106 (1982): 471.

56. Cf. the remark of Grabbe, "Josephus and the Jewish Restoration," see n. 3 above, 262 that the only aspect of the story now demonstrated to be reliable is the construction of the Samaritan temple in the late 4th century B.C.

JOSEPHUS' ATTITUDE TOWARD THE SAMARITANS:
A STUDY IN AMBIVALENCE

Louis H. Feldman

1. The Samaritans as Independent of the Jews

The Samaritans represent an excellent case study of the limits of tolerance which the mainstream of Judaism demonstrated toward the challenging movements which grew up within it.[1] Other divergent movements, such as those mentioned in the Bible--Dathan, Abiram, and Korah (Numbers 16), or the Rechabites (Jeremiah 35)[2]--apparently disappeared within a short time or are shrouded in mystery. Though Josephus claims (*Ant.* 18.11) that the Essenes, who received so much attention in antiquity, particularly from him (*War* 2. 119-161), as well as the Sadducees, existed from the most ancient times (*ek tou panu arkhaiou*), we have no actual evidence of the existence of these sects prior to the second century B.C.E. In any case, we have no references to them after the destruction of the Temple in the year 70. The Samaritans are the only such group (prior to the emergence of the Karaites in the eighth century) for whom we have a continuous history covering many centuries to the present day.

Though the Samaritans regard themselves as within the mainstream, our concern here is to delineate the attitude of the mainstream of Jews or Israel toward the Samaritans. To do so we have eight major sources--the Bible, pagan writers, Josephus, the New Testament, Church Fathers, the Talmudic rabbis, inscriptions, and the writings of the Samaritans themselves.[3] Each of them presents problems. Most of these are brief, late, apologetical, and/or polemical.

The Bible uses the name *Shomronim* once (2 Kings 17:29), but probably with the meaning "Samarians" rather than "Samaritans." The references in pagan writers are extraordinarily few and brief. Such a passage as that in the first-century Curtius Rufus (*Histories of Alexander the Great* 4.8.34.9-11) does establish the independent existence of the Samaritans.[4] He mentions the Samaritans as such. He, like other pagans, must have been aware of the separate existence of the Jews, who were so numerous and influential at this time. The references in the New Testament (Matthew 10:5; Luke 9:52, 10:29-37, 17:11-19; John 4:1-42, 8:48; Acts 8:25) are few and in a polemical context. The reference in the third-century Church Father Origen (*Against Celsus* 2.13), which states that after the Emperor Antoninus Pius had removed the prohibition of circumcision for Jews he still forbade the Samaritans to circumcise their sons, indicates that he chose to differentiate Jews from

Samaritans. The references to Samaritans in the Church Father Epiphanius, dating from the fourth century, are certainly in a polemical context.

Those in the rabbinic writings are more numerous. The redaction of the works is at the end of the second century at the earliest and, in the case of many of the *midrashim,* well into the Middle Ages; they, too, are in a polemical context. Even the dramatic discoveries of papyri at Samaria[5] and the references to Samaritans in an inscription on the island of Delos in the Aegean Sea add little to our knowledge of the Samaritans, let alone to our perception of how they were regarded by the mainstream of Jews.

In the case of the Samaritans' own literature, very little of it, with the exception of the Scriptures, Targumim, and liturgies, can be definitely ascribed to the older period,[6] prior to the Middle Ages. Thus, we are left with Josephus as the main source for knowledge of the Samaritans over a period of centuries and, in particular, for the attitude of the Jews toward them. Even in Josephus, we cannot always be sure that the word which is translated "Samaritans" may not refer to "Samarians," that is, the inhabitants, not necessarily Samaritans, of Samaria. Josephus, too, has his prejudices; but he is less prejudiced than some have thought, particularly in the *Jewish War*. In any case, we shall note a good deal of ambiguity in his attitude.

Josephus would have us believe that he attempted to be objective: he tells us (*Life* 10-11) that he made a thorough investigation of the Pharisees, Sadducees, and Essenes, submitted himself to hard training while passing through each of the three, and spent three years with a hermit named Bannus. The fact that he says (*Life* 10) that there are three sects--namely the three which he successively joined--indicates that he did not regard the Samaritans as a Jewish sect. The fact that in his rebellious youth he did not experiment with living as a Samaritan confirms this. Though the Jerusalem Talmud (*Sanhedrin* 10.6.29c) speaks of twenty-four sects of heretics, Josephus speaks of the sects as three in number, despite the fact that, on three additional occasions (*War* 2.119-166, *Ant.* 13.171-173, 18.11-22), he refers to *the* sects. He adds the Fourth Philosophy sect only to the last description as a background for the events leading to the Jewish uprising against the Romans in his own day.

One common characteristic of the three sects is their antiquity. According to Josephus (*Ant.* 18.11), they have existed from the most ancient times; the other sects of which the Talmud speaks were apparently of more recent origin or they were apparently much less important or influential. The Samaritans, even according to their most bitter opponents, possessed antiquity and certainly in Josephus' day were numerous, important, and influential. Indeed, one would have thought that Josephus would include the Samaritans as one of the sects of Judaism, since they are similar to the Sadducees, who likewise did not accept such a basic principle as the Oral Torah. In terms of basic philosophy, one might argue that they are no more different from the mainstream of Judaism than the monastic-like Essenes, the main portion of whom refused to obey the crucial commandment of "be fruitful and multiply" and who, like the Samaritans, refused to offer or were debarred from offering sacrifices in the Temple (*Ant.* 18.19).

There are a number of indications that Josephus looked upon the Samaritans as a nation (*ethnos*) (*Ant.* 10.184, 17.20, 18.85), fully parallel to, and independent of the Jews, with political aspirations of their own. Hence, Samaritanism was unlike Christianity, which did not thus define itself. The very fact that he calls the Samaritans an "ethnos" is itself significant. An exhaustive examination of Josephus' use of this word indicates that he generally reserves it for either the Jewish nation or the Jewish people, whether in Judaea or in the Diaspora (253 times); or for other nations[7] (124 times)--Idumaeans, Arabs, Gauls, Parthians, Pamphylians, Africans, Philistines, Alani, Medes, Cappadocians, Ethiopians, Moabites, Canaanites, Amalekites, Sikimites, Assyrians, Ammanites, Syrians, Ituraeans, and Germans. He speaks (*Ant.* 17.20) of someone of Samaritan origin "ethnos," where the term implies a categorization that depends upon birth in a nation, not upon adherence to a creed or a set of practices, hence, not as a variety of Judaism. On three occasions he uses "ethnos" to indicate tribes within the Jewish nation--namely the Hebrew tribes ruled by Saul and David (*Ant.* 6.63, 7.390) and the kinsmen within the Jewish state at the time of the outbreak of the revolution against the Romans (*War* 4.278). On seventeen occasions he employs it to indicate ethnic groups within a geographical entity, whether in the Persian Empire (*Ant.* 11.186, 187, 194, 215, 216, 272, 283, 285); in Egypt (*Ant.* 10.222, *Against Apion* 1.137); in Batanaea (*Ant.* 18.106); in Galilee (*Ant.* 12.331, *Life* 44, 45, 82); or the tribes allegedly removed from Cuthos which became the Cuthaeans (Samaritans, *Ant.* 9.279, 288). The last two cases indicate that Josephus looked upon the Samaritans as an ethnic entity rather than as a religious group or sect. In fact, and again very significantly, Josephus, despite the fact that he uses the word "ethnos" very frequently--401 times to be exact--he never employs it to refer to one of the sects of Judaism--whether Pharisees, Sadducees, Essenes, or Fourth Philosophy--or any other religious grouping.

In his account of their origin (*Ant.* 9.279, 288-291), Josephus clearly looks upon the Samaritans as non-Jews who were brought from Persia to

Samaria by the Assyrians. They are coupled with the Idumaeans and the people of Coele-Syria and are distinct from the Jews. We find confirmation from the fact that the Persian king, Darius I, commands them to give up the villages which they had taken from the Jews (*Ant.* 11.61). It is clear that they are not Jews, inasmuch as they are listed (*Ant.* 11.174) with the Ammnites, Moabites, and all those living in Coele-Syria as continually plotting against and killing the Jews. And there is no indication either in the Bible or in Josephus that they were ever converted to Judaism through circumcision or through any other formal way.

The Bible (2 Kings 17:25) states that the Samaritans at first did not worship the Hebrew God. It states that the king of Assyria took the initiative to send them one of the priests of the ten tribes of Israel in order to teach them how to fear the Lord. Josephus, despite his obvious prejudice against the Samaritans, assigns the initiative to the Samaritans (*Ant.* 9.289): it is they who consult an oracle which tells them that they will gain deliverance from the pestilence that has afflicted them if they will worship the Hebrew God. It is they who send envoys to the king of Assyria asking him to send priests from the captives that he has taken in the war with the Kingdom of Israel. The implication is that they are genuinely seeking to be properly converted to Judaism. Josephus then editorializes (*Ant.* 9.291), and bitterly remarks that the Samaritans alter their attitude according to circumstance: when they see the Jews prospering they call them kinsmen, claiming (obviously falsely, from Josephus' point of view) that they are descended from Joseph; but when they see that the Jews are in trouble they declare themselves to be of a different race having nothing in common with them.

Further indication that Josephus regarded the Samaritans as being distinct from the Jews may be seen in the statement (*Ant.* 11.88.97): when the Jews were rebuilding the city of Jerusalem, the Samaritans accused them of fortifying the city for the purpose of revolt. Moreover, Josephus adds an extra-Biblical account (*Ant.* 11.114) of the Samaritans inflicting injuries upon the Jews in Palestine upon this occasion, and the consequent appeal of the Jews to King Darius of Persia.

That Josephus looked upon the Samaritans as utterly distinct from the Jews may also be seen in his account (*Ant.* 11.302-303) of the marriage of Nikaso, the daughter of the Samaritan Sanballat (*Ant.* 11.392) to Manasseh, the brother of the high priest Jaddus (Jaddua). Josephus adds that Sanballat's motive was to win the goodwill of the entire Jewish nation. Therefore, it is clear that Sanballat himself, as a Samaritan, was not a Jew. Josephus, moreover, goes further (*Ant.* 11.306) in stating explicitly that the Samaritan woman whom Manasseh had married was a foreigner (*allophuloi*, "of another race"). This same word is used frequently in the *Septuagint* with reference to the Philistines, indicating that Josephus regards the Samaritans as being utterly different from Jews. Indeed, Josephus states (*Ant.* 11.307) that the elders in Jerusalem regarded this marriage as the beginning of intercourse with foreigners (again using the same word, *"allophulous"*).

Josephus would have us believe that the Samaritans looked upon themselves as distinct from the Jews. When Sanballat petitioned Alexander the Great to grant permission for a temple to be built (*Ant.* 11.322), he explained that he had a son-in-law who was the brother of the high priest of the Jews. The clear implication is that Sanballat himself did not identify with the Jews. Furthermore, when Sanballat says that many others of Manasseh's countrymen (*homoethnon*)[8] wish to build a temple, again the implication is that many members of the ethnic group known as Jews (since Manasseh was a Jew), in contrast presumably to Samaritans and other non-Jews, wished to build the temple.

Another indication that, in Josephus' eyes, the Samaritans are utterly distinct from the Jews is to be found in his account (*Ant.* 12.7-10): in the latter part of the fourth century B.C.E., Ptolemy Soter took many captives in Judaea and Samaria and settled them in Egypt. Josephus proceeds to differentiate between the Jews whom he brought and the others who joined them and, on the other hand, the Samaritans. The Samaritans, he says, quarreled with the descendants of the Jews, the chief point of contention being the sanctity of their respective temples in Jerusalem and on Mount Gerizim. The Jews and the Samaritans were each determined to keep alive their fathers' way of life and customs.

We are told (*Ant.* 12.156) that the Samaritans did much mischief to the Jews a century later by laying waste their land and by carrying off slaves. It is again clear that they are separate groups: if the Samaritans were a Jewish sect in Josephus' eyes, he would have said that the Samaritans did mischief to *other* Jews. Again, when describing (*Ant.* 13.74-79) the quarrel between the Jews in Alexandria and the Samaritans with respect to the merits of their respective temples, Josephus cites this as a case of *the* Jews vs. *the* Samaritans.[9]

We may further ask, as does Mor,[10] why, if the Samaritans were a sect of Jews, and if they both suffered the same fate during the persecutions enacted by Antiochus Epiphanes, they did not co-operate and join together with the Maccabees against the Seleucids. It is clear that the two groups had different goals and could not co-operate even when facing a common enemy. Indeed, according to Josephus (*Ant.* 12.258-261), when the Samaritans appealed to Antiochus Epiphanes, they clearly sundered themselves off from the Jews by explaining that their ancestors had observed the day called the Sabbath by the Jews and by commending the king for having dealt with the Jews as their wickedness deserved. In turn, they petitioned Antiochus not to punish them for the charges of which the Jews were guilty, insisting that they were distinct in race (*genei*) and customs.

Moreover, in view of the support which the Samaritans apparently gave to Antiochus Epiphanes, one would have expected Judas Maccabee to undertake to punish them as he did renegade Jews (1 Maccabees 7:6). And yet, neither 1 Maccabees nor Josephus says anything about such a campaign, perhaps because Judas regarded them as being non-Jews in the first place.[11]

That the Jews and Samaritans are distinct from one another is again evident from Josephus' account (*Ant.* 13.74-79) of the quarrel, as he states it, between *the* Jews in Alexandria and *the* Samaritans who worshipped at the temple on Mount Gerizim: each group asserted that its temple had been built in accordance with the laws of Moses.

Further evidence that the Samaritans are distinct from the Jews may be seen in Josephus' account (*Ant.* 13.275) of King John Hyrcanus' attack on Samaria in the second century B.C.E.: Hyrcanus did so because he hated the Samaritans on account of the injuries which they had inflicted upon the people of Marisa, "who were colonists and allies of the Jews." The fact that Josephus contrasts the Samaritans with allies of the Jews indicates that he regards the Samaritans as non-Jews.[12]

There is another indication (*Ant.* 17.319) that the Samaritans are not regarded as Jews by Josephus: after the death of Herod, the Emperor Augustus treated them differently from the Jews. A fourth of their tribute was remitted by the Emperor because they had not joined the rest of the people in revolting. Inasmuch as political status, at least at that time, was an integral part of Judaism, failure to join the Jews was tantamount to a declaration that they were not Jews.

A further indication that they are thought of by Josephus as distinct from the Jews is the fact that on at least two occasions (*War* 2.111, [=*Ant.* 17.342], 2.239-245 [=*Ant.* 20.132-136]) they send delegations separate from the Jews to Roman authorities; and in neither the *Jewish War* nor in the *Antiquities* do the Samaritans, in either the first century B.C.E. or in the first century C.E., give any indication of claiming kinship with the Jews.[13] There is likewise a contrast between the Jews and the Samaritans in Josephus' statement (*War* 2.111, *Ant.* 17.342) that on coming to power, the ethnarch Archelaus, himself the son of a Samaritan woman, treated not only the Jews but even the Samaritans with great brutality, whereupon, we are told, both parties sent deputies to the Emperor to denounce him. That the Samaritans are not merely a sect within Judaism would seem to be indicated by the fact that we never hear of separate delegations of, for example, Pharisees and Sadducees.

Moreover, it seems most probable that the Samaritan leader (*Ant.* 18.85-87) who, in approximately the year 36, attracted such a large crowd and who was ruthlessly suppressed by Pontius Pilate was viewed by him as having messianic pretensions and hence as a political rebel somewhat similar to John the Baptist as portrayed by Josephus (*Ant.* 18.116-119). The fact that his followers appeared in arms (*Ant.* 18.86), and that when the procurator Pontius Pilate came with his armed forces they fought him in a pitched battle (*Ant.* 18.87), would support the hypothesis that they intended to revolt against the Romans and to establish an independent state.[14] The fact that the Samaritans (*Ant.* 18.88) had their own council (*boule*) is further indication that they were independent of the Jews. If, immediately thereafter, the Samaritans (*Ant.* 18.88) appealed to Vitellius, the Roman governor of Syria, charging Pilate with reckless slaughter, this does not prove that the real aim of those who gathered at Mount Gerizim was not messianic independence; it may indicate only that the Samaritan leaders did not share the enthusiasm of the messianic pretender and of the multitudes who followed him. Or, alternatively, it is simply that after the fact they tried to argue that Pilate had misconstrued their aims.

We may wonder, as does Coggins,[15] that Josephus, in recounting this episode, shows almost no sign of anti-Samaritan feeling, this despite the fact that the Samaritans, in being armed, were certainly reminiscent of the Fourth Philosophy revolutionaries and despite the fact that in the *Antiquities,* as Schwartz[16] has noted, Josephus is far more anti-Samaritan than in the *Jewish War;* but in this respect Josephus is similar to Tacitus, who though bitterly anti-Jewish, nevertheless is careful to give the impression of writing *sine ira et studio,* that is impartially, by noting (*Histories* 5.10.1) the responsibility of the procurators in provoking the Jews to rebellion. Moreover, Josephus may well have been influenced to adopt a more positive view of this incident in view of the fact that the Samaritans did not apparently, after all, join the Jews in the great rebellion against the Romans in 66-74--still another indication that the Samaritans did not regard themselves as Jews and were not so regarded by the Jews, inasmuch as the revolutionaries, as we are told (*War* 2.562, *Gittin* 56a), forced those Jews who were lukewarm or opposed to the uprising to join them.   This is particularly revealing, inasmuch as we hear (*War* 3.308), though this may reveal Josephus' animus against the Samaritans, that they were themselves contemplating the prospect of revolt.   The fact, however, that early in the war the Samaritans on Mount Gerizim were slain in such large numbers--11,600, according to Josephus (*War* 3.315)--and to a man by the Roman general Cerealius would seem to indicate that they were armed and that they offered resistance.

Still another incident which would seem to confirm that the Samaritans are distinct from the Jews is recounted at length by Josephus in both the *War* (2.232-246) and the *Antiquities* (20.118-136), and confirmed by Tacitus (*Annals* 12.54), where we are told of a conflict between the Galilaeans and the Samaritans which resulted in the murder of some Galilaeans and the sack of several Samaritan villages in revenge. The fact that the attacks occurred while the Galilaeans were on their way through Samaritan territory to the Temple at the time of one of the three pilgrimage festivals would serve to indicate that the conflict was not between those Jews who lived in Galilee as against those who lived in Samaria but rather between the adherents of the Temple in Jerusalem and those who refused to accept the sacrificial cult, namely, those who did not accept the centrality of the Jerusalem Temple, that is, one must assume, the Samaritans.   Moreover, it seems unlikely that the words "Galilaeans" and "Samaritans" are mere geographical terms, inasmuch as we do not hear elsewhere of any such dispute, whereas, according to Josephus (*Ant.* 20.118), it was the "custom" of the Galilaeans to pass through Samaritan territory on their way to the Temple, indicating that they frequently did so. That Tacitus (*Annals* 12.54.2), in connection with this incident, speaks of the feud between the Jews and the Samaritans as longstanding shows, at the very least, that he regarded them as being separate from one another.

The fact that the Galilaeans, in revenge for the murder of several of their number by the Samaritans, urged the Jewish masses (*Ant.* 20.120) to resort to arms would indicate that the conflict was between Jews and non-Jews; we must draw the same conclusion from Josephus' remarks (*Ant.* 20.122) that the procurator Cumanus armed the Samaritans and marched out against the Jews, that (*Ant.* 20.125) the leaders of the Samaritans met with Ummidius Quadratus, the Roman governor of Syria, and accused the Jews of sacking their villages, and that the Jews, in turn (*War* 2.240, *Ant.* 20.127), blamed the Samaritans.   In his decision (*War* 2.242-243, *Ant.* 20.132) Quadratus speaks of the dispute not as being between the Samaritans and the Galilaeans but rather as being between the Samaritans and the Jews; likewise, the Emperor Claudius himself hears the case as presented by the Samaritans and the Jewish leaders (*War* 2.245, *Ant.* 20.135) and orders three of the most prominent leaders of the Samaritans to be executed. It is hard to believe that if the Samaritans were Jews the Jews would have accused them thus, knowing that if they won the Samaritans would, in all likelihood, be put to death.

If Josephus views the Samaritans in religious terms and emphasizes, in particular, the centrality for them of Mount Gerizim, this may be due to two factors in particular. In the first place, Josephus was himself a priest and, as we can see from the tremendous amount of attention that he gives to the Temple and the priesthood in the *Antiquities,* he looked upon the sacrificial cult as central. Moreover, he viewed them in religious rather than in political terms because he defined Judaism thus, opposed as he was to those groups, notably the Sicarii and the Zealots, who looked upon Judaism as primarily a political entity. But we may guess that this is a misreading of the Samaritans, who, as we can see from their several revolts to establish their independence, regarded themselves, as did the Jews, as a nation.

Finally, we may remark that there is pagan evidence, albeit from a later date, namely from the beginning of the second century, that the Samaritans constituted a separate religion; for we read (*Historia Augusta,*[17] *Quadrigae Tyrannorum* 8.3) a letter ascribed to the Emperor Hadrian, who reigned from 117 to 138, that there is no chief of the Jewish synagogue, no Samaritan, and no Christian presbyter who is not an astrologer, soothsayer, or anointer; here the Jews, Samaritans, and Christians are distinct and separate groups. A similar distinction is evident from the declaration (*Historia Augusta, Antoninus Heliogabalus* 3.5) of the Emperor Elagabalus, who reigned from 218 to 222, that the religions (*religiones*) of the Jews and the Samaritans and the rites of the Christians must be transferred to the temple which he built on the Palatine Hill in Rome.

2. The Samaritans as a Jewish Sect[18]

And yet, there are a number of indications outside of Josephus that the clear-cut division between the Jews and the Samaritans so emphasized by Josephus had not taken place until a later period. The Samaritans themselves, according to their *Sefer Ha-Yamim,* insist that they are the direct descendants of the Joseph tribes, Ephraim and Menasseh, and that they are, in fact, the true Jews. Presumably, they realized that inasmuch as in ancient times there was such great respect for antiquity[19] their legitimacy as a religious movement would be questioned unless they could prove their antiquity. Thus, Coggins[20] has noted that the Jewish community at Elephantine in the fifth century B.C.E. apparently felt no qualms about appealing[21] to the authorities in both Jerusalem and Samaria, untroubled, it would seem, by the fact that the Jews and the Samaritans were at odds with one another.

It is often stated that the fact that the Samaritans built their own temple on Mount Gerizim brought about the final break with Jerusalem. However, the mere fact that the Samaritans did not accept the Temple in Jerusalem but worshipped at their own temple on Mount Gerizim was in itself not sufficient to have them declared to be non-Jews, as we see in the case of the Temple of Onias in Leontopolis in Egypt. In that case we are told (*Mishnah, Menahoth* 13:10) that while the priests who have ministered there are disqualified from serving in the Temple in Jerusalem the sacrifices themselves in Leontopolis are not to be considered as offerings to idols.[22] We may further note, as does Hall,[23] that in no tractate of the *Mishnah* is there the slightest suggestion that the practice of idolatry exists among the Samaritans. Nor, for that matter, do the Samaritans receive any attention in the Talmudic tractate *Avodah Zarah*, which deals with idol worship among non-Jews.

The rabbis themselves were quite clearly ambivalent with regard to the status of the Samaritans, as numerous writers, most recently Schiffman,[24] have shown.[25] As late as the second century we find a dispute (*Qiddushin* 75b) between Rabbi Akiba, who says that the Samaritans embraced the Torah, that is, converted to Judaism, out of conviction, and Rabbi Ishmael, who declares that they did so out of fear and presumably were not legitimate proselytes, whereupon Rabbi Eliezer offers a midway position in stating that some of them are true proselytes while others are not.[26] Somewhat later in the century we find a dispute (*Tosefta, Terumah* 4:12 and 4:14) between Rabbi Judah the Prince and his father Rabbi Simeon II ben Gamaliel II, in which the former declares that a Samaritan is like a non-Jew, whereas the latter insists that he is like a Jew in all respects; the fact that, according to the latter, a Samaritan is *like* a non-Jew indicates that he is really a Jew.

Moreover, the *Mishnah (Berakhoth* 7:1) rules that a Samaritan may be counted as one of the three necessary for reciting a special formula in the grace after meals--an indication of their acceptance, *de facto* at least, as Jews. The ambiguous status of Samaritans is reflected in the statement ascribed to the first-century Rabbi Eliezer ben Hyrcanus (*Mishnah, Qiddushin* 4:3) that one who is of doubtful status, such as a foundling or a Samaritan, may not marry a Jew. Moreover, an anonymous passage in the *Mishnah (Kethuboth* 3:1), which may be attributed to the second-century Rabbi Nehuniah ben ha-Qanah,[27] requires a monetary penalty from a man who has sexual relations with a Samaritan girl; since non-Jewish girls are excluded from this law, apparently the Samaritan girl is regarded as Jewish or, at any rate, is not definitely a non-Jew.

That the Samaritans are not non-Jews would seem to be indicated by the anonymous *Mishnah (Sheqalim* 1:5), which states that it is not permitted to accept from a non-Jew or a Samaritan the half-shekel which all Jews are required to contribute to the Temple. Schiffman,[28] who notes that a similar passage, but not mentioning the Samaritans by name, is to be found in the *Tosefta (Sheqalim* 1:7), where it is attributed to the early second-century Rabbi Akiba. He concludes that the reference to the Samaritans was introduced into the *Mishnah* by Rabbi Judah the Prince at the end of the second century, since the view here expressed agrees with that of Judah the Prince, as noted above, in the *Tosefta, Terumah* (4:12, 4:14).

The important point, it would seem, is that the Samaritans, even though they are not treated as Jews, are here enumerated separately from non-Jews. Similarly, when it comes to the question as to whether one can assume that tithes have been taken, the Samaritan is coupled (*Mishnah, Demai* 3:4) with the *'am ha-'aretz,* who is certainly a Jew, albeit one who is not careful in such matters. In both cases, they can be relied upon not to replace the already tithed produce with untithed produce. According to this passage in the *Mishnah,* if produce is left with a non-Jew it is definitely considered to be untithed.

The anonymous ruling (*Tosefta, Pesahim* 2:1), dated to the end of the second century,[29] states that Samaritans have an obligation to abstain from eating leaven during Passover and that their leaven, if owned during Passover, may not be eaten by Jews thereafter; we must conclude that the Samaritans, at least so far as this law is concerned, are regarded as Jews or, at any rate, are not regarded as non-Jews, inasmuch as non-Jews are permitted to own leaven during Passover.

The *Mishnah (Rosh Hashanah* 2:2) states that "once the Samaritans[30] became corrupted," the rabbis decreed that the new month should be announced through messengers rather than through torches. This indicates that the Samaritans had changed in the course of time and that at some time before the end of the second century, when the *Mishnah* was redacted, the Samaritans were apparently more trustworthy. A similar point of view is reflected in the dialogue (*TJ, Avodah Zarah* 5.4.44d) between some Samaritans and Rabbi Abbahu (ca. 300 C.E.). They asked him why he regarded them as Gentiles in all ritual matters whereas the previous generation of Jews had found their food and wine acceptable. His reply was that their fathers had not corrupted their ways whereas they had. Inasmuch as the wine of Gentiles is prohibited (*Mishnah, Avodah Zarah* 2:3), it would seem that at one time, presumably before the fourth century, the Samaritans were not regarded as non-Jews.

For Josephus, as a priest, the Temple in Jerusalem was central. Even so, there are indications that he is ambivalent on the question of whether the Samaritans are really separate from Jews. Someone who did not worship at the Temple was not excluded, *ipso facto,* from the Jewish fold. We call attention to the fact that the exclusion of the Essenes from the Temple in Jerusalem (*Ant.* 18.19) did not prevent Josephus from including them in every one of his listings (*War* 2.120-161, *Ant.* 13.171, 18.18-22) as one of the sects of the Jews. Furthermore, there is every reason to believe, as Dexinger[31] remarks, that in Judaism there was more tolerance for non-fulfillment and yet belonging than in a religion such as classical Christianity, where the rational denial of religious truths leads to exclusion.

It would seem significant that Josephus, despite his numerous allusions to the Samaritans, did not regard the difference in the text of the Pentateuch or the rejection of the Oral Torah or the difference in the calendar as being of sufficient importance to even mention them. The fact that the Samaritans had a text of the Pentateuch which differed from that of central authorities of Judaism in Jerusalem in approximately six thousand places[32] is not in itself grounds for their being excluded from Judaism. We now see that the Dead Sea Sect had a text of the Torah which likewise differed in numerous places from the text which has come to be known as the Massoretic Text. As to the rejection of the Oral Torah, the same was true of the Sadducees, who are not read out of the Jewish fold but are regarded by Josephus as one of the Jewish sects in each of his enumerations (*War* 2.119, *Ant.* 13.171, 18.16-17). As to having a different calendar--an issue which would seem to be so central in Judaism--the Dead Sea Sect likewise, with their solar calendar, differed but were apparently not read out of the fold.

Furthermore, in Josephus there are indications that the Samaritans looked upon themselves as Jews. In the first place, we may note a significant and--in view of Josephus' anti-Samaritan prejudice--a surprising change in Josephus' paraphrase of the Biblical account of the origin of the Samaritans. Where the Bible (2 Kings 17:33) states that the Cuthaeans feared the Lord but also continued to worship their own gods, in Josephus (*Ant.* 9.289-290), once the Cuthaeans are informed by an oracle that they should worship the Most High God, they ask the king of Assyria to send them some priests from the captive Israelites; and they proceed, after being instructed by them, to worship this God. Hence, this would imply that they had been fully converted to

Judaism. There is thus no indication in Josephus that the Samaritans practiced any kind of syncreticism, whereas if there were we would have expected Josephus, in view of his hostility to the Samaritans, which is much stronger in the *Antiquities* than in the *War,* to mention this.

Furthermore, we are told (*Ant.* 9.291) that when the Samaritans see the Jews prospering they call them their kinsmen (*"suggeneis,"* that is related by birth), on the ground that they are descended from Joseph and thus are related to them through their common origin, but that when they see that the Jews are in trouble they say that they have nothing in common with them and declare that they are aliens of another race (*alloethneis*). The fact, as noted by Hall,[33] that in neither the *War* nor in the *Antiquities* does he give any examples where the Samaritans, during the century before and after Jesus, deny their kinship to the Jews shows that in Josephus' own day the Samaritans had not yet broken away completely from Judaism, at least in their own perception.

In addition, we hear (*Ant.* 11.85) that when the Jews, after the return from Babylonian captivity, were rebuilding the Temple, the Samaritans approached the chiefs of the Jewish families and asked to have a share in the building. Their argument was that they had been no less loyal than the returning Jews in their worship of God, that is, in effect, that they were sincere converts. Their help is declined on technical grounds, namely that the kings of Persia had granted permission only to the returnees. The very fact, however, that the high priest (*Ant.* 11.87) says that he will allow them to worship in the Temple is evidence that he regarded them as Jews, inasmuch as non-Jews were forbidden to enter the Temple precincts (*War* 5.194, 6.125; *Ant.* 15.417).

The marriage of Manasseh, brother of the high priest, to Nikaso, daughter of Sanballat the Samaritan (*Ant.* 11.302-312), presents another illustration. A close reading of the fact that the elders in Jerusalem considered this marriage a stepping-stone for those who might wish to marry foreigners would indicate that they regarded the marriage itself to be legal. Perhaps they looked upon the Samaritans as one of the groups whom the high priest and his family were forbidden to marry, but they feared that it would lead others to go beyond the law and marry outright foreigners.[34]

Further indication that the Samaritans were, indeed, part of the Jewish people may be seen in Josephus' explanation (*Ant.* 11.340): when the Samaritans came to court Alexander, they are described as apostates (*apostaton,* "deserters, rebels") from the Jewish nation (*ethnous*), clearly implying that they were, in origin, part of the Jewish people but that they had defected. We may note that in all the other six (or seven) occasions (*Ant.* 10.220, 221; 11.22, 24; 14.433 [alternate reading]; *Against Apion* 1.135, 136) when Josephus uses the word "apostates," it always refers to a rebel, hence one who is originally part of a nation or empire. The fact that Josephus refers to the Samaritans here as apostates and hence not as foreigners but as heterodox Jews who are, indeed, of Jewish origin seems to be in direct contradiction to his statement elsewhere (*Ant.* 9.290) that they were Cuthaeans from Persia and therefore non-Jews. That Josephus is, however, biased against the Samaritans seems to be evident from the fact that Josephus not only calls them apostates but regards them as liars in that they assert that they are Jews when they see the Jews prospering.

Josephus goes on to say that when the Samaritans saw that Alexander had singularly honored the Jews, they decided to admit (*homologein*) that they were Jews. The implication is that the Samaritans really were Jews but that up until that time they had declined to acknowledge it. Josephus, with his anti-Samaritan bias, then proceeds to say (*Ant.* 11.341) that the truth is that they have no kinship with the Jews (clearly implying that others thought that they were related) but that when they see some good fortune come to the Jews, they grasp at the connection (*koinoniai*, "communion, association, partnership") with them, and say that they are related, and trace their descent from Ephraim and Manasseh, the sons of Joseph.

When, according to Josephus (*Ant.* 11.343-344), Alexander the Great asked them who they were, they replied that they were Hebrews (*Hebraioi*) but were called Sidonians of Shechem. Apparently this answer did not satisfy Alexander, or perhaps it surprised him, since he had been briefed by the Jews to regard them as non-Jews. He asked them again whether they were Jews (*Ioudaioi*).[35] Thereupon apparently drawing a distinction between Hebrews (presumably the descendants of Abraham) and Jews (the descendents of Judah in particular), they denied that they were Jews.

A hint that the Samaritans are Jews but rebellious in their views may be gathered from the fact that, according to Josephus (*Ant.* 11.346-347), after Alexander's death whenever anyone was accused by the people of Jerusalem of eating unclean food or violating the Sabbath or committing any other sin, he would flee to the Samaritans, saying that he had been unjustly expelled. It would seem unlikely that a Jew, after being expelled, would feel at home in an environment that was intrinsically removed from Judaism.

Likewise, according to Josephus (*Ant.* 12.257), when the Samaritans saw the Jews suffering misfortunes at the hands of Antiochus Epiphanes in the second century B.C.E., they no longer admitted that they were kin (*suggeneis*). The implication was that they were really related to them by birth. Similarly, in the *Second Book of Maccabees* (5:22-23), Antiochus Epiphanes regarded the Jews and the Samaritans to be a single group, inasmuch as we read that Antiochus left viceroys to maltreat the people (*to genos*), mentioning viceroys for Jerusalem and Gerizim.[36]

Again, in the dispute between the Jews and the Samaritans in the presence of Ptolemy Philometor (*Ant.* 13.74-79), it is significant that there is no reference in the remarks of the Jewish representatives to the foreign origin of the Samaritans; and both the Jews and the Samaritans assert that their respective temples had been built in accordance with the same laws of Moses.

Still another indication that they were regarded as Jews is the fact that John Hyrcanus, whose policy it was to convert non-Jews in Palestine to Judaism (*Ant.* 13.257), did not do so with the Samaritans but rather destroyed their temple (*Ant.* 13.281).

The fact that Herod, who was so eager to dispel the innuendoes of his non-Jewish ancestry, married a Samaritan (*War* 1.562, *Ant.* 17.20),[37] Malthace, indicates that he felt confident that Jewish public opinion would not look upon her as a non-Jew. Herod (*Ant.* 16.225) showed his regard for Jewish sensibilities by making the marriage of his sister Salome with Syllaeus the Arab conditional upon Syllaeus' conversion to Judaism,[38] but he apparently had no fear of adverse reaction on the part of the people to his own marriage to Malthace. There is no indication that Herod made her conversion to Judaism a condition of the marriage nor is there an indication that she converted to Judaism. Presumably she did not have to do so. Furthermore, when the son named Joseph, of Herod's brother, also named Joseph, married Olympias (*War* 1.562, *Ant.* 17.20), the daughter of Herod and Malthace, there is no indication that Herod or his brother insisted on her conversion to Judaism. Nor is there any indication that their daughter Mariamme (*Ant.* 18.134) converted to Judaism to marry Herod, the brother of Agrippa I and the grandson of Herod the Great. Apparently, the reason was that she was already regarded as Jewish.

The fact that Herod (*Ant.* 17.69) appointed a Samaritan named Antipater as his agent to take care of his son, also named Antipater, indicates that relations between Jews and Samaritans were not so strained. Herod, generally careful to avoid antagonizing his subjects without reason, would not have appointed a Samaritan if the Samaritans were regarded as clearly non-Jewish or if they were utterly hated.

Both Jews and Samaritans objected to Archelaus, son of Herod the Great by the Samaritan Malthace, on other grounds (*War* 2.111, *Ant* 17.342), but there was no objection to him as a non-Jewish king, at least as reported by Josephus, even though the Bible (Deuteronomy 17:15) specifically requires that the king be "one from your brethren," which the Talmud interprets to mean a born Jew.[39] Furthermore, there is no indication that Archelaus showed favoritism to the Samaritans; indeed, both Jews and Samaritans complained about him to the Emperor Augustus (*War* 2.111, *Ant.* 17.342).

Relations between Jews and Samaritans were not as strained as would seem evident from the statement in the New Testament (John 4:9) that Jews have no dealings with Samaritans. For example, a contemporary of Jesus, Agrippa I, later to become king of Judaea, was able (*Ant.* 18.167) to borrow the huge sum of a million drachmas from a man of Samaritan origin who happened to be a freedman of the Emperor.

Most recently further evidence has come to light indicating a Samaritan presence at Masada. This suggests that the Samaritans joined the Sicarii in the defense of Masada. Talmon[40] has now published a papyrus fragment in Samaritan handwriting which was found in a room near the synagogue at Masada. The fragment contains a reference to Mount Gerizim written as a single word, as the Samaritans write it.[41] Inasmuch as it is practically certain that this is a Samaritan fragment, the most likely conclusion is that the Samaritans were among the revolutionaries who co-operated in the defense of Masada.

In summary, the period of the Second Temple was, as Baron[42] has remarked, without doubt a prolific period in the history of Jewish sects-- twenty-four sects, according to the Jerusalem Talmud (*Sanhedrin* 10.6.29c). These sectarian movements show both great strength and variety, and we would have expected Samaritanism to be included as one of these. However, Josephus, like the rabbis, is ambivalent with regard to the Samaritans, at times referring to them as a separate national entity and at other times looking upon them as a variety of Jew. Finally, though the *Antiquities,* written a decade and a half after the *War,* is more strident in its anti-Samaritanism, there is no discernible difference between the two works on the question of whether the Samaritans are or are not an entity separate from the Jews. It would appear that the separation of the Jews and the Samaritans, like that of the Jews and the Christians, was not sudden but took place over a considerable period of time and was accompanied, as we would guess, since we are talking about Jews, by considerable debate.

Endnotes

1. Despite the profusion of scholarship on the Samaritans (see my *Josephus and Modern Scholarship (1937-1980)* [Berlin, 1984], 528-541, 946), there has been nothing like a systematic attempt to assess Josephus' attitude toward the question of whether they were or were not part of the Jewish people.   James A. Montgomery, in entitling his fundamental work *The Samaritans: The Earliest Jewish Sect* (Philadelphia, 1907), came to a premature conclusion. Recently Rita Egger, *Josephus Flavius und die Samaritaner: Eine terminologische Untersuchung zur Identitätsklarung der Samaritaner* (Freiburg and Göttingen, 1986), after systematically examining all the passages in Josephus in which he refers to Samaritans and the people who inhabited Samaria, concludes that Josephus knew that the Samaritans were not identical with the other people who lived in Samaria but that confusion was created, at least in part, by his assistants and by the translation of his work from the original Aramaic into Greek. We may respond, however, that the major references to the Samaritans are in the *Antiquities,* and that it is in the *War* and not in the *Antiquities,* as we learn from Josephus himself (*Against Apion* 1.50), that Josephus had assistants. She concludes that Josephus himself, contrary to the view generally held by scholars, was not anti-Samarian but rather viewed the Samaritans as part of the Jewish people and was objective in commenting on them; on the other hand, he was anti-Samaritan and regarded their ancestors as Persians who had settled in Samaria. But, as Egger herself admits, Josephus sometimes uses "Samarians" for both of these groups, and it would seem that Jews deliberately obscured the difference in their desire to distance themselves from both. Moreover, if, as Josephus (*Life* 12) asserts, after experimenting with the other sects, he chose to identify with the Pharisees, we would certainly expect that he would adopt the strong anti-Samaritan stance that, on the whole, marked the Pharisaic attitude, based primarily on their refusal to accept the Oral Torah and the primacy of Jerusalem.

2. Diodorus Siculus (19.9), in the name of Jerome of Cardia, speaks of the asceticism, particularly the prohibition of drinking wine, of the Nabataeans at the end of the fourth century B.C.E. in language very similar to that used by Jeremiah in describing the Rechabites.   Moreover, the *Mishnah* (*Ta'anith* 4:5) indicates that the seventh of the month of Ab was reserved for the wood offering of the family of Yonadab, the son of Rechab, the founder of the group, thus indicating that the family still survived; and we hear (*Genesis Rabbah* 98.13) that Jose ben Halafta, in the second century, claimed to be a direct descendant of the Rechabites. But there is no indication that the Rechabites survived as an organized sect.

3. To these may probably be added the reference in Ecclesiasticus 50:25-26 to the foolish people who dwell in Shechem, who, says the author, are no nation [*ethnos*]. The general interpretation, as Ferdinand Dexinger, "Limits of Tolerance in Judaism: The Samaritan Example," in E. P. Sanders et al. eds., *Jewish and Christian Self-Definition,* vol. 2:

Aspects of Judaism in the Graeco-Roman Period (Philadelphia, 1981), 104 and 335, n. 92, remarks, is that the Samaritans are here referred to.

4. The Samaritans are here mentioned as having burned the Macedonian governor, Andromachus, who had been placed in charge of Syria during Alexander the Great's sojourn in Egypt. According to Curtius Rufus, those Samaritans who were responsible were punished by Alexander after his return in 331 B.C.E. Because we know from Josephus (*Ant.* 11.321-345) that the Samaritans and the Jews went to great lengths in vying with one another in courting Alexander's favor, we may assume that Curtius Rufus knew enough to distinguish the two groups.

5. See Frank M. Cross, "The Discovery of the Samaria Papyri," *Biblical Archaeologist* 26 (1963): 110-121; "Aspects of Samaritan and Jewish History in Late Persian and Hellenistic Times," *Harvard Theological Review* 59 (1966): 201-211; and "Papyri of the Fourth Century B.C. from Daliyeh," in David N. Freedman and Jonas C. Greenfield, eds., *New Directions in Biblical Archaeology* (Garden City, 1969), 60-64.

6. See the discussion by R. J. Coggins, "Samaritan Traditions," in his *Samaritans and Jews: The Origins of Samaritanism Reconsidered* (Atlanta, 1975), 116-131.

7. Salo W. Baron, *A Social and Religious History of the Jews,* vol. 1 (New York and Philadelphia, 1952), 168, is incorrect when he states that next to the Jews the Samaritans are the only group in Palestine's heterogeneous population to merit the designation *ethnos* in Josephus' *Antiquities.* The term is also found with reference to the Idumaeans (*War* 1.123, *Ant.* 14.300), the Philistines (*War* 5.384), the Moabites (*Ant.* 1.206, 10.182), the Canaanites (*Ant.* 3.301, 4.3, 4.300, 5.49, 5.55, 5.58, 5.88), the Amalekites (*Ant.* 6.138, 9.188), and the Ituraeans (*Ant.* 13.319).

8. Dexinger (1981), n. 3, 103, argues that the use of this term indicates that the Samaritans regard themselves as fellow countrymen of Jews, but a closer look at the context indicates that the fellow countrymen are either Manasseh's fellow countrymen or perhaps (if we read *heautoi*) his own fellow countrymen, but with no indication that the Jews and Samaritans are fellow countrymen.

9. Stanley J. Isser, *The Dositheans: A Samaritan Sect in Late Antiquity* (Leiden, 1976), 5-11, argues that this narrative is clearly not historical but a typological legend: the story of rivals arguing before a ruler on condition that the loser be put to death.

10. Menachem Mor, "Samaritan History: The Persian, Hellenistic and Hasmonaean Period," in Alan D. Crown, ed., *The Samaritans* (Tübingen, 1989), 15.

11. James D. Purvis, *The Samaritan Pentateuch and the Origin of the Samaritan Sect* (Cambridge, Mass. 1968), 112-113, speculates that perhaps the Samaritans supported the Maccabean revolt and notes that, according to Samaritan traditions, there were three significant religious movements in Palestine during the Hasmonean period, namely the Pharisees, the Sadducees, and the Hasidim, and that the last of these was made up of Samaritans. According to 1 Maccabees (2:42), at the beginning of the revolt, Mattathias

received the support of the Hasideans or Hasidim. Purvis suggests two other possibilities, namely that the Samaritans might have been dealt with harshly by Judas or that the silence of Josephus at this point indicates that the Samaritans were of no great concern to Judas.

12. R. J. Coggins, "The Samaritans in Josephus," in Louis H. Feldman and Gobei Hata, eds., *Josephus, Judaism, and Christianity* (Detroit, 1987), 267, is here unnecessarily skeptical about the translation "Samaritans," and says that the Greek word here, *Samareusin,* may also mean "Samarians," that is, merely inhabitants of Samaria, many of whom, of course, were not Samaritans.

13. Coggins, 267, is consequently mistaken when he declares that all the allusions to the Samaritans in the period of Roman rule that have survived imply that they were a religious group within the broader spectrum of Judaism.

14. Coggins, 267-268, objects to my translation (*Josephus,* vol. 9, Loeb Classical Library [London, 1965], 61) of the word "ethnos" as used by Josephus with regard to the Samaritans (*Ant.* 18.85) by "nation," arguing that this seems too limited and precise; he says that "people" would probably convey the sense more satisfactorily. But if my appraisal of this particular incident is correct, it is precisely a political uprising that Josephus is describing; and the Samaritans themselves certainly looked upon themselves as a nation, albeit a nation in subjection. In an unpublished paper, "Josephus on Jewish-Samaritan Relations under Roman Rule (63 B.C.E. - 70 C.E.)," which he has been kind enough to send me, Aryeh Kasher argues that the Samaritans were armed not because of fear of the Roman procurator but rather because of their desire to take precautions against a possible attack by their domestic rivals, the citizens of the Sebastean *polis.* But we may remark that the fact that they had been gathered by a messianic-like leader would indicate that their aim was nothing less than complete independence.

15. Coggins, 268.

16. Seth Schwartz, *Josephus and Judaean Politics* (Leiden, 1990), 83, n. 100. We may note that the whole incident is omitted from the account of Pilate's procuratorship in the *War* (2.169-177). That Josephus is more favorably inclined toward the Samaritans in the *War* than in the *Antiquities* may also be seen in the fact that he omits from his account of Coponius' procuratorship in the *War* (2.117-118) the incident, so damning to the Samaritans, of the scattering of human bones in the Temple precincts by the Samaritans (*Ant.* 18.29-30). Similarly, a comparison of the account in the *War* (2.232-246) with the account in the *Antiquities* (20.118-136) of the conflict between the Galilaeans and the Samaritans during the procuratorship of Cumanus reveals the same greater damning of the Samaritans in the *Antiquities;* thus, for example, in the *War* (2.233) Cumanus treats the request of the Jews to punish the Samaritan murderers as less important than other affairs on his hands, whereas in the *Antiquities* (20.119) Cumanus is actually bribed by the Samaritans and consequently neglects to punish them.

17. To be sure, Ronald Syme, *Ammianus and the Historia Augusta* (Oxford, 1968), 219, argues at length that the *Historia Augusta* is a historical romance by a fraudulent author, but he admits (177) that a wealth of valuable details can be disengaged from it. The author, he remarks (204), "comports himself as the new Suetonius, and he enters into competition with the historians, modestly adding novel and precise detail, the product of scholarly research."

18. Coggins, see n. 12 above, 258, says that it is certainly possible that the fact that Samaria is included in Josephus' description of Jewish territory (*War* 3.48-50) is evidence that the Samaritans were not distinguished from the rest of the Jews except insofar that they were heterodox. But we may counter by saying that the fact that Samaria is included in Jewish territory does not mean that there was no separation between Samaritans and Jews. Rather, this indicates that the province of Samaria was in Jewish hands.

19. Cf. the remark of Celsus (ap. Origen, *Against Celsus* 1.14) equating "ancient" with "wise." Indeed, for Celsus, as Henry Chadwick, *Early Christian Thought and the Classical Tradition: Studies in Justin, Clement, and Origen* (New York, 1966), 23, remarks, it is axiomatic that nothing can be both new and true. Hence, Origen's repeated insistence in that treatise that Christianity is not new but rather a continuation of Judaism.

20. Coggins, see n. 12 above, 264.

21. See James R. Pritchard, *Ancient Near Eastern Texts,* 3rd ed. (Princeton, 1969), 492.

22. It is also possible that there was a temple at 'Araq el-Emir in Transjordan. A palace built there by Hyrcanus of the House of Tobias in the early part of the second century B.C.E. that has been excavated has been thus identified by Paul W. Lapp, "The Second and Third Campaigns at 'Araq-el-Emir," *Bulletin of the American Schools of Oriental Research* 171 (1963): 8-39; and by Edward F. Campbell, "Jewish Shrines of the Hellenistic and Persian Periods," in Frank M. Cross, ed., *Symposia Celebrating the Seventy-Fifth Anniversary of the Founding of the American Schools of Oriental Research 1900-1975* (Cambridge, Mass., 1979), 162-164. Menahem Haran, *Temples and Temple-Service in Ancient Israel: An Inquiry into the Character of Cult Phenomena and the Historical Setting of the Priestly School* (Oxford, 1978), disputes this view, inasmuch as, he says, it does not fit in with the historical circumstances of that time, since, unlike Leontopolis, which was some distance away from Jerusalem, 'Araq el-Emir was not. But, in any case, we do not hear anywhere that those who built such a temple or sacrificed there are declared to be non-Jews.

23. Bruce W. Hall, *Samaritan Religion from John Hyrcanus to Baba Rabba: A Critical Examination of the Relevant Material in Contemporary Christian Literature, the Writings of Josephus, and the Mishnah* (Sydney, 1987), 302.

24. Lawrence H. Schiffman, "The Samaritans in Tannaitic Halakah," *Jewish Quarterly Review* 75 (1984-85): 323-350.

25. A major difficulty in considering the question of the rabbinic attitude toward the Samaritans is that in the printed editions of rabbinic texts. Christian censors substituted the word *"Kuthim"* (i.e. Samaritans) for various terms for non-Jews. See William Popper, *The Censorship of Hebrew Books* (New York, 1969), 59.

26. In the tractate *Kuthim* (Higger, 66) even Rabbi Ishmael agrees that originally the Samaritans were genuine proselytes.

27. See Schiffman, 333.

28. Schiffman, 337.

29. See Schiffman, 348.

30. The Cambridge manuscript has *"ha-minim"* rather than "Samaritans," but, as Schiffman, 345, n. 85, remarks, this must be an error.

31. Cf. Dexinger, 112: "Put in Christian theological terms, this would mean that Judaism can have not only a church of sinners as in Christianity, but also a 'church' of heretics."

32. Most of these are, to be sure, superficial and often merely of an orthographical nature, but there are a number of variants of a more fundamental kind. See Martin J. Muller, "The Transmission of the Biblical Text" in Martin J. Muller and Harry Sysling, eds., *Mikra: Text, Translation, Reading and Interpretation of the Hebrew Bible in Ancient Judaism and Early Christianity* (Assen, 1988), 95-96.

33. Hall, 167.

34. See Schiffman, 334.

35. A similar distinction is apparently made by Theodotus, the author of an epic poem, which, according to Alexander Polyhistor (fragment 1, lines 3, 5-6, as cited by Eusebius, *Praeparatio Evangelica* 9.22.1), is entitled "On the Jews" (*Peri Ioudaion*); but in the poem itself the term used to describe the Jewish people, both in his own summary of the contents (fragment 2, line 1, as cited by Eusebius, *Praeparatio Evangelica* 9.22.2) and in the lines of poetry actually quoted from Theodotus (fragment 4, line 18, as cited by Eusebius, *Praeparatio Evangelica* 9.22.6), is not "Jews" but "Hebrews" (*Hebraioi*). It is usually said that Theodotus was a Samaritan, inasmuch as the poem seems to be preoccupied with Shechem, the "sacred city" (fragment 1, line 16, as cited by Eusebius, *Praeparatio Evangelica* 9.22.1) of the Samaritans; but this view is no longer unchallenged, and there is good reason to think that the author was a Hellenistic Jew. For an exhaustive summary of the arguments on this issue see Carl R. Holladay, *Fragments from Hellenistic Jewish Authors*, vol. 2: *Poets* (Atlanta, 1989), 58-68.

36. This is the conclusion of Morton Smith, *Palestinian Parties and Politics That Shaped the Old Testament* (New York, 1971), 189-190.

37. We may guess that Herod favored Samaritans because they had a common enemy, the Hasmoneans. In the case of the Samaritans, they apparently had not forgotten that it was the Hasmonean king John Hyrcanus who had razed their temple on Mount Gerizim.

38. Aryeh Kasher, *Jews, Idumaeans and Ancient Arabs: Relations of the Jews in Eretz-Israel with the Nations of the Frontier and the Desert during the Hellenistic and Roman Era (332 BCE-70 CE)* (Tübingen, 1988), 163-164, argues that Herod's motive in insisting on Syllaeus' conversion was not consideration for public opinion in Judaea but rather a clever stratagem, namely his hope to demonstrate his senior status in the political partnership which was about to be formed between Syllaeus and himself. Syllaeus' reason, namely that if he submitted to conversion he would be stoned to death by the Arabs, was just an excuse, says Kasher. However, if we may judge from the similar statement (*Ant.* 20.39) by Helena, the mother of Izates of Adiabene, that his conversion would produce much disaffection among his subjects, presumably because it would entail denying all other deities, we may, it would seem, take Syllaeus' explanation at face value. Kasher, in his unpublished paper (above, n.14), says that Herod should not be suspected of wishing to respect Jewish religious law in that he did not even refrain (*Antiquities* 15.253-254) from giving his blessing to the marriage of his sister Salome to Costobar the Idumaean, an idolater dedicated to the Cos rite. But a close examination of the passage in Josephus shows that it was not Costobar but his ancestors (*Antiquities* 15.253) who had been priests of the Cos (*Koze*) rite. Moreover, Josephus (*Antiquities* 15.254) states that Hyrcanus a century earlier had altered the way of life of the Idumaeans and had forced them to adopt the customs and laws of the Jews, that is, he had converted them forcibly to Judaism. Hence, Costobar was, it would seem, a Jew at the time of his marriage to Salome.

39. That this law was clearly meaningful at this time is to be seen from the rabbinic passage (*Mishnah, Sotah* 7:8) that when Agrippa I, a generation later, reached this passage in Deuteronomy, he burst into tears, presumably because he was part-Edomite.

40. Shmaryahu Talmon, "Fragments of Scrolls from Masada," *Eretz-Israel* 20 (1989): 283-284, (in Hebrew). Talmon, in a letter to the author for which I am grateful, notes that Yigael Yadin, the excavator of Masada, did not identify the fragment as Samaritan but rather suggested that its lettering be compared with the writing on the coins from the revolt. To date none of the fragments found at Masada has been submitted to a Carbon 14 test, and there is no plan to do so. The technique cannot be easily applied to very small fragments, inasmuch as some of the material is destroyed in the process. In addition, the margin of error is too large when one is concerned with comparatively restricted time spans. A new method of applying the Carbon 14 test has been used on some Qumran fragments which allows for a margin of error of no more than 25 or 30 years, but the results of these tests, taken in July, 1990, have not yet been made known. As to palaeographical criteria, they cannot be easily established, since we have no examples of the early Samaritan script on soft material. Lapidary inscriptions from Mount Gerizim which are available cannot easily be compared with the Masada papyrus, inasmuch as the writing technique is very different. Talmon cautiously declines to conclude from this small find that the Samaritans joined the Sicarii in the defense of

Masada, though he is convinced of a Samaritan presence at Masada, just as the fragment of *Shirot Olat Hashabbat* found at Masada, as well as some other small fragments which he has published, appear to indicate the presence of Qumranians at Masada. Pummer, in a letter to the author for which I am grateful, has expressed doubt as to whether the writing on this papyrus is distinctively Samaritan. He thinks that the writing is a palaeo-Hebrew script that was used in other writings of the time from Qumran.

41. For a similar spelling see the inscription discovered in 1979 in Delos and published by Pierre Bruneau, "Les Israélites de Delos et la juiverie délienne," *Bulletin de Correspondance Hellénistique* 106 (1982): 465-504; and commented upon by A. Thomas Kraabel, "New Evidence of the Samaritan Diaspora Has Been Found on Delos," *Biblical Archaeologist* 47 (1984): 44-46; and "Synagoga Caeca: Systematic Distortion in Gentile Interpretations of Evidence for Judaism in the Early Christian Period," in Jacob Neusner and Ernest S. Frerichs, eds., *"To See Ourselves as Others See Us": Christians, Jews, "Others" in Late Antiquity* (Chicago, 1985), 220-224. Reinhard Pummer, "Argarizin: A Criterion for Samaritan Provenance?," however, argues that the mere fact that Mount Gerizim is written as a single word, *"Hargerizim,"* is not necessarily proof of Samaritan provenance, especially since the *Vetus Latina,* which is certainly not a Samaritan document, twice (2 Maccabees 5:23 and 6:2) has the form *"Argarizim,"* and since the fragments of Giessen papyri (13, 19, 22, 26), which most probably do not belong to the Samareitikon, have the form *"Argarizim."* I wish to express my gratitude to Reinhard Pummer for calling my attention to his article on this subject.

42. Baron, *A Social and Religious History,* see n. 7 above, 2.26.

SAMARITANISM—JUDAISM OR ANOTHER RELIGION?

Benyamim Tsedaka

According to early sources, the ancient Israelite religion was created as a consolidation of oaths and covenants. The promise which G-d made to Abraham, Isaac and Jacob concerned the nature of ties between the Israelites and their land: the Mount Sinai Covenant concerned itself with the significance between the Israelites and their Pentateuch; the Moab Covenant uniting the two substances into one essence was renewed in the Shechem Covenant between Joshua and the Israelites. Hence was the original religion of Israelites consolidated, and its patterns were determined in the ancient period of the crystallization of the people.

Initially, it was a religion designed as a covenant between the people of Israel and their G-d. Only later was the religion influenced by historical events and conflicts characterizing the materialization of the nation itself. Sources in the Bible clearly describe the historical development of the controversies creating the first schism inside the ancient Israeli religion.

The two leading forces in the ancient people of Israel--the sons of Joseph on one hand, and the tribe of Judah on the other hand--created two spiritual centers that competed with each other. The Pentateuch is character-ized by the creation of the religious foundation of the people in the northern part of the land of Israel: the building of the first altars in Shechem and its surroundings, the ceremonies of blessings and cursings on Mount Gerizim and on Mount Ebal, and the erection of the first altar in the period of settlement in a new country. But the sources also tell us about the second spiritual center founded on the other tribe's land, namely Judah on the Temple Mount in Jerusalem, which vied for the loyalty of the people of Israel. Two traditions branched out from these rival geographical and political centers. The singular tradition in the North vied with the other distinctive tradition in the South. When the southern spiritual center was created, the ancient religion of the Israelites became a "mother religion." This was the turning point in the existence of the Israeli religion.

These two traditions used different calendars, different methods of establishing the dates of the holidays, and different structures of religious and political leadership. They differed in various manners, and differed in the materialization of the text of the Pentateuch; the North presenting an "Ephraimic" version, the South a "Judaic" version.

Researchers today tend to follow the fingerprints of one of the versions in various texts of the Bible. There is special interest in the tradition impeded in the second book of Kings, chapter 17: The king of Assyria brought foreigners to Samaria to study the Manner of the G-d of that land. Less than 50 miles away from Samaria, priests serving in the Temple in Jerusalem would gladly comply with requests to teach the Pentateuch in Samaria. The king, however, sent to them priests of the Israel diaspora in Babylon, thousands of miles away from Samaria. It would seem that the unique tradition of the northern Israeli kingdom made the Assyrian king reach his decision to send priests who served in the spiritual centers there.

Differing traditions and different geographical conditions created different identities. The kingdom of Judea in the south was called "Man of Judea," and the kingdom of Israel in the north was called "Man of Israel." The Israelites in the north were called "Samaritans" because the site of the Israel kingdom was in Samaria. In the south they were called "Jews" because the site of the southern kingdom was in Judea. After the destruction of Samaria in 722 B.C. and the destruction of Judea in 586 BC, the two different names--"Samaritans," as compared to "Jews"--followed the nations to the places of exile. These names developed from one Israeli identity whose source is in the Pentateuch. We read this in Leviticus Chapter 24, verses 10-11:

> verse 10: And the son of an Israelite woman, whose father was
> an Egyptian went out among the children of Israel: And this son
> of the Israelite woman and the man of Israel strove together in
> the camp.
> verse 11: And the Israelite woman's son blasphemed the name
> of the Lord, and cursed. . . .

Already in the original stratum of the version there is a clear distinction between the title of one whose two parents are Israelites, (therefore, he is an "Israelite," or a citizen of Israel) and between one whose only one parent is from Israel (and therefore, is a "stranger"). The distinction is further seen in the Chapter 24, verse 22: Ye shall have one manner of law, as well as from the stranger, as for one of your own country.

Many hundreds of years after these verses were written, two dedication addresses, discovered on the Island of Delos in the Aegean Sea and written in Greek, identify an "Israelite" as one of the people of Israel. One address belongs to the third century B.C. The other, belonging to the second century B.C., is written: "We are Israelites who give offerings to Argarizim" (Thus the name in one word--"Argarizim").

So, as early as the third century B.C., a small and proud community of economic and political brokers on the Aegean island of Delos, far from the land of Israel, point out their national identification: "We are Israelites . . ." "We give offerings to Argarizim" is a statement of their religion. If we would find dedication addresses of the Jewish congregation in Delos, it seems would open with a similar sentence: "We are Israelites, who give offerings on the Temple Mount in Jerusalem." These dates are important for researchers to distinguish when Samaritanism and Judaism were first created as different religious traditions of the people of Israel. A Biblical researcher who determines that Judaism is the "mother religion" framework out of which other Jewish units were developed during the first centuries of the period of the Second Temple, clearly bends the historical truth.

Conditions created outside the land of Israel led to the identification of Jews and Samaritans among the people of Israel. This description of the exiled people was made by foreigners. Thus, those who were exiled from Judea were routinely called "Jews," until this identification was adopted by the exiles of Judea themselves. They were called "Jews" from then on, and identified themselves as a separate nation with traditional exclusivities that were formed during the Diaspora period and afterwards.

All the years the immigrants from Babylon in the Diaspora spent in exile before they immigrated to Jerusalem with Yeshua and Zerubbabel, and the 160 years in which the people who immigrated with Ezra and Nehemiah were in the Babylonian Diaspora, created the "Jewish Togetherness" which was founded and consolidated in Babylon. The first exiles, who returned to Jerusalem with Yeshua and Zerubbabel, experienced the last years of the kingdom of Judea, and saw the land of their forefathers before it was destroyed in 586 B.C. The last exiles returning to Judea in 428-424 B.C. were led by Ezra and Nehemiah. These two leaders were models of the Diaspora experience; their traditional life style was based upon the patterns formed and consolidated in exile. These patterns created the "Jewish Togetherness" in the Diaspora, the predecessor of the separate Jewish tradition developed from the ancient Israelite religion, and which continues in this form to our very day.

Several groups of exiles from various countries brought this "Jewish Togetherness" to Babylon. A group identity was formed out of exile life, far away from the traditional framework of life in the homeland. This "togetherness" identification defined those who did not endure the exile process as not belonging to the community. The attitude is unique to the immigrants returning to Israel with Ezra and Nehemiah.

By comparison, the people returning to Jerusalem in the sixth century integrated with the indigenous Israelites. Even their priests intermarried with these returnees, as is described in Nechemiah, Chapter 13, verse 28. But the immigrants who arrived in Jerusalem towards the end of the fifth century took strong steps to remain distinct and separate from the native people, and to eliminate any remaining ties with the native people.

The unique identity of "Jewish Togetherness" created in the Babylon diaspora was not only a social step. Distinct spiritual values enforced the "togetherness," and led to a consolidation of the group identity. This consistent position of separatism served to emphasize the identity of the group, whether one refers to differing traditions and customs, or with the actual manuscripts of the books of laws and commandments.

The gradual transformation of the Samaritan writings in the Pentateuch also results from this pattern of separatism. In Israel, other inhabitants still held to the original text of the Pentateuch. Neither these inhabitants nor their forefathers were ever exiled from the country. Their spiritual foundation relies on the books of commands and laws of the Pentateuch written in the language of the land of Israel, a language which did not reflect the spirit of the diaspora experience. In their minds and hearts, their spiritual foundation, their elders, and the ancient Israelite kingdom are all irrevocably connected with the homeland.

It is true that some of the forefathers of these inhabitants were exiled by the Assyrians and possibly by the Babylonians. In the diaspora they were called "Samaritans" because they were brought forth from Samaria. However, those Jews who returned from Babylon met the descendants of the kingdom of Samaria who were not exiled.

The members of the small community of merchants and politicians on the Island of Delos identified themselves as Israelites. That the community continued to adhere to the traditions of the land of Israel implies that it did not undergo the long period of exile which would have affected those traditions. The situation of the past can be projected on the present. Many do not differentiate between "Judaism" and "Israel" and consider the terms synonymous. Those known as Samaritans do not, as their forefathers did not, recognize the expression "Samaritan," which was made up by outsiders. They continue to adhere to the original identification of "Israelites."

During the period of the Second Temple, the people of Israel developed separate group identities and separate traditions--"Jews" and "Samaritans", "loyal to Jerusalem" and "loyal to Argrizim." The ancient Israelite religion imbedded in the Torah scrolls is the unifying element. The dividing elements, different interpretations of this same religion, brought about the two separate traditions. The Jewish tradition was formed through a lengthy process. Researchers tend to characterize the Israel-Samaritan tradition as a separate religion. One opinion among the researchers of the period of the Second Temple is that Samaritanism, as one expression of the Jewish religion, must be rejected. This results in a patronizing attitude of Judaism towards Samaritanism. The sages of the Mishnah and Talmud devoted extensive entries to the Samaritan presence, proving that they were concerned about the influences derived from Jews and Samaritans living together in the land of Israel. The sages of the Mishnah and Talmud even attributed a foreign origin to the Israeli-Samaritan, calling him by the notorious name of *Kutim.* This was intended to shunt the Jew away from the Israeli-Samaritan, and to keep the Israeli-Samaritan tradition from influencing the Jewish-Jerusalemite tradition.

However, living together for many generations in Israel also brought about occasional military and political cooperation between Jews and Samaritans against foreign rule. It also caused the formation of common traditions, found in both Jewish and Samaritan sources. Quite frequently researchers find that the Samaritans copied traditional Jewish symbols such as the menorah, the shofar, and trumpets in their material. This can be seen in archaeological excavations dating back to the Second Temple. However, the menorah, the shofar and the trumpets were not exclusively Jewish symbols, but part of the accessories of the Holy Temple of the Ark of Covenant which Moses erected in the Sinai Desert. These were the accoutrements of the ancient Israelite religion, out of which the two different and parallel traditions have developed.

The presentations of one tradition copying from the other one, expresses a patronizing attitude towards Samaritanism which exists in the Judaic research. Both traditions grew up from the common ground of the ancient Israelite religion. It is not the "Jewish religion" nor the "Samaritan religion" posed before us, but a "Jewish tradition" and a "Samaritan tradition," both daughters of the Israelite religion.

JEWISH-CHRISTIAN SECTS
AND THE JEWISH-CHRISTIAN DEBATE*

Richard A. Freund

I. "Debate and Conflict" as Models for Studying Jews and Christians in the First Four Centuries C.E.

Generally, the relations between the Jews and Christians in the first four centuries of the Common Era are described in terms of "conflict," "debate," or clear and distinguishing polemics. This model of extremely well-defined conflicts between extremely well-defined religious groups is also maintained in the investigation of the relations between Christians and Pagans in these same centuries. A. Momigliano in his 1963 work, *The Conflict Between Paganism and Christianity in the Fourth Century*,[1] for example, established the concept of "conflict" and especially "religious conflict" as an important element in the understanding of the relationship between Paganism and Christianity in the fourth century C.E.[2]

In his 1987 work, *On Pagans, Jews and Christians*, Momigliano continued to use the model of the earlier work, but goes further and gives the impression that clear religious conflict existed between three totally different and recognizable groups.[3]

Often, in studies which investigate the relationship between Judaism and Christianity in the first four centuries of the Common Era (C.E.), the "Jewish-Christian Debate"[4] is the methodological framework or terminology used to describe the way in which Jewish and Christian self-definitions functioned in this period. There have been a growing number of recent attempts to reassess this model of extreme religious conflict from a number of fronts.[5]

Those who wish to reassess the model of extreme religious conflict or debate between well-defined groups do not ignore negative pagan[6] and Jewish[7] reactions to Christianity preserved (for the most part) in Christian sources. The reinvestigation of these sources centers upon contextualizing the Christian materials and reading these materials in light of varying groups of pagans, Christians and Jews rather than a single unified "Paganism," "Judaism," and "Christianity" throughout the entire Roman empire.

The model of understanding the relationships between strictly defined Christianity and Paganism, Paganism and Judaism, and Judaism and Christianity is paralleled by other studies in Jewish and Christian relations in the first through the fourth century C.E., which also highlight extreme and well--

defined religious conflict.[8] Some writers have used the model of conflict and suggested that Christianity and Judaism were in a common struggle against paganism while simultaneously Christianity was engaged in a debate with Judaism in the first four centuries of the Common Era.[9] Others have suggested that Judaism and Paganism joined together in a common struggle against Christianity.[10]

This paper will deal with the nature of a Jewish-Christian Debate especially in light of the existence of varying definitions of Jews and Christians in the first four centuries of the Common Era. This paper questions the model of extreme religious conflict between strictly defined Jews (read: Rabbinic) and Christians (read: Nicean) as both anachronistic as well as misleading in understanding the relationship between Judaism and Christianity in these early centuries. The existence of numerous Jewish-Christian sects and their role in the self-definition process of Jews and Christians in this period may explain some problematic aspects of the early history of the Jewish-Christian debate. The problematic aspects include the total lack of evidence for a Jewish component in the Jewish-Christian debate in Jewish literature of this period, and conflictive themes raised in the early Christian polemic.

The Jewish-Christian debate is defined more clearly by the medieval example where named rabbis and church authorities actually debated (in writing or in mock trials) fundamental principles of Christian theology and biblical theology.[11] The polemical literature from both the Jewish and Christian sides in the first three (and perhaps four) centuries of the Common Era suggests an internal Jewish and Christian self-definition process rather than the medieval model of actual "debate" which pitted Jews against Christians.

II. The Jewish-Christian(s) Debate: One Debate or Two?

David Rokeah, in his dissertation at the Hebrew University in 1968, stated the following:

> Scholarly literature dealing with the polemic presents the opinion that the Jews participated in it during the period from the Bar-Kochba revolt to the days of the Emperor Julian (and even afterwards) in no less a degree than in the Hellenistic period and during the first hundred years of Christianity. Some scholars suggest that the Jews were fighting the Church for the souls of the pagans; others argue that there existed a pagan-Jewish alliance to fight Christianity, their common foe. Still other scholars admit the existence of a Christian-Jewish polemic,

but emphasize that while the Christians and Jews fought each other, both were waging a fierce battle against idolatry. However, after reading the sources themselves, I reached the conclusion that such explanations are not compatible with the simple meaning of the pagan writings, and that even the character of the Christian treatises "Adversus Judaeous" does not necessarily testify to the existence of a Christian-Jewish polemic.

He goes on to state:

In the Hellenistic-Roman period, the pagans composed special polemical treatises against the Jews, and were answered by them, whereas from the second century A.D., *no work of such a character is extant, and not even the title of such a work is mentioned in the sources.* This hiatus is filled by pagan and Christian polemical-apologetic writings. It is difficult to explain this fact unless one assumes that is reflects the polemical reality. This analogy is somewhat weakened by the existence of the Christian writings "Adversus Judaeos;" However, *no Jewish work has been preserved which might have caused their composition or which reacted to them.* If one examines the content of these writings against the Jews and their schematic construction, it becomes clear that they were not addressed to the Jews in particular but to the pagans, sectarians, heretics, and even catechumens.[12]

The existence of numerous references to the doctrines of Jewish-Christian sects in conjunction with theological issues of particular concern to Jewish-Christians and Gentile Christians preserved in Christian (Nicean) literature raises many questions. Those who wish to reassess the Jewish-Christian debate in light of the existence of varying Jewish-Christian groups must begin to question whether Christian polemical literature of the period is directed towards the Jewish/Rabbinic tradition (to which it is often compared) or to the Jewish-Christian traditions of the same period. This paper argues that the Christian polemical literature of the period, for the most part, is directed towards Jewish-Christians **and not towards Rabbinic Jews** who did not have an interest in the Christological questions raised in this literature. This may be one of the reasons why no exact Jewish component for a Jewish-Christian debate can be clearly identified in rabbinic or Jewish literature of the period. The first form of the Jewish-Christian(s) debate is, therefore, a debate between Jewish-Christian sects and other forms of Christianity developing in the period.

Additionally, this perspective does see the Jewish-Christians in a debate with Rabbinic Jews who did not have an interest in Christological questions but did have an interest in other aspects of Jewish-Christian interpretation, practice and authority within Judaism. As we shall see, this perspective presents Jewish-Christian groups of the first four centuries as involved in a two fold debate. The second form of the Jewish-Christian(s) debate is, therefore, a debate between Jewish-Christian sects and Rabbinic Jews and authority.

Not only were Jewish-Christian groups found to be heretics by differing groups of Gentile Christians (especially those who had little or no interest in historical Jewish customs and traditions), but also, almost simultaneously, they found themselves involved in a polemic with Jews who had little or no interest in Jesus but did have an interest in other areas of interpretation, practice and authority. In this two-fold Jewish-Christians debate a direct "(rabbinic) Jewish"-"Christian" confrontation is obviated or at least postponed until the internal status of the Jewish-Christians within Judaism and Christianity, was resolved.

III. The Jewish Christians Sects

The use of the term "Jewish-Christian" is itself problematic.   In general, Jewish-Christians are known by a nomenclature unique to their group, goals or leader. So for example there are Ebionites, Sethians, Nazareans, etc. not "Jewish-Christians." They are Jews in so far as they observe elements of rabbinically defined Sabbath, festival and other Jewish legal questions and Christians in so far as they have integrated some form of belief in Jesus. While many of the different Jewish-Christian groups differed as to their Jewish observance and specific belief in Jesus, all the groups mentioned in classical sources shared these characteristics.   The working definition of a Jewish-Christian in this paper will therefore be:

> 1. One who observes Jewish law, holidays and customs (generally defined by rabbinic texts-especially Saturday observance of the Sabbath, circumcision, and 14th of Nisan Passover),

2. One who professes a belief of some kind in Jesus as an important prophet, divine or super-human character, or oftentimes in an ambiguous role as simply "Messiah,"

3. A Jew (either by birth, conversion or identification).

Not much is known about the existence of specific groups within the earliest ranks of Christianity in the late first century and early second century C.E. The designation "Jewish-Christians" is problematic even in the early second century C.E. and often anachronistic or anticipatory when speaking of the first generations of Jewish followers of Jesus, James, the brother of John, and Peter. The extreme diversity of the different groups by the mid-second century C.E. makes a single designation misleading. Also, among the Christian writings about heresies are many groups which had little to do with Jewish practices or Judaism but are primarily differentiated by their philosophical conceptualizations of Jesus. Gnostic groups, for example, represented a separate but equal challenge to the defining principles of Christian self-definition. These groups with varying gnostic tendencies could also be Jewish-Christian if they maintained Jewish practices.

The use, therefore, of the ambiguous concept of "Jewish-Christians" even up until the second century C.E. is fraught with inherent problems but does have some advantages. Some Jewish-Christian groups, for example, drew upon already existing religious and political terminology to distinguish their group. The designation of Paul's group as *"Nazoraioi,"* for example, in Acts 24.5 should be distinguished from a Jewish-Christian sect of the same/similar name used by later fourth century Church writers. In short, in the confusion of varying religious self-definitions in the first four centuries of the Common Era it is extremely difficult to simply state "Jews" or "Christians."

Some of the early terminology does warrant investigation. Paul, in Galatians 2.7, describes his own commitment to the "uncircumcised" and Peter's to the "circumcised," but little more about these divisions (as well as other distinctions found among later groups) or the exclusivity of these missions is revealed. It is not clear, for example, if Paul was the first to originate this "mission" or whether he was following an already existing pattern.

The divisions of "ethnei" for non-Jew and Paul's designation in Romans[13] of the non-Jewish followers as "Israeli" as opposed to Jew, bears witness to an early attempt to make a new/old designation. Other divisions such as those between (Greek-speaking) "Hellenists" and (Aramaic/Hebrew-speaking) "Hebrews" for example, in Acts 6.1, do not seem to represent the major doctrinal questions of Jewish law (associated with Paul) but do represent some form of internal societal distinctions of the period. Other designations such as Pharisees and Sadducees in the Gospels, for example, do not necessarily designate absolutely clear antagonist groups either, especially in light of the variants extant in the different Gospel accounts. The confusion among the different groups and their distinctions continues into the second century C.E. Even among the earliest records of the different Jewish-Christians groups there are disagreements as to the details of their genesis, leaders, doctrines etc.

Hegesippus, a writer of the second century C.E., whose writings are preserved in the fourth century *Ecclesiastical History* of Eusebius, for example, states the following concerning the different Jewish Christian groups (HE 4.22.3-5):

> There was Thebouthis who, soured at not having been made a bishop, began to disseminate corruption in the midst of the people, propagating the theories of one of the Jewish factious sects, to which he belonged. From them too came Simon, head of the Simonians; Cleobius, head of the Clebians; Dositheus, head of the Dositheans; Gortheius, the head of the Gortheians and Masbotheians. From these then originated the Marcianists, the Carpocratians, the Valentians, the Basilidians, the Satornilians, every one of whom aired on his own the most foolish eccentricities.

A contemporary, Irenaeus, also records the names of many other groups of which we have little or no information. There is no listing of Simon's group, for example, emerging from any other source other than from Simon even though Hegesippus lists Theobuthis as the founder. This may mean that these sources do not share the same information about these groups in either quantity or quality. Many of the sources of these early Jewish-Christian sects should also be differentiated according to geographic location. For example Irenaeus, whose *Against Heresies* is one of the most important early sources of information, was born in Asia Minor but did his writing at a more advanced stage of his career, clearly after coming to take up his post in Europe (Western Christianity).[14] Hegesippus, who had lived in Jerusalem (Eastern Christianity), however, does not even mention the Ebionites as having emerged from a separate person.

The appearance of clear, definite, and separate origins of a group such as the Ebionites and their doctrines in the writings of Irenaeus does indicate that by the second century C.E., certain Jewish-Christian groups had firmly established themselves and were considered by Western thinkers as extremely dangerous. So Irenaeus writes concerning the Ebionites:

> Those who are called the Ebionites agree that the world was made by God; but their opinions with respect to the Lord are similar to those of Cerinthus and Carpocrates. They use the Gospel according to Matthew only, and repudiate the Apostle Paul, maintaining that he was an apostate from the law. As to the prophetical writings, they endeavour to expound them in a somewhat singular manner: they practice circumcision, persevere in the observance of those customs which are enjoined by the law, and are so Judaic in their style of life, that they even adore Jerusalem as if it were the house of God.[15]

IV. The "Anonymous" Jewish-Christians Debate in Christian Literature

The point of the preceding pages was to demonstrate that many of the debates among Jewish-Christians and non-Jewish Christians in Christian literature by the second century C.E. were well known and sometimes conducted using the unique nomenclature; i.e. Ebionites, Simonians, Clebians, etc. In other cases, however, a similar debate seems to have been going on in Christian literature of the late first and second century C.E. which did not employ the specific names of the sects. Instead this literature chose to leave the "enemy" unnamed or used terms such as "Hebrews" and sometimes "Jews" to designate Jewish-Christians.

Despite the importance of Paul and Pauline materials in the corpus of the New Testament, Jewish-Christians seem to be a major flash point for early Christianity even in the first century C.E. In the earliest literature, the Jewish-Christians appear to have formed (a) cohesive and irregularly defined group/s by the end of the first century C.E. It appears that some of the earliest materials of Christian literature, including perhaps the Fourth Gospel allude to the controversy over Jews who continued to observe the law and held varying beliefs about the nature of Jesus and his messianship. These controversies should be called a "Jewish-Christians debate" rather than a "Jewish-Christian debate" since they include Jesus as an article of their faith.

This type of understanding clarifies some of the content of the Fourth Gospel (according to John), which apparently presents another version of the life, mission and meaning of Jesus. This gospel has a few parallel traditions which are common to all four gospels, only a couple reflect the same controversies as those present in the Synoptics. In fact, the controversies of John are quite different from those of the Synoptics. In order to see their differences, we shall first examine the similarities.

In John 2.13-25, we find the controversy over the cleansing of the Temple. Matthew 21.12-17; Mark 11.15-19; and Luke 19.45-48 have a similar incident. In Matthew, Jesus enters the temple of God, drives out those who sold pigeons, and overthrows the tables of the money-changers. In all three accounts he quotes the verses in Isaiah 56.7 and Jeremiah 7.11 as proof-texts for his actions. "The chief-priests and scribes" in the Synoptics hear his exegesis and do not debate him, but rather keep silent. In the account of John we have an actual debate, as the "Jews" ask him: "It has taken forty-six years to build this temple, and will you raise it in three days?" The question of Jesus in the Synoptics and his exegesis of the verses of the Prophets are mixed in the account of John. This controversy of the Synoptics was not connected to the issue of Christology. In John, we find the controversy linked to the question of Jesus' resurrection on the third day.

In John 3.1-21, we find an encounter rather than controversy with the Jews. In this encounter, Nicodemus, "a man of the Pharisees, a ruler of the Jews," proclaims that Jesus is "a teacher come from God; for no one can do these signs that you do." The agreement is almost startling in comparison with the number of controversies reflected in John.[16]

In John 4.46-54, there is the healing of the official's son, which is similar, in general, to the healing of the Centurion's slave in Matthew 8.5-13 and Luke 7.1-10. As with the Lucan version, there is no controversy concerning this healing. The controversy which is reported in Matthew 12.9-14; Mark 3.1-6; and Luke 6.6-11 concerning the question of healing on the Sabbath, is similar to the controversy in John 5.1-18, where a paralyzed man is healed on the Sabbath. According to John 5.16-18:

> This was why the Jews persecuted Jesus, because he did this on the sabbath. But Jesus answered them, "My Father is working still, and I am working." This was why the Jews sought all the more to kill him, because he not only broke the sabbath but also called God his own Father, making him equal with God.

In the Synoptic account of the same story the controversy was also over healing on the Sabbath, but Jesus' answer is characteristically connected with his overall eschatological view of the Sabbath and other Jewish laws in the coming end. Thus he answers in the Synoptics: "Is it lawful on the sabbath to do good or to harm, to save life or to kill?" In John we find the controversy based on the christological question of whether Jesus was equal to or was the son of God.

Typical of all the controversies in John, no matter what the issue, the basis for the controversy with the Jews will ultimately be the christological question. In John 6.41, the Jews murmur at Jesus, who proclaimed himself "the bread which came down from heaven." In 6.52 the Jews dispute the nature of "the flesh he gives to eat." In John 9.48-58 we find another parallel with a Synoptic tradition, but the christological interpretation of John gives it new meaning. In John 9.48-58:

> The Jews answered him, "Are we not right in saying that you are a Samaritan and have a demon." Jesus answered, "I have not a demon; but I honor my Father, and you dishonor me. . ." The Jews said to him, "Now we know you have a demon. Abraham died, as did the prophets' and you say, 'If any one keeps my word, he will never taste death'. . . Who do you claim to be? . . ." It is my Father who glorifies me, of whom you say that he is your God . . . ." The Jews then said to him, "You are not yet fifty years old and have you seen Abraham?" Jesus said to them, "Truly, truly, I say to you, before Abraham was, I am . . ."

The partial parallel in the Synoptics is found in Matthew 12.22-30; Mark 3.19-22; Luke 11.14-16. In the Synoptic Gospels, however, the charge is made that "He is possessed by Beelzebub, and by the prince of the demons he casts out demons." This is connected with the charge of Jesus performing healings and casting out demons. The argument in John is linked to whether Jesus is of divine stock.

In John 9.13-34, Jesus heals on the Sabbath. Like the examples of Jesus' healing on the Sabbath in the Synoptics, this causes controversy. In the Synoptics, however, the link is between Jesus' eschatological plan and the nature of the Sabbath[17]. In John 9.14-34 we find the following argument:

> They brought to the Pharisees the man who had formerly been blind. Now it was a sabbath day when Jesus made the clay and opened his eyes. . . . Some of the Pharisees said, "This man is not from God, for he does not keep the sabbath." But others

said, "How can a man who is a sinner do such signs?" There was division among them . . . for the Jews had already agreed that if any one should confess him to be Christ, he was to be put out of the synagogue . . . If this man were not from God, he could do nothing.

What is amazing in this argument is that the original controversy of the Synoptic tradition has completely disappeared. Instead of "Is it lawful to heal on the Sabbath," the question is a christological question as to Jesus' act; i.e. are they linked to a good or evil power. Unlike the Synoptic gospels, there is suddenly a dogmatic statement concerning the nature of Jesus in the synagogue: ". . . for the Jews had already agreed that if any one should confess him to be Christ, he was to be put out of the synagogue." This type of statement reflects a completely different Jewish-Christian debate from the Synoptic Gospels account. In the Synoptics, the nature of the divinity of Jesus is barely touched upon, and certainly is not a part of a debate. In the Gospel of John, we find a group of Jews who do not address the question of the legality of Jesus' healing on the Sabbath, but rather question the source of the authority for the healing. If, however, one would like to compare John's question of authority to the Synoptics' question of authority, we find that they are addressing completely different questions. In the Synoptics, as we have seen, Jesus' authority is God. In the Gospel of John, all recognize that the authority of Jesus is divine, but the question is the nature of the divinity. The milieu of John's Gospel is completely different from that of the other Gospels. The audience is also different in John's Gospel. In John 10.19-21 we read the following:

There was again a division among the Jews because of these words. Many of them said, "He has a demon and he is mad; why listen to him?" Others said, "These are not the sayings of one who has a demon. Can a demon open the eyes of the blind?"

The community that John is addressing appears to be Jewish-Christians, i.e. Jews who had accepted different parts of Jesus' works as basically true, and others who accepted other parts. This is evident from 8.31, 11.45, 12.11, and other citations. This group, in particular, did not accept the divinity of Christ and therefore their debate is based on questions concerning the divinity; good or evil. Kümmel, in his *Introduction to the New Testament*, writes the following:[18]

Already in the time of Irenaeus (Haer. III.11.7) it was assumed that Jn is polemicizing against the Gnostic Cerinthus, and this view finds supporters today.   But what we know about Cerinthus--separation of a God above from a God below; separation of the Spirit from Jesus before his passion--is not the target of Jn's polemic . . . so the statement by Irenaeus is scarcely true.

Among Jewish-Christian sects, Cerinthus was not only the originator of the heresy listed by Irenaeus, but also other heresies. His basic premise as shown in Eusebius[19] was that the kingdom would be set up on earth, similarly denying the ultimate divinity of Jesus' mission and ministry. L. Martyn, in his book, *History and Theology in the Fourth Gospel,* proves that the controversy between the Jews and Jesus reflects the situation of the Christian community in the time of the author of the Fourth Gospel. That is to say, that the Jewish-Christians were now being put "out of the synagogue" as the controversy over the divinity of Christ grows.[20]

The question is whether Christians were put out of Jewish synagogues, or whether orthodox Christians were being put out of Jewish-Christian synagogues? If in fact, L. Martyn is correct, and the author of the Fourth Gospel is representative of the situation in the Christian community of his time, there is every indication that the problem and debate going on in the Gospel of John is not "Judaism" vs. "Christianity," but "Jewish-Christianity" vs. "Christianity," or variant forms of Jewish-Christianity and Christianity.

In the discussion in John 9.13-41 we see the nature of the debate between the Jewish-Christians and the Christians:

Now it was the sabbath day when Jesus made the clay and opened his eyes . . . Some of the Pharisees said, "This man is not from God, for he does not keep the sabbath." But others said, "How can a man who is a sinner do such signs."

It is clear that both groups in question accept the healings as fact. The question remains as to whether the power is from God or some other source. In 9.18 this is even clearer:

The Jews did not believe that he had been blind and had received his sight, until they called the parents of the man who had received his sight.

The "Jews," whoever they are in this case (as opposed to the aforementioned Pharisees), accept the healing as fact. The "Jews" here, however, accept that Jesus has the power to do the healings, but that he is not the Christ. This is clear from 9.22: ". . . for the Jews had already agreed that if any one should confess him to be Christ, he was to be put out of the synagogue."

This controversy becomes clearer in 10.19:

There was again a division among the Jews because of these words. Many of them said, "He has a demon and he is mad; why listen to him?" Others said, "These are not the sayings of one who has a demon. Can a demon open the eyes of the blind?"

The division between the Jews is not as to Jesus' ability to perform miracles (which all these Jews accept) but as to his claim of divinity. 10.31 confirms this view:

The Jews took up stones again to stone him. Jesus answered them, "I have shown you many good works from the Father; for which of these do you stone me!" The Jews answered him, "It is not for good work that we stone you, but for blasphemy; because you, being a man, make yourself God."

The Jews, therefore, must be assumed to be believers in the good works of Jesus, and opposed to the claim of Jesus' divinity.

Returning to the claims of Cerinthus, they are remarkably similar to those made by "the Jews" in John. We find, therefore, in an account of Epiphanius the following account of Cerinthus and his followers.[21]

verse 1: Cerinthus from whom the Cerinthians received their name came to bring the venom of his beastly seed into the world. He does not differ much from the above-mentioned Carpocrates but he pours out the same malicious poisons in the world.
verse 2: For, speaking blasphemously against Christ in the same way as the one mentioned above, he also declares that Christ was born of Mary and the seed of Joseph, and likewise that the world was made by angels.

verse 3: For this one did not differ in any way from the first one in the elements of his doctrine, except that he adhered to Judaism only partially. For he said that the Law and the Prophets have been given by angels and that the legislator is one of the angels who created the world . . . after Jesus, born from the seed of Joseph and Mary, had grown up, Christ, that is the Holy Spirit, descended upon him in the form of a dove in the river Jordan and that he to him and through him to them were with him revealed the unknown Father.

verse 6: And therefore, since a power from above came upon him, he performed these mighty works. And while he himself suffered and rose again, but Christ--that means he who descended upon him in the form of a dove--who came from above upon him flew away without suffering. And Jesus is not supposed to be Christ.

The Christian community had changed over the course of time since Jesus' death. The debate between the Jews and the Christians of John's day, however, was not arguing the same issues as in the accounts of Matthew, Mark, and Luke. The purpose of this short survey of the different Gospel accounts is to show the changing nature of the Christian and Jewish community in the earliest stages of Christianity. It is significant, however, that John recognizes the official position of Judaism towards the Roman government. The political pragmatism of Judaism is antithetical to the political eschatology prevalent at this period in the church. In John 19.12-15:

Upon this Pilate sought to release him, but the Jews cried out, "If you release this man, you are not Caesar's friend; every one who makes himself a king sets himself against Caesar." When Pilate heard these words, he brought Jesus out and sat down on the judgment seat at a place called The Pavement, and in Hebrew, *Gabbatha*. Now it was the day of the Preparation of the Passover; it was about the sixth hour. He said to the Jews, "Behold your king!" They cried out "Away with him, away with him, crucify him!" Pilate said to them, "Shall I crucify your king?" The chief priests answered: "We have no king but Caesar."

By the beginnings of the second century C.E., a form of Jewish-Christian debate was, therefore, being carried on in Christian literature. This is especially true in the literature known as the Apostolic Fathers and Ante-Nicean Fathers. The literature of the Ante-Nicean Fathers is both voluminous and varied. This study, will occupy itself with three different early sources which although they appear to represent a Jewish-Christian debate, in fact represent a Jewish-Christians debate in the course of the second century C.E. The three sources to be evaluated are:

1. *The Epistle of Barnabas* (referred to: *Barnabas*),
2. Justin's *Dialogue With Trypho (Dialogue),*
3. Tertullian's *Adversus Judaeos.*

These three works represent a link between the extant literature in chronology, argumentation, audience, and world-view. We begin with *The Epistle of Barnabas.*

A. Lukyn Williams, in *Adversus Judaeous* (page 19), states the following concerning Barnabas:

> What then were the aim and purpose of the writer? Plainly his object was not, as with writers of a hundred years later, to establish certain doctrines of the Faith, or to oppose the views of certain heretics. His aim is at once wider and simpler than that. He has in his mind the twin dangers of Judaism and Antinomianism. He fears the influence of the Jews and the laxity of the heathen, and, from the very first, he has before his eyes both these rivals to true Christianity, although the former is more prominent in chapters i-xvii, and the latter of chapters xviii-xxi. Yet it should be observed that with regard to the former he never shows bitterness against the Jews and Judaism. He may write contemptuously, but he never writes bitterly.

When reading *Barnabas*, one is immediately struck by one rather unusual fact. In both the Greek and Latin versions the appellation "Jews," "Judaism," and "Pharisees" are nowhere to be found. This rather unusual lacuna provides an interesting insight into the inner workings of *Barnabas* and the purposes of its author. Though much can be said about the audience of *Barnabas,* it is probable that the omission of the appellation "Jews" is indicative of the community in which Barnabas was preaching. His attack as Williams put it against the "twin dangers of Judaism and Antinomianism," is not as clear as Williams would have us believe. It is clear on the one hand that Barnabas is aware of certain "commandments" which can in no way be linked with Jewish writings from this period or any other (chapter 7). Furthermore, Barnabas has a completely different perspective on the laws of the Sabbath (chapter 15), circumcision (chapter 8), and of clean and unclean animals (chapter 10) than any other Christian author prior to his time.   As Barnabas states: "Is then there not a command of God that they should not eat (these things)?   There is, but Moses spoke with a spiritual reference" (chapter 10).   While Barnabas reflects the concept raised by Paul of "transference" of the heritage, he is so oblique in his presentation, that it warrants investigation. In chapter 13 we read the following: "But let us see if this people is the heir, or the former, and if the covenant belongs to us or to them."

As we have mentioned before, the Jews are not mentioned by name, so it is difficult to identify who is the "us" here, and who is the "them."   At the end of chapter 12, which directly precedes this above-mentioned section, however, we have a clue as to their identity.   There it states:

> Behold again: Jesus who was manifested, both by type and in the flesh is not the Son of man, but the Son of God.   Since therefore, *they* were to say that Christ was the son of David, fearing and misunderstanding the error of the wicked, he saith, "The Lord said unto my Lord, Sit at My right hand, until I make Thine enemies Thy foot-stool."   And again, thus saith Isaiah, "The Lord said to Christ, my Lord, whose right hand I have holden, that the nations should yield obedience before Him; and I will break in pieces the strength of kings."   Behold how David calleth Him Lord and the Son of God.   But let us see if this people is the heir, or the former, and if the covenant belongs to us or to *them*.

It is clear that the "they" of the preceding end of chapter 12 is the only syntactical antecedent to the "them" of chapter 13.   Since this is the case, it is interesting to note that the "they" refers to a group which recognizes that Christ was the son of David, while the "us" refers to those that say that David called him the Son of God.   Referring to this exact group of people, Tertullian states the following:[22]

> So then, even as he is made less than the angels while clothed in manhood, even so he is not less when clothed with an angel. This opinion could be very suitable for Ebion who asserts that Jesus is mere man and only the seed of David, that means not also the Son of God . . .

It is obvious that the *Barnabas*, which left its opponents purposely unnamed, is attacking not Jews and Judaism, but the Jewish-Christian sect called "Ebionites."   Irenaeus explains concerning the Ebionites:[23]

. . . they practice circumcision, persevere in the customs which
are according to the Law and practice a Jewish way of life, even
adoring Jerusalem as if it were the house of God.

In chapter 16 of *Barnabas* we find the following description of the
opponents of Barnabas:

Moreover, I will also tell you concerning the temple, how the
wretched, wandering the error, trusted not in God Himself, but
in the temple as being the house of God.

The parallel language is remarkable. The arguments of Barnabas
cannot be used to deduce a "Jewish-Christian debate." This distinction is
significant, since it seems to indicate that Christianity was not interested in
carrying on an open debate with Judaism or Antinomianism, but rather at the
early stages of the second century C.E. was still debating the issues of the
meaning of Jesus' ministry among themselves. Sequentially, therefore, the
advent of a Jewish-Christian debate could not occur, nor should it have be
expected to occur until Christianity had defined itself to itself.

A. Lukyn Williams, in *Adversus Judaeos* (page 35), outlines Justin's
Dialogue with Trypho as the following:

I. The Old Testament itself looks forward to the Law being
superseded. To this is added a more detailed study of the
various ordinances of the Law.

II. The Old Testament itself looks forward to the Coming of the
Messiah and even predicts details about Him, which are in fact
fulfilled in Jesus. It tells us also of His two Advents (not only
of one); of His pre-existence and His Divine nature; and His life
on earth. In connection with this Justin deals particularly with
the Coming of Elijah; the Virgin Birth, which, as he rightly
insists, has nothing in common with heathen myths; the Holy
Spirit descending on Him at His Baptism; His humiliation in
general; His Crucifixion and His Resurrection.

III. Justin informs us of certain interesting facts about
Christians, and mentions some of their beliefs. He himself "and
all other entirely orthodox Christians believe in the Millennium,
in a Jerusalem built up and adorned and enlarged as the prophets
Ezekiel and Isaiah and all the rest acknowledge." Again, he

tells us of false Christians; the observance of the Law by some Christians; and Evil Angels.

IV. He also dwells at some length on the Call of the Gentiles, and God's present relation to the Jews, with their behavior towards Him.

It is interesting to note that in the entire 142 chapters of Justin's *Dialogue,* the designation "Jews" appears only four times. The description of the "Jews," appears only once. In the beginning of the *Dialogue,* Trypho states the following:

> "Trypho" says he, "I am called; and I am a Hebrew of the circumcision, and having escaped from the war lately carried on there, I am spending my days in Greece, and chiefly at Corinth."

In much of Christian literature of this period the designation "Hebrew" is used by some writers to refer to distinguish between Jews and converts to Christianity and often Jewish-Christians.[24]

In the only clear reference to "Jews," we find that the real purpose behind the *Dialogue* is expressed (chapter 80):

> . . . I signified to you that many who belong to the pure and pious faith, and are true Christians, think otherwise. Moreover, I pointed out to you that some who are called Christians, but are godless, impious heretics, teach doctrines that are in every way blasphemous, atheistical, and foolish. But that you may know that I do not say this before you alone, I shall draw up a statement so far as I can, of all the arguments which have passed between us; in which I shall record myself as admitting the same things which I admit to you. For I choose to follow not men or men's doctrines, but God and the doctrines (delivered) by Him. For if you have fallen in with some who are called Christians, but who do not admit this (truth) and venture to blaspheme the God of Abraham, and the God of Isaac, and the God of Jacob; who say there is no resurrection of the dead, and that their souls, when they die, are taken to heaven; do not imagine that they are Christians, even as one, if he would rightly consider it, would not admit that the Sadducees, or similar sects of Genistae, Meristae, Galilaeans,

Hellenists, Pharisees, Baptists, are Jews (do not hear me
impatiently when I tell you what I think), but are (only) called
Jews and children of Abraham, worshipping God with the lips,
as God Himself declared but the heart was far from Him.

A major trend of the *Dialogue* is the following (chapter 80):

. . . some who are called Christians, but are godless, impious
heretics, teach doctrines that are in every way blasphemous,
atheistical, and foolish. But that you may know that I do not
say this before you alone, I shall draw up a statement so far as
I can, of all the arguments which have passed between us; in
which I shall record myself as admitting the same things which
I admit to you.

The *Dialogue* may be intended, therefore, as a defense of the "true"
Christians, (of which Justin is assuredly one). The nature of the dialogue is
not to confute Judaism, necessarily, but rather to differentiate "Christianity,"
from other pretenders to the title. The "statement" that Justin refers to in the
preceding citation (chapter 80) is apparently the account which he has made
throughout the remaining chapters. It is clear that the one reference to the
Jews is used by him to differentiate what he sees as one heterodox belief from
another orthodox belief. The very use of the word "sects" in describing the
Sadducees and the Pharisees recalls the original Greek sense of "heresies;" i.e.
divisions or identifiable groups (here among the Jews), and not as Justin uses
it; i.e. in the sense of "heretical" or "heterodox" vs. orthodox. It is clear
from this use of the Sadducees and Pharisees as "sects," that the intention of
Justin's *Dialogue* is not an attack upon Judaism, but rather an attack upon
heterodox movements within Christianity and a defense of the orthodox
position. In chapter 47, the defense is set in the context of several "your race"
passages which point not to Jews, but to those who have accepted Jesus as the
Christ in some form and maintain Jewish law:

But if some, through weak-mindedness, wish to observe such
institutions as were given by Moses, from which they expect
some virtue, but which we believe were appointed by reason of
the hardness of the people's hearts, along with their hope in this
Christ, and (wish to perform) the eternal and natural facts of
righteousness and piety, yet choose to live with the Christians
and the faithful, as I said before, not inducing them either to be
circumcised like themselves, or to keep the Sabbath, or to
observe any other such ceremonies, then I hold that we ought to

join ourselves to such, and associate with them in all things as kinsmen and brethren. "But if, Trypho," I continued, "some of your race, who say they believe in Christ, compel those Gentiles who believe in this Christ to live in all respects according to the law given by Moses, or choose not to associate so intimately with them, I in like manner do not approve of them."

The emphasis here is on the "some of your race that compel those Gentiles who believe in Christ to live in all respects according to the law of Moses." It seems that Trypho's "race" believe in the Christ, (and observe the law given to Moses) but "some" of them are compelling Gentiles who believe in Christ to live also according to the law of Moses.

The difference between the heterodox view of Trypho and the orthodox view of Justin is expressed in chapter 48:

For there are some, my friends, . . . of our race, who admit that He is Christ, while holding Him to be man of men; with whom I do not agree nor would I, even though most of those who have (now) the same opinions as myself should say so; since we were enjoined by Christ himself to put no faith in human doctrines, but in those proclaimed by the blessed prophets and taught by Himself.

The orthodox Justin believes that the "true Christian" is one which will accept "weak-minded" individuals who observe the "law of Moses," but believe in Christ, and do not compel Gentiles to observe the "law of Moses" and do not believe that Christ is a "man of men." The heterodox Trypho, on the other hand, is of a race which believes in Christ, accepts the law of Moses, but presumably induces others to keep the law. Similarly, the designation of the term "Christian" is, in Justin's view, only the "true Christian." In chapter 96 he states the following: "For you curse in your synagogues all those who have become Christians from Him."

The Christian designation for Justin is one who has separated himself from the heterodox beliefs of the Jewish-Christians. To Justin it simply was unimaginable that a person who held Jesus in high regard could allow Christians to be cursed. Quite possibly, however, the distinction for a Jewish-Christian was that "they" did not consider themselves Christians and therefore did not see this as a particularly problematic.

Tertullian's *Adversus Judaeos,* the third source of the Jewish-Christians debate in the early second century C.E. Christian literature, represents the overall influence of the Jewish-Christians in the shaping of Christian views. It is a more passive, perhaps negatively defined influence with clear rhetorical precedents in classical Greco-Roman sources of the period. It presumes the existence of a group: "those that say x," and presents its arguments as refutations of these principles. This emerging form of the Jewish-Christian debate does not necessarily involve active Jewish-Christian participants from the second century C.E. This form of Jewish-Christian debate is a theoretical debate. It is found in Origen's *Contra Celsum,* for example, and often is a method for developing an argument.[25] This form of Christian argumentation does not necessarily involve an active Jewish or Jewish-Christian participant, but rather an imagined argumentation and opponent. It is interesting to note that by the time Tertullian wrote *Adversus Judaeos,* a great change had occurred in the polemic tractates. By the end of the second and beginning of the third century C.E., we find page after page in his tract the appellation "Jews." It can be said that the "Jewish-Christian debate," as described by Schoeps, first began at the end of the second century C.E. with this form of rhetorical debate. Unfortunately, it was probably was still directed towards those who kept Jewish practices and therefore can be seen as a form of Jewish-Christians debate.

In the *Adversus Judaeos,* Tertullian sets up a debate form (chapter 4):

For the Jews say, that from the beginning God sanctified the seventh day, by resting on it from all his works which He made and that thence it was, likewise, that Moses said to the People: "Remember the day of the Sabbath, to sanctify it: every servile work ye shall not do therein, except what pertaineth unto life." *Whence we (Christians)* understand that we still more ought to observe a Sabbath from all "servile work" always not only every seventh day, but through all time. . . . But the *Jews are sure to say,* that ever since this precept was given through Moses, the observance has been binding. . . . Whence it is manifest that the force of such precepts was temporary, and respected the necessity of present circumstances; and that it was not with a view to its observance in perpetuity that God formerly gave them such a law (emphasis my own).

The debate format is quite uniform in the argumentation of Tertullian. It must be noted, however, that the proofs brought to substantiate his claims are not necessarily the same as his predecessors. In the case of the Sabbath observance, for example, Tertullian brings an obvious exception to the law of cessation from servile work from the Maccabees:

> For in the time of the Maccabees, too, they did bravely in fighting on the Sabbaths, and routed their foreign foes, and recalled the law of their fathers to the primitive style of life by fighting on the Sabbaths.

This type of argumentation, while totally rhetorical in nature ("But the Jews are sure to say . . .") represents a new stage of Jewish-Christian relations. Christianity by this point was sufficiently defined internally to turn its attention beyond the apologetic tractates of internal feuding, to the vindication of Christianity in addition to Judaism.   In *Adversus Judaeos,* (chapter 9) we read the following:

> *Accordingly the Jews say:* Let us challenge that prediction of Isaiah, and let us institute a comparison whether, in the case of the Christ who is already come, thee be applicable to Him, firstly, the name of Isaiah foretold, and secondly the signs of it which he announced of Him. *Well, then,* Isaiah foretells that it behoves Him to be called Emmanuel; and that subsequently He is to take the power of Damascus and the spoils of Samaria, in opposition to the king of the Assyrians. "Now,"'*say they, "that (Christ) of yours,* who is come, neither was called by that name, nor engaged in warfare. *But we,* on the contrary, have thought they ought to be admonished to recall to mind the context of this passage as well . . ." (emphasis my own).

Tertullian sets up the challenges and retorts of the Jews and Christians in a form which can only be called a debate. It must be said, however, that the whole device of the debate in this case is literary in nature, for the original pretext of the *Adversus Judaeos* had been "a dispute between a Christian and Jewish proselyte." This pretext quickly retreats into the background revealing a disputation arranged "point by point . . . that the pen should determine, for reading purposes, the question handled" (chapter 1).

Whether or not the Jewish-Christian debate as reflected in Tertullian's *Adversus Judaeos* actually took place the way he described it is not essential to this study. What is important is that Tertullian raises many of the issues which Schoeps described as those which "Jews of all centuries have bitterly contested. . . ." We find, for example, in chapter 18 of *Adversus Judaeos,* the connection between the death of Jesus and the destruction of Jerusalem.[26]

Finally, Tertullian's contribution to the Jewish-Christian debate is distinguished by his new Christian synthesis. He refers to the "clue" (ducatum) to the error of the Jews in his Two Advent theology. The Two Advent theology must be seen as the synthesis of Christians who believed that there was an earthly mission, which ended in suffering and death, and a second mission which will end in glory and judgment. In combining the two Christian positions, he has successfully integrated the outstanding heresies into Christianity. In the end of his tractate, he offers a challenge to Judaism:

> For at the present day nations are invoking Christ which used not to know Him; and peoples at the present day are fleeing in a body to the Christ of whom in days bygone they were ignorant, you cannot contend that is future which you see taking place. Either deny that these events were prophesied, while they are seen before your eyes; or else have been fulfilled, while you hear them read; or, on the other hand, if you fail to deny each position, they will have their fulfillment in Him with respect to whom they were prophesied.

V. Jewish-Christians in Fourth and Fifth Century Christian Literature

Ephiphanius of Salamis, a fourth century C.E. Christian writer born in Palestine near Gaza, has the most complete and informative list of over forty separate Jewish-Christian groups in his *Panarion*.[27] He lists groups such as the Elkasites; Sampsaeans; followers of Marthus and a Marthana; Messalians; four separate sects of Samaritans (Essenes; Sebuaeans; Gorothenes; Dositheans); seven sects of Jews (Sadducees; Scribes; Pharisees; Hemerobaptists; Nasaraeans; Ossaeans; Herodians); Simonians; Meandrians; Satornilians; Basilideans; Nicolaitans; Gnostic sects (Secundians; Stratiotics; Phibionites; Socratists; Zacchaeans; Coddians; Borborites); Carpocratians; Cerinthians (also known as Merinthians); Nazoraeans; Ebionites; Valentinians; Ptolemaeans; Marcionites; Marcosians; Colorbasians; Heracleonites; Ophites; Cainites; Sethians; Archontics; Cerdonians; Lucianists; Apelleans; Severians; Tatianists.

Eusebius,[28] the Church historian, makes the following comment concerning the early Jewish-Christians debate:

> The first preachers of our Saviour himself called them by a Hebrew name Ebionites, indicating them to be poor of understanding. They say the know one God and do not deny the

body of the Saviour, but they do not recognize the divinity of
the Son.

This note, and others like it in Eusebius and other Patristic literature,
indicates that a group of Jewish Christians existed very early in the life of the
early Church ("the first preachers of our Savior himself called them by a
Hebrew name Ebionites.") They were not "normative" Christians by virtue
of the fact they rejected the divinity of Christ. Writing in his *Ecclesiastical
History,* 3.27.1-6, Eusebius explains that others by the same name preached
other controversial doctrines:[29]

> verse 3: There were others, however, besides them, (the
> Ebionites) that were of the same name but avoided the strange
> absurdity of the former, and did not deny that the Lord was
> born of a virgin and the Holy Spirit. But nevertheless in as
> much as they also refused to confess that he was God, Word
> and Wisdom, they turned aside into the impiety of the former,
> especially when, like them, they did their best to observe strictly
> the bodily worship of the law.

Continuing, Eusebius presents another controversy of a Jewish-Christian
group:[30]

> verse 1: We have learned that at this time Cerinthus became the
> author of another heresy . . . And he says that after the
> resurrection the kingdom of Christ will be set up on earth, and
> that in Jerusalem the body will again serve as the instrument of
> desires and pleasures. . . .
> verse 6: But Irenaeus in the first book, *Against the Heresies,*
> adds some more hidden false doctrines of the same man, and in
> the third book he relates a story which deserves not to be
> forgotten. He says, on the authority of Polycarp, that the
> Apostle John, once entered a bathhouse to bathe. But learning
> that Cerinthus was within, he left the place and rushed out of
> the door, for he could not bear to remain under the same roof
> with him. And he advised those that were with him to do the
> same, saying: "Let us flee, lest the bathhouse falls down, for
> Cerinthus, the enemy of the truth is within."

It is clear that the later Church recognized this controversy to be quite
early (at least in the time of the earliest apostles). Epiphanius lists a number
of early combatants of the Church and their respective heresies:

verse 28: The Cerinthians, also called the Merinthians. They take their name from Cerinthus and Merinthus, being Jews they are proud of circumcision. They say the world was created by angels and that Jesus was called Christ because of his progress (in virtue).

verse 29: The Nazoraeans. They confess that Jesus is the Christ, Son of God, but they live in every way according to the Law.

verse 30.1: The Ebionites. They are similar to the above Cerinthians and Nazareans. The heresy of the Sampsaeans and the Elkesaites joined with them. They say that Christ was created in heaven, and also the Holy Spirit. Christ dwelt in Adam and put him on again. They say that this brought him to perfection at his coming in the flesh. They are Jews. They use Gospels. Eating meat is abominable to them. They consider water to be divine. As I said, Christ put on a man at his coming in the flesh. They often baptize themselves in water, summer and winter for sanctification, like the Samaritans.[31]

Epiphanius also provides insights into the controversy going on between the Jews and the Christians and the Jews and the Jewish-Christians:

verse 7.1: These heresies, just mentioned, of which we here are giving a brief sketch, passing over the name of Jesus did not call themselves Iessaeans and did not keep the name Jews; they did not call themselves Christians, but Nazoraeans, taking the name from the place Nazareth . . . For such people make a fine object to be refuted and are easy to catch, for they are rather Jews and nothing else. However, they are very much hated by the Jews. For not only the Jewish children cherish hate against them but the people also stand up in the morning, at noon and in the evening, three times a day and they pronounce curses and maledictions over them when they say their prayers in the synagogues. Three times a day they say: "May God curse the Nazoraeans," for they are supposed to believe more than these because they proclaim as Jews that Jesus is the Christ which runs counter to those who still are Jews who do not accept Jesus.[32]

This notation indicates that the debate of the Jews was not with the Christians who accepted Christ, but rather those Jewish-Christians who accepted Christ and were trying to remain Jews. This indicates that perhaps there was a Jewish-Jewish/Christian debate, though not a Jewish-Christian debate. It does in fact recognize that the Jews and the Christians alike hated the Nazoraeans, and that the only debatable point raised by the Jews in their controversy is that the Nazoraeans were not Jews. This is not surprising, since from the developing Church's point of view, they also were not Christians.

VI. The Jewish-Christians Debate in Early Rabbinic Literature?

R. Travers Herford, in his book, *Christianity in Talmud and Midrash,* collected all the potential references to Christianity from the Talmud and Midrash. His work, which was a landmark achievement, when it appeared in 1903, provides a good point of departure. This paper, which deals only with the first four centuries of the Common Era, will isolate the issue of a Jewish-Christian debate to Tannaitic literature, the earliest rabbinic pronouncements, which include *Mishnah, Tosefta,* Tannaitic Halachic Midrashim, (*Mechilta, Sifrei* on Numbers and Deuteronomy and *Sifra* on Leviticus), and some Baraitot from the Talmudim. Even some of this material goes beyond the pale of fourth century C.E. Judaism and includes pronouncements from Babylonian rabbis who may not have had first hand information on Christianity. Herford's statements concerning Christianity in the Tannaitic period will be considered. Herford states the following (page 351):

> Considering, for the present the traditions of the Tannaite period, it will be noticed that the *Mishnah* does not contain the names Jeshu, or Ben Stada, or Ben Pandira. *Tosephta* contains all three, but not the form Jeshu ha-Notzri. Neither *Siphri, Siphra,* nor *Mechilta* contain, so far as I know, any allusion to Jesus. *Tosephta* contains a covert reference to Jesus in certain questions put to, and answered by, R. Eliezer ben Horqenos. These scarcely add any details to the tradition, because they are so obscure that their meaning is very uncertain.

The unearthing and collecting of the references cited by Herford is in itself a monumental and important task. In this case, however, it must be said that the work of Herford systematically produces an error of the grossest sort in textual research. In the case of the Tannaitic period, it is obvious that Herford is reading the clearer references of the Amoraic period into the more obscure references of the Tannaitic period. In the case of two references found in the *Mishnah,* and three citations found in the *Tosephta,* this is especially true. In the first case, Herford cites a reference from the *Mishnah* in tractate *Yevamot* 4.13 as proof of the allegation that Jesus is a *"Mamzer."*

Unfortunately, he fails to cite this *Mishnah* in full, and ultimately misses the whole point. The *Mishnah* in *Yevamot* states:

> Who is deemed to be a bastard? (The offspring of the union with) any consanguineous relative with whom cohabitation is forbidden. This is the ruling of R. Akiba. Simeon the Temanite said: (The offspring of any union) the penalty for which is *Kareth* at the Hands of Heaven. And the *Halacha* is in agreement with his view. And R. Joshua said: (The offspring of any union), the penalty for which is death at the hands of Beth Din. Said R. Simeon b. 'Azzai: "I found a role of genealogical records in Jerusalem. And therein was written, 'So-and-so is a bastard (having been born) from (a forbidden union with) a married woman,' which confirms the view of R. Joshua."

First, it is quite evident that the name of Jesus does not appear, in any form, in this *Mishnah*. Second, judging from Herford's analysis of the *Mishnah*, it is obvious that he was not sure that the reference was to Jesus (page 44):

> When, therefore, Shim'on b.'Azai reported that he had found a book of pedigrees, in which it was stated that "a certain person" (*peloni*) was of spurious birth, it is *certainly probable* that the reference is to Jesus (emphasis my own).

Finally, it is clear that because Herford only cites the latter part of the *Mishnah*, he inadvertently misinterpreted the meaning. He states (pages 44, 45): "And R. Jehoshua had laid it down that a bastard is one .who is condemned to a juridical death."

This is a complete misreading of the *Mishnah*. The *Mishnah* in fact states that R. Akiba defined a bastard as a product of the union of the Levitically prohibited relatives. Simeon the Yemanite brings the opinion that a bastard is defined as even the product of the union of a woman and a man whose crime can be punished by Divine Justice. R. Joshua, however, brings the opinion that a bastard is the product of the union of a woman and a man whose crime (of the woman and the man) is punishable by death at the hands of the earthly court. The *Mishnah* is not speaking at all about the juridical death sentence of the child, rather the parents who were committing adultery! Herford, however, brings this *Mishnah*, and misinterprets it, in order to lend credence and longevity to the Amoraic traditions of the death sentence of Jesus. As he states on page 45:

> Now Jesus undoubtedly had been condemned (though not on account of his birth) to a juridical death, as the Talmud recognizes. (See passages given subsequently, 80, 83).

It is obvious that even Herford recognized that Jesus was not given a death sentence because of his birth, but he obviously tried to find a basis for the sentence of death given in the Amoraic sources to Jesus. Additionally, it is clear that Herford is relating the concept of bastard found in the *Mishnah* to the Amoraic tradition of the *BT Shabbath* 104b, which points to the illegitimate parentage of Jesus. Unfortunately, these are the opinions of third and fourth century C.E. Babylonian sources. Herford has read the late Amoraic concept of Jesus' illegitimate birth into a Tannaitic piece, and, in doing so, completely misinterpreted the *Mishnah*.

In citing the *Mishnah Sanhedrin* 10.2, Herford makes some interesting revelations. The *Mishnah* states:

> Three kings and four private men have no part in the world to come; the three kings are Jeroboam, Ahab, and Manasseh . . . the four private men are Balaam, Doeg, Ahitopel and Gehazi. (translation by Herford, page 64-65).

Herford states in his commentary to this *Mishnah* (page 66):

> Moreover, Balaam was not an Israelite, and therefore could not logically be included in a list of exceptions to a rule which only affected Israelites. It is evident that Balaam here does not mean the ancient prophet of Num. XXII fol., but some one else for whom that ancient prophet could serve as a type. From the Jewish point of view there was considerable likeness between Balaam and Jesus. Both had led the people astray; and if the former had tempted them to gross immorality, the latter, according to the Rabbis, had tempted them to gross apostasy.

Herford then goes on to cite a piece of the *BT Gittin* 56b, 57a. In this section, the Amoraim bring opinions from Titus, Balaam, and Jesus. What is obvious *prima facie,* is that Balaam and Jesus are not synonymous, since the Rabbis themselves distinguish them. Similarly, Herford himself makes the statement that Balaam is not an Israelite, while Jesus is a Jew. Again, nothing about Christianity or its founder can be found in these passages.

In the references to Jesus found in the *Tosephta,* two of the citations refer to a Ben Stada, two refer to Ben Pandira (Pantiri) and one to an unnamed man who was crucified. Though it is quite possible to link the events as recorded in those citations to events in the life of Jesus; i.e. healing powers, crucifixion, etc., the fact remains that these were elements of ancient society which could be connected to any religious or philosophical movement in antiquity. The names of the individuals involved in these citations, also give rise to many questions. Herford, himself, is forced to admit (page 40):

> I cannot satisfy myself that any of the suggested explanations solve the problem; and being unable to propose any other, I leave the two names Ben Stada and Ben Pandira as relics of ancient Jewish mockery against Jesus, the clue to whose meaning is now lost.

Although Herford readily admits that the meanings of the names are lost, he links the different accounts in the *Tosephta* using these names with the accounts in the *Talmudim.* In a footnote on page 345 (note 1), Herford clearly recognizes that the Tannaitic source, R. Eliezer, differentiates between the two figures Ben Stada and Ben Pandira; yet, Herford persists in presenting the later Talmudic account of *BT Shabbat* 104b and *BT Sanhedrin* 67a, which in fact connect the two.

Unfortunately, Herford deals with Talmudic materials as if they all represent a continuous historical tradition. In the Talmud, however, there is a tendency to unify traditions in a method which is not always sensitive to their historical origins. The traditions concerning Ben Pandira and Ben Stada, however, cannot be seriously considered as a recognition or polemic with early Christianity since the connection of these names to a crucifixion is tenuous and historically not found in the Tannaitic period. Furthermore, the citation which Herford cites concerning the crucifixion of Jesus in the *Tosephta, Sanhedrin* 9.7 does not mention Jesus, Ben Stada, or Ben Pandira. To be fair, the Talmud mentions cases of crucifixions, but none of these events are in any way remotely connected to any of these names. In the Talmudic references which Herford relates to Jesus' crucifixion, there is in fact no crucifixion, but rather a hanging. It cannot be argued that the Rabbis did not know the difference, since the distinction clearly exists. This is not to say that the Rabbis of the Amoraic period are not alluding to Jesus' crucifixion. If they were, however, it can only be said of their references that they are not debating the validity or implications of Jesus' crucifixion, but rather mocking an account or accounts which they had in their possession. At the time of their redaction into the Talmud, in Babylonia, it seems that they no longer had any connection with actual historical events.

Another significant part of Herford's book must also be discussed in the context of a possible Jewish-Christian debate in the Tannaitic period. This is the question of the meaning and the significance of the word *"min."* On page 365, Herford writes:

> We have seen that the term *"min"* denotes an unfaithful Jew, one who was not loyal at heart to the principles of the Jewish religion, and who either in thought, word, or deed was false to the covenant between God and Israel. We have now to inquire whether the term was applied to all Jews tainted with heresy, or whether it was restricted to the adherents of one particular heresy and, if so, which heresy? (page 367). The question who were the persons called *minim* practically resolves itself into the choice between Jewish Gnostics and Jewish Christians. That they were Jews is beyond dispute. A Gentile is never called a *"min".* . . .

Herford's presentation of the materials where the word *"min"* appears is complex. In re-examining the sources, one realizes the terrible disadvantage Herford had in collecting such materials. First, many of the texts that Herford used had previously in the Middle ages been censored by officials whose understanding of the Hebrew/Aramaic sources was limited.   Secondly, Herford's investigation of the materials was not totally systematic. Of the estimated thirty five times that the word *"min"* (with the meaning "heretic") appears in all Tannaitic literature, some references are missing in Herford's work.   A review of the compete list of *"min"* and its derivatives in this literature reveals the original meaning during the Tannaitic period.   In the entire *Mishnah,* the word *"min"* appears nine times. In the tractate known as *Yadayim 4.8,* the translation is as follows:

> A Galilean Min said: "I complain against you, O ye Pharisees, that you write the name of the ruler of divorcement."   The Pharisees said: "[Do] we complain against you, O Galilean Min, that you write the name of the ruler above and the Divine name below?" [It is said] And Pharaoh said, "Who is the Lord that I should harken unto His voice to let Israel go?" But when he was smitten what did he say? "The Lord is righteous."

This version is supported by the earliest and best manuscripts of the *Mishnah*. The question is obviously between two Jews concerning the place of non-sacedotal information (i.e. official state information) in a (Jewish) religious document. The distinction, however, between the Pharisee and the *min* is not entirely clear, judging from the remarks of the Pharisee. It seems that these *minim* do write God's name together with the name of the ruler, even preceding the name of God with the name of the ruler. It would appear, however, that they do not do so on religious documents. This *Mishnah* clearly shows that the *Mishnah* had some concept of a *"min,"* but this case shows that the concept was limited to "religious exclusivists."

In an example of the word, *"minuth"* in the *Mishnah*, tractate *Sotah* 9.15 reads the following:

> In the footsteps of the messiah insolence will increase and honor dwindle; the vine will yield its fruit (abundantly) but wine will be dear; the government will turn to Minuth.

Before approaching the interpretation of this section, a word must be said about the text. Y.N. Epstein, in *Mavo Lenusah HaMishnah*, states:

> Many things have been added to the ends of tractates from Tannaitic and Amoraic material. There are those (who were added) in order to end up a good note, others that supplement the with laws from the *Tosephta;* There are those that are found in our editions and others which cannot be found except in manuscript form. There are, however, some endings which are already from the time of the *Mishnah* and its redactors. . . . In this category is the end of tractate *Yadayim* . . . And thus, "pseudo-Tannaim" and scribes after them acted in a similar fashion adding legendary materials at the end of a tractate in order to end it upon a good note. . . In this category is the end of tractate *Sotah* . . . they added from the *Tosephta*, chapter 15.3-5 (also *PT Sotah* 24c and *BT Sotah* 49b end) and from *Baraithot* which are found in *BT Sanhedrin* 97a (pages 974-976).

Epstein clearly points out that the material at the end of tractate *Yadayim* is indigenous to the *Mishnah*, while the material found at the end of tractate *Sotah* is not. This is important, since in judging the meaning of the word *"min"* in the *Mishnah*, this source should not be included. It is possible, however, to interpret the *Sotah* passage in light of the reference found in tractate *Yadayim*. In the *Sotah* passage, when the messiah will come, (as representative of the Divine Kingdom), the abundance of Nature will continue, but the labor of man necessary to turn Nature into a product will not. The conclusion being: the political government of this world will turn to *minuth*. The interpretation of *"minuth"* in *Sotah*, like that of *Yadayim*, is inherently political in nature. *"min"* in *Sotah* implied dissatisfaction with a mixing of religion and politics. *"minuth"* in the government would mean the political regime moving totally to religious concerns: i.e. religious exclusivism. The view was held that the political state insures the smooth production of commodities. With the coming of the messiah, the earth would still produce its fruits, but the government which used to oversee the smooth production of the fruits into wine will turn to totally religious concerns, and "wine will be dear" (i.e. smooth production of commodities would be interrupted). In both these instances, however, the meaning of *"min"* and *"minuth"* is clearly "religious exclusivism" as opposed to the political concerns of the world. This meaning of *"min"* is associated with a number of references in the *Mishnah*. Though many varied opinions are associated with *"min,"* none clearly point to either Jewish Gnostics or Jewish Christians.

Of the other seven references to *"minim"* or derivatives, the meaning of the designation falls into one of three different categories:

1) either the reference is to a *min* whose comments are unintelligible,[33]
2) or not easily linked to a clear religious designation,[34]
3) or linked to a certain religious system.[35]

Of the one remaining reference to *minim* in the *Mishnah*, a special designation must be made. In the twenty-five references to *minim* throughout the rest of Tannaitic literature, only one reference appears in the *Mishnah* and in three of the four other collections of Tannaitic literature. This *Mishnah* must be viewed in comparison with the other parallel citations in the hopes of achieving an overall Tannaitic meaning for the word *"min"*:

Parah 3.3: Having arrived at the Temple Mount, they alighted. Beneath the Temple Mount and the courts was a hollow which served as a protection against a grave in the depths, while at the entrance of the court the jar of the ashes of the sin-offering was provided. A male from among the sheep was brought and a rope was tied between its horns, and a stick or a bushy twig was tied at the other end of the rope, and this was thrown into the jar. The male (sheep) was then struck so that it started

backwards when (a child) took the ashes and mixed as much of
it as could be visible on the water. R. Jose said: "Do not give
the *minim* an opportunity to cavil, but (a child) himself took it
and mixed it."

Herford explains:

The literal meaning of the phrase is clear; but the application of
it is very difficult to understand . . . . The discussion upon
them was therefore purely academic. Accordingly the difficulty
arises. What reason there to fear the Minim? From all that we
have learnt hitherto, it does not appear that the Minim took part
of interest in the discussions upon Halacha in the Rabbinical
assemblies (page 317).

Herford could not interpret this *Mishnah* correctly because he had
convinced himself that the Amoraic conclusions about *minim* (which possibly
linked them with the Christians, though this needs clarification) were in total
consonance with the Tannaitic views concerning *minim*. It is clear that this is
not the case, and even in the Tannaitic period the title *"minim"* was applied to
different heresies, or perhaps a variation upon one theme. *"Min"* appears in
the rest of Tannaitic literature as follows:

Tosephta: 15 independent citations
Mechilta: 1 independent citation
Sifre Devarim/Bamidbar: 8 independent citations
Sifra: 1 independent citation

"Independent" indicates that two appearances (or more) of the word
"min" (or derivatives) in the same sentence or in one complete pericope does
not constitute more than one citation. In all the different meanings which can
be found concerning the *"min,"* only one citation appears in three of the four
Tannaitic collections listed above. However varied the other references to *min*
and its derivatives may be, the original meaning can probably be found in this
unique citation:

Shimon B. Azzai said, "Come and see what is written in the
Torah concerning all the sacrifices. Neither 'Elohim,' nor
'Elohecha,' nor 'Shaddai,' nor 'Z'vaot,' rather 'YHVH,' the
particular name, *so as not to give the minim occasion to
cavil"*[36] (cited from *Sifre Bamidbar*, 143, Horovitz edition,
191).

The citation appears in the *Tosephta* twice, *Sifre* once, and *Sifra* once. The meaning, however, is disputed by a number of notable sources. In the *Tosephta Yoma* 3.2, the section on the *minim* appears in a completely different context. Saul Lieberman in his book, *Tosephta Ki-Fshutah*, Part 4, order Moed, page 766, deals with an interpretation of this section. In *Yoma* chapter 4, the issue is, as stated in the first *Mishnah:* "He [the High Priest] shook the urn and brought up the two lots (for the sacrifices as described in the book of Leviticus 16), on one was inscribed: "for the Lord," and on the other: "for Azazel."

Tosephta Yoma 2.9-10 (Manuscript Erfurt: 3.1-2):

He shook the urn and brought up the two lots. One in his right hand, and one in his left. If the right hand brought up ("for the Lord") all Israel was happy. If it ("for the Lord") was brought up on the left hand, all Israel was not happy. (10) They asked R. Akiba: What does it matter to change left to right? He said to them: Do not give occasion to the *minim* to cavil.

Lieberman here links the worship of ancient pagan deities and their rites to the question of why one should not make a distinction in favor of the right.[37] Other opinions have been raised on this question,[38] but the simple meaning of the entire pericope indicates that in fact the people had, perhaps, a preference for the lot marked, "for the Lord," to be brought up by the right hand. If there is room for the *minim* to question, cavil, or rebel,[39] it was probably from the arbitrary nature of being able to exchange right and left without any concern for the on-lookers' belief that the act was somehow affected by God. This, perhaps, does give us a meaning which links the *Mishnah* text(s) and the citation which appears here and in the *Sifre Bamidbar* 143 quoted above.

The *min* was a "religious exclusivist," one who saw religion (and especially his/her brand of religion) as the most important function of life. The *min* would have occasion to question if sacrifices were given to a God of many names. A *min* would have reason to question a God who arbitrarily ordained ritual. A *min* would cavil at the putting together of the name of Moses and the name of the ruler on a religious document. Whatever the original meaning of the word *"min,"* it is unquestionably a very general term for one whose religious convictions came first, and who opposed political intervention in religious matters.

There are in fact more specific definitions of "min" to be found in Tannaitic Literature.[40] It seems, however, that they are secondary to this meaning. If in fact something can be learned from this short survey of the Tannaitic literature's definition of min, it is the following: The meaning of min and its derivatives does not necessarily indicate a Jewish-Christian. The representation of a Jewish-Christian debate which is based on citations concerning the minim in the Tannaitic literature, is counter-productive and misleading. The evidence of an active Jewish-Christian debate, dialogue, face-to-face confrontation or interaction between Rabbinic Jews and "Nicean"-like Christians, cannot be legitimately cited from Tannaitic literature.

Three other Jewish sources of information from the period should be investigated: Josephus, Philo, and the Papyri. Josephus has an interesting place in the Jewish-Christian debate, since he recorded in great detail the events of the first century C.E. This citation has been the subject of much debate and questions have been raised concerning its authenticity because of its odd placement in Book XVIII.[41] It does provide information on Jesus, in a formula-like way:

> About this time there lived Jesus, a wise man, if indeed one ought to call him a man. For he was one who wrought surprising feats and was a teacher of such people as accept the truth gladly. He won over many Jews and many of the Greeks. He was the Messiah. When Pilate, upon hearing him accused by men of the highest standing amongst us, had condemned him to be crucified, those who had in the first place come to love him did not give up their affection for him. On the third day he appeared to them restored to life, for the prophets of God had prophesied these and countless other marvellous things about him. and the tribe of the Christians, so called after him, has still to this day not disappeared (63-64).

Again in *Antiquities XX,* Josephus writes:

> And so he convened the judges of the Sanhedrin and brought before them a man named James, the brother of Jesus who was called the Christ, and certain others . . ." (Josephus, *Antiquities,* trans. Louis Feldman, [London, 1960], 200.)

These two references are the only evidence in Josephus of his knowledge of a "Jewish-Christian debate," since *Wars* lacks any references.

Concerning Philo, Mr. R. H. Colson, in the general introduction to the Loeb edition of Philo, writes the following:

> It has been generally held that he (Philo) was born about 20 B.C. The date of his death is uncertain, but it has been seen that his lifetime covers the lifetimes of Jesus Christ and John Baptist, and much of that of St. Paul. *There is no intimation that he knew anything of their work* (1:ix-x) (emphasis my own).

The papyri, from Jewish sources of the early Roman period, yield no information concerning Jesus or any of his disciples.   The following, therefore, is a summary of our conclusions concerning the literature of the Jewish-Christian debate from the Jewish perspective:

1. There is no clear mention of Jesus or his disciples in any of the Tannaitic literature.

2. The references to *minim* in the Tannaitic literature do not refer specifically to Christians but perhaps to Jews with varying views on different issues such as interpretation, practice and authority. Some of these groups could be Jewish-Christians.

3. From the period of the first century C.E. Philo and the papyri do not reflect any knowledge of Jesus, his disciples or Christians. Josephus, however, does present a Jewish view concerning Jesus, his disciples, and Christians. His view, if it is to be considered authentic, reflects not a debate, but an acceptance by some Jews, and condemnation (for no apparent reason) by others. If Josephus is considered in the context of all the other Jewish sources of the period, it is difficult to accept the account as authentic.

4. In light of the entire corpus of Jewish material extant from this period, the conclusion is that the Jews were not debating the Christians, in writing at least, nor can it be said that the Jews felt that they were being debated. The fact that Josephus and Philo do have tractates confuting pagan charges, it would be natural to assume that they would have composed similar tracts answering Christian charges had they thought that these questions were damaging. Since the Christian literature is extant, it is possible to examine to see if the charges were necessarily directed against the Jews or not.

VII. One More Rabbinic Source: The *Birkat HaMinim*

After reviewing the early rabbinic sources relating to the *minim,* and coming to the conclusion that Jewish-Christians, Gnostics or other groups are alluded to in these passages but certainly not Christians, one more rabbinic source relating to the *minim* needs review. This is the so-called *Birkat HaMinim,* the curse or blessing of the *minim* found in the thrice repeated daily *Shemonah Esrei* prayer and which is generally understood to be a condemnation of Christians and a significant part of the evidence for an active Jewish-Christian Debate in the first four centuries of the Common Era.[42] This prayer, according to the Babylonian Talmud in a *baraita* (attributed Tannaitic statement) in tractate *Berachot* 28b ff. states:

> Our Rabbis taught: Simeon HaPakoli ordered the Eighteen Benedictions before Rabban Gamliel at Yavneh. Rabban Gamliel said to the Sages: Is there no one who knows how to compose a benediction against the minim? Samuel HaKatan stood up and composed it. Another year, he forgot it and tried to recall it for two or three hours yet they did not remove him.

If this is Rabban Gamliel II of Yavneh (as it is presently understood), this would place a certain composition of the *Birkat HaMinim* in the beginning of the second century C.E. The unusual redactional questions concerning the composition and recomposition of the blessings may account for Samuel HaKatan's inability to remember the exact formulation that he had used. More importantly, the inexact nature of the content of the benediction here and the entire designation of *min* in Tannaitic literature may indicate the nature of the problem; i.e. the fluid nature of the definition of *min* and the changing status of the Jewish-Christians within rabbinic Judaism in the first three centuries of the Common Era. In fact, it seems to be, in its earliest form a condemnation of a certain group of Jewish-Christians and for certain specific reasons.

The twelfth blessing of the so-called 18 (later 19) blessing prayer or *Shemonah Esrei* ("Standing" prayer or *Amidah*) is referred to as the *"Birkat HaMinim."* It is preceded by a blessing (blessing #11) for the political leaders in ancient times: "Restore our judges as in days of old, restore our counsellors as in former times . . ." and it is followed by blessings (#13 and #14) which also speaks about the leaders of ancient Israel. So, blessing #13 reads: "Let your tender mercies be stirred for the righteous, the pious, and the leaders of the House of Israel. . . ." Blessing #14 reads: "Reestablish there the majesty of David, Your servant. . . ."

One may ask what blessing #12 against the Jewish-Christians is doing juxtaposed between blessings for the leadership of ancient Israel? In its present form, it "curses" only a group of "slanderers" (*malshinim*): "Let there be no hope for the slanderers . . ." and the references to the *minim* are not part of the current liturgy. In earlier versions which circulated from the late rabbinic/geonic period, however, the *nazoraeans* and the *minim* are mentioned in this blessing. Most studies of this section have concentrated on the actual blessing and its meaning. It is important to note the **placement or context** of this blessing in relation to the preceding and following blessings to understand how this "curse" was perceived. In all likelihood, from the placement of this blessing in between two blessings concerning the political leadership of ancient Israel, the "curse" in its original form was directed against a group which was presenting an alternative political leadership within ancient Judaism or against groups which were undermining the leadership of the period. More importantly, in most of the extant versions of the prayer, the *"minim"* are accused not of theological crimes but rather of slander, treachery and alliance with an evil kingdom; i.e. political crimes.

This idea that the blessing/curse is directed at political usurpers or crimes and not theological questions at all is expressed by a number of different contemporary writers. D. Flusser[43] argues that the original prayer pre-dated the Christians (he places it in the period of the Hasmoneans) and others argue that the blessing may have originally included became part of the ruling (non-Jewish) government. Y. Liebes also suggests the political implications of the blessing and that the rabbinic term for this group, *"min,"* is derived from the Palestinian Aramaic dialect word, *"mina,"* referring to a unique or separate nation or people.[44] An inscription on the mosaic floor of the ancient synagogue at Ein Gedi provides a general benediction of similar quality and content to the *Birkat HaMinim* without the mention of *"minim."*[45] The inscription's general content and the absence of the *"minim"* formula suggest that in its earliest form the benediction was a generic benediction covering a multitude of sins, (many of which were political) and that later this generic benediction was directed more specifically against any new or perceived internal political usurper depending upon the political climate.[46]

This political meaning is also suggested by the most ancient forms of the blessing which survive in the Genizah fragments. These fragments which derive from the 6th and 7th century C.E. may be more indicative of this later period rather than a representative of the first four centuries of the Common Era, a fact which may be of crucial importance given the changing nature and target of this benediction. One ancient form of the blessing, for example, reads:

> May the apostates have no hope and may You uproot the wicked
> government quickly in our day. May the Nazoraeans and the
> Minim disappear in a moment. Let them be erased from the
> book of life and not be inscribed with the righteous.[47]

The Sephardic, Yemenite, Persian versions of the blessing all include the *minim* together with informers, collaborators, and enemies of the Jews. At the present time, in most prayer books of Ashkenazic (Eastern and Western European) origin, there is no mention of the words *"minim"* or *"Nazoraeans"* as is found in most ancient versions of the benediction apparently because of the way that certain Church fathers linked the *minim* to the Christians.[48] This paper will not attempt to sift through the different references to *"minim"* in rabbinic literature.   It is obvious from even a cursory investigation of the differing uses of *"minim"* in rabbinic literature that a single, all encompassing, designation of *"minim"* is difficult. In the absence of such a definition, it is more prudent to assign a specific designation to a specific usage if the text allows such a distinction. Such seems to be the case regarding the text of the *Birkat HaMinim.*

In the extra-Judaic sources, Justin Martyr, in his *Dialogue with Trypho* (written around 150 C.E.), states in a number of passages that the Jews curse the Christians (or Christ, or both) in their synagogues.[49]   Another second century C.E. source, Origen, also raises the issue of the cursing of Jesus.[50] It is difficult to know whether they are speaking about a formal part of the synagogue service (i.e. the *Birkat HaMinim*) or whether more informal derogatory statements are alluded to here. In the final pronouncement in the *Dialogue*, for example, Justin states:

> Assent, therefore, and pour no ridicule on the Son of God; Obey
> not the Pharisaic teachers, and scoff not at the King of Israel as
> the rulers of your synagogues teach you to do *after your*
> *prayers,*[51]

indicating that this was just an informal practice.

A more exact reference which clearly establishes the benediction as directed against Jewish-Christians, the Nazaraeans, can be found in the writings of Epiphanius who states:

> For not only the Jewish children cherish hate against them but
> the people also stand up in the morning, at noon and in the
> evening, three times a day and they pronounce curses and

maledictions over them when they say their prayers in the synagogues. Three times a day they say: "May God curse the Nazaraeans."[52]

It is clear that he understood the curse to be directed against the Nazoraeans and not the Christians. In the same section he described the Nazoraeans:

These heresies, just mentioned, of which we here are giving a brief sketch, passing over the name of Jesus did not call themselves Iessaeans and did not keep the name Jews. They did not call themselves Christians but Nazoraeans, taking this name from the place Nazareth. But actually they remained wholly Jewish and nothing else. For they use not only the New Testament but also the Old, like the Jews. For the legislation and the Prophets and the Scriptures which are called the Bible by the Jews are not rejected by them as they are by those mentioned above. They are not at all mindful of other things but live according to the preaching of the Law as among Jews: there is no fault to find with them apart from the fact that they have come to believe in Christ.[53]

Another fourth and fifth century C.E. Church figure, Jerome, however, appears to have conflictive information regarding this cursing. In four passages[54] (three of which are found in the same commentary on Isaiah), for example, he states that the Jews blaspheme the Christians under the name of "Nazarenes." In what appear to be conflictive statements, Jerome mentions a Jewish-Christian group, the Nazaraeans, three times in the same commentary on Isaiah, and makes clear that members of this group are not Christians.[55] In his other writings, Jerome makes a finer distinction which seems to explain the confusion. He explains:

Until now a heresy is to be found in all parts of the East where Jews have their synagogues. It is called "of the Minaeans" and cursed by the Pharisees up to now. Usually they are called Nazaraeans. They believe in Christ, the Son of God born of Mary the virgin, and they say about him that he suffered and rose again under Pontius Pilate, in whom also we believe, but since they want to be both Jews and Christians, they are neither Jews nor Christians.

It is possible that Jerome differentiated between Nazarenes and Nazaraeans,[56] but the association of the names in Augustine and other writers[57] as well as the varied transliterations and variant readings found in earlier and later works makes this possibility difficult.

According to Jerome, in the East, probably in fourth century C.E. Palestine (where he lived), the benediction probably employed the word *"minim"* to designate Jewish-Christians. In the West, or perhaps among other groups in the East, these *"minim"* were generally referred to as "Nazaraeans." In either case, though Jerome recognizes that the specific intent of the curse was directed towards specific Jewish-Christians, his personal suspicion is that the general import was directed towards all Christians. Jerome's experiences with and pronouncements about "the Jews" were manifold and complex but mostly negative, especially in the East. With the exception of Jews converted to Christianity who helped him with his knowledge of Hebrew, he rarely has positive things to say about them, and it is not surprising that he is suspicious of the overall intent of the benediction in his period.[58]   In short, the information that Jerome supplies confirms the basic thesis of Jewish antipathy of certain Jewish-Christians and even more so identifies them specifically with the rabbinic term *"minim."*

VIII. The Political Implications of the Jewish-Christians Debate

Hans Schoeps, in *The Jewish-Christian Argument,* wrote the following:

The anti-Semitic polemic of the nations of the world goes back to early antiquity--to be exact, to Haman's vexation that here was a nation with laws differing from the law of every nation. Similarly, the arguments of Christian polemic against Judaism have been the same for over nineteen centuries; they can be traced back to the earliest period of history of the Christian Church. They consist of the following statements, belonging to the doctrinal basis of every Christian might and Jewish historical impotence, in ever-repeated exegeses of certain Old Testament passages.
1. The Messiah, foretold in Genesis 49.10, Isaiah 53, and numerous other passages of Scripture, was Jesus of Nazareth, who was nailed to the cross under Pontius Pilate.
2. Since the rejection and crucifixion of the Messiah, Jesus of Nazareth, the election of Israel has been transferred to the Christian Church; henceforth the Church is to be called the true Israel.

3. The punishment resulting from the crucifixion of Jesus is the destruction of the Jerusalem temple. This is an expression of God's consequent rejection of the people of Israel, who, because of their hardness of heart, must wander through the world until the Lord's return. Then all Israel will be converted, enter into knowledge of Jesus, and find salvation through him.
4. According to the witness of Paul, the Jewish law has been abrogated through faith in the new revelation. Jews of all centuries have bitterly contested all four statements. The growing Church was not taken seriously during the first centuries of this era. For this reason, remarkably few passages can be found in the Talmud referring indisputably to the historical Jesus; and the knowledge which the Babylonian rabbis had in general of the whole course of events in Galilee was scanty and legendary (18-19).

Schoeps points out some of the major points in the Jewish-Christian debate (or the lack thereof), and is quick to point out that the "Jews of all centuries have bitterly contested all four statements." Although he is probably correct about most of the past millennium, Schoeps seems to recognize that perhaps he is reading the events and literature of a later period into an earlier period, when he writes: "The growing Church was not taken seriously during the first centuries of this era. For this reason, remarkably few passages can be found in the Talmud referring indisputably to the historical Jesus . . ."

After reviewing the Tannaitic literature, the situation lends itself to the question; If not with the Jews, then with whom were they disputing? The issues of the early church were real issues, debatable issues, but the New Testament authors and the early Church Fathers realized from the outset that the success or failure of the church would be decided not by the Jews, but by the Roman authorities. The issues, which Schoeps so expertly defined, were still the issues. The question is "for whom were they issues?" The early church itself may have been debating these issues. This would imply that, very early in the first century C.E., the changing nature of the church gave rise to what might be called a "Jewish-Christians debate."

Shlomo Pines presented some new and interesting facts about the Jewish-Christians in the early Church.[59] The translation of the Arabic manuscript in question is quoted as follows:

(71a) After him, [i.e. after the death of Jesus] his disciples (*ashab*) were with the Jews and the Children of Israel in the latter's synagogues and observed the prayers and the feasts of [the Jews] in the same place as the latter. [However] there was a disagreement between them and the Jews with regard to Christ. The Romans (al-Rum) reigned over them. The Christians [used to] complain to the Romans about the Jews, showed them their own weakness and appealed to their pity. And the Romans did pity them. This [used] to happen frequently. And the Romans said to the Christians: "Between us and the Jews there is a pact which [obliges us] not to change their religious laws (adyan). But if you would abandon their laws and separate yourselves from them, praying as we do [while facing] the East, eating [the things] we eat, and regarding as permissible that which we consider as such, we should help you and make you powerful, and the Jews would find no way [to harm you]. On the contrary, you would be more powerful than they." The Christians answered: "We will do this." [And the Romans] said: "Go, fetch your companions, and bring your Book (kitab)." [The Christians] went to their companions, informed them of what had taken place between them and the Romans and said to them: "Bring the Gospel (alinjil) and stand up so that we should go to them." But these [companions] said to them: "You have done ill. We are not permitted [to let] the Romans pollute the Gospel." (71b) "In giving a favorable answer to the Romans, you have accordingly departed from the religion. We are [therefore] no longer permitted to associate with you; on the contrary, we are obliged to declare that there is nothing in common between us and you" (14).

This description of the early Church's beginnings is unparalleled in Church histories, and with good reason. The main thrust of it indicates that the Jews and the Christ followers were still worshipping together after the death of Christ. The nature of the controversy between the Jews and the Christians was not any of those listed by Schoeps, but rather the "Romanization" of the Christ act. The politization of Christianity here characterizes the split between those "companions" who are obviously Jews with positive sentiments towards the Christ and the Christians who are complete adherents.

This manuscript is critical, however, to an understanding of the Jewish-Christian debate for two reasons. First, the implication is that the Jews and the Christians could have remained together despite their disagreement concerning Christ. The problem and ultimate split was caused not by the disagreement over the Christ act, but rather by the outside involvement of the Romans.   Secondly, it is not the Jews and the Christians who separate following the intervention of the Romans, but the Jewish-Christians who remained with the Jews (apparently) and the Christians who "abandoned their laws, prayed and ate as the Romans." This may provide the beginnings of the answer to the question of what happened to the Jewish-Christians. According to this document it was the Roman intervention which ultimately decided the fate of the Jewish-Christians, not all the debates or polemics of the Jews or the Christians. They may have given up their Jewish practices in the hopes of being finally accepted by the Romans and the other Christians. In doing so, however, they gave up their own unique religious identity and the controversies associated with it. With their demise, the medieval Jewish-Christian debate may have indirectly been initiated.[60]

Endnotes

* I began my recent work on the Jewish-Christian Sects while participating in an NEH Summer Seminar at Columbia University, June-July, 1990. The bulk of the research was done during my tenure there. I am grateful to Professor A.Cameron, director, for his insights and the NEH for its support.

1. A. Momigliano, ed., *The Conflict Between Paganism and Christianity in the Fourth Century* (Oxford, 1963).

2. This conclusion can be reached by the use of the title: *The Conflict Between Paganism and Christianity in the Fourth Century,* although only H. Bloch's "The Pagan Revival in the West at the End of the Fourth Century," (193-218) appears to expressly address the issues of conflict.

3. A. Momigliano, *On Pagans, Jews, and Christians* (Middletown, CT, 1987).

4. Most studies reflect the existence of a real debate, despite the absence of clear Jewish textual evidence. So, A. Lukyn William, *Adversus Judaeos* (Cambridge, 1935).

5. A. Harnack, for example, takes Justin Martyr's *Dialogue with Trypho* as directed to a Greek public and not the Jews. "Die Altercatio Simonis Iudaei et Theophili Christiani nebst Untershungen über die antijüdische Polemik in der alten Kirche," in *Texte und Unterschungen* (Leipzig, 1883) 75ff; and Harnack, *The Mission and Expansion of Christianity in the First Three Centuries* (New York, 1960).

6. Certainly the existence of Christian rebuttals to pagan argumentation and pagan reactions (preserved albeit in Christian works) is substantial. Works such as Origen, *Contra Celsum;* Tertuillian, *Apoligeticum;* the *Acta Martyrum; Acta Cypriani; Acta Maximiliani;* Arnobius, *Adversus Nationes;* the fragments of Porphyry, *Contra Christianos* preserved in Eusebuis' writings; and the fragments of Julian, *Contra Galileos*

preserved in Cyril of Alexandria, *Contra Julian* demonstrate a strongly negative pagan reaction and argument against Christianity. Most of the independent (non-Christian) sources of this conflict have not been preserved. In one of the few independent pagan sources, Symmachus, *Relatio* to the Emperor Theodosius in 384 concerning the debate over the removal of the Altar of Victory from the senate house, the statements made by Symmachus do not reflect the negative, argumentative style reflected in most of the fragments of statements of earlier pagans preserved in Christian traditions. In fact, Symmachus' statement in the *Relatio:* "Man cannot come to so profound a mystery *by one road alone,"* cited from B. Croke and J. Harries, *Religious Conflict in Fourth Century Rome: A Documentary Study* (Sydney, 1982), 38.

7. Justin Martyr, *Dialogue with Typho;* Origen, *Contra Celsum;* and other Christian works do suggest a negative Jewish reaction to Christianity. M. Simon, *Versus Israel* (Paris, 1948), has collected most of the references for this negative reaction. Similarly, most of the independent (non-Christian) sources of this conflict have not been preserved in Jewish writings.

8. H. J. Schoeps, *The Jewish-Christian Argument* (New York, 1963), for example, includes a chapter entitled: "The First Centuries of Conflict"; J. Parkes, *The Conflict of the Church and the Synagogue* (New York, 1969); A. Alföldi, *The Conversion of Constantine and Pagan Rome,* trans. H. Mattingly (Oxford: 1948); E. R. Dodds, *Pagan and Christian in an Age of Anxiety* (Cambridge, 1965); B. Croke and J. Harries, *Religious Conflict in Fourth Century Rome: A Documentary Study* (Sydney, 1982); Robin Lane Fox, *Pagans and Christians* (Harmondsworth, 1986); D. Rokeah, *Jews, Pagans and Christians in Conflict* (Jersualem, 1982), page 47, used the word "conflict" but cautiously distinguishes between a "polemic" and a "debate." However, he states: "The two religions disregarded each other, and did not confront each other in an active polemic." The dissertation and the book are cited separately because contents vary.

9. Y. Baer, "Israel, the Christian Church, and the Roman Empire from the Time of Septimus Severus to the Educt of Toleration in A.D. 313," *Studies in History,* ed. A. Fuks and I. Halpern, *Scripta Hierosolymitana,* 7 (Jerusalem, 1961): 79-149.

10. See D. Rokeah, *Jews, Pagans and Christians,* see n. 8 above, 49.

11. For example, the debate between Nachmanides and Fra Paulo in 1263.

12. David Rokeah, Ph.D. Dissertation (Hebrew University, 1968), I, IV. The English translation is from the English abstract by D. Rokeah.

13. So too, Justin in the *Dialogue with Trypho, The Ante-Nicene Fathers,* ed. A. Roberts and J. Donaldson (Grand Rapids, Michigan, 1979 reprint), 1:267, chap. 135.

14. *The Anti-Nicene Fathers,* see introductory notes on 1:309-314 and 1:451 n. 11.

15. *The Anti-Nicene Fathers,* 1:352.

16. W. G. Kümmel, *Introduction to the New Testament*, trans. H.C. Kee (Nashville, 1975), 202-203.

17. Matthew 12.9-14; Mark 3.1-6; Luke 6.6-11.

18. Kümmel, *Introduction to the New Testament*, see n. 19 above, 229-230.

19. See Kümmel, 199 n. 109.

20. J. L. Martyn, *History and Theology in the Fourth Gospel* (New York, 1968), 17, 55, 127ff.

21. A. F. J. Klijn and C. J. Reinink, *Patristic Evidence for Jewish-Christian Sects*, Supplements to N.T. 26 (Leiden, 1973): 163; Also Hippolytus, 121; and others; 1-19.

22. Klijn and Reinink, *Patristic Evidence*, 109.

23. Klijn and Reinink, 105.

24. The use of the term "Hebrew" as opposed to a "Jew" in the writings of Origen and Jerome demonstrate that they had different uses for the term. See N. R. M. De Lange, "Origen as a Source for Jewish History," *Proceedings of the Sixth World Congress of Jewish Studies*, ed. M. Jagendors and A. Shinan (Jerusalem, 1975), 2:4-5. Using a common method of transliterating Hebrew words to Greek, some writings seem to have derived the designation *"Ebraioi"* from *"Abra(m)on"* or the followers of Abraham, possibly linking themselves to the Abrahamic covenant rather than the Mosaic covenant. See M. Stern, *Greek and Latin Authors on Jews and Judaism* (Jerusalem, 1980), 2:161.

25. One finds for example: "A Jew introduced as an imaginary character would not have said . . ." quoted in R. L. Wilken, *Judaism and the Early Christian Mind* (New Haven, 1971), 28.

26. H. Schoeps, *The Jewish-Christian Arguments*, trans. D. Green (New York, 1963), 19, 32-40.

27. Latest edition and notes in: *The Panarion of Epiphanius of Salamis*, Book 1, trans. F. Williams (Leiden, 1987).

28. All the Patristic material cited in this section will be cited according to: A. F. J. Klijn and C. J. Reinink, *Patristic Evidence for Jewish-Christian Sects*, 151.

29. Klijn and Reinink, *Patristic Evidence*, see n. 21 above, 141.

30. Klijn and Reinink, 141-142.

31. Klijn and Reinink, 161.

32. Klijn and Reinink, 173-175.

33. E.g., *Mishna Megillah* 4.8-9 in (Herford, *Christianity* 199-200).

34. E.g., *Mishna Hullim* 2.9 in (Herford, 178).

35. E.g., *Mishna Rosh Hashanah* 2.1 in (Hereford, 328).

36. See: J. Neusner, *The Tosefta* (New York, 1977), 175. (*Tractate Parah* 3.3).

37. S. Lieberman, *Hellenism in Jewish Palestine* (New York, 1950), 167 n. 21.

38. E.g., *The Babylonian Talmud,* Seder Moed, trans. Rabbi Dr. Leo Jung, (Yoma), (London, 1938), 3:191 n. 9.

39. *The Babylonian Talmud,* 191-192, see above, n. 38.

40. E.g., *Mechilta* 37b in (Herford, 301), Gnostic? *Tosephta Sanhedrin* 8.7: ". . . that the Minim might not say there was a companion with Him in the work." This might suggest 'Demiurge' found in Plato's *Timaeus,* 40c.

41. On this question see the enormous bibliography on the question collected by L. Feldman, *Josephus, A Supplementary Bibliography* (New York, 1986).

42. K. L. Carroll, "The Fourth Gospel and the Exclusion of Christians From the Synagogues," *Bulletin of the John Rylands Library* 40 (Manchester, 1957/58): 19-32; D. Flusser, *Judaism and the Origins of Christianity* (Jerusalem, 1988), 637-642. E.E. Urbach, like D. Flusser, argues that the original benediction (prior to 70) included a curse against the *perushim,* those leaving the community, and that this curse later was directed against *Minim* and eventually after the Bar Kokhba revolt included *Notzrim,* whom he sees as Christians. *The Sages: Their Concepts and Beliefs,* 1:401ff; also, E.E. Urbach, "Self-Isolation or Self-Affirmation in Judaism: Theory and Practice in the First Three Centuries," in *Judaism from the Maccabees to the Mid-Third Century,* ed. E. Sanders and A. I. Baumgarten (Philadelphia, 1980); and J. Heinemann, *Prayer in the Talmud: Forms and Patterns* (Berlin and New York, 1977); L. Finkelstein, "The Development of the Amidah," *JQR* 16 (1925/6): 1-43, 127-70; W.D. Davies, *The Setting of the Sermon on the Mount* (Cambridge, 1966), 272-277, sets the date of the composition of the *Birkat HaMinim* in 85 C.E.

43. Flusser, *Judaism and the Origins of Christianity,* 637-642. He bases himself, in part, upon the reading of *Tosefta Berachot* 3.25. S. Lieberman, in his commentary on this *Tosefta* states: "We learn that this blessing was initially a curse against sectarians and people who had the habit of removing themselves from the community in difficult times. This curse was directed at all the sects and individuals who endangered the unity of the public, and the benediction of *perushin* existed long before Shmuel Hakatan. *Tosefta Kifeshutah, Order Zeraim,* part 1 (New York, 1955), 54.

44. Y. Liebes, "Who Makes the Horn of Jesus to Flourish?" *Immanuel* 21 (Summer 1987): 55-66.

45. B. Binyamin, "*Birkat HaMinim* and the Ein Gedi Inscription," *Immanuel* 21 (Summer 1987): 68ff.

46. See, for example, Schäfer, "Die Sogenannte Synode von Jabne zur Trennung von Juden und Christen in Ersten/Zweiten Jh. n. chr.," *Judaica* 31 (1975): 58-59.

47. G. Mann, *HUCA* 2 (1925): 306, from a Geniza fragment.

48. See L. Finkelstein, *JQR*, New Series 16:156.

49. *Ante-Nicene Fathers*, 1:202, 218 (with emendations of note #6), 246, 247, 253, 257, 268.

50. Hom. II. 8 in Ps. 37 (PG XII, 1387).

51. See n. 50 above, 268, chapter 137: ". . . *meta tein prosuchein.*"

52. Cited from *Patristic: Evidence for Jewish-Christian Sects,* by A. F. J. Klijn and G. J. Reinink, 174-175. Jerome in his commentary on Isaiah, Chapter 52, verses 4-6, uses similar language to distinguish this group; Ibid., Klijn, 219, 221, and 225. It is even possible to distinguish perhaps another group, Minaeans, as Jerome states in his *Epistola:* "Until now a heresy is to be found in all parts of the East where Jews have their synagogues; it is called 'of the Minaeans' and cursed by the Pharisees up to now. Usually they are named 'Nazoraeans.' They believe in Christ, the Son of God born of Mary the virgin, and they say about him that he suffered and rose again under Pontius Pilate, in whom also we believe, but since they want to be both Jews and Christians, they are neither Jews nor Christians." This view of the Minaeans does not exactly coincide with the views of the Nazoraeans recorded elsewhere in Jerome. Klijn and Reinink, 201.

53. Klijn and Reinink, 173.

54. In his commentary on Amos 1.11-12; Isaiah 5.18-19; Isaiah 49.9; and Isaiah 52.4-6; Klijn and Reinink, 219, 221, and 225.

55. Isaiah 8.11-15; 8.19-22; 40.9-11; Klijn and Reinink.

56. L. Schiffman, *Who was a Jew?* 59-60. Klijn and Reinink claim that the designations are varied from Greek, Latin and Synraic transliterations. So, *"Nazoraioi," "Nazarenus," "Nazaraenus," "Nazaraeus," "Nazareus,"* for example.

57. Augustine, *de baptismo,* 7.1.1; Klijn and Reinink, 237; and also 50 n. 1.

58. See J. Barr's, "St. Jerome's Appreciation of Hebrew," *Bulletin of the John Rylands Library* 49 (1966): 280-302. Letters and commentaries also reflect this complex relationship between his love for the *veritas hebriaca* and his general dislike for the Jews; see Letter 84.3 and commentaries on Psalms 72 and 110 (among many other possible examples) which demonstrate this general view.

59. S. Pines, "The Jewish Christians of the Early Centuries of Christianity According to a New Source," *IASHP* 2, no. 13 (1966): 1-2.

60. There is evidence for a clear Jewish component to a Byzantine Jewish-Christian Debate. See N.R.M. De Lange, "A Fragment of Byzantine Anti-Christian Polemic," *Journal of Jewish Studies* 41.1 (Spring, 1990): 92ff. There are also materials in the Babylonian Talmud and later *Midrashim,* for example, dating from 4th and 5th century Babylonia which are garbled and clearly negative treatments of Jesus and/or Christianity (e.g. Babylonian Talmud, *Avodah Zarah 4b*) but these cannot be used as evidence of systematic "debate" materials.

WHO WERE THE JEWISH SECTARIANS UNDER EARLY ISLAM?

Steven M. Wasserstrom

The history of Jews and Judaism in the first centuries after Muhammad will remain a pastiche of speculations and extrapolations until the pluralism of the Geonic period has been thoroughly reinvestigated. Thus, though a "pan-Karaite" theory held sway early in this century, we still do not understand even such rudiments as the social setting of the origins of Karaism. The imperative to reopen this investigation seems in certain respects all the more pressing in the case of *extra-Karaite* Jewish sectarianism. In short, a rethinking of Jewish group organization at the end of antiquity is required. It was with this desideratum in mind that I undertook a systematic analysis of Muslim heresiography of the Jews. In that work, I analyzed the surprisingly rich range of classical Arabic sources concerning Jewish sectarianism.[1] The present essay presents some of the results of that research, supplemented by subsequent discovery and analysis of texts.

The first problem one encounters in this field of research is the paucity of datable Jewish sources. We possess almost no Rabbanite sources which specify the identities of other Jewish groups. The Geonim were famously disciplined in giving the silent treatment to their opposition and rivals: they did not "name names." Thus, aside from a few *responsa* and indirect statements, as well as some allusions in *piyyutim* and other poems, no Jewish sectarians are specified by name by the Geonim. Some Rabbis do refer to contemporaneous *minim;* Saadia cryptically criticized a group of *"anashim she-nikraim Yehudim"* ("people who are called Jews"); and, occasionally, a polemicist referred to *apikorsim,* or in Arabic, *Khawarij.*[2] These derogations often simply referred to Karaites, or to dissident Rabbanites.[3] Rarely can any other firm sectarian identity be teased from these oblique clues.

A second point with regard to Jewish sources is in order. The Cairo Geniza, which one might expect to be as rich a source on this subject as it is on so many other realms of Judaica, seems almost as silent as were the Geonim with reference to sectarians. Exceptions from the Geniza include the few texts (such as the Damascus Document) associated with the Qumran Jews;[4] a fascinating tenth-century polemical text of unknown origin studied only, and incompletely, by Jacob Mann;[5] some miscellaneous hints gleaned from documents;[6] and some works claimed by Shlomo Pines and his students to be Jewish-Christian.[7] This apparent paucity of Geniza evidence, however, may be misleading. We have reason to believe that important texts relevant to the study of Jewish sects under Islam exist in the Fircovitch collection in Leningrad. Still, even with *glasnost,* these texts have not been catalogued fully, much less published.

The following, then, represents an attempt based largely on Muslim sources--as well as on Karaite, Christian, and Rabbanite sources, though only secondarily--to survey the state of the question concerning the smaller Jewish sects under early Islam. I have searched for groups who are called or call themselves Jews; those that were considered to be or considered themselves to be somehow Jewish; and/or those that were neither Rabbanite, Karaite or Samaritan. Thus, this article particularly concerns Jewish groups possessing a distinctive body of doctrine and practice, whose organization and whose self-definition set them apart from being Rabbanites, Karaites and Samaritans, but not necessarily apart from being *"Jews."*

Given these general criteria, one could argue respectably for the existence of a handful of groups. On my reading of the sources, however, sufficient evidence exists to assert seriously the historicity of only three of these. Moreover, the study of one of these, the Jewish-Christians, involves methodological problems so knotty that I have decided not to attempt to untie them here. This leaves only two substantial, (and possibly interconnected), sects. They are generally referred to as the *"Isawiyya"* and the "Jewish-Gnostics.

The *'Isawiyya*

The first group I wish to discuss is also the only one to possess all of these characteristics in their fullest form. Abu 'Isa Al-Isfahani, as he was commonly known, was by far the most significant Jewish prophet-figure of early Islam.[8] Indeed, Abu 'Isa was the most influential Jewish "prophet" between Bar Cochba in the second century and Shabbetai Tzvi in the seventeenth century. In fact, this charismatic sectarian played on Jewish messianic expectations in an almost-successful attempt to create a new political Judaism along the lines of Shi'ism. His political creation, the *'Isawiyya,* was nothing less than the most important Jewish sect (after the Karaites), in the millennium from the rise of Islam until the sixteenth century. And the impact of this group was registered in dozens of works of medieval Muslim literature as well as in all substantial works of modern Jewish historiography dealing with Judaism under early Islam. In these works, Abu 'Isa remains notorious for his relativization of revelations--the doctrine that Muhammad and Jesus were genuine prophets, but only to their own communities and *not to the Jews.*

I do not have the time to today to analyze the full range of evidence concerning this group.[9] Thus I will not now elaborate their origins in the eighth century, their armed battles against the Muslims, or the numerous connections between them and the proto-Shi'i revolutionaries. Let me just say this concerning their doctrine and practice: Abu 'Isa forbad divorce; he required 7 or 10 prayers a day; he retained the Rabbanic forms of the *Shemone Esre* and the *Shema;* he exalted the Rabbis almost as high as the prophets; and he forbad the consumption of meat, fowl and wine. He allowed intermarriage with Rabbanites, because they celebrated the same holidays. And he used the same Torah text as did the Rabbanites.

Finally, a recently rediscovered chapter from the earliest Persian heresiography provides these precious additional details, heretofore unknown to the scholarship on Abu 'Isa:

> He imposed 10 ritual prayers in every 24 hour period. He said, "one to whom a nocturnal emission occurs and does not perform ablutions will not be pure for 7 days." He established a tax of 2/5ths: 1/5 for the Community and another 1/5 for the treasury of the Messiah (in such a manner that it remains in the treasury until the manifestation of the Messiah).[10]

This last, enticing detail, which evokes the Shi'i system of *khums* (1/5) tax for the Imam, provides strong new evidence for an hypothesis first put forward by Israel Friedlaender just before World War I.[11]   Friedlaender argued that the *'Isawiyya* were a product of a mid-eighth-century milieu which simultaneously spawned Shi'ism. I have recently provided additional evidence to support this proposition: most notably, I have compared this Jewish rebellion with that of its precise contemporary, the so-called *Mansuriyya*. I have adduced nine features of dating, doctrine and practice which they shared in common.[12]   I shall return to the general question of this formative Shi'i milieu in my remarks below.

The *'Isawiyya* eventually were widely, if sparsely, distributed over the lands as well as over the centuries of classical Islamicate civilization. From his hometown of Nisibis, Abu 'Isa took his movement to Isfahan. Subsequently, still in the Persian orbit, we find these sectaries in Rayy (present day Teheran) Hamadan, Qumm and Arrajan,whence they may have spread as far as Transoxania. In the central Islamicate lands, they seem to have settled in Palestine (if that is where the Palestinian Rabbi Jacob ibn Ephraim encountered them), as well as in Damascus, where Qirqisani certainly knew of a group of them. Remarks made by Shaybani and Maimonides suggest their possible presence in Mesopotamia. And, finally, that presence may have extended to Andalusia: ibn Hazm tells us that he met many Jews who held such doctrines.

Therefore, we have evidence of the *'Isawiyya* surviving through the eleventh and twelfth centuries, with some possibility that they survived even later than that. Spread to the far corners of the Islamicate world, this group endured for at least 300 years. This reconstruction militates against the consensus of modern scholarship, that the sect was merely an ephemeral aberration. Indeed, for eighty years, since Poznanski asserted that the preKaraite Jewish sects under Islam sprang up and died away "like mush-rooms,"[13] there has been little historiographic progress in this connection.

The *'Isawiyya,* in short, were not a mere flash in the crucible within which Islam was forged and Judaism was transmuted. They were, rather, a comparatively long-lived Jewish reaction to Islamicization. And in a sense they persist to the present. On the one hand, Abu 'Isa even is enshrined in some Karaite traditional texts as a progenitor (which, incidentally, is a fascinating misapprehension; though our encyclopedias still tell us that the Karaites "subsumed" the preKaraite sects such as the *'Isawiyya,* a claim which these Karaite texts seem to share, there is in fact no evidence to support such an assertion). On the other hand, the *'Isawiyya* are consistently listed as a major Jewish sect by Muslim scholars into the twentieth century. Thus, the *'Isawiyya* do survive even today, but only as a kind of scholastic spectre, a shadowy reminder of their ultimate failure.

Jewish-Gnostics

Of the three kinds of Jewish sectarians I have noted, it is arguable that only one left an indelible mark not only on the memory, but also on the practice of subsequent Judaism. In this regard I follow the hypothesis of Gershom Scholem: Jewish Gnostics produced the work known as *Sefer ha-Bahir,* which in turn was instrumental in the origins of Kabbalah. Scholem emphasized this theory throughout his sixty-year career, from his 1923 dissertation on the subject,[14] to the final proofs of the English translation of *Origins of the Kabbalah* prepared at the end of his life,[15] but he never identified the Eastern Jewish gnostics he posited so insistently.

Several kinds of (variously persuasive) evidence suggest that Jews and gnostics actively interacted during the first centuries of Islam. The best evidence of this kind is, of course, that of the Mandeans. While the Mandeans would appear to have shed any but the most vestigial Judaity by the Islamic period, physical remains seem to prove that Jews and Mandeans were still actively involved with one another in the first century or so of Islam. The evidence is that of the celebrated Mandaic incantation bowls. These magic bowls have been shown to be produced by and for both Jewish and Mandean professional magicians and customers.[16]

What evidence, aside from Mandaic bowls, do we possess concerning "Jewish-Gnostics," if there ever were such creatures? First of all, I remind you that Mesopotamia gave rise to, and long sustained, the most successful episodes of gnostic prophesying activism. The great Mesopotamian gnostic prophets of late antiquity, Elchasai and Mani, both emerged from Jewish--Christian communities.[17] The subsequent Manicheans retained strongholds here for centuries after they had fully rejected whatever marginal Jewishness Mani had picked up from his Elkesaite upbringing. We know that, further east, the Persian uprisings before and after Muhammad gave rise to prophets to whose suasions Jews were periodically susceptible. The great revolt against the Sasanids on the part of the gnostic Mazdak, just prior to the rise of Islam, both garnered Jewish supporters and fed into the rise of Shi'ism, with its own Jewish spinoffs such as the 'Isawiyya (Yar-Shater).

Heterogeneous sources refer to the presence of Marcionites, Manicheans, Mandeans and various other gnosticized pagans in seventh and eighth century Iraq.[18] This "sectarian milieu," to use John Wansborough's phrase, linguistically in transition from Aramaic to Arabic, was marked by its seemingly fluid interconfessionalism, most especially among its prevalent magicians and gnostics[19]. Moreover, work on the phenomenon of conversion shows that Islamicization developed slowly, even here in the Muslim heartlands. In other words, in the first century, and well into the second century of Islam, we know that gnostic sectarians, some with more or less visible Jewish roots, subsisted in this region. Among these, I suggest, we should include groups whom Gershom Scholem termed Jewish-Gnostic.[20] Two detailed reports, in particular, testify to a certain degree of Jewish--Gnostic syncretism in the period of the rise of Islam. Theodor bar Khonai, 8th-century Nestorian bishop of the Central Asian city of Kashgar, and Ibn al-Nadim, the assiduous 10th-century librarian and bibliophile, provide evocative information concerning such syncretism.

In the following, I will try to show how these reports may clarify the emergence of *Sefer ha-Bahir*.

In the *Fihrist* of Ibn al-Nadim, the fullest and most reliable source on gnosticism surviving after antiquity, we read that the followers of a sectarian named Khusraw al-Az-Rumanqan lived on a canal of the Tigris. This group "cursed and belittled Jesus" and sang ritually, "It is we who have dug the channel in the world and have stolen from the world this great treasure."[21]

Moreover, Ibn al-Nadim also explicitly associated this group with a revolutionary group known as the *"Khurramiyya."* This report is relevant for several
reasons: First, the "channel" and "great treasure" are gnostic technical terms,
which are taken up in *Sefer ha-Bahir* (and extensively analyzed as such by
Scholem). Second, the *Khurammiya* were a post-Islamic manifestation of the
Mazdakites, who fed into the proto-Shi'i rebellions, and who are said to have
had Jewish followers. Most significantly, once it is reexamined in light of a
report by bar Khonai concerning the so-called Kanteans, Ibn al-Nadim's report
reveals something new concerning "Jewish" sectarians.

According to the eleventh chapter of bar Khonai's *Liber Scholiorum,*
the Kanteans were a Perso-Mesopotamian gnosticizing sect who were reformed
by one Battai during the reign of the Sasanid emperor Peroz (459-487):

> The people of this sect had a leader named Papa, son of Klilaie
> of Gaukay. This Papa owned a slave named Battai. Out of
> laziness, he fled servitude. He hid among the Jews and left
> there for the disciples of Mani. He collected and arranged some
> of their words and some of the mysteries of their magic . . . he
> had stolen from the Jews the prohibition of eating pork-meat,
> from the Pentateuch the name of the Lord God, and from the
> Christians the sign of the cross . . . [as for his doctrine]: . . .
> the Lord God spoke seven words, and seven powers emanated
> from him. Then seven demons rose up and opposed the Lord
> God and the seven powers coming from him; after having
> shackled these adversaries, they stole from the Father of
> Greatness the principle of the Soul. The demons then began to
> cleanse and scour Adam, the first man. But the Lord God
> came, and destroyed Adam and remade him.[22]

Are these Kanteans "Jewish gnostics"? I would give four reasons to
associate this particular gnostic group with Jews. First, bar Khonai himself
cites no less than three explicit associations with Jews. Second, the immediate
followers of the Kanteans, the Mazdakites and the Khurramiya, included Jews
and converted Jews among them.[23] Third, Ibn al-Nadim describes several
groups very closely related to the Kanteans, whom he links with the Khurramiyya: as Bar Khonai does with the Kanteans, Ibn al-Nadim describes these
groups as being *explicitly but only partially* Jewish in orientation. Finally, the
association of Battai with Jewish magic plausibly may be more than a mere
polemicizing cliché. I have found the names of the ten heavens cited by Battai
on a Mandaic incantation bowl, in a context in which incantations were used
(if not authored) by Jews.[24]

This last point may be a crucial one, for the putative Urtext of *Sefer haBahir,* the so-called *Raza Rabba,* is twice cited in the tenth century in the specific context of books of magic.[25] This context did not surprise Scholem, who concluded that "[the] combination of the various elements would suggest that the *Raza Rabba* dates from roughly the same period as [the incantation bowls], that is, between the fifth and eighth centuries."[26]

The question that remains, then, is this: where can we locate *Sefer haBahir* in such a sectarian milieu? It seems reasonable to assert a general location amidst the interpenetrated cosmologies of Mandeans, Kanteans and Mazdakites. I can describe this setting with some further specificity, as follows: First, these Jewish-gnostics flourished in the century or two before and after Muhammad, in present day Iraq and the areas of nearby Iran. Moreover, some supported gnosticizing rebellions were initiated at the end of the Sasanid and continuing into the second century of Muslim rule. They incorporated aspects of Judaism, Christianity, Islam and Zoroastrianism, though both Christian and Muslim sources do emphasize their Jewish social connections, a connection confirmed by the magic bowls.

Finally, I can make one specification concerning these Jewish-gnostics, which may be of critical significance. I have identified a text from this milieu which strikingly parallels aspects of both the form and the gnostic content of *Sefer ha Bahir.* This text is the *Umm al-Kitab,* authored in the eighth century boomtown of Kufa, the home-base of the Shi'i gnostics. Concerning this setting, Josef van Ess has recently observed:

> Muslim authors are rather stingy with their references to Jewish influence . . . but if there was any direct contact it would have been with the early Shi'i Gnostics. . . . Was Islam, then, the continuation of Judaism, as has been suggested anew in recent studies? Perhaps in Kufa, but only there.[27]

Finally, Van Ess' fellow Tübingen Islamicist, Heinz Halm, who has translated and annotated a section of the (originally) Kufan gnostic *Umm al-Kitab,* characterizes its background this way:

> [The earliest stratum of the *Umm al-Kitab*] appears to be a strongly Jewish-colored gnosis, to which its special character is indebted. It is therefore to be taken seriously that the [later Shi'i] polemic [against the earlier Shi'i gnostics] named a converted Jew as the author of [*ghuluww*] [gnostic Shi'ism], one 'Abdallah ibn Saba'.[28]

It is into this general context that I would argue for a future comparison of *Sefer ha-Bahir* and *Umm al-Kitab:* I believe that it provides an
important missing link in the history of Jewish sectarianism under early Islam.
And so, in the end I follow Scholem's conjecture:

> It is in the neighborhood of Mandean and Manichean communi-
> ties in Mesopotamia where gnostic materials were kept alive in
> such varied forms, that we could most easily imagine the
> existence of such Jewish Gnostics . . . [but] we must not
> underestimate the difficulties raised by such an hypothesis.[29]

One such difficulty, to be sure, is that it may well not even be
legitimate to call these people "Jews" at all! But since the sources emphasize
their relations with Jews, and since they would seem to have made an impact
on subsequent Jewish thought and practice (through *Sefer ha-Bahir*) I have
treated them (provisionally) as constituting a sectarian syncretism between
Judaism and gnosticism.

The Shi'i Connection

I have argued that the two most significant secondary Jewish sects
under early Islam both were insinuated into the gnostic and interconfessional
setting of formative Shi'ism. If this *were* the case, how are we to make
historical sense of this fact? I would remind you of the historical context.
Shi'ism was not clearly defined until the early tenth century. The years of
tentative self-definition before that time were filled with absorption, experiment and innovation. Shi'is, indeed, were not only vigorous proselytizers, but
also voracious mythological consumers. Thus until the ascendancy of the
Twelvers (*Ithna Ashariyya*), so-called "Shi'ism" was at most a scattered
commonwealth of variegated groups and subgroups. To survive, much less
thrive, these sects often idiosyncratically accommodated themselves to the
senior religions of their environment. All the while, Jews lived under or
alongside the dominion of such *parvenu* groups for perhaps two full centuries.
I find this a plausible scenario: some threatened Jews under the new Muslim
rule felt the need to accommodate themselves to their neighbors, as did
Muslim minorities, such as the Shi'i groups. The resulting syncretism
between Muslim and non-Muslim minorities would seem to represent an
intelligible common cause shared between them.

It should be remembered, as I have already noted, that certain
influential trajectories of early Shi'ism were indisputably gnosticized.[30] Such
interreligious amalgamation was not historically unfamiliar. Gnosticism in this

region, after all, had for centuries specialized in what Nock called "the formation of blended worships with a capacity for success in the world at large."[31] That is, gnostics burrowed inside established religious practice by means of their vaunted protective coloration. That gnostics did camouflage themselves within Judaism as well as camouflage themselves inside Islam may seem strange. But in fact what might be called the "reAbrahamization" of gnosticism, along with its aggressive politicization, constituted a distinctive phenomenon of the early Islamic period.[32] This syncretism inherited and, to some extent, perpetuated a discernible and even tenacious social formation of the end of antiquity, the syncretized Jewish sect.

Both Rabbanites and Sunnites soon successfully mounted opposition to such syncretism. In fact, Sunni subsequently, insistently, and tellingly, portrayed the Shi'is as being a Judaizing intrusion into the Islamic community: the Shi'a by this (and other) means became irremediably marginalized.[33] Rabbanites likewise forced into oblivion the boundary-blurring apostates of their community. In the end, it was due to the success of such reaction that we know so little about the groups discussed here.

Conclusions

Who were the Jewish sectarians under early Islam? In part, they comprised self-defined, identifiable and sustained factions between the eighth and tenth centuries who interpenetrated with Shi'is and gnostics. I would argue that the syncretism I have described amounted to a fourth force in Judaism under early Islam (after the Rabbanites, Karaites, and Samaritans). Few of the dozens of Muslim sources say anything to contradict this hypothesis. Muslim heresiographers thus almost invariably mention Rabbanites, Karaites, Samaritans and 'Isawiyya together as the four predominant factions of the Jews.

The 'Isawiyya, indeed, became the most substantial Jewish minor sect of the Middle Ages. And the Jewish-gnostics may have created the most influential pre-Kabbalistic masterpiece, Sefer ha-Bahir. Both of these groups seem to have been interpenetrated with Shi'i thought. Still, in the end I confess that the evidence I have presented remains very much open to reinterpretation. I will consider myself successful if I have succeeded in arguing that Jewish sectarianism under early Islam deserves that closer inspection.

Endnotes

1. Steven M. Wasserstrom, *Species of Misbelief: A History of Muslim Heresiography of the Jews*, PhD. Dissertation (University of Toronto, 1985); "The Moving Finger Writes: Mughira ibn Sa'id's Islamic Gnosis and the Myths of its Rejection," *History of Religions* 25 (1985): 1-29.

2. Jacob Mann, "An Early Theologico-Polemical Work," *The Collected Articles of Jacob Mann*, vol. 3 (Gedara, Israel, 1971), 411-459.

3. Bruno Chiesa, "Il Guidaismo Caraita," *Correnti Culturali e Movimenti Religiosi de Guidaismo*, ed. Bruno Chiesa (Roma, 1987), 163-169.

4. Louis Ginzberg, *An Unknown Jewish Sect* (Revised and updated translation of *Eine unbekannte jüdische Sekte*, [New York, 1922]) (New York, 1976).

5. Jacob Mann, see n. 2 above.

6. Mordechai Friedman, "Menstrual Impurity and Sectarianism in the Writings of the Geonim and of Moses and Abraham Maimonides," *Maimonidean Studies* vol. I, ed. Arthur Hyman (New York, 1990), 1-23 (Hebrew section, in Hebrew).

7. Steven M. Wasserstrom, "Jewish Pluralism in the Geonic Period: The Case of the 'Jewish-Christians'," *Journal of the Society of Rabbis in Academia* 1 (1991): 75-79, at p.78 n. 10; Patricia Crone, "Islam, Judeo-Christianity and Byzantine Iconoclasm," *Jerusalem Studies in Arabic and Islam* 2 (1980): 59-95; Yehudah Liebes, "Who Makes the Horn of Jesus to Flourish," *Jerusalem Studies in Jewish Thought* 3 (1984): 313-348 (in Hebrew); Menahem Kister, "Plucking the Grain on the Sabbath and the Jewish-Christian Debate," *Jerusalem Studies in Jewish Thought* 3 (1984): 349-366, (in Hebrew).

8. Wasserstrom, "The 'Isawiyya Revisited," *Studia Islamica* 75 (1992): (in press). Sources and details for what follows can be found in this article.

9. Wasserstrom, "The 'Isawiyya Revisited."

10. My translation from Guy Monnot, *Islam et religions* (Paris, 1986).

11. Israel Friedlaender, "Jewish-Arabic Studies," *Jewish Quarterly Review* 1 (New Series 1910-1913): 183-215; *Jewish Quarterly Review* 2: 481-516; *Jewish Quarterly Review* 3: 235-300.

12. Wasserstrom, see n. 8 above.

13. Samuel Poznanski, "Philon dans l'ancienne litterature judéo-arabe," *Revue des études juives* 50 (1905): 22.

14. Gershom Scholem, *Das Buch Bahir*, Ph.D. Dissertation (Munich, 1923).

15. Gershom Scholem, *Origins of the Kabbalah*, trans. Allan Arkush from *Ursprung und Anfange der Kabbala*, 1962, (Princeton, 1987).

16. Jonas Greenfield, "Notes on some Aramaic and Mandaic Magic Bowls," *The Journal of the Ancient Near Eastern Society of Columbia University* 5 (1973): 149-156.

17. John C. Reeves, *Jewish Traditions in Manichaean Cosmogony in Light of New Evidence from the "Book of Giants,"* Ph.D. Dissertation, HUC-JIR (Cincinnati, Ohio, 1989).

18. Michael G. Morony, *Iraq After the Muslim Conquest* (Princeton, 1984), 280-431.

19. John Wansborough, *The Sectarian Milieu: Content and Composition of Islamic Salvation History* (Oxford, 1978); Wasserstrom, "The Moving Finger Writes: Mughira ibn Sa'id's Islamic Gnosis and the Myths of its Rejection," *History of Religions* 25 (1985): 1-29.

20. Gershom Scholem, *Jewish Gnosticism, Merkabah Mysticism and Talmudic Tradition* (New York, 1960).

21. Ibn al-Nadim, *The Fihrist of al-Nadim*, 2 vols., trans. Bayard Dodge (New York, 1970).

22. My translation from the French translation by R. Hespel and R. Draguet of Theodor Bar-Konai, *Theodore bar Koni, Livre des scolies (recension de Seert)*, 2 vols. (*CSCO* 431-432), (1982), 256-257.

23. Wilferd Madelung, "Abu 'Isa al-Warraq über die Bardesaniten, Marcioniten und Kantaer," *Studien zur Geschichte und Kultur des Vorderen Orients*, eds. H.R. Roemer and A. Noth, (Leiden, 1981), 210-224; Erik Peterson, "Urchristentum und Mandaismus," *Zeitschrift für die neutestamentliche Wissenschaft und die Kunde der älteren Kirche* 27 (1928): 55-98; E. Yarshater, "Mazdakism," *Cambridge History of Iran*, vol. 3, ed. E. Yarshater (Cambridge, 1983), 991-1024.

24. James Montgomery, *Aramaic Incantation Texts* (Philadelphia, 1913), 141.

25. Scholem, *Origins of the Kabbalah*, see n. 15 above, 106.

26. Scholem, *Origins of the Kabbalah*, see n. 15 above, 107.

27. Josef Van Ess, "The Youthful God: Anthropomorphism in Early Islam," *The University Lecture in Religion at Arizona State University* (1988): 12-13.

28. My translation from Heinz Halm, "Das 'Buch der Schatten'," *Der Islam* 58 (1981): 15-86 at p. 54.

29. Scholem, *Origins of the Kabbalah,* see n. 15 above, 193.

30. Halm, "Das Buch der Schatten," *Der Islam* 55 (1978): 219-266; "Das Buch der Schatten," *Der Islam* 58 (1981): 15-86; *Die Islamische Gnosis,* (Zurich and München, 1982); Wasserstrom, "The Moving Finger Writes," see n. 1 above.

31. Arthur Darby Nock, (Oxford, 1933 [reprint,1967]).

32. Wasserstrom, "The Moving Finger Writes," see n. 1 above.

33. Wasserstrom, "'The Shi'a are the Jews of our Community'--An interreligious Comparison Within Sunni Thought," Paper delivered at the Annual Meeting of the American Academy of Religion (1990).

THE SABBATEAN MOVEMENT IN SMYRNA:
THE SOCIAL BACKGROUND

Jacob Barnai

In their introduction to the section on Sabbateanism in *Christians and Jews in the Ottoman Empire,* which appeared in 1982, the editors, B. Lewis and B. Braude, wrote the following:

> The social background and social impact of Sabbateanism have not been as thoroughly examined as the spiritual. It has been claimed that in the aftermath of exhaustion and disappointment, Ottoman Jewry reinforced the power and authority of rabbinic leadership, and in the process, lost the wellsprings of its cultural and economic vitality.[1]

Gershom Scholem's monumental study of Sabbetai Zevi and the Sabbatean movement during Sabbetai Zevi's lifetime[2] demonstrates extensive historical and social knowledge. Nevertheless, it concentrates mainly on the theological background of Sabbateanism, and on the religious aspect of the movement itself. In his extensive discussion of the background of the development of Sabbateanism, Scholem stressed the religious and spiritual factors: the dissemination of R. Isaac Luria's version of the *Kabbala* in the sixteenth and seventeenth centuries, and the continuity and internalization of the messianic idea in Jewish history.

Scholem generally attributed secondary or marginal importance to the social and economic factors that led to the outbreak of Sabbateanism in Jewish and other circles, although these factors were discussed by several previous investigators. An example is the association of the Marranos with Sabbateanism.[3] An additional example are the pogroms in Eastern Europe during 1648-49, to which Scholem did not attach much weight.[4] There were some social factors to which Scholem ascribed more importance, such as the hostile confrontations among the rabbis in Smyrna[5] (which I will discuss later). Only recently has more extensive attention been paid to this aspect. Social aspects of Sabbateanism were discussed by the sociologist Sharot in his book, *Messianism, Mysticism and Magic.*[6]

In this lecture I will discuss the social aspect as a factor and background for the outbreak of the Sabbatean movement and its transformations. There are several relevant questions:

1. Is there a connection between the social and economic background and the growth and decline of the Sabbatean movement?

2. How did Sabbetai Zevi and Nathan of Gaza work within Jewish society for the furtherance of their messianic mission?

3. Was the reaction of Jewish society to Sabbetai Zevi's message based purely on ideological and theological considerations, or were these considerations accompanied by social and economic motives as well?

4. How did the Sabbatean movement, its eventual failure, and the conversion of its "messiah" to Islam affect Jewish society?

The subject is very broad, and the questions quite comprehensive. A proper discussion of all these questions would have to encompass the entire Jewish diaspora in the seventeenth and eighteenth centuries. I do not pretend to be able to do this, certainly not within the framework of a paper which I see as being an invitation to discussion rather than being a preemptive conclusion. I have thus chosen to investigate some of these basic issues with respect to the Jewish community of Smyrna, which was a centrally located Jewish community in the seventeenth century. Smyrna is particularly important in the history of Sabbateanism because it is the city in which Sabbetai Zevi and many of his followers were born, grew up, and carried out many of their activities.

We must briefly analyze the social structure of the Jewish community in order to discuss the question of whether there was a connection between the social background in Smyrna and the Sabbatean movement. The city did not have a Jewish community at the end of the Byzantine period or during the Ottoman occupation in the fourteenth and fifteenth centuries. Even the Spanish exiles did not go there at the end of the fifteenth century or during the sixteenth century. The reason was simple--Smyrna was a small, insignificant town until the end of the sixteenth century. Under the aegis of European companies for the Levant at the end of the sixteenth century and during the course of the seventeenth century, Smyrna did begin to develop. Its port became a focus of widespread international trade, and Jews began to immigrate.

The Jewish migration to Smyrna, beginning at the end of the sixteenth century, was mainly a migration of Spanish and Portuguese Jews. These were not of the generation of the expulsion from Spain, but their third and fourth generation descendants. Marranos from Portugal returned to Judaism and emigrated to Smyrna during the seventeenth century as well. The Portuguese Marranos, whose counterparts arrived at various communities in Western Europe during the seventeenth century, were a very important element in Smyrna's developing community.[7] These Jews were joined by others from

Italy and from many different communities in Turkey, the Balkans, and other vicinities in the Ottoman Empire.[8] The Smyrna community was thus unlike the communities of Spanish exiles during the sixteenth century. The exiles who arrived in Smyrna brought with them traditions that had been consolidated in various Jewish communities within and outside the Ottoman Empire. In the seventeenth century, the traditions and customs of Istanbul, for example, were already different from the traditions and customs of Salonika. These differences were reflected in the conflicts among the traditions in Smyrna.[9] This very heterogeneous population of immigrants attempted to consolidate patterns of behavior and tradition through harsh confrontations in the society and in the community leadership of Smyrna.

Smyrna's international mercantile character was very prominent in the seventeenth century. Our sources say little about Jewish manual workers there, but much about Jewish merchants and traders. In this respect, Smyrna differed from other cities in the Ottoman Empire. Istanbul, Bursa and Salonika had many Jewish artisans and manual laborers in that century. The Jewish community in Smyrna maintained connections with the communities of origin and with other European communities. The fact that many of the Smyrna's Jews were engaged in international trade and brokerage strengthened these connections. Sabbetai Zevi's father and brothers arrived in Smyrna from the Balkans in the early seventeenth century. They were soon engaged in trade as independent brokers and merchants, and they became very wealthy.

During the first half of the seventeenth century this pluralistic community of immigrants did not yet have a solid, stable leadership. R. Joseph Escapa (d. 1661) was a very dominant rabbi who overshadowed the others, but he faced fierce opposition, and had to struggle to maintain his standing.[10] In the middle of the century he did succeed in imposing his authority and legislated regulations for the entire community on matters of taxes, property rights, and the like. During the first half of the century, six congregations were established in the city to represent the arriving waves of immigrants. Two of these congregations, the richest and most prominent of the six, were congregations of Portuguese Marranos (which seem to have been joined by other Jews from all over the Ottoman Empire and outside, most of the Sephardaim, as well). Another congregation consisted of Jews who immigrated from neighboring areas to Smyrna. The remaining congregations consisted of immigrants from Salonika, Istanbul and other places.

The Gabbai family, owners of a printing house in Livorno who had immigrated to Smyrna, set up a printing house in Smyrna in 1658. From 1658 to 1665, (the year Sabbetai Zevi returned to Smyrna as a "messiah"), ten books, mainly on *Halakha,* were published in the city.[11]

It was in this society that Sabbetai Zevi was born and raised, and here his personality was formed. Several of his close friends and fellow students were from families of Portuguese Marranos. I believe that this is a significant factor in Sabbetai Zevi's messianic interests. Historians have pointed out that in communities of Portuguese Marranos, such as those in Livorno, Venice, Ancona, Hamburg, and of course Amsterdam, the Sabbatean message was accepted by extensive portions of the community.[12] The fact that the Jewish community there was not consolidated permitted Sabbetai Zevi's strange activities to take place, both in his youth and after he returned to the city as a "messiah" in 1665-66. When he first began his strange activities during the sixteen-forties and fifties, R. Joseph Escapa exiled him from the city, but he returned again and again. One of Sabbetai Zevi's close friends who became his ardent disciple, R. Moses Piniero (a characteristic Portuguese name), was a troublemaker who was forced to leave the city for Livorno at the end of the sixteen-fifties.[13] In 1665-1666, the tense social situation and the hostile rivalry within the community's leadership permitted Sabbetai Zevi's intensive activity in Smyrna, when he returned as a "messiah."

This rivalry was accompanied by violence between the various groups and by the handing over of rivals to gentile courts or consulates. When R. Joseph Escapa died, Sabbetai Zevi and his supporters exploited the unstable social situation in the community. They took over the Portuguese synagogue on the Sabbath, deposed R. Aaron Lapapa, and crowned R. Haim Benveniste its sole rabbi. While there were true believers and opponents of Sabbetai Zevi in the city, many people supported him out of fear and calculated self-interest. This caused his supporters to outnumber his opponents. The feelings in the city during this period were described well by an anonymous author of responsa (who I believe was R. Solomon ben Ezra, one of the pillars of the community at that time):

> I well remember how we used to live in the protection of our
> great rabbi and teacher R. Joseph [Escapa] who ruled over us.
> . . . But when he grew old . . . differences and quarrels arose
> between the members of the community . . . and the fire of
> controversy burned like an oven.[14]

After describing the attempts to find authorized candidates for the city rabbinate, and the compromise that was finally achieved between R.Benveniste and R. Lapapa on the division of the rabbinate, the author of the responsum describes Sabbetai Zevi's return to Smyrna as a "messiah":

> On the sixth of Tevet 5426 [January 1666] a proclamation was suddenly announced . . . that everyone should go to the Portuguese congregation and kiss the hand of R. Haim [Benveniste]. . . . And in the name of our rabbi and teacher it was announced that the spirit of the prophet Samuel would be bestowed upon him. Everyone who thirsted to see God's salvation, thinking that God was redeeming His people, ran together to this place. . . . And even those who did not believe this announcement went there as well, out of fear of the masses, that they should not rise up against them and say, "You are rebelling against the words of the Messiah of God." . . . Our rabbi, R. Aaron Lapapa, was persecuted and hid . . . for he was afraid to go outside, even to go to the synagogue to pray with a quorum of ten, because they were persecuting him for not being a believer [in Sabbetai Zevi].[15]

Sabbetai Zevi's domination of the Smyrna community in early 1666--which was an important factor in the movement's spread among the other Jewish communities--would not have been possible if he had not exploited the divisiveness and fierce hostility in the society and in the community leadership at that time.

There were also some paradoxes in the division between his supporters and his opponents in Smyrna. Sabbetai Zevi appointed R. Haim Benveniste as rabbi of the city. R. Benveniste was an outstanding *Halakhic* scholar, perhaps the greatest decider of *Halakha* in Turkey in the seventeenth century. In all his books there is almost no mention of *Kabbala,* and when he does mention it, he adds reservations. His fierce opponent in the community, R. Solomon Algazi, was one of the most important Kabbalists in Turkey. Moreover, it is not known whether R. Haim Benveniste actually arrived at his belief in Sabbetai Zevi out of pure motives. One may speculate that his intense desire to be appointed the sole rabbi of the congregation led him to support Sabbetai Zevi.

Another important question is how the vicissitudes of Sabbetai Zevi's life and his eventual conversion affected Jewish society in the seventeenth and eighteenth centuries. In Smyrna, at least, they undoubtedly had a great impact. One piece of evidence informs us that the Pinto congregation divided in two during 1666,[16] and that this division occurred as a result of the struggle between the Sabbateans and their opponents. The Sabbatean "prophet" Daniel Bonafus was active in the Pinto congregation during the 1670s.[17] Many Jews in Smyrna continued to believe in Sabbetai Zevi and his teachings after he left the city for Istanbul, and years later, after his conversion and death.[18] Some of his friends, teachers and supporters did indeed repudiate this belief, at least in public. For example, R. Haim Benveniste beat his breast in repentance in a letter to the Tire community on the eve of the fast of the Ninth of Av in 1667: "Last year we all sinned like straying sheep by making the Ninth of Av into a day of feasting and rejoicing."[19] He accepted upon himself the penance of fasting every Monday and Thursday for a whole year to atone for his belief in Sabbetai Zevi. Nevertheless, his attitude towards Sabbateanism at this time is not totally clear.

Sabbetai Zevi's first teacher of *Kabbala*, R. Isaac da-Elba, a Smyrna rabbi whose original attitude towards Sabbetai Zevi's messianism is unknown, was also among his opponents after his conversion.[20] On the other hand, there is much clear evidence of many people in Smyrna who remained overt Sabbateans in the late seventeenth and early eighteenth centuries. There were dozens of such believers, some of them from noble or wealthy Smyrna families. It is not surprising that the Sabbatean Michael Abraham Cardozo found refuge in Smyrna for several years. Even some of the well-known rabbis of Smyrna in the late seventeenth century and during the eighteenth century continued to believe in Sabbetai Zevi. For several decades after his conversion, echoes of the controversies and debates between his supporters and his opponents could be heard within the city. It is unsurprising that the best seller *Hemdat Yamim* ("Delightful of Days")[21] was written, edited and printed in Smyrna in the eighteenth century by a group of rabbis with connections to Sabbateanism. All these rabbis held key positions in the leadership of Jewish community, although by this time they were no longer acting on behalf of Sabbateanism in public, and the publication of this book took place in secret and in a very sophisticated, conspiratorial manner.

Even in the nineteenth century, Sabbetai Zevi and Nathan of Gaza did not incur the same reservations or opposition that they incurred in other Jewish communities throughout the world. In the middle of the nineteenth century, R.Haim Palagi of Smyrna, the greatest Turkish rabbi of that century, who collected manuscripts about Sabbetai Zevi, was still defending Nathan of Gaza and the book *Hemdat Yamim,* attributed to him. R. Palagi praised the pilgrimages to Nathan's grave in Skopje and noted:

If you are angered by [Nathan's] belief in Sabbetai Zevi, that does not affect his teachings, for R. Akiva was one of our greatest sages even though he was mistaken about Bar-Kokhba.[22]

This is an amazing comparison, and it tells us a great deal about R. Palagi's view of Sabbateanism. We can see how the influence of Sabbateanism on the Smyrna community continued well into the nineteenth century, with a largely sympathetic attitude to the founders of the movement and to their teachings.

I would like to end on the note with which I began: We saw that, alongside the religious causes for messianic belief, social forces in Smyrna were also active in the background of the Sabbatean movement. We also saw that the influence of Sabbateanism on the Jewish society in Smyrna reached as far as the nineteenth century, well past the period in which Sabbetai Zevi himself was active.

We must also consider the contentions of Lewis and Braude that the Sabbatean crisis did not bring about the economic and spiritual decline of the Jews in the Ottoman Empire, but rather the decline was a social, spiritual and economic process that had begun before, and was merely accelerated by, the appearance of Sabbateanism.

It seems to me that, as far as the economic situation is concerned, this is not accurate. Indeed, there had been a certain decline in the economic status of the Jews in Turkey and in the rest of the Ottoman Empire in the seventeenth century, but the Jewish community in Smyrna was growing and flourishing during the years preceding Sabbetai Zevi's appearance. Even in the following years, there were no signs of decline in the economic status of the Jews of Smyrna *and the Sabbatean crisis did not affect their situation in the slightest*. The economic decline of the Jews of Smyrna was associated with another event entirely: In 1688 the city was destroyed by an earthquake.[23] Thousands of people were killed and the harbor was unusable for years. In the early eighteenth century, the city was rebuilt. When the Greeks and Armenians started to become prominent in its economic life and in international trade, the Jews were edged out.[24] The claims that have been made about the economic situation are thus inaccurate with respect to Smyrna.

The social and spiritual aspects are considerably more complicated. We saw that Sabbetai Zevi exploited the fact that the Smyrna community had not been consolidated at the time of his activities. It was *after* the terrible upheaval that occurred in the community (1665-1666), and after Sabbetai Zevi's conversion that the community calmed down somewhat and became more united than it had been before. It also seems that all the important communities did not develop uniformly. In Salonika, for example, the mass conversion of the Doenme sect in 1683 led to a severe social and spiritual crisis. This issue requires more extensive clarification.[25]

As far as the spiritual aspect is concerned, I'm not sure that the great decline in the creativity and cultural level of the Turkish Jews began before the advent of Sabbetai Zevi. In the seventeenth century there were a number of great Torah scholars in Salonika, Istanbul and Smyrna. R. Haim Benveniste in Smyrna, his cousins Moses and Joshua Benveniste in Istanbul, and R. Haim Sabbetai and others in Salonika all maintained a very high level of Torah study, and their books are studied as *Halakhic* works to this very day. It is true that there was a noticeable decline in the area of *Halakhic* innovation in the generation following Sabbetai Zevi; there may be a connection between that crisis, and the Turkish scholars' seclusion and their immersion in the study of *Kabbala.* However, creativity in the fields of *Midrash* and *Kabbala* developed and reached a peak in Smyrna in the eighteenth century: the books, (for example *Midrash Talpioth* and *Shevet Musar*),[26] of the homilist and Sabbatean R. Elijah Hacohen Ha'itamari became known throughout the Jewish world in the eighteenth and nineteenth centuries, and continue to be read today. The book, *Hemdat Yamim,* is entirely a product of the Sabbatean crisis.

For all these reasons I am not sure that the Sabbatean crisis caused the decline of the rabbis' status. Beginning in the late eighteenth century, a decline in their status did occur. It seems that *this* decline was caused by the economic deterioration, the severe social polarization, the prevailing ignorance, and the general influence of the society surrounding them.

Endnotes

1. B. Braude and B. Lewis, *Christian and Jews in the Ottoman Empire* (New York and London), 26.

2. G. Scholem, *Sabbati Sevi: The Mystical Messiah* (Princeton, 1973).

3. See D.S. Katz, "Menasseh ben Israel's Christian Connection: Henry Jessey and the Jews," in *Menasseh ben Israel and His World,* ed. Y. Kaplan, H. Mechoulan and R. Popkin (Leiden, 1989), 117-138; E.G.E. van der Wall, Petrus Serrarius and Menasseh ben Israel, "Christian Millenialism and Jewish Messianism in 17th-Century Amsterdam," in G. Scholem, *Sabbati Sevi . . .* 164-190; J. Barnai, "Portuguese Communities in Smyrna," in *Nation and History,* vol. 1, ed. M. Stern (Jerusalem, 1983), 289-298 (in Hebrew).

4. I am planning to publish a paper on this topic in the near future.

5. Scholem, *Sabbati Sevi*, see note 2 above, 371-416; see also D. Tamar, *Studies on the History of the Jews in Palestine and the East* (Jerusalem, 1981), 119-135 (in Hebrew); J. Barnai, "R. Yosef Escapa and the Smyrna Rabbinate," *Sefunot* 18 (1985): 53-82 (in Hebrew).

6. Stephen Sharot, *Messianism, Mysticism, and Magic:* A Sociological Analysis of Jewish Religious Movements (Chapel Hill, 1983).

7. Barnai, "Portuguese Communities," see n. 3 above; Kaplan et al., *Menasseh ben Israel,* see n. 3 above; Y. Kaplan, *From Christianity to Judaism* (Oxford, 1990); Y.H. Yerushalmi, *From Spanish Court to Italian Ghetto* (New York and London, 1971).

8. J. Barnai, "The Origins of the Smyrna Jewish Community in the Ottoman Period," *Pe'amim* 12 (1982): 47-58 (in Hebrew); D. Goffman, *Izmir and the Levantine World, 1550-1650* (Seattle and London, 1990), 77-92.

9. J. Barnai, *Organization and Leadership in the Jewish Community of Smyrna in the 17th Century* (Brandeis University, in press).

10. Barnai, "R. Yosef Escapa," see n. 5 above.

11. A. Ya'ari, "The Hebrew Press in Smyrna," *Areshet* 1 (1959): 91-222 (in Hebrew).

12. Barnai, "R. Yosef Escapa," see n. 5 above.

13. Scholem, *Sabbati Sevi,* see n. 2 above, 110-116.

14. R. Abraham Palagi, *Avraham Ezkor* [I Will Remember Abraham] (Smyrna, 1889), 35. On this responsum see J. Barnai, "A Document from Smyrna Concerning the History of Sabbateanism," *Jerusalem Studies in Jewish Thought* 2 (1982): 118-131 (in Hebrew).

15. Palagi, *Avraham Ezkor.*

16. Tamar, *Studies on the History,* see n. 5 above, 149.

17. A. Freimann, *Inyaney Shabbetai Zevi* (Issues on Sabbetai Zevi) (Berlin, 1912), 10.

18. J. Barnai, "On the History of the Sabbatean Movement and its Place in the Life of the Jews in the Ottoman Empire," *Pe'amim* 3 (1979): 59-72 (in Hebrew); M. Benayahu, "The Sabbatean Movements in Greece," *Sefunot* 14 (1977): (in Hebrew).

19. R. Ya'akov Sasportas, *Zizat Novel Zevi* (The Withering Flower of Zevi), ed. I. Tishbi (Jerusalem, 1954), 208.

20. J. Barnai, "Two Documents Concerning the History of Sabbateanism in Tunis and Smyrna," *Zion* 52 (1987): 191-202 (in Hebrew).

21. A. Ya'ari, *The Mystery of the Book* (Jerusalem, 1954) (in Hebrew); I. Tishbi, *The Paths of Belief and Heresy* (Ramat Gan, 1964) (in Hebrew).

22. R. Haim Palagi, *Kol Hahaim* (All the Living) (Smyrna, 1974), 17-18 (in Hebrew).

23. E. Bashan, "Fires and Earthquakes in Smyrna," *Miqqedem Umiyyam* 2 (1986): 13-28 (in Hebrew); C. Iconomos, *Étude sur Smyrne* (Smyrne, 1868), 128-131.

24. N. Ülker, *The Rise of Smyrna, 1688-1740*, Ph.D. Dissertation, (University of Michigan, 1974), 42ff.

25. Benayahu, "The Sabbatean Movements," see n. 18 above, 77-108.

26. J. Barnai, "Connections and Distinctions Between the Sages of Turkey and Those of Poland and Central Europe in the 17th Century," *Gal-Ed* 9 (1986): 13-26 (in Hebrew).

HASKALAH AND THE ROOTS OF JEWISH RADICALISM IN NINETEENTH CENTURY RUSSIA

Erich E. Haberer

In his autobiography, the Yiddish poet and song-writer Eliakum Zunser relates the story of the arrest of Arkadii Finkelshtein and members of his Vilna socialist circle in 1872. This being the first manifestation of socialist radicalism among Russian Jews, the Governor-General of Vilna chastised Jewish community leaders: "To all the other good qualities which you Jews possess, about the only thing you need is to become Nihilists too." Adding insult to injury, the General blamed this state of affairs on the "bad education" they were giving their children. Rejecting this accusation, the spokesman of the Jewish notables replied: "Pardon me General, this is not quite right! As long as we educated our children there were no Nihilists among us; but as soon as you took the education of our children into your hands they became so."[1]

Such a response was fair enough, but what the notables failed to recognize--or were perhaps reluctant to admit--was that the arrested Vilna radicals, and those who continued their socialist propaganda later on, were as much a product of internal Jewish circumstances and conflict as they were a phenomenon fostered by external non-Jewish influences and tsarist educational policy. More specifically, the origins of the Finkelshtein circle, and of Jewish radicalism in general, were rooted in the volatile ideological and sociological transformation of the Jewish community under the impact of the *Haskalah*.

The connection between the *Haskalah* and the rise of Jewish radicalism in Russia has so far received little attention from historians. For instance, while scholars have generally recognized that Russian Zionism was in many ways a radical extension of the Jewish Enlightenment, and as such a nationalist ideology of modernization, they have virtually ignored that a similar process was at work with respect to pre-Zionist expressions of Jewish radical behavior. Indeed, even more so than in the case of Zionism, these expressions of radicalism were directly and integrally linked with the penetration of the *Haskalah* into the communities of Russian Jewry between the late eighteenth and mid-nineteenth century.[2]

Most crucial for demonstrating this vital connection is the history of the formation of an enlightened, secularized Russian Jewish intelligentsia. Arising in conditions of conflict, both vis-a-vis Jewish traditional society and Russian autocratic regimentation, this intelligentsia became radicalized to such a degree that many of its members eventually were assimilated into the Russian revolutionary movement. It is probably for this latter reason that Jewish historians especially, have failed to pay attention to the phenomenon of early Jewish radicalism even though it belongs to the Jewish historical experience. Indeed, this radicalism was so deeply rooted in the social milieu and cultural world of the *Haskalah* that its youthful exponents retained aspects of Jewishness even as they were absorbed into the Russian revolution.

The Enlightenment was, of course, a European-wide phenomenon which arose in the late 1600s when rationalist thinking, empirical analysis, and utilitarian ethics came to the fore and culminated in an ideology of reason. Ushering in the making of modern European civilization, the proponents of this new ideology rejected medieval religious dogmas and supernatural explanations of the nature of man and his worldly environment. For them, man and his striving for happiness and social usefulness was the measure of all things in the realm of religion, morality, economics, and politics. Relying on reason alone--the assumed rationality and civic virtue supposedly shared by all human beings--man could discover the laws of nature and create for himself a world in harmony with his own "true nature." He could, in other words, reform society to conform with his natural desires for individual liberty, moral goodness, secular knowledge, and unrestrained creativity: all of which would benefit the "common good." In short, humanity, rationality, and utility, interpreted and defined in terms of universal human nature and universal natural law, became the hallmarks of the Enlightenment and its prescriptions for the education of mankind and the reformation of society.

As the Age of Reason wore on and found its luminaries in the French *philosophes,* these ideas gained general currency in Europe and began to influence all areas of cultural, social, and political life. The Jews were not to be excluded from the tremendous impact of the Enlightenment which, "because it strove to be universal, . . . perforce had to include even the Jew."[3] It was, however, not until the flowering of the German *Aufklaerung* in the latter half of the eighteenth century that this truth was fully recognized, and that moreover, Jews themselves were drawn to the Enlightenment, and--in the person of Moses Mendelssohn (1729-86)--articulated a corresponding Jewish ideology: the *Haskalah.*

It is one of these imponderable ironies of history that Germany was not only the land of the Holocaust, but also the country in which the idea of emancipation and the practice of acculturation in the spirit of the Enlightenment gave birth to the modern Jew.[4] It was in Berlin, among the outstanding representatives of the *Aufklaerung,* that, as one historian phrased it, "Mendelssohn was granted the unique opportunity of being accepted by the gentile world as no Jew before him."[5] Here that Mendelssohn set out to make this opportunity available to all Jews by bringing them into the mainstream of European civilization.

The *Haskalah* was a direct result of his efforts to convince Gentiles as well as Jews that the Enlightenment and its all-inclusive concepts of rationality, humanity, and utility made Jewish exclusiveness irrational, inhumane, and useless. The twofold ghetto of Jewish existence and bondage-- the external ghetto of legal disabilities imposed by medieval Christianity and the internal ghetto of religious tradition maintained by rabbinical Judaism--had to be abolished to release the Jew into the modern world. Mendelssohn's equation was as simple as it was convincing: rationalism in religion, society, and government required the emancipation of Jews on the one hand and the reformation of Jews on the other.

It was the latter part of the equation, however, the transformation of Jewish life according to the dictates of the Enlightenment, that claimed the attention of Mendelssohn and his disciples. Though strenuously lobbying for Jewish civil rights, the Mendelssohnians believed that as long as the Jewish community itself remained locked into a medieval way of life, which for them was characterized by ill-mannered ignorance, religious intolerance, and xenophobic exclusiveness, Jews could not expect to be accepted into Gentile society. Thus, while leaving the public promotion of Jewish civil emancipation in the hands of their *Aufklaerer* German friends, like Gotthold Lessing and Christian Dohm, they concentrated on the dismantling of the ghetto from within by propagating the use of German, the teaching of secular subjects, the restriction of rabbinical authority, and the adoption of so-called useful occupations.

Education, or rather re-education, of the Jews was the essential ingredient of the Mendelssohnian Enlightenment. The acquisition of European cultural and social norms would prepare the Jew to enter the world of the Gentile. In order to break the stranglehold of tradition, he had to be taught first the language of the land. Acquisition of the medium of communication, German, would free him from the spiritual and material tutelage of Orthodox rabbis and conservative elders who ruled the Jewish community (*kehillah*). By the same token, he would abandon Yiddish, the Judeo-German language which symbolized for the Mendelssohnians all that was offensive about Jewish behavior and ghetto mentality. Replacing Yiddish with German would have the salutary effect of purifying the Jew culturally and liberate him socially from the traditional oligarchic controls of rabbinical-communal authority which had kept the light of reason from penetrating Jewish consciousness.

Language, however, was only the first step towards inner reform. Besides advocating German, there was a whole array of reformist measures the *maskilim* deemed necessary for "Europeanizing" the Jews. Demonstrating their own desire for acculturation, and thereby setting an example for their reluctant coreligionists, the Mendelssohnians adopted European dress and customs as an outward sign of reform. Less visible, but more fundamental, was their campaign for radical changes in the occupational habits of Jews-- habits which, according to the physiocratic bias of the Enlightenment, were directly responsible for the supposedly moral corruption of contemporary Jewry. It was by discouraging Jews from money-lending, inn-keeping, peddling, and other petty commercial activity, and by redirecting them into "useful" trades like farming and manufacturing that they would escape their pariah status and prove eligible for citizenship. In this, as well as in their general reformist attitude, the *maskilim* became *nolens volens,* the opponents of traditional Jewish elites, and the allies of enlightened absolutist govern- ments. While blaming Jewish backwardness on the former, they turned to the latter to legislate an end to the temporal powers of rabbinical authority and solicited its enlightened officials to assist their own plans for recasting the Jewish people in the image of the European Enlightenment.[6]

Spreading outward from Berlin to the German and Austrian principali- ties, the *Haskalah* reached Russia via East-Prussia and Galicia. One of the first places of Mendelssohnian influence in Russia was the estate of Joshua Tseitlin (1742-1822) in Uste, Belorussia. Representing the commercial and spiritual aristocracy of Lithuanian-Belorussian Jewry that was well connected to Berlin and St. Petersburg, Tseitlin happened to be the grandfather of the first revolutionary Russian Jew--the Decembrist Grigorii Peretts (1788-1855).[']

Thus, at the very inception of the *Haskalah* in Russia, we find the beginnings of Jewish radicalism in the person of Peretts, who was educated by Russia's foremost Jewish enlighteners, at first on his grandfather's estate and later in his father's St. Petersburg residence. Indeed, Peretts was a child of the *Haskalah* and a prototype of its most radical expression: the secular educated Jewish intellectual, who, alienated from traditional Judaism and isolated from official Russian society, sought salvation in revolution.[8]

Sketching the outline of Perett's odyssey from *Haskalah* to revolution, we find that Tseitlin's estate in Uste resembled a "free academy" where Jews-- learned rabbis, talented talmudists, and maskilic writers--conducted scientific experiments and generally met for study and dialogue in the spirit of Mendelssohn.[9] It was from among these people that the *Haskalah* recruited its early, albeit sparse, following in Russia, including the friends and tutors of the Tseitlin family: Mendel Satanover, Lev Nevakhovich, Nota Notkin and last, but not least, Abram Izrailovich Peretts--the father of the Decembrist Grigorii Peretts.

Abram Peretts, the son of a Galician rabbi, had come to Tseitlin's attention because of his intelligence and learning. Convinced that Adam Izrailovich was "destined to become an outstanding rabbi," Tseitlin provided for him to study at his "academy" and later arranged to have him marry his daughter. The first and only child of this marriage was Grigorii. But the enlightened atmosphere of Uste and Tseitlin's own desire to promote the material well-being of his son-in-law, completely transformed the erstwhile talmudist into a *maskil* dedicated to worldly pursuits of happiness. By introducing Abram to Prince Potemkin as his successor in their business dealings, Tseitlin paved the way for Abram's brilliant career as an eminently successful financier at the imperial court in St. Petersburg. In the mid-1790s, Empress Catherina II (1762-96), appreciative of his commercial expertise in serving the crown, permitted Abram Peretts to reside permanently in the capital. She also granted the privilege to his close friends Nota Notkin and Judah Nevakhovich. This signified the beginning of the St. Petersburg Jewish community. The three notables also became known as the founding fathers and leading spokesmen of Jewish Enlightenment and emancipation in Russia.[10]

While Abram Peretts and his friends ascended the ladder of social prestige and political influence, Grigorii--or "Grisha," as he was affectionately called--grew up on his grandfather's estate in Uste. His education, determined by the old Tseitlin, was moderately Mendelssohnian in its combination of traditional religious and modern secular learning. Grisha's principal tutor was Mendel Satanover, the most outstanding pioneer of the early Russian *Haskalah*.

Satanover, as Semen Dubnov noted sarcastically, "had been privileged to behold in the flesh the Father of Enlightenment in Berlin."[11] Thoroughly saturated with the philosophy of the *Haskalah* as propagated by Mendelssohn and his circle, Satanover had made it his mission to bring Enlightenment to the Jews of Russia. Writing both in Hebrew and Yiddish, he promoted secular learning and popularized scientific knowledge in such diverse fields as medicine and geography, all of which enjoyed much success in conveying contemporary European culture and the need for modernizing Jewish education. Needless to say, his pupil Grisha was the direct beneficiary of his teachings.

In 1803, at the age of fifteen, Grigorii left Uste in the company of Mendel Satanover to live with his father in St. Petersburg. For Grigorii this meant growing of age in a household which, as his biographer stated, was "dominated by western *Haskalah* (Berlin) culture."[12] The Peretts' residence was a novel and disturbing experience for a boy who had been raised in a setting which, although touched by the powerful rays of Mendelssohnian Enlightenment, was still securely embedded in a traditional Jewish milieu. Unlike Tseitlin's Uste, the secluded abode of erudite talmudists and moderate *maskilim,* the fashionable salon of Peretts' St. Petersburg was the meeting-place of liberal-minded Russians and enlightened Jews who embodied "Berlinerdom" at its most extreme.

In a sense, the Peretts abode stood suspended between two worlds--traditional Jewish and official Russian society, each equally unprepared to accept the outlandish ideas of its *maskilic* residents. Their isolation was made painfully evident during the 1802-1804 deliberations of Alexander I's "Committee for the Organization of Jewish Life" and subsequent developments which petrified Jewish disabilities in Russia until the revolution of 1917.[13] As partisans of reform and enlightenment more than willing to cooperate with the tsarist government, Peretts and company found no resonance in the Jewish community. While its deputies to the Committee appreciated their help in dealing with St. Petersburg officialdom, as representatives of Jewish conservatism, they rejected the Mendelssohnian heresy of the *Berlinchiki.* Shunned by their coreligionist, the disciples of *Haskalah* put all their hope in the Committee's apparent determination to legislate an end to Jewish separateness by appropriate legal, social, and educational reforms.

Alas, the resultant Jewish Statute of 1804 did not bring solace to its Jewish well-wishers. The Statute failed to ameliorate Jewish life and in practice, retarded, rather than advanced Jewish emancipation. Its "enlighten-ment" provisions, such as promoting education, manufacture, and agriculture among Jews were left largely unattended by the tsarist government which found it easier and politically more expedient to implement the Statute's restrictive measures to curb "Jewish exploitation" of the native population.[14]

Even more disappointing and personally irksome for the *maskilic* advocates of reform was the fact that the Statute left intact precisely those structures of Jewish life which, in the first place, prevented the integration of Jews into Russian society: the *kahal* and the *Pale.* The former, Jewish communal self-government, preserved the power of traditional elites who opposed the secularizing and liberalizing ideology of the *Haskalah.* The latter, Jewish settlement restrictions, prohibited the departure of Jews from their communities to advance themselves socially in the larger Gentile society. Abolishing both would have opened the floodgates of cultural and political change, leading ultimately to social integration and civic emancipation. As it was, neither was forthcoming. This left Peretts and his friend in the unenviable position of superfluous men, stranded on Russian shores without hope and purpose.

Estranged from their own community and frustrated by their anomalous status in a society that rejected them as Jews, Peretts and Nevakhovich acquired for themselves and their children the proverbial "ticket of admission to European culture:" they embraced Christianity by converting to the Lutheran faith.

Having thus "carried 'Berlinerdom' to that dramatic *denouement,* which was in fashion in Berlin itself," the St. Petersburg *maskilim* defaulted on their own enlightened aspirations for emancipation.[15] Their *denouement* for the sake of personal salvation terminated their *maskilic* mission, now thoroughly discredited in the eyes of pious Jews. But their history of prematurely pioneering the *Haskalah* in Russia conjures up all the elements which characterized the ideas and behavior of subsequent, and much more numerous, generations of Russian *maskilim*. In this milieu, a politically radicalized Jewish intelligentsia came to view emancipation as a universal task of revolution.

Grigorii Peretts was an early manifestation of the radicalizing potential of the Russian *Haskalah,* preceding the actual formation of a secularized Russian-Jewish intelligentsia by several decades. He was not only its first representative, but also the archetype of the nineteenth-century Russian Jewish radical whose personality was shaped by the novel phenomenon of the Jewish Enlightenment and whose revolutionary engagement was rooted in this modernizing ideology and its unsettling sociological consequences.

As we had occasion to observe, Tseitslin's Uste laid the foundation for his rebellious intellectual development. There, in the care of the *maskil* Satanover, he acquired an education in the spirit of the Mendelssohnian school, which, though not necessarily in conflict with traditional Judaism, removed him by one step from the conventional modes of Jewish existence. Abram Peretts' St. Petersburg, already socially and culturally remote from the *Lebenswelt* of the Russian Jewish community, signified a radical extension of his *maskili* upbringing. There, in the company of his father, he experienced the private and public commitment of Russia's foremost *maskilim* to realize their ideal of enlightenment and concomitant goal of Jewish emancipation. But as he was to learn, there was as yet no place for them and their vision in either Jewish or Russian society. Grigorii's personality and consciousness remained deeply molded by the threefold sequel of his formative years: enlightenment ideology, elusive emancipation, and social marginality. The combination of the three, a recurrent combination in the radicalization of Jews, was the recipe making Peretts a Decembrist revolutionary.

In the revolutionary society of the Decembrists, Grigorii Peretts found a fellowship held together by shared ideas and objectives corresponding to his own lofty ideals of enlightenment and political commitment to emancipation. Last but not least, it answered his psychological need for social communion in an otherwise alienating environment that negated his identification with established Jewish or Russian society. But it was a sign of his Jewish background and *maskilic* education that, in joining his fate with Russia's nascent radical intelligentsia, Grigorii identified with its most moderate representatives, whose views closely coincided with his own *Haskalah* derived German-Jewish *Weltanschauung*.

The "Society of Peretts," as the group of people he organized was known, considered itself a party of "pure constitutionalists" who utterly opposed the revolutionary republicanism propagated by the more radical Decembrist Pavel Pestel, the spokesman of Russian Jacobinism.[16] Moreover, as a *Jewish* Decembrist, Peretts also differed from his fellow conspirators in that he arrived at his revolutionary destination along a different path and experience than they did: namely, via the Mendelssohnian *Haskalah* and his father's futile politics of emancipation. Hence, it was from within this Jewish context, that Grigorii Peretts decided to join the Decembrists while rejecting republican government and Jacobin violence. He favored constitutional monarchy and gradual reform to be realized through enlightened civic education and the institutionalization of the rule of law. Political enlightenment and *Rechtstaat* philosophy in the German sense, rather than revolution and republicanism in the Franco-American sense, were the basic motifs determining Peretts' Decembrist activity--an activity which, like its motifs, originated in his *maskilic* upbringing and alienating experience. In this, as well as in his pattern of social disengagement from traditional Jewish life and political reengagement in modern Russian revolutionary affairs, Peretts resembled the socio-political evolution of subsequent generations of revolutionary Jews in Russia.

Indicative as Grigorii Peretts is for our recognition that the *Haskalah* stood at the cradle of Jewish radicalism, it is important to remember that his Decembrist story was merely a preview of this fact. The necessary conditions for its incomparably more potent "repetition" later on were created only during the reign of Nicholas I, which commenced with the Decembrist uprising in 1825 and ended with Russia's defeat in the Crimean War in 1855. It was during this period that the Russian *Haskalah* came into its own as a vibrant Jewish modernization movement.

This development, the transformation of Jewish society in Russia, can be divided into two phases. The first, roughly from the mid-1820s through the 1830s, led to the consolidation of the *Haskalah* as more and more Jews declared their allegiance to the ideas of the Mendelssohnian Enlightenment. The second, beginning in the early 1840s, further solidified the movement by welding a still incoherent collection of *maskilim* into a social group that signified the institutionalization of the *Haskalah* in the form of a "self-conscious and self-confident intelligentsia, dedicated to creating a new life and culture for Russia's Jews."[17] Taken together, the process was symbiotically connected with Nicholas' policies in Jewish education, socio-economic regulations, and army conscription. It generated a definite cultural and political rift in Jewish society which steadily deepened with the consolidation of the voices of conservatism on the one side and of modernity on the other. The unending conflict between the two caused the eventual disaffection of *maskilic* youths from Judaism altogether, and drove them into the arms of revolutionary Russia.

The first signs of conflict were, as we know, already evident during the preliminary phase of the *Haskalah*. True, the period was marked by much "fluidity between traditionalism and enlightenment,"[18] best exemplified by Joshua Tseitlin. Tseitlin bridged both worlds by maintaining excellent relations with the leaders of rabbinical conservatism while patronizing the pioneers of *Haskalah* such as Mendel Satanover. Nonetheless, the potential for conflict between the two positions was clearly apparent in the refusal of the *kahal* deputies to support the St. Petersburg *maskilim's* cooperation with Alexander I's reformist endeavors. Instead of confrontation, however, Abram Peretts and Lev Nevakhovich converted to Christianity and thus left the traditionalists in complete control of internal Jewish affairs.

Several decades later, this hegemony came to be increasingly challenged by a new generation of *maskilim*. What made this challenge particularly forceful was the fact that the *maskilim* had not only grown in numbers and confidence, but that in the late 1830s, they began to enjoy the support of the tsarist government.

In 1838, Nicholas I's Minister of Education, Count Uvarov, sought the cooperation of the *maskilim* to institute a new educational programme for the Jews of Russia. "Give us a finger," he told them, "and we shall stretch out our whole hand."[19] With this approach, Uvarov reversed the previous tsarist Jewish policy which had been largely repressive in its social, economic, and military measures to force the Russification of Jews through conversionist assimilation. In arguments strikingly similar to that of leading proponents of Jewish amelioration in the West, the tsarist Minister had concluded that this coercive policy was counterproductive to the avowed goal of changing Jews into "virtuous," "useful," and socially integrated subjects of the Russian state. Only positive educational measures, namely the re-education of Jews in *Jewish* schools--schools based on *Haskalah* principles and operated with the assistance of enlightened Jews--would lead to their "gradual rapproachment (*sblizhenie*) with the Christian population and the eradication of superstitions and harmful prejudices instilled by the study of Torah."[20]

Uvarov vigorously pursued the implementation of his reform project while he simultaneously elicited the support of prominent German and Russian *maskilim*. His determination culminated in the convocation of a Rabbinical Commission. From May 6 to August 27, 1843, the proposed new schools were discussed with the implicit understanding of sanctioning their establishment in Jewish communities throughout the empire. The Commission prevailed over hassidic and rabbinic objections, and in November 1844, it cleared the way for the government's new law "On Establishing Special Schools for the Education of Jewish Youths."[21]

The law stipulated that, in addition to traditional Jewish education in kheders, yeshivas, and talmud Torahs, Jews would now receive their own modern public system of primary and secondary education, as well as state rabbinical seminaries for training Jewish teachers and crown rabbis. The actual implementation of this program began in 1847 with the transfer of previous private *maskilic* schools to the public domain and the establishment of two Rabbinical Seminaries in Vilna and Zhitomir. Thereafter, the number of Jewish primary and the less prevalent secondary schools rose close to 100, reaching a student population of approximately 3,500 by 1855.[22]

Thus within a decade of the new law on Jewish education, the Pale of Settlement was spun with a network of *Haskalah*-based schools. On the one hand, this raised the ire of the traditionalists to an unprecedented pitch but, on the other hand, provided the *maskilim* with an institutional framework to pursue the "Europeanization" of Russian Jewry.

The long-standing conflict between traditionalists and *maskilim* was henceforth focused on the new schools. The former boycotted them as "heretical" institutions unfit for the education of Jewish children; the latter supported them as vehicles for their own advancement, superbly suited for the preaching of *Haskalah a la* Mendelssohn. Neither scored an unqualified victory, but the struggle further intensified the antagonism between traditionalists and reformers. It produced a permanent and highly volatile fission in Jewish society which continuously kept Jews in a state of discord and recrimination. While the reformers relied on the schools in their uncompromising crusade against the "forces of darkness," the conservatives became even more intransigent in their fight against the unholy alliance between tsarism and *maskilim*. Rightly sensing the potentially destructive impact of this alignment on their position of authority, the anti-modernist rabbinical and hassidic elites--and with them the bulk of tradition-bound Russian Jewry-- overcame their century-old divisiveness and united into an Orthodoxy singularly determined to resist the intrusion of "goyish norms."[23] This happened none too soon.

Even though religious traditionalism retained its hold over the majority of Jews in Russia, the *maskilim,* now in collaboration with the tsarist government, emerged as a powerful secular counter-elite in Jewish life. They came to represent a coherent, self-perpetuating movement for change, which indeed threatened to undermine the traditional status quo by penetrating and making converts in every substantial Jewish community in the Russian empire.

The single most important reason which transformed the *maskilim* into "a potent force within Russian Jewry" was precisely that institution which caused the traditionalists to gather their forces into an Orthodox camp: the new school system.[24] The new schools fortified the staying-power of what had previously been a scattered, persecuted, and ostracized *maskilic* minority. Now employed by the Russian state as teachers and administrators of the newly established schools, the *maskilim* were finally in possession of an institutionalized "power base" which rivaled the traditional *kahal* institutions of their Orthodox opponents and made them economically and socially independent of Jewish communal authority. Operating from such a position of strength, the enlightenment movement educated the next generation of *maskilic intelligenty* and proliferated. In spite of the intense opposition of the Orthodox, a steady stream of Jewish youths passed through the crown schools and state rabbinical seminaries in the 1850s and, in the following decade, they re-entered these institutions as teachers or went on to graduate in Russian gymnasiums and universities. The end result of this "institutionalization" of the *Haskalah* was the formation of a full-fledged Russian-Jewish intelligentsia that was to shape modern Jewish cultural life well into the 1870s.[25]

The historical significance of this new intelligentsia for the evolution of Jewish radicalism was enormous. The state schools--especially the rabbinical seminaries--furnished the Russian revolutionary movement of the 1860s and 1870s with its first recruits. Aside from that fact, the intelligentsia nourished by these schools created the ideological and social atmosphere that enveloped a rising generation of Jews. It imbued them with an activist, *maskilic Weltanschauung* which turned many of them into rebels opposed to anything resembling the life-style, religion, and politics of traditional Jewry. Indeed the very word, *"intelligentsia,"* conveys, *par excellence,* the character of the *maskilic* movement, a potent cultural force.

The word "intelligentsia," originally coined from the contemporaneous Russian phenomenon of *intelligenty,* was appropriately applied to the *Maskilim* from the 1850s onward. Although the term has been variously defined, most scholars agree that it designates a group of people who were not simply intellectuals in a professional or academic sense. Rather it designates a select congregation of individuals who sought to change the world around them in accordance with their dichotomized images of good versus evil, truth versus falsehood, justice versus injustice, education versus ignorance, and so on. As Isaiah Berlin wrote in his characterization of the Russian intelligentsia:

> Its members thought of themselves as united by something more
> than mere interest in ideas; they conceived themselves as being
> a dedicated order, almost a secular priesthood, devoted to the
> spreading of a specific attitude to life, something like a
> gospel.[26]

The gospel of the *maskilic* intelligentsia was, of course, the German-Jewish Enlightenment which constituted a special mission for them to "Europeanize" Russian Jewry through secular education and general socio-cultural self-regeneration.

This sense of mission and concomitant ideological outlook was effectively transmitted from one generation to another through the medium of the new schools. Every student in these institutions, wrote one of its more illustrious graduates:

> . . . regarded himself as no less than a future reformer, a new
> Mendelssohn, and therefore, in quiet worked out a plan of

action which he jealously guarded from his friends. [They] were thoroughly convinced that they were going to bring about a complete revolution in the world view of the Jewish people, and they impatiently awaited their moment of action.[27]

This, then, was the frame of mind fostered by the new Russian-Jewish intelligentsia.

The phenomenon was not restricted to the Jewish youth in the crown schools. It also penetrated the high-castles of rabbinical Judaism, the *yeshivas,* and claimed converts to the *Haskalah* among its talmudic students. Even among the teachers of the *kheder,* the bulwark of Jewish elementary religious education, there were Germanophil *melamdim,* who, in their wanderings from one shtetl to another, had become infected with the Mendelssohnian virus spread far and wide by the *maskilic* intelligentsia.[28] Still, the revolutionary strain of this virus had not yet made its appearance. Although the "culture" for breeding it was sufficiently developed at the end of the 1850s, it was only in the following decade that external conditions were propitious for creating the right revolutionary off-spring.

The revolutionization of Russian Jews was the result of intellectual, social, and political currents, which, given the right historical context and momentum, allowed for the fusion of *maskilic* aspirations with Russian radicalism. The first instance of such a fusion occured in the case of Grigori Peretts. Another instance arose in the 1860s, but now the context and scale were vastly different from that of the Decembrist experience of Grigorii Peretts. The Great Reforms of Alexander II (1855-1881) drastically changed the intellectual and political landscape of Russian society. These reforms, and the dynamic developments initiated by them, did not by-pass the Jewish Pale of Settlement and its *maskilic* intelligentsia who, as we shall see shortly, were profoundly influenced by the Russian renascence of the 1860s.

Alexandrian succession came as a great relief to the Jews of Russia. On the very day of his coronation in 1855, Alexander II inaugurated what has been called "the golden age" of Russian Jewry by abolishing juvenile conscription. Under Nicholas I, this cruel recruitment of boys, some as young as seven, had caused untold grief in Jewish homes, pitting Jew against Jew in a vicious struggle, as the rich and powerful sought to save their children from life-long military service at the expense of the children of the poor and underprivileged.[29] This edict was followed by a series of decrees which, between 1859 and 1865, improved Jewish rights of residence: guild merchants, licenced artisans, and post-secondary students were granted the privilege to settle anywhere in Russia.

The new aura of liberalism and its ameliorative effects were welcome by all Jews. The *maskilim* and those Jewish parents, rich as well as poor, who availed themselves of the new educational opportunities of Alexander's reign were the real beneficiaries of the reforms. For them, rather than for Russian Jewry in general, who continued to live in a state of abject poverty and legal disabilities, the period of the Great Reforms was indeed a "golden age" in that it gave their offspring, the children of the *Haskalah*, the long-sought possibility to advance socially and economically in Russian society. But the opportunity thus created--and eagerly exploited--brought with it a profound change in the physiology and ideology of the *maskilic* intelligentsia. It initiated a process which eventually led to the political radicalization of Jews.

Alexander's educational reforms in general, and his Jewish policies in particular, gave rise to what Elias Tscherikower called a "modern diploma intelligentsia" (Jews who studied for and received a university, or comparable professional, degree).[30] The creation of this new social stratum progressed rapidly in the 1860s and 1870s. The quasi-emancipatory atmosphere of the Alexandrian era exerted such a powerful influence on the thinking and behavior of Jews that many were willing to override Orthodox objections to secular culture and public education. Crucial for this change in attitude was the November law of 1861. It made Jews graduating from post-secondary schools be eligible for state employment throughout Russia, as well as permitting them to pursue professional and commercial careers outside of the Pale of Settlement. Promulgated in the same year as the statutes on the emancipation of the serfs, the law gave the impression--as did the whole tenor of Alexander's Jewish legislation--that Jewish emancipation was in the offing, and that education could make it an immediate reality.

This article of faith acted as an irresistible stimulus for Jews to enter Russian schools in the hope of claiming an academic degree or professional certificate. The first to make good on this promise were the students of the rabbinical seminaries who had been allowed to continue their education in Russian universities since 1856. Next in line were the hundreds of students who had graduated from Jewish crown schools or from Russian gymnasiums prior to 1861, followed finally by the thousands of Jewish students who entered Russian secondary schools after 1861.

There was a dramatic increase of Jews attending secondary and post-secondary schools. In 1853 there were only 159 Jews enrolled in Russian gymnasiums, constituting little more than one percent of the total student population. Their numbers quickly climbed to 552 (3.2%), 2,045 (5.6%), and 7,004 (12%) for the years of 1863, 1870, and 1880 respectively.[31] The entry of these students into diploma granting institutions of higher learning began to show up statistically in 1865. In that year, 129 or three percent of all students attending post-secondary schools were Jewish. By 1876, this figure increased to over 300 and, finally, settled at around 2000 or approximately 15 percent of the population in the mid-1880s. Jewish presence was particularly pronounced in the faculties of medicine and law. For instance, in 1886, over 40 percent of law and medical students at the Universities of Kharkov and the University of New Russia in Odessa were Jewish.[32] This trend was as true for the 1860s and 1870s as it was for the 1880s, and duly reflected the tendency of Jewish youth to study for a diploma which held out the prospect of a professional career in government service or in Russian society at large. It also reflected the Russian cultural orientation of the new "diploma intelligentsia."

The decade of the sixties witnessed, in fact, the transformation of the old *maskilic* intelligentsia into a Russian educated intellectual elite whose outlook and aspirations were closely tied to contemporary liberal and radical elements in Russian society. In other words, the new *diplomirte yidishe inteligenz* and its numerous aspirants in the rabbinical seminaries, gymnasiums, universities, medical schools, and vocational institutes superceded the old-fashioned *maskilim* of the '40s and '50s. It transformed the *Haskalah* from a German-Jewish phenomenon into a Russian-Jewish ideology of assimilation and emancipation. Education *a la russe,* or rather, "Russification," was now seen as a fair prize for gaining civil liberties. "Europeanization" now came to be understood as "the enlightenment of Jews through Russian language and *in the Russian spirit.*"[33] This was accompanied by an unprecedented surge of pro-Russian sentiment and loyalist gratitude towards the beneficent Tsar-Liberator. But while this attitude was widely shared in *maskilic* circles, and persisted even after Alexander's "official liberalism" gave way to renewed conservatism, the *Russian spirit* of the "new enlightenment" produced more than loyal, educated, and "useful" Jewish subjects of the tsarist state: it also produced Jewish cadres for the Russian revolutionary movement.

The long-term revolutionary consequences of the *Haskalah* were related to the very process of its "Russification." Two interrelated and mutually reinforcing socio-ideological developments were at work in this fateful transformation: namely, the already mentioned formation of a Russian educated Jewish youth, and the still to be discussed concomitant fusion of *maskilic* tradition with Russian "nihilism."

The nihilist phenomenon was the most radical and spontaneous expression of the vibrant Russian renascence of the 1860s. Comparing this renascence with the philosophical and ideological excitement produced by the French Enlightenment, Alexander Vucinich observed that in Russia:

> The role of the *philosophes* was assumed by the *raznochintsy*, a class born in the crevices of the growing urban community and epitomizing the inexorable decay of Russia's estate system anchored in the institutions of autocracy and feudalism. The clamour for "the destruction of all authority" . . . and "the ridiculing of all *res sacrae*" best expressed the *raznochintsy* movement. . . . [Its leading exponents] echoed the *philosophes'* conviction that the scientific study of man, realism in art, humanitarian goals in legislation, and unalloyed faith in the perfectibility of institutions and social relations are the main sources of social progress.[34]

The Russian *philosophe* par excellence was Nikolas Chernyshevskii. More than any other exponent of *raznochintsy* ideology, he was a true encyclopedist who made contemporary Western social and political thought accessible to the inquisitive minds of Russia's youthful intelligentsia. Perhaps most significant in expressing and shaping the ideals of the latter was his 1862 novel, *What is to be Done? The Tales of the New People*. The principal characters of the novel embodied all the redemptive social and spiritual virtues of the "new people of the sixties." Their communal life-style of work, free love, and learning made them perfect role models of emancipated men and women. The baptism of these "new people" was performed by the great Russian writer Ivan Turgenev. In his novel, *Fathers and Sons*, Turgenev christened them "Nihilists," and thus made the label "nihilism" stick as the ideological denominator of Russian radicalism in the 1860s.

It was Dmitri Pisarev who gave nihilism its final polish as the ideology of the *raznochintsy* movement. Pisarev fashioned nihilism into a philosophy that emphasized the role of the "rational egoist." As an agent of progress, the "rational egoist" would effect his own, as well as society's emancipation through the acquisition of critical reason and a strictly scientific and utilitarian education. Science, both as an educational experience and as a useful profession, was seen as "a panacea for all social ills and the only path to a better society."[35]

The point of departure for this journey along the road of progress was the "emancipation of the individual" by virtue of his own volition, his own desire to enrich his personality in the pursuit of socially applicable knowledge such as medicine, chemistry, biology, engineering, and jurisprudence. These vocations were to be the ambition of the neophytes of the "nihilist enlightenment" which promised the making of a new society. The promise, especially in its Pisarevian pronouncements, rung a familiar note for Jews brought up in the tradition of the *Haskalah*. They, and more directly, those already studying in Russian gymnasiums and universities--the spawning ground of nihilist beliefs and life-style--were psychologically and intellectually prepared to absorb the ideas of a kindred ideology.

The potential for merging the nihilist off-shoot of the Russian cultural renascence with the post-Nicholavean *Haskalah* is readily apparent. As a philosophy of emancipation, Russian nihilism can be viewed as an extension of the Jewish Enlightenment: it reinforced and radicalized its ideals of secular learning, self-improvement, and social responsibility. The ideas of the *Haskalah,* especially as propagated by its more zealous representatives, predisposed young Jews to embrace nihilism with its emphasis on "the secularization of wisdom" and "the utility of knowledge" in liberating the individual and society from supposed medieval institutions and prejudices. Indeed, as Jonathan Frankel points out, "the 'nihilist' movement in the Pale was, in fact, only a *reductio ad absurdum* of the earlier [Jewish] Enlightenment movement, for both fathers and sons prized modern education above else."[36]

What the "sons" appreciated more than anything else was the fact that, in contrast to the idealist *maskilim* of the *Haskalah*, the Russian *philosophes* of nihilism thought of education in terms of scientific knowledge that held out the prospect of a "new society" governed by egalitarian and rationalist principles. The pillars of the "nihilist value system" were scientism, utilitarianism, and individualism.[37] These provided the sort of moral and intellectual support sought by the "sons" in their revolt against what they saw as the hypocritical religious and social order in the Pale. Scientism answered their existential needs for a rational ontological ideology which harmonized with their ingrained respect for secular education. Utilitarianism confirmed their philanthropic ethics in making it morally obligatory to acquire socially applicable knowledge. Individualism encouraged their emancipatory, if not assimilationist, tendencies as a legitimate and necessary means of forming an authentic progressive personality.

Indeed, it was truly phenomenal how nihilism took hold of the Jewish youth and how easily it coalesced with their *maskilic* thinking. Contemporaries, who themselves were caught up in this movement, have vividly described the ease with which nihilist ideas and mannerisms captured the imagination of the young. One of them wrote:

> Together with the spread of Russian (and in some cases German) literacy and the striving towards, and taste for, enlightenment, . . . [there] developed in the local Jewish community, too, a conflict between "fathers" and "sons." Among the youth arouse and grew the desire to liberate themselves from the despotism of parental authority, . . . to escape from the yoke of religious tradition, to digress more or less from the old commands and requirements of Orthodoxy.[38]

Not even students of traditional Jewish learning were immune to the novelty of nihilism. Perhaps somewhat exaggerated, but still revealing, is the observation of another participant:

> The magic of nihilist views was such that even . . . *eshibotnikov* [yeshiva students], wrapped up in the study of the Talmud and other ancient Hebrew texts, fell under their influence: two-three conversations with a nihilist was often enough for a *eshibotnik* to give up all his patriarchal beliefs, as well as his specifically [talmudist] appearance and habits. . . . Turning away from sterile talmudic learning, . . . he then took up studying various sciences in which he, not infrequently, displayed great ability.[39]

The author of these lines was from Kiev where, we are told, he belonged to "a fairly large group . . . of Jewish students of both sexes who adopted all the views and habits acquired by the nihilists."[40] These students were a familiar and provocative sight with their plaid cloaks, long hair, and thick staffs or, in the case of girls, with their extremely plain dress, cropped hair, and dark glasses. Often this general defiance of conventional modes of behavior implied also--and often primarily--a rejection of specifically Jewish forms of social and religious life. Girls would rebel against the dictate of prearranged marriage and their parents' refusal to provide them with an education. Often demonstrating their own choice of life-style, they would live together in a communal setting and make it their favored pasttime to insult traditional sensibilities by parading in the streets holding hands, eating non-kosher food, and smoking on the Sabbath.[41] For many, nihilism exhausted itself in this superficial juvenile rebelliousness or meant little more than a fierce desire to learn foreign languages in preparation for entering Russian schools to study "goyish" sciences. But for others it led to a much more serious--and typically *maskilic*--endeavour: namely, to seek an education, to become "thinking individuals" for the sake of enlightening the Jewish masses, to promote "Europeanization" and consequently, social progress.   What occurred was a fusion of *Haskalah* and nihilism in the person of the *maskilic nihilist*.

Jewish nihilism took the form of a cultural movement composed of numerous informal study circles.   These circles organized "libraries" and schools, and generally engaged in all sorts of unauthorized educational activity. Here the concept of "Europeanization" was subsumed under the new mission of a populist crusade to bring the fruits of European civilization in general, and Russian culture in particular, to the Jewish people. Spearheading this crusade were Jewish gymnasium students and rabbinical seminarians. In places like Vilna, Mogilev, Zhitomir, and Kiev, they formed "circles of self-education" which, in turn, proliferated by attracting talmudists, pupils of Jewish crown schools, and privately educated children of wealthy Jewish merchants.   Meeting more or less regularly, its members would read and discuss Russian literature, articles from the Russian-Jewish periodical press, and works of the German-Jewish *Haskalah*. Some ventured to write their own Russian, Hebrew, and Yiddish compositions criticizing and satirizing Jewish life and its Orthodox leadership. These they circulated in manuscript form or, on occasion, were able to get published in local newspapers. Eventually, as the groups matured and increased in size, they applied themselves to the task of popular education as volunteer teachers of free literary schools of their own creation or, more frequently, in the *talmud-torah* institutions of the Jewish community. The popularity of literary schools within and outside of *talmud-torah* establishments and the radicalizing potential of this activity has been widely attested in the memoir literature.[42]

What is equally apparent is that the Russifying "enlightenment propaganda" of the *maskilic nihilists* evolved from their own *Haskalah* inspired self-education and critique of traditional Jewish life.   Facilitated and strengthened by nihilist influences, it also signified a radical continuation of the perennial conflict between traditionalists and modernists: up to a certain degree,   the rebellious "sons" enjoyed the tacit support of the *maskilic* "fathers."[43]

Yet, the very nature of this uncompromising struggle and the expansive character of nihilist activity in terms of personal emancipation and social obligation soon diverted the "sons" from the mainstream of Jewish life into the turbulent waters of Russian radicalism.

The journey which led Jewish nihilists to anchor their ship in the harbour of Russian revolution cannot be dealt with here. It suffices to state that the *maskilic* subculture of nihilist dissent (study circles, student communes, literary schools, and *talmud-torah* activity) served as an apprenticeship for practicing socialism, revolutionary propaganda, and "underground" living later on. Those who partook in this experience were tested for a new life which brought them into conflict with established authorities, both Jewish and Gentile. They discovered that their social activism was not only opposed by Orthodox Jews, but also by tsarist officials who intimidated their *maskilic* well-wishers and took stern measures to suppress their literary schools and special *talmud-torah* classes.

On almost every level they had to struggle against unyielding opponents who viewed their unconventional behavior and unauthorized activity as subversive to the established order of traditional Jewish and official Russian society. For those who persevered, this was a "school of dissent" which imbued them with a sense of mission, gave them the stamina to fight on, and trained them to operate in a hostile environment.[44] There was also the reward of intimate comradeship, of unbound optimism, and, last but not least, the feeling of belonging to a select group of people who self-consciously viewed themselves as the vanguard of progress. All these things, and the corporate spirit fostered by their *kruzhkovaia zhizn'*, their life in circles and communes, contributed to their radicalization and prepared them to cope with the travails of the future. In attracting and socializing numerous youths, the subculture of Jewish nihilism created a reservoir of prospective socialist Jews who became active in the 1870s as the propagandists, technicians, and organizers of revolution in the Russian Populist movement.

Conclusion

The Finkelshtein circle of 1871-72 stood at the threshold between *maskilic* nihilism and revolutionary populism. It was a typical example of *Haskalah* inspired radicalism which in due course absorbed Russian nihilist ideas. Subsequent socialist circles in Vilna and other cities of the Pale of settlement underwent a similar process. Having discovered in socialism a new secular faith, they were poised for revolutionary action already upon entry into the populist movement.

The largely autochthonous character of Jewish radicalization within the context of the *Haskalah* continued to influence the outlook and behavior of Jews even after their assimilation into the Russian revolutionary milieu. In its socialist transformation, their Jewishness expressed itself in a uniquely a-

populist, cosmopolitan *Weltanschauung*. Jewish motives, such as enlightenment and emancipation, retained their hold on revolutionary Jews who, for the
most part, were unable to identify with the romantic peasantism and Russian
particularism of their populist comrades. First and foremost, they viewed
themselves as cosmopolitan socialists who had left *di yidishe gas* not for the
sake of the Russian peasantry, but in the belief that socialism, as an international movement, would build the "churches of the future" which would
"conquer the whole world," attain "universal happiness, freedom and
equality," and elevate mankind to "a new, infinitely higher degree of
civilization. . . ."[45] These visions of "universal brotherhood" and "universal
emancipation" did not derive from Russian populism. Like the Decembrist
Peretts, populist Jews looked westward, to Germany, to find the signposts that
would guide them to the promised land of salvation.

More concisely, German Social Democracy with its Marxian promise
of the millennium and its more immediate appreciation of bourgeois liberties,
was the source of inspiration for Jews to serve the "universal church" of
socialism. This German orientation, already evident in Grigorii Peretts'
maskilic upbringing and revolutionary career, originated in the Mendelssohnian
Haskalah and its quest for the "Europeanization" and emancipation of the
Jewish people in a world governed by reason, humanity, and creativity.
Jewish cosmopolitan socialism not only retained these universals of the
enlightenment, but also transmitted them to the Russian liberation movement
of the 1870's and 1880s. For having entered the "universal church" through
the open gates of revolutionary populism, the Jewish socialist became an agent
of westernization among his Russian peers who, in typical populist fashion,
rejected bourgeois (European) politics as being incompatible with social
revolution and the communistic instincts of the peasantry. In this role, his
uniquely Jewish contribution to Russian revolutionary history consisted in
redirecting populism towards an appreciation of political freedom and civil
liberties, on the one hand, and in pioneering social democracy in Russia, on
the other.[46]

Endnotes

1. E. Zunser, *A Jewish Bard*, ed. A.H. Fromenson (New York, 1905), 32.

2. This criticism also applies to J. Frankel's excellent work, *Prophecy and Politics,
Socialism, Nationalism, and the Russian Jews, 1862-1917* (Cambridge, 1981). While
recognizing that Jewish socialism and nationism were both rooted in the *Haskalah*,
Frankel does not develop this theme and its historical significance for originating and
shaping Jewish radicalism in Russia.

3. M. Meyer, *The Origin of the Modern Jew: Jewish Identity and European Culture in Germany 1749-1824* (Detroit, 1967), 13.

4. For a penetrating historical analysis of the tragic connection between emancipation, antisemitism, and the Holocaust, see R. Tuerup, *Emanzipation und Antisemitismus. Studien zur "Judenfrage" der bürgerlichen Gesellschaft* (Göettingen, 1975); Tuerup, "Jewish Emancipation and Bourgeois Society," *Leo Baeck Institute Year Book* 14 (1969): 69-91.

5. Meyer, *The Origin,* see n. 3 above, 18.

6. A. Springer, "Enlightened Absolutism and Jewish Reform: Prussia, Austria, and Russia," *Californian Slavic Studies* 11 (1980): 237-67.

7. The term Decembrist derives from the December uprising of 1825. Sometimes called the "First Russian Revolution," it marked the beginning of the Russian revolutionary tradition. The Decembrists were primarily tsarist officers who in the aftermath of the Napoleonic War founded secret societies aiming to transform Russian autocracy into a constitutional monarchy with more radical elements advocating the establishment of a republican government. For an account of the Decembrist movement, see: A. Mazour, *The First Russian Revolution 1825. The Decembrist Movement: Its Origin, Development, and Significance* (Berkeley, 1939); and M. Raeff, *The Decembrist Movement* (Englewood Cliffs, NJ, 1966).

8. There are two principal works on Peretts: Ia. D. Baum, "Evrei-dekabrist," *Katorga i ssylka,* kn. 25 (1926): 97-128; and V.N. and L.N. Peretts, *Dekabrist Grigorii Abramovich Peretts* (Akademii Nauk SSR, 1926). He is also mentioned in the Soviet bio-bibliographical dictionary of revolutionary activists (*Deiateli revoliutsionnogo dvizhenia v Rossii. Bio-bibliograficheskii slovar',* 1:142), which contains a short entry on him with additional bibliographical information.

9. J. Meisl, *Haskalah, Geschichte der Aufklärungsbewegung unter den Juden in Russland* (Berlin, 1929), 40-42; J. Raisin, *The Haskalah Movement in Russia* (Philadelphia, 1913), 118-19. There is also a short biographical note on Joshua Tseitlin in *Evreiskaia entsiklopedia* 15:789-90.

10. Baum, "Evrei-dekabrist," see n. 8 above, 98-99; Peretts, *Dekabrist,* see n. 8 above, 8-9. On the lives and careers of Peretts, Notkin, and Nevakhovich, see their respective biographical entries in *Evreiskaia entsiklopediia* (12:394-95; 11:801-2; 11:633-24).

11. S.M. Dubnov, *History of the Jews in Russia and Poland,* 3 vols. (KTAV Publishing House, INC, 1975 [Reprint of the Jewish Publication Society edition, 1916]), 1:388.

12. Baum, "Evrei-dekabrist," see n. 8 above, 101.

13. On the Jewish Committee and A. Peretts', Nevakhovich's, and Notkin's role in it, see J. Klier, *Russia Gathers Her Jews. The Origins of the "Jewish Question" in Russia, 1772-1825* (Dekalb, IL, 1986), chapt. 5.

14. Klier, *Russia Gathers Her Jews,* 135-45, 183-84; Dubnov, *History of the Jews in Russia,* see n. 11 above, 1:142-45.

15. Dubnov, *History of the Jews in Russia,* 1:388.

16. For Peretts' activity and disposition in the Decembrist movement see Baum, 103-112. As for the "Society of Peretts": this was the first organization in the Russian revolutionary movement to bear the name of a Jew. Another sign of Jewishness was the password of the society--*Heruth.* Peretts was also in the habit of buttressing his arguments for constitutionalism with citations from the Old Testament.

17. M. Stanislawski, *Tsar Nicholas I and the Jews: Transformation of Jewish Society in Russia, 1825-1855* (Phildelphia, 1983), 188. This is by far the best study of Russian Jewry during the reign of Nicholas I. My own analysis of the formation and revolutionary potential of the Russian-Jewish intelligentsia during this period draws heavily on Stanislawski's work.

18. Stanislawski, *Tsar Nicholas I,* 50-51, 55.

19. Stanislawski, *Tsar Nicholas I,* 63.

20. Stanislawski,*Tsar Nicholas I,* 67.

21. On the Rabbinical Commission and the new law, see Stanislawski,*Tsar Nicholas I,* 76-85; Dubnov, *History of the Jews in Russsia,* see n. 11 above, 2:50-59.

22. Stanislawski,*Tsar Nicholas I,* 98-101; Iu. Gessen, *Istoriia evreiskogo naroda v Rossii,* 2 vols. (Leningrad, 1925-27), 2:119-21.

23. Stanislawski, *Tsar Nicholas I,* 186-87.

24. Stanislawski, *Tsar Nicholas I,* 108.

25. Stanislawski, *Tsar Nicholas I,* 109.

26. I. Berlin, *Russian Thinkers,* ed. H. Hardy and A. Kelly (New York, 1979), 117.

27. M. Margulis, "Iz moikh vospominanii," *Voskhod* 15 (1895): no. 2:116. Also cited by Stanislawski, *Tsar Nicholas I,* 108-9.

28. G.E. Gurevich, "Zapiski otshchepentsa," *Voskhod* 4 no. 5 (1895): 14.

29. For a detailed account of juvenile conscription under Nicholas I, see Stanislawski, *Tsar Nicholas I,* 13-34.

30. E. Tscherikower, "Yidn-revolutsionern in rusland in di 60er un 70er yorn," in *Historishe Shriftn,* vol. 3 (Vilna, 1939), 63.

31. L. Greenberg, *The Jews in Russia. The Struggle for Emancipation,* two volumes in one (New York, 1976), 1:83; Gessen, 2:179; *Evreiskaia entsiklopediia* 13:49-50. For the gymnasia and progymnasia located in the Pale of Settlement, these figures translated in the case of the Odessa school district to 286 Jews (11.7%) in 1863, and 2,724 or almost 30% of all students in 1885. Less staggering, but still impressive was their increase in the districts of Vilna and Kiev which, in 1884, reached 24% and 12.4% respectively. In fact, some schools turned out to be predominently Jewish, as for example the 2nd Odessa Gymnasium and the Kherson Gymnasium where Jews made up more than 75% of the student body.

32. *Evreiskaia Entsiklopediia,* 13:50; Tscherikower, "Yidn-revolutsionern in rusland," see n. 30 above, 64, 112.

33. Dubnov, *History of the Jews,* see n. 11 above, 2:215.

34. A. Vucinich, *Social Thought in Tsarist Russia: the Quest for a General Science of Society* (Chicago and London, 1976), 2. Literary, *"raznochintsy"* means "people belonging to various estates." But historically the term has been associated with students and professionals of non-noble background, who, by the mid-19th century, formed a new urban social stratum known for its progressive views and revolutionary potential.

35. Vucinich, *Social Thought,* 4-5.

36. J. Frankel, *Socialism and Jewish Nationalism in Russia, 1892-1907,* Ph.D. Dissertation (Cambridge University, 1961), 43-44.

37. Vucinich, *Social Thought,* see n. 34 above, 3-5.

38. P. Akselrod, *Perezhitoe i Peredumannoe* (Berlin, 1924), 44-45.

39. L. Deich, *Rol' evreev v russkom revolutsionnom dvizhenii* (Berlin, 1923), 30.

40. Deich, *Rol'* 33.

41. Deich, *Rol',* 28-34; Akselrod, *Perezhitoe,* see n. 38 above, 45-46; Gurevich, "Zapiski," no. 6:86-99; Frankel, "Socialism and Jewish Nationalism," see n. 36 above, 38-39.

42. Gurevich, "Zapiski," no. 5:19-22; Akselrod, *Perezhitoe,* 54-55; L. Deich, *Za Polveka,* 2 vols. (Berlin, 1923), 1:19-23.

43. Gurevich, "Zapiski," no. 5:21; and Deich, *Rol',* 31; and Gurevich, *Za Polveka,* 1:22-24.

44. The "school of dissent" term was coined by D. Brower in his excellent book, *Training of the Nihilists: Education and Radicalism in Tsarist Russia* (London, 1975)--see especially chapters 5 and 6.

45. Akselrod, *Perezhitoe,* see n. 38 above, 71-73.

46. On the participation of Jews in, and their contribution to, the Russian revolutionary movement, see: E. Haberer, *The Role of Jews in Russian Revolutionary Populism, 1868-1887,* Ph.D. Dissertation (University of Toronto, 1987).

THE JEWISH YOUTH MOVEMENTS
AS AN HISTORICAL PHENOMENON[1]

Chaim Schatzker

The beginnings of Jewish youth movements go back to 1907, with the establishment of the first group of hikers in Breslau, from which would sprout in 1912 the first large movement, Blau-Weiss, or The Blue-White movement. Initially Jewish youth groups were established on the model of the German youth movement; indeed, they acquired the latter's ways of thinking, forms of organization, and methods of education. Between the two world wars, the Jewish youth movement expanded throughout Germany[2] and spread to Czechoslovakia and Eastern Europe.[3] These groups played an important, and at times a very central, role in the following historical domains:

(a) Germany Jewry from the beginning of the century,
(b) History of Zionism in Western and Eastern Europe,
(c) Pioneering fulfillment,
(d) History of the Kibbutz movements,
(e) The Holocaust and resistance,
(f) The surviving remnant.

In each one of these areas, youth movement activity was unique, distinct from other organizational activities--even from other youth organizations, such as the young guard of various political parties, student organizations, and so on. It is important, therefore, to define what is meant by the uniqueness of the Jewish youth movement as an historical phenomenon.

The Jewish youth movements, throughout their various periods and geographical dispersion in Western and Eastern Europe, were distinct from one another in outlook, political orientation, social composition, level of Jewish identity or assimilation, ways of realizing their ideas, and their road to Israel and activities in the Homeland. The primary question remains, therefore: is it possible to speak of "youth movement" as a single, defined historical phenomenon, or only of "youth movements," because the distinctive features of each group surpass the similarities? Do we, on the weight of philosophic argument over general concepts, accept the nominalist approach, which argues that in actuality there are only different youth movements and that the general term, "youth movement," is used only for convenience of speech? Or do we accept the approach of the realists, who argue that there does indeed exist a general concept, "youth movement," from which the various types of youth movements draw both their definition and their legitimacy as individual movements and also their affinity to it as an overall reality? If this is the case, what is the definition of this overall concept?

What is the nature of the affinity of the various movements emanating from it?

As an initial thesis, I shall adopt the second approach--that of the existence of an overall youth movement as a unity within a multiplicity. This may be compared (as it was done before by Martin Buber and Max Brod) to the Hassidic movement, which is also very complex. The Hassidic movement has streams, factions, courts, and dynasties, which more than once have contended with one another. Still, there is one Hassidic movement, since there are components that make it become so and that remove from the whole whatever is not Hassidic, such as *Misnagdim*.

The development of every youth movement is similar. One may see in time a uniformity, which enables us to speak of an individual youth movement as a crystallized phenomenon within the multiplicity of movements. This uniformity, found in the circumstances of its creation, in its stages of development, in its aims, its content, and its influence wielding, was not felt at the time by the movement members themselves, among whom there generally grew a strong recognition of the singularity of their movement. Research on movements based on the sources, reveals a uniform social and historical phenomenon, the ways of imminent development being common to all movements.

We find it difficult to define this unity phenomenon. In any discussion of the youth movement, the broadest possible definition must be found, one that will include the spectrum of youth groups. The definition must also be narrow enough to exclude youth and young people's organizations that are not strictly youth movements. I would exclude the Pioneers (*Hehalutz*), which may have been composed of youth movements but was not in and of itself a youth movement. This semantic matter is important. The fact that there are youth movements today--although utterly different from those we are discussing--has caused many historians to take the phenomenon for granted, as something needing no other word of explanation. This attitude is a roadblock to understanding the phenomena and its significance.

An attempt will now be made to define the phenomenon of the youth movement according to seven characteristics,[4] exercising a clear, explicit reservation that we are talking here about an ideal, Max Weber-type of entity. In actuality, these characteristics are not always so fully noticeable, and their appearance in the various movements is variable. These seven characteristics were not determined arbitrarily. The determination was preceded by many years of research, in the course of which the texts of the various movements were examined for their motivations and characteristics. An analysis of these elements may then explain the essential character or essence of the different youth movements and their behavior in various historical situations, including the Holocaust, in which the reaction of youth belonging to a movement differed from that of unorganized youth.

Discontent with "Society" and the Striving for "Community"

In its critique of society, the youth movement deplores the atomization of men in the age of technology; the dissolution of organic relationships and bonds; loneliness and heartlessness; the ugliness and constriction of the large cities; modern technology and the rational industrial society which, through its one-sided emphasis on the development of the intellect, leads to the spiritual and emotional impoverishment of mankind. Dissatisfaction with this state of affairs prompts the striving for a new life style, for a community, a collectivity in which all those frustrated and withered vital shoots can thrive and blossom out in a new and satisfying life.

Inner Truth as an Ontological Criterion

The endeavour to "fashion life in the spirit of inner truth," proclaimed in the Meissner Formula, indicates the crucial importance of this theme within the total concept of the youth movement. In the youth movement's critique of society, the one feature most frequently pilloried was the lies and falsehood behind the facade of social norms and conventions. They were confronted with "inner truth" or the "spirit of truth" as a criterion of a fulfilled and righteous life conducive to strengthening community bonds. The movement sought the key to the discovery and recognition of this truth in the intuition, the subjective inner stirrings of the individual and the community, while rejecting rational, objective criteria as inadequate and misleading. It was art rather than science, sentiment rather than reason, intuitively grasped rather than externally established norms that were considered the effective instruments in a genuine search for truth.

The Bund

This organizational cell of the youth movement also owes its origin to a collective emotional experience. "For the constitution of the 'Bund' emotional experiences are vital, they form its 'foundation.'" "The flame of the 'Bund' only leaps up when those stirred to their depths as individuals meet, mutually recognize the common direction of their 'feeling' and on that basis kindle one another's enthusiasm."[5] The collective will (*volenté générale*) is forged at the Bund rally, mostly through strong emotional attachments focused on the personality of an inspiring leader. Born as a flash of intuition, the collective will is subsequently spelled out in statutes and resolution. Any deviation from that collective will must end either in separation from the Bund or in a recantation. Discussions may well take place within the Bund, but decisions are arrived at by the rising into consciousness of an "inner truth," not by the mechanistic method of democratic vote-counting. Sparked by the emotional ambiance of the Bund rally, this "liberating" idea illuminates the road ahead.

Totality of Commitment

Although activities accounted for only a small proportion of the time of its members, the youth movement was not content with the role of an subsidiary instrument of education, but endeavoured (on the whole with success) to totally dominate the lives of its members. Actually, the striving for "wholeness" and total commitment follows from the characteristics of the youth movement already described here. In its critique of society the youth movement deplored the fragmented, mechanistic relations between men, and its search for communion was expressed in a yearning for a pattern of organic, harmonious and all-embracing relations between the members of the community. Thus, there is a straight line leading from the principle of "inner truth" and the attempt to translate it into real life to the principle of the "totality" of the youth movement. "Inner truth," as it was truth in its purest form--in contrast to all externally imposed norms--demanded unconditional compliance, irrespective of society and social circumstances. It was bound to be regarded as indivisible and exempt from the need to enter into compromises with other "truths," exempt from the need to iron out differences and find a middle way. The more that "inner truth" was felt to be an elementary phenomenon of nature, the more complete was its demand for total submission. The educational approach chosen by the youth movement to translate its postulate into reality and to harness the total identities of its members consisted in the endeavour to mold their "conviction" and their "bearing."

Molding "Conviction" and "Bearing"

The youth movement based its approach on the assumption that in education the relationship between cause and effect, challenge and response, is never a straightforward and direct one, but that human reactions and modes of behavior in real situations are determined by psychological predispositions, classified as *Gesinnung* and *Haltung,* conviction and bearing. These predispositions in turn are derived from certain value judgments.

Having adopted this concept, which is diametrically opposed to that of modern behaviorism, the youth movement proceeded with faultless logic to draw a conclusion that is vital for an understanding of the movement. Once it is accepted that an individual's mode of behavior is governed entirely by convictions and bearing, there is little point in attempting to influence behavior directly in the course of the educational process. What matters instead is to dominate convictions and bearing. This would then spontaneously and without any further outside intervention--perhaps with redoubled efficacy as a result of refraining from exerting any external pressure--direct behavior into the desired channels. An unshakable faith in the inner logic and inevitability of this process confirmed the youth movements in its tendency to concentrate almost exclusively on the molding of the convictions of its followers, while the customary "schoolmasterly" methods of behavioral drill were spurned with ridicule and contempt, as they appeared to be based on a confusion of cause with effect in the sphere of education.

The same interpretation was applied to social processes. All the sections of the youth movement, representing a broad spectrum of different hues and diverging tendencies, were united in the belief that a transformation of the social order could only be effected by human beings who themselves had been transformed beforehand, and that only a "different" type of man would be able to ensure the survival of a new order. On the other hand, a genuine transformation could never be brought about by the use of violence to enforce changes in external circumstances, unless such changes were preceded by a spiritual transformation of the human beings concerned.

"Indirect" Education

The youth movement looked upon "indirect " education as the most effective means of influencing the conviction and bearing of its followers. In place of the "direct" education practiced in the schools, which endeavoured to transmit to the pupil information, opinions, skills and modes of behavior, the youth movement sought to affect the conviction and bearing of its followers indirectly, not by preaching the word, but through the mysterious workings of symbols and allusions, and above all through the participation in experiences charged with emotion; not through the impact of outside influence, but through the inward force of moved hearts and souls.

Contrary to the educational principle of rationality, which took it for granted that rational thinking will of necessity engender rational, and thus "positive" action, the youth movement believed that if only the youngster was exposed to the "right" type of experience, if he became "moved," his convictions and bearing would be molded the "right" way and appropriate action was bound to follow in due course.

The Movement and the "Moved"

The features listed here suggest a new and unconventional definition of the youth movement, summing it up primarily not as an organization of young people but rather as *Jugendbewegtheit,* youth's state of being moved, of being emotionally gripped by the sense of being young. This interpretation in terms of a movement of the human spirit appears to be supported by the general usage of the youth movement, which in referring to its followers never spoke of "members," but of *Jugendbewegte,* the "youth-moved" or "moved youth."

By understanding these characteristics, we can arrive at a deeper insight into the activity of the Jewish youth movement in each of those historical domains that I cited at the outset of my remarks.

(A) The third generation after the emancipation of the Jews in Germany at the beginning of the century, unlike what is commonly thought, displayed no harmony and balance in the confrontation between its Jewishness and its Germanness. It was, instead, fractionalized. The youth movement posed a challenge, and it is the way of Jewish youth who know their Judaism from introspection as internal truth to mold their lives in its light as an attempt to realize this truth. Against this concept of synthetic Judaism, the youth movement set up the ideal of the whole person, who comes to Judaism, not through intellectual and doubting analysis, but through an inner experience animating one's whole being.

The issue not raised (or only partially brought up by teachers, rabbis, parents, and various Jewish organizations) was raised by the Jewish youth movement--the return of Jewish youth to its Judaism.

(B) Like the transformation process to Judaism, which was internalized, grounded on deep spiritual experience, so too the transformation to Zionism, to socialism, and to pioneering was undertaken through the characteristic and special components of the youth movement. It is against the background of these special components that one must view the relationship of the youth movement with the *Hehalutz* organization and its method of pioneering fulfillment. They were motivated by the longing for "fellowship" and for "inner truths." Under pressure of the revolution, inflation, the impoverishment of the middle class, and anti-Semitism, which came in the wake of the war in the period between the two wars, all the Jewish youth groups underwent a process of transformation both to socialism and to Zionism. They had a special conception of these two "isms" as spiritual attitudes, as frames of mind, and as ethical decisions. At this stage, the Jewish youth movement remained anti-political, or at least a-political. The choice of socialism and Zionism stemmed in the main from its being a youth movement seeking to fashion its life in the light of inner truth.

The worsening economic situation of the 1920s, economic crisis, unemployment, hunger, the workers' economic and spiritual distress, and the growing politicalization of life in Germany, on the one hand, and increasing anti-Semitism on the other, had the effect of putting the Jewish youth movement face to face with reality. Once again, it could not remain merely in the realm of spiritual attitudes and frame of mind. The socialist parties presented the youth with a social challenge; the ascendancy of national-socialism placed before them a challenge of national self-identity; and the establishment of the *Hehalutz* movement set before them the challenge of personal pioneering fulfillment.

On these different challenges, the Jewish youth groups broke up into three rival factions:

1. one faction sought to translate the socialist spiritual attitude into actual socialist-communist deed;
2. a second wanted to translate the Zionist position into actual Zionist pioneering activity;
3. a third group was content with remaining a German-Jewish youth group and nothing more, a kind of "youth haven."

The arguments among these factions constituted the principal feature of the Jewish youth movement at this stage. It is against the background of the special characteristics of the youth movement that one must see its relationship with Hehalutz and the path to pioneering fulfillment.[6]

The youth movement and *Hehalutz* remained intertwined in the consciousness of the Jewish settlement in Palestine after the Second World War. As the two main youthful bearers who implemented the idea of Zionist pioneering fulfillment, they are for the most part mentioned in a single breath. In fact, organizational treatment of them is united in one department of the

Jewish Agency. Their roots and the beginnings of their histories, however, do not at all testify to a single identity of idea or of purpose or of organization. Furthermore, the history of their relations up to the outbreak of the Second World War is replete with contrasts rooted in their very essence.

Like the process of transformation to Judaism and Zionism, the process of transformation to socialism would be aided by those characteristic components and mechanisms of the youth movement, especially a revulsion for "society" and "civilization" and the longing for fellowship. After this objection to the socialist and communist idea seemed like a spirit of renewal, bringing equality and meaning back to the world.

This idea, taken from the German youth movement, appears in various guises in the Jewish youth movements. Moreover, the common disgust expressed by socialism and the youth movements at the extant capitalist world brought the two together. It also created in the hearts of youth movement members a feeling of identity, as they imagined they saw in socialism and the kibbutz a kind of extension of the fellowship of their movement. What these two transformation processes, to socialism and to Zionism, shared in common was this: their point of origin was not rooted in reality, in the real world and its demands, but in the experience of the youth movement, which remained self-centered even in light of, and at times in contrast to, Zionist or socialist demands.

In 1933 and in the years that followed, therefore, the youth movement could not find satisfaction in the large numbers of new members who joined or who joined *Hehalutz,* being motivated by the force of reality and the power of political and economic constraints. Even then, it saw its principal role in maintaining "spiritual training," which appeared to it to be more important than "physical training," and was looked upon as a necessity.[7]

We find repeated references in the written sources of all of these youth movements describing the low point reached in 1933. This was a deep and nearly total spiritual caesura--not a physical one--between Jewish young people and their German external environment as a result of its having rejected them. This is what emerges from the testimonies, among them even of seven-year-old children who were rejected by their non-Jewish classmates and friends. Such was the pattern in all the educational and social spheres--at school, in the streets, and in the professions. The situation of young people living in small towns was especially bad in this regard, and we find very urgent requests to get these children away from these areas.

The upshot was the ties of Jewish young people with their peer group were broken, as were their relations with role models and their bonds of identity, all of which play an essential part in the process of socialization. They also experienced a breakdown in the scale of stable values, which is of special significance for an adolescent in need of ordering his or her personality. In looking around, Jewish youngsters could find no valid and binding values offered by the environment; all that could be seen was a world in which values were being degraded, an *Entwertung aller Werte*. Everything seemed relative, so that they did not even try to discover alternate values in either themselves or their relationship with their environment. In a lecture entitled 'Education Problems in Our Work,' a teacher who was active in *Habonim* reviewed his experience of the change being manifested by Jewish youngsters as a result of the events in those years. He spoke of the threat of psychological crippling, of the prospect of a general given to superficial actualization and unable to form personal ties of any lasting value. Others spoke of the possibility of the emergence of feelings of inferiority attended by aggressive and arrogant behavior that might result from the loss of psychological equilibrium. Still another potential danger was that Jewish youngsters might internalize anti-semitic doctrines in the course of adapting themselves to the patterns of Nazi thought and argument, notwithstanding the fact that these doctrines were being directed against them.

It would appear, therefore, that the intellectual and psychological support which was the sole means for personality to develop harmoniously-- and which Jewish youngsters had been deprived of by their force of circumstance--could only be obtained by young Jews within the milieu of the youth movement. This was virtually the only ambiance available at the time to young Jews in which they could live as Jews without risking depression, humiliation, disorientation, or damage to their personalities. A *Habonim* manual compares the benefits of such an ambiance with the advantages of a compass on a journey: it gave a fixed point needed for orientation. In contrast to the parental home, where a young person met with reproaches, irritation, and tensions, the youth movement offered security, warmth, courage, the spirit of action, the joy of youth and existential values. The memoirs of Ora Borinski, Jizchak Schwersenz,[8] and others repeatedly testify to the conception of a society of young people that took the place of the family in inspiring a feeling of belonging and security in a shattered and ruined world. And as conditions steadily grew worse, and even reached the unmitigated disaster of Auschwitz and Birkenau, the individual's sense of merging totally with the society of his fellows and with the movement would grow to an extent never dreamed of the by the youth movement.

Perhaps man really needs something like a barbed-wire fence so that he should always feel conscious of the value of living day to day in the group (*Gemeinschaft*), until every person, even if he should remain alone, will feel that he himself is a society in each of his decisions.[9]

And in the cruel and hard decision of whether to join one's parents or remain with the group, it is often the group which tips the scale: "If only we could stay together, that is the wish that motivates us most strongly these days."[10]   At Auschwitz, one member of the movement gathered others together in order to "try through arguing, talking, parties, and inquiries into the issues that concern us, to take their minds off the terrible ordeal of day-to-day existence."[11]   And in the shadow of the crematoria of Auschwitz, a seventeen year old girl who was a member of the movement wrote:

> . . . In my thoughts I am always with you. . . . We never despair of the hope of one day seeing you again. Often we sing and talk amongst ourselves. And we still try to study. I have only one request: always take us into your circle at the hour of parting and never forget us. . . .[12]

Ora Borinski and Jizchak Schwersenz tell of nearly identical symbolic rituals that were practiced at parting, in which the pieces of torn flag and broken chain were given for safe keeping to members as a symbol and token of the continuity of the fellowship and its activity.

The great range of activities of the youth movement fell into two major categories: "internal work," which followed the special pattern that had always been a traditional part of the youth movement; and "external work," which the circumstances of the times called for, an which consisted of work within the community, social work, education, work on behalf of political parties, propaganda, vocational retraining, and involvement in a variety of other activities of a similar type. There were four major contexts within which vocational training was undertaken. In three of which the youth movements played a significant and possibly even a crucial role:

1. Youth *Alijah*;
2. Intermediate and *Hehalutz hachscharah;*
3. Vocational training for those going to other countries (apart from Palestine);
4. Individual and non-collective vocational training.

But of the widest scope and greatest importance were the activities that the youth movement carried out together with *Hehalutz*.[13]

Many articles and books have been written about the role that the Jewish youth movement and *Hehalutz* played in the time of the Holocaust, one of the most significant and responsible missions ever entrusted to youth, an about the greatness of their deeds, which "can be properly judged only against the background of the reality of those times."

Here I confine myself to one of the most significant phenomena that characterized the perception of the youth movement at that time, namely, the unusual, surrealist interaction between the domain of reality and that of imagination.

During the time of the Holocaust, those youth movements underwent a gradual process of disassociation between their former patterns of ideology and educational work, and reality. *Eretz Yisrael,* on the one hand, and assimilation in the national entity of their countries on the other, became increasingly unachievable and unrealistic ideals. Nevertheless they continued within the realm of imagination alone, to take a perhaps even more important part in the life of their adherent than they ever had before in the realm of reality. In order to understand this phenomenon, we have to go back to one of the most significant characteristics of the youth movement.

The youth movement based its approach on the assumption that in education, the relationship between cause and effect, challenge and response, is never a straightforward and direct one, but that human reactions and modes of behavior in real situations are determined by psychological predispositions, classified as *Gesinnung* and *Haltung,* convictions, inclinations, and attitudes. These predispositions are in turn derived from certain value judgments. Indeed, the youth movement had always maintained that the decisive element for an man is not reality, but consciousness of inner truth and the mental attitudes that derive from it.

In concentrating on mental attitudes and the shaping of a model of existence in conformity with them, the Jewish youth movements were not able to reduce the role of external reality or dismiss it from consciousness. Believing that attitude of mind and individual choice overpowered external reality, they worked toward a complete disassociation between those two domains.[14]

While Zionist movements sought to steer the mental attitude of their members in a practical and creative direction, the non-Zionist youth movement was intent on ignoring a reality they found unacceptable and beyond bearing. But they chose to escape, as though to a remote island in a sea of reality, seeking their refuge in a state of intellectual narcosis that could offer no solution or way out. In the tension between "reality" and "inner truth," they chose the latter and paid the price of abandoning the domain of reality. After all efforts of those groups to integrate into the "new order" of the Third Reich ended in failure and after they had to admit that their hope of joining the *voelkisch* German order was untenable, "to support it despite everything" was in perfect keeping with the movement's *Haltung,* since it was "not external success but a person's inner choice which is decisive." The total elimination of *Gesinnung* from the domain of real events now took the form of surrender to a despair from which there was no more thought of escape, a despair that was like a "universal seal".[15]

In eastern Europe also,[16] the Jewish youth movements stuck to their former ideologies. The newspapers of the Zionist and socialist movements with their various factions, continued to devote considerable space to *Eretz Yisrael* affairs and to socialistic theory. At the beginning, the youth movements might have been "confident that the troubled times would pass and then the nation would need a young generation that was bodily strong and spiritually sound, which would be the one to lead the Jewish masses to different future, a better future."[17] Those hopes became increasingly unrealistic. Nevertheless, the youth movements went on with their Zionist programs:

> Like a blind musician plucks the strings of his harp, so do we
> pluck the strings of our dream. Since we are crushed by chains,
> we dream of flying. Since we are living as slaves we dream of
> a life of freedom. Instead of songs of sadness, let us give
> expression to our dream by crying, just as prisoners express
> their dream of freedom by weeping.[18]

Reading letters from *Eretz Yisrael* became "a moment of forgetting, of disassociation from reality."[19]

The second astonishing phenomenon which characterized the youth movement within the domain of interaction between reality and imagination, but in the opposite direction, was the acceptance of the most remote and most unthinkable impression as reality. Images, which in normal times would have exceeded even the wildest nightmares, were perceived as reality by organized youth long before this was the case with the adult Jewish world. Various Jewish youth groups and movements were among the first to see through the camouflaged activities of the Germans and to recognize the bitter reality of the Nazi plan to annihilate all the Jews; this at a relatively early date near the start of the gassings at Chelmno and the mass murder at Ponary. The youth movements' underground papers gave the first news about the mass killing and published the first call for resistance. Rather than being perceived on the basis of factual information, it was quite in line with the patterns of thinking and feeling of the youth movement that this conception was perceived mainly by intuition and brutal inner realization. thirty years before, Jewish students and youth movements had been among the first to recognize the real meaning hidden behind the slogans of modern anti-semitism, or A-semitism, as it was called in circles of the German youth movement.[20] Furthermore, the call to resistance that came from youngsters of pre-military age who had never touched any kind of weapon before, was not based on logic or any real prospects for success or victory, but on an inner decision in spite of reality.

The story of the deeds of the youth movement has been told many times.[21] This paper has sought to show that certain reactions and patterns of behavior of the Jewish youth movement could not be explained by external circumstances only, or by the fact that its members were more flexible and footloose, not being burdened by familial responsibilities, but also by the nature of its being a "youth movement." It is true that young people are regarded as not being fond of rigid thought patterns, more open to new ideas and innovative ways of thinking, and more receptive to revolutionary actions than adults. But as Gutman has pointed out: "In order to crystallize such an inner decision, people need both mental and spiritual daring and a sense of community with others of similar aspiration."[22] Both were anchored in their very being a "youth movement."

This chapter cannot be concluded without discussing the central role of the youth movements in organizing and leading the surviving remnant of the Holocaust. The youth movement was the only Jewish organization that was not utterly destroyed in the Holocaust. Jewish youth movements existed prior to, during, and after the Holocaust.

Immediately after the liberation and at times even before it, the youth movements renewed their activities both in collecting children, taking them out from the monasteries and Christian families, gathering them together in children's homes, educating them, and so forth. All this took place at least a year before the arrival of the first emissaries from Israel (Palestine). These Youth *Aliya* emissaries were to encounter a very confused and complex reality.

Most of the Jewish children and youths, refugees of the Holocaust and potential candidates for immigration to Palestine, were concentrated in Germany. According to an UNRRA count, in Germany in October 1946 there were some 22,000 Jewish children and youth whose numbers grew to 24,000 soon afterwards; 2500-2600 of them were orphans. In other European countries the concentration of Jewish children survivors was much smaller. Most of the Jewish youth came from Poland, some of them having escaped to Russia during the war and returned to Poland afterwards. Those who were not absorbed there were transferred to Germany. But children and youth who had hid out during the war years with Christian families or in the forests, in bunkers, and caves were also brought to Germany although a minority was sent to Austria, Italy, France, Switzerland, and England. Among the last were 250 children, evacuees of Theresenstadt. So, too, children from Poland constituted 35 to 40 percent of the Jewish youth who had been gathered in Holland, most of the youngsters with Dutch citizenship having spent the war years hidden in Christian homes. In Switzerland, children of German, Italian, Hungarian, and Yugoslavian origin were collected. Despite all the prohibitions and regulations, there was great mobility of children and youth among the different areas of Allied occupation in Germany and the various European countries. In a youth village that was later set up on Cyprus, there were more than 1,760 children and youths gathered from various countries.

Youth movement leaders and counselors from among the survivors collected these masses of children, organized them, and cared for them. At times they even accompanied them from the camps and forests. One Youth *Aliya* official, soon after arriving in Germany, described the activity of the youth group leaders in these words:

> It is hard to know the main factor that propels these people into action. At a time when they themselves are weary, after having undergone the seven circles of hell in the death camps or on the roads of vast Russia, suffering famine, cold, and other misery, at a time when they themselves are in need of aid and sustenance was there here a human-humane factor that pushed them to round up children that they found wandering without care and education. Was there here, on the one hand, love for the weak and suffering creature who could not yet fight the battle for existence and, on the other, an instinctive feeling of fatherhood or motherhood? Was there here the will of the movement to acquire souls for the movement? It is possible that many and various motives drove these youth leaders and it is possible that all of them combined together and generated their

actions. The fact is, though, that all these anonymous leaders saved for us thousands of children, orphans and unaccompanied children, who were later educated in various children's homes. Were it not for them, who knows what fate would have awaited thousands of Jewish children who today are being educated in the Youth *Aliya* framework.[23]

Endnotes

1. On the Jewish Youth Movement, see Herman Meier-Cronemeyer, "Jüdische Jugendbewegung," *Germania Judaica*. Kölner Bibliothek zur Geschichte des deutschen-Judentums, Folge 27/28, 8 Jahrg., Heft 1-4 (1969); Chanoch Rinott, "Major Trends in Jewish Youth Movements in Germany," *Leo Baeck Institute Year Book*, 19 (1974); Chaim Schatzker, *Tnuat Hanoar Hayehudit BeGermania bein Hashanim 1900-1933* (The Jewish Youth Movement in Germany Between the Years 1900-1933), unpublished dissertation submitted to the Hebrew University of Jerusalem (1969).

2. The most famous Jewish Youth movements in Germany were: the "Blau-Weiss," the "Jung-Jüdischers Wonderbund" (JJWB), "Esra," "Kameraden," "Werkleute," "Kadima," "Habonim-Hanoar Hachaluzi," "Brith Haolim," "Jüdischer Pfadfinderbund," "Hashomer Hazair," "Betar," "Brith Hanoar of Zeirei Misrachi," "Noar Agudati," "Makkabi Hazair."

3. The most famous were: "Hashomer Hazair'," "Dror," "Bnei Akiva," "Zionist Youth," "Gordonia," "Beitar," "Haschomer Hadati."

4. On the characteristics of the German Youth Movement and their transformation to the Jewish situation by the Jewish Youth Movement see Chaim Schatzker, "Buber's Influence on the Jewish Youth Movement," *Leo Baeck Institute Year Book*, 23 (1978): 154-163.

5. Hermann Schmalenbach, "Die soziologische Kategorie des Bundes," in *Die Dioskuren, Juhrbuch für Geisteswissenschaften* (München, 1922), 58.

6. On the cooperation between the Jewish Youth Movement and the *Hechalutz* Organization see Chaim Schatzker, "Chaluziut Vehagshama Halutzit shel Tnuot Hanoar Hayehudiot BeGermania Hanazit" (The *Chalutz* Ideal and its Realization by the Jewish Youth Movement in Germany), *Yalkut Moreschet* 30 (November, 1980): 59-82.

7. Chaim Schatzker, "The Jewish Youth Movement in Germany in the Holocaust Period (I). Youth in Confrontation with a New Reality," *Leo Baeck Institute Year Book* 32 (1987): 157-181.

8. See the description and testimonies concerning the period in Anneliese-Ora Borinski, *Erinnerungen 1940-1943* (Germany, 1970); and Yitzhak Schwersenz, *Machteret*

> 00000000000000000000000000000000000000000000000000000000000000000000000000000000000000000000000000000000000000000000000000000000000000000

THE SECT OF CATASTROPHE:
MAHANE ISRAEL-LUBAVITCH 1940-1945

Gershon Greenberg

One of the striking religious responses to the Holocaust (*Khurbn*) during the war itself was that of *Mahane Israel* (MI) of Lubavitch or "HABAD" (i.e. *Hokhma, Bina, Da'at*) Hassidism. MI separated itself from the rest of Judaism in the religious, if not physical sense. It set out to prevent the *Khurbn,* to rescue Jews from it once the *Khurbn* began, to accelerate its passing and to introduce redemption. It did so on existential and cosmic levels simultaneously.

Based at 770 Eastern Parkway in Brooklyn, MI had branches in Canada, England, Australia, the Land of Israel, Paris, Shanghai and in the Oswego, New York refugee camp.[1] I would estimate there were no more than 1,500 members at any given time--there were 670 participants at its *Mishna*-conclusion celebration on June 20, 1943. MI's founding leader was Joseph Isaac Schneersohn (JIS) (1880-1950), the Rav of Lubavitch. The members came from within and without HABAD. It described itself in July 1941:

> We are not any kind of organization in the usual sense of the word. We ask no membership fee, we distribute no membership cards. We do not keep records of completely inactive members. We are no paper organization. We have no meetings, we distribute no honors. We have no glory seeking officers and we discredit no activities. Whoever wants to work voluntarily in awakening Jews to the demands of the days of redemption, which Admor Shlita has done since last 1-2 October 1940, can come to help us. He will become a member of our MI automatically.[2]

In this paper I will focus on three aspects of MI: secret knowledge, activities to accelerate the end of the *Khurbn,* and the negation of Judaism outside MI's bordered encampment.

Esoteric and Exoteric Knowledge

MI delineated its community from the rest of the world. Calling itself "Goshen" ("Only in the land of Goshen, where the children of Israel were, was there no hail." Exodus 9/26). The community was veiled in secrecy. MI members claimed to be privy to the great secret contained in Joseph's last words *"pakod yifkod,"* i.e. "surely remember:"

I die and God will surely remember you and bring you out of
the land [of Egypt] unto the Land which He swore to Abraham,
Isaac and Jacob (Genesis 50/24).

Serah inherited the knowledge of the secret from her father Asher, who had
inherited it from his brother Joseph, who had inherited it from his father
Jacob. She knew that the pairing of words meant the Land would combine
religious and national dimensions and she could identify Moses as the deliverer
(*Midrash Exodus Rabba* 5/13)[3] The secret made its way over the generations
to JIS. It meant to him that death implied life, exile implied Land-centered
redemption, and that messianic sufferings (*Hevlei Moshiah*) implied the coming
of the messiah. It created a secretive mentality--MI members were enjoined
to keep their membership hidden even from friends and family members.[4]

From October 20, 1940 through July 20, 1943, MI's journal *Hakeriyya
Vehakedusha* (from "Reading and holiness for eternal life" in the Yom Kippur
liturgy)[5] published upside down acronymic codes about the future. For
example, the one of September 21, 1941 was decoded on July 20, 1944, and
meant:

The tyrant Hitler's end is in his ongoing cruel threat to
annihilate all individuals in Europe and America on both sides
of the ocean. All the horrible, violent German actions will be
impeded when they confront the furious volcanoes which are
now boiling with a vengeance against German Nazism. They
will overcome Hitler's victorious and abhorrent land of Nazis
like fire. They will annihilate its population's existence as
Nazism has thirsted to annihilate Jews. In summer around *Ellul*
[i.e. August - September] when America will be involved in its
November [1944] [added in July 1944] elections, there will be
great troubles in Europe and Hitler will make his abominable
threats.[6]

As Joseph did not proclaim the words until he was sure to die, so the
esoteric knowledge would become exoteric only after the realities of *pakod
yifkod* were underway, after death was imminent and irrevocable. On October
2, 1940, MI members were instructed, "Do not spread [the secret] among
strangers. [And] do so only when the exile oppresses you so severely that
your very existence is endangered."[7]

As it turned out, as soon as secrecy was established, it was broken.
During October 1940, JIS announced "Immediate *Teshuva* (penitent return)--

Immediate *Geula* (redemption)."[8] The decision to make the knowledge public was JIS', as it was once Elijah's--to whom JIS was compared in terms of suffering isolation because of zeal for God (I Kings 19/14).[9] Beginning May 20, 1941, JIS published four proclamations (*Kol Kore*) in Yiddish and English periodicals in Chicago and New York.[10] Their intent was to shatter the epistemological resistance to *pakod yifkod*--one manifestation of the *Hevlei Moshiah* era was a defilement (*Tuma*) atmosphere which clouded perception of apocalyptic truth. Hopefully, Jews would hearken and act appropriately by doing *Teshuva*--i.e., become aware of their heavenly root, be sincere towards God, mindful of His presence, love Him through one's neighbors and serve Him in all concrete situations and with modesty.[11] MI counted on its women to help JIS communicate the knowledge; for the women were more sensitive than men to the onset of crisis and apocalypse.[12] Given their intent, observed the *Hakeriyya Vehakedusha* (HK) editor who kept his own identity secret, the *Kol Kore*s constituted a crystallization of prophetic teaching about the end of days, they were Holy Scripture.[13]

Behind the *Kol Kore*s lay an apocalyptic ideology. Exile (*Galut*) which resulted from sin, became increasingly worse because there was no *Teshuva*. It reached its worst point with *Khurbn*-Hitler. There was no caesura in history prior to the *Khurbn* nor any after it when *Teshuva* would channel history into apocalypse. The *Khurbn* placed the people of Israel face-to-face with collective death. A small number would necessarily turn to God and populate *Goshen,* and would work to save the universe and bring about redemption. This imminent redemption, expected in terms of months, would rebalance the universe after Hitler. In the *Kol Kore*s, the Rav proclaimed that God had imposed Hitler upon history as He once imposed Haman, to evoke *Teshuva*. Jews had to recognize their own ignorance and become aware how they faced a choice between life and death. They had to choose *Teshuva* for the sake of life or be destroyed. If there was awareness, confrontation of the choice, correct choice and then implementation, a fortress for *Goshen* could be established to resist the catastrophe in Europe as well as in America. The existential process would have corresponding cosmic ramifications: the *Hevlei Moshiah* would be lessened and redemption would be accelerated.[14]

Activities to End the *Khurbn*

Beyond the work directed towards awareness, MI had a number of activities directed to bring others into Goshen. It assigned teams to rescue youths vulnerable to Christian missionary efforts, diverted Jewish adults from Christian Science offices, distributed informational materials to Jewish soldiers and chaplains, and sent ritual items to Displaced Persons in the American and British zones in Europe.

Within the HABAD community, MI established a *Bikkur Holim* society to visit hospitals to console the ailing and provide copies of HK and JIS' *Conversations* (*Sihot*). It sent delegates to private homes to persuade parents to send their children to proper Talmud Toras and Yeshivas. MI organized a division of women in summer 1941 to tell *midrashic* stories to children and explain the enduring validity of Tora and *Mitzva,* and it established the *Eishel* (*Agudat Shiurei Limud Torah*--Organization for Tora Study Sessions) to enroll students in HABAD's *Tomkhei Teminim* Yeshivas.

MI also established *Psalm* and *Mishna* fellowships. The *Psalm* Fellowship was established May 22, 1942, to reinforce MI messianism through Psalm recitations. Centered in Jerusalem and directed by Shlomo Y.L. Eliezerov, the fellowship was led by Ashkenazi Chief Rabbi Isaac Halevy Herzog (1888-1959), Sephardi Chief Rabbi Benzion Meir Hai Usiel (1880-1953), and Ultra-Orthodox *Agudat Israel* leader Joseph Zevi Ben Israel Dushinsky (1868-1948). The three led a group of elders at the Western Wall or at the grave site of King David near Mt. Zion in reciting the 150 Psalms at dawn. MI believed that the recitations would awaken Jews throughout the world to *Teshuva* and thereby ease the *Hevlei Moshiah.* Elders were chosen because God cherished the activities of the elders at the time of the redemption from Egypt, and He would do so again. MI aimed to make the recitations a world-wide activity, and groups (including males and females) were set up in America and Canada in synagogues and *Bathei Midrash.* There were "elder fellowships" to recite the complete book of Psalms over a seven day period before *Shaharit;* "daily fellowships" to recite them over a thirty day period; and "Sabbath fellowships" to recite Psalms 119-150 either before *Shaharit* or between *Minha* and *Ma'ariv* on Sabbaths. On the first day of *Shavuot,* the holy day of the granting of Tora, all the fellowships throughout the world held simultaneous recitations and there was a celebratory meal at King David's gravesite. The fellowship functioned for at least two years, through the first day of *Shavuot,* May 28, 1944.[15]

The Oral *Mishna* Fellowship was established April 9, 1942 and lasted at least through May 20, 1945, the day after *Shavuot.* Fellowship members had cards which associated recitation of *Mishna* text with *Teshuva* and *Teshuva* with the end of exile and onset of redemption. Tractates were assigned by lotteries (May 24, 1942; June 24, 1942; June 20, 1943; and June 18, 1944) such that all six were completed within the year. Assignees were expected to repeat their sections over and over to the point of memorizing them. Upon completion, a celebration (*Siyyum*) was held (June 20, 1943; June 18, 1944; May 20, 1945). Menahem Mendel Schneersohn (MMS) (b. 1902) had the leading role in the *Siyyumim*.

JIS explained the function of the recitation in terms of purifying the air. He offered an example of the way in which words affected the air, which he attributed to the medieval philosopher Levi ben Gershom (1288-1349):

> When a person is walking in the street and suddenly has a good idea about Tora, *Mitzva* or good behavior, it means that he met someone who studied Tora, kept *Mitzvot* and behaved properly. Someone awakened a good (atmosphere) around him. Similarly if he has a bad idea, it means that a bad person with evil thoughts affected him.

The air of the world had become clouded, poisonous and sickening because Tora-speech (Tora refers to holy literature in the broadest sense) was absent. Because of this, Jews were numbed to feeling God and were obsessed with materiality. In a cyclical process, absence of Tora speech produced a barrier to God, which in turn intensified the absence and increased the difficulty of overcoming it. Through Tora-speech the air would become pure and communication with God would be possible. Indeed, Tora-speech as *Mishna* repetition constituted a *Teshuva* which could lighten the *Hevlei Moshiah*. The need was greatest in markets, streets, and public conveyances; speech in synagogues was comparatively pure.

Why did *Mishna* in particular purify the air? Having the same letters as soul (*Neshama*), *Mishna* was potentially identifiable with the essence of the individual. For example, Shneour Zalman of Lliady (1745-1813) told a follower that if he learned *Mishna Kelim* by heart, he would develop a powerful intellectual apparatus (*Kelim*), and he did. Shmuel ben Menahem Mendel Schneersohn (1834-1883) called someone "*Shabbat,*" because he studied the *Mishna* by that name. The soul could expel the materialistic dust which clung to it as with a slingshot (I Samuel 25/29). If it was filled with *Mishna,* the individual would have the power to contest the evil forces and clear the air for communing with God. R. Eleazar had observed that *Mishna* was a "pillar of iron" *(Barzel),* equivalent numerically to *Safek* (doubt) and *Amalek.* (More precisely, "*Barzel*" is 239 and "*Safek*" or "*Amalek*" is 240.) This meant that a *Mishna* personality could neutralize the doubt brought on by "*Amalek*" (*Midrash Vayyikra Rabba* 21/4).

MMS elaborated the theory behind *Mishna* recitation according to traditional sources in a separate treatise written in summer 1944:

1. Of all factors in the universe, air affected the personality most. It was possible to survive up to seven days without eating or drinking, as Moses himself had (Exodus 24/16, *Yoma 4b,* Rambam, *Mishne Tora Hilkhot Shavuot* ch. 5, *Halakha* 20), but without air a person would die within the hour (*Yoma* 75b, Rambam, *MT Hilkhot Deot* ch. 4 beginning: *Shulhan Arukh. Even Ha'ezer* paragraph 17, part 32; Menahem Mendel Schneersohn [1789-1860], *Tzemah Tzedek, She'elot U'teshuvot Mi'shulhan Arukh Even Ha'ezer nr. 78*). It was for this reason that "man should praise the Creator for every breath he takes" (*Midrash Genesis Rabba* ch. 14 end). Food and drink had a serious affect upon personality. For example, Elisha ben Abuyya rebelled against God because when his mother was pregnant with him she passed by a temple of idolatry, ate some of the food and "it spread through her like the venom of insects" (*Midrash Ruth Rabba* 6/4). If such was the impact of food, how much more seriously would air affect the personality?

2. Air was affected by speech, and good speech expelled defilement (*Tuma*) in the air. R. Judah ben Bathyra told a disciple:

> My son, open thy mouth, [do not mumble] but let thy words be clear, for words of Tora are immune to uncleanness, as it says, 'Is not My word like as fire?' (Jeremiah 23/29). Just as fire is immune to defilement, so words of Tora are immune to defilement (*Berakot* 22a.)

Rambam commented that Ezra's enactment that a person who had a nocturnal pollution may not read Tora never took effect, because Tora words were immune to defilement (Rambam, *Mishne Tora Hilkhot Keriyyat Shema* ch. 4, *Halakha* 8).

3. Of all the words of Tora, *Mishna* was the best suited practically to purify the air. For it could be spoken even without a text, while Hebrew Scripture could not (*Gittin* 60b).

4. *Mishna* was able to transform the exiled world into a redeemed world. According to R. Isaac, Tora was given in fire and darkness to show that someone constantly occupied with it would be saved from the fire of *Gehinnom* and the darkness of exile. Thus, God told Abraham:

As long as thy children shall be absorbed in the Tora they will
be saved from punishment. But should they turn from her and
forget her paths, the fire of *Gehinnom* will have dominion over
them and they will be subjugated by the nations of the earth
(*Zohar* 2, 83b).

Mishna was the primary instrument of Tora-rescue. Thus God stated that if
Israel engaged in the oral law while among the nations, He would gather them
up (*Hosea* 8/10). Joseph Caro pointed out that it was the tribe of Asher that
responded to cries for rescue from *Gehinnom.* The tribe promoted study
(*Horayot* 13b, *Menahot* 85b), and Asher responded to the cries with "Did you
read?" If the answer was "yes," the person was rescued (Joseph Caro, cited
in Elijah ben Solomon Abraham [d. 1792], *"Anaf Efod," Midrash Talpiot*).

Beyond rescuing Israel from exile, *Mishna* was the instrument for
bringing redemption. When Israel returned from the first exile, the Temple
was not fully restored because the Jews did not have the right intention: they
engaged in Tora but did not bless it or study it for its own sake. *Mishna*
provided the right intention (*Sota* 36a with Rashi, *Nedarim* 81a with Nissim
ben Reuben of Gerondi). Redemption was also conditional upon social unity
and the removal of groundless hatred--the sort of hatred which caused the fall
of the second Temple (*Yoma* 9b). The Pentateuch could not promote unity
because it had no *Halakhic* differences to be resolved while the *Gemara* had
them and left them unresolved, *Mishna* provided a single basis traceable to
Moses and did promote social unity (*Kiddushin* 30b, *Sanhedrin* 33a, Shneour
Zalman of Lliady, *Shulhan Arukh Yore Dea. Hilkhot Talmud Tora* ch. 2
beginning, and *"Kuntres Aharon,"* (1815/1816) and *Idem, "Ve'ele Shemot"*
paragraph 6, *Shemot Torah Or* (1837).[16]

The Negative World Beyond Goshen's Borders

MI related to the rest of Israel solely in negative terms. Goshen's
truth--the secret knowledge of apocalyptic events was radical in character, and
left no neutral ground between it and the rest of the world. JIS expressed it
thusly:

Now is the end of the *Asshalta degeula* (the onset of
redemption). Now our duty, our concept of *Teshuva* is
different. The destroyer has come to obliterate everything bad
and betraying in the world. Accordingly, the old forms of
betrayal and the old, neutral form of *Teshuva* no longer hold for
Jews. The call [for *Teshuva*] demands a fiery awakening to

receive the countenance of our righteous messiah. One must now stop planning new centers of exile under the mantel of neutral piety, neutral faith, and neutral Tora-parties.[17]

Accordingly, MI denounced assimilation (Reform, Enlightenment), secular nationalism, the *Agudat Israel* and *Agudat Harabbanim* organizations of the Orthodox (while they supported HABAD)[18] and even ultra-Orthodoxy *per se*.

For their part, MI declared, assimilationists were the contemporary Hellenists, the contemporary Yeshurun:

But Yeshurun grew fat and thick. Thou art grown fat, thou art become thick, thou art obese. Then he forsook God who made him (Deuteronomy 32/15).

Assimilationists falsely deduced that since God did not help Tora-true Jews in Europe it was pointless to be pious in America. They regarded the drama of *Asshalta demeshiha* as a fairy tale. They were obsessed with the anticipated victory by democratic nations instead of recognizing that the entire catastrophe was under divine direction, and they were concerned with a second military front but not with *Teshuva*. MI included the American Jewish Conference:

The destructive satan has penetrated weak-minded Judaism [in America] in the guise of false speech about creating unity (August 29 - September 1, 1943, New York City).[19]

MI attacked secular nationalists for disregarding Tora as the basis for a Jewish state. The restoration, for MI, was to be a holy event which turned on *Teshuva*. Otherwise, it would eventually be destroyed, no matter how much physical building had taken place (see Rashi to *Yoma* 86b). In May 1944, JIS reminded his listeners that Israel was "a Land which the Lord your God looks after, on which the Lord you God always keeps His eye, from year's beginning to year's end" (*Deuteronomy* 11/12). Thus, God detested the fact that the Land was now being led mostly by people who were Godless and were opposed to Tora and *Mitzvot*. In part of the Land, the Sabbath was being desecrated, family purity and practical *Mitzvot* were being ridiculed, Tora scholars and Yeshiva students were laughed at, people ate unkosher food. In November 1944, the HK editor brought forward the traditional argument against wresting control of establishing the state away from God. God cast Israel into exile, commanded her to be true to the governments under which she found herself (see *Ketubot* 111a), and promised to end the exile with His hand at the right time. Israel has suffered, served the governments and waited. At this point, this whole program should not be changed such as to make divine redemption into something political-worldly. The redemption of faith may not be separated out, the *"Al ha'purken"* (on account of the redemption) may not be detached from the *Al ha'nissim* (on account of the miracles) ("We thank Thee for the miracles, for the redemption, for the mighty deeds and triumphs, and for the battles which Thou didst perform for our fathers in those days, at this season." [*Mussaf* for *Hanuka.*]) In any case, the editor was sure, a separation would fail: "because even if the nations should give us all the Land of Israel and allow us to establish there a real independent government, the Jews themselves would remain true to the oath not to precipitate the end, and most would not want to leave exile."[20]

In 1941 and 1942 Orthodoxy was criticized as well. In JIS' first *Kol Kore* (May 26, 1941), he stated that the *Agudat Harabbanim's* call for a day of prayer and fasting on May 12, 1941 was insufficient, if not without value, under contemporary conditions. Those being called upon were deaf--precisely because until now the "spiritual leaders" of Orthodoxy failed to enunciate the call prescribed by the Sages for times of despair: "When catastrophe comes to the world, expect the onset of the messiah,"[21] or to tell the masses that Judaism included belief in the messiah and *Hevlei Moshiah* and that the current troubles were possibly those very sufferings.[22] The HK editor stated on May 26, 1941, that *Aguda's* call after its April 29-30, 1941, bi-annual convention, concluding that all hope for worldly salvation had been extinguished, was as old as exile and not sufficiently relevant to the contemporary crises. A categorical declaration was needed:

> Imagine what would happen if the same hundred rabbis of the convention would come forth with a *Kol mivasser* (harbinger of things to come) [proclaiming] that the total redemption was near, that the Jewish troubles were *Hevlei Moshiah*. What a great awakening this would call forth among all classes of Jews! If this would be stated in all homes, stores and offices! And published by the entire press so that kith and kin knew of it! The synagogues would be packed by thousands of Jews. Even the non-religious would fast and recite Psalms.

Such a call would be correct, the *Teshuva* and prayer it evoked would be correct, and so would the help of Heaven. The convention did not issue such a call, because its members did not realize that we were at the eve of the redemption. If they did, it would have been impossible not to state so and offer consolation. Left to themselves, it was no wonder that the Jewish masses still thought that God remained high in heaven, redemption was distant, salvation was possible from other sources and that the Tora should be sent back to Sinai.[23]   In October 1941, MI criticized even the ultra-Orthodox (*Yereim ve'haredim*) for not appreciating the apocalyptic drama underway. That left them in the same camp with heretics, outside of Goshen:

> You really want to stand together with those who are totally heretical about the messiah . . . [so that] if the messiah indeed did not come you would *win* with them? If the messiah did, you would *lose* with them? This is quite bizarre--that one way or the other the *Yereim ve'haredim* should stand on the same platform with heretics . . . instead of with [JIS] who opposed them, *against* them if they won, *against* them if they lost.[24]

On June 23, 1942, JIS expressed his concern in writing to the *Agudat Harabbanim* annual convention then taking place in Atlantic City. The *Aguda* understood that the time had come of which God said: "I shall set before you a king whose decrees are as severe as Haman's so that Israel will do *Teshuva*" (*Sanhedrin* 97b). But would its leaders "Pick from each of your tribes men who are wise, discerning, and experienced, and I will appoint them as your heads," (Deuteronomy 1/13), who bear the responsibility, evoke the *Teshuva?* The crisis was one of God's strong hand and of "Turn back, turn back from your evil ways, that you may not die" (*Ezekiel* 33/11). Either the rabbis should give an ultimatum to do *Teshuva* and return to Tora, or they should renounce their spiritual leadership lest they bear the terrible guilt for silently witnessing heresy. They must declare "Darkness shall cover the earth and thick clouds the people; but upon you the Lord will shine" (Isaiah 60/2); that no matter how difficult, Jews must not despair but hope in the Creator. The cry of "Turn back," JIS wrote, must enflame the point of Judaism within each heart. "Everyone must be consoled with the sense of *Teshuva,* which can diminish the *Hevlei Moshiah* and bring the complete redemption closer."[25]

The letter had no apparent effect. After the convention, the HK editor expressed regret that the leaders had not yet declared the *Hevlei Moshiah* which preceded redemption, necessitating *Teshuva* for as long as it was possible.   By their silence, they had implicitly rejected MI's call for "Immediate *Gelva*--Immediate *Teshuva*." They were, thereby, indirectly responsible for the *Hillul Hashem* (desecration of God's name) among the masses. The editor concluded: "Even as late as 1942 the rabbis here still have not acknowledged [JIS'] two-year old call, 'Immediate redemption.' We will not forget this. Still we will not forget to pray for forgiveness [and that] at next year's convention the rabbis will have a different view."[26]

Finally in September 1942, "Ish Yehudi" wrote about the fact that the world-rabbinate--presumably World *Agudat Israel*--still did not believe in the present reality of *Hevlei Moshiah*:

> Does the world-rabbinate think that the Jews have still not fallen low enough in the religious sense? That the troubles the Jews are going through all over the world are insufficient to be the *Hevlei Moshiah*? Does the rabbinate anticipate that there will be Jews who are even worse in terms of their Judaism? Troubles which are greater than the ones we have now, before recognizing redemption?

The call for *Teshuva* without "Immediate redemption" was not enough. For the *Agudat Harabbanim's* call for a return to *Mitzvot* to succeed, it needed to state that the time for choosing *Teshuva* had passed and that the *Hevlei Moshiah* were now forcing Jews to *Teshuva*. The principle was not, as the *Aguda* presented it, merely an appeal:

> But if from thence thou shalt seek the Lord thy God thou shalt find Him, if thou seek Him with all thy heart and with all thy soul. When thou art in tribulation and all these things are come upon thee, even in the latter days, if thou turn to the Lord thy God, and shalt be obedient unto his voice (*Deuteronomy* 4/29, 30).

It was a matter of "Better return to God out of goodness (i.e. good will), because if not, you will have to do so out of badness (i.e. catastrophe)."[27]

Mainline Orthodoxy: Perception and Reality

The perception that the Orthodox leaders did not acknowledge the *Hevlei Moshiah*, the apocalyptic crisis, the either/or situation, was, in fact, largely without basis. Elhanan Wasserman of Baranowitch had published his classic *Ikvassa Demeshiha* in New York in 1939 and it was cited by the Orthodox leadership. In April 1941, for example, it was excerpted in *Idishe Shtime, Argan fun Agudat Israel in Amerika* in New York.[28] Upon Wasserman's request in 1941, Shimon Schwab of Baltimore published a complementary volume of verifying texts from *Tenakh, Hazal, Zohar*, the Vilna Gaon, and Wasserman's treatise (including the *Hofetz Haim* citations), saying that he prepared *The Fountainhead* so that:

The thirsty ones could drink of the water of the life of faith and trust, and draw from it the pure spirit which awakens *Teshuva,* to prepare themselves to receive the countenance of the *Shekhina* ("Prepare to meet your God, O Israel." Amos 4/12).[29]

In October 1940, Israel Halevi Rosenberg, Eliezer Silver and Dov Arye Levinthal, representing the *Agudat Harabbanim* presidium, stated that the same divine hand which had brought war against millions would fulfill the promises of prophets and Sages about redemption, that "Prayer and *Teshuva* remove the evil decree."[30] (the *Nissane tokef,* in the Rosh Hashana liturgy).   Nissan Telushkin, editor of *Hamessila* following which was published by the Va'ad Harabbanim of Greater New York said in the spring of 1941 that the slavery and redemption of Egypt were reflected in the bitter life of contemporary Israel.   Pharaoh was again out to persecute Israel, while sea and desert again separated Israel from the Land.   But the people did not protest, for "they knew that their redemption was before them, and that the sufferings were but the *Hevlei Geula* which cleansed and purified the defilement (*Tuma*) of the destroyed land which had stuck to them."[31]

Jacob Rosenheim (1870-1965) was President of the *Agudat Israel* World Organization.   On February 12, 1941, while still in London, he had spoken of the terrible suffering in Europe as one which only the prophetic voice of a Jeremiah could adequately describe.   But the very triumph of radical evil guaranteed the rule of Providence in history.   For it was the ultimate universal crisis between Amalek and Israel, between evil/*Sitra ahra* ("other side") and the Jewish people as God's herald in history.   The simultaneous concentration towards the Land (*Kibbutz Galuyyot*) and dispersal of Israel confirmed that the mysterious gathering of holy sparks towards the center was underway, and this implied redemption.[32]

Rosenheim came to America on July 4, 1941.   In February 1942, at the Jewish Center of New York, he said the war was the external expression of metaphysical powers, Amalek's war against God ("The Lord will be at war with Amalek through the ages." Exodus 17/16).   Hitler was evil, and by reason of their natural law of existence, the powers of evil had to hate the world-center of holiness.   Hitler's attack on Israel proved that Israel was disseminated by God and suffering for the historical aim of uniting mankind under divine sovereignty--which was the sole remedy for the disasters of history.[33]   In May 1942, in Washington Heights, after cautioning against mathematical calculations about the coming of the messiah, R. Samuel b. Nahmani said in the name of R. Jonathan:

Blasted be the bones of those who calculate the end. For they would say, since the predetermined time has arrived, and yet he has not come, he will never come. *(Sanhedrin* 97b).

Rosenheim stated that Israel, as God's witness--"My witnesses are you, declares the Lord." (Isaiah 43/10)--which suffered for mankind, was now involved in the last phases of God's battle with Amalek.[34] In August 1942 Rosenheim spoke of the *Khurbn* as the Yom Kippur of the world. On Yom Kippur satan concentrated all his efforts to have Israel sin on a single representative, the High Priest, but the High Priest miraculously averted calamity *(Midrash Leviticus Rabba* 21/4). Now Hitler, epitome of historical evil, the *Sitra ahra*, was concentrating on Israel--but holy Israel would avoid the calamity. In the *"Gog-Magog"* cataclysmic war between Germany (see "Gomer" as "Germania" in *Yoma* 10a) and Israel, Germany would be destroyed by "hailstones" when American bombs destroyed Hitler's armies on the earth of the Land of Israel (see Ezekiel 38 and 39), and the light of eternal peace would ensue. Rosenheim pointed to the contemporary signs of *Asshalta degeula* and *Ikvassa demeshiha*:

1. All the world was at war.
2. Divine sovereignty was replacing sovereign nationalism, which was being recognized as the cause of *Khurbn.*
3. Dispersion of Israel over the world which Israel would unite in God's honor (Genesis 28/14, Psalm 113/3).

Rosenheim even stipulated the end of history in another 297 years, the world having entered the desolations of the last of its six millennia *(Rosh Hashana* 31a).[35]

Eliezer Silver, president of *Agudat Israel* in the United States and Canada, stated in April 1941 that the secret to resistance against Nazism was faith in imminent redemption, drawn from faith in the divine promise of ultimate redemption. The time was that of *Ikvassa demeshiha*, and it was necessary to be clear and decisive about being either for God or for Baal. There was no room for compromise. The difficult choice for Tora-Judaism would, he assured, lead to victory because that was the path of Jewish eternity.[36] In August 1942, Silver reiterated a 1939 statement blaming Israel for the fact that Tora was replaced by world-chaos. When he heard cries to Heaven over the destruction of great European *Kehillot* ("My tents are ravaged." Jeremiah 10/20), he turned to the Jews who severed their bonds with the Patriarchs, God and Torah ("All my tent cords are broken." Jeremiah 10/20). Silver called for self-examination: ("If a man sees that painful sufferings are visiting him, let him examine his conduct, for it is said 'Let us search and try our ways and return unto the Lord'." *Lamentations* 3/40, *Berakhot* 5a) and *Teshuva*. When the world turned volcanic and Jews pleaded "Until when, God? How much longer will You let Your people Israel be victim to catastrophe and humiliation? How much longer will You tolerate the vultures and the wild animals, the vile ruler's lies and deceptions?" they had to look into themselves and respond to God's call for *Teshuva*.[37] He assured the *Agudat Israel* at its Special Conference on Strengthening the Jewish Religion, August 20, 1942, that it was not too late: "If the limbs of animal offerings burst off from the altar before midnight, they can be put back" (*Yoma* 20a).[38]

To what could MI's misperception be attributed?

1. While *Agudat Israel* and *Agudat Rabbanim* were concerned with contemporary political and social dimensions to developing the Land of Israel,-[39] MI categorically rejected getting involved with the political issues of peace congresses and democratic governments.

2. Although HABAD was engaged in rescue--*Tomkhei Temimim Yeshiva* personal, *Pidyon Shivuim* Emergency Fund, food shipments to the starving in Europe[40]--MI apparently was not. The Orthodox leaders were--e.g. Va'ad Hatzala. Thus, Silver told the *Agudat Israel* August 24, 1941 convention in Baltimore that the task was not only to search the soul (*Heshbon ha'nefesh*) but to work out a plan for rescue, that *Teshuva* and actions came together.[41] For MI, *Teshuva* was the exclusive center, and man's role in history was passive under God. For the Orthodox, *Teshuva* shared the center with Tora and there was greater room for human activity.[42]

3. While the Orthodox leaders remained vague about the timing of the messianic coming, MI was specific. For example, the liturgical year which began September 11, 1942 was identified as the last year of exile,[43] and MI even prepared a special *Sefer Tora* to welcome the messiah.[44]

Still, however, leading Orthodox spokesmen did address the crucial elements--*Hevlei Moshiah, Teshuva,* either/or choice--contrary to MI criticisms. One can only surmise that JIS and MI needed to annul the validity of Orthodoxy because it lay outside Goshen.

Concluding Observations

From the perspective of the history of religious thought, it is of interest to note MI's aura of "Gnosticism." Hans Jonas described Gnosticism as a dualistic, transcendent religion of salvation in which knowledge was the means for attaining salvation. Its object was to transform the knower so as to make him partake in divine existence. The knowledge was about God, the history of the upper world and the salvation of man which issued from it. Truth was received through sacred and secret lore. The dualism of the Gnostic world was between the world and God, and between those men who had the knowledge and the rest of the world. The unknowing world embodied the negative of knowledge.[45]

MI did bear these traits in its own way, but also went beyond them. Goshen inhabitants were intent upon transforming the universe, ending the *Khurbn* and bringing redemption. This was an act of incredible religious courage--possibly unique during the *Khurbn* era.

Endnotes

* MI = Mahane Israel. JIS = Joseph Isaac Schneersohn or Admor Shlita MMS = Menahem Mendel Schneersohn. HK = *Hakeriyya Vehakedusha*. I am grateful to the staff of the Library of Congress Hebraica section, R. Moshe Kolodney of the Agudat Israel Archives in New York and R. Nehemia Kessler at the R. Levi Yitzhak Library in Brooklyn for help in obtaining the materials for the study.

1. Shlomo Duber Levin, *History of HABAD in the United States* (Brooklyn, 1988), 304-312 (Hebrew title, Yiddish text); JIS, "Letter 3/375 (27 January, 1949)," *Iggerot Kodesh X 5709-5710* (Brooklyn, 1984), 70-71 (Hebrew); JIS, "Letter 3/384 (8 February, 1949)," *Iggerot Kodesh X 5709-5710* (Brooklyn, 1984), 80 (Hebrew). JIS, "Letter 3/447 (31 March, 1949)," *Iggerot Kodesh X 5709-5710* (Brooklyn 1984), 138 (Hebrew); MMS, "Letter 2/467 (10 August, 1944)," *Iggerot Kodesh VII 5704-5705* (Brooklyn, 1984), 375-379 (Hebrew); Ed., "Hagrala fun Mishnayot be'al pe," *HK* 2/23 (14 July, 1942): 2; JIS, "Yom Alef, 17 Sivvan [5703]," *Sefer Ha'sihot 5703-5704-5705* (Brooklyn, 1986), 132-135 (Hebrew title, Yiddish text).

2. MI, "Le'alter le'geula," *HK* 1/11 (24 July, 1941): 7, 9, 10.

3. *Midrash Exodus Rabba* 5/13. Serah bat Asher also helped Moses locate Joseph's coffin, which was indispensable to redemption (Genesis 50/25); Cf. Deuteronomy Rabba 11/7 and *Yalkut Shimoni* 1/965; ed., "Tevet, the month of public introspection," *HK* 4/41 (27 December, 1943): 1; ed., "Tevet, der monat fun heshbon ha'nefesh ba'tsibbur," *HK* 3/28 (8 December, 1942): 1-2.

4. Levin, *supra.*

5. The phrase came from "Ha'aderet veha'emuna" of the Yom Kippur liturgy, drawn from *Hekhalot Rabbati* (Pietrkov 1884 ed.), ch. 26, paragraph 7.

6. Ed., "Nit veyt fun sof," *HK* 4/48 (20 July, 1944): 1-2. The original acronym appeared in *HK* 2/13 (21 September, 1941): 4.

7. Ish Yehudi, "*PT7'PT10* Let there be light, *PT7'PT10*" *HK* 1/1 (2 October, 1940): 8-10, (Hebrew title, Yiddish text).

8. Ed., "Fun der redaktsie, fun 5701 biz 5703," *HK* 3/34 (3 June, 1943): 10-11.

9. Ed., "*Kol Kore* to our brethren the children of Israel," *HK* 2/14 (21 October 1941): 11 (Hebrew title, Yiddish text).

10. The first *Kol Kore* also appeared as: JIS, "*Kol Kore* fun Lubavitsher Rabbin--Le'alter le'geula," *Der Teglikher Yiddisher Kurier* (30 May, 1941), 11; JIS, "*Kol Kore* fun Lubavitsher Rabbin--Le'alter le'geula," *Der Morgen Zhurnal* 40 nr. 12,034 (27 May, 1941): 8.

11. JIS, "Last discussion of Passover (9 April, 1942)," *Sefer Hama'amarim PT5\ PT10 Kuntresim 3* (Brooklyn, 1986): 80-84 (Hebrew title, Yiddish text); JIS, *Tractate on the Teaching of Hassidism* (Brooklyn, 1945), 23-24 (Hebrew).

12. MI, "*Kol Kore* fun der *PT7'PT10* MI *PT7'PT10* tsu di Idishe froyen," *HK* 1/11 (24 July, 1941): 12-13; cf. MI Women's Division, "Sehr geehrte froy," cited in Levin, *supra;* also JIS, *Reyd tsu froyen, fun Rabbin Shlita* (Brooklyn, 1943?) listed in ed., "Seforim un broshuren tsu bakumen dem farlag *PT7'PT10* kehot*PT7'PT10,*" *HK* 3/34 (3 June, 1943): 13.

13. Ed., "Fun der redaktsie. Der ferten *Kol Kore* fun Admor Shlita," *HK* 3/26 (11 October, 1942): 8-10.

14. JIS, "*Kol Kore* fun'm Lubavitsher Rabbin," *HK* 1/9 (26 May, 1941): 15; an English version appeared as JIS, "To the nearing redemption," *HK* 1/11 (24 July, 1941): 2-3; a slightly altered Hebrew version appeared as JIS, "Le'alter le'geula," *Netzah Israel* 3 (Munich, August 1948): 6-7; JIS, "Tsveyter *Kol Kore* fun'm Lubavitsher Rabbin," *HK* 1/10 (25 June, 1941): 9; also JIS, "Tsu di gleykhgiltige. Letter 1/455 (11 June, 1941)," *Iggerot Kodesh V 5700-5701* (Brooklyn, 1983), 377-386; JIS, "Driter *Kol Kore* fun'm Lubavitsher Rabbin," *HK* 1/11 (24 July, 1941): 5-7; JIS, "Call for prayer and penitence by the Rabbi of Lubavitch," *HK* 1/13 (21 September, 1941): 1; JIS, "*Kol Kore* from the Admor of Lubavitch," *HK* 1/13 (21 September, 1941): 4 (Hebrew); JIS, "Ferter *Kol Kore* fun dem Lubavitsher Rabbin Shlita. Sisu ve'simhu be'simhat Geula! Der driter front," *HK* 3/25 (11 September, 1942): 12-14; ed., "Fun der redaktsie. Der ferten *Kol Kore* fun Admor Shlita," *HK* 3/26 (11 October, 1942): 8-10.

15. When Moses selected elders to advise him, God was so pleased that He descended from heaven and permitted the spirits of prophecy to come over them (Numbers 11/24-25). Louis Ginzberg, *Legends of the Jews* 3 (Philadelphia 1911): 248-251. It was unclear why Psalms 119-150 were selected.

16. See Gershon Greenberg, "An active messianic response during the Holocaust, Mahane Israel-Lubavitch," *Proceedings of the 19th Scholars Conference on the Holocaust,* ed. Alan Berger (New York, 1991). On recitation in 16th century *Kabbala* see Lawrence Fine, "Recitation of *Mishna* as a vehicle for mystical inspiration. A contemplative technique taught by Haim Vital," *Revue des Études Juives* 146 nrs. 1-2 (January-June 1982): 183-199.

17. JIS, "*Kol Kore* fun'm Lubavitsher Rabbin," *HK* 1/9 (26 May, 1941): 15.

18. For example, see Eliahu Simpson (of HABAD), "Der Pidyon Shevu'im Emoyrdzhshensi Fond fun Lubavitsher Rabbin," *Idishe Shtime* 2 nr. 2 (March, 1941): 13; ed., "The Gaon the Tsaddik the Admor of Lubavitch Shlita (has come to settle in America)," *Hapardes* 13 nr. 12 (March, 1940): 4, 5 (Hebrew); ed., "Gathering of Agudat Hasidei HABAD. 16 April 1941. 770 Eastern Parkway, Brooklyn, N.Y.," *Hapardes* 15 nr. 3 (June, 1941): 26-27 (Hebrew); ed., "Pidyon Shivuim (of the Admor of Lubavitch for the rescue of Tomkhei Temimim Yeshiva Personnel), *Hapardes* 15 nr. 4 (July, 1941): 13 (Hebrew). ed.], "The Yeshiva and Mesivta *PT7'PT10* Tomkhei Temimim Lubavitch *PT7'PT10* in Brooklyn," *Hapardes* 15 nr. 6 (September, 1941): 19-20 (Hebrew); ed., "Gathering of HABAD on 10 August 1941 at the central house at 770 Eastern Parkway, Brooklyn, N.Y.," *Hapardes* 15 nr. 7 (October, 1941): 2 (Hebrew); JIS, "Our beloved and dear brethren in America [concerning the new building for the Lubavitch Yeshiva in New York]" and "Proclamation of Agudat Harabbanim [in support of the building campaign]," *Hapardes* 15 nr. 9 (December, 1941): 8-11 (Hebrew); ed., "On the arrival of the Rabbi of Lubavitch Shlita in Chicago," *Hapardes* 15 nr. 10 (January, 1942): 9-11 (Hebrew); ed., "Celebration of Lubavitch Yeshiva (14 June 1942)," *Hapardes* 16 nr. 4 (July, 1942): 22-26 (Hebrew).

19. Ed., "Fun der redaktsie. Ahdut bey di hige Iden," *HK* 3/35 (3 July, 1943): 4-5.

20. Ed., "Fun der redaktsie. Z'man Herutenu 5704," *HK* 4/44 (24 March, 1944): 4-5; JIS, "Our rabbis teach us. A statement of the sanctified, honorable Admor Shlita of Lubavitch," *HK* 4/39 (29 October, 1943): 2-3 (Hebrew title, Yiddish text); JIS, "Oystsug fun ma'amar ha'segira mi'lubavitch ([at the annual celebration of the center of Tomkhei Temimim Yeshivas 9 March 1944)," *HK* 4/46 (7 May, 1944): 3, 7; ed., "Fun der redaktsie. Ve'al ha'nissim ve'al ha'purkan," *HK* 5/52 (15 November, 1944): 4-5.

21. "Poranut ba'a le'olam, tsipa le'raglin shel moshiah." I have been unable to find the source.

22. JIS, "*Kol Kore* fun'm Lubavitsher Rabbin," *HK* 1/9 (26 May 1941): 15. The fast was called for 12 May 1941. At a large gathering that day at the Hatam Sofer Synagogue in New York, Eliezer Silver gave a sermon for the purpose of "awakening

Teshuva, rescuing souls, and redeeming those who were imprisoned (*hatzalat nefashot u'pidyon shivu'im*)." See ed., "Great fast," *Hapardes* 15/3 (June 1941): 2 (Hebrew).

23. Ed., "Der emes vegen dem itztigen Idishen *Khurbn,*" *HK* 2/14 (21 October, 1941): 11 (Hebrew title, Yiddish text).

24. MI, "*Kol Kore* to our brethren the children of Israel," *HK* 2/14 (21 October 1941): 11 (Hebrew title, Yiddish text).

25. JIS, "Brief vos Admor Shlita mi'lubavitsh hat tsugeshikt tsu tsvey hey-yahrige Idishe konvenshons," *HK* 2/23 (14 July 1942): 6.

26. Ed., "Di konvenshon fun der Agudat Harabbanim," *HK* 2/23 (14 July, 1942): 10.

27. Ish Yehudi, "Bakent zikh mit der varnung *PT7'PT10* Le'alter le'geula *PT7'PT10,*" *HK* 3/25 (11 September, 1942): 15-17; and MI, "Di *PT7'PT10* MI *PT7'PT10* apelirt, ruft, makht bekant un varent," *HK* 1/11 (24 July, 1941): 13-14.

28. Elhanan Wasserman, *Ma'amar Ikvassa Demeshiha Vema'amar al Ha'emuna. A belakhtung fun der yetztiger tekufa* (New York, 1939); Elhanan Wasserman, "Gedanken vegen Yahadut," *Idishe Shtime* 2 nr. 3 (April, 1941): 2-3; see Gershon Greenberg, "Orthodox theological responses to Kristallnacht: Haim Ozer Grodzensky (*PT7'PT10* Ahiezer *PT7'PT10*); and Elhanan Wasserman," *Holocaust and Genocide Studies* 3 nr. 4 (1988): 431-441 and 4 nr. 4 (1989): 519-521.

29. Shimon Schwab, *The Fountainhead. Collection of statements about Ikvassa demeshiha.* Including Pesukim, Midrashim and statements by Hazal, with Peirushim from Rishonim and Aharonim zts'l. Together with several notes and explanations regarding the matters of Ikvassa demeshiha. This is a book of awakening for those expecting salvation. It is not concerned with secrecy, rather precisely with matters which are simple and open to everyone. And it does not come, God forbid, to reveal what the Ancient of Days has hidden, nor to contemplate the end of days which is hidden from the eyes of all the living. (New York, 1941), 1 (Hebrew-Aramaic). On Schwab cf. Shimon Schwab, *Selected Writings* (Lakewood, New Jersey 1988). R. Wasserman's son Elozer Simha told me that soon after *Ikvassa Demeshiha* was published, an Orthodox synagogue in Baltimore held weekly readings of the text. Interview with R. Elozer Simha and Rebbetzin Wasserman in Jerusalem, 21 August 1989.

30. Eliezer Silver, Israel Halevi Rosenberg and Arye Hacohen Levinthal, "Proclamation of Agudat Harabbanim to the Jews of America," *Hapardes* 14 nr. 7 (October, 1940): 2 (Hebrew); cf. Israel Halevi Rosenberg, "Address of the Gaon Israel Halevi Rosenberg Shlita at the first session of the Agudat Israel Committee," *Hapardes* 13 nr. 5 (August, 1939): 10-12 (Hebrew); see Asher Zelka Rand, "The Rabbi, the Gaon R. Israel Rosenberg [at] seventy years old," *Edot Le'Israel* (New York, 1949), 5-14 (Hebrew).

31. Nissan Telushkin, ed., "Contemporary questions. *PT7'PT10* And all the firstborn of my children shall I redeem *PT7'PT10*," *Hamessila* 6/3 (March-April 1941): 1 (Hebrew) On Telushkin see Yehuda Rubensteyn, "The Rabbi Nissan Telushkin (1881-1970)," *Index to the Rabbinical Periodical PT7'PT10* Hamessila *PT7'PT10* (New York, 1977), 15-17 (Hebrew).

32. Jacob Rosenheim, "The Fateful Hour," *Ha'or. Organ of the Orthodox Jewish Youth* 2 (London, 12 February, 1941): 3-4; cf. Jacob Rosenheim, *Comfort, Comfort My People* (New York, 1984); Joseph Friedenson, ed., *Ya'akov Rosenheim Memorial Anthology. A Concise History of Agudat Israel* (New York, 1968).

33. Jacob Rosenheim, *Jewish Future. Address to a meeting [at] the Jewish Center of New York*, 1 February 1942 (Mss. held at *Agudat Israel* Archives, New York City).

34. Jacob Rosenheim, *Agudat Israel in Wartime.* (Address held at Audubon Hall, Washington Heights, 3 May 1942.) (Mss. held at *Agudat Israel* Archives, New York City); cf. Jacob Rosenheim, *The Right Answer to Hitler's Challenge* (n.d., n.p., mss. held at *Agudat Israel* Archives, New York City); and Jacob Rosenheim, *The War in the Light of Jewish Tradition* or *The Battle of God against Amalek* (n.d., n.p., mss. held at *Agudat Israel* Archives, New York City).

35. Jacob Rosenheim, "Concerning war in general and the present war in particular, from the perspective of Jewish life [Excerpted from address at *Agudat Israel's* Special Conference on Strengthening Judaism, Belmar, New Jersey, 20 August, 1942]," *Hapardes* 16 nr. 6 (September 1942): 17-19 (Hebrew).

36. Eliezer Silver, "Der Yom Tov fun Idisher eybikeyt," *Idishe Shtime* 2 nr. 3 (April 1941): 1. On Silver see Aaron Rakeffet-Rothkoff, *The Silver Era in American Jewish Orthodoxy* (New York, 1981).

37. Eliezer Silver, "Shuva Israel. Yamim-noraim ruf fun Harav Eliezer Silver tsum Amerikaner Identum [on 20 August 1942]," *Address Delivered by Rabbi Eliezer Silver, President of Agudat Israel of America at the Opening of the Special Conference of Agudat Israel for the Strengthening of the Jewish Religion, Belmar, New Jersey, 20 August 1942* (New York, 1942), inside covers. This statement was adapted from Eliezer Silver, "Awaken you slumberers from your slumber. Arise. Gird yourselves to grow stronger in Tora and religion, to do *Teshuva* and good deeds," *Hapardes* 13 nr. 6 (September, 1939): 2-3 (Hebrew).

38. Eliezer Silver, "Di derefenungs-rede fun nasi fun Agudat Israel in Amerika," *Address Delivered, supra,* 4-17.

39. See for example Jacob Rosenheim, "Agudist world-problems. Introductory address delivered to the convention of *PT7'PT10* Agudat Israel of America *PT7'PT10* in Baltimore on 23 August, 1941," *Agudist World Problems* (New York, 1941?), 3-16.

40. See Shlomo Duber Levin, *History of HABAD in Soviet Russia* (Brooklyn, 1989), (Hebrew title, Yiddish text); Eliahu Simpson, *supra;* ed., "Gathering of Agudat Hasidei HABAD. 16 April 1941," *supra.*

41. Eliezer Silver, "When thou criest, let thy companies deliver thee," *Idishe Shtime* 2/5 (August 1941): 1 (Yiddish).

42. For a mainline Orthodox interpretation of *pakod yifkod* see Joseph Eliahu Henkin, "The strength and existence of Israel among the nations," *Hamessila* 6 nr. 2 (March, 1940): 2-4 (Hebrew); on Henkin (1881-1973) see Yosef Fridenzon, "Tsu der petira fun ha'gaon R. Yosef Eli Henkin zts'l. A fartseytisher Id," *Dos Idishe Vort* 168 (September-October 1973): 3-4.

43. Ed., "*PT7'PT10* Ala Elokim ba'terua, Hashem be'kol Shofar! *PT7'PT10* (Psalm 47/6). Ven der Gott fun din u'mishpat iz oyfgegangen durkh a shalen tsu milhama, kumt der Gott fun rahamin tsu oysleyzen zeyn folk durkh lozen heren dem shofar shel moshiah," *HK* 3/25 (11 September, 1942): 1.

44. Ed., "A spetsieler *Sefer Tora* mit velkhen tsu mikabel panim zeyn moshiah tsidkeinu," *HK* 2/14 (20 October, 1941): 12; ed., "Committee for the *Sefer Tora* to welcome the countenance of the messiah. 770 Eastern Parkway. Members of the committee: R. Shmuel Halevi Levitan, R. Eliahu Simpson, R. David Shifrin," *HK* 2/25 (11 September, 1942): 5 (Hebrew title, Yiddish text).

45. Hans Jonas, *The Gnostic Religion* (Boston, 1963), 32, 320-341.

INTERSECTING SPHERES: FEMINISM AND ORTHODOX JUDAISM

Rela Geffen Monson

Until the recent past, certain areas of the synagogue and many roles within it were considered male "turf." The best description of this phenomenon is found in Sam Heilman's book, *Synagogue Life,* where he writes:

> Perhaps the most important role to consider in the setting is the sex role. As already stated, Kehillat Kodesh Jews, for all their modernity, segregate the sexes quite strictly among adults, especially within the sanctuary. . . . The scope and nature of this sex segregation, however, goes beyond moments of prayer . . . that is, whenever the members get together to affirm in some way their collective membership in the Jewish world, they segregate the sexes. This affirmation need not be the manifest purpose of the gathering. For example, although there are no formal restrictions on mixing during the *kiddush* after services, the men and women continue for the most part to remain segregated. . . . When a woman breaks this barrier, she does so with obvious display of purpose; the same thing is true for men. . . . Segregation of sexes also occurs during shul-government meetings. Not only do women then sit separately; they are also assigned tasks different from the men's. While men make policy decisions, women implement them.[1]

The gender segregation, described by Heilman in the context of an Orthodox synagogue, accurately reflects the general traditional patterning in synagogues. This patterning was a diffuse one. The exclusion of women from ritual roles carried over to the exclusion from leadership in the polity of the congregation. Conversely, any new partnership in ritual will impact other spheres of synagogue life.

Within the Conservative or Reform synagogue which grants women ritual equality, egalitarian treatment in the polity is never far behind, in fact, sometimes it precedes ritual inclusion. There are signs that within Orthodoxy, equality in the polity is sometimes substituted for ritual inclusion to demonstrate that the Orthodox establishment is not "sexist" but rather bound by immutable *Halakhic* restrictions which do not reflect ill on a woman's status. Thus Saul Berman, in an article in *Tradition,* stated that:

> . . . we may suggest that on one hand, the exemption from communal presence seems to be a central element of women's

status in Jewish law, necessary to ensure that no mandated or preferred act conflict with the selection of the protected role. But, on the other hand, many of the elements of the three areas of problems . . . are accidental side effects of the status conferral, which in themselves contribute nothing, and may ultimately interfere with, the attainment of the central social goal. If such be the case, it is the unavoidable responsibility of religious leaders to do all within their power to eliminate these detrimental side effects.[2]

Berman is suggesting that what is not immutably ordained must be responsibly changed by Orthodox leaders to insure the commitment of traditional Jewish women which is necessary to the future of Orthodox Judaism.

Within the centrist Orthodox community, then, one can expect that male "turf" will be more specific and less diffuse in character than it was in the past. Restrictions on women will be limited to those documented legally, while issues not demonstrably *Halakhic* (legal) in nature will be decided more in consonance with the spirit of the age. Moreover, women may seek, within the religious sphere, to develop new rituals or adopt old ones not clearly proscribed by the law. Thus, the newly developed birth rituals for girls have been accepted and even written by some Orthodox rabbis, though there have been dissenters on this issue.[3]

In various parts of the United States, grown Orthodox women meet in women's *minyanim* (prayer quorums) so that they may have the experience of leading a congregation in prayer, participating in the Torah reading service and teaching in the context of prayer. Sometimes, they don prayer shawls to complete the experience. This is not greeted with derision by all leaders, though it is by many. Berman represents the sympathetic neo-Orthodox rabbinate when he notes:

A small number of religious women have begun donning *tallit* and *tefillin* daily, and have, in so doing, discovered a vital source of religious expression and strength. . . . Constantly increasing numbers of women are attending synagogue services with some regularity, and that trend can be expected to intensify with the increasing liberation of women from the home and with the spread of *eruvin* in religious communities. Under the circumstances, relegating women to the back of the synagogue, both physically and spiritually, will only assure their gradual disappearance from religious life. Building committees must be sensitized to the necessity of designing structures which demonstrate that in the appearance before God, men and women are equal.[4]

Berman is reflecting a new sensitivity, which though by no means universal, bodes well for bringing women into the Orthodox synagogue as an institution albeit in a special place. Though as of yet, the data are suggestive rather than conclusive, the clear implication of the qualitative and quantitative evidence is that the women's movement has had a subtle but profound impact on American Jewish Orthodoxy. When Daniel Elazar and I did a study of synagogue life in the mid-1970s, and included a grid on synagogue participation for women in Reform, Conservative, and Orthodox synagogues, some of our hypotheses were given a jolt.[5]

Among the variables which we expected to predict the participation or non-participation of women in given synagogues was the age structure of the membership. It was predicted that the younger the age of the average member, the more likely a synagogue would be to move away from traditionalism. Among Orthodox synagogues, this hypothesis was not borne out. On some issues, Orthodox congregations with a young membership were more traditional than those with older or mixed ages predominating. For example, seven percent of Orthodox congregations with most members between the ages of twenty-five and thirty-nine permitted women to lead English readings in the service, while twelve percent with most members forty to fifty-nine year old members predominating did so. Perhaps young people choosing the Orthodox way of life today are more fervent and ideologically consistent than their parents. There is a substantial body of evidence to that effect in other contexts.[6]

In an article describing American Jewish denominationalism, Lazerwitz and Harrison suggest that the trend is toward more sharply defined groups with greater homogeneity within each. They state that:

> . . . the tendency of increasing numbers . . . to eschew affiliation with organized religion may sharpen denominational differences. . . . As the least committed drift away from religious affiliation, they will leave behind those for whom matters of belief and behavior have the most significance.[7]

In the fifties and sixties, marginally traditional Jews who felt comfortable in the service or in their congregation of family of orientation stayed affiliated with Orthodox synagogues. By the end of the seventies, personal observance patterns were expected of members and enforced by social contract, and the nominally Orthodox drifted away. Thus, at the same time that some Orthodox women were seeking to change the status quo in their institutions, many of those same institutions were becoming more homogeneous and less flexible.

Given this background, let us examine several spheres of influence in which the American feminist movement and certainly the Jewish feminist movement has made itself felt within Orthodoxy.

1. Rhetoric

In October of 1983, the principal of the Orthodox Beth Jacob School tried to market his school to the Philadelphia Jewish community this way:

> There are girls in this community who want to study Talmud and participate in Judaic studies and are discouraged by the fact that Orthodoxy doesn't ordain women . . . Beth Jacob has a tough program with students spending 10 forty-five minute periods in class. . . . At the end of four years, each girl will be proficient in all aspects of Judaic studies. She will be able to open a Bible and discuss both medieval and contemporary commentary of the text with any scholar. She will know how to prepare a sermon as well as any rabbi. We are building scholars, giving them the key to Jewish life. They will be able to function as literate knowledgeable Jews.[8]

This rationale would not have been written even a decade earlier. It reflects the response of the Orthodox movement through rhetoric and action to feminism. Both the curriculum and the "pitch" for entry to the schools has changed. The headmaster of the school is arguing that women have distinct but equal roles within Orthodox Judaism, yet he states that they are now being encouraged to plunge into the world of Jewish scholarship in a new way.

2. Spirituality and Prayer

Other types of involvement of Orthodox Jewish women are focused in the area of prayer and spirituality and include such innovations as giving a Torah to women to dance with on *Simhat Torah;* passing the Torah or marching with the Torah around to the women's section in the processions on the Sabbath morning prior to and just after the reading of the Torah; and designing synagogues with greater thought given to the placement and design of the women's section.[9] Other innovations which have affected synagogue life include the development of women's prayer groups which meet regularly on *Shabbat* in synagogues and monthly women's prayer groups on the new moon which has traditionally been considered a women's holiday. These women's *tefilah,* or prayer groups, are on the cutting edge of the Jewish women's movement within Orthodoxy.[10]

In 1984, a Rabbinic responsum was issued by four rabbis from Yeshiva University which banned women's prayer groups. This ban, and the language of the rabbis by whom the ban was pronounced, has provoked great controversy within the centrist Orthodox community. The responsum was directed toward traditional women trying to express their spirituality within a *Halakhic* (Jewish legal) framework. The women maintained that these groups were not "prayer quorums" (*minyanim*), and that they did not include prayers which may only be said when such a quorum is present.[11] Nevertheless, the Yeshiva University rabbis took a strong stand against the existence of the prayer groups. As a result of the disappointment and anger of women who were involved in *tefilah* groups, the Women's Tefilah Network was organized in the summer of 1985 and women's prayer groups continue to grow in size and number.

Contributing to the consternation caused by the responsum was the fact that several Orthodox rabbis in New York were sponsoring women's prayer groups and personally guiding them so that their mode of prayer would be within the norms of *Halakha.* The controversy even spilled over to Israel where an acrimonious debate over the legitimacy of the responsum took place in the letters to the editor section of the *Jerusalem Post.*[12]

From the sociological point of view, the women's prayer groups are a functional alternative serving as a safety valve, or holding back a demand for greater equality within the context of the Orthodox *minyan,* while allowing the participants to expand their religious experience within a *Halakhic* framework. *Rosh Hodesh* (New Moon) groups which study and pray together once a month perform a similar function.

At this point, one cannot predict the ultimate effect of the prayer ban on Orthodox synagogue life. For some women it may be the final push toward leaving the Orthodox framework for prayer, while for others it may become the motivation to push for change within their congregations. By wearing prayer shawls in the women's section of the synagogue, individual Orthodox women have chosen to publicly display their commitment to positive time-bound commandments within the synagogue. While these individual actions do not change the structure of the synagogue or its service, they do, by their public nature, have an effect on the consciousness of all the men and women who are present. An analogous symbolic statement was made earlier by those women within Orthodox synagogues who stood and said the *Kaddish* prayer aloud when they were in mourning, even though they were not required to do so. Saying the *Kaddish* is both a verbal and physical symbol in synagogues where only the mourners stand. In like fashion, wearing a prayer shawl is a physical symbol which cannot be ignored by the rest of the congregation.

3. Life Cycle Rituals

In addition to rhetoric and spirituality expressed primarily through prayer, a major impact of the Jewish feminist movement has been felt in the area of life cycle rituals.[13] Baby-naming ceremonies called *Simhat Bat* have also been developed within centrist Orthodoxy.

When analyzing the impact of the women's movement on Orthodoxy in particular, it is necessary to look at different indicators than one would in the examination of Conservative or Reform synagogues and families. The life cycle rituals provide a useful way to look at changes which actually have occurred in all of the movements. The introduction of ceremonies welcoming baby girls into the world is one of the impacts of the Jewish women's movement which was felt in the Orthodox community. In addition, the Bat Mitzvah ceremony which previously had been identified with non-Orthodox movements became incorporated into the normative fabric of modern Orthodox life. The Bat Mitzvah was always celebrated in Israel, however in the United States it was avoided in order not to associate Orthodoxy with the innovations of Mordecai Kaplan. Today, women who themselves never celebrated their Jewish coming of age arrange elaborate teas and other ceremonies for their twelve year old daughters. These ceremonies go beyond the social, often including delivery of a learned speech by the young girl and sometimes recitation by her of *havdalah*. Sometimes the occasion of the Bat Mitzvah is publicly announced in the synagogue and in the girl's honor the father and brothers of the Bat Mitzvah are given Torah honors. Although the performance of the girl does not take place in the context of a synagogue service, the occasion is still one which is connected to synagogue ritual. In a few synagogues the *d'var Torah* (learned speech) may be given at the close of the service in the sanctuary and in others a women's *tefila* group provides the context for the Bat Mitzvah.

4. Study of Rabbinics

The fourth critical area of impact of the women's movement on centrist Orthodoxy is in the area of study. Within the traditional community this development may ultimately yield the greatest ramifications. While there still rages a debate about women studying Talmud, it is a fact that over the last decade institutions of higher learning for women who are newly observant or have always been so have been established in the United States and in Israel. Vanessa Ochs has written recently of some of the leaders of these Yeshivot for women in Israel.[14] At the high school level hundreds of Orthodox teenage girls have studied rabbinics in schools like Flatbush Yeshiva and Ramaz. The opening up of the study of classics on secular and Hebrew College campuses has also made an impact on the advanced knowledge base of women. And make no mistake about it, with or without ordination, knowledge of rabbinics is one key to power in the traditional community.

In sum, the thesis of this paper has been that centrist Orthodoxy has been significantly influenced by the Jewish and general feminist movements in at least four key areas: rhetoric; prayer and synagogue roles; life cycle rituals; and study (Talmud Torah). In subtle ways, even the more right wing of Orthodoxy has been touched by the societal changes in the status of women. This paper has focused on American Judaism, however, it is clear that these changes have reached Israel and Europe as well.

Appendix

EXAMPLE OF RHETORIC AND STUDY

Women in/and Halakha

A Conference sponsored by the Jewish Studies faculty of Yeshiva University in cooperation with Stern College Alumnae Association and Torah Activities Committee (Stern College)

Sunday, December 16, 1984   22 Kislev 5745

at Koch Auditorium
Stern College for Women
245 Lexington Avenue (at 35th Street)
New York, N.Y. 10016

Morning Session:
9:30 a.m. — Coffee

10-12 Noon
Rabbi Saul Berman, Stern College
"Women and Talmud Torah"

Dr. Sara Reguer, Brooklyn College
"Women and the Development of Halakha"

Commentators:
Mrs. Miriam Cohen, Prospect Park High School
Rabbi Ephraim Kanarfogel, Stern College
Questions and Discussion (Audience)

Afternoon Session:
1:30-4:00 p.m.
Dr. G.E. Ellinson, Bar-Ilan University
"The Question of Obedience"

Dr. Moshe Meiselman, Torat Moshe, Jerusalem
Yeshiva University of Los Angeles
"Women and the Synagogue"

Commentators:
Dr. Rivka Ausubel Danzig,
Director of Group Homes FACA, Philadelphia
Rabbi Mordechai Willig,
Mazer Yeshiva Program, Stern College
Questions and Discussion (Audience)

For Further Information, call: (212) 960-5347

INCLUSION OF WOMEN
AMONG RIGHT-WING ORTHODOX FOR STUDY

ב"ה

פישו ושמחו בשמחה גמר משנה תורה

JOIN IN THE
GRAND "SIYUM"*
OF MAIMONIDES
MISHNEH TORAH

Monday, March 10
7:30 pm
Lower Merion Synagogue
123 Old Lancaster Rd.
Bala Cynwyd

Distinguished Rabbis and Roshei
.Hayeshivos will Participate

ALL ARE WELCOME!
A special section has been reserved for women and children

·Join us for this special celebration of learning.
Program includes music and refreshments

*Ten of thousands of Jews all over the world will be completing
the text of Rambam's Mishneh Torah for the second time*

for more information call
the Philadelphia Lubavitcher Center 725-2030

ORTHODOX WOMEN & MODERNITY: PRAYER GROUPS

Rabbinic 'will'

Survey of women's preferences would clarify halachic 'way'

EMANUEL RACKMAN

An event worthy of celebration is the publication in England of a volume by the principal of Jew's College, Dr. Jonathan Sacks. It is called "Traditional Alternatives: Orthodoxy and the Future of the Jewish People." Every Jew ought to read it--whether Orthodox, non-Orthodox, Zionist or secularist. I marvel at how, in a few hundred pages, the author is able to describe so well the Orthodox Jewish scene today.

I offer no review of the book: I have always declined to write reviews of book in which I am mentioned. However, a number of points in it evoked reactions in me that I felt impelled to share with others.

For example Rabbi Sacks cites Blu Greenberg's famous remark that "where there is a rabbinic will there is a halachic way," but adds that "Does not entail that where there is a halachic way, there is a rabbinic will."

It is precisely this "rabbinic will" that merits more attention than he has given it. Who are the rabbis whose will we are to consider? And is it not possible that the will of even the best of them derives from sources no altogether impeccable-- mistakes of fact, mistakes in judgment and even personal feelings not necessarily saintly?

Sacks refers to the "modern Orthodox" thinkers of the 1960s, most notable Eliezer Berkovits and myself as "controversial." And nothing has made us more controversial than our insistence that all rabbis ought to "will" the several problems of Jewish law that are not only agonizing innocent, devout Jewish women but also alienating thousands more from any respect for Jewish law because of the inertia of those who know the "way" but will not take it.

Sacks is by no means unaware of the problem. But he tries to be fair to the other side. The way available to solve the problem, he writes, "would weaken the struc-

ture and sanctity of Jewish marriage as a whole." Is this assumption valid? I know it has been said so often that no one any longer questions its truth. My experience and that of many other rabbis who have served in pulpits is that the failure to use the "halachic way" to correct evils is doing tremendous damage to Jewish family life, and instead of inducing an appreciation of the sanctity of Jewish marriage it is evoking feelings of revulsion.

Perhaps I err. But instead of relying upon unproved assumptions, why not risk a survey? This would be a fairer way to arrive at the "rabbinic will" instead of relying upon an intransigent few who in most countries resort even to intimidation to frighten bolder younger rabbis into submission to a sickening inertia.

A few years ago, at a rabbinical convention, I proposed a way to solve many problems in Jewish family law. I felt that this could be accomplished by changing basic presumption of the halacha that may no longer be valid. It was the presumption that women prefer any kind of marriage to no marriage at all. On this presumption are based a number of significant halachic conclusions that it would be to the advantage of women to change.

Under pressure from those who still cling to the myth that the halacha never changes, Rabbi Soloveitchik--who learned of what I had said only by hearsay--expressed his disagreement publically and forcefully. When I later met with him to argue about his disagreement, he said: "Rackman, you may be right and I may be wrong. You view the halacha historically and I like to view it mets-historically." Thus, for him, the presumption as stated by our sages was the statement of an ideal-- no a presumption of fact. Yet he could not explain why that particular presumption about a woman's preference differed from other presumptions that change in history. And I was quite certain that in the modern age, many women would prefer no marriage to a bad marriage. Certainly, the question deserved a new look. And, as with many other presumptions, a change might be in order. Many famous halachic authorities agreed with me. And

even Rabbi Soloveitchik appeared to have second thoughts about the meta-historical character of the presumption.

Certainly, a survey as to how most Jewish women feel today is not difficult to make. It would be more difficult perhaps to take a survey as to whether the present state of Jewish law is contributing to the "structure and sanctity of Jewish marriage as a whole." But certainly the survey would open the eyes of many rabbis who prefer to mouth assumptions without seeking any verification whatsoever.

I do not happily accept the characterizations of Rabbi Berkovits and myself as "controversial." I would prefer being called a gadfly. I do not try to create quarrels. But I do not like to sweep facts under the carpet. I want to expose them, especially when continued human suffering is the price paid for silence.

THE JEWISH WEEK, INC.
JANUARY 12, 1990

WOMEN'S PRAYER GROUPS

To the Editor of
The Jerusalem Post--

Sir, -- I read with interest your article of September 11, "Orthodox women fume at rabbis." One may no longer remain silent. I have read carefully the responsum of the five talmudist at Yeshiva University, forbidding prayer services by women. I wish to state unequivocally that their so-called "T'shuva" has nothing to do with Halacha.

People will have to realize that knowledge and understanding are not identical. One may know a lot and understand very little.

There may be a great deal of Orthodoxy around. Unfortunately, there is only very little halachic Judaism.

May God grant to the women of Women's Tefilla Network strength and courage to continue their efforts to the best of their abilities.

Rabbi Eliezer Berkovits, Jerusalem

ORTHODOX BAT MITZVAH INVITATION: LIFE CYCLE

Please join us when our beloved daughter

Shira Israela

שירה ישראלה

will recite Havdalah and give a D'var Torah

on the occasion of her becoming a Bat Mitzvah

Motzaei Shabbat, the seventh of March

Nineteen hundred and eighty-seven

at seven forty-five in the evening

Beth David Synagogue

39 Riverside Drive, Binghamton, New York

Shira will share her Bat Mitzvah with her friend

Yuna Royak, of Bendery, Russia

daughter of Viacheslav and Rianna Royak

who is unable to live according to the

precepts of her Jewish heritage

A reception will follow the service

Steven and Rebecca Katz

ORTHODOX BAT MITZVAH PROGRAM

BAT MITZVAH
OF
TAMAR DINA RASKAS

We are pleased that you are joining us for Shabbat in honor of Tamar's Bat Mitzvah. Listed below is the schedule for this joyous occasion.

Friday, May 23

4:00 - 6:30	Check in at the Marriot Airport Hotel
6:45 - 7:00	Candle Lighting
7:00	Kabbalat Shabbat
7:30	Shabbat Seudah

Shabbat, May 24

8:00 - 9:30	Coffee, Juice & Danish
9:30	Davening
11:30	Kiddush
12:30	Shabbat Luncheon
5:00	Shabbat Discussion Group
6:30	Mincha
7:00	Shalosh Seudos
8:45	Mariv followed by Havdalah
10:00	Melave Malka

LIFE-CYCLE RITUALS: INTERNATIONAL IMPACT, ENGLAND

ואבגיל היתה טובת־שכל ויפת תאר

Celia and Elkan Levy

have much pleasure in inviting you

to the Bat Chayil ceremony of their daughter

Abigail Deborah

at the Stanmore Synagogue,

London Road, Stanmore, Middlesex

on Sunday, 23rd October, 1983 at 3 p.m.

יום א׳ פר׳ חיי שרה

and at Home

22 Glanleam Road,   Supper 7.30 p.m.

Stanmore, Middlesex   R.S V.P.

FEMINISM: IMPACT ON THE ORTHODOX SYNAGOGUE IN NON-RITUAL ROLES

Orthodox women gaining in synagogue posts

GITELLE RAPOPORT

Amid continuing controversy about the public role of women in Orthodox Jewish life, a handful of female pioneers are achieving quiet success as administrators in Orthodox synagogues.

At Lincoln Square Synagogue, for example, the current program coordinator, acting executive director and outgoing director of outreach are all women. "I had the opportunity to exciting creative work there and to broaden my professional skills," says Suri Kasirer, the former outreach director who was the first woman on Lincoln Square's professional staff. "Rabbi [Saul] Berman and the congregants were very supportive. Countless people came up to me and said, 'So you're the woman listed on the synagogue stationery!'-- with pride that a woman had such a high position in an Orthodox synagogue."

Ronnie Beecher, the first woman executive vice president at the Hebrew Institute of Riverdale, "is a very powerful person in the shul," according to Rabbi Avi Weiss. "Two years ago she gave the public appeal on Yom Kippur, and it was the best we've ever done."

■

While women have long held administrative jobs in Orthodox schools, a woman in Shoshana Jedwab's position is less common. As education director of The Jewish Center on Manhattan's Upper West Side, she develops the synagogue's education programs as well as teaching classes. Like Kasirer, she derives satisfaction from being a role model for other women.

"A few women have told me they really appreciate having a woman Torah teacher," Jedwab says. "I wouldn't mind giving a sermon . . . at times, but I'm not pushing for it. I think [teaching] allows for a more . . . sophisticated rendering of material."

Two of Manhattan's Orthodox synagogues have female executive directors. Toby Einsidler, who worked her way up from part-time secretary to executive director at Park East Synagogue never doubted her chances of achieving such a position. "I was always told you can do whatever you want," she says, "if you set your mind to it."

. . . Although all these women stress the encouragement they have received from rabbis and congregants, ripples of opposition have surfaced from time to time. Ovadiah reports that at first "there were some people who didn't think a woman should be hired for this position, for historical reasons. We're the oldest Jewish community in America, and they [were] resistant to change. . . ." Misgivings about women in leading roles may be expressed as discomfort rather than antagonism. "Men in shul positions are accustomed to dealing with each other," says Becher. "Being in [this kind of position] is more than just coming to board meeting; there's a camaraderie, a feeling of brotherhood among the men in a synagogue . . . Perhaps unconsciously, they're not accustomed to including women in that. There must be a conscious effort [to do so]. . . . The men in my shul are better at this than most."

Kasirer says she felt "very appreciated" at Lincoln Square. But she admits that "there was a limit to how far I was going to go . . . If I had been a rabbi, I would have been viewed with a certain deference, because he has that title. They feel he has more knowledge and more expertise."

Although there are more women on Orthodox synagogue boards than ever before, higher-ranking women officers such as Beecher, who are elected by the membership and serve on a volunteer basis, are still relatively rare. According to Rabbi Ephraim Sturm, executive vice president of the National Council of Young Israel, may women hold office in the national organization, but in member shuls they usually are limited to the secretary positions "by practice, thought not by policy." Two women have been presidents of Young Israel synagogues in the past five years, said Sturm, by they did not sit in front of the con-

gregation or make announcements from the pulpit.

Rabbinic authorities differ on whether it is halachically permissible for a woman to be a synagogue president. Several years ago a halachic commission of the Rabbinical Council of America ruled against it. Young Israel synagogues "leave it up to the individual rabbi" to decide the question, said Sturm. A few New York Orthodox rabbis said that they would not object to a woman president in their synagogues, but that so far the issue hasn't come up.

∎

"We've gone out of our way to bring women on staff who are key players," says Weiss. Most rabbis, however, do not specifically recruit women for synagogue jobs. Still, they are optimistic about women's long-term opportunities, at least in non-rabbinic positions. According to Shearith Israel's Rabbi Marc Angel, "In an Orthodox synagogue, women would naturally not gravitate toward positions that involve [communal] ritual," but women will continue the work they always have done "in administration,

community service and social services."

Berman predicts that women eager to "utilize their knowledge . . . for the benefit of the Jewish community will play an increasingly important role in the governance of Jewish communal life."

"What I see as exciting is women teaching Torah in an Orthodox synagogue," says Rabbi Jacob J. Schacter at The Jewish Center. "Women have been under-utilized as a resource within Orthodoxy, especially in education."

If there is a trend toward more women in synagogue positions of authority, Park East Synagogue's Rabbi Marc Schneier views it as a reflection of "more women in the work force . . . After losing [so many Jews] to the Holocaust and assimilation," he emphasizes, "we have to maximize whatever leadership and whatever talent we can harness."

"LIVING JEWISH," *The Jewish Week, INC.* JANUARY 12, 1990

IMPACT ON THE SYNAGOGUE
Synagogue Combines Halachah, Women Rights

Boston (JTA) - Women reading the Torah, giving the Saturday sermon and participating in the Talmud class may not be news to most Reform and Conservative synagogues, but it is a novelty in the Orthodox community. Nevertheless, that is exactly what is taking place at the Orthodox synagogue Shaarei-Tefillah of Newton, Mass.

"In no other Orthodox synagogue I have ever been involved with could women participate to the same extent," says Rochelle Isserow, a member and frequent participant.

Synagogue President Alan Feld is quick to point out, however, that "women participate fully within the framework of Orthodox Halachah," meaning they do not lead services, nor read from the Torah during the regular service.

As in all Orthodox congregations, men and women sit separately during services, but during lectures and classes there is mixed seating.

Women's participation at Congregation Shaarei-Tefillah has included giving Shabbat morning and afternoon sermons, as well as on special occasions such as during the all-night study session that accompanies the holiday of Shavuot. These sermons are always on religious issues and always gender neutral, "with no distinction in the subject matter," Mr. Feld says.

On the holiday of Simchat Torah and at a bat mitzvah, there are women's services where women read from the Torah. While men are free to observe, and, as Ms. Isserow says, *shep nachs,* they do not participate.

Ms Isserow, the first woman to give a Saturday morning sermon, sees the participation of women in the synagogue as a real benefit to the whole community.

"Our participation," she said, "provides credibility to women as serious thinkers on Torah." Ms Isserow believes that women's participation makes them better role models, particularly to the young men of that community.

Mr. Feld explains that women's participation has been successful because of the high level of education in the congregation. "Men and women in the community are yeshiva graduates," says Mr. Feld, "so we are starting with a group of people who are knowledgeable in religious matters."

Many of the women are also professionals, which makes them more willing to take a leadership position in the congregation.

"There is a strong tradition of women learning in our community," Ms Isserow said.

Ms Isserow explained that the purpose of the congregation is not simple to increase the participation of women, but "to increase all participation."

Mr. Feld concurred, saying that "our main goal is preserving as forcefully as we can the idea of men and women performing mitzvot."

To do this, Shaarei-Tefillah has instituted democratic reforms to allow all members of the congregation to participate equally. This has included one vote per person rather than per family. What has resulted is an executive committee that is gender blind and currently includes a woman vice president.

Although the synagogue was formed only six years ago, it has grown considerably over that time and now includes 90 families. Halachic decisions for the congregation, including those concerning the role of women, are made by a council of members, all of whom are ordained rabbis.

SPIRITUALITY: WOMEN'S PRAYER GROUPS

Orthodox Jewish Women Push Role in Prayer

By CHARLES AUSTIN

Rivka Landau's clear voice filled the room with the flowing tones of traditional Hebrew prayer. As she chanted, "Baruch atah Adonai, Elohenu melech haolam" ("Blessed be Thou, our Lord, King of the Universe"), more than 100 women, some of them wearing prayer shawls, stood to join in the response. For the 30 minutes that she led the service, opening a daylong conference yesterday on "Women, Prayer and Tradition," the 12-year-old from Teaneck, N.J., was at the center of a growing development in Orthodox Judaism--prayer groups led by women.

Although the number of women taking part in prayer groups is small, the mere presence of the groups had prompted discussion and controversy among Orthodox Jews. Orthodox Judaism generally limits the religious responsibilities of women.

Most of the women attending the conference, at the headquarters of the American-Israel Friendship Association on East 39th Street in Manhattan, considered themselves Orthodox Jews and spoke of their high regard for Halacha, or Jewish law. But without violating the main precepts of the law, they are seeking, through the prayer groups, ways to expand their roles in the religious life of their communities.

'Not looking for Equality'

"It is not equality we are looking for, but ways for women to be more devout," said Claire Mendelson, who attends a women's prayer group in Manhattan.

In Orthodox Judaism, women are not obligated to say the same prayers in synagogues as their husbands and brothers. Although they attend synagogue, they are separated from men during worship and take no part in leading prayers or reading from the Torah, the sacred scrolls containing the Scriptures. The rules are more liberal for women in Conservative and Reform Judaism.

The prayer groups meet regularly, often in members' homes, and the women pray and read from the Torah as prescribed by Jewish ritual. Organizers of the conference said there were at least nine such groups in the New York area and more in other cities.

Dr. Judith Hauptman, assistant professor of Talmud at the Jewish Theological Seminary of America and keynote speaker at the conference, said new interpretations of Jewish law could support the groups. To avoid problems, however, women in some groups omit parts of the prayers that are specifically designated for men.

Question of a Minyan

Most of the women do not object to the physical barrier that separates them from men during worship. And they do not all agree on whether the prayer groups constitute the minyan, or quorum of 10 Jewish males, that the law requires for public worship. Some of the women argue that a minyan simply requires 10 Jewish adults. They do not advocate ordination for women.

Women who have joined the prayer groups say they do so out of a deep spiritual need to pray with other Jews and read the Torah.

"The first time we say the inside of a Torah," said Arlene Agus of Manhattan, describing her feeling reading the Scriptures during worship, "our eyes went blind with tears."

THE NEW YORK TIMES
MONDAY, JUNE 6,1983

Endnotes

1. Samuel Heilman, *Synagogue Life: A Study in Symbolic Interaction* (Chicago, 1976), 69-70.

2. Saul Berman, "The State of Women in Halachic Judaism," *Tradition* 14 (1973).

3. Meiselman, Moshe, *Jewish Women in Jewish Law* (New York, 1978).

4. Berman, "The State of Women," see n. 2 above, 123-4.

5. Elazar, Daniel J. and Rela Geffen Monson, "Women in the Synagogue Today," *Midstream* 27, no.4 (April, 1981).

6. Charles S. Liebman, *Aspects of the Religious Beliefs of American Jews* (New York, 1974).

7. Bernard Lazerwitz and Michael Harrison, "Denominationalism in American Jewish Life," *American Sociological Review* (1979), 665.

8. Jewish Exponent (Appendix, P. for flyer publicizing conference at YU demonstrating similar rhetoric).

9. Elazar and Monson, "Women in the Synagogue," see n. 5 above; and Berman, "The State of Women," see n. 2 above.

10. See Appendix, 192 above, for illustrative materials.

11. Larry Cohler, "Women's *Tefilah* Group Finds Torah Connection Exhilarating," *Jewish World* (January 25-31, 1985).

12. See Appendix, 195 above, for *Jerusalem Post* letter from Rabbi Eliezer Berkovits.

13. For examples of Orthodox Bat Mitzvah invitations, see Appendix, 196, 197, 198; for examples of Bat Torah invitations, see Appendix, 193.

14. Vanessa L. Ochs, *Words on Fire* (New York, 1990).

INTERPRETING ADULT BAT MITZVAH:
THE LIMITS AND POTENTIAL OF FEMINISM
IN A CONGREGATIONAL SETTING

Stuart Schoenfeld

Judith Plaskow, in her recent book, speaks for many Jewish women when she writes, "I am not a Jew in the synagogue and a feminist in the world. I am a Jewish feminist and a feminist Jew in every moment of my life."[1] This chapter will examine the extent to which the same heightened dual consciousness of being both a feminist and a Jew is found in a major contemporary innovation in Judaism--the participation of adult women in the ritual of bat mitzvah.

Adult bat mitzvah, like its male counterpart, adult bar mitzvah, became common in the mid-1970s. Both the journalism[2] and the scholarship[3] on adult bat mitzvah agree that women go through the process of preparing for the ceremony and enacting it as a significant and successful rite of passage which changes their relationship to Judaism and to the religious communities in which they participate. Adult bat mitzvah has become quite frequent, and women often prepare and go through the ritual in groups.

The innovation of adult bat mitzvah has happened at the same time as the development of Jewish feminist literature and as feminist-inspired changes have happened within Jewish practice, so it might be expected that adult bat mitzvah would be understood as a Jewish feminist ritual. In particular, it might be expected that women who choose to have bat mitzvahs as adults are identifying with the kind of self-conscious Jewish feminism that Plaskow and others articulate--that they are making public statements about the right of Jewish women to participate in Judaism in a way which fully recognizes them as Jews and as women. However, research on the experience of going through adult bat mitzvah in two different settings in the late 1980s indicates that its links to Jewish feminism are indirect and complex.

In 1986, Miriam,[4] a woman in her mid-twenties who worked for a Jewish organization, arranged her bat mitzvah at a small, liturgically traditional but unaffiliated congregation which had become gender egalitarian two years before. At this congregation, gender egalitarianism meant no distinction in ritual privileges. The traditional prayers were only partially changed.[5] Miriam was called on a Saturday morning, Miriam was called to the reading of the *maftir* and *haftorah,* and she delivered the *d'var Torah.*

The second bat mitzvah studied, which occurred in 1988, involved eighteen women who participated in two groups of nine on the first two days of Passover at a large Reform temple.[6] At the morning service, each woman gave a brief commentary on a section of the day's Torah reading, was called to an *aliyah,* and read or chanted a section from the scroll.

In the both settings there was some reluctance to have the event understood as a feminist statement. Some understanding of the indirections and complexities in the relationship of Jewish feminism to adult bat mitzvah may be gained by placing this ritual innovation in the context of some common issues which social movements face. In the analysis which follows, some general comments about social movements will be made first, followed by a discussion of Jewish feminism as a social movement, and the responses of the branches of Judaism. We will then turn to the data about the adult bat mitzvahs studied and see how they fit into the larger pattern.

Social Movements, Established Organizations and Cooptation

Social movements mobilize people around broad objectives which cannot be incorporated into the issue by issue process of organizationally structured change. These movements bring together a coalition of individuals and interest groups who feel themselves subject to systemic subordination. Established patterns of social relationships discriminate against them, deny them prestige by negative stereotypes, and frustrate their attempts to band together to pursue their common interests. As outsiders in common opposition, those who participate in the coalition which comes together in a social movement develop feelings of solidarity. Mutual support gives the participants in the movement freedom to speak out and behave in ways which they would otherwise not dare to do.

When established patterns of social relationships change in response to the grievances expressed by the social movement, the solidarity and momentum of the movement are threatened. Polarization diminishes and identification with the movement is less attractive. This process is one aspect of the classic dilemma of cooptation.[7] Established organizations may take over enough of the agenda of a social movement to eliminate the pressure for more radical change.

This observation is neither a moral criticism nor a theory of elites conspiring to subvert innovative movements. Leaders of established organizational structures and leaders of social movements understand the need for change in rather different ways. They are each in competition for the allegiance of the same people and will want to appear responsive to them. Unless the relationship between a social movement and established organizations degenerates to polarized hostility, one can expect some sentiment in each camp for borrowing and adapting from the other. One would also expect that the borrowing and adapting would have to appear to follow the inherent logic of each camp and would often be rhetorically unacknowledged.

Feminism and Judaism

The process of changing women's status within Judaism has conformed to this pattern. The emergence of a feminist movement within Judaism was followed by compromise, accommodation and cooptation on the part of Judaism's various branches. This pattern may be seen by examining the feminist critique of Judaism, the varied agenda which has emerged from this critique and the types of responses the branches of Judaism have made.

Jewish feminists have identified with each other on the basis of common feelings of subordination. The feminist critique of Judaism emerged from the open discussion of these feelings. The feminist critique of Judaism is not homogeneous; there are strong differences of opinion among Jewish feminists. What they share is a willingness to support other women's right to explore these ideas and the agenda which flows from them. The feminist critique of Judaism contains various assertions, which it may be helpful to review at this point.[8]

The Bible, it is argued, reflects a patriarchal society. When taken as divine revelation, its laws, stories and rhetoric justify male superiority and female subordination. Since the biblical text is sacred, the role models of female religious and political leadership which did find their way into the Bible could not be erased, but post-biblical male writers have overlooked later female leaders--writing them out of history. Traditional interpretations of Torah and other biblical texts, exclusively written by men, elaborated and consolidated anti-female views and laws, and portrayed God and public religious activities as male. Male authorities consistently denied women ritual equality, higher level study and participation in positions of authority. Some respected Jewish authorities expressed a fear of sexuality, associating women with sexual impulses and the threat of physical and moral impurity.

Jewish feminists argue that anti-female bias of Judaism is only partly redressed by formal equality in ritual participation and access to positions of authority. Feminism, they argue, will only be successful when the informal conservatism which keeps women out of positions of real influence is overcome and when mainstream Judaism incorporates new ideas and rituals which reflect the female as well as the male experience. Jewish feminists re-examine the sacred texts through theology and new *midrashim* to bring out the feminist potential in Judaism. Historical scholarship writes women back into Jewish history. New rituals relate turning points in women's lives, female solidarity and female imagery of God to Jewish sources.

It is also important to note that there is a feminist movement within Christianity, groups of women exploring female spirituality outside of the limits of Christianity and Judaism, and feminists who have renounced religion in favor of humanistic values.[9] Many Jewish feminists are aware of these ideas, feel sympathetic to them, and cooperate with the women involved. From the perspective of Jewish feminists, the options available to Jewish women are more than either changing Judaism or accepting a continuing subordination. Jewish women also have the option of responding to the feminist critique cf Judaism by rejecting Judaism and the Jewish community altogether in favor of non-Jewish female spirituality or non-religious feminist humanism.

The different branches of Judaism have expanded the role of women. Some Orthodox authorities risk the censure of their colleagues by promoting increased opportunities for female scholarship and worship.[10]   Formal equality is found in the other movements. The Conservative movement, after lengthy deliberations, admitted women to the rabbinate.[11]   Reform and Reconstructionist Judaism have no ideological barriers to full female equality; female applicants were simply accepted to their seminaries and female rabbis and cantors are now common. Reform and Reconstructionist Judaism are also theologically open, permitting the entry of ideas from the feminist critique of Judaism into theological discussion on an equal status with other ideas. Theological ideas and ritual practices such as those promoted by Plaskow and in the collection edited by Adelman remain highly unconventional.[12]

The response of the various branches of Judaism to feminism may be characterized as a combination of accommodation, compromise, and cooptation. During this period, adult bat mitzvah has become common.[13] It has not generated the controversy that other innovations have. The elites of each branch have neither debated it nor encouraged it.[14] Jewish feminist writing does not promote adult bat mitzvah as an important ritual initiative. The ritual has developed at the congregational level in all but the Orthodox branch, where it is not found at all. The reasons for its wide spread are to be found in the dynamics of congregational life.

Adult Bat Mitzvah as a Congregational Ritual

Congregations have their own agendas--to encourage and maintain the enthusiasm and commitment of their members. By responding to their needs and giving them a fuller understanding of the beliefs and practices of Judaism, they enable their members to better participate in congregational activities. Congregations have found it relatively easy to respond to the motivation of women to have adult bat mitzvahs because these rituals fit so well into the overall congregational agenda.

In understanding the meaning of the ritual to the women who participated, it may be significant to note that none of them came to the decision to have a bat mitzvah through feminist involvement. Their passage took another route. Making Judaism an important part of their lives brought them into contact with similar Jewish women. Miriam related her experience when she went away to university:

> It was the first time I had non-Jewish friends. They were beautiful people, caring people, and they began to question me deeply about my religious identity, something that my Jewish friends and I never discussed, it was just something taken for granted. . . . I identified myself in a very Jewish way, and yet I couldn't answer basic questions about Judaism. . . . [These] non-Jewish people were . . . spiritual and religious but not in an established religion. . . . I began to find myself liking their ways and their spirituality but yet I didn't want to lose my traditional past. . . .

After university, Miriam's non-Jewish friends put her in contact with a compatible woman who led a Jewish women's group that studied together and held periodic retreats in the city to which Miriam was moving. After being part of this group, Miriam decided to have a bat mitzvah, in large part to express to her family the religious direction her life had taken and to have them participate in it.

The temple b'not mitzvah came for a variety of reasons: more interest in exploring religious issues than other members of their families, a felt need to make up for an inadequate Jewish education, the desire to learn along with their children, a follow-up to conversion, or some combination of these reasons. These reasons express motivation in personal terms. They do not express ideological self-consciousness about being part of a movement or the desire to make a public statement about the role of women in Judaism. For some in the group, the learning, which extended over eighteen months, was the initial focus. These women did not decide to participate in the ritual until the rabbi's assumption that all would participate and the group solidarity that had developed brought them along.

The ritual innovations which Jewish feminists have proposed express events in a woman's life in the presence of other women using female religious language. In both adult bat mitzvahs, in contrast, the specifically female dimension of the ritual was not part of its formal structure. The adult bat mitzvahs were, in form, like the bar or bat mitzvahs of thirteen year olds or the bar mitzvahs of adult men, consisting of reading from the Torah (and in Miriam's case the *haftorah*) and delivering a commentary. The rituals took place in mixed gender congregations which were not part of the feminist movement. The small independent congregation was still self-conscious about its gender egalitarianism but, like the temple, had other issues on its agenda, which were reflected in its weekly services and associated activities. The temple announcement of the program invited both men and women, although the one man who initially enrolled soon dropped out.

The congregational rather than female focus of the adult bat mitzvahs can be further seen in those attending. At both congregations about half of those attending were invited to the bat mitzvahs. Miriam belonged to a Jewish women's group which held periodic retreats. She could have held a female-only ritual at one of the women's group retreats, but chose instead to have a congregational ritual. She chose a congregational ritual because she wanted her bat mitzvah to be attended by a larger group of about forty-five people--her parents, other friends and friends of her parents that she thought of as family. Members of the women's group did take liturgical leadership roles at the service on the day of the bat mitzvah, but within the context and limits of the normal congregational service. None of the eighteen women at the temple reported being part of a feminist group. Each invited about twenty guests, some less, some a few more--immediate family and close friends. Like conventional bar/bat mitzvahs, these adult bat mitzvahs brought individuals and their families into congregational sanctuaries. Female solidarity, though, was in the background, and more will be said of this later.

In addition to the mixed gender, congregation and family context of the rituals in both settings, the temple service was one in which males occupied the senior authority positions. Although the temple previously had a female rabbi as part of its staff, this was not the case at the time of the bat mitzvah. The rabbi and cantor who led the service and helped the women prepare were both male. The relationship with the senior rabbi, as interpreter of the tradition and guide to Jewish life, was particularly close. Other women acted only as Hebrew language teachers. Their help was appreciated and acknowledged, but the Hebrew teachers were not a part of the ceremony. One of the b'not mitzvah was more feminist in her language and approach than the others. She expressed her discomfort to the class about having men conduct the rest of the service. On the day on which her group of nine had their bat mitzvahs, they also participated in other parts of the service, taking over tasks that would otherwise be done by the rabbi.

At the small congregation service, other women besides Miriam did take important ceremonial roles, but not all of them. The leader of the women's group led the Torah service and a close female friend prepared a commentary for presentation during the kiddush. Miriam did turn to a male, a co-worker whose values she respected, to teach her the technical skills needed for chanting the Torah and haftorah. Like the Hebrew teachers at the temple, Miriam's tutor did not participate in the ceremony.

The bat mitzvahs, while contributing to the process of enlarging female participation, did not otherwise challenge conventional gender relationships. Of the eighteen commentaries written by the temple class, only one spoke about the women's movement and changes in the female role. Another noted, without commenting on the issue of gender, that the class had "twinned" with a group of women refusniks.[15] A third closed with a reference to her daughters.

In contrast to this tentative acknowledgement of women's issues, the commentaries of the temple group contained many references to conventional ideas about gender relationships: the importance of family observances, the centrality of the Jewish home, the responsibility of parents to pass on tradition to children. These conventional references reflected the women's role relationships. Almost all of the women were married, with children. They did not want the bat mitzvah to disrupt these relationships, but to enhance them. In a few cases, involvement in the bat mitzvah was not supported by other members of the family. The affirmation of conventional relationships in the commentaries may be seen as a message of reassurance.

Miriam was more articulate about gender issues. Her social relationships were mixed in gender and age. She was unmarried, with a circle of male as well as female friends, fond of her parents and their friends. Her personal accommodation was expressed in her d'var Torah. She quoted Jewish feminists and traditional commentators, speaking of women as leaders in learning and politics by extending the role of being a "mother of Israel" beyond giving birth and nurturing children to all those acts which nurture and sustain the community.   By this strategy she associated herself with the conventional imagery of motherhood, but stretched its implications.

What we have seen so far illustrates the compromise and accommodation that occurs when established organizations respond to a social movement.   Comparing the two settings, it seems clear that Miriam's bat mitzvah contained more elements drawn from Jewish feminism than the one at the temple.   These feminist elements, though, were incorporated into a ritual which also had strong congregational and familial themes.   The comparatively greater public feminism of Miriam's bat mitzvah may reflect her point of view, the self-consciousness about gender issues in the congregation or the greater salience of feminist language in 1986 than in 1988.   The congregation at which Miriam's bat mitzvah took place also thought of itself as marginal to the religious establishment.   It thought of its practices as innovative and remained unaffiliated with any of the branches of Judaism, making it easier for participants to express somewhat unconventional opinions.

While adult bat mitzvah has not been high on the agenda of Jewish feminists, it has become common as a way for congregations to incorporate enhanced female participation.   As a congregational event, adult bat mitzvah encourages congregational and family ties, highlights women's links to religion and spirituality within conventional Judaism, and may take place in settings where real and symbolic authority remain concentrated in male hands.   One might ask whether Jewish feminism has been coopted through these compromises, whether the women were permitted only what was not threatening to the institution and encouraged to be happy with that.

The Feminist Dimension of Adult Bat Mitzvah

This conclusion, however, could only be reached if the analysis stopped at this point.   There are other data from the research which support a more nuanced interpretation.   The women's accounts of their experiences in both settings showed that they did not think of the bat mitzvah as an end, but as part of a larger process of raising women's status and opportunities.   They were aware of the more challenging issues that feminism raises for Judaism and used their relationships with other women involved in their bat mitzvahs to explore these issues.   The support that they received from other women as they went through their bat mitzvahs helped them push out the boundaries of what they considered themselves capable of doing.   The other side of the reluctance of almost all involved to view the bat mitzvah as a feminist statement was the feeling of having personally broken through a gender structured limitation as part of a group of women.

As we have seen, Miriam's bat mitzvah was held in a congregational and family context. On the other hand, she was able to present herself before congregation and family only because of her female associations, which gave her emotional and practical support. Similarly, the temple class spoke of the support that they gave to each other. One commented on the feeling of "sisterhood" that they retained after the ceremony and another summed up the emotional consequences with the statement, "I've made life-long friends." Since most friendship networks remain gender based, one has to wonder whether such a feeling would have developed in a mixed gender group.[16]

In both settings, the women were aware that support from other women gave each individual strength to accomplish tasks that had seemed too hard. The women's group in which Miriam participated, through its retreats, study and ritual creativity, played a mediating role between traditional female role models and new opportunities for Jewish women. The temple class was composed of some women who had known each other and some who met the others for the first time. They reported that they learned to trust and rely upon each other as the class progressed. They opened up to each other when discussing their feelings about Judaism. Those who had felt isolated or whose interest in Judaism was questioned by their families were reassured by having like-minded companions. When those who were beginning the study of Hebrew were anxious, the more experienced women calmed and reassured them. After the portions for the bat mitzvah ceremony were assigned, those who had not intended to participate felt that they were strongly committed to the group and had to go through with it. As the date approached, the women discussed ideas for their commentaries together and those who were strong in Hebrew assisted those who needed help with their Torah portions. The feeling of mutual interdependence and valuing each one's special contribution was strongly expressed in the following statement: "Everybody had a strength or skill that they brought to the group in some way. I don't know what it was, but everybody contributed something at some point or another and gave something special."

The feeling that the group supported each individual was expressed in the decision that they had to make about seating. Normally, b'nai mitzvah sit on the *bimah* through the service. The women decided, however, that they would sit in the first two rows, with the nine having the bat mitzvah on that day in the front and the nine having the bat mitzvah on the other day in the second row. They explained that they wanted each person to have the chance to be the center of attention by herself and that they wanted to be in front so that they could see and hear the others. One of the women described their feelings at the actual event:

> I can still remember as each person went up, we were all excited and we followed . . . at the end, the rabbi and the cantor called the . . . group up and they did the *shechechiyanu*. Everybody--tears were just--we were crying. Then they came down--I'll never forget this--it was like we were in a football huddle. We were hugging each other and kissing each other and wishing each other *mazel tov*. There was a feeling there, I can see it like it was yesterday. . . .

Despite the fact that much of the language of the bat mitzvahs reflected an accommodation to congregational and familial needs, the experience of female bonding was important in each setting. Similarly, while the congregational focus emphasized the bat mitzvah as female participation in established practices, the broader feminist agenda of transforming Judaism did become part of the experience.

Miriam was explicit in her *d'var Torah* about the modern Jewish woman "going through a period of rebirth and renewal." She associated the biblical role models of Deborah and Miriam with the legitimacy of female communal leadership, spiritual creativity, and a leadership style of compromise and teamwork. She spoke about *Rosh Chodesh* groups, all-women prayer groups, and the ordination of women. In the interview, she spoke about her quest for spirituality within Judaism. In neither the interview nor in her *d'var Torah*, though, did Miriam make any direct reference to the feminist critique of Judaism as a patriarchal religion which requires many changes in its theology and practice.

Interestingly, some of the women in the temple class who were circumspect in their public commentaries did address this issue indirectly during the interview, perhaps because the interview was a lengthy, wide-ranging group discussion. Latent feminism came out early in the interview when one women was describing her motivation:

> We had a woman rabbi a few years ago who had a short study session for women about being comfortable with the Torah. She said most women are afraid of touching the Torah. . . . She made all of us go up and hold the Torah. It was an incredible experience because I'd never touched the Torah before that. . .

My husband comes from a Conservative background and women don't touch the Torah. Not that he'd say "No," but there was a subliminal message somewhere. I wanted to prove that I could do all these things and I did.

This woman was describing a movement which has preached gender equality for over a hundred years, but in which conventional practice has had an inhibiting effect. That the husband, like many current members of Reform congregations, has a more traditional background suggests one reason for the continuation of the gap between theory and practice. The importance of a female rabbi encouraging other women to overcome their reluctance to use their rights is also apparent.

In addition to this expressed awareness of latent sexism in the Reform movement, the women found that others outside the temple perceived the bat mitzvah to be promoting women's changing status in Judaism. One women commented on her surprise at how many women asked how they could do it. Another continued in vivid detail:

I took my kids swimming. . . . Women came up to me saying, "I saw your picture. It was wonderful. Tell me how you did it." [interjection: the picture was terrible, but you were wonderful] A woman came up to me and said, "How can I get bat mitzvahed at [the temple]?" I said, "They're starting another class." It turns out that she was a member at [an Orthodox synagogue]. She said, "There is no way they are ever going to do this for us. I admire you women for what you have done. I would give my eye teeth." I said, "You'll have to join. [the temple]; that's the only way you can do it." A lot of Conservative women, more towards Orthodox really, that were swimming there were really excited about it, really moved by it, in terms of "How do I get it going? What happens?" I was in [a Jewish book store], picking out a book and somebody said *"Mazel Tov."* Someone else asked me what happened and I told them I'd had a bat mitzvah at [the temple]. Out of the clear blue, behind the stacks, somebody said, "Only at [the temple] would you find anything like this happening." This young man, with a *yarmulke* on, came up to me and said, "It's wonderful," and he really gave it to that man. He said, "I belong to an Orthodox synagogue. We have a lot of very young Jewish women studying and learning and going on." He says, "Mark my words, in the next fifteen, twenty, thirty years you're going to see a big change in Orthodox women because they want this. They want to learn. The feminist movement is taking hold on our Orthodox Jewish women." I hope he's right.

Specifically women's perspectives came up in an aside when one of the women spoke about the "personal honor" of standing before the Torah and doing "what all other Jews do--read a part." Another woman interjected, "All other male Jews." She went on, contrasting the female and male experience of reading Torah, "Because we're women and so connected with time, and so connected with generations, emotionally, I think it was even much more meaningful."

The issue of God's gender also came up in the interview when one of the women said, "I have a very simple minded approach to God . . . I just talk to Him . . . Her." There was laughter over the indeterminate end, but another continued seriously, "God has to be female. There's not enough compassion in God to be male. God has to be female." Another replied, "I wish He were female, but I somehow don't think He is. I wish I could get myself around that thought." Later, a woman talking about how to talk to her children about God said, "I guess the only way I'll really know if there really truly is a God is when I die that maybe one day She will be there to welcome me to the heavens."

The women were asked directly about the feminist implications of their bat mitzvahs. Did their public participation as women in Jewish worship spill over into other aspects of their lives as women? Their answers to this question had a certain parallel to the toning down of feminist rhetoric in public while being more open to women's issues in their talk with each other. The first answer was a simple "No." A second woman explained, "My participation as a bat mitzvah is a result rather than a cause. . . . I simply feel that I've taken advantage of what there is rather than being a pioneer." A third woman added, "Absolutely."

However, a fourth took the answer in a different direction, seemingly without noticing. "I felt similar," she said, "I think it refueled my feeling of power. It added to my inner strength to do whatever I want to do and carry my family along with me." "I like that, 'inner strength'," commented another. This elicited the remark, "I didn't let A. use the word 'empowerment' [in her commentary]. It sounded like real feminist jargon." A number of women added approving comments about the "inner strength" that came from the process.

A further comment referred back to the centrality of reading from the Torah, "Being able to get up and do that is sort of an indication of, not only our inner strength, but our ability to take the bull by the horns, to forge this class, to make this gesture and assert our power (but that's not our expression), to show how we really felt about doing something we wanted to do." Another continued, to expressions of general agreement, "You hear a lot about people complaining about how things should be. . . . Here is a group that doesn't talk about what should be, or could be, or shouldn't be, but did. I felt very, very strongly about that, . . . that we made things happen."

In this conversation there is an initial rejection of links between the bat mitzvah and a broader feminist agenda. This rejection is followed by immediate agreement that, of course, the success of the bat mitzvah had implications for self-confidence in other settings. This agreement is followed by the explicit rejection of feminist jargon to describe the implications. There is subsequent talking around the topic to say in conventional language what feminist jargon says succinctly. It sounds as if the b'not mitzvah want to identify with the agenda of the feminist movement without being labelled. They are, after all, wives, mothers, and members of the congregation as well as women. They seem to feel, probably with good cause, that a public label as feminists would cause them problems in these other relationships without any benefits.

Conclusion

This analysis has moved through three possible interpretations of the now common practice of adult bat mitzvah. First, the initial view that the women involved saw bat mitzvah as a feminist statement just wasn't supported by the data. There was some explicit rejection of it being a feminist statement, and where it was present it was partial and subordinate to other aspects of the experience. Second, this analysis examined the way in which adult bat mitzvah could appear to have coopted the energy brought out by feminism for nonfeminist congregational purposes. While the ritual did affirm family and congregational roles, this finding of cooptation was not the whole story either. Third, the research led to the conclusion that despite cooptation, the bat mitzvahs brought out potential for further change. The women went through experiences which made them more competent, confident participants in Judaism and which encouraged them to think of Jewish issues in feminist terms.

It is indeed possible that we are entering into a new era in religious history. Within liberal Judaism and Christianity, in ways unprecedented in the past, authority structure has changed to accommodate women in positions of authority, and theology is changing to recognize female spirituality. Feminism may be moving from an opposition that critiques religion from the margins to one of the currents in the main stream, which flows into and blends with the other currents, continually modifying them.

Both the uncertainty about where the blending may take Judaism and the awareness that it is happening were caught in an interchange between two members of the temple bat mitzvah group. The interchange is a little cryptic, but the explication of the text will be left to the reader. Towards the end of the interview, after the women had distanced themselves from feminism only to find feminist issues surfacing in their conversation, one woman was commenting on the effects of the bat mitzvah. "There is," she said, "a sisterhood, if you will, in that when we get together a certain feeling stays with us." Another woman asked, "Are you talking about feminism?" The first replied, "Just a little bit." And then they all laughed.

Endnotes

1. Judith Plaskow, *Standing Again At Sinai* (New York, 1990), ix.

2. Ruth Mason, "Adult Bat Mitzvah: A Revolution for Women and Synagogues," *Lillith* 14, no.4 (Fall, 1989): 21-24.

3. Stuart Schoenfeld, "Integration into the Group and Sacred Uniqueness: An Analysis of Adult Bat Mitzvah," in *Persistence and Flexibility: Anthropological Perspectives on the American Jewish Experience,* ed. Walter Zenner (Albany, NY, 1988), 117-135; Stuart Schoenfeld, "Ritual and Role Transition: Adult Bat Mitzvah as a Successful Rite of Passage," forthcoming in *The Uses of Tradition: Jewish Continuity Since Emancipation,* Jack Wertheimer, ed. (Cambridge, MA).

4. A pseudonym; for a fuller account of Miriam's bat mitzvah and an interpretation of other issues, see Schoenfeld, "Integration into the Group and Sacred Uniqueness."

5. The congregation continued to use the Orthodox *siddur* edited by Birnbaum; the person leading public prayer, however, was instructed to add the name of the corresponding matriarch whenever a patriarch was mentioned and to add *"imoteinu"* (our mothers) whenever *"avoteinu"* (our fathers) was in the text. The reader's repetition of the *musaf amidah* was shortened, and the text of the prayer for the welfare of the state of Israel was slightly modified, notably by changing the opening approved by the Israeli Chief rabbinate "Our Father" to "Our God." Otherwise, the traditional texts remained.

6. For a fuller account of the group adult bat mitzvah and an interpretation of other issues, see Schoenfeld, "Ritual and Role Transition."

7. First discussed by Robert Michels in *Political Parties: A Sociological Study of the Oligarchical Tendencies of Modern Democracy* (New York, 1966).

8. There is now an extensive literature, with its own internal debates, by Jewish feminists. The sources consulted in the preparation of this chapter were Susannah Heschel, ed., *On Being a Jewish Feminist: A Reader* (New York, 1983); especially the chapter by Arleen Stern, "Learning to Chant the Torah," 182-185; and the contrasting chapters by Cynthia Ozick, "Notes Toward Finding the Right Question," 120-151; and Judith Plaskow, "The Right Question Is Theological," 217-222; Susan Weidman Schneider, *Jewish and Female: Choices and Changes in Our Lives Today* (New York, 1984); Penina Adelman, *Miriam's Well: Rituals for Jewish Women Around the Year* (Fresh Meadows, N.Y., 1986); Plaskow, see note 1. above; and *Lillith* magazine.

9. See Carol P. Christ and Judith Plaskow, eds., *Womanspirit Rising: A Feminist Reader in Religion* (New York, 1979), for an inter-religious collection of feminist writing.

10. Within Israeli Orthodoxy, increased opportunities for higher level female study are found at Midreshet Lidenbaum, Nishmat, and the Shalom Hartman Institute. In the United States, Drisha offers advanced study for women; Blu Greenberg, the wife of Orthodox rabbi Irving Greenberg, has written on the possibilities of changes in gender roles within Orthodoxy. Norma Joseph in Montreal combines a public commitment to both Orthodoxy and feminism.

11. And is in the process of admitting women to the cantor's association.

12. See n. 1 and n. 8 above.

13. Paula Hyman, in "The Introduction of Bat Mitzvah in Conservative Judaism in Postwar America," *YIVO Annual*, 19 (1990): 133-146, cites a case in 1950 where the mother of one of the girls in a bat mitzvah class participated in their group ceremony. Although further work on the evolution of congregational practices is required to document the diffusion of adult bat mitzvah, it appears to have been uncommon until the late 1970s. See Schoenfeld, "Ritual and Role Transition."

14. On the distinction between elite and folk Judaism, see Charles Liebman, *The Ambivalent American Jew* (Philadelphia, 1973); and Stuart Schoenfeld, "Folk Religion, Elite Religion and the Role of Bar Mitzvah in the Development of the Synagogue and Jewish School in America," *Contemporary Jewry* 9 (1988): 67-85.

15. Soviet Jews who had applied for exit visas and had their applications refused. Many bar and bat mitzvahs in the 1970s and 1980s were "twinned" with refusnik children of bar/bat mitzvah age, the bar/bat mitzvah outside the U.S.S.R. acknowledging the one inside during the ceremony.

16. See the film, *When Harry Met Sally*.

HALAKHAH AND HOLOCAUST THEOLOGY:
PERSPECTIVES ON POWER

G. Philip Points

Jews are no exception to the characterization that living in the late twentieth century is living as "children of modernity" in post-modern times, seeking to draw from and remain faithful to pre-modern traditions. Indeed, Nimian Smart has elaborated upon some of the alternative perspectives upon modernity as a way of comprehending the dynamics of present historical existence. With real insight, his analysis includes the differentiation of various ways in which traditions are influential in our era.[1] There are precritical, critical, and post-modern ways of relying upon tradition in the effort to meet and deal with modernity; yet in a very real sense, the modern era has passed. In its passing, there are pervasive energies which continue to nag at us, to inspire us and to threaten us, as we come to realize that a new era--a postmodern era--has been born.

The modern era said that traditions were not important and were to be surpassed in the freedom of autonomous existence. This autonomy included free minds which could be trusted to provide critical appraisals of virtually every issue confronted, and allowed for completely satisfying resolutions which set the conditions for the full flowering of humanity. The post-modern reality amidst which we now seek to live, bears as its "perhaps most significant" assumption" a growing appreciation of the thoroughgoing, radical interdependence of life at all levels and in every imaginable way."[2] This post-modern sensibility also includes an openness to other religious options and an openness to the rise of those dispossessed because of gender, race and class.

Whether one accepts the label of "post-modern" as a fruitful designation for our present living, it seems obvious to me that there is a new situation and a new sensibility which must be taken into account as we try to understand the importance of tradition in human living. Even though traditions are the outcome of human interpretation and construction, tradition is not valueless, as modernity would have us believe. More importantly, traditions must be managed in interdependence with each other. The autonomy envisioned by modernity has been called into question. We now seem to understand that the interpretations rendered are effected by the living conditions of the interpreter. Hence, the managers of traditions need to give as much attention to the conditions of their own living as they give to the responsibility of managing. Gender, race, and class are of crucial significance in qualifying the sort of autonomy envisioned in modernity.

We have then, the double and even triple challenge to sensibility and perspective of modernity with respect to tradition and autonomy. Not only is tradition our "natural," humanly-created habitat (and so a qualification upon our autonomy), but also traditions are interdependent with each other, and the management of traditions is inseparable from the gender, race and class of the managers. Acknowledgment of these facts about tradition and the actual conditions of human living gives concrete meaning and body to the phrase often repeated by Blu Greenberg: "Where there has been a rabbinical will there has been a way." With this awareness she presses for interpretation and management of tradition (*Halakhah*), directly seeking to address the needs of Jewish women who have found themselves in sympathy with various emphases in the women's movement.

Likewise Marc Ellis is attentive to the actual conditions of living, and urges that Jews come to see the extent to which they are captive to the trauma of the Holocaust, and have been blind to the need to work on behalf of justice for the oppressed and the underclass in the world. For Ellis, uncritical acceptance of modernity and Jewish commitment to the independent nation-state renders impossible the Jewish witness to its own tradition of justice and fairness on behalf of the poor and the oppressed. He believes that, because of their absorption with the Holocaust, the Jewish people have come to accept the secular state and political solutions of Israel. Israel has become the expression of Jewish power and presence in the world, a political power and presence which is far more real and viable from the perspective of modernity. Ellis wants to challenge this modernity just as Greenberg wants to challenge precritical traditionalism. For Greenberg and Ellis, tradition is far too valuable to be relinquished in such fashion. Management of tradition in a spirit of post-modern sensibility is what is needed and what is offered.

In discussing these two patterns of thinking, I am directing attention to two matters which have shared the first line attention of Jews in America for the last decade: Jews in America have been more concerned with questions raised by the women's movement and with affairs in Israel than with any of the other issues.[3] The feminist movement has generated fears about the survival of the Jewish people and of religious living for Jews. The survival of the Jewish people is, to an astonishing degree, perceived to be tied to the survival of Israel.

In an odd sort of way the two came together when Greenberg attended the First International Jewish Feminist Conference in Jerusalem in November, 1988. While there, Greenberg, an Orthodox Jew from America, was at prayer along with other women at the Western Wall. These women were harassed by ultra-Conservative Jews in the male section.[4] This incident symbolizes both the perceived threat to Jewish existence present in the freedoms to women expressed in the women's movement, and the perceived threat to Israel present in any deviance or criticism with respect to Israeli life. In Greeenberg's thinking, the perceived threat to Jewish existence is the result of the absence of rabbinical will. In Ellis's thinking, the perceived threat to Israel results from the Holocaust mentality and a surrender to the secularity of modernity. Looking at the struggles with tradition and the representations of tradition in the work of Greenberg and Ellis provides the occasion to explore perspectives on power. The exercise of power has a dialetical relationship with tradition's qualities of support and recalcitrance, a relationship between reformative energy and the absence of tradition. In this exploration of tradition and power, we can see that the endeavors of Greenberg and Ellis point to the "general phenomena which have characterized Judaism throughout the ages."

First, in living and working with tradition, Greenberg and Ellis are concerned about pluralism in opposition to sectarianism in the Jewish experience. Anyone with even a minimum awareness of Jewish history and the role of *Halakhah* would realize that pluralism characterizes the history of life with *Halakhah*. Beyond this *Halakhic* existence, there are those other Jews who have now sought to remain identified and identifiable as Jews without the discipline of *Halakhah*. Greenberg acknowledges that such discipline appears sectarian to others and that her effort to bridge feminist concerns and observance of Jewish law stimulates divisiveness among Orthodox Jews and even elicits sectarian resistance on the part of some. Nonetheless, she seeks to sustain a "dialectical tension" between tradition (which she wants to protect with "the fierceness of a mother protecting her young"), and the new value of women's equality (which she also knows she can "never yield").[5] She believes that the *Halakhic* system "has tried to maintain the balance of needs between community and individual, Jew and non-Jew, authority and freedom, religion and society." However, in this century, says Greenberg, "*Halakhic* authorities have been concentrated overwhelmingly in the change-resistant sector of society." She seeks an "authentic Jewish women's movement," one which tries to provide new approaches within *Halakhah,* one which can include women's concerns and which can in turn, shape women's concerns according to Jewish values.[6]

The feminist values are carried in, and give birth to, the "feminist ideology" which Greenberg summarizes in four propositions:

1. Women have the same innate potential, capability, and needs as men, whether in the realm of the spirit, the word, or the deed.

2. Women have a similar capacity for interpretation and concomitant decision-making.
3. Women can function fully as "outside" persons, in broader areas of society beyond the home.
4. Women can, and should, have some control over their own destinies, to the extent that such mastery is possible for anyone.[7]

She then transforms these general statements into "a theology of woman as Jew," which is summarized below:

1. A woman of faith has the same innate vision and existential longing for a redemptive-covenantal reality as a man of faith. She has the same ability and need to be in the presence of God alone and within the context of the community. Such a woman is sufficiently mature to accept the responsibilities for this relationship and the rights that flow from these responsibilities. If these spiritual gifts do not flow naturally from her soul, she can be educated and uplifted in them in much the same fashion that Jewish men are.

2. Jewish women, as much as men, have the mental and emotional capacities to deal directly with the most sacred Jewish texts and primary sources. Jewish women are capable of interpreting tradition based on these sources. They can be involved in the decision-making process that grows out of the blending of inherited tradition with contemporary needs.

3. Some women, as some men, are capable of functioning in the positions of authority related to the religious and physical survival of the Jewish people.

4. Women as a class should not find themselves in discriminatory positions in personal situations. In such matters as marriage and divorce, a woman should have no less control or personal freedom than a man, nor should she be subject to abuse resulting from the constriction of freedom.[8]

Greenberg believes that these propositions make "a fundamental claim about women contrary to the model generated in *Halakhah.*" *Halakhic* living "inhibits women's growth, both as Jews and as human beings;" it "continues to delimit women." In light of "the primary model of Jewish woman as domestic creature--as wife, mother, dependent, auxiliary--all other roles and responsibilities that seemed to conflict with the primary model simply were eliminated."[9] Persistent generation of the traditional *Halakhic* pattern for women promotes sectarianism. On the other hand, Greenberg rejects the generation of measures which would coerce all women into restrictive models that exclude wives and mothers.[10]   She is convinced that, as in the past, where there is rabbinical will there is a way--in this case, as way to avert sectarianism with respect to women's equality and to encourage the development of a free and full humanity for women. The "free and full" of course, acknowledge that there will be, and there should be encouraged, a variety of paths for this development under the guidance of *Halakhah*

Just as Greenberg confronts the pre-critical traditionalism of *Halakhic* facing of feminism, so Ellis addresses the uncritical modernism which seems to control current Jewish living in relationship to the State of Israel.   "To speak publicly on issues of the Holocaust and Israel in a critical manner," says Ellis, "is to court suspicion and raise the specter of treason. The results may be excommunication from the Jewish community, or worse, the accusation that one is supporting the climate for another Holocaust." The "dilemma in which the Jewish people of North America and the State of Israel--the two most articulate and politically powerful Jewish communities--presently find themselves" is that "prophets and villains appear at every turn, defined by angles of vision and experience that depend upon various propensities and points of view."[11]   From the perspective of modernity, an economically, politically, and militarily powerful nation-state is the only viable mode of existence for Jews in the world today. The nation-state is the place for people today and Israel is the place for the survival of Jewish living. This, according to Ellis, seems to be the point of view of Jews who are held captive to the experience of the Holocaust, and the to propensities which emerged in its aftermath.

Ellis believes that an authentic witness out of Jewish tradition calls for a primary consideration of the historic commitment to justice and peace. This witness is possible only when the sincere voice of Diaspora Jews is received. This voice declares that the State of Israel is one voice, but not the primary and certainly not the only voice, but one among several voices. As Jews welcome many voices, even those which are critical of particular Israeli policies, Jews will be saved from a sectarian existence grounded in the conceptions of power which come out of modernity. In short, the voice of tradition on behalf of justice and peace can save Jews from the sectarianisms of modernity with its notions of self-serving, autonomous power. Greenberg attracts attention to the possibility that *Halakhic* existence for Jews might become sectarian. Ellis is convinced that modernity might create a sectarian mode of existence for a people whose history has honored plurality in Diaspora committed to justice and peace on behalf of the oppressed and the trampled. Ellis calls attention to the "Jewish prayers said each morning that thank God for making one a Jew and calling one to be free." These prayers represent for him a hope that his faith "can lead to authentic solidarity with all those who struggle for human dignity and justice."[12]

There was a time in the recent past when the State of Israel was opposed by some Jews. Only with the Six-Day War in 1967 did North American Jews come to the "uncritical consensus one sees today." Prior to that time, Orthodox, Reform, and Conservative Jews had opposed the formation of the new nation-state as the center of Jewish attention. Then, says Ellis, Jewish theologians slipped from presenting the story of Israel as "intrinsic to the renewal of Jewish life" into refusal of "the pious sphere of prayer and good deeds and spoke publicly about the need for empowerment as a religious response to destruction." A sense of "pride that an empowered Jewish community, once dependent on the protection of others, could go it alone and win decisively" is, according to Ellis, one reason North American Jews came to view Israel as "singularly important." Ellis believes that Holocaust theology might have responded to, and helped form a consensus which "blunted the theology's critical edge."[13] This theology came from such persons as Elie Wiesel, Richard Rubenstein, Emil Fackenheim, and Irving Greenberg--from the periphery of organized Jewish power. Ellis concurs that it belongs with the Exodus event and the rabbinic interpretations in its scope and honesty.[14] Nonetheless, this consensus has come to have the power to excommunicate those who are critical of policies in the State of Israel.[15]

Ellis is not primarily concerned with obvious sectarianism however. Rather his effort is toward the movements of ethical concern and renewal which portend the more important form of survival for the people of Israel. This form of survival can come only from a base in pluralism and an authentic witness toward a renewed form of solidarity with all those who would serve justice and peace for humankind. Ellis believes it must come from the periphery of Jewish existence prepared "to challenge a consensus that admits of little dissent."[16] Unlike the sectarianism which Blu Greenberg confronts in change-resistant Orthodoxy, the resistance faced by those such as Marc Ellis is more wide-spread among Jews. There is intense community opposition to public discussion of Diaspora Jewish concerns with particular policies of the Israeli government, whereas the sectarianism addressed by Greenberg is formed primarily among Orthodox Jews. In both cases, we have patterns of thinking which touch the core of Jewish existence.[17]

A second way in which their work touches the core of Jewish existence is in the careful consideration of religiosity versus secularity. As I read her books and listen to her lecture, I sense that Blu Greenberg is a hesitant, sensitive, dedicated and thoughtful person who has profound appreciation for the sacredness of tradition as manifest in *Halakhah*. For her, there is a divine essence in *Halakhah* which provides discipline for living. On the other hand, she recognizes that *Halakhah* is time-bound in that its decisions and instructions have been those rendered at particular times by particular persons whose discernment, judgement, and interpretation have made *Halakhah* a very human (albeit male) "divine essence." Greenberg does not want to threaten or shatter that divine essence; she wants to preserve it while insisting that rabbinical will is crucial both in preserving the divine essence and in serving human need. She wants to address the needs of women as they have been touched by the women's movement, yet she does not want an interpreter to lose the sense of the sacredness of *Halakhah*.

The sacredness of *Halakhah*, for her, seems to be related to the fact that Torah has always been for men, as the study of Talmud has been for men, being part of *minyan* has been beyond her and other women. The otherness, the distance, the experience that *Halakhah* provided for her seems to be part of its sacredness.[18] This sense of sacred religious reality is elicited also in the experience of stability, the experience that with Torah and *Halakhah* there is only imperceptible change. Sacred means other and permanence.[19] Her profound appreciation for the system in its entirety is stated this way:

> Its ability to preserve the essence of an ancient revelation as a fresh experience each day; its power to generate an abiding sense of kinship, past and present; its intimate relatedness to concerns both immediate and other-worldly; its psychological soundness; its ethical and moral integrity. On the whole, I believe that a Jew has a better chance of living a worthwhile life if he or she lives a life according to *Halakhah*.[20]

Nonetheless, as we have seen, Greenberg believes that this system delimits women in unacceptable ways. She does not want to break the chain of tradition which holds her and guides her; however *Halakhic* Jews are at a crossroads where they have three options:

1. Jews can revert to the fundamentalist pole, where hierarchy of male and female remains unchallenged in most areas of human life.

2. Jews can allow the new value system to penetrate our civil lives but not our religious lives. In other words, women may be encouraged to see themselves as equals in social, economic, and political spheres. This is the current stance of modern Orthodoxy.

3. Jews can find ways within *Halakhah* to allow for growth and greater equality in the ritual and spiritual realms, despite the fact that there are no guarantees where this will lead us.[21]

Greenberg acknowledges that she has come to a sense of crossroads because of "the contemporary Western humanist liberation philosophy of the secular women's movement." Yet she is convinced that it is not the source of the insight which is at issue; it is the rightness, the fairness, the wholesomeness of what is proposed that is to be judged. She believes that there are "unique Jewish ways in which we appropriate positive ideas, customs and values"; she believes "we can enhance our system by these new accretions." She believes changes can be made which are "continuous with the essence of Judaism."[22]

In a telling passage, she reveals the depth of her conviction about the importance of a guiding will in managing tradition. Though the original impulse toward equality for women comes from feminism, she says:

I still would like to think that a creative pondering of the ideals of Torah Judaism might lead to the same conclusions. Thus, the central concern of the observations has to do with organic, internal changes, changes in our private Jewish lives, unmediated by society, quotas, affirmative action, and the like-- changes based on intrinsic Jewish values and brought about because the *Halakhic* way of life calls them forth.[23]

She acknowledges that *Halakhic* life has been delimiting for women, yet she is convinced that were there is rabbinic will there is *Halakhic* way. It is human will rather than *Halakhah* which has created barriers for women, and Blu Greenberg's discussion of Jewish attitudes toward divorce gives clear evidence that the will to remain faithful in religious practice need not be broken by the secular modes of existence wherein fairness and encouragement for women are to be found. She seeks ways wherein it will be possible for even Jewish women, committed to equality for women, to be aware that every sweep of their lives "should be experienced properly within the framework of a holy community."[24]

For Ellis, the dynamic between religiosity and secularity goes in the reverse direction. Greenberg seeks to manage the religious strain of Jewish existence in such a way as to satisfy the secular valuing of the equality of women, whereas Ellis seeks to free the theological tradition from its captivity to secularity. Obviously, at least from a Reform perspective, Holocaust theology did not originate in secularity. It was a powerful witness which came out of the tradition as a response to the devastation--a response which was able to see the Holocaust as more than a secular event. But, as noted previously, Ellis suspects that the critical theological edge was lost in the energy which was focused by the thought. Power, secular power, power as seen in modernity in the form of political, economic, and military strength, displaces religious and theological insight and practice. Ellis believes that it is time to move on; political solutions and revolutions to solve problems of Jewish living are not enough today. Yet, the theology which holds the day is little more than raw secularity.

To suggest that for Marc Ellis, Holocaust theology is captive to secularity is to underscore that the secularity of Holocaust theology was not willed and chosen. Jews have come to acknowledge the revelatory significance of the Holocaust, but Jews have not thoughtfully and freely chosen to combine raw secular expression of power with theological justification. On the other hand, it was in part because of the focus of attention upon the Holocaust that the acceptance of modernity's power occurred. His theory is that Holocaust theology represents Jews when they were weak and cannot speak of the people who are today becoming powerful and even oppressive. Holocaust theology presents a rationale for gaining power and cannot investigate the cost of that empowerment. Holocaust theology speaks well about struggle for human dignity in the death camps and about the question of God and Jewish survival, but it cannot speak about the ethics of a Jewish state with nuclear weapons which is expropriating land and torturing children. Ellis seeks, above all, to demonstrate the need for a theological and religious perspective upon Jewish life, yet he urges that often Holocaust theology simply does not accept that such problems and exercises of power exist. These occurrences which are "facts" to the world community are, when considered from the perspective of Holocaust thinking, "deemed outside of Jewish discourse *as if they are not happening because it is impossible that Jews would do such things.* Thus, a community that prides itself on its intelligence and knowledge is on its most crucial issue--the future of our people--profoundly ignorant."[25] Ellis believes that the reason for this weakness in Holocaust theology is that it comes from a time when Jews were weak; what is needed now is a pattern of thinking which is grounded in present realities.

Today, Jews have been empowered, and a theology adequate to the present living conditions of Jews must be able to offer directives for the exercise of enormous power. A new ethical dimension is needed if that power is to be in the service of the classical Jewish witness for justice and righteousness rather than simply a modern nation-state's need for security.

Ellis develops the idea that solidarity needs to be at the core of a Jewish theology of liberation. Jewish thinking and practice, as a people empowered and through a modern nation-state, needs at its core the pursuit of solidarity with victims of oppression, aggression, and neglect. Jews need to be attentive to the trust, partnership, and commitment which have been extended toward Israel and toward Jews by the United States of America and by christians. Behavior in Israel needs to be judged according to the adequacy of its attentiveness to these bonds of solidarity. Relationships between Israel and the government of South Africa need to be qualified by a bond of solidarity which results in support for the struggle of South African blacks. The theology which is needed can come from the Exodus and prophetic themes which are "at the heart" of Jewish tradition. "A Jewish theology of Liberation is our oldest theology, our greatest gift to the world, which has atrophied time and again, only to be rediscovered by our community and other communities around the world."[26] The solidarity generated by such thinking is more than a basis for criticism of abuses of power; it can also decrease the sense of isolation and abandonment. This understanding of solidarity for Jews restores the religious dimension with its particularity and points toward another dynamic in Jewish existence.

The third phenomenon characterizing historic Judaism is universalism facing separation. Jews have lived with the historic mission of being "a light unto the nations." This, of course, has rendered a clear sense of place in relationship to the other peoples of the earth. This particular role however, depends upon an internal unity among Jews. This means that the universalism-separation dynamic has always been lively within the Jewish tradition itself. It means further, that the place and connection for Jews in the midst of others and the togetherness of Jews among each other are interrelated. It is *as a people* that Jews have had a place in the world, and it is as this particular people that Jews have a universal bond with non-Jews. Those who are "a light unto the nations" are not to withdraw into separatist ways. They are to maintain a mode of existence in which they can acknowledge that they are a people whose identity includes active participation in the universal human community.

For Greenberg, this means being a corrective within the larger society. She sees an opportunity to help set the priorities of the women's movement by directing attention to concerns of family in face of those of career. Specifically, developing equitable possibilities for part-time as well as full-time employment can be a way to convey very effective messages about the importance of family. This would counter the "antifamily bias" which has been "subtly" communicated by the feminist movement as it has sought "equal pay for equal work for full-time jobs," but not for part time jobs. For many women the care of family is a matter of choice as well as tradition; this is especially true for Jewish women, she believes. Yet the emphasis upon full-time employment values career over family. "Thus the Jewish community, and particularly the Jewish agencies involved in employment policies, should press for decent pay for part-time jobs everywhere."[27] In addition, wherever possible, efforts could be made to restructure jobs so they could be shared and could fit part-time needs of mothers. This, she says, is a path which would not include an emphasis upon day-care center. Instead, family concerns have priority in directing social change. The aim is not to discourage full-time employment and careers for women, but to provide an option for women and relieve them from the pressure to view employment and family in opposition to each other.

Blu Greenberg also points to weakness in the popular notion of self-actualization. Her concern is to note that the ideal of self-actualization seems to include a denial that "there can be self-fulfillment in the process of giving to others." Perhaps women, especially in previous generations, have been "overly generous in their yielding of self," but any "relationship of intimacy, if it is to last, requires the surrender of some of the self-disclosing, sharing, making compromises, yielding."[28] The time, energy, sacrifice, and generosity of spirit necessary in marriage and in the parent-child relationship are the opposites of instant gratification. The stress upon self-actualization in the feminist movement needs the correction which can come from the traditions of family living which have emerged among Jews.

In these two instances, we see how Greenberg seeks to provide qualifications for the frame of social values by infusing cherished Jewish values into social constructions of the feminist movement. Perhaps her most basic correction is offered when she speaks of "the production-value system" which has been created by males through the generations. She proposes that women ought not simply step into that system and its society. Rather, "Jewish feminists must affirm the basic Jewish principle that the human being is valuable in his or her very being." In this discussion, Greenberg is speaking of her concern that the feminist movement has simply adopted and underscored the materialistic orientation of the society created by males. She urges correction of the notion that one's worth is "determined by what and how much" one produces, what kind of job one has, one's titles, one's earnings.[29] In contrast to this orientation, the universal witness which Jews must continue to make is that one's values and character are the real marks of who one is, and what value one has. In going beyond the production-value system, society can liberate both men and women for more human living.

Greenberg believes "that ultimately Judaism will emerge stronger and not weaker" as a result of the encounter with feminism.[30] She will not be satisfied, however, unless there is a *Halakhic* way to achieve the ends which have been awakened. Greenberg will not settle for a separation between the values of civil life and the values of religious life when it comes to the equality of women. Rather, this is at least one place where the bridge must be present, where the universalism of historic Judaism must be actual.

Marc Ellis provides an equally sensitive and extraordinarily bold handling of the dynamic between universalism and separation within Jewish existence. He too speaks in the imperative in making his case for relinquishment of uncritical theological support for Israel. Greenberg seeks a way beyond the guilt experienced by a Jewish woman in the face of the feminists' valuing of career over homemaking and family raising. Ellis seeks a way beyond the self-hate experienced by Jews, or allocated toward Jews who question the exercise of power in and through Israel. Ellis also seeks a way to avert allegations of Christian anti-Jewishness turned upon Christians who are critical of the behavior of Israel. He wants to find a way in which criticism of Israel does not separate Jews from one another, for this would weaken the Jewish testimony as a light unto the nations. Simultaneously, he wants to preserve and behave fairly with the universal bonds between Jews and non-Jews, especially Christians, South African Blacks, and the United States.

Ellis sees this issue in relationship to the ongoing question of Jewish identity. He says that the State of Israel must be "de-absolutized" in order to adequately address the matter of Jewish identity in the contemporary world.[31] Largely under the vision of Holocaust theology, with the Holocaust and the State of Israel at its center, the notion of the practicing Jew has been altered "from one who engages in ritual and observance of the Law to one who cherishes memory, survival, and empowerment." A Jewish theology of liberation, such as Ellis envisions, would add to this new-found identity the vigorous "critical and efficacious pursuit of justice and peace." Yet there is a serious problem of identity underlying the presence of secular Jews who are active in matters of justice while feeling estranged from "religiosity" and Orthodox Jews who contribute to injustice while feeling self-righteous about their "religiosity."[32] The problem to be addressed is that those who seek Jewish particularity and those who pursue a more universal identification have increasingly derived their identity within the context of Holocaust theology and the State of Israel.

Jews will not be able to shed this dual event in Jewish history; Jews of today will not be able to become pre-Holocaust Jews. It is necessary for Jews think about the situation now rather than as it was forty or fifty years ago. Those two important parts of Jewish history cannot be allowed to prohibit Jewish thinking from being thinking in the present. Those events which are not to be shed from the Jewish present must be reinterpreted in the present. The Holocaust and Israel cannot be allowed to draw Jews into a separatist position in the handling of power. "In both events there is, among other things, an underlying theme of solidarity with our own people as well as others who have come into solidarity with us."[33] So Holocaust and Israel urge Jews to embrace the world "with the hope that our survival is transformative for our own people and for the world." The key to fulfillment of this hope and to Jewish identity is in the handling of power.

> To celebrate our survival is important; to realize that our empowerment has come at a great cost is another thing altogether. Can we at the fortieth anniversary of the State of Israel realize that the present political and religious chauvinism can only lead to disaster? Can we argue openly that the issue of empowerment is much broader than an exclusive Jewish State and that other options, including autonomy with confederation, may be important to contemplate for the fiftieth anniversary of Israel? Can we openly articulate that, as American Jews, we can no longer ask American foreign policy to support policies that contradict the ethical heart of what it means to be Jewish?[34]

The realities of living in the nuclear age compel Jews to restore the light of universal mission to Jewish existence as the appropriate witness in living together with non-Jews.

> In order to be effective, the universal witness must overcome a fear which is "deeply imbedded in the Jewish community." It is a fear which elicits repression of insights and sympathies of the people, as well as the teachings of the tradition. No matter the extent of reform and modification needed in the tradition, Jewish people cannot afford to drive away those who are critical of some of the ways in which recently acquired Jewish empowerment is being handled. "If it is true that a totally ethical people cannot survive, it is also true that we may be in danger of being a people void of ethics," says Ellis.[35] His concern is that unless Jews discern and reassess the theology which underlies the present situation of empowerment, the Jewish presence in the world will become ever more problematic as a light to the nations.

> Israel has been considered to be "the most powerful single image of the continued working of God's power in history" and the "symbol of Jewish

faithfulness to the command to survive."[36]   Another has said "my faith, salvation, and future as a Jew are indeed bound up in large measure with the existence and survival of the Jews and the Jewish State on a portion of the Holy Land. It is only an earthly and mortal instrument but nevertheless it is real--real as a haven, real as a vibrant example of the Jewish return to history, and real as one particular expression of Judaism, and Jews trying to grapple in day-to-day terms with modernity."[37]   Yet another has been reported to have said that "Israel is a God in the Jewish community."[38]   Such statements as these point to the need for assessing the theological significance of Israel for the Jewish people.   Such statements also feed the fear of, and intensify resistance to, those who would seek to engage in a rational discussion of the place of Israel in Jewish identity and in the world today. The ironic situation seems to be that precisely the sort of discussion that is needed to brighten the universalism and its light to the nations is the sort of discussion which separates Jews from each other and so makes the universal light grow more dim. On the other hand, the converse is the case also. The absence of that open discussion about Israel seems to allow the Jews to hold together as a people, albeit a people who by their own traditional norms are not a good light to the nations.

Ellis, like Greenberg, has called for recognition of the connection between traditional values and present possibilities. Greenberg will not accept a separation between the values of civil life and the values of religious life in the matter of the equality of women. The text and the tradition must be reinterpreted in order to preserve continuity of present demand with the directive of tradition. Though Orthodoxy is a system basically resistant to change, and reinterpretation generates an openness wherein we cannot be sure where we are headed, Greenberg insists that traditional values and present possibilities can be held together. Acceptance of equality of women does not mean relinquishment of *Halakhah,* and the movement for equality of women can be enhanced by correctives found in *Halakhah.* A similar pattern is found in Ellis' proposals. Theological insights rooted in a time of powerlessness cannot be allowed to weaken the universal bonds with humanity which have characterized the tradition's understand of the place of Jews in the world. Rather, theological directives are needed which can enhance the interdependence between Jews and non-Jews. Acceptance of a modern nation-state as part of Jewish identity does not mean relinquishment of the ethical guidance which is also one of the marks of Jewish identity. Indeed, a people which knows powerlessness and victimization by the powerful is to be the bearer of a concrete solidarity with others who are victims of injustice. As in the matter of equality of women, the universal bond of Jews with non-Jews can be sustained only if there is open discussion among Jews themselves.

In both instances, the matter of empowerment is crucial. How are Jewish women to understand and exercise power equal to that of men? How are Jews to acknowledge and direct a modern nation-state when all Jews do not live in that state, yet they accept that state as in some measure definitive of who they are as Jews and as human beings? The theme of empowerment is crucial for any people whose experience has been both marginal and on the boundary. Speaking out of the experience of a people whose historic path has been just that, Greenberg and Ellis are important voices on behalf of all such people in an age which is learning to reconceive power and its uses in the service of justice and peace within the human community. There are three specific insights which deserve our attention.

First, we have our treasures in earthen vessels. To see *Halakhah* as time-bound and humanly managed seems to be a first step in acknowledging the responsibility of empowerment. For Greenberg, it is a step which has been carefully taken. In struggling to become fully a member of the community, she has participated in "a revolution which has changed the course of Jewish life in America."[39] Not only do our treasures get reappraised, but they also can be lost, broken and traded. If we accept the judgment of Lucy Dawidowicz that a woman as rabbi "undermines the very essence of Jewish tradition," then Greenberg's efforts can be viewed as contributing to the collapse.[40] If *Halakhah* is time-bound in the matter of female empowerment, then all *Halakhah* is historicized. Further, this historicized *Halakhah* is to be treasured and touched by the minds of women as well as men, and women are to do their own thinking rather than to rely on the thinking of men. Women, that is, would speak from the far edge of the margin about matters which they see as formative. Women would show ways in which the human will could manage tradition so as to address the needs of women and the new human treasures which should be in the making.

Others, of course, look at the earthen vessel from a different perspective. According to Cynthia Ozick, feminism among Jews is rooted in the Holocaust rather than in secular feminism. Because of the loss of life during the Holocaust, "every Jew will be more a Jew than ever before."[41] In the past, women have been prohibited from identifying the treasure and interpreting its value for human living. Now such endeavor must be undertaken by every Jew (and by every human creature). Ozick says that the failure of the Jewish treasure to provide justice for women is a scandal, that the Torah does not speak against the abuse of women in the world. "The relation of Torah to women calls Torah itself into question." She wants to know where in Torah is the commandment which speaks against the lessening of the humanity of women. Torah needs help, and women must give that help

This, according to Ozick, is the right motivation for women and not something drawn from the modern world.[42]

Perhaps a more direct and more radical appraisal of the human treasure is provided by Judith Plaskow. In her judgement, the plight of women is not the result of *Halakhah*; the real issue is the maleness of God. The maleness of God makes *Other* of woman just as the Otherness of woman makes maleness of God.[43] Her concern is to point at the magnitude of the required change if proper appraisals of human lives are to emerge. The value which humans see in human lives is interdependent with the way in which humans identify God. According to this view, Greenberg is trying to repair particular laws or traditions; more than this first step is needed. More even than encouraging female empowerment in the interpretation of the tradition is needed. As Susannah Heschel notes, only theology can "offer the solution to the present problem, determining the role of rabbinic tradition in contemporary Judaism and its application to the lives we lead."[44] Heschel seems to want removal of the rabbinical and denominational system together with the creation of the opportunity for each individual to do his or her own inquiry. One's relation should be with "the diversity and totality of Jewish tradition, unmediated by one of its modern forms."[45] In short, let each one of us participate in the naming of values which are to shape our existence on earth.

The second insight which emerges from the work of Greenberg and Ellis is that we must be on guard against the judgments of the captive mind. Ellis's proposal suggests the possibility that in rejecting open, critical discussion of policies in Israel, Jews are doing precisely what was done by Christians, by nations, by institutions and by governments in failing to intervene in the Nazi action against the Jews. Perhaps Jews are as much captured by the world's celebration of nationalism and its values (especially economic independence) as the world was captivated by the values of the Nazi era. If the ethos which emerged over the centuries made possible the institutionalization of the moral acceptability of the notion that Jews are evil (so that no one would interfere when efforts were made to eliminate the Jews), it could also be the case that the ethos in which Jews live today is one which has institutionalized the moral acceptability of Jews' murdering and torturing innocent Palestinians and using Christians and Americans to support the unbridled independence of Israel. We must look seriously at the question whether Jews are becoming captives of an unacceptable moral ethos. In that earlier case the ethos had led to an institutionalized expression of an underlying attitude against the Jews, whereas in the present time. We seem to be moving toward the institutionalized expression of an attitude among Jews--the world owes us a place, and we will take it at any cost. Is there something which Jews have learned from their experience at the margin and on the boundary which can correct this repetition of a earlier pattern? Ellis seems to say "yes," Jews have learned to beware the judgement of the captive mind.

Greenberg's work suggests a similar disclosure. The handling of power within Orthodoxy has shaped a disposition toward equality in power such that it is acceptable for the rabbis not to find a *Halakhic* way for that equality of power to become real. What the women's movement sees as humanly and morally unacceptable is quite satisfactory from the perspective of the traditional managers of Orthodoxy. A traditional understanding of female power simply blocks the birth of a counter attitude. What is remarkable in Blu Greenberg's work is that she is trying to continue in Orthodoxy when other Jewish women are convinced that Orthodoxy is a lost cause. Just as a "good Jew" was not possible in the mind of "a world which did nothing," so "feminist Orthodox" seems also to be impossible. Greenberg's efforts remind all of us to beware the judgments of the captive mind. What we begin to ask here we also ask in the matter of the handling of power in the setting of government policies in Israel. How does it happen that, in the course of human affairs, an ethos can emerge in which victimizing other humans is utterly acceptable?

Greenberg says that such victimization is unnoticed when the Orthodox premise is introduced, i.e. divinity and stability go together (and are virtually interchangeable), and the human will is devoid of the impetus toward change. Ellis says the victimization of human life can occur without sufficient objection so long as victims persist in seeing their suffering as special and fail to find their bond with other victims. Jewish Holocaust theology formed quickly and deeply to focus and articulate something which had germinated during preceding generations; the previous experience of Jews as a guilty and evil people was confirmed in what the Holocaust delivered. The imprisonment of the persistent victim has eyes for only one thing--how to escape. Power is the way to escape from the victim's role. That power, though, takes one into a new prison which is devoid of awareness of its own victims.

The third insight which deserves our attention is that monotheism can contribute to the making of community in a post-modern era. This seems to demand deliberation because of the possibility of religious persecutions and hatreds among and within the three monotheistic traditions. Both Greenberg and Ellis are trying to reshape religious and ethical practice. What, though, is the significance of such perspectives for a people who cannot readily identify with religion, who in large numbers do not profess belief in God, and whose identification with Jewishness is largely ethnic? "Historical rootedness, family ties, and especially communal feeling and activity (aided by occasional flare-ups of antisemitism) motivate" a Jewish identification for most Jews, according to Elliot N. Dorff. "The key is the strong sense of Jewish Peoplehood that Jews inherit, a sense that is made even stronger by its interdependence of land and governmental structure."[46]

It seems to me that Dorff is correct in saying that "the real question is how long such an ethnic Jewishness can last."[47] For how many generations can the *memories* of religious identity persist? How long will the religious endowment of others last? How long and with what efficacy can discussion of the religious and ethical dimensions of Jewish experience continue? Have the Jewish people come to a point in their history wherein the non-religious ones find little or no appeal in the issues identified and addressed by those Jews who are religious?[48]

The question is not intended to engender further consideration of the matter of Jewish unity. Rather, the question is about the relevance of religion and theology for Jewish experience and Jewish living. Religious and secular Jews are together; they were drawn together by the Holocaust. The Holocaust holds them together and makes necessary the pursuit of communal norms which can satisfy both groups of Jews. It seems obvious that a "strong sense of Jewish peoplehood" is connected with, and has its particular character because of, the Diaspora existence of Jews. It is a peoplehood which emerged without land or governmental structure. It seems equally obvious that as the issues of land and government become more important in Jewish existence, the peoplehood which came with Diaspora existence will dissipate. What bearing do religious and theological considerations have on this occurrence?

In their concern for community, solidarity and survival, Greenberg and Ellis exemplify their support for one of the two primary themes to emerge in the Jewish response to the Holocaust. As Peter Haas understands it, Jews have come to reject the modernist emphasis upon the individual in favor of service to survival and to solidarity "for their own sake" and not in order to serve race or nation: "human community is a value in its own right and is to be pursued everywhere for its own sake."[49] In this concern, we see the expression of the most fundamental post-modern theme, that of the radical interdependence of life. This means that the very Holocaust theology which Ellis questions is itself already expressing the theme which Ellis wants to uphold. My concern is not with interpretations of the Holocaust, but with directives for Jewish living in a time which stresses equality of women and Jewish negotiations concerning identity.

It seems to me that the convergence of Post-Holocaust Jewish themes with post-modern themes presents the opportunity for Jews to bear witness in the present from their centuries-old roots. The directive toward solidarity and survival for their own sakes is a contemporary rendering of the idea of human community in covenant with God. Survival and solidarity present for the Jewish people *a place to be* in the community of the world; it is a sense of place with roots in the ancient Jewish tradition; it is a place in a world which is coming to realize that it is interdependent in all its parts. The post-modern awareness presents an opportunity for the Jewish community to shed it "the world hates me" sensibility, and to be formed by the other ancient Jewish theme that "the world is one" as God is one. The people of Israel can now move toward equality for all and community with all, and the people can do this without relinquishing the ancient, ethical identity of those whose struggle is with God, and not a struggle with women or with other nations, or with the world.

Perhaps Haas is correct that the "reevaluation of the relationship between Judaism and the West is one factor in the increasing conservatism of Judaism." Such a movement blocks the will of *Halakhic* way and closes the bridge into the world of interdependence which is in the making. As Haas notes, the move "away from too-close association with Western liberal culture, combined with the pull toward Jewish survival, has moved the center of contemporary Jewish life away from accommodation with the West and toward reexamination of traditional values."[50]

This, it seems, presents the opportunity for Jewish reexamination to be undertaken with an open door to the winds of change which are active in the world wherein Jewish survival is to occur. The questions are whether the *Halakhic* way can contribute and whether the open, self-critical dialogue can prevail in a world which sorely needs equal participation by all to move toward solidarity and community. The community envisioned both by post-modern developments and by the religious deliberations of Greenberg and Ellis is a community in which differences are valued and a transcendent aim is pursued (amidst struggle for survival) by each, with all, for its own sake.

Endnotes

1. Ninian Smart, *Worldviews: Crosscultural Explorations of Human Beliefs* (New York, 1983); and *Religion and the Western Mind* (Albany, 1987), especially chapter 5.

2. Sallie McFague, *Models of God: Theology for an Ecological, Nuclear Age* (New York, 1983); and *Religion and the Western Mind* (Philadelphia, 1987), x.

3. See Susannah Heschel, ed., *On Being a Jewish Feminist* (New York, 1983), xxv; also Eugene B. Borowitz, "Freedom," in *Contemporary Jewish Religious Thought,* ed. Arthur A. Cohen and Paul Mendes-Flohr (New York, 1987), 261-267.

4. I regret that I cannot recall the source of the report on this incident.

5. Blu Greenberg, *On Women and Judaism: A View from Tradition* (Philadelphia, 1981), 36.

6. Greenberg, *On Women and Judiasm,* 5-6.

7. Greenberg, *On Women and Judiasm,* 39.

8. Greenberg, *On Women and Judiasm,* 39-40.

9. Greenberg, *On Women and Judiasm,* 39-41.

10. Greenberg, *On Women and Judiasm,* 14.

11. Marc H. Ellis, *Toward a Jewish Theology of Liberation: The Uprising and the Future* (Maryknoll, New York, 1990), 4.

12. Ellis, *Theology of Liberation,* x.

13. Ellis, *Theology of Liberation,* 111. See especially the discussion in note 1.

14. Ellis, *Theology of Liberation,* 110.

15. Ellis, *Theology of Liberation,* 111, note 2.

16. Ellis, *Theology of Liberation,* 111.

17. Borowitz, "Freedom," 266, see n. 3 above.

18. Borowitz, "Freedom," 266.

19. Ellis, *Theology of Liberation,* 142-143.

20. Ellis, *Theology of Liberation,* 40.

21. Ellis, *Theology of Liberation,* 42.

22. Ellis, *Theology of Liberation,* 42.

23. Ellis, *Theology of Liberation,* 42-43.

24. Ellis, *Theology of Liberation*, 140. The emphasis upon rabbinical will and community is strikingly similar to the thinking of Socrates as he comes to the end of his trial, hears the verdict, and while in prison, reconsiders his relationship to the law. Socrates is ready to die. His mind is clear. He does not want to follow the advice of his friend and escape to another country. Socrates imagines the laws saying to him, if you go away, "you will go away a victim of the injustice, not of the laws, but of men" (*Crito*, XVI). Translation by F.J. Church, revised by Robert D. Cumming, in *Euthyphro, Apology, Crito*. The Library of Liberal Arts (Indianapolis, 1956), 65. Greenberg notes the existence of an unmistakable pattern toward equalization in Jewish divorce law and urges that rabbis today can no longer think themselves unable to move along toward rectification. "To say that their hands are tied or that they can resolve an individual case, but cannot find a comprehensive solution is to admit that they are unworthy of the authority vested in them. Worse, it bespeaks a lack of rabbinic will to find a *halakhic* way" (Greenberg, 47).

25. Marc H. Ellis, "Theology, Politics, and Peace: A Jewish Perspective," in Theodore Runyon, ed., *Theology, Politics and Peace* (Maryknoll, New York, 1989), 94. Italics are in the original text.

26. Ellis, "Theology, Politics and Peace," 96.

27. Greenberg, *On Women and Judiasm*, 161.

28. Greenberg, *On Women and Judiasm*, 16.

29. Greenberg, *On Women and Judiasm*, 19.

30. Greenberg, *On Women and Judiasm*, 37.

31. Ellis, "Theology, Politics, and Peace," 104.

32. Ellis, *Theology of Liberation*, 118.

33. Ellis, "Theology, Politics, and Peace," 104.

34. Ellis, "Theology, Politics, and Peace," 105.

35. Ellis, *Theology of Liberation*, 36.

36. These are statements by Peter Haas characterizing the thought of Eliezer Berkovits and Emil Fackenheim. Peter J. Haas, *Mortality After Auschwitz: The Radical Challenge of the Nazi Ethic* (Philadelphia, 1988), 222-224.

37. Ben Beliak, "A Jewish Response to John Cobb: The Earth and Humanity: A Christian View," in *Three Faiths--One God: A Jewish, Christian, Muslim Encounter*, ed. John Hick and Edmund S. Meltzer (Albany, 1989), 131.

38. Ellis, *Theology of Liberation*, 90.

39. Heschel, *On Being a Jewish Feminist*, xvii, see n. 3 above.

40. Heschel, *On Being a Jewish Feminist*, xx.

41. Heschel, *On Being a Jewish Feminist*, 135.

42. Heschel, *On Being a Jewish Feminist*, 143-150.

43. Heschel, *On Being a Jewish Feminist*, 227.

44. Heschel, *On Being a Jewish Feminist*, xxxii.

45. Heschel, *On Being a Jewish Feminist*, xxxii.

46. Elliot N. Dorff, "This is My God: One Jew's Faith," in Hick and Meltzer, *Three Faiths*, see n. 37 above, 11.

47. Dorff, "This is My God.," 11.

48. Among the helpful resources for thinking about this question would be the following: Jacob Neusner, *The Way of the Torah: An Introduction to Judaism* (Belmont, CA, 1979); Abba Eban, *Heritage: Civilization and the Jews* (New York, 1984); Lucy Dawidowicz, *The Jewish Presence: Essays on Identity and History* (New York, 1978); Alfred Kazin, *A Walker in the City* (New York, 1951); Karl Marx, "On the Jewish Question," in *The Marx Engles Reader*, ed. Robert C. Tucker (New York, 1972), 24-51.

49. Haas, *Mortality After Auschwitz*, 216, see n. 36 above.

50. Haas, *Mortality After Auschwitz*, 216.

TO BE A PART OF, NOT APART FROM AMERICA:
AMERICAN REFORM JUDAISM AND SOCIAL JUSTICE

Joel D. Gereboff

"The social entity is the starting point for a religious system. Religious systems begin not in canonical writings but in the social entity. It is the social entity that defines fundamental categories and classifications. It derives, invents, integrates and shapes a discourse. Once defined, these categorical givens impart substance and define boundary to the collective life of the social entity, its worldview and its way of living. These fundamental categories impart to the system in social reality that rigor, coherence and self-evidence which make the system work."[1] These assertions by Jacob Neusner succinctly express the notion that any particular Judaism, or in Neusner's terms, any Judaic system, results in the definition of the boundaries of a social entity called Israel. Judaisms, like other religions, thus are social phenomena, acts of shared imagination. Religions are among the most significant forces shaping human history. Therefore, one of the key contributions that the study of the history of Judaism can make to the humanities is increasing the understanding of how humanity forms society, creates culture and sustains civilization.

This paper investigates the ways in which one group of Jews, the lay leadership of the American Reform movement, have defined themselves and their relationships to other people. The particular evidence that we will analyze to map these efforts at social boundary formation are the Social Action Resolutions that the Union of American Hebrew Congregations has passed at its General Assemblies.[2] These statements are an interesting group of writings. By their very nature, they reflect an attempt by Jews to establish relationships with non-Jewish groups. The fact that they are the products of the Union of *American* Hebrew Congregations (UHAC)--a group of Jews who in their own title describe themselves as Americans--makes these works a particularly useful set of data for investigating how these Jews define the parameters and overlappings of their Americanness and their Jewishness.

It is additionally significant that these writings reflect the views of lay people and not the views of a rabbinic elite. As a result, the writings allow one to investigate the history of Judaism in a manner not often accessible for earlier periods of Jewish history. In sum, our findings are meant to contribute to the field of the history of American Judaism, but also, and especially, to the history of religions, as it is pursued by scholars who draw upon the discipline of the sociology of knowledge for significant theoretical frameworks and theories. We, accordingly, shall now briefly describe some of these theories and identify their methodological implications for our analysis and interpretation of the resolutions of the UAHC.

The sociology of knowledge treats culture as socially constructed. A culture, in the words of Clifford Geertz is:

> . . . a historically transmitted pattern of meaning embodied in symbols, a system of inherited conceptions expressed in symbolic forms by means of which human beings communicate, perpetuate, and develop their knowledge about and attitudes toward life.[3]

Howard Clark Kee, a leading New Testament scholar using the insights of the sociology of knowledge, puts matters this way:

> Human knowledge is a socially shared phenomenon. Knowledge is social in nature and oriented within a community sharing convictions and assumptions.[4]

According to Kee, the interpreter of the texts of a cultural group:

> . . . must endeavor to read behind the words of a text in order to seek at the underlying and unspoken assumption of the writer. One must attempt to discern the writers implicit sense of the community and to do so with reference to the specific historic context of the writer or group.[5]

Scholars who have applied such notions to the study of early Christianity and of the Judaisms of that era, have focused on the rhetoric of the writings of those communities as a key indicator of their sense of their boundaries.[6] How a group talks about issues and the range of issues it considers, reveal much about what the group takes for granted about itself and its context. Thus the study of religion, as the study of social systems, amounts to the analysis of symbol-change. Tracing alterations in the meaning and use of symbols, for example in the denotations of terms like "Jew" and "American," allows the researcher to analyze the larger religious systems to which such words belong. That effort, in turn, brings one to the description of the social entity that expresses and legitimizes itself by means of such a system of symbols.

In our exploration of the resolutions of the UAHC, we will describe and analyze three of their features. First, we will comment upon the choice of issues that the resolutions address. We will show that over the course of more than one hundred years there have been dramatic changes in the agenda of the UAHC, particularly with regard to the relative interest of that body in matters that relate exclusively to Jews versus those pertaining to other groups as well. Second, we will investigate the tone of the resolutions. Our analysis here will indicate that, over time, the writers of these documents wrote with more resolve and in a more forceful manner when pressing for their causes. Third, and of most importance, we will look at the reasoning and the justifications offered in the resolutions for the positions that are advocated. We shall argue that the frequency of the invoking of Jewish and non-Jewish reasons to substantiate proposals drastically changes. Moreover, the meanings of the terms "Jewish," "Jew" and "Judaism," change. The relationship between such phrases and words like "American" and "human" also changes. These alterations point to significant shifts in the boundaries these lay Reform writers implicitly draw for themselves as Jews and as Americans.

Before detailing these results, we first must note some of the general features of the resolutions and several assumptions we make with regard to them in this study. Between 1874 and 1985, the UAHC approved two hundred and fifty-two resolutions relating to issues of social justice.[7] These statements served several purposes, above all expressing the official views of the Union. They were also meant as works that would shape the thinking of the members of Reform congregations. Furthermore, they served as the platform for actions to be pursued by individual Reform Jews, congregations and the movement as a whole. Finally, these documents were frequently disseminated to people outside the Reform movement, both to non-Jews and to other Jews. In light of these purposes, the texts can be read as expressions of the authors' self understanding, the understanding these writers intended for other Reform Jews, and the views that the leadership of the UAHC hoped that others would come to hold of Reform Judaism.[8]

The resolutions point to three phases in the thinking of the UAHC regarding the meaning of, and the relationship between, being Jewish and being American. In all three periods (1874-1946, 1948-1964, 1966-1985), Reform Jews saw themselves as both Jews and as Americans, but the understanding of these elements of their identities differed.

During the first period, from 1874 until the year after the conclusion of the Second World War (1946), the explicit pronouncements of these people seemed to be at some variance with what they actually appeared to think. The writers declared that they were Americans by nationality, Jewish only in terms of their religious persuasion. Because of the latter, they were deeply committed to social justice for all. The themes and the rhetoric of the resolutions, however, suggest that their authors were fairly insecure in their acceptance as Americans. They continued to show concern almost exclusively for Jews and make very few pronouncements with regard to other people. Toward the end of this period they were still are fairly hesitant to forcefully assert their Jewishness, but they identified themselves with the Jewish people.

In the second phase, from 1948 until the mid-1960s, the authors of the resolutions seemed very comfortable to be both Jews and Americans. This derived from their sense of the fundamental sameness of American and Jewish values. Both systems, above all, call for efforts to better the opportunities of disadvantaged and oppressed peoples. Even during this period however, these Reform Jews often seemed to feel a need to justify to themselves and to others their legitimacy as Americans who were also Jewish.

The mid-60s marks the beginning of the third stage in the self-understanding of Reform Jews. They now appeared to be confident that they were acceptable Americans. They continued to show a concern for non-Jews, although the focus and the basis of their efforts shifted substantially from that of the preceding period. Finally, they now sawe themselves in a serious way as connected to other Jewish people, both of the present and the past. The remainder of this paper will support these claims by interpreting the general characteristics of the resolutions of each of the periods and by citing selective examples that typify their argumentation and rhetoric.

The majority of the resolutions (50 of 78) prior to 1948 pertain to matters affecting only Jews. For the most part, those that relate to non-Jews were issued between 1919 and 1946. In fact, up until 1907, no statement of the UAHC addresses an issue involving non-Jews. Most of the resolutions on Jewish matters either calls for actions for the amelioration of the political, social or religious situation of Jews or praises non-Jewish individuals for having acted in that vein. In the early years, the UAHC was concerned about the persecution of Jews in Russia and the improvement of the condition of Jewish immigrants to America. In the 30s and 40s, the focus shifted to the policies of the Nazis towards Jews. The resolutions on matters affecting non-Jews cluster around two issues: endorsing programs for world peace (7 resolutions), and objecting to restrictions on immigration into the United States (2 resolutions). In 1941, the UAHC passed three resolutions expressing its commitment to the United States' war efforts and to democracy in general. The remainder of the resolutions reveal very limited ongoing interest in the situation of non-Jews. In 1907, the UAHC called for aid for stricken Jamaicans in Kingston. Two years later it condemned child-labor practices.

It returned to the issue of employment only in 1946 when it deplored discrimination against minority groups in matters of employment. A further statement, passed in 1935, is connected to the treatment of minorities. In it, the UAHC urged the enforcement of measures to curb lynching.

What accounts for these disproportionate interests of the UAHC? Subtle features of the rhetoric and argumentation of the resolutions, as well as some general information regarding the situation of Jews in the United States up until the late 1940s, explain these patters better than do the overt declarations of the UAHC regarding self-understanding as Jews and as Americans. Let us first turn to the explicit remarks of the UAHC on its sense of identity, and then we shall examine more closely the actual phraseology and tone of the resolutions.

Until 1937, the lay leaders of the UAHC declared that they were Americans by nationality and Jewish in religion alone.[9] The latter component of their identity gives rise to two particular commitments: a concern for the "material, mental and moral conditions"[10] of other Jews, and a universal mission of service to mankind as a whole, through the propagation of the "great and lofty moral and religious principles of Judaism."[11] When the UAHC addressed the first of these tasks, it referred to other Jews as either co-religionists or brethren. On the surface, the concern for the well-being of other Jews, the responsibility to protest oppression, and the denial of rights to other Jews, both in America and abroad, stemmed from the notion that members of the same religious community have particular obligations to each other. This way of understanding the entailments of belonging to the same religious group is not very typical for most religious communities. It seems that the leaders of the UAHC continued the practices that characterized Jews for centuries, practices grounded in the conviction that Jews are a religiously defined *people*. The Reform leaders, however, felt compelled to pursue such actions only on the basis of religious mandates, and not on the grounds of membership in the same nation. Thus, the UAHC had seemingly redefined the meaning of being Jewish. Below we shall suggest that the care expressed for other Jews also flowed from the insecurity of these American Jews regarding their acceptance as Americans.

We need to add one further point on the explicit meanings assigned to the term "Jew" by the drafters of the resolutions. In 1937, the year that the sister organization of the UAHC, the Central Conference of American Rabbis, passed the Columbus Platform, the UAHC, for the first time referred to itself as part of "the Jewish People." The members thereby explicitly redefined their relationship with other Jews. The phrase "Jewish people" appeared in a resolution urging the financial and moral support of Jews in Palestine. To quote the text itself:

> The UAHC expresses its satisfaction with the progress made by the Jewish Agency in the building up of Palestine. We see the hand of Providence in the opening of the Gates of Palestine for Jewish people. The time has now come for all Jews, irrespective of ideological differences to unite in the activities leading to the establishment of a Jewish homeland in Palestine.[12]

It is worth noting that two years earlier, in 1935, the UAHC had already endorsed the efforts of the Jewish Agency, but in that resolution called those Jews fleeing to Palestine "co-religionists."[13] In other resolutions passed between 1937 and 1946, the UAHC used the word "Jews" by itself. We can assume that the drafters took it for granted that as Jews, they belonged to the same religion and the same people. The drafters of these later resolutions, however, did not go out of their way to stress this new understanding. The data we shall introduce below suggest that the composers of those statements did not want to accentuate the fact that American Jews are related to other Jews as more than just co-religionists.

Before we take up this matter, let us briefly comment upon the second aspect of the meaning assigned to the idea of being Jewish in this period: the concern for mankind as a whole.

Declarations explicitly articulating this notion were first passed only in 1919. This late date is somewhat curious since the concept of "The Mission of Israel" was a cornerstone of the thinking of the UAHC since its inception. The founder of the UAHC, Rabbi Isaac Meyer Wise, strongly endorsed this idea, as did the Pittsburgh Platform of 1886. Interestingly, in 1919, when the UAHC explicitly declared its allegiance to the "Mission of Israel," it did so in a resolution on the centenary of the birth of Rabbi Wise. In that resolution, as well as in one from that same year calling for the creation of the special Department of Synagogue and Social Service, the UAHC professed its "dedication to the development of the Jewish religion, a great religion with a universal message for humanity." It reasserted its commitment to "the ideal to which this Union owes its being and to which it has been steadfastly devoted, namely, the promotion of the Mission of Israel, to serve mankind through the propagation of the great moral and religious principles first enunciated by our prophets."[14]

Similarly, in 1929, in a resolution that called for the creation of "The Committee on Social Justice," the UAHC defined that body as one:

> . . . designed for the pronouncement and preservation of the traditionally sympathetic attitude of Judaism toward those who are struggling for more equitable and just conditions of life in fields of industry, commerce and social relations and toward progressive efforts in the realm of industrial, economic and sociological aspects of human relationships.[15]

The commitment to non-Jews is central to the definition of Jewishness, but it is striking to see how little concern the resolutions overtly expressed for non-Jews. This reluctance can best be explained by a desire on the part of these Reform Jews to maintain a very low public profile. They were not so secure in their acceptance as Americans that they wished to be in the forefront of the pursuit of controversial policies. An analysis of the rhetoric of the resolutions passed prior to 1946, both those regarding Jews and those regarding non-Jews, and the locating of these efforts in their larger historical contexts, points to this conclusion.

One would surmise that the statements that articulate the most general principles of the UAHC would justify the proposals on the basis of Jewish teachings or principles. To the contrary, in almost all instances, the UAHC appealed to general humanitarian and ethical considerations to support its recommendations. It is not until 1935 that the phrase, "in accord with the historic Jewish" actually is cited to undergird a specific proposal.[16] The first citation of a Jewish text occurred only in one resolution, and this dates from 1946. This statement, which called for aid to the victims of war, ends with the remark that the UAHC "prays that the day may speedily come when men shall learn war no more."[17] Of note, these words appear without a notation indicating that they come from the book of Isaiah. After 1948, the UAHC frequently cited explicit biblical passages to justify and explain its positions. But up until 1946, the UAHC legitimized its directives by appealing to humanitarian values or to the national interests of America.

Let us look in more detail at the actual wording of some of these earlier resolutions in order to reinforce our assertion that prior to 1946, Reform lay people avoided highlighting their uniqueness as Jews.

Several favorite phrases conveyed the commitment of the drafters to general humanitarian values. The writers often referred to the oppression and suffering of their co-religionists. They commented on the denial of their civil and religious rights. They noted how the brutal treatment of Jews contradicted the enlightened tendencies of the modern era and how these deeds were contrary to the great mission and values of the United States. Remarks of this sort do show an unwillingness to advocate policies on explicitly Jewish grounds, particularly those policies beneficial to Jews. However, they do not, by themselves, suggest any hesitancy on the part of the leaders of the UAHC to press their case for their concerns.

Other phrases that appear quite commonly in these texts do point to the conclusion that these Jews cowered before non-Jews. For example, in a number of instances the authors go out of their way to underscore that aiding Jews will in the end, benefit the United States. In a proposal calling for resettling Jewish immigrants to the western parts of the United States, the authors claimed that such a policy would reduce "congestion in the East that breeds immorality and crime and that perpetuates undesirable exclusiveness."[18]   Even more telling is the frequent declaration that the authors of the texts are "loyal Americans."[19]   On several occasions the drafters feel compelled to introduce the caveat that the proposed policies should be pursued "so long as they are not incompatible with public interests."[20]

Most indicative of the insecurity of these writers are remarks that read like an obsequious expression of gratitude to others for the help they have given to Jews.[21] Such statements are especially striking when they appear in resolutions from the 40s. The actual historical record shows something less than an aggressive endorsement of Jewish causes. In these same resolutions the UAHC also went out of its way to state that it was not only concerned for the Jews in Germany but considerate of all those who suffer.

It seems to me, that these authors felt constrained to note that their concern for fellow Jews is never at the expense of their broader, universalistic commitments. A series of resolutions beginning in 1933 and running to 1946 on the situation of the Jews under Nazi control point to these conclusions.

In the opening paragraph of a resolution from 1933, the UAHC declared that "their hearts go out in this hour of trial to our brethren who are undergoing unspeakable suffering in Germany." The paragraph continues by noting, among other things, "the exclusion of German Jews from participation in the common life of the country in which they have taken a notable part for generations." The next paragraph immediately switches matters when its authors state: "We are highly gratified that many Christians of this and other countries, and numerous secular and professional bodies, have nobly expressed their condemnation of the unjust actions of the constituted authorities of Germany."   The authors also noted that they "are gratified that the representatives in both Houses of Congress have voiced the indignation of the American people regardless of race or creed."[22]

Two years later the UAHC, along with passing a resolution urging the non-involvement of the U.S. in case of war, returned to the issue of Jews in Germany. The statement notes that "the unspeakable suffering in Germany has continued." It goes on to state that they must return to the subject and "avow our steadfast purpose." The next remarks, however, are:

> We commend the manifestation of a helpful official attitude and
> renew our grateful acknowledgment of Jewish and non-Jewish
> support. As loyal Americans we are mindful of the problems
> which confront those who must determine our national policy,
> but we call upon the enlightened public of a right thinking, right
> feeling world to condemn and continue to combat, as a blight
> upon civilization, the barbarity that seeks to deny to worthy
> Jews all that is cherished in life.[23]

Resolutions from the time of the American entry into the war continue to present the case for the Jews in a less than demanding manner.   For example, in 1941 the UAHC declared that: "Since Judaism emphasizes the supreme worth of the individual and exalts the democratic way of life, that we again affirm our opposition to all forms of government which deny these religious, humanitarian ideas.   These include communism, nazism and fascism."[24] The UAHC felt the need to state in a second resolution from that year that it "give[s] maximum support to all those who rise in defense of embattled democracy."[25]   Most interesting is a third resolution from 1941. In it the writers noted their "profound sympathy for the victims, *both Jewish and non-Jewish,* of the ravages of war, and with all who are denied their elemental human rights by aggressor nations"[26] (emphasis added).   Even in 1943, and again in 1946, at a time when the Nazi atrocities were already well known, the UAHC seemed uncomfortable at singling out Jewish victims and also appeared to bend over backwards to thank others for their assistance.   In one resolution from 1943 it declared that "while the Four Freedoms must be applied to all persons of whatever faith, the UAHC is deeply concerned with the fate of Jews who are suffering special hardships."[27]   A second statement from 1943 begins with the words:

> Of all the sufferers at the hands of the enemies of civilization,
> Jews have met with the cruelest fate. Hundreds of thousands of

them have already been massacred and millions more face imminent annihilation.

Before the authors' call for "prompt and resolute action to avert the extinction of the European Jewish communities," they inserted the following remarks:

> We have been profoundly moved by the universal outpouring of sympathy for our martyrs and by the moral indignation which have been expressed by all free peoples of the world. We are deeply grateful for these evidences of compassion and human solidarity.[28]

It is apparent that thanks must be offered for an effort, (which we now know was far from extensive), before the authors were willing to call for a campaign to avert the annihilation of Jews.

The resolution of the UAHC from 1946 on the victims of war repeats the above themes. It opens with the declaration: "Because we worship a universal God we are concerned with the suffering and injustices of all men everywhere. We are mindful of the large number of displaced persons and suffering people of many nations and of all faiths." It is only in the second paragraph of this document that its authors declared, "We cannot adequately express our sense of profound grief over the calamity and tragedy which has annihilated some six million European Jews." In the very next sentence. however, the authors stated, "We are appreciative of the sympathies of men of good will everywhere." After calling upon the British to abrogate the White Paper and to make available Palestine for the settlement of Jewish homeless, the authors repeat their gratitude for the efforts of non-Jews. They assert, "We commend our Christian brethren, speaking recently through the World Council of Protestant Churches, for their forthright condemnation of anti-semitism."[29]

Our detailed examination of the resolutions from the years 1874-1946 reveals a pattern suggestive of the defensiveness of their authors regarding their status as Americans. This lack of certainty, one would argue, also accounts for the record of the UAHC, in the period prior to 1948, on matters of social justice. Other scholars who have commented upon the activity of the Reform movement before 1946 have noted that, even in those instances in which any of the constituent bodies of the Reform movement took a stand on matters of social justice, other American groups, for example, progressivist politicians or the Federal Council of Churches, had already endorsed those positions.[30]

Recent work on anti-semitism in American, well summarized in Leonard Dinnerstein's book, *Uneasy at Home,* argues that Jews in America have always been overly concerned about anti-semitism and have frequently been victims of it. A typical response by Jews to these phenomena has been the attempt to keep a low profile. Dinnerstein documents this well, especially in the case of Southern Jews.[31] The tenor of the UAHC resolutions, as well as the range of issues upon which it was willing to take an explicit stance, was consistent with this pattern of behavior of American Jews.

In summary, the leaders of the UAHC, until the end of the first third of the twentieth century, thought of themselves as loyal Americans and as Jews in a religious sense alone. They, however, were not very confident that they were looked upon in this way by their non-Jewish neighbors. They did not even want to highlight particular Jewish reasons as justifications for their proposals. They were willing to speak on matters that are like "mom and apple pie" issues. They needed to underscore continually, that even when they showed a concern for Jews, it was because of humanitarian or American considerations. Even after they had gone on record asserting that they were part of the Jewish people, they did not subsequently highlight this element of their self-understanding. It is finally important to note, that as one would expect, the lay leaders of the UAHC seemed far more reserved than did the rabbinic leaders of the Reform movement. The Central Conference of American Rabbis, for example, already in the 1920s expressed a far more activist concern on matters of social justice. Numerous resolutions were adopted by the CCAR on a whole host of practices relating to social justice. Reform rabbis also were more vociferous in their support of Zionism. On some occasion the two organizations within the Reform movement came into conflict regarding their views of issues of social justice.[32] These divergent positions, I would suggest, stem from the slightly different definitions each gave to their being Americans and Jews. Beginning in 1948 the UAHC started to move closer to the stance of the CCAR, and we have claimed that a second phase in the thinking of the UAHC can be dated from that year.

1948, the year of the creation of the state of Israel, was also the first year in which resolutions were brought to the General Assembly after the formation of the Joint Commission on Social Action of the CCAR and the UAHC. The charge of this commission was "to suggest to affiliated congregations ways and means of applying and implementing the prophetic teachings of Judaisms." A full time director was also appointed to head the Joint Commission. Some aspects of the resolutions of the UAHC from 1948 onwards are attributable, to a degree, to these institutional changes. The experiences of World War II and the creation of the State of Israel also played some role in shaping the activities of the Union. We will suggest, however, that it was not until the mid-60s, the date we have chosen to mark the end of the second phase in the history of the UAHC's involvement with social justice, that these two events came to have a significant impact on the drafting of resolutions. It was, rather, some broader developments within American society in general that contributed most to the agenda and the tone of the statements of the UAHC between 1948 and 1965.

The central idea conveyed by the resolutions is the total compatibility of being a Jew and an American. Jews and Americans subscribe to the same basic ethical values; Jews in fact originated these values. Jews, accordingly, can take an active part is pursuing matters of social justice, for in doing so, they are serving both Jewish and American ideals. The resolutions of the UAHC, in short, seem fully consistent with Will Herbergs's characterization, in *Protestant, Catholic and Jew,* of the nature of religious identification in America in the 1950s.

Sixty of the resolutions passed between 1948 and 1965 pertain to non-Jews, while only twenty-four, just over one-quarter, deal with matters directly affecting Jews alone. Both groups of texts focus upon certain issues. Nearly one-third of those on policies affecting non-Jews, seventeen of the sixty, support efforts in behalf of the civil rights of minorities, blacks in particular. Another key concern of the UAHC in this period was the pursuit of peace and the control of arms. Eleven resolutions relate to this matter. Three other issues repeatedly draw the attention of the UAHC. Six pronouncements call for the government to respect free speech, even when this might impinge upon national security. Five resolutions endorse upholding the separation of church and state; four pertain to immigration policies. All other issues of social justice are the topics of only one resolution. These include pronouncements on birth control, divorce, population control, education, ecology, the aged, capital punishment, labor relations and world hunger. This agendum itself suggests a broadened understanding of the matters that fall under the category of social justice. It also indicates a willingness on the part of the UAHC to take a stand on such matters.

The UAHC in general supported fairly strongly a liberal understanding of political, civil and economic rights, and seemed eager to insure their extension to all Americans. It was also in favor of a liberal immigration policy. These positions can of course be interpreted as flowing not only from the values to which these Jews subscribed, but also from their own self-interest as Jews. The argumentation in the resolutions, however, never phrased the endorsements in terms of Jewish self-interest. This, as we shall see, is in contrast to the position of the UAHC in the period after 1965. Another basic commitment of the leaders of the UAHC in the period between 1948 and 1965 was to the role of the federal government as the insurer of civil rights. The federal government, or at least a component of it, was seen as the natural ally of the UAHC, and the organization looked to Washington to promote the interests of all Americans. On the whole, the UAHC positioned itself on the left side of the American political spectrum, but not in an extreme way. While the UAHC was now willing to stake out its positions more forcefully than before, it did not, in general, adopt radical proposals that other "mainline" groups in America would find objectionable.

During most of this second period, the UAHC justified its resolutions by appealing to the basic values of America, the role America plays in the world, and the American dream. These core American values were, according to our authors, fully consonant with the highest traditions of Judaism. This conviction was best conveyed by what can be treated as the charter of the Commission on Social Action which was adopted in 1955, "The Statement of Basic Principles on the Synagogue and Social Action."[33] It states:

> Judaism gave to the world the concept of the sanctity and dignity of the individual. All men are equal in that they are created in the image of God.

The formulators of the text supported this claim with an appeal to Num. 15:16: "One law and one ordinance shall be both for you and for the stranger that so journeth with you." This text also asserts that "respect for the civil rights of all men is each man's duty to God. We are challenged by our religion to support the basic human rights of every one." This last conviction, according to the authors, derives from the Talmudic statement, "What is hateful unto thee, do not do unto thy neighbor." In light of these Jewish teachings, the authors concluded this paragraph of their statement of principles by asserting:

> As Jews and as Americans dedicated to the democratic tradition, we are impelled to join with our fellows in overcoming bigotry and prejudice, in seeking through education and legislation the elimination of discrimination and segregation because of race, religion and national origin, in demanding for ourselves and for all other Americans equality of opportunity in work, home, health and education.

This one paragraph, which I have quoted in full, reveals the basic posture and thinking of the UAHC during the second period. The authors saw themselves as Americans and as Jews. Phrases of this sort appear in a number of documents from this era. A second theme found in the above remarks is the claim that Jews are the fellow citizens of other Americans who support policies for social justice. In a number of texts the authors appeal to this claim. They stated, for example, in a document on racial justice in 1963 that: "Cognizant of the failure of our nation to achieve full and equal rights for all its citizens, *and recognizing the special potential of religious groups to lead in the correction of this failure,* we hail the National Conference on Religion and Race" (emphasis added).[34] They further reported at that conference, that: "for the first time in our nations history, ranking representatives of the countries major religions bodies, including the UAHC and the CCAR, met to confront the issue of race and to bring to bear upon it the religious principles of their denominations." The tone of these and other remarks in the resolutions passed between 1948 and 1965 indicated that the UAHC saw itself now as one among equals. No longer do we find the almost sniveling expressions of gratitude and platitudes bestowed upon others, like those in resolutions prior to 1948.

The conviction that Reform Jews are equal partners in the pursuit of the American dream is revealed as well by the frequent citation of Jewish teachings, including explicit biblical texts, as support for the positions of the UAHC. Numerous resolutions open with phrases like, "Judaism teaches," or "Jewish tradition conceives of." The citation of biblical texts was an additional means for conveying the synonymous nature of the basic teachings of Judaism and other American religious groups. Infrequent references to *rabbinic* sources, similarly, underscored the compatibility of Jewish and American values. The Religious Action Center, created in Washington in 1959 in order to effectuate the religious aims of the UAHC, is consistent with this new self-understanding. The resolution of 1961, detailing the goals of the Center, contains the lines:

> Many Christian groups, both Protestant and Roman Catholic, have long maintained social action offices in the nation's capital. These bodies have hailed the establishment of our center as an opportunity to consult and cooperate in Washington with their counterparts in the Jewish religious agencies on the great moral issues which face our nation and the world.[35]

The UAHC thus saw itself as the equal partner of other mainline religious groups who were dedicated to the realization of the American dream for all members of that society.

The paragraph we cited above from the 1954 "Statement of Basic Principles" includes a phrase (that appears in a number of resolutions from this second period) which points to a third component of the thinking of the UAHC at this time. The quoted paragraph opens with the words, "Judaism gave to the world the concept . . ." This expression suggests that, in order to legitimize to themselves the necessity of the continuation of the Jews as a separate group, these authors had to note apologetically that Judaism was the first religion to subscribe to enlightened, democratic values. Another feature of the texts that suggests an attempt both at identifying with other mainline groups and at maintaining a distinction between Jews and them is the avoidance of the term "Judeo-Christian." I assume the phrase is consciously not used, for it appears in only one of all the resolutions passed by the UAHC, in a statement from 1959 advocating non-segregated housing.[36] The UAHC, in this period of interfaith cooperation, did not wish to collapse Judaism into Christianity. Some distinctions between the two must remain. What most distinguishes Jews from Christians are the facts that Jews were the first to advance the great and lofty moral principles of mankind, and the concern Jews have for other Jews. But in the statements from this second period, the leaders of the UAHC were generally not yet willing to appeal to the second of these features distinctive to Jews.

An examination of the resolutions from 1948-65 on matters pertaining only to Jews also points to this conclusion. In the texts at hand there is virtually no reference to the idea of Jewish peoplehood. This is interesting in light of the endorsement of this idea by the UAHC in 1937. Even after 1948, the lay leaders were not yet fully comfortable with the claim that Jews, as a group, have no need for a special justification for their ongoing existence. Only in the mid-60s, the years we have chosen as the concluding dates for this second period, do we see, for the first time, appeals to the idea of the self-validating legitimacy of the Jewish people and to the notion that Jews--because they are members of that people--have obligations to help one another and to work together for the unity and survival of the Jewish people.

Between 1948 and 1965, the UAHC focused upon four matters effecting Jews. The first of these matters, liberalizing immigration laws, was the topic of two resolutions, one in 1948 and one in 1953. In both cases there was not even any mention of the fact that the authors endorsed these measures so that Jews might be admitted more easily to the United States. The style of these two resolutions thus is similar to that of many of the pronouncements from the previous period. The one significant difference is that the proposal from 1953 does open with the words, typical of this era: "The highest traditions of Jewish and American life affirm the moral worth of every man."[37]   Concern for Israel and concern for Jews in the Soviet Union, the second and third topics on Jewish matters, were each the subject of four resolutions. The interest of the UAHC in these subjects, and its willingness to work on them with other Jewish groups increased during this period. The positions of the UAHC on these topics also became more forceful and demanding as the years progress. Several examples provide evidence of these patterns.

The first statement of the UAHC on the State of Israel dates from as late as 1955--seven years and three meetings of the UAHC General Assembly after the establishment of that country. The authors in that statement express their gratitude to the government of the United States, call upon it to exercise its most earnest efforts to bring about a permanent peace between the Arab states and Israel, and "resolve that the United States do nothing to jeopardize the government of Israel or weaken its position as a bulwark of democracy in the Near East."[38]   In a second resolution on Israel from that year, the UAHC restates "their sense of moral and spiritual solidarity with and tangible support of our [their brethren] in the historic land of Israel."[39]

Two years later, in 1957, following the Suez Crisis, the UAHC issued two new statements on the Middle East. The statements, again, have a moderate tone. In the first of these, a resolution on the admission of Egyptian Jewish Refugees into the U.S., the authors began by asserting: "We feel constrained to express our deep disappointment over the decisions of the Administration not to admit to the United States a fair number of refugees from Egyptian persecution."[40]   They go on to note that "this indifference to the tragic plight of innocent victims of Nasser's inhumanity stands in sharp contrast to the prompt and generous succor offered to those who fled the Communist tyranny in Hungary."   The authors then contrast the actions of the U.S. with those of the Canadian government, and ended by urgently requesting the President to reconsider the decision. The tone of this resolution is more forceful and lacks the apologetic strains found in documents from the era of the Second World War. This resolution, however, still does not make strong demands; for example, it does not appeal to the failure to rescue Jewish refugees during the period of the Second World War as the grounds for the requested assistance.

The second resolution from 1957 on Israel, one that refutes the accusations of the American Council for Judaism, is also instructive regarding the self-understanding of the leaders of the UAHC. In that document, the UAHC claims that the American Council "misrepresents historical Judaism, as well as what it calls classical Reform Judaism."[41] The writers then simply state, "There is no antithesis between Judaism as a religion and Jews as a people." They also remark that, "The Jews of the United States and Canada are properly interested in and concerned for the State of Israel without, in the slightest degree, diminishing their abiding loyalty to their respective countries." The UAHC felt no need to defend or explain these statements. This silence can be taken to indicate, that in the UAHC opinion, it was now self-evident that Jews were both a people and a religious community. The growth of the self-confidence of these Jews is best illustrated by their resolution from 1965 on the Middle East. In it they noted the danger of new aggression in the Middle East and then state, "They believe firm measures *must be taken* by our government to halt the drift toward a new outbreak of armed hostilities" (emphasis added).[42] It is also worth observing that the authors first make their demands upon the Administration and only then go on to express their gratitude to Congress for its support. It seems that these Jews, in 1965, did not feel the need to grovel before governmental authorities before urging actions.

The various resolutions of the UAHC on the matter of Soviet Jewry also reflected the change in attitude and self-understanding of the leaders of that group. The first statement on this issue, passed in 1959, was similar in tone to earlier pronouncements protesting the treatment of Jews in foreign lands. It states simply that, "The UAHC has traditionally expressed its deep concern for the welfare of our brethren throughout the world."[43] As a result, they "request the State Department to protest through proper channels the denial of equal rights and privileges to Jews in the Soviet Union." Four years later, in 1963, the UAHC returned to the matter of Soviet Jewry. The resolution from that year signaled some new departures that are portentous of the kind of resolutions that would follow in the period from 1967 onwards. It opens with the remarks, "American Jewry can no longer ignore the impending spiritual extermination of the Jewish community of the USSR."[44] The writers then note that the approach of quiet diplomacy had failed. An expression that had not been used in previous UAHC documents appears: "The commandment of *pidyon shevuyim,* the redemption of the captives, is a religious imperative which we can ignore only at the perils of our souls." Classifying Judaism as a religion of commandments and using Hebrew words were novel departures for the UAHC. These innovations would become typical features of the wording of UAHC-resolutions in the 70s and 80s.

Also noteworthy in this resolution was the remark that the UAHC should "initiate or cooperate fully in an effort to bring all of the organizational elements of the American Jewish community to a common table." This call for unified action on the part of American Jews had an urgency to it that it was missing in earlier resolutions on inter-organizational cooperation. It was true that in 1955 the UAHC had endorsed working with NACRAC "in recognition of the historic solidarity of the House of Israel."[45] But that document did not see closer coordination between agencies as a critical need. The text on Soviet Jewry from 1965 did so, and was typical of later views of the UAHC. From that time forward, the UAHC had no compunctions about potential negative consequences that might result from combined public activities of American Jewish organizations.

The UAHC, in fact, was strongly supportive of such unified efforts. This is evident from the resolution of 1965 that urged the strengthening of the coordinating bodies of the American Jewish community, including the President's Conference. The UAHC, in a statement on this matter, endorsed the recommendation of the President's Conference that proposed "the sphere of interest and involvement [of that body] extend to both national and international issues of Jewish concern affecting the well-being of fellow Jews throughout the world."[46] Jewish unity and unified public, Jewish actions were welcomed now by the leaders of the Reform movement. They had come to see themselves as part of the people of Israel, as members of religiously defined people, that spokes in its own idiom and that had nationalistic interests.

Because these Jews had no doubts about their status as Americans, they were willing to press and protest for their demands. These characteristics would appear far more frequently in the resolutions from 1967 onwards. In those texts, a phrase that appeared for the first time in a 1965 UAHC resolution on discrimination in housing would become a key expression. In the resolution on housing, the authors explained their view by remarking, "Jewish history has a special sensitivity to the horror of the ghetto."[47] By the use of this statement, the UAHC indicated that the values and sensitivities Jews hold derive not only from religious teachings, from the words of the prophets, but also from the historical experience of Jews. To say this, the leaders of the UAHC now took it for granted (contrary to what they had claimed in 1919), that Jews were in fact "bound together in the past and present by political ties and by common cultural aims that are not incidental to the dominant purpose to which Israel has been consciously dedicated from the beginning, namely the development of the Jewish religion."[48] By 1965 the UAHC thought of Jews as a people in more than a religious sense, and, to a degree, the actions that Jews should pursue could be deduced from the past history of their common ancestors. Let us now look more carefully at the resolutions from 1967 and observe the greater frequency of this self-understanding.

As we have noted, the statements from the most recent period emerge from Jews who are fully confident of their acceptance as Americans and who identify themselves as members of a historic, international religious, ethnic, national group. This latter component of their identity makes significant demands upon Jews and, for no reason beyond that identification with the Jewish people, calls for actions on behalf of other Jews. From 1967 and forward, the leaders of the UAHC place a great deal of emphasis on their needs *as Jews*. This is indicated by both the range of topics and the rhetoric of the resolutions from this era. Nearly 40% of the pronouncements of the UAHC after 1967 relate to matters directly affecting Jews alone. While this means that sixty percent of this proposals still pertain to other peoples and groups, the increase in the number of statements on Jews indicates a significant shift in the priorities of the UAHC. As we shall see, there are, moreover, important differences in the agenda of the UAHC of the different eras, on matters relating to non-Jews.

In this most recent period, the Jewish agendum of the UAHC focuses upon issues affecting the survival of Jews and the Jewish people more broadly. Over twenty resolutions pertain to the State of Israel. Many call for ongoing support by Jews and by the government of the United States. Others deal with the status of Reform Jews in Israel, the roles of Reform rabbis and synagogues in particular. These statements often stress the need to maintain the unity of the Jewish people. The well-being of *klal yisrael,* (a phrase that appears a number of times in these most recent documents) is a matter of concern for all Jews. The self-assurance of these writers regarding their status and responsibilities as members of the people of Israel is revealed by their growing willingness to challenge the policies of the State of Israel. The basic conviction of the UAHC is that Jews form one people, but are pluralistic in their religious and political views.

The conditions of Soviet Jewry is the other distinctively Jewish matter that continues as a focus of the UAHC during the period between 1967 and 1985. Resolutions call for the equal treatment of Soviet Jews and for their right to emigrate from the Soviet Union. The UAHC, in this period, addresses, as well, the situation of two other groups of Jews, those in Arab land and those in Ethiopia. In both cases the UAHC seeks to alleviate their deplorable conditions and "to bring them home to Israel."[49]

The rhetoric of these resolutions on Jewish matters suggests that the writers see their belonging to the Jewish *people* as a central component of their identities. It also suggests that the UAHC is preoccupied, to an extent, with the survival of the Jewish people in general, and not merely with the well-being and rights of individual Jews. The composers of these newest resolutions speak, for example, of the "eternal ties that bind Jews together as a community."[50] They claim that it is a *mitzvah* to work for "the continued safe and creative existence of the Jewish people."[51] This last remark is typical for this period in that it reflects the tendency to think of Judaism as a religion that gives rise to obligations, to commandments, incumbent upon Jews, that exceed ethical teachings. The use of Hebrew words, and explicit references to classical Jewish texts as justifications occur in a significant number of resolutions. Furthermore, these documents employ phrases like "historic Jewish destiny," "the drama of Jewish history," and "Jewish people"--all of which indicate that the actions Jews ought to follow derive both from religious texts and from the actual events that comprise the historical experience of the Jewish people. Such phrases appear in texts directed at non-Jews, as well as in those speaking only to Jews. They communicate to non-Jews that even gentile endeavors on behalf of Jews should be consistent with the self-understanding of the latter group.

Now it is true that the writers do appeal sometimes to American values, American political interests, and general humanitarian values as reasons for non-Jewish support of causes affecting Jews alone. But such considerations do not appear with the same degree of frequency as they do in texts from earlier periods. In a similar vein, the authors of only three of the most recent texts go out of their way to thank non-Jews for their help in supporting Jewish interests. In sum, the UAHC from 1967 onwards consists of individuals who proudly affirm their identification with the larger Jewish community and are also fully at home in America. Let us now look, in more detail, at how these Jews define themselves as Americans.

Many of the rhetorical features just noted appear in the resolutions on matters affecting non-Jews. The authors, even when addressing such issues, often open by appealing to Jewish values and teachings. These texts, in addition to employing terms like "prophetic tradition" and "teachings of Judaism" invoke the idea that Jews are a people with a particular history. They speak of the insights of Jewish tradition, the lessons of Jewish experience and the values of Judaism. Jewish religious and historical experience yields commandments, obligations and *mitzvot*. Biblical texts appear frequently in these statements on matters dealing with non-Jews. At the same time, the authors do not often need to note explicitly their allegiance to America. They take their loyalty for granted. As Jews, they see themselves as having every right to make demands of the American people. Now it is true that these documents do cite frequently American and humanitarian considerations as the bases for their proposals. This, however, should not be of surprise. It is understandable that when lobbying Americans, Reform Jews would attempt to convince them on the basis of ideals and laws to which Americans subscribe. The wording of the texts, however, do not give primacy to such considerations. Their phrasing, on the contrary, suggests, but no longer needs to state overtly, that their authors see a significant degree of agreement between their American and their Jewish identities. The drafters can invoke freely, and without apologetic overtones, both kinds of factors as the grounds for their positions.

The way in which the composers of these text refer to the support given by non-Jews to Jews can serve as an example of this new style of rhetoric. Writers of proposals in earlier periods often seemed to appeal to such endorsements in order to legitimize the involvement of Jews in the issues under discussion. The earlier texts did not wish to highlight that Jews were in the forefront of the pursuit of many causes. In the most recent proposals, references to the views of other groups are more incidental, that is, these pronouncements tend merely to report that other groups happen to agree with the UAHC on the issue at hand. The UAHC seems happy to form coalitions with other groups, but it does not appear to limit its efforts when such common purpose cannot be achieved.

A further feature of the rhetoric of the proposals on non-Jewish matters that points to the emergent self-confidence of the UAHC is the overt reference to Jewish self-interests. For example, in a resolution from 1971 on the problem of poverty in the United States, the authors note that there are also a sizable number of poor Jews. Federal anti-poverty programs thus serve Jews and non-Jews.[52] Even more telling of the new significance these authors ascribe to the self-interests of Jews are the explicit declarations of these interests in the resolutions. In a resolution from 1981 on right wing extremism the authors assert, "They see these developments as a threat to the future of American life, to a democratic society, to Jewish values and to the security of American Jewry."[53] This willingness to note explicitly how the adoption of a policy, that largely deals with non-Jews, also benefits Jews is a dramatic change in the thinking and argumentation of Reform leaders. We argued above that, in earlier times, when the UAHC advocated policies because of the concern for Jews, they avoided references to these Jewish interests and instead cited American and humanitarian considerations. After 1967, the era of ethnic acceptability in America, Reform Jews are willing, perhaps even eager, to be far more assertive of their uniquely Jewish concerns.

A brief review of the range of issues effecting non-Jews that the UAHC addressed between 1967 and 1985 also indicates shifts in the self-understanding of the leaders of this group. The UAHC passed proposals on a wide range of issues during these years. Numerous matters were taken up that were previously not considered, and at the same time, some earlier priorities were downplayed. These developments point to alterations in the thinking of the UAHC regarding identification with other groups. The UAHC between 67 and 85 continued to be interested in matters of peace and limitations on armaments, especially nuclear weapons. Concern for social justice now encompasses the rights of groups hitherto not discussed. Resolutions now address the needs and rights of women, "boat-people," hispanic-Americans, Native-Americans, central-Americans, Japanese-Americans, homosexuals and Palestinians. On the other hand, the interest in the civil rights of blacks diminished substantially during the 70s and 80s. This was reflective of the growing rift between blacks and Jews in America. Similarly, the commitment to improving interfaith relations also decreased. Already in 1969, two years after the Six Day War, the UAHC remarked, "We have reached a new turning point in American interreligious relations. Some affected by events subsequent to the Six Day War now counsel retreat and withdrawal from Christian-Jewish involvement."[54] The proposal under review ends by "urging that a special committee be approved, and in conjunction with the CCAR, immediately undertake a *searching* reexamination of our present interfaith structure and program" (emphasis added).

One might argue that this call for reassessment in the area of interfaith relations, this call, because of Jewish self-concern and pride, for a realignment of the relationships between Jews and others, points to some important changes in the dedication of the UAHC to social justice. This conclusion is supported by what can be interpreted as the lack of persistent interest by the UAHC in most matters of social justice that do not deal with Jews. While the UAHC did pass resolutions between 1967 and 1985 on a broad range of topics, it generally addressed each matter only once. Nothing comparable to the intense commitment, in the 60s, to the civil rights of blacks is apparent in these more recent documents. The concern of these writers for their own well-being as Jews, seems to play a far greater role in the shaping of their agenda. They make no apologies for this. Their loyalty to America is not even raised. In fact, the willingness of these authors to challenge forcefully the actions of the American government increases in this period. This development underscores the above conclusions.

Not only are the writers of the most recent resolutions unabashed in their criticisms of American policies on such matters as Central America and nuclear weapons, but, on at least two occasions, they gave limited endorsement to disobeying federal law.   In 1967, in a paper on selective service, they noted, "It is possible under unusual circumstances for an individual to find himself compelled by conscience to reject the demands of a human law which, to the individual in question, conflicts with the demands made upon him by a higher law."[55] The authors underscodre the validity of their position by noting that "many of the greatest prophets and rabbis are revered precisely because they placed the imperatives of conscience above the dictates of the state."   In 1985, the last year of this third period, in a pronouncements endorsing the providing of sanctuary to Central American refugees, the UAHC again legitimized the disobedience of the policies of the Administration.   In this instance, the text cites the actions of the prophet Nathan as an example of a person who "confronted a state wielding its power unjustly and abusively."[56] Now it is true that on several occasions, in policy statements on Jewish vigilantism and on religious deprogramming, the UAHC, during these years condemned breaking laws, even when done to aid Jews. These last two texts, however, are not particularly strong in tone and do not reflect any defensiveness on the part of these authors regarding their status as Americans.   The invoking of Jewish considerations as the reasons for disregarding American law, as occurs in the two noted texts, is a dramatic indication of the shift in the self-understanding of these American Jews. They had moved from being a group, who, even when interested in the desperate situation of Jews, avoided appeals to Jewish texts and convictions, and instead humbly requested the help of others on humanitarian grounds, to people, who because of both their historic experience and their religious values assertively called for non-Jews to alter their treatments of both Jews and non-Jews.

Leonard Fein, in his recent book on American Jews, *Where Are We,* opens his chapter on the tension Jews experience between their concerns for universalism and particularism with the observations:

Each generation finds its own formulas for the expression of Jewish particularism. *Landsmanschaft* and lobby, language and cuisine, neighborhood and synagogue, all these and more offer opportunities and reinforcement for the expression of the distinctive mores that define the community. They are among the ways in which boundaries are drawn, among the devices that enable us to know who stands within the community, who outside.[57]

Our exploration of the resolutions on social justice of the Union of American Hebrew Congregations adds another chapter to the understanding of the ongoing drama of the efforts of Jews to work out the sociological and ideational boundaries of their collective lives.

Endnotes

1. J. Neusner, "'Israel': Judaism and Its Social Metaphors," *Journal of the American Academy of Religion* 55 (1987): 331-33.

2. In order to base our discussion on the identical type of evidence, we omit resolutions passed either by the Board of Trustees or by the Executive Committee of the UAHC. It is possible that had such statements been submitted to the wide range of laypeople attending General Assemblies, they might not have been passed by that body.

3. C. Geertz, *The Interpretation of Cultures* (NY, 1989), 89.

4. H. Kee, *Knowing the Truth. A Sociological Approach to New Testament Interpretation* (NY, 1989), 6.

5. Kee, *Knowing the Truth*, 75.

6. In addition to the works of Neusner and Kee, see among others: W. Meeks, *The First Urban Christians*. The Social World of the Apostle Paul (New Haven, 1988); J. Lightstone, *Society, the Sacred, and Scripture in Ancient Judaism. A Society of Knowledge* (Waterloo, IA, 1988); and Segal. J. Neusner and C. Goldscheider, *Social Foundations of Judaism* (Englewood Cliffs, NJ 1990), contains essays that apply these insights to later periods in the history of Judaism. Also see A. Eisen, "The Rhetoric of Chosenness and the Fabrication of American Jewish Identity," in *American Pluralism and the Jewish Community*, ed. S.M. Lipset (New Brunswick, NJ, 1990), for an analysis, of writings by American Jews, that focuses upon rhetorical features to discern the self-understanding of these people.

7. The Commission on Social Action of Reform Judaism compiled these statements in 1985 and printed them under the title, *Where We Stand*. We, therefore, follow self-designation of the Reform movement in treating these, and only these texts as those expressing their views on social justice.

8. Union of American Hebrew Congregations (henceforth UAHC), *Where We Stand. Social Action Resolutions Adopted by the Union of American Hebrew Congregations* (NY, 1985). Our analysis is based almost exclusively on the documents themselves. We have not looked at debates surrounding their passage. We also did not attempt to identify resolutions that either never made it to the floor of the General Assembly or that were rejected by that body. We also made no effort at trying to determine what issues the UAHC might have addressed. We merely assume that the omission of such matters from the resolutions of the UAHC indicates either that those Jews thought such issues were not

their concern or that because of their implicit sense of identity, they did not even explicitly consider such matters. In the latter instance, because of the ways in which they defined themselves as Jews and as Americans, they already excluded certain matters from conscious consideration.

9. UAHC, 8,14,17.

10. UAHC, 6.

11. UAHC, 14.

12. UAHC, 25.

13. UAHC, 24.

14. UAHC, 14-15.

15. UAHC, 19-20.

16. UAHC, 22.

17. UAHC, 30.

18. UAHC, 6.

19. UAHC, 23,26.

20. UAHC, 4.

21. UAHC, 3, 10, 15, 21, 23, 28, 29, 30.

22. UAHC, 21.

23. UAHC, 23.

24. UAHC, 26.

25. UAHC, 27.

26. UAHC, 26.

27. UAHC, 27.

28. UAHC, 28.

29. UAHC, 30.

30. See M. Meyer, *Response to Modernity. A History of the Reform Movement in Judaism* (NY, 1955), 287-88; M. Raphael, *Profiles in American Judaism. The Reform, Conservative, Orthodox, and Reconstructionist Traditions in Historical Perspective* (San Francisco, 1984), 49; R. Gittelsohn, "The Conference Stance on Social Justice and Civil Rights," in *Commemoration of the Seventy-Fifth Anniversary of the Founding of the Central Conference of American Rabbis,* ed. B.W. Korn (NY, 1965), 103-104; L. Mervis, "The Social Justice Movement and the American Reform Rabbis," *American Jewish Archives* 7 (1955): 122-24.

31. L. Dinnerstein, *Uneasy at Home. Antisemitism and the American Jewish Experience* (NY, 1987), 1-8, 257-64.

32. I make these observations on the basis of the discussions of the work of the CCAR by Mervis, Gittelsohn, and Meyer, see n. 30 above. Meyer, in particular, notes the differences between the views of the CCAR and the UAHC but does not explore in detail the resolutions of the latter body.

33. UAHC, 43-46.

34. UAHC, 63.

35. UAHC, 59-61.

36. UAHC, 52.

37. UAHC, 34.

38. UAHC, 41-42.

39. UAHC, 42.

40. UAHC, 46.

41. UAHC, 48.

42. UAHC, 72.

43. UAHC, 55.

44. UAHC, 67-68.

45. UAHC, 42-43.

46. UAHC, 69.

47. UAHC, 70.

48. UAHC, 14.

49. UAHC, 144.

50. UAHC, 145.

51. UAHC, 146.

52. UAHC, 104-105.

53. UAHC, 61-62.

54. UAHC, 91.

55. UAHC, 78-79.

56. UAHC, 184-85.

57. L. Fein, *Where are We? The Inner Life of America's Jews* (NY, 1989), 177.

THE STATUS OF THE NON SABBATH OBSERVER:
THE RABBINIC RESPONSE TO NONCONFORMITY

Morris S. Gorelik

This paper will explore the attitudes of Rabbinic authorities towards the non-conformist as reflected in the Responsa literature. The analysis will focus primarily on the theological tendencies and sociological awareness of the decisors. The purely *Halakhic* dialectics will not be subject to the analysis. Since the object of this study is to probe attitudes, an examination of the exegetical and legal methodology would deflect from the primary purpose. The boundary between religious motifs and objective *Halakhic* considerations must be preserved. In this way, one can more easily single out the non-legal considerations in the shaping of a *Halakhic* decision.

As a point of departure, the study will be confined to the exploration of a single area of *Halakha,* the *Halakhic* status of the public Sabbath desecrator. Sabbath observance is referred to in the Bible as the "external sign between G-d and Israel."[1] Its holy character is preserved by abstention from proscribed activities. If profaned, the Bible prescribes capital punishment for the desecrator. "Those who desecrate it shall be put to death."[2]

In Rabbinic literature the Sabbath is ranked as a supreme religious value. Talmud materials abound in promoting the meticulous adherence to the minutiae of the *Halakhic* requirements. No stone is left unturned by the Rabbis in their teachings on the complexities of Sabbath rules. Sabbath observance was looked upon as the weathervane of religious commitment. Willful Sabbath desecrators are virtually excluded from the community until they have repented. Their integrity is suspect and their association is discouraged. Sabbath violation is tantamount to idolatry. Since the Sabbath is the sign of the covenant, its desecration is akin to violating the contractual relationship with the Creator. This attitude will become more apparent at later junctures in this paper.

Thus, when the rabbinic authorities were confronted with the ever increasing rejection of the heretofore traditional norms of Sabbath observance during the nineteenth and twentieth centuries, (which is the key focus of the present study), they were confronted with a complex dilemma. Were the public Sabbath desecrators to be ejected from the community or was it legally possible and religiously desirable to mitigate the severity of the law? What follows will be an examination of selected specimens from Rabbinic and Responsa literature dealing with the challenge of non-conformity. More so, the response will reflect diverse attitudes vis-a-vis the larger society which is essentially pluralist. Hopefully, the analysis will contribute to a clearer understanding of an aspect of the encounters within the contemporary American Jewish community.

Two Talmudic sources touching upon the status of the public Sabbath desecrator give rise to the post-Talmudic deliberations on the subject. The following passage in the Talmud clearly spells out *Halakhic* directive:

> It is written *Of you,* (Leviticus 1:2) but not all of you, thus excluding the apostate. *Of you,* that is, among you Israelites, does this distinction apply, but not among other nations (that is, from other nations all may bring offerings to the Temple, no distinctions are made). *Of the cattle* includes persons who are devoid of merit, like animals; hence, the Rabbis have declared: One should accept sacrifices from the transgressors in Israel, so that they may be inclined to repent, but not from an Israelite apostate, or from one who offers a wine libation to idols or from one who profanes the Sabbath publicly.[3]

The law is unequivocal. A public Sabbath desecrator is equated with an apostate. His sacrificial offering must be rejected, whereas the offering of a transgressor in other areas of *Halakha* is acceptable.

The above ruling is also cited elsewhere in the Talmud in regard to the law of *Erub.* An *Erub* is the setting up of an enclosure around one or more properties in order to permit occupants to carry or transfer items from one property to another. Three conditions are required: first, a fence or wiring must encircle the open area; second, the ritual requires the endorsement of all residents within the enclosure. This may be effected either by the individual renouncing ownership of his property for the purpose of carrying objects on the Sabbath, or by renting the property for a minimal rental fee. The third requirement is the placing of a Sabbath meal in the home of one of the residents who serves as the "Sabbath owner" of the area. *Erub* means the merger of the properties. Fulfillment of these requirements effects the conceptual fusion of the involved properties forming one *Halakhic* property for the Sabbath. With regards to the renouncing of ownership of one's property, the Talmud added an important condition, namely, this method is permitted only for a Jewish person. Since he is aware of the significance of an *Erub,* one may rely on the sincerity of his renunciation. However, since a non-Jew is not subject to these rules, he may not fully grasp the significance of the concept, therefore he may only assist by renting his property for a nominal sum for such a purpose. In conjunction with this subject, the Talmud cites Rav Huna's ruling relating to the public Sabbath desecrator, "Who is regarded as an Israelite mumar (whose renouncing is invalid)?, He who desecrates the Sabbath." In an extended discussion of this ruling, the Talmud cites the above-quoted Tannaitic passage equating the public desecrator with the idolater; consequently, the desecrator's act of renunciation is invalid. Renting the desecrator's property for the Sabbath purpose is the only means for effecting the *Erub*.[4] In the post-Talmudic literature, this Talmudic principle is virtually universally accepted and recorded in the classical codes of the *Mishna Torah* and *Shulchan Aruch* as normative *Halakha*.[5]

Subsequent discussions on this subject in Responsa literature center about the explanation of the Talmud's stringent ruling by the classic commentator, Solomon B. Isaac (1040-1105), popularly known as Rashi. He writes as follows:

> An Idolater denies the Holy One Blessed is He and the desecrator of the Sabbath denies His creation and testifies falsely that He did not rest on Sabbath.[6]

Rashi adds an important dimension to the discussion. Although it is a grave offense, the act of Sabbath desecration by itself is not sufficient ground to equate the desecrator with an idolater. For, were the act of desecration by itself an adequate reason, the Talmud would not differentiate between the public and the private offender. Thereupon, Rashi points out that the public desecration is viewed as a public declaration of rejection of the theological doctrine represented by the Sabbath observance, namely an affirmation in the doctrine of creation and is, therefore, equivalent to an act of idolatry. Since the private offender is not guilty of public demonstration against fundamental doctrines, his *Halakhic* status remains unchanged.

In the nineteenth century, Rabbi Jacob Ettlinger (1798-1871) writes at length on the status of the public Sabbath desecrator. Following his prefatory remarks underscoring the stringency of the Talmudic Law, he then proceeds to consider the contemporary public desecrator:

> Behold, until now we have discussed the basic law(as to) how to judge (or view) the public Sabbath violator but with regards the transgressors of our times, I do not know how I should consider them since because of our many sins, the leprosy has greatly spread, for with most of them, the desecration of the Sabbath has become permissible . . . and there are amongst them who recite the Sabbath prayers and recite Kiddush of the day and after this they desecrate the Sabbath whether with

activities prohibited by the Torah or [prohibited] by the Rabbis and behold, a violator of the Sabbath is deemed an apostate only because one who denies the creation and this one acknowledges through prayer and Kiddush.   And what [about] also their children who arose after them who have not known and have not heard the laws of the Sabbath.   They are similar to the Sadducees who are not considered to be apostate even though they desecrate the Sabbath because they emulate their forefathers [literal translation: because the actions of their father is in their hands].   And they are like children who are raised among idolaters [literal translation: children who were kidnapped amongst non-Jews] . . . and so did the Mabit write may his remembrance before a blessing.   Perhaps, also, the Sadducees who were not accustomed [to reside] among Jews and they do not know the fundamentals of the law and are not arrogant towards the learned of the generation and they are not considered willful unquote [literal translation: till here].   And many of the transgressors of the generation are like them and they are even better than them.   For what [reason] R. Shimshon is stringent regarding them to consider their wine as heathen wine is not because of the desecration of the holy days similar solely to the Sabbath but because they denied also the principles of the faith.   They circumcise but do not uncover the corona and they do not have [probably: practice] the laws of marriage and divorce, for because of this, their children are mamzerim.   And regarding this, most transgressors of our times have not made a breach.   And therefore, according to my humble opinion, one who is stringent to consider the contact of wine of these transgressors as *Stam Yayin* [Rabbinically prohibited wine] may the blessing come upon them.   But also for those who are lenient, they have [authorities] on whom to lean upon if it is not certain for us that he [Sabbath Desecrator] knows the law of the Sabbath and arrogant to desecrate in the presence of ten Jews together for this [one] is certainly an absolute apostate and his touching of the wine is prohibited.[7]

R. Ettlinger was compelled to cope with the ever increasing changes in religious observance particularly with regard to the rampant Sabbath desecration. Large segments of German Jewry were then undergoing radical alterations in religious attitude and behavior. Traditional style of religious observance was challenged by a non-ghetto cultural milieu coupled with attractive economic, academic, and professional opportunities. Modification of religious outlook was therefore a natural consequence of societal and cultural inducements.

In response to the circumstances, R. Ettlinger contributed two basic insights. The first relates to the Talmudic ruling that Sabbath desecration is as grave as idolatry. He opines that the disqualification is contingent upon the motive, that is, "a desecrator of the Sabbath denies his Creator and testifies falsely that he did not rest on the Sabbath." The act of desecration is not by itself a reason to classify the desecrator as an idolater. Motive is the determining factor. The second contribution is his assessment of the social changes. Convincingly, he writes that the Sabbath desecrator of his day is not a denier of fundamental dogmas. The desecrator recites the Sabbath prayers and the Friday night *Kiddush* that proclaim G-d as Creator. His act of desecration does not represent a theological rejection of the Creation motif, but it is a reflection of changing patterns of religious behavior.

R. Ettlinger applies a relativistic perspective to the Talmudic ruling. He does not, however, shed his reservations. One may surmise that he was conscious of making a historic decision. His ruling is lenient, yet he writes:

> And, therefore, according to my humble opinion, one who is stringent to consider the contact of wine of these transgressors as *Stam Yayin* [Rabbinically prohibited] may the blessing come upon them.

Apparently, he did not want to open the floodgates to indiscriminate Sabbath desecration, so he conferred his blessing upon those who preserved a strict position. This caution is underscored in the concluding passage of his responsum when he declares unequivocally that the permissible ruling applies only to those who don't know about the Sabbath and arrogantly profane the day. Thus, R. Ettlinger is cautiously lenient.

R. David Hoffman (1843-1921) endorses the thesis proposed by R. Ettlinger. He was asked whether an individual who publicly desecrates the Sabbath and does not recite *Kiddush* may be included in a *minyan,* the basic quorum for public prayer. At the outset of the responsum, he declares that the *Halakha* disqualifies a public Sabbath desecrator for such purpose but then he admits that "indeed, in this age, the practice is to be lenient even in Hungary and certainly in Germany." Furthermore, upon inquiring about the practice of a synagogue where such an individual was permitted to lead the public prayer, he was informed by an officer that the practice was in vogue for many years. R. Hoffman surmises that the Rabbinic authorities associated with the synagogue relied upon the precedent established by R. Ettlinger. He does add however, in the spirit of the latter, that wherever possible one should pray at synagogues where this leniency is not required. In conclusion, he suggests that the present day transgressors are not to be classified as public offenders. A public offender is one who arrogantly defies the normative communal observance of the Sabbath. His act of desecration represents a rejection of basic doctrine, thus, he withdraws from the community of the believers. In our day, he reasons, the conditions are reversed. Most are not Sabbath observers. On the contrary, the minority who are Sabbath observers are deemed to be outsiders. A public desecration in the community of non-observers is not *Halakhicly* disqualifying. He adds that this interpretation may not be the sole ground for a lenient ruling but only in conjunction with other factors. R. Hoffman inches ahead, but very cautiously.[8]

The last rav of Pinsk, R. Aaron Walkin (1865-1942), received an inquiry from a rabbi of another community whether a *kohen* who was a public Sabbath desecrator could discharge his priestly duty of reciting the priestly benediction at public prayer services. Furthermore, the inquirer adds that it would be incongruous for a transgressor of serious sins to bless a "holy nation." R. Walkin replies:

> In this matter, it is not my desire to discuss at all for it is necessary to be cautious in order to establish the law for it is well known our Sages may their memory be for a blessing 'at all times the left [hand] should reject and the right [hand] draw near'. . . Maimonidies and already the Sages may their memory be for a blessing that a transgressor if he has transgressed against the Lord [but] when he comes to the Synagogue to pray we receive him and don't behave towards him in a contemptuous manner. Look up carefully there that even Sabbath desecrators it is not proper to reject them but [one should] draw them near and encourage them to perform mitzvahs and so in responsa of the Ridvaz [R. David B. Zimra] concludes 'and however a leader of a generation should be cautious in matters as these and attract them with words until he repents little by little.' Look it up there.[9]

Since he is sensitive to the human condition and to societal changes, R. Walkin is hesitant in replying to the inquiry. He wishes to maintain the integrity of the Talmudic rule, while he doesn't wish to banish the transgressors. He is mindful of the Rabbinic dictum that a transgressor shall not be embraced warmly, but at the same time, signals should be sent out welcoming him to repent and rejoin the community. Therefore, R. Walkin prefaces his responsum by underscoring the necessity of caution and restraint and, not withstanding his reservation, he proceeds to pursue the *Halakhic* ramifications of the query. The responsum is a masterful account of a decisor seeking to establish moral perspectives on firm *Halakhic* grounds. He is fair and objective. He cites sources that at first glance would oblige the decisor to take a rigid stance. However, his analysis of relevant materials delimits what would otherwise lead to severe conclusions. His key conclusion is that the present generation is analogous to "a child who was kidnapped [and raised] among gentiles." In his summation he adds the following:

> From all these reasons [listed above], it appears to me that those who breach [the barriers] in our times who are accustomed in this one should not widen the schism by rejecting them totally and since they come to the Synagogue and wish to recite the priestly benediction they shall not drive them away by force and perhaps they will pay heed during the priestly benediction as they conclude with Sholom to correct and better their ways. [10]

In his summation, R. Walkin introduced an additional motif. The chasm between the observant and the non-observant must be narrowed. The transgressor may be induced through tolerance and understanding to mend his ways. A spirit of optimism prevails in the responsum. The transgression of the Sabbath is an extremely serious offense and must not be taken lightly, but by keeping the doors open, the transgressor may return to the fold.

The three rabbinic authorities quoted above were alert to the changing religious sociological scene. In order to cope with non-traditional religious norms, they searched for alternate solutions while at the same time they retained the integrity of the *Halakha*. At first they had tread gingerly as they put forward their ideas but as time passed their steps became sturdier and convincing.

R. Ettlinger's *Halakhic* stance or attitude was not universally accepted. At an earlier period, R. Moses Sofer (1762-1839), the spiritual mentor of Hungarian Jewry, forged an extreme formulation of an absolutist attitude. In one responsum he writes:

> That which emerges from all that was stated above that is prohibited to anyone who is called a Jew is to open his store on Sabbath . . . and if he does not pay heed and it is not possible to compel by means of the offices of the county, behold, he is

removed and separated from the congregation of Israel and he
has no religion at all and is disqualified for testimony. . . .

Or, as he writes in the same responsum:

Behold, he is separated from the congregation of Israel and he
is considered as one who left the religion and he is not a Jew
nor a Christian nor a Turk [Muslim], therefore it is prohibited
for any Jew to eat in his home and his slaughtering is
prohibited.[11]

R. Sofer strongly insists upon expelling the public Sabbath desecrator
from the community. He strips him of his privileges so that fellow Jews must
shun his society. He even entertained the possibility of denying him his
Jewish personal status, that is, ascribing to him the status of a non-Jew. This
notion was put forward by other Rabbinic authorities, but at this point, R.
Sofer, basing his arguments on earlier *Halakhic* sources, demurred. The
Halakha may impose penalties and disqualifications in matters of kosher
slaughtering, acceptance in the prayer quorum and the like, but the personal
status remains unchanged.

Such a strict approach as advocated by R. Sofer has its echo in the
responsum of the Lithuanian decisor and famed headmaster of the Yeshiva of
Volozhin, R. Naftali Zvi Hirsch Berlin (1817-1893). He takes as
uncompromising a stand as that of R. Sofer. In response to a query whether
one may participate in the pre-Zionist BILU movement working for the
reclamation of Palestine whose members were public Sabbath desecrators, he
writes:

Heaven forbid to join with them in matters of service of G-d.
Since their sacrificial offering is rejected, for they are equated
with idolaters, their prayer is an abomination, and post factum,
the prayer is unfit.[12]

He also cautions: "But one must be on guard not to stumble into their
society." R. Berlin himself was an ardent supporter of efforts to reclaim the
Land of Israel and encouraged others to join in this national enterprise,
nevertheless, he refused to alter the definitive *Halakha* regarding transgressors
of the Sabbath.

A leading proponent of the absolutist position is R. Chaim Eleazar
Shapiro (1872-1937). He vigorously champions non-conditional adherence to

the Talmudic ruling.   Following are revealing excerpts from his pivotal
responsum:

> I am astonished about what he [R. Ettlinger] wrote that a
> Sabbath desecrator is deemed an apostate only because that one
> who denies the Sabbath denies the creation and the Creator that
> which is not so [about] this one who acknowledges through
> prayer and Kiddush even [if] he desecrates it willfully...this
> [opinion] is not evident to me.   In the commentary of Rashi
> [for] this *Tanna* the desecration of the Sabbath is very strict [i.e.
> regarding defining the status of the transgressor] like idolatry
> because one who desecrates the Sabbath denies the actions of the
> Name *may* it be blessed implying that the Holy One blessed be
> He did not rest during the creation. . . . And if so when one
> publicly desecrates the Sabbath willfully behold he is a denier
> of the resting of the Holy One blessed be He on the Sabbath for
> the resting was all night and the whole of the seventh.   And
> what benefit is the Kiddush that he does and is then a rest for a
> half of day. The words shall be drowned because of this with
> his wine . . .

> And what he states with regards to the *Mabit* that the Sadducees
> were not accustomed amongst Israel and they did not know at
> all then they are not considered willful behold the *Mabit* wrote
> there only that they are not [considered] willful and they are
> disqualified only from [the standpoint] of the Rabbinic [law i.e.
> not from the standpoint of the Torah Law] if so, one must be
> concerned about his marriage act [i.e. it is valid, for were his
> disqualification Torah sanctioned then the marriage is invalid]
> and even regarding this *Mabit* wrote perhaps . . .

> And also the deniers because of our many sins in our days also
> in the German lands are not completely similar to the Karaites
> who live in lands where there are no Jews for the Karaites are
> not amalgamated at all with the Jewish people. And they are a
> people unto themselves and it is not possible for them to know
> at all of the customs of Israel because in addition they reside at
> a distance from the Jewish cities therefore the *Mabit* entertained
> the question not to consider them as willful as prescribed
> [defined] by Torah only as Rabbinically disqualified but this is
> not a matter at all to permit in our case and the publisher of the
> *Binyan Zion* did well by placing that responsum number 23

which was printed previously from that time on [amongst] the decisions which are for teaching but not [for] practice . . .

And what R. Yehuda Asad wrote there [in his *Responsa Yoreh Deah*, number 50] "as of today in our times that the generation is exceedingly licentious, one should not reject them so much nor to push them [away] with both hands Heaven forbid so they should not become licentious. And it is better to draw them close with strength." And I am amazed for this is against the ruling that is explicit in the *Shulchan Aruch Yoreh Deah* 334:1 in the [annotation] of R. Moses Isserles, "we excommunicate one who is guilty of excommunication . . . even [if] there is concern that though he may go out to bad way [yet] one should not be concerned." And certainly in this [case] one should not permit drinking the wine of a Sabbath desecrator because that he shall not become more licentious . . . If so, certainly with regards to *Stam Yayin*, its prohibition is very strict according to everyone to drink [it] even at a loss of money and its loss is certain, certainly they shall not be lenient regarding to drink it ourselves in order to draw the transgressors close . . . On the contrary, this is the concern that our Sages may their remembrance be for a blessing decreed in order he shall not learn from his actions and that we should arise and invalidate this with unfound opinions and to permit in order we should befriend them and through this they will learn from his ways. A Jewish athiest is certainly more licentious [than a non-Jew] and there is more concern they will learn from his actions when they will associate with him more than what they will learn from the actions of a worshipper of stars and constellations.[13]

Several crucial objections were raised by R. Shapiro. In the first place, he vehemently disputes R. Ettlinger's thesis that the theological motive of the transgressor as the determining factor in disqualifying a Sabbath desecrator. The act of desecration in itself affects the status. Since he commits such a serious offense, he is classified as a "worshipper of stars and constellations." Its offensive character cannot be mitigated by the recital of Sabbath prayers and the *Kiddush*. For R. Shapiro, the above quoted Rashi's comments on the Talmudic ruling are a clarification but not a condition. The motif is inconsequential. In the second place, he refuses to look upon the public Sabbath violators of his day as "children who were kidnapped and raised among non-Jews." He claims that present day violators, unlike the Karaites, do not live in isolation. Social intercourse between observant and non-observant Jews are common in contrast to Karaites who resided in areas uninhabited by the Rabbanites. Since the transgressors of today as well as their children are exposed to Jewish style of living, they cannot be compared to "children who were kidnapped . . ." A most telling feature of R. Shapiro's attitude is his definition of a "child who was . . ." His definition is restrictive. On the other hand, R. Ettlinger contributed a far reaching interpretation. Social conditioning, home environment and the like are factors to be taken into account.

And third, R. Shapiro vigorously protested R. Asad's lenient attitude in reaching with a hand of friendship toward the transgressor in the hope of drawing him closer to observance. R. Shapiro opined that such an approach would backfire, since a friendly attitude would only encourage the transgressor to continue straying from traditional observance. He is also fearful that close association with such transgressors would have an adverse influence on the traditionalist. In order to preserve the integrity of the community and guard its members from negative influence, it is imperative to avoid relationships with the transgressor until he repents. The penalty of ostracism, therefore, must remain in force. R. Shapiro's responsum thus summarized in vigorous tones a stringent adherence to the Talmudic ruling.

Turning to the latter half of the twentieth century, refrains of the nineteenth century conflicts are still heard loudly and clearly. Similar concerns and similar convictions are reiterated. Two schools of thought endure without interruption. It appears that the catastrophic chapter of World War II and the restoration of the State of Israel have not modified perspectives. Perhaps here and there, additional observations are contributed, but the core of the debate rages on as in yesteryear.

For example, joining the absolutist circle is R. Moses Sternbuch who is currently a member of the *Beth Din-Rabbinical Court*--of the *Edah Haredit*-- the extreme Orthodox community of Jerusalem. While in Johannesburg, South Africa, he served as dean of a *Kollel*, a school for advanced Talmud studies. During his tenure in Johannesburg, he received numerous religious and ritual queries, among which was a series of questions pertaining to the status of the Sabbath desecrator. His comments, aside from purely *Halakhic* consider- ations, are revealing. While he leaned toward a strict interpretation of the Talmudic ruling, he displayed a sensitivity to contemporary dilemmas. In one responsum, he was asked by the Rav of a small community whether he (the Rav) might fulfill the *mitzvah* (religious obligation) of hearing the sounds of the Shofar on Rosh Hashona sounded by a public Sabbath desecrator. R. Sternbuch's reply was negative, since a public Sabbath desecrator is equivalent to an idolater.   Were the desecrator to be classified as "a child who was kidnapped and raised among idolaters," it would then be permitted if a Sabbath observer were not available. Still he remained perplexed. Perhaps the ruling that a public Sabbath desecrator is like an idolater did not apply in the present situation because the Rav would not be able to fulfill the *mitzvah* obligation without the assistance of the desecrator. The Talmudic ruling of labeling a Sabbath desecrator as an idolater would, in his opinion, apply only in circumstances where the latter's services would not be required to enable the fulfillment of a *mitzvah* by a Jew. R. Sternbuch concluded by advising the Rav to spend the holidays elsewhere.

In another responsum, he was asked whether a public Sabbath desecrator may be included in a *minyan*. At the outset, he declared that he did not favor closing the doors of those synagogues which lack a quorum of Sabbath observers. Thus, he was led to suggest that the ruling of equating Sabbath desecration with idolatry would not apply if it would lead to negative consequences, namely, no public prayers or reading of the Torah. Furthermore, he buttressed his position by reminding the reader that many authorities endorsed the lenient view of R. Ettlinger. On the other hand, he was concerned lest a permissive ruling in this situation would lead to undesirable results. In the course of time, people may forget that the permissible ruling was essentially a stop-gap measure. Thus, he cautioned the inquirer to return after a year for a review of this decision. Otherwise, he advised people to avoid such situations.

May one invite a Sabbath desecrator to recite the blessing at the Torah reading?   R. Sternbuch responded by stating that in their country, the desecrators don't commit violations for spite, but solely for convenience. On the other hand, how may one recite a blessing "who has chosen us from among the nations and has given us the Torah," while he does not observe the law of the Torah? Is this not a blessing in vain? In order to prevent hatred, one may invite him to recite the blessing but only after seven people have been given the opportunity. The rationale for this was that the basic number for Torah reading is seven, additional numbers are optional. He concluded that in general, however, one should avoid honoring such people.[14]

R. Sternbuch seems to be caught on the horns of a dilemma.   He adheres unquestionably to an absolutist interpretation of the Talmud ruling in the tradition of R. Sofer and R. Shapiro.   However, he is mindful of uncomfortable consequences if absolute rigidity prevails. He is hesitant to call for suspension of public prayer, to close the doors of the synagogue, to provoke hostility, etc. His sensitivity impels him to search for solutions within the parameters of an absolutist religious philosophy, even though the solutions may be not entirely to his liking.

The Debretzin Rav, R. Moshe Stern, who currently resides in Boro Park, New York, is spiritual mentor to large segments of extreme Orthodox Jews. An erudite scholar and prolific writer, he deals with the status of the non-public Sabbath desecrator at great length. His attitude is unswervingly absolutist, being generally unimpressed with societal developments. He is very protective of the status quo and seeks to extend the Talmudic ruling to its logical conclusion. His literary style is direct and demanding, and he pulls no punches. In one responsum, he quotes the words of an early post-Talmudic authority, *"'Israel shall observe the Sabbath'* one who observes the Sabbath is called an Israelite but one who doesn't observe the Sabbath is not called an Israelite." He follows this with a quote from a nineteenth century source: "It was asked of the Chatam Sofer whether it is permitted to invite a Sabbath desecrator 'to recite a blessing' at Sefer Torah, and he replied that G-d forbid to invite him to the Torah and to include him in the minyan." He adds one should not invite a *Kohen* who is a desecrator to the Torah even if there are no other *Kohanim* present because this is regarding the Torah with contempt. In his analysis of the Talmudic ruling, he endorses R. Shapiro's conclusion though he concedes there are classic decisors who side with R. Ettlinger. Though he is not oblivious to seeking solutions, he does not appear as conversant of the contemporary nuances as R. Sternbuch. Some of his conclusions are as follows:

- a public Sabbath desecrator may not be included in the basic quorum for public prayer,
- one must not respond "amen" to his blessings,
- a Sabbath-desecrating *Kohen* may not be invited to recite a blessing at the Torah even if there is no other *Kohen* available,
- and may not participate in the public recitation of the priestly blessing.

He advises Rabbis to prevent such desecrators from receiving honors during the public services.[15] R. Stern is the reincarnation of R. Shapiro, and like the latter, he espouses a religious philosophy of separatism.

Two outstanding contemporaries of R. Sternbuch and R. Stern differ with their perspectives. One is the late R. Moshe Feinstein (1895-1986) who, during his lifetime, was the doyen of American decisors. His arguments are insightful and impelling. The following is a summary of his thesis: The act of Sabbath desecration, whether committed publicly or privately, is an equally serious offense; yet the Talmud distinguishes between the two instances. In the former instance, the desecrator is condemned as an idolater. This is because he has willfully and arrogantly committed the offense. Were he to commit the offense privately, one need not suspect he did so in defiance. One may assume he violated the Sabbath for economic gain or for any other purpose that would not cast suspicion on his belief in G-d and His creation. If there is reason to assume that even a public desecration was committed for non-theological reasons, then the disqualifications would be inapplicable. And since today "most Sabbath violators desecrate because of economic reasons and there are many who pray, they are not considered as non-Jews." However, he prefers to discourage such *Kohanim* from reciting the public priestly benediction in order to underscore the seriousness of the offense, whatever its reason may be.[16]

In concurrence with R. Feinstein's attitude, the former Sefardic Chief Rabbi of Israel, R. Ovadiah Yosef (1900-), is deeply critical of the negative posture towards the non-observant, and supports his critique with numerous references. He also points out R. Shapiro's historical errors. The Karaites were *not* isolated from the Jewish community. They were exposed to the religious observances and the practices of the Rannanites, yet they were treated as "children who were kidnapped. . . ." Therefore, our attitude toward the non-observant of our day should be similar. His responsum is a masterful defense of the thesis initially proposed by R. Ettlinger.[17]

In the above survey, the evidence points to two trends in dealing with non-conformity. Proponents of both sides search for *Halakhic* sources to support their respective stances. Both insist that the integrity of the *Halakha* must be preserved. The pivotal issue, then, is to what degree do meta-*Halakhic* considerations share in advancing a decision without affecting its *Halakhic* integrity. The stakes are high, and ultimately history will be the final arbiter.

Endnotes

1. Exodus, 31:13.

2. Exodus, 31:16.

3. *B. Hullin*, 5a.

4. *B. Erubin,* 69a.

5. See e.g. Rambam, *Hilkhos Erubin*, 2:16; *Shulchan Aruch, Orach Chaim* 385:3.

6. *B. Hullin*, 5a, s.v. Elah Lav.

7. *Teshuvot Binyan Tzion - Hahadoshot*, no. 23.

8. *Teshuvot Melmed Lehoil, Orach Chaim*, no. 29.

9. *Teshuvot Zekan Aaron I, Orach Cahim*, no. 12.

10. *Teshuvot Zekan Aaron I, Orach Cahim*, no. 12.

11. *Teshuvot Chatam Sofer, Chosen Mishpat*, no. 195.

12. *Teshuvot Mashiv Davar I*, no. 9.

13. *Teshuvot Minchat Eleazar I*, no. 74.

14. *Teshuvot Vehanhagot, Yoreh Deah*, nos. 468, 469, 472.

15. *Teshuvot Beer Moshe V*, nos. 90-94.

16. *Igros Moshe, Orach Chaim*, no. 33.

17. *Teshuvot Yabia Omer I, Yoreh Deah*, no. 11.

IMAGES OF THE MOVEMENTS:
PERCEPTIONS OF AMERICAN JEWISH UNIVERSITY STUDENTS

Mervin F. Verbit

The Issue

Liberal religious movements can be understood in two ways. From one perspective, they are as deeply committed as are more traditional movements, but to a different doctrinal interpretation and ritual regimen. In this view, they are profoundly sincere attempts to comprehend ultimate truth and to implement its imperatives, and they reach their non-traditional conclusions with an intellectual rigor and spiritual integrity equal to those of traditionalists. From the other perspective, liberal religious movements are compromising attempts in a largely secular culture to have both one's penny and one's cake. In this view, they are not sincere attempts to construct authentic religious life, but rather ways of rejecting genuine religious commitment while continuing to enjoy the respectability, the aesthetically and emotionally pleasing occasions, and the social connectedness that can accompany involvement in religious activity.

The truth of the matter is that both perspectives need to be taken seriously. Ideological movements attract people on the basis of both intrinsic motives rooted in intellectual and spiritual acceptance of principles and extrinsic motives having to do with the political, economic, social and psychological benefits that participation offers. Adherents to liberal religious movements reach their positions out of varying mixtures of the two kinds of motives, and the movements themselves, therefore, reflect both. Traditional religious movements, of course, also have both intrinsic and extrinsic attractions which are manifest in the conduct of those movements.

Any religious movement's ideological leaders--that is, the thinkers whose written and oral statements formally define the movement--will naturally focus on its (intrinsic) principles. That same movement's style, however, will inevitably be shaped in significant measure by the extrinsic factors which influence not only its "rank and file" members, but also its lay leaders and clergy.

Much to the chagrin of the leadership of the Conservative and Reform Movements in American Judaism, there seems to be considerable acceptance of the notion that those movements are somehow "less"--rather than "differently"--religious than Orthodoxy. The "elites" of Conservatism and Reform assert that their movements are just as legitimately Jewish and religious as is Orthodoxy, perhaps--if their interpretations of Jewish history and thought are valid--even more so. The "folk," however, often seem at best ambivalent about that claim. It is this ambivalence which the present paper explores. It reports perceptions of the movements by a sample of American Jewish university students and changes in those perceptions over the decade between 1975 and 1986.

Method

The data for this report were gathered at two major American universities, one a private institution in an eastern city, the other a midwestern state university in a college town. Both have several undergraduate, graduate and professional schools, and both offer a wide range of options for all levels of Jewish self-expression available on or near campus. Data were collected in 1975 (under the sponsorship of the Institute for Jewish Policy Planning and Research of the Synagogue Council of America) and again in 1986 (with support from the American Jewish Committee). Both surveys used the same sampling technique and the same questionnaire, except for about five percent of the items which were changed to reflect new conditions.

The 1975 survey yielded 641 usable responses; in 1986, there were 691 usable responses. In both years the samples were about evenly divided among lowerclassmen, upperclassmen, and graduate or professional students, and in both years about 54% of the overall sample were women. The samples were demographically what we would expect regarding the education and occupations of parents and the proportion of parents and grandparents that were native-born.

With regard to Jewish identity, on the other hand, the samples were purposely biased. The surveys were not designed to get "profiles" of Jewish student identity because doing so would have required a far more expensive sampling technique than was possible, and because, in any case, "profiles" are likely to become outdated very quickly. Rather, it was decided to explore the structure of Jewish identity and the relationship among its components as these are manifested in various "types" of Jews. For that kind of study, a longer and more detailed questionnaire was needed, thereby reducing the response rate, and a larger than representative proportion of positively involved Jews was required in order to provide a sufficiently large sub-sample for analysis.

The sample's positive bias is reflected in the fact that 24% of the 1975 respondents and 29% of the 1986 respondents reported having attended summer camps that were Hebrew-speaking or had "other strong Jewish content." Twenty-eight percent of both samples claimed at least some

Hebrew-speaking ability, and 35% reported having taken some university course(s) in Jewish studies. Forty-one percent of the 1975 and 53% of the 1986 sample had visited Israel. As a result, the marginals from these data can be read only as upper limits. The data allow us to compare sub-groups within the sample, as well as to trace changes over the decade, but they do not enable us to know what proportion of Jewish university students in general reflects any given pattern of Jewish identity.

As part of the questionnaire, students were asked to indicate whether they believed that each of eight adjectives was "very appropriate," "somewhat appropriate," or "inappropriate" as a description of each of four religious approaches. The eight descriptions were: "internally consistent," "authentic," "emotionally satisfying," "sincere," "modern," "parochial," "assimilationist," and "hypocritical." The four religious approaches were: Reform, Orthodox, Conservative, and "Chassidim."

It is likely that almost all non-Orthodox respondents saw the Orthodox as divided into two basic categories: those who dress in standard Western styles and participate broadly in the society's cultural life and institutions, and those who generally do not. It is also likely that most non-Orthodox respondents, unaware of the differences within Orthodoxy's "right wing," view the Chassidim simply as "Ultra-Orthodox." Consequently, the presence of Chassidim as a separate approach on the questionnaire suggests that the ratings of Orthodoxy were probably based largely on perceptions of "Modern" or "Centrist" Orthodoxy, and it is to that part of Orthodoxy that we refer when we use the term Orthodoxy, unmodified, below. For the same reasons, perceptions of Chassidim can probably be read better as perceptions of what most respondents saw as "Ultra-Orthodoxy," and, therefore, that term is used, despite its imprecisions and ambiguities, in reporting the findings.

Because of the nature of the sampling and because of the purpose of the analysis, the data are presented separately for the children of Orthodox, Conservative, and Reform homes. In the 1975 sample there were 65 respondents from Orthodox homes, 311 from Conservative homes, and 187 from Reform homes. The comparable numbers for 1986 were 48, 373, and 228, respectively. (In order to simplify language, we shall refer to Orthodox, Conservative, and Reform students, but we mean students who reported having been raised in Orthodox, Conservative, and Reform homes. There were not enough students from Reconstructionist homes in the sample to permit separate analysis for them, and the same holds true, of course, for students from Chassidic or other "Ultra-Orthodox" homes.)

The data are reported in "standardized scores." These scores are averages, standardized as percentages of the total possible agreement with a description. In other words, "very appropriate" was scored 100, "somewhat appropriate" as 50, and "inappropriate" as 0, and means were calculated for each description for each student group. Table I and Table II show the 1986 sample; Table III and Table IV show the differences between the 1975 and 1986 responses. In all tables the data are ordered in two different ways for ease of comparison.

It should be kept in mind that, because of the bias in the sample, no one mean score should be taken as representative of American Jewish university students raised in a given movement. The comparisons among the means, however, *are* probably representative, since the selective bias is likely to have had similar influence on all three sub-groups of students. As with most attitudinal data, imprecisions inherent in the method suggest that small differences be ignored. Larger differences and consistent patterns, on the other hand, should be taken seriously.

Some of the descriptions are obviously more likely to be applied, whether in praise or in criticism, to some movements than to others. Specifically, we would expect "modern" and "assimilationist" to be seen as more appropriate as we move toward the liberal pole of the continuum and "parochial" to increase in the reverse direction. The other descriptions-- "internally consistent," "authentic," "emotionally satisfying," "sincere," and (negatively) "hypocritical"--do not have an obvious relationship to the traditional-liberal continuum, and as a result, respondents might be expected to see their own movements in the most favorable light with regard to these characteristics. The extent to which they do so is what the analysis reported here was designed to learn.

Findings

"Internally Consistent"

Students from all three movements responded that Orthodoxy is more internally consistent than Conservatism, and Conservatism more than Reform, and the differences were not small. The difference narrowed among the more liberal students, not because they saw Orthodoxy as less internally consistent, but rather because they saw Reform as more internally consistent. It is interesting that Conservative and, especially, Orthodox students, but not Reform students, saw Ultra-Orthodoxy as less internally consistent than Orthodoxy. (Recall that, here and throughout, we assume that by Orthodoxy we can mean "Modern" or "Centrist" Orthodoxy.) There was considerable consensus (variations of no more than six points) among the three groups of students regarding the internal consistency of the four approaches. The only exception was that Reform students were much more likely to see the Reform Movement as internally consistent than were Orthodox and Conservative students, but even the Reform respondents saw Reform as less internally consistent than Ultra-Orthodoxy, Orthodoxy, and Conservatism.

The students in the 1986 sample were more likely than those in the 1975 sample to see their own movement as internally consistent. The only significant change in the perceptions of other movements was that in the later sample Reform students gave higher scores for internal consistency to Conservatism. What is especially worth noting is that by far the largest change between the perceptions of 1975 and those of 1986 was that the later group of Orthodox students was much less likely to view Ultra-Orthodoxy as internally consistent.

"Authentic"

Students in all three movements saw authenticity decline as one goes from Orthodoxy to Ultra-Orthodoxy to Conservatism to Reform.   The differences in the evaluations of Orthodoxy and Ultra-Orthodoxy as authentic were small, though consistent in direction, but the perceived differences between Orthodoxy and Conservatism, and between Conservatism and Reform were remarkable. Indeed, they were the largest among the five descriptive characteristics which are not clearly related to the traditional-liberal continuum. Again, the differences in the perceptions of the four approaches were smallest among the Reform students, but only because they evaluated Reform as more authentic than did Orthodox or Conservative students, and-- again as with internal consistency--they gave their own movement lower ratings than they gave the other three approaches.   There was consensus among students in the three movements regarding Orthodoxy and Ultra-Orthodoxy. While Conservative and Reform students had similar and more positive perceptions of Conservatism, Conservative students did not return the compliment regarding Reform, whose authenticity they viewed pretty much as did the Orthodox students.

Perceptions of authenticity tended to increase across the board from 1975 to 1986, but many of the changes were small.   The only notable increases were in Orthodox students' perceptions of Reform and in Reform students' perceptions of Orthodoxy and Conservatism as authentic.

"Emotionally Satisfying"

Students in all three movements viewed Ultra-Orthodoxy as the most emotionally satisfying approach, followed, in order, by Orthodoxy, Conservatism, and Reform. The more liberal the student group, the less variation there was in its perceptions of the four approaches' emotional satisfaction. This was due almost entirely to the fact that reform students saw the Reform Movement as significantly more emotionally satisfying than did Orthodox or Conservative students (but still as less emotionally satisfying than Orthodoxy or Conservatism). Regarding this characteristic, Conservative students evaluated Orthodoxy as favorably as did Orthodox students, and their perceptions of Reform were much closer to the perceptions of Orthodox students than to those of Reform students.

Comparing the 1986 sample with the 1975 sample, we see that in the later sample Orthodox students gave all four approaches higher scores for being emotionally satisfying and that the increase was greatest regarding Reform and, next, Orthodoxy. Conservative students' evaluations in the later year were more favorable only regarding Conservatism, and Reform students' ratings increased for Conservatism and Reform.

"Sincere"

Perceptions of the "sincerity" of the four approaches showed basically the same pattern as did perceptions of the extent to which they are "internally consistent," "authentic," and "emotionally satisfying." Perceived sincerity declined as we move from the traditional to the liberal pole, and that was the case for students in all three movements. As before, the perceptions of the Reform students showed least variation, primarily due to the fact that they gave the Reform approach higher ratings for sincerity than did students from the other two movements. Orthodox and Reform, but not Conservative students, gave Ultra-Orthodoxy slightly higher ratings for sincerity than they gave Orthodoxy.

Changes in perceptions of sincerity from 1975 to 1986 were small and showed no consistent pattern.

"Modern"

Unlike the characteristics already considered, "modern" is inherently related to the positions taken by the four approaches on the issue of how appropriately to deal with conflicts between Jewish traditions and contemporary cultural norms. As would be expected, the more liberal the approach, the more likely it was to be seen as modern, and that was true for all three student groups. The three groups were virtually identical in their ratings of Reform. The perception of Conservatism as modern increased with the traditionalism of the students. Conservative and Reform students agreed in their views of Orthodoxy and Ultra-Orthodoxy, but Orthodox students were far more likely to see Ultra-Orthodoxy and, even more so, Orthodoxy, as modern than were Conservative and Reform students.

As compared to the 1975 sample, in the 1986 sample Orthodox students were more likely to see all four approaches as modern, and the differences were especially pronounced for perceptions of Orthodoxy and Conservatism. Conservative and Reform students were more likely to see Conservatism as modern.

"Parochial"

In some meanings of the term, parochialism does not differentiate the inherent positions of the movements from one another. However, to the extent that parochialism is defined as the tendency of a group to look within to its own history and classical ideology for norms rather than to the contemporary standards of larger societies, it *is* a stronger characteristic in the more traditional approaches.

All three groups saw Orthodoxy as more parochial than Conservatism and Conservatism as more parochial than Reform. Conservative and Reform students saw Orthodoxy and Ultra-Orthodoxy as equally parochial, but Orthodox students viewed Orthodoxy as considerably less parochial than Ultra-Orthodoxy. The average perceptions among the three student groups were the same for Ultra-Orthodoxy and Conservatism. By contrast, as already pointed out, Orthodox students saw Orthodoxy as less parochial than did Conservative and Reform students. Also, perceptions of Reform as parochial increased somewhat as we move from Orthodox to Conservative to Reform respondents. This last finding, surprising at first, may reflect different meanings of "parochial" and/or different criteria for judging a movement to be parochial.

Although the changes in perceptions from 1975 to 1986 were generally small, they showed an interesting pattern. Orthodoxy's image as parochial declined, and perceptions of Conservatism and Reform as parochial increased. The only large change was that Orthodox students were clearly less likely to see Orthodoxy as parochial in the later sample.

"Assimilationist"

The more traditional movements often accuse the more liberal movements of being "assimilationist," that is, of accepting or even encouraging the assimilation of Jews into the larger society, thus leaving behind their Jewishness. The more liberal movements do not see themselves this way and, in fact, argue that by making Jewish life compatible with contemporary cultural norms and styles, they serve as bulwarks against what would otherwise be large-scale assimilation by Jews, most of whom are unwilling to live in fully traditional ways.

All three student groups saw Reform as considerably more assimilationist than Conservatism and Conservatism as considerably more assimilationist than Orthodoxy and Ultra-Orthodoxy.   Perceptions of Orthodoxy were the same in all three groups. Conservatism was viewed as assimilationist to the same extent by Conservative and Reform students, but more so by Orthodox students. The perception of Reform as assimilationist clearly increased with the traditionalism of the students' group.

The only difference between the 1975 and the 1986 samples was that in the later year Orthodox students were clearly more likely to apply the "assimilationist" label to Conservatism and Reform. To a smaller degree, they were less likely to apply it to their own approach and to Ultra-Orthodoxy.

"Hypocritical"

"Hypocritical" is like the first four descriptive terms in that it has no intrinsic relationship to the positions of the four approaches about which students were asked to give their impressions. It is unlike them in that it is negative rather than positive.

Perhaps the first observation to be made is that the perceptions of the four approaches by the three student groups showed less overall variation for "hypocrisy" than for any other descriptive term in the study. Also, each student group saw its own movement as the least hypocritical of the approaches (with the exception that Orthodox students viewed Ultra-Orthodoxy as slightly less hypocritical than Orthodoxy). For Orthodox students, the movements increased in hypocrisy as they move from traditional to liberal, but the differences were not large. For Reform students, they increase, also by small amounts, in the opposite direction (except that, as did Orthodox but not Conservative students, they saw Ultra-Orthodoxy as less hypocritical than

Orthodoxy).   Conservative students were more critical of Reform than of Orthodoxy regarding this characteristic.

Between 1975 and 1986, Orthodox students became less critical of Reform as hypocritical, and Conservative and Reform students became more critical of Orthodoxy and Ultra-Orthodoxy.

Summary

The only characteristic on which students gave their own movement the most favorable (or, more precisely, the least unfavorable) ratings was "hypocritical," but the students were not all that much less critical of their own movements than of the others in this regard.

On all of the other descriptive characteristics in the study, the movements were ranked in order along the traditional-liberal continuum by students in all three movements. All three groups of students saw Orthodoxy as more internally consistent, more authentic, more emotionally satisfying, more sincere, and more parochial than Conservatism, and Conservatism as more appropriately described by these terms than Reform. Similarly, all three groups saw Reform as more modern and more assimilationist than Conservatism and Conservatism as more modern and assimilationist than Orthodoxy.

Orthodoxy elicited the greatest consensus among the children of the three movements. The only exceptions to the general similarity of scores given to Orthodoxy by the three student groups were that Orthodox students were more likely to view Orthodoxy as modern and less likely to view it as parochial than were Conservative and Reform students, and the more liberal the student group, the more likely it was to consider Orthodoxy hypocritical. All three groups gave Orthodoxy similar and very high ratings for being internally consistent, authentic, emotionally satisfying, and sincere, and similar and very low ratings as assimilationist.

On all the characteristics, Conservative and Reform students gave Ultra-Orthodoxy virtually identical ratings. On most of the characteristics, Orthodox students rated Ultra-Orthodoxy more favorably than did the more liberal students, though some of the differences were small.   The only dramatic differences in the perceptions of Ultra-Orthodoxy by Orthodox students on the one hand, and Conservative and Reform students on the other, were that Orthodox students were clearly more likely than the more liberal groups to view Ultra-Orthodoxy as modern and less likely to view it as hypocritical.

The greatest disagreement among the three student groups concerned the Reform Movement. Except for the general agreement that Reform is modern, the average scores for the Reform Movement showed more variation than did the scores for the other three approaches for which respondents gave their perceptions. It is also worth noting that, while the view of Reform tended to become more favorable on most characteristics as we move from the Orthodox to the Conservative to the Reform sub-sample, the Conservative students were much closer to the Orthodox students than to the Reform students regarding the extent to which Reform is internally consistent, authentic, emotionally satisfying, and hypocritical. By contrast, they were about at the halfway point between Orthodox and Reform students regarding the extent to which Reform is sincere, parochial, and assimilationist. Therefore, the dissent over Reform was mostly the result of the tendency of Reform students to view their own movement more favorably than did Orthodox or Conservative students. Nevertheless, even the Reform students viewed Reform as considerably less internally consistent and authentic than Orthodoxy or Conservatism.

If the patterns reported here reflect the consciousness of American Jewry beyond our sample, and there is good reason to believe that in general they do (perhaps a bit more here and a bit less there), then the challenge to the leadership of the Conservative Movement, and especially, the Reform Movement is clear.

Table I   STUDENTS' PERCEPTIONS OF THE CHARACTERISTICS OF THE MOVEMENTS, BY MOVEMENT OF HOME
(STANDARDIZED SCORES)

	INTERNALLY CONSISTENT	AUTHENTIC	EMOTIONALLY SATISFYING	SINCERE	MODERN	PAROCHIAL	ASSIMILATIONIST	HYPOCRITICAL
Orthodox on Ultra-Orthodox	77	89	91	92	21	84	8	18
Conservative on Ultra-Orthodox	81	84	85	86	7	84	12	37
Reform on Ultra-Orthodox	80	85	81	84	9	85	13	36
Orthodox on Orthodox	85	94	83	84	39	70	13	25
Conservative on Orthodox	85	89	83	87	18	84	12	33
Reform on Orthodox	79	91	76	79	14	85	15	40
Orthodox on Conservative	54	56	68	70	74	52	56	39
Conservative on Conservative	62	66	74	80	68	49	42	31
Reform on Conservative	60	66	72	77	56	52	40	35
Orthodox on Reform	37	31	47	50	89	23	83	45
Conservative on Reform	42	35	54	61	88	26	71	44
Reform on Reform	56	57	70	75	87	32	60	28

Table II   STUDENTS' PERCEPTIONS OF THE CHARACTERISTICS OF THE MOVEMENTS, BY MOVEMENT OF HOME
(STANDARDIZED SCORES)

	INTERNALLY CONSISTENT	AUTHENTIC	EMOTIONALLY SATISFYING	SINCERE	MODERN	PAROCHIAL	ASSIMILATIONIST	HYPOCRITICAL
Orthodox on Ultra-Orthodox	77	89	91	92	21	84	8	18
Orthodox on Orthodox	85	94	83	84	39	70	13	25
Orthodox on Conservative	54	56	68	70	74	52	56	39
Orthodox on Reform	37	31	47	50	89	23	83	45
Conservative on Ultra-Orthodox	81	84	85	86	7	84	12	37
Conservative on Orthodox	85	89	83	87	18	84	12	33
Conservative on Conservative	62	66	74	80	68	49	42	31
Conservative on Reform	42	35	54	61	88	26	71	44
Reform on Ultra-Orthodox	80	85	81	84	9	85	13	36
Reform on Orthodox	79	91	76	79	14	85	15	40
Reform on Conservative	60	66	72	77	56	52	40	35
Reform on Reform	56	57	70	75	87	32	60	28

Table III CHANGES FROM 1975 TO 1986 IN STUDENTS' PERCEPTIONS OF THE CHARACTERISTICS OF THE MOVEMENTS, BY MOVEMENT OF HOME (STANDARDIZED SCORES)

	INTERNALLY CONSISTENT	AUTHENTIC	EMOTIONALLY SATISFYING	SINCERE	MODERN	PAROCHIAL	ASSIMILATIONIST	HYPOCRITICAL
Orthodox on Ultra-Orthodox	-16	+7	+6	+1	+10	+2	-7	-1
Conservative on Ultra-Orthodox	-3	+2	-2	-5	-3	-2	+1	+12
Reform on Ultra-Orthodox	-2	+2	-3	-7	-6	-3	+3	+9
Orthodox on Orthodox	+9	+4	+14	-1	+18	-11	-7	-4
Conservative on Orthodox	-1	+4	0	-2	+2	-3	+2	+7
Reform on Orthodox	+4	+13	+2	-3	+3	-2	-3	+11
Orthodox on Conservative	-1	+4	+9	+1	+20	+4	+16	-1
Conservative on Conservative	+7	+4	+10	+8	+10	+3	+5	-4
Reform on Conservative	+7	+11	+7	+5	+10	+1	0	+1
Orthodox on Reform	+3	+12	+17	+4	+9	+6	+19	-9
Conservative on Reform	-2	0	+2	-1	+3	+3	+3	+2
Reform on Reform	+6	+7	+6	+6	0	+6	-2	0

Table IV   CHANGES FROM 1975 TO 1986 IN STUDENTS' PERCEPTIONS OF THE CHARACTERISTICS OF THE MOVEMENTS, BY MOVEMENT OF HOME (STANDARDIZED SCORES)

	INTERNALLY CONSISTENT	AUTHENTIC	EMOTIONALLY SATISFYING	SINCERE	MODERN	PAROCHIAL	ASSIMILATIONIST	HYPOCRITICAL
Orthodox on Ultra-Orthodox	-16	+7	+6	+1	+10	+2	-7	-1
Orthodox on Orthodox	+9	+4	+14	-1	+18	-11	-7	-4
Orthodox on Conservative	-1	+4	+9	+1	+20	+4	+16	-1
Orthodox on Reform	+3	+12	+17	+4	+9	+6	+19	-9
Conservative on Ultra-Orthodox	-3	+2	-2	-5	-3	-2	+1	+12
Conservative on Orthodox	-1	+4	0	-2	+2	-3	+2	+7
Conservative on Conservative	+7	+4	+10	+8	+10	+3	+5	-4
Conservative on Reform	-2	0	+2	-1	+3	+3	+3	+2
Reform on Ultra-Orthodox	-2	+2	-3	-7	-6	-3	+3	+9
Reform on Orthodox	+4	+13	+2	-3	+3	-2	-3	+11
Reform on Conservative	+7	+11	+7	+5	+10	+1	0	+1
Reform on Reform	+6	+7	+6	+6	0	+6	-2	0

FACTIONS WITHIN A FACTION:
ISRAEL'S COMMUNIST MOVEMENT

Sondra M. Rubenstein

Introduction

Israel's communist movement can trace its ideological roots to the *Po'ale Zion* in 19th century Eastern Europe and Russia. A small faction of the *Left Po'ale Zion* in Palestine formed the *Mifleget Poalim Sotsialistim* (the Socialist Workers' Party, the MPS) in 1919 and assumed the impossible task of merging Zionist-proletarianism with (or rather into) liquidationist anti-Zionism.[1]

In December 1920, when the *Histadrut* was founded, the MPS changed its name to the *Mifleget Poalim Sotsialistim ha-Ivriyim* (the Hebrew Socialist Workers' Party, the MPSI). This group, blamed for instigating violent anti-Jewish demonstrations and riots in 1921, was outlawed by the British. Shortly thereafter, a new bloc emerged within the *Left Po'ale Zion*. Called the "Workers' Fraction," this was the front for a new clandestine Palestine Communist Party (PCP), which split into rival factions at its Fourth Party Congress in 1922. Out of 450 members, one-third took the slogan "Leave the Zionist hell!" They set up a rival communist party, giving it the Yiddish (and hence symbolically anti-Zionist) name of *Komunistishe Partey fun Palestine* (KPP), and established the "Proletarian Fraction" as its front organization.

Moscow considered the larger PCP "progressive" because it was striving to develop a revolutionary consciousness among Jewish workers and because it remained more conciliatory than the KPP toward Zionism, immigration, and *Binyan ha-Eretz* (the policy of building and developing a Jewish homeland). On the other hand, Moscow considered the KPP an uncomfortable and embarrassing manifestation of the "infantile disease" of left-wing communism denounced by Lenin when he introduced his New Economic Policy (1921).

Actually, differences between the KPP and the supposedly more moderate PCP were more a matter of timing than of substance. In July 1923, after ten months of destructive rivalry, the two groups were reunited at the Fifth Party Congress. On August 1, 1929, dubbed "Comintern Day" by the PCP, the party introduced new slogans calling for Arab agrarian revolt, land distribution, war against the bourgeois and clerical leaders of the Arab national movement, and the establishment of a workers' and peasants' government. When violence erupted at the Western Wall in Jerusalem and spread, the communists were again blamed for incitement. British police arrested many;

others hid, and some fled to the Soviet Union. Initially welcomed as staunch supporters of communist internationalism, they were ultimately condemned as Zionist spies and sentenced to death or to long prison terms. Most disappeared into Stalin's gulag.

The PCP's temporary reunification collapsed in 1943 with the emergence of various splinter groups. In addition to the Arab faction, the National Liberation League (NLL), there were three Jewish groups:

> (1) the "official" communist party led by Shmuel Mikunis, Meir Wilner, and Esther Wilenska;
> (2) the Communist Educational Association (soon to be called the Communist Union and later the Hebrew Communists) led by Meir Slonin, Simha Tsabri, Kalman Gelberd, Eliezer Preminger, and Shmuel Ettinger;
> (3) *Am ve Olam* (The People and the World), which saw itself as a socialist society, led by Chanoch Bzoza.

Subsequent attempts at reunification were partially successful, but disintegration seemed inevitable as differences emerged over the post-war order in Palestine. As the British mandate unraveled in the fall of 1947, the Palestinian communists--both Jews and Arabs--continued in disarray, a condition which had characterized much of their pre-statehood existence.

I. Toward Statehood and a Reunified Communist Party

1. For years Moscow remained aloof, recognizing no group as the "official" party. As statehood approached, each group functioned separately, adapting to new realities. Among the Jewish communists, the Communist Union (formerly the Communist Educational Association) again changed its name. At a "founding" meeting in October 1947, CU leaders announced formation of the "new" Hebrew Communist Party. The new party soon had greater influence among academic youth and the younger generation than did the PCP led by Mikunis, Wilenska,[2] and Wilner. It was, however, the Mikunis group which retained control of the party apparatus. Since Moscow recognized neither as the communist party in Palestine, both continued to send delegations to the Soviet satellite countries.

Meanwhile, two factions developed within the Arab NLL over the issue of partition. When fighting began in November 1947, the group led by Fu'ad Nassar and Emil Habibi was active in areas occupied by Arab armies.[3] Still supporting the Soviet position on partition, they tried to convince Arab workers to accept the U.N. decision.   Many were arrested by Egyptian authorities and detained in a Sinai camp until the Israeli offensive in the winter of 1948-1949.   On their return to Israel, they joined those who had, since August 1948, been engaged in talks with the Jewish communists which ultimately led to the party's reunification.[4]   The other NLL faction, led by Emil Touma and Musa Dajani, opposed partition.   They joined the Haifa National Committee to organize a struggle against the Jewish state.   Later, many escaped to Lebanon.   Some returned and collaborated with those who were working toward a unified Arab-Jewish communist party.[5]   Reunification talks, begun during August 1948, led to a meeting in Haifa in October at which the communists announced formation of MAKI, the "New All-Israel Communist Party," the result of a PCP-NLL merger.[6]   They were joined by the Hebrew Communists and the Arab communists returning from Lebanon and the Sinai.

All groups were given representation on MAKI's Central Committee (CC), which proclaimed the party's renewed unity would strengthen Israel's "fight for independence and [would] intensify the struggle to ensure a democratic regime . . . and to protect the interests of the working class."[7]   Its announced aim was to secure implementation of the partition resolution.   The party's merger was said to restore the communists to their "international status."   The statement added: "While the war continues, and the Israeli Army is hammering at the invader in the Negev and Jerusalem, Haifa is the scene of a fusion between Jewish and Arab workers."   Supposedly, this showed that the war being fought "at the instance of British and American imperialists and Arab reactionaries" ran counter to the interests of those involved.   The Arab communists," the statement concluded, are "bravely fighting the reactionaries who are striking at the Jewish state and are preventing the establishment of an independent and democratic Arab state."[8]   Despite MAKI's much heralded beginning, reunification did not last.   The Hebrew Communists were expelled in early 1949, some joining the pro-Soviet MAPAM, others completely retiring from the political scene.   The Arabs, too, would break away and ultimately they would again form a separate communist party, RAKAH.

2. Israel's communists achieved an aura of respectability on May 14, 1948 when Prime Minister David Ben-Gurion invited PCP Secretary General Meir Wilner to co-sign Israel's Declaration of Independence.   Wilner refused because the document's last paragraph invoked "the God of Israel."   Only when the text was altered to "the Rock of Israel," did the communists agree to sign.[9]

Israel's independence began a new era for the country's communists, now able to use political channels open to recognized parties in a parliamentary democracy. In their campaign for seats in the First Knesset, they called on workers to support the communists against the "reactionary forces in Israel," described as property owners and the right-wing and center parties which "aimed at lowering the [workers'] standard of living."[10] In the election of January 28, 1949, communists won four Knesset seats (out of 120), receiving 3.5% (15,148) out of a total of 505,567 eligible votes cast.[11] MAKI was second with Arabs (after MAPAI's two allied Arab lists),[12] taking 22.2% of approximately 33,000 eligible Arab votes.[13] The communist Knesset members now freely expressed opposition to MAPAI policies. On conclusion of the Rhodes Peace Talks, *Kol Ha'am* (long-time communist organ in Palestine) objected to creation of a neutral zone between Egypt and Israel on the grounds that it could be seen as the "granting of military bases to the Imperialist Powers."[14] Even the Armistice Supervision Commission set up to function near the Lebanese border was criticized as providing an American foothold in the Middle East. MAKI warned against American maneuvers in this sector.[15] On April 4, 1949, the Armistice with Trans-Jordan, leaving conquered Samaria and Judea on the West Bank in Jordanian hands, also came under attack. The communists joined with MAPAM in a motion to repudiate the agreement[16] on the grounds that: the Armistice Agreement referred to "the Hashemite Jordan Kingdom," implying recognition of King Abdullah's expansionist aims;[17] it made possible the establishment of British bases on Palestinian soil (a reference to Jordan's origins on Palestinian territory); and, it was not a move toward peace, but rather created a perpetual threat of war.[18]

3. Israel's application for U.N. membership set off another round of debate focusing on Israel's future alignment. "It is our duty upon entering the U.N.," *Kol Ha'am* stated, "to adopt a steady and unequivocal policy supporting democracy and encouraging world progress and freedom." The paper eschewed neutrality, saying there were "no problems on which we can remain neutral," citing: the Indonesian people's war for independence, the question of atomic energy, disarmament, and Israel's relationship with "fascist" states.[19] In foreign policy debates, MAKI representatives denounced Great Britain for opposing Israel and the United States for the failure of the Lausanne talks on the Arab refugee problem, Israel's budgetary problems, and for "trying to extract territorial concessions," while praising the Soviet Union's unswerving support.[20]

The Knesset debates also signaled another communist split. Eliezer Preminger (Hebrew Communist Party), voted with his fellow members in support of a MAPAM-initiated resolution containing fourteen policy points,[21] but he disassociated himself from a statement made in Bucharest by MAKI leader Shmuel Mikunis, then touring Eastern Europe. Foreign Minister Moshe Sharett charged that Mikunis had said emigration from Rumania should be held up until there was a democratic regime in Israel. After Preminger expressed his deep concern over the suspension of immigration,[22] Meir Wilner, representing MAKI, rose to defend Mikunis. He called the Sharett quotations[23] mere lies and said he resented Sharett's warning that defamation of Zionism could not be reconciled with expressions of loyalty to the state. About the trials of Zionists in Budapest, Wilner said he had no wish to interfere in the internal affairs of Hungary. He recalled that during World War II, the British had tried to discredit Jewish emigration on the pretext that it might be a cover for Nazi agents while after the war the British charged that emigration was a cover for communist agents.[24] On his return to Israel, an angry Mikunis refuted the charges against him and denounced Moshe Sharett and "the press that served Wall Street by repeating the lies." While denying he had said the Israeli government was a U.S. puppet, he charged Ben-Gurion with having "hitched its cart to the American wagon."[25]

II. Domestic and Foreign Policy Challenges

1. Freedom to operate within the Israeli political system created new opportunities for MAKI members to voice their opinions. At the same time, open participation made them a target for criticism. On Army Day, July 17, 1949, *Kol Ha'am* sang the praises of Israel's "friends in the camp of world peace and progress, headed by the USSR and the Peoples' Democracies," while condemning "the military, economic, and political help which our enemies received openly from the British Imperialists and covertly from American capitalists and oil magnates." Despite the alignment of Israel's elite, the article noted, the army "drew its strength from its strong ties with the masses." On the other hand, when in late July 1949 a number of unemployed immigrants and ex-servicemen demonstrated in Haifa, Tel Aviv, and Jerusalem, the government condemned the party, despite its denial, for instigating anti-government demonstrations.[26] Replying, the communists blamed the country's serious unemployment situation on the actions and attitude of the capitalists who had restricted production and had undermined the state economy for personal gain. It was the communist position that instead of criticizing the demonstrators, the government should force the capitalists to direct their profits into productive channels, creating public work programs which would employ the now unemployed.[27]

The communists also warned against an arms race which would seriously affect Israel's budget and economy. *Kol Ha'am* drew attention to this issue when Washington lifted the arms embargo against Israel. Somehow the communists made a connection between the American plan for the return of Arab refugees to Israel and the lifting of the embargo:

> American propaganda machinery is now endeavoring to convince Israel that armaments are necessary for reasons of her "internal security," which will be threatened by the admission of the refugees. Washington warmongers intend to turn the Middle East into an imperialist military base. This plan is opposed to the interests of Israel and her security.[28]

MAKI lamented budget allocations for the police and the Department of Religions while insufficient allocations were made for health, education, labor, and immigrant absorption. On tax policy, *Kol Ha'am* noted that while the income tax, the absorption tax, and taxes on imported goods were paid largely by the worker-consumer class, the property tax was ridiculously low.[29]

There was no shortage of issues for the communists to raise and their positions were predictable on the arms race, unemployment, taxes, the economy. However, the controversy over the internationalization of Jerusalem created problems for them and resulted in another of their customary flip-flops as they struggled once again to fall into line with Moscow. On August 8, 1949, MAKI warned against American pressure to internationalize the city. *Kol Ha'am,* in line with other Israeli newspapers, asked the government to resist all such pressure.[30] A subsequent *Kol Ha'am* article, commenting on the Palestine Conciliation Commission's (PCC) plan for the internationalization of Jerusalem, repeated the party's belief that the U.S. intended to create an "imperialist enclave within the State of Israel."[31] On September 17, 1949, the party issued an appeal for immediate government action to include Jerusalem in the State of Israel.[32] Three days later, the communists organized a demonstration against the internationalization plan.

Both MAKI members and communist-leaning fellow travelers in MAPAM were therefore shocked by the party's turnabout, which apparently was signaled by Soviet representative M. Semyon Tsarapkin's statements during a U.N. debate on December 9, 1949. Tsarapkin charged that the PCC plan was the latest Anglo-American imperialist effort to prevent full implementation of the partition plan. Russia, he said, insisted on the creation of an independent Arab state and on an international Jerusalem under the

Trusteeship Council. It was Britain who had provoked the Arab Legion aggression which resulted in the division of the Holy City, and "we are now asked to legitimize this seizure." There was no evidence, he continued, that the people of Arab Palestine wish to be "subjected to the occupation regime of Trans-Jordan."[33] Tsarapkin also introduced an amendment to the internationalization proposal abolishing the PCC.[34]

When Australia introduced a resolution giving Jerusalem self-government under the Trusteeship Council (on which the Soviet Union was represented), *Kol Ha'am* immediately announced its support.[35] The paper now warned against an "Israel-Abdullah-Bevin agreement" and declared that only the eviction of the Jordanian invaders from Palestine and the establishment of a democratic Arab state in the Arab sector would promote peace and security in the country.

During the Knesset debate on December 13, 1949, dealing with the government's decision to transfer the administration from its temporary seat at HaKirya (in Tel Aviv) to Jerusalem, Meir Wilner spoke in support of the internationalization plan. He said that the plan was not designed against Israel but was intended to eject the Jordanian Arabs "with their British guns from the Old City and the rest of Palestine to assure peace for the people of Jerusalem."[36] Wilner and General Secretary Mikunis were later excoriated by MAPAI's organ *HaDor* (December 20, 1949), which noted the communist party's "complete capitulation to the position of the Cominform regarding Jerusalem," and reported that "a member of the Cominform had arrived in Israel recently to investigate the actions of the party leaders." The change in the party's stand was therefore attributed to instructions brought from Moscow by its envoy.

For their part, the party leadership published a resolution in *Kol Ha'am*,[37] regretting the party's previous program favoring the inclusion of Jerusalem in the state of Israel and which now was recognized as an "opportunistic mistake" because the party had failed to understand "that the rejection of part of the November 29 U.N. partition plan must be followed by the rejection of the whole plan." The party had, the CC explained, neglected to see the connection between this one aspect of the Palestine problem and the problem as a whole, as well as the relationship between the entire Palestine problem and British and American imperialism in the Middle East.

MAKI's leaders were again caught by surprise when the chief Soviet delegate to the U.N. announced on April 19, 1950, in a letter to U.N. Secretary General Trygve Lie, "It has become clear that the General

Assembly's resolution does not satisfy the Arab or Jewish populations of either Jerusalem or Palestine as a whole." The USSR was therefore withdrawing its support for the now doomed internationalization plan.[38] *Ha'aretz* (the organ of the Liberal Progressive Party) succinctly analyzed the Soviet action: "[T]he Russians are realistic and must have come to the conclusion that there were no prospects of implementing the internationalization scheme and their stand could therefore have no consequence but the handicapping of the Israel Communist Party [MAKI]."[39] After taking a deep breath, the Israeli communists again accepted Moscow's lead, and patted themselves on the back with: "The people of Israel will never forget that in the days of the establishment of the State decisive help was extended it by the Soviet Union and the Peoples' Democracies. The masses in Israel will not let the people forget the share which the Israel Communist Party had in the recruiting of help from those countries." They then warned against Israel joining an anti-Soviet Middle East bloc and permitting the establishment of foreign military bases on Israeli soil.[40]

2. While Jewish communists were agonizing over the Jerusalem issue, Arab communist leaders were working in Arab communities in Israel and among Arab refugees. An issue of extreme importance to Arab refugees was the Abandoned/Absentee Property Bill. On March 1, 1950, Tewfik Toubi, working with Dr. Moshe Sneh of MAPAM and Amin el Jarjura of the Nazareth Democrats, sought to soften the bill by exempting from its jurisdiction property of Arabs who returned lawfully to Israel. In response to this proposal, the chairman of the Finance Committee, Mr. D. Z. Pinkas (Orthodox Religious Party), said the property could not automatically revert to returning Arabs because this "would impose hardship upon people who had developed it for years."[41] Toubi continued to oppose the bill. On March 8, 1950, he, Jarjura, Sneh, and Eliahu Eliasha (Sephardi Party) sought without success to exempt the properties of persons returning to Israel.[42] When the bill became law on March 14, 1950, the vote was 39-12, with the opposition including MAKI, MAPAM, and Jarjura, the Nazareth Democrat.[43]

3. The constitutional debate was one of many issues which attracted communist involvement. *Kol Ha'am* said that absence of a constitution affected relations between the state and the Zionist movement, resulting in the dominance of Zionism in all aspects of Israeli life. MAKI advocated supreme state control, saying immigration and absorption should not be handed over to "non-national institutions."[44] The communist attitude toward "non-national institutions" was linked, at least in part, to actions of the Jewish Agency's Department of Agricultural Settlement. The communists had protested alleged discrimination against them in cooperative settlements. The Agricultural

Workers' Union (AWU) decided on February 9, 1950, that communist members of cooperative settlements (*moshavim*) had to form a separate village "as the right of every settlement movement to establish one-party villages, has been traditionally recognized."[45]   This AWU decision was a reaction to communist attempts to form cells in several villages.   A spokesman of the Co-operative Settlements Union (CSU) claimed that communists had almost succeeded "in ruining the settlements by constant political strife."

The communists were trying to break the hold of the Zionist Organization and the *Histadrut*.   They resented the constitution of the CSU because it required all members to belong to both the ZO and the *Histadrut*. There were perhaps 40-50 communist families in *moshavim*.   In some places, relations between the communists and non-communists became so strained that the communists received no help from other members of the cooperative and complained about discrimination in the distribution of seed.[46]   Communists resented this attempt to isolate them and saw this non-governmental settlement and absorption policy as directly challenging a traditional left-wing socialist base of communist support--the agricultural settlement.   They sought relief through a national constitution which would formally institutionalize state control in the complex areas of settlement, absorption, and political protection.

The issue was resolved by a Knesset vote (50-38) on June 13, 1950 to adopt a state constitution by evolution over an unspecified period.   Laws would receive individual approval, and at a later date, they would be combined to form a constitution.[47]   *Kol Ha'am's* reaction was a stinging condemnation of the coalition vote, seen as a betrayal of the electorate, a "confirmation of the mandatory constitution, and a continuation of the emergency regime promulgated in 1936."[48]

4. Four other domestic issues (some with foreign policy implications) are of interest: the law of return, the austerity and rationing program, acceptance of U.S. aid, and German reparations.

(1) The Law of Return: On July 5, 1950, the Knesset unanimously passed the Law of Return, affirming every Jew's right to settle in Israel.   The MAKI-MAPAM faction supported the principle but were concerned the government, seeking to keep dissenters (such as communist sympathizers) out of the country, might abuse the law. MAPAM's proposed amendments (supported by MAKI and by Menachem Begin's right-wing *Herut* coalition) provided that no Jew may be deported from Israel and made the clause affirming every Jew's right to migrate to Israel irrevocable.   David Ben-Gurion fought these amendments, arguing the question of deportation had

no place in the Law of Return and would be dealt with through separate legislation. He said the government would not permit abuse of the Law of Return by criminal and (undefined) undesirable elements, even if they were Jewish. The proposed liberalizing amendments were defeated.

(2) The Austerity and Rationing Program: Rationing of shoes and clothing went into effect on July 31, 1950, and brought immediate condemnation in *Kol Ha'am* and *Al HaMishmar.* The MAKI and MAPAM newspapers saw the government policy as hurting the workers' living standard. They said that restriction of consumption would cause serious unemployment and argued with the government's contention that the present state of affairs was inevitable. They blamed the government for having permitted the waste of foreign currency on non-essential commodities. *Kol Ha'am* interpreted the new policy as a plan to transfer a considerable part of the available supplies to the black market and concluded: "Had imports been nationalized and foreign currency wisely spent, rationing of this kind would not have been necessary."[49]

The *Histadrut's* organ, *Davar,* justified the rationing system as intended to save Israel from bankruptcy. The paper warned against a threatened merchants' strike and explained it had become necessary to bring the standard of living into line with the country's income. Israel's sterling balances and loans from the U.S. were diminishing, and income from various foreign donations had decreased.[50] *Kol Ha'am* ignored these explanations, calling instead for full employment, increased production, and nationalization of foreign concessions and imports.[51] MAKI's program was designed to appeal to the working class and small business owners, those hardest hit by the austerity and rationing program.

In the Knesset debate of August 7, 1950, Meir Wilner blamed Israel's economic problems on the fact that "94% of Israel's foreign trade was with the United States and her satellites," who demanded payment in foreign currency and who wanted to suppress the new state.[52] When these charges were repeated by Wilner's fellow communist, Esther Wilenska, at a *Histadrut* council meeting on September 7, 1950, she was hooted down with cries of "fifth columnist" and "trouble-maker."[53] *Kol Ha'am* kept the issue alive, predicting lower wages for workers and higher profits for employers.[54]

The economic situation, combined with religious issues, caused a government crisis leading to Ben-Gurion's resignation on October 15, 1950, and the scheduling of new elections (to be held in July 1951). In the Knesset debate of October 17, Shmuel Mikunis charged that the governing coalition had reduced the standard of living, given rise to profiteering and clericalism, and shown itself incapable of precise economic planning. He called for a united labor front to deal with Israel's economic plight.[55] *Kol Ha'am* blamed the economic impasse facing Israel on: the coalition's anti-labor internal policy, its anti-Israel foreign policy, and its failure to solve Israeli problems in agricultural development and immigrant absorption.

(3) Acceptance of U.S. Aid: On January 2, 1951, Ya'acov Geri, Minister for Trade and Industry, proposed freezing wages.[56] To MAKI, this was part of the manufacturers' attack on the workers' standard of living. In the debate on Israel's economic plight, Finance Committee Chairman Pinkas raised the subject of U.S. aid under the Truman Point Four Program. MAKI and its MAPAM supporters opposed acceptance of funds, saying it would inhibit Israel's political and economic independence. MAPAM objected to the provision that the funds should be spent for American goods. Sneh specifically focused on U.S. Secretary of Defense George C. Marshall's statement that Israel would do its share to combat the spread of communism and therefore deserved help. Pinkas, responding to Sneh and the communists, said nothing in the agreement prejudiced Israel's political and economic independence and if any East European country were to offer Israel credits similar to the Export-Import Bank credits, Israel would willingly sign on.[57] The debate on acceptance of Point Four technical assistance was continued when Sharett presented his foreign policy report.[58] The MAKI-MAPAM opposition repeated the usual criticisms and charges to which Knesset members had already grown accustomed. When the Point Four aid package was signed on February 26, 1951, by Sharett and U.S. Ambassador Monett Davis, the MAKI-MAPAM reaction was predictable: This was "one more step towards Israel's inclusion within the strategic and economic plans for the Western bloc."[59] Israel's acceptance of U.S. aid placed her "at the disposal of the warmongers."[60]

(4) German Reparations: This involved a highly emotional and complex blending of domestic, economic, political, and psycho-social concerns with strong foreign policy implications. The issue brought together the communists, MAPAM, Menachem Begin's Herut coalition, the religious groups, and many apolitical survivors of Hitler's death camps. The idea that Jews could be compensated for their material losses may have grown out of a speech made by Kurt Schumacher, the post-war leader of the German Social Democratic Party. Schumacher spoke to the delegates of the American Federation of Labor at San Francisco in October 1947, and repeated what he had said to his own people about the moral necessity of admitting the crimes committed against the Jews.[61] On January 16, 1951, the Israeli government

presented a note to the governments of the United States, Great Britain, France, and the USSR, regarding Jewish claims against Germany. The note dealt with individual claims. To that point, no contact had been made or sought by the Israeli government directly with the Bonn government.

Indirectly, Bonn signaled that it "would like" to establish direct relations with Israel, adding that the "initiative" must come from Israel, since the Israeli public was still unwilling to end the "moral boycott of Germany."[62] Yet, within days, the Social Democratic wing of the German federal parliament urged the Bonn government to indemnify the Jews dispossessed by the Nazi regime and to pass a law recognizing Israel as the legal heir of unclaimed Jewish property.[63] On February 22, 1951, a Socialist bill, giving Israel title to all unclaimed Jewish property in Western Germany, was introduced in the Bonn parliament.[64]

There followed heated Knesset debates over Israel's request for $1.5 billion in German reparations.[65] Begin charged the Ben-Gurion government with preparing to sell out the Jewish people and with having implied recognition of the Bonn government if reparations demands were met.[66] While Begin organized emotional anti-reparations demonstrations held on March 25, 1952,[67] the communists also worked the issue. *Kol Ha'am* saw the opening day of the Hague negotiations as "one of the blackest days" in Israel's history. The purpose of these talks, the paper stated, was not restitution and compensation, but "an attempt to open the door to Israeli and Jewish recognition of Germany's inclusion in the neo-Nazi aggressive Atlantic Pact." MAKI's paper demanded a halt to the negotiations and the recall of the Israeli delegation.[68] In July, Bonn offered $107 million,[69] sparking more debates which resurrected emotions of holocaust survivors who refused to accept payment for their losses. When Moshe Sharett and Bonn's Conrad Adenauer signed the Reparations Agreement on September 10, 1952, *Kol Ha'am* claimed the agreement was "a victory for the neo-Nazis who were preparing a new world war."[70]

MAKI was not alone on this sensitive issue; nor was it alone on certain other domestic issues. Its stand on jobs and housing for new immigrants attracted support of those from North African and Middle Eastern countries who felt European Jews were discriminating against them. Also, certain Arab groups took note of MAKI's position on equal rights for Arabs and its opposition to the Abandoned/Absentee Property Bill. As we shall see, these and other domestic issues dominated the election campaigns through the 1950s.

5. Despite Israel's self-proclaimed policy of non-identification with either West or East, the new state found itself drawn into the cold war after its first national election in 1949. Since the U.S. State Department suffered from the same misperceptions as had the British with regard to left-wing, particularly communist, strength in Israel, the general expectation within the Truman administration was that Israel would move to the left and align itself with the Soviet Union. President Truman, aware of Soviet aid to Israel in its struggle for independence, was therefore gratified when MAPAI, the labor party, received a strong plurality, and the communists won only four out of 120 seats. Perhaps, Ben-Gurion's reward was *de jure* recognition and a $100 million, long-term, low-interest loan,[71] setting off an immediate controversy within the Knesset as to U.S. motivation for the sudden generosity. MAKI saw ominous designs for American military bases and unrealistically called for rejection of the loan. Ben-Gurion tried to maintain a policy of neutrality, but the Korean conflict forced the Israeli Cabinet to take sides.

When, on July 2, 1950, the Israeli Cabinet adopted a resolution supporting the U.N. Security Council vote to intervene in Korea, a leftist opposition bloc attempted to unseat the government. Although the MAKI-MAPAM no-confidence motion was easily defeated (79-19), the debate remains of interest because it highlights some major differences between the MAKI-MAPAM bloc and the governing coalition. MAPAM's Yitzhak Ben-Aharon and Ya'akov Riftin agreed with MAKI's Meir Wilner that there were legal grounds on which to dispute the validity of the Security Council decision. The Korean affair, they said, was a civil war and American intervention was aggression. MAKI-MAPAM argued that Israel had, by this Cabinet decision, abandoned its policy of non-identification. Pinhas Lubianker (MAPAI) responded that non-identification never meant Israel would take no position on controversial issues. Rather, it meant that there should be "no total identification with either bloc in the cold war."[72]

Most Israeli newspapers, including *Ha'aretz* (Liberal Progressive) and *Davar* (*Histadrut,* General Federation of Jewish Labor), endorsed the government's statement in support of the Security Council resolution,[73] while MAPAM's *Al HaMishmar* interpreted Security Council efforts not as directed towards peace, but in support of U.S. intervention in an internal dispute. *Kol Ha'am* criticism of the Cabinet resolution was even stronger. It denounced the U.S., "whose armies, fleet, and air force were cruelly attacking the Korean people." Citing Israel's support for the "illegally passed" Security Council resolution, the article said this meant that Israel had decided to join the "camp of the Anglo-United States Imperialists."[74] So consistent with Moscow was

MAKI on this issue, that the *Kol Ha'am* article could have appeared in Pravda.

The Knesset debate on Korea set off an extended debate on Israel's foreign policy and alignment. The communists attacked the American presence in Formosa, calling it an "occupation" and an act of aggression. Noting Israel's "recognition of Republican China," *Kol Ha'am* drew the conclusion that support for Security Council actions in Korea meant that Israel was betraying that recognition and abandoning its neutralism.[75] Foreign Minister Sharett responded that "Israel had therefore to choose between becoming a second Albania or a second Denmark."[76] *Kol Ha'am* further criticized the government for having failed to cancel British oil concessions and for preparing to grant new concessions to U.S. firms.[77]

Sharett's speech at the U.N. General Assembly on September 27, 1950, added fuel to MAKI criticism. *Kol Ha'am* noted the many "non-committal phrases" and said that only on the issue of U.N. membership for the People's Republic of China did Sharett come close to expressing the feelings of the Israeli people. Yet, even on this point, "He tried to hide the fact that it was the U.S. government which was sabotaging the proposal."   On the "reconstruction of neo-Nazi Germany," the paper commented that Sharett had "shilly-shallied," for he had forgotten to vehemently protest U.S. action in the rehabilitation of Nazism in Western Germany.

6. German rearmament and the prospect of its being included in NATO set off a torrent of criticism from MAKI. The communists, supported by MAPAM, attacked the government's acceptance of a remilitarized West Germany, while pointing out Soviet restraint in not arming East Germany, identified as "an important base for peace" and headed by anti-Nazi leaders.[78] Mikunis and MAPAM's Yitzhak Ben-Aharon initiated the protest on December 25, 1950, calling for a full debate and describing the Brussels agreement as a new phase "in the preparations for a Third World War." Mikunis said the Germans would betray the Western powers, turning their arms against the West "just as they did against Russia in 1941 after the Soviets armed them."[79]

MAKI-MAPAM coordinated protest meetings in Tel Aviv and Haifa on December 30, 1950.[80] In Tel Aviv, Esther Wilenska and three MAPAM Knesset members (M. Sneh, Y. Riftin and I. Bar Yehuda) spoke to a few thousand, while MAPAM's Ben-Aharon spoke at a World Peace Movement meeting in Haifa. Ben-Aharon contrasted the decision of the Brussels conference to rearm Western Germany with the decision taken at Prague by the East European states. The latter called for continued demilitarization of

Germany. Another Knesset debate held on January 10, 1951, resulted in the passage (54-16) of a resolution protesting the rearmament of both West and East Germany. MAKI and MAPAM members who voted against it objected to the "distortion" and proposed a formula specifically attacking the twelve North Atlantic powers.[81]

7. The MAKI-MAPAM working relationship became strained when the resolutions of MAKI's Twelfth Annual Conference (in May 1952) signaled the party's return to its traditional anti-Zionist line. MAKI recognized the existence of Israel, but not its borders. It demanded the ceding of Israeli-occupied territory (something over one-third of the Israeli-held territory) which was originally designated for an Arab Palestinian state by the U.N. decision of November 29, 1947. It resolved that Arab refugees be readmitted and returned to their former property and called for the disbanding of the Israeli Army and, in its place, the creation of a "People's Army," with only a one-year military service requirement. Female conscription would be abolished.[82]

Typical of the Zionist reaction was the editorial entitled "Communist Call for Dismemberment of Israel."[83] Once again MAKI found itself on the defensive and was even forced to deny the Mikunis description of East European immigrants as deserters. MAPAM's reaction took the form of an apology. It explained MAKI's failure to understand the application of communism to the peculiar situation inherent in the "territorial concentration" of the Jewish people in Israel.[84] However, within MAPAM, various factions of the left (the anti-Zionist wing of *HaShomer HaTza'ir,* including M. Sneh and Y. Riftin, along with *Mishmeret Zeire,* the MAPAM youth movement) and the right (the pro-Zionist wing of *HaShomer HaTza'ir*) as well as the left *Po'ale Zion* group and the more "centrist" *Ahdut Avoda,* began to debate MAPAM's acceptance of "orthodox" Marxism and its closeness to Stalinism. The Ahdut Avoda group in MAPAM, for instance, argued against MAPAM's support for the Moslem Brotherhood and its unconditional support for the "People's Democracies" and socialist states established in post-war Europe under Soviet hegemony.

The bitterness of the debate within MAPAM and the doubts many had over their party's close association with MAKI increased when news of Mordecai Oren's arrest in Prague reached Israel. Oren, a leader of MAPAM's extreme left wing,[85] was charged by the Czech communist regime with having "carried out criminal acts against the security of the state,"[86] and with being an agent of Zionist imperialism, a spy for the British Intelligence Service, and a "sympathizer of the Fascist gang of Tito."[87] Labeled an international criminal with "the face of an international Apache,"[88] Oren was presented as the missing link between Zionism and the Czech "traitors" (including R. Slansky, O. Fischl, R. Margolius--all Jews), who had been high officials in the Czech communist party. His confession of his "crimes" before a Czech tribunal made matters worse for his friends on MAPAM's CC who, in a state of shock, voted to issue an immediate call for his release.[89] They reaffirmed support for the communist world and stressed solidarity against the anti-communist wave of propaganda brought on by the Prague trials.[90]

MAPAI's charge of anti-Semitism against the Czech regime was initially met with silence from MAKI and from MAPAM members who tried to defend themselves by claiming MAPAI's attacks were aimed at discrediting them in the eyes of the Israeli public.[91] The communists, however, soon fell in line with Moscow, accepting the guilt of those on trial in Prague. In the debate on November 25, 1952, preceding the resolution condemning the Prague trials, Meir Wilner presented a defense of the Czech prosecution. Yet, when challenged to state clearly whether or not Oren was guilty, he did not reply.[92]

Within MAPAM, the earlier fissure was widening between the all-out pro-Stalinist wing of Sneh and Riftin and the more moderate socialist-Zionist types headed by M. Ya'ari. When MAPAM convened on December 25, 1952, the vote was 232 to 49 in favor of a strong condemnation and rejection of the Prague trial of Oren as an anti-Semitic outrage.[93] Sneh's written justification of the events in Prague were rejected by MAPAM's *Al HaMishmar,* but did appear in *Kol Ha'am* and in *Hador.*[94] He argued that there was no intention at Prague to incriminate working-class Jews, but only those "exploiters" found in the Jewish bourgeoisie whose Zionism was a counterrevolutionary force. Sneh portrayed the Prague trials as an important contribution to world peace. Czechoslovakia, he said, had been threatened by a Titoist coup. The Czech leadership had no choice but to weed out these dangerous elements.[95] In response, Ya'ari asked: "Was it so necessary for the defense of Czechoslovakia . . . to emphasize the Jewish origin of assimilated Jewish communists who had betrayed their own people and who hated Zionism . . . ?" While Ya'ari was ready to accept the guilt and "treachery of Slansky and his comrades,"[96] he firmly rejected the contention of the communists and Sneh that bourgeois Zionism was somehow different from a national liberation movement of the Jewish people. Therefore, he argued, if Sneh condemns the former, he clearly also rejects the latter.

For Sneh, there was little to do but eventually leave MAPAM. However, at first, on January 17, 1952, he formed a new Left Socialist

Faction within MAPAM. Demanding that MAPAM leave the Zionist Executive and create a united front with the communists, he continued to astound his former comrades by leading his group in a vote with MAKI[97] during the Knesset debates on Kremlin charges in the "Doctors Plot."[98] MAPAM expressed no opinion as to the guilt or innocence of the Moscow doctors. They took the position that the matter was an internal Soviet affair. On the other hand, the communists accepted the doctors' guilt but said that the Soviets had not identified them with the Jewish nation.[99] MAPAM's leadership demanded dissolution of Sneh's Left Socialist Faction and called for the resignation of their six (out of MAPAM's 13) Knesset seats on the grounds that they no longer represented MAPAM policy.[100] While some Zionist publications outside Israel[101] misread Sneh's intentions and predicted that the Sneh-Riftin group would not join forces with MAKI because of the unpleasant, anti-Semitic "new winds blowing from Moscow,"[102] Sneh not only joined the communists in 1954 but brought to MAKI a level of leadership and intellect which had been missing since the earliest days of Daniel (Wolf Auerbach), one of the Comintern's most important agents and organizers.[103]

8. The Slansky-Oren trials, the "Doctors' Plot," and the increasing anti-Semitic nature of Soviet propaganda led to a backlash in Israel. The Soviet Embassy in Tel Aviv was bombed on February 9, 1953, and despite a formal apology from the Israeli government condemning those responsible, the Soviets broke relations with Israel three days later. Ya'acov Ro'i attributed the deterioration in relations to domestic problems in Russia and its satellites, rather than to any Israeli action or policy or to any development within Israel.[104]

In fact, Soviet attitudes toward Israel had begun to change as early as the fall of 1948 when, during the Jewish High Holy Days, the Soviets were surprised and angered by the emotional welcome given Golda Meyerson (later Meir) outside the Moscow synagogue.[105] Within weeks, Jewish theaters were closed, the Yiddish press was suppressed, many Jews were removed from positions of influence and the campaign against "cosmopolitanism" was intensified.[106] Israel's first ambassador was warned not to cultivate relations with Soviet Jews, and her subsequent return to Israel in the spring of 1949 was linked to rumors of an official Soviet demand for her recall.[107] In June 1949, the Soviet Orientalist, Vladimir Lutsky, addressing a Moscow symposium on the "colonial and semi-colonial countries," analyzed Israel's orientation toward the West: with Britain's ouster from Palestine, Israel exhausted its anti-Western potential and attention should be redirected towards the Arabs and their latent anti-Western feelings. Thus, while Soviet international support for Israel was initially turned into Soviet impartiality (expressed in Soviet abstentions on Security Council votes concerning the Arab-Israeli conflict), the Soviet domestic approach was uncompromisingly aimed at discrediting Israel, Zionism, and Soviet Jews who wished to emigrate.

With Stalin's death in March 1953, the new leadership repudiated the allegations against the doctors. On the very day the doctors were declared innocent, MAKI members were distributing pamphlets with extracts of a Mikunis speech praising their trial.[108] Forced to perform another about-face, the party hailed the "excellence of socialist justice."[109] This, as much as anything else, showed that, while the puppet may have been in Israel, its strings led directly to Moscow. In July, the Soviets resumed relations with Israel followed by a number of bilateral trade agreements (during 1954-1956), and the granting of permission to hundreds of Russian Jews to emigrate to Israel. Although these actions during the Khrushchev "Thaw" appeared to signal smoother relations, they were soon overshadowed by the Czech arms deal with Egypt in 1955.

9. Following the coup and subsequent abdication of Egypt's King Farouk, General Mohammed Naguib, on September 7, 1952, assumed the Egyptian premiership and took over the Ministry of War and Marine. In subsequent moves, Naguib purged the Egyptian political system, eliminated dissidents from the army, and had himself proclaimed by decree of the Egyptian Cabinet the president and supreme authority in Egypt. On December 9, 1952 the Egyptian Cabinet was reshuffled to contain mainly Naguib-appointed technicians to implement agrarian and industrial reforms. The Egyptian Constitution of 1923 was then jettisoned. However, in February 1954, it appeared that President Naguib was in trouble, and by November he was out.

The Revolutionary Command Council charged him with having plotted with the Moslem Brotherhood to assassinate Colonel Gamal Abdel Nasser, then premier. Nasser launched his own cleanup campaign, first against the Brotherhood and other political opponents and then against an "espionage ring" which included ten Jews who were tried on December 11, 1954. When two of the ten were sentenced to death, *Kol Ha'am* blamed the American imperialists: "They want these sentences to expedite their military pacts in the Middle East"[110] aimed against the Soviet Union. Seeking to legitimize his own regime, Nasser focused attention on Egypt's external enemies. He criticized the British for their presence in Suez and the Americans for their refusal to sell arms to Egypt and for the harsh terms tied to loans needed for the proposed Aswan Dam project; and, fedayeen attacks across Gaza into Israel became an almost daily occurrence.

Meanwhile, MAKI concentrated on the "Lavon Affair" dealing with a "security mishap" which was somehow connected to the espionage trials just ended in Egypt.[111] *Kol Ha'am* not only determined the guilt of Defense Minister Pinhas Lavon, but described him and Ben-Gurion as "military adventurers" endangering Israel's existence.[112] In the debate on the day Lavon resigned, Mikunis announced his party's satisfaction with the resignation, but said he was just as much opposed to Ben-Gurion, "the most pro-American man in Israel."[113]

The stepped up border attacks (from Gaza and the Golan Heights) and the news on September 27, 1955 that Nasser had signed an $80 million contract to receive Czech arms, raised Knesset anxiety over Israel's security. On September 29, Sharett asked Soviet Chargé d'Affaires Nikolai Klimov to clarify Soviet Middle East policy.[114] Rumors of the approaching agreement had reached Israel earlier and on September 12, 1955, Ambassador Josef Avidar[115] had called on A. Zaitzev, Director of the Near and Middle Eastern Department at the Soviet Ministry, to inquire about statements by Syrian and Egyptian representatives regarding Soviet preparedness to supply their countries with arms. Zaitzev said he was authorized to state that these "publications and statements were devoid of any foundation and were nothing but fantasies." He added he was unaware of any negotiations conducted by any of the People's Democracies.[116]

The day before its official confirmation, *Kol Ha'am* denounced rumors of the Czech arms deal as "libelous." In the next 24 hours, the party was forced to do an about-face. Esther Wilenska called the transaction a "commercial agreement for Egyptian self-defence against imperialistic pressure." She said arms sale to Egypt would "further peace in the Middle East," and Israel could also receive Soviet bloc arms, "if it would follow Egypt's example."[117]

10. The recurrent flip-flops, Moscow's emergent pro-Arab policies, and the rearming of Egypt unleashed vehement criticism of Israeli communists. Moshe Sneh, by then a MAKI leader, was the subject of articles suggesting that, as a former member of the Jewish Agency Executive, he might attract many followers and "poison many souls with the venom of communism."[118] One article asked "Will MAKI go underground?" and cited the party's "feverish preparations" in anticipation of being outlawed as a subversive enemy agent. Supposedly, members had begun to destroy all "bulk records," including membership lists, address registers, subscription lists, correspondence files and minutes of meetings.[119] It explained the party's four groups of members:

- "Rap-Takers" (Sneh, Mikunis, Wilenska, Toubi, and other "first stringers");
- "Parallel-party members" (who are prepared to resume party work through various front organizations);
- "Apparatus members" (trusted communists engaged in "espionage, sabotage, and   psychological fields" unlinked to the parallel-party system);
- "Sleepers" ("crack agents" who earlier infiltrated rival political parties, police and security services, commerce and industry, army, etc.)[120]

Some articles recounted MAKI's tarnished past, evaluated its power and influence, and reassured readers that the party's numerical strength was small. Still, they were told the danger was in the party's "semi-conspiratorial" character and in the precarious nature of Israel's security.[121]

Because of mounting criticism, there was a decrease in party activity, marked by MAKI's reticence on the cost-of-living struggle and the absence of communist-organized demonstrations. There was increased internal party rumblings, leading to paralysis of MAKI's propaganda machinery. Finally, there were defections in almost all branches, including those of such old-timers as Chanoch Bzoza and Senya Frishberg in Tel Aviv and Shmuel Padua in Jerusalem.[122]

11. MAKI again had to recant its "error" when it initially supported Israel's Sinai operation which began October 29, 1956.[123] *Kol Ha'am* first spoke of "a police action against bloodthirsty marauders and the Pharaoh on the Nile" (an obvious reference to Gamal Abdel Nasser). Within forty-eight hours, it said the operation was "an imperialist collusion."[124] They were, of course, echoing Moscow's line in *Pravda* on November 1. This charged the British, French, and Israeli leadership with "premeditated aggression" conceived "with the object of crushing the national-liberation movement of the Arab peoples and restoring the colonial system throughout the Middle East and North Africa."[125] These events were used to justify the Soviet bloc's continued arms aid to Egypt as necessary to help it "prepare for self-defense against British and French colonial aggression" with the ultimate hope of establishing a "neutralist" Middle East.[126]

III. The Communists in Israel's Knesset Elections: 1951-1969

1. In 1951, MAKI's share of votes rose to 4% (from 3.5% in 1949), giving it five Knesset seats. The party platform dealt mainly with local issues, but also included the following demands: a firm foreign policy that would strengthen peace; a Big Five agreement against German rearmament; cancellation of the "aggressive Atlantic Nazi Pact"; denial of economic and strategic bases to warmongers and abrogation of all concessions.[127] It sought votes in the *ma'abarot* (tent camps) of dissatisfied immigrants awaiting jobs and housing. To attract Arab voters, MAKI touted its binational character, pointing to Tewfik Toubi (second on its candidate list) and Emil Habibi (fourth) as proof of its commitment to Arab interests and its opposition to the government's Arab policy.

In the Third Knesset elections (July 1955), MAKI held its second place standing with the Arabs (after the MAPAI-affiliated Arab lists) although its actual share of votes decreased. Issues separated the new Yishuv from the old, providing much grist for the communist propaganda mill. While European immigrants were mostly settled, newer immigrants from North Africa and Middle Eastern countries had grown resentful over *ma'abarah* conditions, unemployment, the attitude of European-born bureaucrats, queues at government offices, and perceived discrimination. And, they resented those who sat in Jerusalem or Tel Aviv and told them to settle in the Negev.[128]

Analysis of the 1955 election results was complicated by an increase of almost 21% over the total votes cast in the previous Knesset election. MAKI's gain of a mere 0.5% was downplayed by Uri Ra'anan as "their natural increase" sufficing only to maintain their previous position.[129] Still, the small increase was translated into an additional communist seat.

2. MAKI's estimated membership in 1956 was 3,500.[130] Approximately one-third of its 1955 vote came from the Arab sector and one-quarter of its members were Arabs, mostly from Nazareth and its environs, the Triangle, and to a lesser degree from Haifa, Jaffa, Lydda, Ramle. Few Arab members were pure ideological communists; rather, they were primarily fellaheen and workers moved by economic and social grievances and angered by Israeli military presence in their areas. Their support symbolized their resentment and protest against the state of Israel.

As for MAKI's Jewish membership, 80% were new immigrants, mainly from Bulgaria, Iraq, Rumania and Poland. There were few Germans among them. Except for members of the Iraqi intelligentsia, including a number of university students, the majority were "lumpenproletariat." They lived mostly in tent cities, were easy prey for communist anti-government propaganda, but were non-ideological (and non-intellectual). The remaining 20% of Jewish membership was the party's important core. Their backgrounds had much in common with earlier MPS leaders: labor Zionism, East European, from petit bourgeois families who practiced strict religious adherence. Some had come to Palestine as youngsters during the late 1920s or 1930s, and many had acquired a solid education which made them articulate leaders. However, their extreme positions still made it unlikely that they would attract many followers.

During the mid-1950s, MAKI, like communist parties elsewhere, was built on cells, some of up to 20 members. Generally, the cells were much smaller, facilitating work of a conspiratorial nature. The cells were grouped in local branches, which were then included in seven regional organizations. The party's policy-making body remained the CC, which adhered to the old Leninist principle of "democratic centralism." It had 15 members (11 Jews, 4 Arabs) and eight candidate members who, in strict accordance with the Soviet model, lacked voting rights. The CC regularly met once or twice a month to review any instructions from the political committee and to supervise the work of the party. The political committee (the local version of the Soviet Politburo) consisted of seven members (five Jews, two Arabs). Decision-making power was vested in this small group. MAKI's day-to-day affairs were handled by the secretariat, then composed of Tewfik Toubi and Ruth Lubitch (Mordechai Oren's sister-in-law).[131] The MAKI organbureau, which had generally dealt with organizational matters, was eliminated in 1953, when the Kremlin abolished the Soviet equivalent. As noted, the real power of the party was exercised by MAKI's political committee (or politburo). The number of its members varied from time to time. The leaders were deeply committed ideologically and were highly intelligent. Few details are known about their lives because they avoided publicity. Some of these leaders[132] were:

• Shmuel Mikunis, born in Russia in 1903, arrived in Palestine at age 18 and first supported himself as an actor and as a worker in road construction, citrus groves and building trades. He attended the Polytechnic Institute in France, becoming a civil engineer in 1934. A graduate of Moscow's Kutvo, he returned to Palestine, and became active among workers and intellectuals. He was a member of the party delegation appearing before the U.N. Commission on Palestine in 1947, and worked in East European countries gaining support for Israel's struggle in 1948. He wrote numerous articles and pamphlets for the party, served in the party's highest echelons, and was often accused of "personality cult."[133]

• Dr. Moshe Sneh, born in Poland in 1909, was educated at Warsaw University. He was chairman of the General Zionist Organization in Poland

and a delegate to several Zionist congresses, beginning in 1933. After serving in the Polish army as a captain in 1939, he made his way to Palestine in 1940, where he joined the *Haganah*. From 1945 to 1946, he was chief of the *Haganah*, leading that Jewish resistance movement against the British. In June 1946, about to be arrested, he escaped to Paris where he helped organize transport for "illegal" immigrants, made some important contacts and negotiated with several European governments for arms transfers to Israel. A member of the Executive at the World Jewish Congress (Montreux, 1948), Sneh began his political life as a General Zionist, gradually moving left into MAPAM's leadership and then to MAKI, where he became the party's leading theorist. He edited the party paper and authored many articles. Not long after his switch to MAKI, he was made a member of the politburo.[134]   Israeli journalist Samuel Segev, among others, said of Sneh that he was extremely brilliant and could easily have become Prime Minister of Israel had he not moved so far to the left.

• Meir Wilner was born in 1918 in Vilna, where he attended Hebrew high school. He came to Palestine in 1937 and attended Hebrew University in Jerusalem. Wilner wrote many articles and pamphlets for the party and, along with Mikunis, he was often accused of "personality cult." In 1965 he became the leader of RAKAH, the new Arab communist party, and he continued to retain his Knesset seat following the elections in July 1984.

• Esther Wilenska was born in Vilna in 1918 and came to Palestine in 1938. After attending Hebrew University, she taught in Jerusalem and was a member of the executive committee of the General Federation of Labor. She became a member of the PCP's CC in 1944, later rising to the politburo. For a time she also served as the editor of *Kol Ha'am* and wrote articles on the class struggle, political and economic topics. After divorcing Wilner, she married Breitstein.

• Zvi Breitstein came to Israel in 1935. He was also an editor of *Kol Ha'am*, and served as a CC member and as chairman of the control commission. After he was dropped from the control commission in 1972, he and his wife, Esther Wilenska, left MAKI to form a more radical group.

• David "Sasha" Hinin is believed to have been born in Eastern Europe. In 1963 he studied in the Soviet Union on a one-year program, and perhaps because of this was considered a conservative communist, a "Stalinist" who "was guided by Soviet interests alone." However, his devotion to the Soviet Communist Party may have been manifest even earlier, when "he . . burst into tears after the Twentieth CPSU Congress (in February 1954), when his idols were destroyed"[135] by Khrushchev's exposure of Stalin's brutal crimes and cult of personality.

● Tewfik Toubi, born in Haifa in 1922, attended the Bishop Gobut School in Jerusalem, served as a Mandatory official in Haifa, and was the youngest person to win a Knesset seat at that time. An editor of the twice weekly *Al Ittihad* and a member of the World Peace Council, Toubi served as a member of the presidium of the National Committee for Peace while also serving on MAKI's CC and politburo. He wrote many articles on political problems and on the Arab minority in Israel. His Christian upbringing and his perceived "pro-Jewish" tilt (probably because both he and his brother George married Jewish women) earned him the reputation of a "moderate."

● Emil Habibi was born in Haifa in 1922 and was also a Christian. He had a university education and because of his nationalist leanings was suspected for a time of "nationalist deviation." He was a journalist, a member of the CC and the politburo.

3. Funds for MAKI's use were raised primarily through front organizations both in Israel and in the United States. In 1956 it was reported that:

> For the past three years campaigns have been conducted . . . (in the U.S., for instance, by a Polish Landsmannschaft, under the direction of a certain Mr. Vendi, by a Borison Landsmannschaft, and by the Emma Lazarus Women's League) for the ostensible purpose of building a Reuben Breinin Dispensary in Israel. The moneys collected . . . some $60,000 in the past year alone--are transmitted to Shimon Cohen ("Shimmek"), Secretary of the Tarbut La'am (People's Culture) Society, an Israel front organization, who is at the same time Treasurer of MAKI.[136]

The report noted that no sign of the dispensary could yet be seen in Israel. Other fund-raising techniques included subscriptions to the party's press and periodicals and special campaigns for party conferences, to which "a full fortnight's wages must be contributed by every member."[137] The party also operated commercial ventures, including a bookbinding workshop in Jaffa, a metal and souvenirs enterprise in Tel Aviv, a distribution agency for books and periodicals in Tel Aviv and another in Haifa.[138] These enterprises also provided employment for party members.

4. Israel's Fourth Knesset election was held in July 1959. Participation of both Jews and Arabs was high--81% (969,337 valid votes were cast). An important event affecting this election was the riots which broke out in Haifa's Wadi Salib quarter, later spreading to Beersheba and Migdal Ha'emek. These were of a distinct communal character and had their origin in the economic distress and lack of integration of newly-arrived immigrants from Asia and North Africa. This became a central issue, resulting in changes in some party lists: "Oriental," or Sephardi, candidates being added to attract votes. A second issue was French-Israeli ties. As a result of Arab pressure, France's nationalized Renault cut its ties with Israel, raising questions of Israel's "over-dependence" on France. And there was the issue of Israel's arms deals with West Germany. While this had led to the resignation of Israel's government only a few months earlier, it receded in importance as election day approached. MAKI used these issues to attract Jewish voters.

There were other issues specifically affecting Arab voters. But here MAKI miscalculated. The Iraqi revolution in August 1958 deposed the Hashemite monarch, a British legacy, and brought to power 'Abd al-Karim Qasim. Because this followed the Syro-Egyptian union of February 1958 so closely, it unleashed dreams of Arab unity and liberation from Israeli rule. Many Israeli Arabs believed that Qasim would join the United Arab Republic under Nasser's leadership. When MAKI followed Moscow's line in supporting Qasim in his subsequent conflict with Nasser, Israeli Arabs became alienated. While they approved of MAKI's anti-Zionist stance, denial of communist support for Nasser was tantamount to betrayal of the promise of pan-Arabism.

Under Moscow directives, MAKI attempted to organize young Arab nationalists into a popular front. This effort coincided with the brief honeymoon between the UAR and the Soviet Union. Together, *El Ard* (The Land) Nationalists and MAKI staged protest meetings against the Israeli Nationality Law,[139] the appropriation of Arab land, and the military administration. Co-operation between the two groups was short-lived, as the young pro-Nasser leaders of *El Ard* broke away from the communists in the wake of the split between the UAR and Iraq. Increased politicization of Israel's Arabs was a result of a number of factors, including Egypt's defeat in 1956, the tragic Kafr Kassem incident,[140] and the activities of the *El Ard* group. When this group left MAKI, its leaders urged non-participation for Arabs in the election. In the meantime, MAKI continued to stress Arab non-cooperation with the Zionists, using the slogan "6 against 114"[141] (referring to the number of communists in the Knesset against all the other members). The Arab electorate was faced with the choices of (a) non-participation/boycott advocated by the *El Ard* nationalist group or (b) participation in the election but non-cooperation with MAPAI, advocated by the communists.   The result was surprising to both nationalists and communists.   Approximately 85% of the eligible Arab voters exercised their franchise despite the call to boycott;[142] and MAPAM nudged aside MAKI, taking second place to MAPAI with Arab voters.[143]   MAPAM stole the show from MAKI among Arab voters by, among other efforts, its call for full Arab membership in *Histadrut*.   This strategy was in line with the recent *Histadrut* decisions for which MAPAM had pressed.   A comparison of results taken from purely Arab polling places shows the shift:

	1951	1955	1959
MAPAI	67.9	64.7	49.0
MAKI	15.1	15.6	11.2
MAPAM	5.6	7.3	14.0

Source: Based on information provided by Yosef Waschitz, "Arabs in Israeli Politics" in *New Outlook,* March-April 1962; and Atallah Mansour, "Israel's Arabs Go to the Polls" in *New Outlook,* January 1960, 23-26.

The Soviet loss of prestige resulting from continued disclosures of Stalinist atrocities, suppression of the popular will in Poland and Hungary, and Moscow's intimidation of the Ben-Gurion government during the Suez Affair of 1956 hurt MAKI among its potential Jewish supporters.   In addition, after ten years of election experience, Israeli Arabs were learning to differentiate between various Zionist trends.   They now chose to encourage one, by increasing the strength of MAPAM, and to desert the other, by not voting MAPAI.   In this election, MAKI was not the beneficiary of Arab grievances, and the party emerged more than a bit scathed: it lost three of its six seats, representing a decrease in electoral support from 4.5% to 2.8%.

5. Thus, MAKI ran three campaigns for the Fifth Knesset elections on August 15, 1961.   The first was aimed at the Jews and focused on:

> (a) Nazi war criminal, Adolf Eichmann's trial then nearing its
>   conclusion.   Tied to this was Israel's relations with West
>   Germany, portrayed as the equally wicked heir of the Nazi
>   regime.

(b) Wage increases for skilled workers, said to be justified by existing conditions of full employment and shortages of skilled workers. MAKI identified itself with skilled and unskilled workers in all industries and branches of the economy, supporting all calls for strikes (including that of the rabbis).[144]

(c) Dissatisfaction of new immigrants awaiting full absorption.

MAKI ignored the revived issue of the Lavon Affair, as well as the controversy dealing with the *Histadrut's* power and influence. The party's second campaign was aimed at the Arab voters and included:

(a) Issues of Arab nationalism and political equality. MAKI portrayed itself as the Arab's ultimate voice in Israel.

(b) Demand for abolition of military administration.

(c) Opposition to expropriation of Arab lands either for reasons of security or irrigation works.

(d) Support for Moslem and Druze religious autonomy.

(e) Demands for health and sanitation facilities, better roads and schools, and generally improved working and living conditions for Arab peasants and workers.

(f) Advocacy of the right of all Arab refugees to return.

The party's support for the Arab refugees' right to return attracted many votes among Israeli Arabs. MAPAM was left behind even though it disassociated itself from the official line of "not a single refugee shall return." Instead MAPAM advocated an Arab-Israeli agreement on repatriation of a specific number of refugees, within the framework of a peace settlement.[145]

MAKI's third campaign focused on issues of interest to both Jews and Arabs: tax reduction; an increase in the real wages of workers at the expense of company profits; abolition of social polarization; and concern for working women, such as availability of state-supported child care centers.

In both communities, MAKI also emphasized recent Soviet successes in space as achievements of a progressive and peaceful nature. The party made enormous organizational efforts, opened new branches in immigrant areas, held rallies in various locations, launched a special fund-raising drive, and used every front organization to reach voters. Results were impressive compared to the 1959 losses: MAKI won five seats, representing a 4.2% share of the 1,006,964 valid votes cast.[146] The party took 22.5% of the

Arab votes cast in purely Arab localities.[147] This moved it back into second place, after MAPAI (49.2%) and ahead of MAPAM (11.7%).

6. Despite impressive gains in the Fifth Knesset elections, internal strains relating to Stalinism, neo-Stalinism and the Sino-Soviet dispute caused a small group of the party's younger members to form a dissident group within MAKI. In the early 1960s, cliques of disaffected young members, impressed by the radical revolutionary lines of Maoism and frustrated with Moscow's apparent turn from Marxism, met in parlors and coffee houses, formed cells of their own, and soon identified themselves as the Israel Socialist Organization (ISO). They called their paper *Matzpen* (Compass); and, in turn, they were so identified. *Matzpen* has been compared to the New Left groups which appeared in Europe and the U.S. during the 1960s.[148]

Their commitment to Marxism and its basic tenet of the inevitability of revolution, combined with the Trotsky-Maoist belief in permanent revolution, made them balk at the slogan "peaceful coexistence" and at Soviet resolve to open relations with the capitalist world. Their main thesis regarding the Arab-Israeli conflict was that national coexistence was impossible because the Arabs could not agree to the existence of a Zionist state linked to the Jewish communities of the world. Their solution: "De-Zionization,"[149] meaning Israel would exist as a local phenomenon, without ties to Jews elsewhere, and would return to the borders designated by the U.N. partition plan. It would be socialist and part of a socialist Middle East. What was the reaction of MAKI's leaders? They ejected the *Matzpen* group from the communist party.[150]

7. In the meantime, MAKI was having other internal problems. In December 1963, Meir Wilner submitted to MAKI's politburo his draft of a proposed speech for the upcoming national convention. Asked to speak on organizational questions, his draft deviated from this topic, dealing instead with Arab-Israeli relations and attacking *Kol Ha'am's* position as too sympathetic to Jewish nationalism. The politburo rejected Wilner's draft, reassigning the main address to Mikunis.[151] When Mikunis spoke at the convention in Haifa a month later, he condemned both Jewish and Arab nationalism, attacked the government and political system with the usual litany of criticisms, and cited MAKI's program compared to that of the other political parties. Given ten minutes, Wilner spoke for an hour attacking the Mikunis conclusions and repeating the anti-Israel arguments in his rejected draft. To avoid exacerbating the situation, Mikunis did not respond. He merely summarized the arguments heard.

This "Haifa controversy" was subsequently discussed and, uncustomarily, the political bureau decided to permit both Mikunis and Wilner to present reports on the Arab-Israeli question at the CC session scheduled for July 1964. The resultant resolutions of the plenary session were vaguely formulated so as to satisfy both factions. Mikunis and Sneh, satisfied MAKI's "moderate" line would hold, left for Moscow to attend the International Youth Forum, scheduled to convene in September. Wilner, meanwhile, consolidated his position, increasing his support among Arab party members. He was initially assisted by the appearance of Mikunis' article, "A Word in Ahmed Ben Bella's Ear," in which the author criticized the Algerian president's anti-Israel attitude.[152] Wilner's faction and the Arab members of MAKI argued that since the article expressed a fundamental political stand it should have been submitted to the party's politburo for approval.

Wilner was next helped by an incident in Moscow. Arab representatives to the Youth Forum submitted a draft resolution proposing delegates express solidarity with the Palestinian Arab struggle for "return to their homeland" and "full restoration of their rights" and condemn "imperialism and its continuing suport of existing aggression, which is hindering the march of Arabs of the Middle East towards true democracy and freedom. . . ."[153] Unwilling to see passage of this proposal because it did not call for "mutual recognition and respect for the just rights of both sides," Mikunis instructed the head of the Israeli Young Communist League delegation to support a counter-proposal submitted by delegations from MAPAM and *Ahdut Ha'Avoda* youth organizations,[154] to vote against the Arab proposal and even to walk out of the meeting. These instructions, Wilner later argued, exceeded Mikunis' authority because they were in direct contradiction to the MAKI political bureau decision that its delegation not vote against Arab proposals and not support the left-wing Zionist resolution (prepared before the Israeli delegations left for Moscow).

On his return, Mikunis discovered that MAKI's seven-member politburo was split four to three: Wilner, Toubi, Habibi, and Hinin were aligned against Mikunis, Sneh, and Wilenska. The hardbitten debate continued for months, dividing first the CC and then the membership. In January 1965, Sneh, as editior of the party's paper, again tried to unify the party by walking the ideological tightrope in his editorial: "The source of [conflict] lies in refusal of each side to recognize the rights of the other--in the refusal by Israel's rulers to legitimate the rights of the Arab people of Palestine and in the refusal by the Arab leaders to legitimate the State of Israel and its rights."[155]

Wilner and his supporters argued that *Kol Ha'am,* with Sneh as editor, no longer reflected the party line. In February 1965, Toubi proposed that Sneh be replaced by Zvi Breitstein (of the Mikunis faction) and Ruth Lubitch (of the Wilner faction) and that the secretariat of *Kol Ha'am's* editorial board be expanded with three Wilner supporters. Wilner's advantage of one vote in the politburo passed the resolution, sending it on to the CC for their approval. Mikunis and Sneh, however, turned to the larger MAKI branches in Tel Aviv and Jerusalem, where their supporters rallied and convinced Wilner to avoid a confrontation. Despite attempts to find a common denominator and efforts on the part of Sneh to keep a balance in the party's organ by publishing both sets of views, the Wilner group continued to attack the Mikunis faction for their "nationalist-Jewish" deviation--shades of the old PCP-KPP and *Ha'Emet-Kol Ha'am* disputes of the Twenties and the late Thirties-early Forties.

When the CC met in April 1965, Wilner and his supporters failed to gain a CC condemnation of the Mikunis faction. In May, however, Wilner succeeded in obtaining a majority vote in the CC for a resolution providing for publication of the two points of view. This public airing of an internal ideological dispute (long opposed by Moscow, where such disputes were supposed to be settled definitively), while unusual for an "orthodox" communist party, appears to have been a characteristic of the communist movement in Palestine and Israel. The two points of view, later known as "Opinion A" (Wilner-Tubi) and "Opinion B" (Mikunis-Sneh), appeared in *Kol Ha'am* on May 19, and set off a series of debates at regional conventions, as well as on the pages of the party organ. Since both sides knew that the issues would only be resolved by the Fifteenth Party Conference scheduled for July 1965, an argument arose as to the basis of delegate selection.[156]

At this point, the CPSU delegation arrived, unaware of the depth of the differences between the factions. They assumed a neutral attitude (probably aided by their lack of understanding), and expressed their hope that the propaganda value of a binational Israeli Communist Party could be maintained.[157] When CPSU delegates Georgi Franzeyev and Yuri Mitin met with members of each faction, they stressed the harm a split would cause to the world communist movement, and they succeeded in convincing both sides to concentrate on the coming Knesset elections, postponing the solution to MAKI's problems.[158] Soviet pressure for a compromise resulted in equal representation in all central party institutions and was followed immediately by the departure of the Soviet delegation, under the impression that unity had been preserved. However, as Mikunis later explained: "[F]rom 23 June [the day of the compromise] to 2 August [the last joint session of the CC], the factions continued their acts of deviousness, pressure and factional intervention wherever possible,"[159] in order to determine the choice of conference delegates. In other words, the CPSU delegates, because of their continuing inability to understand the issues peculiar to the Jewish state, accomplished nothing. Finally, on August 3, 1965, *Kol Ha'am* admitted that the CC had failed to resolve the delegate selection dispute, leaving no alternative but for each faction to hold its own conference. This signaled the end of Israel's binational communist party.[160]

8. Two separate and distinct communist parties presented lists for the Sixth Knesset elections of November 2, 1965: MAKI, headed by Mikunis and Sneh, and RAKAH (the Hebrew acronym for the New Communist List), headed by Wilner, Toubi and Habibi. Both parties agreed on:

- support for peoples' liberation movements against colonialism and neo-colonialism;
- an end to the policy of friendship with the "neo-Nazi" rulers of Bonn;
- abrogation of the arms deal with "German militarism";
- support for initiatives to make the Middle East a nuclear-free zone.

They differed on the following:

- MAKI called for an independent Israeli foreign policy, "nonalignment."
- RAKAH called for the abolition of relations of dependency upon NATO, and used the term "positive neutrality" to describe their ideal of an Israeli foreign policy.
- MAKI called for an improvement of Israeli relations with the USSR.
- RAKAH was more explicit, calling for an expansion of political, economic, and cultural ties with the Soviet Union and other socialist countries.
- MAKI wanted the abrogation of the decision forbidding the government to conduct negotiations on the refugee issue on the basis of the U.N. Resolution.
- RAKAH demanded that Israel first recognize the right of Arab refugees to choose between returning to their homeland or receiving compensation.

Israel's recognition of Palestinian rights, RAKAH said, would lead to recognition by the Arab states of Israel and its rights. RAKAH supported an international agreement to end the Middle East conventional arms race by ending all arms shipments to all Middle East countries, from both the Western and Eastern blocs.[161]   During the election campaign, MAKI's leaders accused RAKAH of "Arab chauvinism" and reaffirmed Israel's right to exist beyond question, stating that mutual recognition was the only way to peace. With Arab recognition, MAKI said, must come abrogation of the boycott and free passage through the Suez Canal.   RAKAH responded with charges of "Jewish chauvinism." With the outlawing of the Nasserite *El Ard*, RAKAH's leaders concentrated on organizing Arab cadres.   Toubi and Habibi, Saliba Khamis, Hana Naqqara and Emil Touma expended enormous energy, moving among the Arabs on a daily basis to establish personal contacts.[162] When the *El Ard* leaders requested an alliance, they were rejected out of RAKAH's fear of giving the Israeli authorities any excuse to bar RAKAH's participation.[163]

The New Communist Party could now claim a monopoly on Arab nationalism.   They were even supported by Cairo Radio whose broadcasts reached Israel's Arab population.   The ninth anniversary of the Kafr Kassem tragedy on October 29 provided RAKAH with an opportunity to issue a call to Arabs to vote "against the murderers" so that there would never be another Kafr Kassem.[164] The appeal seemed to work.   When combined with the disappearance of the nationalist *El Ard,* the emergence of RAKAH as an Arab party and the new voter eligibility of some 4,000-5,000 young, educated Arabs, the party's organization and election propaganda efforts succeeded in winning three seats, representing 2.27% (or 27,413 out of 1,206,728 valid votes cast).   MAKI, on the other hand, barely won Mikunis' seat with 1.1% of the vote, as even more votes were drawn off by the New Force, another new party formed by the editors of the weekly *Ha'olam HaZeh:* ". . . thousands of Arabs, mostly young people, gave their votes to a Jewish group that they didn't know personally and from which they couldn't hope for any personal favors."

Journalist A. Mansour believes these votes were a "reward" for a newspaper which was popular among Arabs.   According to Mansour, although it was "sensationalist and pornographic," it was never guilty of catering to the taste for chauvinism or hatred of the Arabs.[165] That may or may not be true, but the "peace caravan" sent into Arab villages is probably what attracted the support of young, first-time Arab voters and others who were either impatient with MAPAM's restraint or uncomfortable with the extremism of RAKAH.   The result: the New Force won almost 3,000 Arab votes (of a total of 14,124), giving it one seat which might have gone to MAKI, whose positions on Jewish-Arab issues were actually quite close to *Ha'olam HaZeh's* new party.[166]

Arab voters again followed the pattern of giving about half their votes to MAPAI (or the Alignment in this case), with the communists placing second, followed by MAPAM. Voting was very heavy, with 83% of the electorate casting valid votes. Of approximately 120,000 eligible Arab voters, almost 100,000 (83.3%, slightly more than the national average) went to the polls. While the Arab communists won 22.6% of the Arab vote, the Jewish communists attracted only 0.5%. In subsequent elections, RAKAH's share of the Arab vote would steadily grow:

$$
\begin{array}{lll}
1969 & - & 29.6\% \\
1973 & - & 36.6\% \\
1977 & - & 49.3\%
\end{array}
$$

Thus in 1977, RAKAH, with close to 50% of the Arab vote, forced MAPAI and its Arab lists into second place among Arab voters.[167]

9. The split in Israel's binational communist party became absolute in 1967 with the Six-Day War. The Soviet bloc (but for Rumania) broke relations with Israel, taking the Arab side. RAKAH followed the Soviet line, demanding Israeli withdrawal, and Meir Wilner voted against a bill calling for an emergency tax, on the grounds that it would finance military action not in Israel's interest.[168] RAKAH's *Al Ittihad* touted Arab military successes until it was clear Israel was winning. Then they condemned the "Eshkol-Dayan-Begin" government and its "adventuristic undertaking," its "policy of force," and its denial of Palestinian nationalism.[169] In July, they were rewarded for their hard line when Moscow recognized RAKAH as the Communist Party in Israel.[170]

On the other hand, Sneh opted for Jewish nationalism, supporting the government's actions and subsequently justifying Israel's position on the occupied territories in terms of self-defense. Mikunis also supported the government, saying: "It was and still is our opinion that unconditional Israeli retreat from the occupied territories would be tantamount to retreating to the situation and conditions which forced the Six-Day War on us; it would be tantamount to inviting another war."[171] However, he added an important qualifier: ". . . we firmly believe that any attempt to annex the occupied territories to Israel also means inviting an Arab war of revenge against Israel." He supported immediate and direct negotiations with the "democratic representatives" of the Palestinian people, noting that "the government of

Israel should reveal such readiness even if there are still no signs of a readiness for peace on the other side of the ceasefire lines."

Thus, almost six months after Moscow had stripped the party of its "legitimacy" by awarding recognition to RAKAH, MAKI's leaders were still trying to walk the tightrope. When MAKI was excluded from preparations for an international conference of communist parties in Moscow, Mikunis appealed, to no avail. Their places were taken by RAKAH delegates, and MAKI's leaders suffered the isolation of other "revisionist" parties. However, with the Soviet invasion of Czechoslovakia in August 1968, the world communist movement split over the issue of Soviet domination, and there followed an improvement in MAKI's relations with both the Rumanian and Yugoslavian parties.

MAKI's leaders also reassessed their party's position in Israel; and when Arab guerrillas launched a series of attacks in the fall of 1968, MAKI's leadership approved Israel's retaliatory raids. This set off a protest from Esther Wilenska and her husband, Zvi Breitstein. They argued that MAKI had strayed from the communist line, gone too far in its support for the "hawkish" government, not made sufficient effort to understand the Arab point of view, and had been too critical of the Soviet Union. These charges were pressed at MAKI's Sixteenth Congress held in October 1968. Despite her failure to alter the party line, Wilenska represented MAKI at "The Berlin Peace Congress" in July 1969. She spoke of mutual recognition but admitted being surprised "when the organizers of a meeting devoted to peace allowed the PLO to distribute propaganda material even denying Israel's right to have been established or to exist."[172]

10. The elections for the Seventh Knesset were held on October 28, 1969, in a general atmosphere of pessimism regarding peace prospects. Economic and social issues ranked first, with "peace policies" relegated to a secondary position. This showed up in the results when three groups identifying themselves with the peace issue had poor showings:[173]

> (1) The Peace List: A group of university professors and other intellectuals set up an election platform based on only the peace issue. This list drew 0.37% (5,138 votes), not qualifying for a seat.
>
> (2) *Ha'olam HaZeh:* Uri Avneri's list received 1.23% (16,853 votes), barely qualifying for two seats (one more than it previously held).

(3) MAKI: Headed by Sneh, the party polled 1.15% (15,712 votes), qualifying for only one seat.

The Arab voters virtually ignored the three peace lists, which attracted only a total of 1,524 Arab votes:[174] The Peace List-350 votes; *Ha'olam HaZeh*-444 votes; MAKI-730 votes. RAKAH ran an anti-Israel campaign and concentrated on the party's natural base, the Arab villages and towns. Significantly, its campaign propaganda ignored the theoretical and ideological aspects of the class struggle, focusing instead on the realities of West Bank life. They emphasized the humiliation of the checkpoints and the communal tension and suspicion in Jewish towns where many young Arabs worked. Their pamphlets advocated immediate and unconditional withdrawal from all occupied areas.[175]

Of the approximately 150,000 valid Arab votes cast, RAKAH received 29.6%,[176] compared to its previous share of 22.6%. They attracted some 10,000 new voters of whom about 1,000 were Druze.[177] Analysts generally agree that the change in the Arab vote in 1969 was among "the most significant findings" in the statistical analysis of that election. Clearly RAKAH's anti-Zionist campaign had attracted many Arab voters away from the Zionist labor parties and their affiliated Arab lists. The party, now overwhelmingly Arab, again won three seats, but its potential seemed greater. MAPAI, faced with the RAKAH challenge, opened its membership to Druze and other Arab veterans of the Israeli Army and moved their Arab Knesset members to prominent positions in the Knesset and onto various committees.

IV. The End of MAKI

1. Danny the Red arrived in Israel in May 1970, when many Israeli youths were questioning the slogan *"ein breira"* (no choice). France's Daniel Cohn-Bendit,[178] the leading representative of Europe's New Left, was invited by the Hebrew University Student Union to speak at their first "peace-in." Seventy high school students had written the Prime Minister questioning the "seriousness" of government efforts to establish peace.[179] Many university students (former soldiers), intellectuals and kibbutz members were raising the same question. Cohn-Bendit's presence in Israel coalesced these individuals and a number of small leftist groups into a New Left movement.

Among those drawn in were two radical groups, *Matzpen* and *Siach*. While *Matzpen* (the Israel Socialist Organization) was a spin-off from MAKI during the early 1960s, *Siach* had begun to take shape after the Six-Day War.

The first *Siach* group had developed in Tel Aviv, formed by disillusioned members of Kibbutz Artzi-HaShomer HaTza'ir who opposed MAPAM's decision to remain in the Alignment, which was part of the government. They were joined by some ex-MAKI members and other previously unaffiliated individuals, while in Jerusalem another--mainly student--*Siach* group was developing. The two groups decided to cooperate, but to maintain their independence. Eventually, similar groups emerged in Hadera, Haifa, and the Negev. There was also an autonomous group of sympathetic high school students.[180]

Through his friend Haim Hanegbi, a *Matzpen* leader, Cohn-Bendit was invited to speak at a kibbutz. His remarks not only unleashed a bitter controversy, but served to split *Matzpen* and then to unify *Matzpen* and *Siach* elements. It thus initiated a new leftist alignment which ran its own list under the name *Moked* (Focus) in the Eighth Knesset election (December 31, 1973). *Moked* is seen as MAKI's direct ideological descendant. MAKI continued to exist, but after the rift of 1965 it grew increasingly weak. This was due initially to further factioning and then to the party's loss in early 1972 of Moshe Sneh,[181] its most formidable theoretician and spokesman.

At the Seventeenth Congress in April 1972, MAKI experienced further problems.[182]   Esther Wilenska condemned MAKI's "moderate" tendencies and called for an alliance with all radical elements. The result was a Left Forum leading to negotiations with representatives of *Olam HADASH* (New World), *Brit HaSmol* (The Left-Wing Alliance) and *Siach*.[183]   In the meantime, a group of Sneh's followers opened negotiations with a new leftist socialist-Zionist group called *Tchelet-Adom* (the Blue-Red movement, blue for Zionism and red for socialism). The resulting coalition in July 1973 also included "the Zionist half"[184] of *Siach*. It was this coalition which took the name *Moked,* under the leadership of Dr. Meir Pa'il, a colonel in the reserves and an expert on military history. In 1974, the more radical Wilenska-Breitstein group would splinter off to join *Meri* (the Israel Radical Camp), consisting of *Ha'olam HaZeh* (led by Uri Avneri) and the radical faction from *Siach*.

2. Outbreak of war on Yom Kippur 1973, the holy Day of Atonement, at first shocked and silenced all critics of the Israeli government. The elections originally scheduled for the end of October were rescheduled for December 31. Before long, both the right-wing LIKUD and the Israeli Left launched their own attacks. LIKUD assailed the government for not pursuing the war more aggressively and for permitting non-military supplies to reach Egypt's trapped Third Army. The Leftists claimed that:

- The government's status quo policy of "no peace, no war" had failed.
- Israelis had been deceived by the false security inherent in the concepts of "strategic depth" and "natural boundaries."
- The government's policies of expropriation, settlement, and annexation had conveyed "the impression that it wanted territories, not peace."
- The government had failed to recognize the existence of a Palestinian people and to accept that "the territory of Israel belonged to two peoples--Jews and Palestinians."
- The government had also failed to realize the necessity for compromise.[185]

In the Knesset debate soon after the start of war, Meir Wilner spoke on behalf of RAKAH, criticizing the government for closing its ears "to all suggestions of peace" and for relying on Israel's military superiority and on American backing. He said that "In contrast . . . the Soviet Union repeatedly suggested a political solution in the direction of a stable and just peace."[186] Shmuel Mikunis spoke for MAKI:

Most . . . except for militaristic right-wing circles and those who crave territorial annexations . . . have realized that political victory can be had by achieving peace, a just peace. . . . We do not ignore the grave significance of the one-sided policy of the Soviet Union in our region which expresses itself these days in a very sharp manner, but we look forward to days to come and therefore we dismiss the extreme remarks of MK Begin against the Soviet Union.[187] (Emphasis mine.)

Despite his implied criticism of the USSR's "one-sided policy," Mikunis' presence on the candidate list would prove to be a burden to MAKI's offspring, *Moked*. Issues of peace and war were expected to dominate the election, but the question of the Labor government's competency intruded. MAPAM members argued the viability of the Alignment and MAPAM's place in it. On election day, MAPAM defectors turned to the five "peace" lists,[188] including RAKAH and the new *Moked* party headed by Pa'il, a non-communist. Altogether the peace movement gained two Knesset seats, giving it a new total of 12. *Moked* won 1.4% out of a total of 1,566,855 valid votes cast, seating only Pa'il.[189] Asked why *Moked* had not lived up to expectations by winning two or three seats, Pa'il mentioned the strongly nationalistic mood in the country, intensified by the Yom Kippur War, and the alignment Tchelet-Adom made with MAKI. He explained that the name Shmuel Mikunis was especially damaging. "I am sure that if not for Mikunis (a known communist and sympathizer of the Soviet Union), we would have two seats in the Knesset."[190]

Clearly, the Jewish communist party had lost its raison d'etre. As noted, MAKI's submersion in *Moked* under Tchelet-Adom and its drift away from communist ideology had been more than the radical Wilenska and Breitstein could accept. In late 1974 it was Mikunis who criticized MAKI, as Moscow had done, for "nationalistic deviation." He abandoned the remnant of the party he had helped build, saying that it had turned Zionist and as a communist he could never be a Zionist.[191] Finally in June 1975, MAKI fulfilled the hopes of Meir Pa'il and dissolved itself,[192] formally passing out of existence. Hence, with the 1973 election, we come to the end of the history of the Jewish communist party in Israel. Before the next Knesset election of 1977, MAKI's offspring, *Moked,* would be even further submerged in still another coalition, "SHELI."

3. RAKAH, the Arab communist party, however, did well in the elections following the Yom Kippur War. Headed by Wilner and Toubi, RAKAH's list won four seats with 3.4% of the total vote and 36.6% of the Arab vote.[193] Its increase from 29.6% of the Arab vote in 1969 was highly significant as an indicator of the change in the Israeli Arab's perception wrought by the recent war. One of its four Knesset seats went to Tewfik Zayyad, later called the "Kremlin Communist" and the "Red Mayor" of Nazareth. Zayyad was born in Nazareth in 1929 and under the influence of some of his teachers, he became an active communist while still in high school. He joined the NLL, which he identified as the Arab counterpart of the Jewish-dominated PCP. In 1949, he was arrested for his participation in a demonstration against unemployment. In 1962, despite an administrative order forbidding him to leave Nazareth without a special permit, MAKI sent him to Russia where he spent two years studying communist ideology and political economy.[194] Zayyad, a Democratic Front candidate, was elected mayor of Nazareth in December 1975, announcing the limited goal of bringing equal rights to Nazareth: "Our struggle is a defined one, a local one, a struggle for the application of Israeli democracy to Nazareth municipal matters."[195]

Yet, on April 2, 1976, Zayyad was "authoritatively" reported "agitating in West Bank cities" just before the outbreak of violence.[196] Indeed, the violence on the West Bank and in the Galilee on March 30, 1976 was attributed to RAKAH instigation, its organizing demonstrations against the government's policy of building Jewish settlements in densely populated Arab areas. Earlier in March, the heads of Arab local councils in the Galilee had signed a statement voicing opposition to government takeover of lands and further Jewish settlement in the Galilee. This was followed by "Land Day" demonstrations, as they became known, with RAKAH being blamed for unleashing a new spirit of confrontation. Thus, the party was now seen as more openly anti-Israel than ever before since statehood. Some even traced links to the PLO through the underground Palestinian National Front (in Judea and Samaria), "affiliated with the outlawed Communist Party of Jordan, and RAKAH in Israel."[197]

4. In 1977, to prepare for the Ninth Knesset elections, RAKAH formed an alliance with the Black Panthers[198] in an effort to regain legitimacy in the Jewish community. Charlie Biton, Panther leader, was given third place--a safe spot--on the RAKAH list, after Wilner and Toubi. This move brought Kochavi Shemesh and other Black Panthers together with RAKAH to form a new coalition, HADASH[199] (*Hazit Democratit Le-Shalom U'le Shivyon*, Democratic Front for Peace and Equality). Also part of HADASH was Hanna Mo'is, a non-communist Christian Arab who was the chairman of the organization of Arab local council heads. Mo'is was given the fifth spot.

The elections of May 5, 1977 brought momentous change to Israel. The Alignment suffered a resounding defeat, bringing Begin's LIKUD coalition to power. RAKAH's Democratic Front took 49.3% of the Arab vote (comprising about 90% of its total), ranking it first among Arab voters. This almost completely reversed the party's position relative to MAPAI, which took 27% of the Arab vote, electing only one Knesset member from its Arab affiliated list.[200] Of 1,747,820 valid votes cast, HADASH won 80,118 (4.6%), giving it five seats. Its peace platform called for:

- Israeli withdrawal from all occupied territories;
- recognition of the Palestinian-Arab people's right to self-determination;
- establishment of an independent state alongside the state of Israel;
- respect of Israel's and all the Arab states' rights to "sovereign existence and development in conditions of peace and security."

It recommended "immediate reconvention of the Geneva Conference . . . with the participation of all parties to the conflict including the PLO. . . ."[201] RAKAH's Democratic Front election success was impressive, but the binational/class emphasis of its campaign failed to attract significant Jewish support. In totally Jewish areas, under 900 voted for the Front out of 80,118 votes.[202]

SHELI, the small political alignment which included *Ha'olam HaZeh,* elements of the Panthers, and *Moked,* completely swallowed Mikunis' MAKI. It won only 1.6% of the total vote, representing two seats for Arie Eliav[203] and Meir Pa'il. Uri Avneri had been ranked third, with Sa'adia Marciano, a Panther founder, in the fourth slot. The party won 2% in large urban centers, less in outlying areas, but polled well on some kibbutzim. However, although its platform was very similar to that of RAKAH's HADASH, SHELI polled only 1% among Arabs.[204]

Differences between SHELI and HADASH were found in SHELI's qualified call for Israel to return to the pre-war lines of June 1967: ". . . except for changes agreed upon by the parties and after settlement of the Jerusalem problem." On this issue SHELI stated that Jerusalem would remain united and the capital of Israel, but the Arab part could, after the establishment of peace, become the capital of a Palestinian Arab state. Calling themselves the SHELI Camp (to emphasize their alliance with various groups dedicated to peace), their campaign was directed toward the leftist supporters of the Alignment (both in MAPAM and in MAPAI). The party was supported by intellectuals advocating an Israeli-Palestinian entente and others who believed negotiations would succeed where military successes had failed to establish peace.

5. The leftists were devastated by Menachem Begin's victory in 1977 and were dismayed by his popularity among Israel's "oriental" Jews. When elections to the Tenth Knesset were held on June 30, 1981, the results were a disaster for Israel's small parties. Begin, still enjoying the prestige which accompanied the signing of the Camp David Accord, had tapped into the Sephardic Jewish community, the "Second Israel," swallowing the potential base of SHELI and other groups. Two large political blocs--LIKUD and Labor (MAPAI)--emerged. Voter participation dropped from 79.2% in 1977 to 78.49%, with 1,937,366 valid votes being cast. SHELI (successor to *Ha'olam HaZeh, Moked* [MAKI], and elements of the Black Panthers) was wiped out, receiving only 0.45% (8,691) of the valid votes cast. RAKAH's Democratic Front for Peace and Equality (DFPE) was also hurt with a drop from 4.6% (five seats) in 1977 to 3.4% (four seats). Their loss was primarily due to a decline in Arab participation in the election, with the Arab abstention rate reaching a record of 31%.[205] Their share of Arab votes fell from close to 50% in 1977 to 37% while, surprisingly, LIKUD more than doubled its strength in the Arab sector from 4,500 votes in 1977 to 10,800. Labor also made impressive gains despite its own history of repressive policies against Israel's Arab population.

Majid Al-Haj and Avner Yaniv argue that the DFPE (HADASH) had:

- outlived its usefulness as a vehicle for Arab dissent;[206]
- undermined its own position among Arab voters by continuing to preach communist ideology while upholding Israel's legitimacy;[207]
- lost credibility in its professed role of supporting Arab nationalism, its place being taken by the new Arab nationalist groups which had succeeded the old *El Ard*.

Interest in Arab nationalist groups was sparked by the Egyptian-Israeli peace agreement; escalation of West Bank tensions; intensification of the Jewish settlements policy; and the dramatic rise in PLO status. Also, the number of Arabs attending Israeli universities had taken a quantum leap from a few hundred to several thousand, thereby considerably raising the level of education among Israel's Arabs. Other factors relevant to the revival of nationalism among Arabs in Israel include restoration of links between Israel's Arabs and their relatives and friends in the West Bank and Gaza territories;[208] and ramifications of the Yom Kippur War. "While boosting Arab morale," the war seemed to have caused "a serious decline in Israel's international position."[209]

While we can understand the increase in Arab nationalism, it is also necessary to say that RAKAH's Front did little to change its strategy to counter these phenomena. The party was hesitant to abandon totally its appeal for Jewish votes, but its list did include one more Arab in a safe position, formerly filled by a Jew. This changed the balance of Arabs and Jews in the first six places on the list (from three-three) to four Arabs and two Jews. However, Wilner still occupied the number one spot; Tewfik Toubi was second. As part of the communist effort to show support for the Arab cause, Toubi had held a much publicized meeting in Bucharest with PLO leader Yasser Arafat, and the DFPE had initiated an Arab congress in Shafa Amir in September 1980. Its purpose was to prepare for the upcoming Arab Masses' General Congress to be held in Nazareth. Although the Nazareth Congress was banned, the communists still hoped to benefit from their efforts. They did not, however, because the overriding Arab perception of RAKAH was that the party had been too content to play a permanent role of opposition within the Israeli establishment.

As for the decline in Arab voter participation, it was primarily due to a PLO call on election eve to boycott the election. This definitely hurt RAKAH's Front. A more interesting question is raised by the increase in Arab votes for LIKUD and MAPAI. This can be attributed to the particularist interests of those educated Arabs who accepted minority status in Israel's political system and hoped to benefit through their political involvement. The Arab voter who had been politically socialized during the 1960s and who was now voting for LIKUD or MAPAI was, in effect, expressing hope for integration and rejecting RAKAH's confusing signals of simultaneous acceptance of and opposition to the Israeli establishment. In addition, this educated voter was ignoring the appeals of the "nationalist/rejectionist" and "abstention/denial" approaches.[210]

To Uri Avneri, the Tenth Knesset was more hawkish than the Ninth. From a parliamentary standpoint, the peace camp was destroyed. Avneri feared the consequences.[211] In light of Israel's subsequent invasion of Lebanon, the losses it sustained, and its subsequent occupation of southern Lebanon (with the obvious hazards to Israeli military personnel), Avneri's fears were realized.

6. As Israel went to the polls on July 23, 1984, the Israeli political scene was far different from any previous time. Almost all the old leaders were gone. A despondent Menachem Begin retired, leaving his party to stand judgment for LIKUD policies which had led to an Israeli presence in Lebanon, a gloomy economic situation with an inflation rate of 400%, and heightened tensions on the West Bank. Suddenly, the Arab, Druze, and Bedouin voters (numbering some 250,000) became very important. In early July, Labor's Shimon Peres treked to Jisr al-Zarqa, a poor Arab village north of Tel Aviv, to persuade several hundred Arabs to vote Labor. "Is there anyone here," he asked, "who wants the LIKUD?" The reply was a unified "No."[212]

However, the Israeli Arabs had set their own agenda and the party which attracted a good deal of their support was the new Arab-dominated list, the Progressive List for Peace (PLP). This new party set forth a nationalist platform which, although close to that of RAKAH, eliminated the old Marxist-Leninist dogma which had become increasingly irrelevant to Israeli Arabs. While lacking the experience and political machinery of RAKAH, the PLP Arab leadership was able to distance itself from past mistakes and benefit from the support of young Arab university graduates whose Palestinian-nationalist orientation the PLP encouraged. Avner Regov traces the PLP's origins to the Committee of Heads of Arab Local Councils, established in 1972. It was a reaction, according to Regov, to the government's refusal to permit the establishment of any nationwide Arab political body. The PLP pulled very strongly in the purely Moslem towns and villages of the Little Triangle and Wadi Ara. Its impressive showing in Kafr Kassem, Tira, and Jatt was at RAKAH's expense. The new Arab party did well in many other large Arab villages, even in the Galilee, placing second to RAKAH's DFPE among Arab voters. The PLP won two Knesset seats with 1.8% (38,012) of the total votes and with 18% of the Arab votes. Together, the PLP and RAKAH won 52% of Israel's Arab votes. This was the first time in Israel's history where more than half of Israel's Arabs supported distinctly non-Zionist parties.[213]

The PLP's two Knesset seats were filled by Mohammed Mi'ari, an Arab nationalist (former member of the banned *El Ard* list) and lawyer from Haifa, and by Matti Peled, a former Air Force general and a member of Israel's General Staff in the Six-Day War. There is a glaring irony here. The PLP had criticized RAKAH for always presenting an ethnically-balanced list with one Jew for every Arab. Wilner always led the RAKAH ticket. The PLP's election propaganda had focused on this, claiming it was done on Moscow's orders and that the communist party was therefore not a truly Arab party. Whatever the PLP strategy which resulted in the positioning of a prominent Jew in the second slot,[214] his presence probably cost the new party many Arab votes.

Mi'ari's background is interesting. Although not a communist himself, he had formed an alliance with two ex-communists, Salim Rashid (a physician) and Kamel Daher (a lawyer),[215] leaders of the Association of Academics in Nazareth which had done well in the previous city elections. Mi'ari had also formed alliances with Riad Abu Al-Asal, the ultra-nationalist Anglican cleric from Nazareth (who was pushing a proposal for an Arab college in the Galilee) and with remnants of SHELI and other defunct leftist groups which had been led by Peled, Uri Avneri, and former SHELI Knesset Member Walid Sadik, a teacher from the Little Triangle.[216]

For Israel's Arab communist party, 1984 seemed to portend an even greater loss of party influence among the country's Arab population than at almost any time in its previous history. With the PLP as a new focal point for Arab discontent in Israel, it appeared that it was now RAKAH's turn to lose its raison d'etre. According to Elie Reches, an expert on Israeli Arab affairs, the PLP clearly represented a formidable challenge to the future of the surviving, small Israeli Arab communist party.[217] Interviewed in September 1985 by *Jerusalem Post* political correspondent Mark Segal, Reches cited the "Palestinization" of the Israeli Arab community since 1967 and the "Land

Day" protest in 1976 as signaling increasing politicization among Israeli Arabs. There appeared to be a new trend toward greater political participation on the part of Israeli Arabs, in the belief that political achievements were possible within the state's legal framework.

Voter participation among Arabs in 1984 reached a high of 72%. With fewer Israeli Arabs heeding the ultra-radical Abna al-Balad's (Sons of the Village) ban against voting for "the Zionist Parliament," it seemed that the Rejectionist Front was weakening. The Progressive List for Peace emerged as the third force in the Arab community, drawing 5% of the vote away from the Labor Party and 4% from RAKAH, with the following results:

Party	% of Arab vote
RAKAH	33%
Labor	24%
PLP	17%

Israel's Eleventh Knesset election in 1984 resulted in a deadlock. Neither the Labor Alignment of Shimon Peres (with 44 seats) nor the LIKUD coalition of Yitzhak Shamir (with 41 seats) was able to gain the support of a majority (61) of the Knesset's 120 members. Lengthy negotiations finally led to a "National Unity" government, initially led by Labor's Shimon Peres, with the understanding that he would step down in favor of Yitzhak Shamir after two years.

7. The November 1988 elections led to still another LIKUD-Labor coalition which was doomed to failure over issues involving peace negotiations with the Palestinians and increasing U.S. pressure from Secretary of State James A. Baker III. When local elections were held in March 1989, the Arab uprising, the *intifada,* was in its fifteenth month and Israel's Arab voters turned out in record numbers. Somewhere between 85% and 90% of those eligible voted, compared with only 50% for the Jewish sector.

In Um el-Fahm, Israel's second largest Arab city and a communist stronghold since the early 1970s, the religious Islamic bloc scored a major victory, ousting the mayor and 11 of the 15 city council members. Among those defeated were HADASH (RAKAH) Mayor Hashem Mahamid, listed fifth on the party's national Knesset slate and Khalid Akbariya, listed twelfth. Akbariya blamed RAKAH's defeat on lack of government financial support to improve the poor level of community services. Voters in Um el-Fahm, he said, were deeply frustrated by their living conditions as compared to what they see in Jewish areas where 90% of them work. Everything from sewage to schools to health clinics, he added, must be improved. Otherwise, he and Mahamid warned, the town would soon become a "little Iran."[218]

The Islamic list took six of the 19 council seats in Nazareth and also did well in neighboring Kafr Kanna. There and elsewhere, candidates on the Islamic list ran on a platform of Islam versus communism. Johny Jahshan, former HADASH city councilman in Nazareth, explained that while members of the Islamic bloc did not attack directly the record of the ruling communists, they did point out the discrepancies between the standard of living in Jewish communities and in Arab communities. They attracted many less-educated Moslem voters and many frustrated youth. Their focus on Islam signaled a change from the traditional struggle between Zionist and non-Zionist parties to one between fundamentalists and the non-Zionist left wing.

In the subsequent run-off elections in mostly Christian Kafr Kanna, the Islamic movement candidate was narrowly defeated by a coalition of communists and three family lists. However, elsewhere the run-offs gave further indication of the growing strength of the Islamic bloc. In Rahat in the Negev and Jaljuliya in the Triangle, Islamic movement candidates were victorious. The result of communist loses in their once "safe" areas, has signaled a formidable challenge to Israel's Arab communists: how to make the party relevant at a time when the international communist movement has lost all credibility and Islamic fundamentalism is on the rise.

While RAKAH's influence has diminished, the party endures. It participated in the mostly peaceful rallies and marches held on March 30, 1989, in observance of the thirteenth annual Land Day and has called for negotiations with the Palestinians and the convening of an international peace conference. Its two Knesset members joined with members of the Arab list and the Labor Party to bring down the National Unity government on March 15, 1990. However, Labor, finding it politically difficult to accept them as partners, proved unable to form a new government. The result was a strengthened, hard-line LIKUD administration.

At the end of July 1990, RAKAH again organized its annual four-day international work camp in Nazareth, kicked off by a peaceful march of thousands carrying placards and shouting slogans calling for the establishment of a Palestinian state alongside Israel. Among those present were delegations from 14 countries, including the USSR, and East and West Germany. The camp also attracted thousands of volunteers from Israel and the territories. Coordinator Raed Nassralla said that the organizers expected many Jewish volunteers from left-wing groups and parties, including peace activists. They would all help to build new roads, lay pavements, erect street lights, and paint school buildings. There was also work on a public garden in the city center, a special project involving the joint efforts of Jewish and Arab youngsters.

Despite these and other efforts, world events appear to have relegated Israel's various communist factions to the proverbial dust bin of history. The old-line communists have retired. Some, such as RAKAH's Meir Wilner, the last of the Jewish communist ideologues, have found it difficult to grasp what has happened. Interviewed after his farewell address to the Knesset on his retirement in January 1990, Wilner refused to acknowledge the reality of events in Eastern Europe and in the USSR "Communism," he said, "cannot fail, because none of the countries has yet reached the ultimate state in which true communism is fulfilled." While admitting that "here and there" mistakes have been made, he exhibited an unrealistic, buoyant hope for the future of communism worldwide. Wilner seemed to be completely ignoring the radicalization of the Palestinian Arabs, the politicization of Israeli Arabs and the growth of Islamic Fundamentalism in the Arab world, as well as the apparent failure of international communism. In fact, his successor in the Knesset is the ousted Um el-Fahm mayor, Hisham Mahamid. Despite his connection to HADASH, Mahamid is more an Arab nationalist than a communist, and it was the HADASH affiliation which hurt him in a community now dominated by the Islamic movement.

MK Tewfik Toubi (from RAKAH's DFPE) retired from the Knesset in July 1990, after serving 41 years. The warmth of the farewell speeches were indicative of the high esteem in which Toubi was held, his long communist affiliation all but ignored. His replacement, Tamar Guzhanski, did not appear to be well known.

V. Conclusion

The success of communists anywhere in the world outside the Soviet bloc has never been measured by the number of members their party attracted, but rather by their ability to influence the policy-making agenda by shaping the issues and focusing the public's attention. In this regard the communist party in Palestine and then in Israel was often successful, despite its small numbers. In the case of an ideological party operating in a hostile environment, there are aspects that are more important than membership size. Rather, commitment of the members to the organization's basic ideology or espoused principles and quality and dedication of the leadership are of great consequence and of greater intrinsic interest. These latter aspects--commitment of the membership and quality of leadership--were crucial because of the inherent conflict between communism and Zionism which inevitably rendered the party's very existence problematic and precarious. Consider the following:

(1) Although special strains were imposed on them by tensions between communism and Zionism, these communists, typically, were not permitted to resolve their problems autonomously. Except for a brief period, late 1930s-early 1940s, they were generally obliged to take their lead from Moscow's agents who carried specific instructions, based on Moscow's own "world view." Thus, Moscow used the party as its own tool to justify and rationalize events which occurred elsewhere, far from the Middle East. In the pre-statehood period, events in Palestine were used to explain and legitimize Soviet policies more relevant elsewhere. And, when Israel came into existence with Soviet backing, the communists and their left-wing supporters in the Knesset were instrumental in neutralizing the strong pro-U.S. element in the Israeli government (at least until the outbreak of the Korean War), encouraging a policy of non-alignment.

(2) Moscow attempted to control its communist sections, which together made up the international communist movement. In this connection, the communist movement(s) in Palestine and Israel emerged as a near microcosm of the communist world--before that world's recent disintegration--reflecting to some degree the broader divisions of opinion, frictions and splits.

(3) Communism never was a monolithic movement. Despite Moscow's past pronouncements to the contrary, there never was one worldwide, Lenin-style, tightly knit party. Still, a comparison of this movement's earliest modus operandi with the Comintern's Twenty-One Conditions (1920)[219] shows how closely the party came to reaching Moscow's standard.

(4) The earlier held myth of world communist unity often led to an over-exaggeration of its influence. This, in turn, led to a distraction from problems within Western societies, to a dissipation of Western energies, and, to a certain extent, to many missed opportunities to capitalize on communist weakness caused by the movement's own internal dissension and fragmentation.

(5) The tendency to judge the success of a political organization by its membership numbers obscured small accomplishments. For example, this particular communist movement was in place and operative when the Soviets

most needed to enlist its help during the difficult period following the German attack. The communist-founded V-League gained legitimacy in the eyes of the *Yishuv* and successfully channeled aid to the Soviets. And, more recently, the vocal peace movement in Israel derived some of its initial impetus from communist and left-wing support.

The following incident illustrates our final point. While the major parties set about forming a government back in 1984, Herut's Transport Minister Haim Corfu and Health Minister Eliezer Shostak challenged Abba Eban for the position of Knesset Speaker on the grounds of their seniority. This led to speculation as to who would be next in line. To the surprise of many, the third and fourth in line for the "longest-serving" Knesset members were the two (now retired) veteran communist leaders Meir Wilner and Tewfik Toubi.[220] Thus perhaps the Party's success should be judged by the mere fact of its ability to adapt to changes and to survive.

With that as a measuring rod, we can conclude that there remains a place for RAKAH in Israeli politics, assuming it continues to adapt. Funding, however, may prove to be a problem in the future. In the past, it was provided by the Soviets, and more recently by the Egyptians. The movement's communist ideology is clearly meaningless, irrelevant to the Israeli and Middle East scene. Israel's increasingly politicized Arab population, for example, is clearly more attracted to the Islamic fundamentalists than to RAKAH. Yet, RAKAH can still be a voice for some segment of the Israeli Arabs and other minority groups, as well as the Jewish political left, the backbone of the Israeli peace movement. However, with the *intifada* in its third year, the Iraqi invasion of Kuwait, Palestinian support for Iraq's Saddam Hussein, and the increasing threat of war, most Jewish Israelis--their numbers increasing daily as a result of Soviet emigration--appear to have moved further to the right and even further away from communist politics than ever before.

Endnotes

1. See Sondra Miller Rubenstein, *The Communist Movement in Palestine and Israel, 1919-1984* (Boulder, CO, 1985), for a detailed history of the party's evolution.

2. Esther Wilenska (Valenska) was soon in a debate over the MAPAM program dealing with domestic and foreign policy issues. See Esther Valenska, "Document: Critique of United Workers Party [MAPAM] Platform," in *Jewish Life* (June, 1948), 27-28. This critique originally appeared in *Kol Ha'am* (Jan. 23, 1948), and argued, uncompromisingly, for: (1) removal of the British military and administration; (2) removal of all military bases and opposition to any future requests for "imperialist"

military bases; (3) rejection of American penetration, including outright opposition to the Marshall Plan; (4) opposition to foreign intervention in the internal affairs of the Jewish state under any pretext, including economic aid; (5) the political independence of the Arab nation; (6) federation "upon which free political unity of the Jewish and Arab states can be based"; (7) complete economic equality "in deeds and not just in words"; (8) the "will to live and to survive" of the Jewish communities of the world in which 95 percent of the Jewish people live. The last position actually represented an anti-immigration position, designed to encourage Jews in the diaspora to remain where they were. For MAPAM's program (which originally appeared in *Le Achdut Ha'avodah*, MAPAM's organ) see Moshe Sneh, "Document: What Orientation for Palestine?" in *Jewish Life* (Mar. 1948), 27-28.

3. Walter Z. Laqueur, *Communism and Nationalism in the Middle East* (London, 1956), 301-302.

4. Laqueur, *Communism and Nationalism*.

5. Laqueur, *Communism and Nationalism*.

6. *Digest of Press & Events* (Jerusalem, Oct. 29, 1948), 26; quoting from *Kol Ha'am* (Oct. 22, 1948).

7. *Digest of Press & Events*.

8. *Digest of Press & Events*.

9. Pinchas E. Lapide, "Hammer and Sickle Over Nazareth," *Jewish Life* (July-Aug. 1963), 9-10. N.B.: Since the source of this periodical is the Union of Orthodox Jewish Congregations, it will hereafter be cited as *Jewish Life, UOJC,* so as to avoid confusion with the communist publication of the same name.

10. *Kol Ha'am* (Jan. 25, 1949).

11. Moshe M. Czudnowski and Jacob M. Landau, *The Israeli Communist Party and the Elections for the Fifth Knesset, 1961* (CA: Hoover Institution on War, Revolution and Peace, Stanford University, 1965), 12.

12. The Workers' Bloc and the Nazareth Arab Democrats polled 51.7% of the Arab vote. See Jacob M. Landau, *The Arabs in Israel* (London, 1969), 110.

13. Landau, *The Arabs in Israel*.

14. *Kol Ha'am* (Feb. 21, 1949).

15. *Kol Ha'am* (Mar. 24, 1949).

16. *Devrai HaKnesset* (Minutes of the Knesset) (Apr. 4, 1949), 290-291, 297-298.

17. MAPAM's Ya'acov Riftin said the Agreement meant "the coronation of Abdullah in [still another] part of Palestine" and that the monarch was only a "symbol of something more sinister." Ibid.

18. MAPAM's Dr. Moshe Sneh noted that Israel had been rushed into this agreement, implying that Israel had acted on orders from Washington.

19. *Kol Ha'am* (May 13, 1949).

20. *Devrai HaKnesset* (June 29, 1949), 862.

21. These expressed MAPAM's views of US diplomatic pressure, the return of Arab refugees, the future of Jerusalem, Gaza and the "Triangle," the Hungarian and Rumanian ban on emigration to Israel, the peace talks and other questions. Ibid.

22. *Devrai HaKnesset* (June 20, 1949), 755-756.

23. *Devrai HaKnesset* (June 20, 1949), 763.

24. *Devrai HaKnesset* (June 21, 1949), 784.

25. *Devrai HaKnesset* (July 18, 1949), 1053-1054. Newspapers, other than the opposition-supported press, subsequently blamed Mikunis for the early closing of the Knesset meeting, charging "Communist Member Causes Uproar."

26. *Digest of Press & Events* (Jerusalem: Jewish Agency for Palestine, Information Section, Aug. 5, 1949), 35-36. The following numbers of demonstrators were reported: Haifa 300, Tel Aviv 200, and Jerusalem 60.

27. *Kol Ha'am* (July 28, 1949).

28. *Kol Ha'am* (Aug. 5, 1949).

29. *Kol Ha'am* (Sept. 2, 1949).

30. *Kol Ha'am* (Aug. 8, 1949).

31. *Kol Ha'am* (Sept. 14, 1949).

32. *Kol Ha'am* (Sept. 17, 1949).

33. *Digest* (Dec. 16, 1949), 445.

34. *Digest* (Dec. 16, 1949), 498.

35. *Kol Ha'am* (Dec. 11, 1949).

36. *Kol Ha'am* (Dec. 11, 1949).

37. *Devrai HaKnesset* (Dec. 13, 1949).

38. *Kol Ha'am* (Dec. 20, 1949).

39. *Digest* (Apr. 28, 1950), 1247.

40. *Ha'aretz* (Apr. 20, 1950).

41. *Kol Ha'am* (Apr. 23, 1950).

42. *Devrai HaKnesset* (Mar. 1, 1950).

43. *Devrai HaKnesset* (Mar. 8, 1950).

44. *Devrai HaKnesset* (Mar. 14, 1950).

45. *Kol Ha'am* (Apr. 19, 1950).

46. *Digest* (Feb. 3, 1950), 839; and (Feb. 10, 1950), 880. On Jan. 22, 1950, some twenty communist members of five cooperative villages, as a protest against alleged discrimination, staged a sit-in at the Jewish Agency building in Tel Aviv. They were finally evicted on Feb. 5, 1950. See *Digest* (Feb. 17, 1950), 914.

47. *Devrai HaKnesset* (June 13, 1950).

48. *Kol Ha'am* (June 14, 1950).

49. *Kol Ha'am* (Aug. 1, 1950); also see *Al HaMishmar* (Aug. 1, 1950).

50. *Davar* (Aug. 2, 1950).

51. *Kol Ha'am* (Aug. 6, 1950).

52. *Devrai HaKnesset* (Aug. 7, 1950).

53. *Digest* (Sept. 22, 1950), 14. Dr. Moshe Sneh, the MAPAM leader, advocated the compulsory use of surplus private capital for the absorption of immigrants, but said that MAPAM would not demand immediate socialization of the country. He also said that "whatever happens," MAPAM would not leave the *Histadrut*.

54. *Kol Ha'am* (Oct. 1, 1950).

55. *Devrai HaKnesset* (Oct. 17, 1950).

56. *Devrai HaKnesset* (Jan. 2, 1951).

57. *Devrai HaKnesset* (Jan. 9, 1951); also see *Kol Ha'am* (Jan. 3, 1951).

58. *Devrai HaKnesset* (Jan. 23, 1951 and Jan. 24, 1951).

59. *Al HaMishmar* (Feb. 26, 1951).

60. *Kol Ha'am* (Mar. 23, 1951).

61. Inge Deutsch Kron, *Bonn and Jerusalem: The Strange Coalition* (Philadelphia, 1970), 18.

62. *Digest* (Feb. 2, 1951), 774.

63. *Digest* (Feb. 16, 1951), 852.

64. *Digest* (Mar. 2, 1951), 919.

65. *Devrai HaKnesset* (Mar. 13, 1951).

66. *Devrai HaKnesset* (Apr. 2, 1951).

67. Michael Bar-Zohar, *Ben-Gurion, A Biography* (NY, 1977), 196-198, for a brief description (from Ben-Gurion's point of view) of a demonstration held on Jan. 7, 1952; and *Digest* (Apr. 4, 1952), 891, for one held on Mar. 25, 1952.

68. *Kol Ha'am* (Mar. 23, 1952).

69. *Digest* (July 25, 1952), 1421.

70. *Kol Ha'am* (Sept. 11, 1952).

71. Chaim Heller, "America, Israel and the Cold War," *Youth and Nation* (Jan.-Feb. 1973), 18.

72. *Devrai HaKnesset* (July 2, 1950).

73. *Ha'aretz* (July 3, 1950); *Davar* (July 3, 1950). *Davar* stated that Israel regarded the U.N. "as essential to the preservation of world peace," and "support for the world organization is one of the mainstays of Israel's foreign policy."

74. *Al HaMishmar* (July 3, 1950), noted that large numbers of South Koreans refused to fight the North Koreans and that the U.S. forces were sent to defend "a reactionary and corrupt regime against a people in revolt against it." Also see *Kol Ha'am* (July 3, 1950).

75. *Kol Ha'am* (July 2, 1950).

76. *Digest* (July 21, 1950), 1695. Sharett responded in an address to Hebrew University students on July 11, 1950.

77. *Kol Ha'am* (July 15, 1950).

78. *Kol Ha'am* (Sept. 29, 1950).

79. *Kol Ha'am* (Dec. 24, 1950), called upon the Knesset to voice horror and concern of Israel at the "criminal decision of the Brussels conference to revive the Nazi Army. . . ." For Knesset debate, see *Devrai HaKnesset* (Dec. 25, 1950).

80. *Digest* (Jan. 12, 1951), 667.

81. *Devrai HaKnesset* (Jan. 10, 1951).

82. "The Communist Party in Israel," *Jewish Vanguard* (Aug. 29, 1952), 4.

83. *Jewish Frontier* (July 1952), 3. The editorial stated: "The Jewish state is to be deprived of Jerusalem, the corridor of land that unites this city with the rest of the country, the bloc of territory which includes Ramla and Lydda, Ber Sheva and a part of the Negev, and Western Galilee."

84. *Digest* (July-Aug. 1952), passim.

85. Oren was previously known as Orenstein. See Rubenstein, *Communist Movement . . .* , 325-327. During WW II, the Palestinian communists founded the V-League, a communist front organization which attracted many non-communists willing to support the Soviet War effort against Nazi Germany. Oren was a V-League delegate, to a trade union congress in Paris in Sept. 1945. On his way there, he met with the Soviet Chargé d'Affaires in Cairo, M. Sultanoff, to discuss the V-League's reorganization and the possibility of Soviet participation in a forthcoming medical and scientific conference in Palestine. See Rubenstein, *Communist Movement . . .* , 265.

86. *Digest* (Apr. 4, 1952), 882.

87. C. Gershater, "The Confessions: A Study of Official Communist Reports of the Prague Trial," *The Zionist Record* (Jan. 30, 1953), 4.

88. Gershater, see n. 87 above.

89. *Digest* (Apr. 4, 1952), 882. On Mar. 26, 1952, the MAPAM Executive, in its first statement on the arrest, said it had caused "grave concern in the camp of progress and peace" in Israel. "We are convinced that Mr. Oren did not commit . . . any premeditated act against the Czechoslovak People's Republic." There had been, the statement concluded, a "tragic misunderstanding." *Digest* (Apr. 4, 1952), 882.

90. Mark Alexander, "Israel's Left Reels to the Shock of 'Prague,'" *Commentary* (Apr. 1953), 379-389.

91. *Devrai HaKnesset* (Nov. 24, 1952); and see *Kol Ha'am* (Nov. 25, 1952), stating that Mr. Sharett's statement was intended as a psychological preparation of public opinion to participate in the aggressive bloc and in a war against the socialist camp.

92. *Devrai HaKnesset* (Nov. 25, 1952). Also see *Kol Ha'am* (Nov. 24, 1952), which described reports of the Prague trial as "the meanest agitation against Czechoslovakia by the propaganda trumpets of American imperialism and the reactionary press."

93. The resolution, however, said nothing about the broader implications of the trials. *Digest* (Jan. 2, 1953), 306.

94. "Sneh's Defection from MAPAM," *Israel Horizons* (Mar. 1953), 10.

95. Alexander, *Israel's Left* . . . . , 381; also see *Kol Ha'am* during this period.

96. M. Ya'ari, "Logic of Our Time," *Israel Horizons* (Mar. 1953).

97. *Kol Ha'am* (Jan. 14, 1953), on the accusations against the Jewish doctors: "It was incredible that despicable Jews have been found willing to serve the American and the British intelligence service and their devilish instructions."

98. A group of Jewish doctors in the USSR were charged by Stalin with conspiring to murder him. The "Doctors' Plot" unleashed a wave of anti-Semitism which only abated after Stalin's death in Mar. 1953. See "How Soviet Sources Played up the 'Doctors' Conspiracy'," *Congress Weekly* (Feb. 16, 1953), 8.

99. *Devrai HaKnesset* (Jan. 19, 1953).

100. "Sneh's Defection. . ." *Israel Horizons* (Mar. 1953), 10.

101. For example, see "Stalin's Sweet Music for Arab Communists," in *Zionist Record* (Johannesburg, South Africa, Jan. 30, 1953), 7. The trials in Prague and Moscow chilled the international Jewish community and led to a spate of articles on communism. See I.L. Kenen, "The Communist Threat to Israel," in *Congress Weekly* (Feb. 16, 1953), 4; M. Zait, "Sakanata Shel MAKI" (The MAKI Danger), in *HaPo'el HaTza'ir* (Feb. 3, 1953), 7 (in Hebrew); Charles I. Glicksberg, "The Jews Versus Communism," in *Congress Weekly* (Feb. 23, 1953).

102. "Stalin's Sweet Music . . .," *Zionist Record.*

103. Daniel Wolf Auerbach was the brother of Alexander Heshen (Zvi Auerbach), the Russian *Po'ale Zion* activist whose friends included Ber Borochov, Yitzhak Ben-Zvi and David Ben-Gurion. Daniel was born in Russia in 1890, and by the age of 15 was involved in revolutionary activities, taking part in the demonstrations of 1905. He is credited with successfully bringing Josef Berger-Barzilai into the PCP from the rival KPP and with the unification of the two Palestinian Communist groups in July 1923. He was

murdered in the Soviet Union in the early 1940s, one of the many Jewish victims of Stalin's purges.   See Rubenstein, *Communist Movement. . . ,* 122-124.

104. Ya'acov Ro'i, "Soviet Policies and Attitudes Toward Israel, 1948-1978--An Overview," *Soviet Jewish Affairs* 8, no. 1 (1978).

105. For a description of the crowd's reaction see "Notes and Comments," *Zion* (Feb. 1953), 2.

106. "Notes and Comments," *Zion,*

107. Ro'i, *Soviet Jewish Affairs,* see n. 104 above.

108. Aryah Rubinstein, "Communist Party in Israel," *The American Zionist* (Oct. 1954), 9.

109. "How Strong Is MAKI?" *Here & Now* (Aug. 15, 1956), 8.

110. *Kol Ha'am* (Jan. 28, 1955).

111. Defense Minister Pinhas Lavon, despite his denials of involvement, was held responsible and was forced to resign.   Prime Minister Moshe Sharett ordered an investigation, the conclusions of which were contained in the Olshan-Dori Committee's report, which was never made public. J. L. Talmon, "Lavon Affair--Israeli Democracy at the Crossroads," *New Outlook* (Mar.-Apr. 1961), 22-30; also see *Decline of Honor* (Chicago, 1976), the controversial account of Avri (Seidenwerg) El-Ad, the former Israeli officer and intelligence operative involved with the effort to establish an Israeli spy network in Egypt.

112. *Kol Ha'am* (Feb. 18, 1955).

113. *Devrai HaKnesset* (Feb. 21, 1955).

114. *Digest* (Oct. 7, 1955), 58.

115. Josef Avidar was the Hagana commander in the Old City of Jerusalem during the riots of 1929.   During the interview with this author in Apr. 1982, he expressed his abiding hatred of the Israeli communists and their Soviet mentors.

116. *Digest* (Sept. 30, 1955), 32.

117. *Devrai HaKnesset* (Oct. 18-19, 1955).

118. Aizik Remba, "The Communists in the Knesseth," reprinted in *The Brooklyn Jewish Center Review* (Feb. 1956), 5.

119. "Will MAKI Go Underground?" *Here & Now* (Feb. 1, 1956).

120. "Will MAKI Go Underground?" *Here & Now.*

121. For example, see: (Author unidentified), "How Strong Is MAKI?" *Here & Now* (Aug. 15, 1956), 7.

122. "How Strong Is MAKI?" *Here & Now,* 9. At that point, Bzoza and Frishberg were attempting to organize a new communist party free of Moscow's pressure.

123. There are many books and articles on the Suez crisis of 1956. Some suggestions are: Michael Adams, *Suez and After--Year of Crisis* (Boston, 1958); Simcha Dinitz, "The Legal Aspects of the Egyptian Blockade of the Suez Canal," in *The Georgetown Law Journal* (Winter 1956-1957); Herman Finer, *Dulles Over Suez: The Theory and Practice of His Diplomacy* (Chicago, 1964); J.C. Hurewitz, *Soviet-American Rivalry in the Middle East* (NY, 1969); Terence Robertson, *Crisis: The Inside Story of the Suez Conspiracy* (NY, 1965). The memoirs of those involved are also of interest: Anthony Eden, *Memoirs--Full Circle* (Boston, 1960); Dwight D. Eisenhower, *The White House Years--Waging Peace (1956-1961)* (NY, 1965); Nikita Khrushchev, *Khrushchev Remembers* (Boston, 1970); Anthony Nutting, *No End of a Lesson* (NY, 1967).

124. See Pinchas E. Lapide, "Hammer and Sickle Over Nazareth," *Jewish Life (UOJC)* (July-Aug. 1963), 10.

125. As quoted in O. M. Smolansky, "Moscow and the Suez Crisis, 1956: A Reappraisal," *Political Science Quarterly* (Dec. 1965), 581.

126. Scott D. Johnson, "Communist Party Politics in Israel," *Studies on Asia* (Lincoln, NE, 1964), 115.

127. Aryah Rubinstein, "Communist Party in Israel," *The American Zionist* (Oct. 1954), 9.

128. Misha Louvish, "Why Did MAPAI Lose Ground?" *Here & Now* (Aug. 4, 1955), 4-5; also see Avraham Schenker, "The Issues in Israel's Elections," *Israel Horizons* (July-Aug. 1955), 7.

129. Uri Ra'anan, "Who Voted For Whom?" *Here & Now* (Aug. 4, 1955), 13. An amusing footnote to the election coverage appeared alongside Ra'anan's article (14), under the title "Pepper & Salt," signed "Salmonides": "Last Thursday was a red-letter (or, rather, Red figure) day for loyal Communists who read nothing but *Kol Ha'am.* While nobody was looking (not even the proofreader), the man who set the election returns for *Kol Ha'am* that morning made the Reds' representation in the Knesset no more and no less than 40.1%. . . . The let-down came the following day, when the paper's editors sadly admitted that the figure should read 4.01%. . . . Don't take it to heart, comrades. We all have our ups and downs."

130. (Author unidentified), "How Strong Is MAKI?" See above n. 121.

131. "How Strong Is MAKI?" *Here & Now.*

132. The sketches of MAKI leaders were culled from various sources, including the *Encyclopaedia Judaica; Who's Who in Israel;* and "How Strong is MAKI?"

133. The Mikunis obituary in the *Jerusalem Post* (May 21, 1982) contained some interesting comments: "Mikunis quit the MAKI leadership in 1975, claiming that it had turned Zionist. As a true Communist, he said, he could never be a Zionist. Thus he refused to join the formal merger between MAKI and Tchelet-Adom, which formed Moked."

134. For Sneh's thoughts as a MAPAM leader see *Youth and Nation* (Nov. 1948), 6-9; on application of the Truman Doctrine to Palestine, see "Document: What Orientation for Palestine?" *Jewish Life* (Mar. 1948), 27-28.

135. See M. Edelstein, "The 1965 Split in MAKI," *Soviet Jewish Affairs* (1974), 36, n. 18, for material on Hinin.

136. "How Strong Is MAKI?" *Here & Now,* see n. 121 above.

137. "How Strong Is MAKI?" *Here & Now.*

138. "How Strong Is MAKI?" *Here & Now.*

139. Citizenship was automatically granted all Jews living in Israel or "returning from exile in the Diaspora" (under the Law of Return), while non-Jews could become citizens by: (1) virtue of residence, (2) naturalization, or (3) birth. The problem for the Arabs living in Israel was their dependence on the interpretation and application of these conditions for citizenship. For example, nationality/citizenship based on residence meant that the Arab had to prove former Palestinian citizenship, continuous presence in Israel from May 14, 1948, and registration as an inhabitant as of Mar. 1, 1952. Many claimed they were unable to prove they met these requirements because the applicable documents were lost, destroyed, or confiscated during the war of 1948.

140. Hal Draper, "The Origins of the Middle East Crisis," *The Israel-Arab Reader,* ed., Walter Z. Laqueur (NY, 1971), 299, calls the incident a pogrom and tells of the Kafr Kassem tragedy which resulted in the death of 46 Arabs at the hands of Israeli soldiers. The incident occurred on Oct. 29, 1956, the day Israel attacked Egypt.

141. Ze'ev Schiff, "Israel's Fourth Elections," *New Outlook* (Jan. 1960), 24.

142. This represented 81,764 out of 96,608 eligible Arab votes. Majid Al-Haj and Avner Yaniv, "Uniformity or Diversity: A Reappraisal of the Voting Behavior of the Arab Minority in Israel," *The Elections in Israel: 1981,* ed., Asher Arian (Tel Aviv University, 1983), 143.

143. MAPAM won its place by its programs and activities in Arab locals. They offered something positive and concrete, as opposed to the negativism of MAKI and El Ard. Arab acceptance of MAPAM's earlier invitation to join as full members had led to the involvement of hundreds of Arab youth who came to MAPAM kibbutzim to participate in training and education in agriculture and other areas. These youths later maintained MAPAM party branches established in Arab villages and cities, taking advantage of the MAPAM-initiated publishing house and cooperatives to gain support for the party. MAPAM's Arabic publications announced the party's campaign to abrogate the military administration, neutralization of the Middle East and an Israeli initiative to solve the Jewish-Arab dispute.

144. Moshe M. Czudnowski and Jacob M. Landau, *The Israeli Communist Party and the Elections for the Fifth Knesset, 1961* (CA, 1965), 38.

145. Yosef Waschitz, "Arabs in Israeli Politics," *New Outlook* (Mar.-Apr. 1962), 40.

146. 81.6% of the general electorate voted. Czudnowski and Landau, 42.

147. In purely Arab localities, 87% of the eligible population voted, 76,918 valid ballots. Czudnowski and Landau, 43.

148. David J. Schnall, *Radical Dissent in Contemp. Israeli Politics: Cracks in the Wall* (NY, 1979), 91.

149. Peretz Merhav, "The Compass Astray," *New Outlook* (Oct. 1969), 49.

150. This did not deter Moshe Machover, who became one of Matzpen's leading intellectuals and organizers. He co-authored "The Class Nature of Israeli Society," in *New Left Review* (1971). Matzpen groups sprang up in various places, including London, England. In Sept. 1972, Matzpen published its "Fundamental Principles," which were uncompromisingly anti-Zionist. Henry Srebrnik, "Matzpen: Anti-Zionism in the 70's," *Youth and Nation* (Summer 1978), 14-16.

151. Edelstein, see n. 135 above.

152. Mikunis had written: "[W]e firmly reject. . . [Ben Bella's] total negation of Israel. In all his references to this topic he has denied her right to existence as an independent state. This view . . . contains not a grain of realism and has not the least prospect of acceptance. It serves only Western imperialism, the Israeli militarists, the reactionary and militarist Arab statesmen, such as the former Mufti of Jerusalem and Ahmed Shukeiri, who themselves played a far from minor role in promoting the tragedy of the Palestine Arab people." See: "ICP Leader Attacks Ben Bella," *New Outlook* (Nov.-Dec. 1964), 76-68 (a reprint of the major part of the Mikunis article). Also see "Letters," *New Outlook* (Jan.-Feb. 1965), 66-67, where Mikunis chides the magazine for omitting certain paragraphs.

153. "Letters," *New Outlook.*

154. "Letters," *New Outlook.*

155. *Kol Ha'am* (Jan. 17, 1965).

156. Wilner, in control of the central committee secretariat, proposed a change in the election system from branch to cell representation. Under the existing branch system, Wilner supporters would have been outvoted, while under the proposed cell system, Wilner (in control of the party apparatus) would have been able to rearrange the cells, strategically spreading his supporters for maximum effect. See Edelstein, n. 135 above, 28-29.

157. The Soviet party had enjoyed being able to cite MAKI support when criticized by Western communists (either Jewish or non-Jewish) for its position on Jewish issues.

158. Edelstein, see n. 135 above, 32, states: "The discussion became emotional; at one point one of the Soviet delegates burst into tears while describing the harm which the split would cause to the world communist movement."

159. Edelstein, see n. 158 above.

160. Significantly, when the Mikunis-Sneh faction opened its conference in Tel Aviv on Aug. 4, 1965, *HaTikva* (the Israeli national anthem) was sung before *The Internationale,* while at the opening of the Wilner-Toubi conference in Jaffa on Aug. 6, 1965, it was sung after *The Internationale* with many of the Arab members remaining silent. The CPSU dispatched greetings at the opening of both conferences, but the Mikunis-Sneh congress also received greetings from thirty-three other fraternal parties. Kevin Devlin, *Communism in Israel* (NY, 1969), 11.

161. For MAKI's position see "Documents: Israeli Parties on Foreign Affairs," *New Outlook* (Oct. 1965), 58-59. For RAKAH: "Documents: Israeli Parties on Foreign Affairs," *New Outlook* (Nov.-Dec. 1965), 64-65.

162. *El Ard* had been outlawed because it was opposed to the existence of the state. Its "Socialist List" was then declared invalid and its court appeal also failed. See Ze'ev Katz, "The Elections--A Defeat for Activism," *New Outlook* (Nov.-Dec. 1965), 17. It subsequently disappeared from the Israeli political scene, leaving the way clear for RAKAH's growth. See Atallah Mansour, "How the Israeli Arabs Voted," *New Outlook* (Nov.-Dec. 1965), 24.

163. Mansour, 24.

164. Mansour, 24.

165. Mansour, 24.

166. In the Israeli political world beyond the two small communist factions the election became a referendum with voters choosing between "military activism," as represented

by Rafi (Ben-Gurion's new Israeli Workers' List) and Gahal (the new *Herut*-Liberal Party bloc) and "anti-activism," as represented by the Alignment (MAPAI and *Ahdut Ha'Avoda*), MAPAM, the Independent Liberals and the two communist parties. Voters were deciding whether to reopen the Lavon Affair investigation, as Ben-Gurion demanded, and whether Levi Eshkol was personally unfit to be Prime Minister, as Ben-Gurion charged. The Alignment won 45 seats, MAPAI's Arab Lists won 4, giving Eshkol an impressive 49 seats.

167. Rael Jean Isaac, *Party and Politics in Israel: Three Visions of a Jewish State* (NY, 1981), 177.

168. Clinton Bailey, "The Communist Party and the Arabs in Israel," *Midstream* (May 1970), 50.

169. Bailey.

170. Bailey, 15.

171. "Questions & Answers," *New Outlook* (Jan. 1968), 52.

172. Esther Wilenska, "Israelis and Palestinians at a Peace Meeting," *New Outlook* (Oct. 1969), 46.

173. The figures for the three "peace" lists were cited by Simha Flapan, "After the Elections," *New Outlook* (Nov.- Dec. 1969), 18.

174. Flapan, "After the Elections," *New Outlook.*

175. "Elections in Israel," *Youth and Nation,* 23.

176. Isaac, *Party and Politics,* see n. 167 above, 177.

177. Bailey, see n. 168 above, 55.

178. At age 17, Cohn-Bendit spent a summer at Kibbutz Hazore'a. See Helen Epstein, "New Arrivals on the Israeli Left," *Midstream* (Oct. 1970), 10.

179. Epstein, "New Arrivals on the Israeli Left," *Midstsream,* 12.

180. The Siach groups ran open weekly discussions. There was no such thing as membership.

181. Philip Hochstein, "Can U.S. afford to hurt Israel? Analysis of mutual helpfulness," *The Jewish Week--American Examiner* (June 14, 1981), 4.

182. Peretz Merhav, *The Israeli Left: History, Problems, Documents* (NY, 1980), 281.

183. David J. Schnall, *Radical Dissent in Contemporary Israeli Politics: Cracks in the Wall* (NY, 1979), 109.

184. "Israel Notes: Another Left Group Emerges," interview with Meir Pa'il, *Youth and Nation* (Oct. 1973), 6-9.

185. Yaron Garmaise, "Our Left on the War," *Youth and Nation* (Jan. 1974), 20-23.

186. "Document: The Knesset Debate," *New Outlook* (Oct.-Nov. 1973), 39-45.

187. "Document: The Knesset Debate," *New Outlook.*

188. The four winning lists were: (1) Independent Liberals (Gideon Hausner)-4 seats, (2) Citizens Party (Shulamit Aloni)-3 seats, (3) RAKAH-4 seats, (4) Moked-1 seat. Uri Avneri's Meri drew only 10,469 votes, too little to qualify for a seat. No doubt his chances for returning to the Knesset were hurt when *Ha'olam HaZeh* party member Shalom Cohen left the Meri coalition to form the Black Panther List which drew 13,332 votes. However, taken together, these two lists drew only 23,801, still missing the one percent minimum. See Nathan Yalin-Mor, "Elections, 1973--The Confusing Elections: Post-Mortem," *New Outlook,* Feb. 1974, 33.

189. *Statistical Abstract of Israel, 1981* (Israel: Central Bureau of Statistics, 1981), 557.

190. Richard Streitfield, "An Interview With Meir Pa'il, An Israeli Socialist, A Socialist-Zionist Party," *Youth and Nation* (Sept.-Oct. 1974), 16.

191. See the Mikunis obituary in *The Jerusalem Post* (May 21, 1982).

192. In an interview with Richard Streitfield in Mar. 1974 published in *Youth and Nation* (Sept.-Oct. 1974), op. cit.), Pa'il said they hoped "that during the next two or three years, MAKI will be dissolved and Moked will be . . . the radical movement."

193. *Statistical Abstract,* see n. 192 above; and also see Rael Jean Isaac, *Party and Politics in Israel: Three Visions of a Jewish State* (NY, 1981), 177.

194. See Moshe Kohn's interview with Tewfik Zayyad in *Jerusalem Post Magazine* (Dec. 19, 1975), 10, on the eve of his election as Nazareth's first communist mayor. Zayyad wrote about his experiences in Russia in *A Nazarene in Red Square.*

195. Kohn, see n. 194 above.

196. Yosef Goell, "Shattered Illusions," *Jerusalem Post Magazine* (Apr. 2, 1976), 7.

197. Goell, "Shattered Illusions," *Jerusalem Post Magazine.*

198. The Black Panthers were a group of disaffected Oriental (non-Western) Jewish youths of deprived background.

199. The acronym "HADASH" means "new." In Sept. 1990, MK Charlie Biton, interviewed by Bill Hutman (*Jerusalem Post*), spoke of himself and his colleagues some thirteen years later. Former Panther member Rafi Marciano is now the director of army preparation programs at the Jerusalem Municipality Youth, Sport and Social Activities Division.

200. Isaac, *Party and Politics in Israel,* see n. 167 above. The Democratic Front polled well in large Arab towns, where it often received 60-90% majorities. See "Election Results--Ninth Knesset," *New Outlook* (June-July 1977), 6.

201. "Elections 1977--Who, What and Why," *New Outlook* (Apr.-May 1977), 22.

202. Majid Al-Haj and Avner Yaniv, "Uniformity or Diversity: A Reappraisal of the Voting Behavior of the Arab Minority in Israel," *Elections in Israel: 1981,* ed. Asher Arian, (Tel Aviv University, 1983), 154.

203. Arieh Eliav was a deputy minister in two Labor governments, as well as a secretary general of the Labor party. Prominent in many vital fields (including immigration and development of new settlement areas), he left the Labor party in the 1970s over an ideological dispute with Golda Meir's cabinet. He then briefly joined Shulamit Aloni's group, and 1977 he agreed to head the new SHELI list.

204. "Elections 1977--Who, What and Why" *New Outlook* (Apr.-May 1977), 21-23, which includes a comparison of RAKAH and SHELI platforms.

205. There was a steady decline in Arab voter participation as follows:

1959	1961	1965	1969	1973	1977	1981
-15%	-17%	-18%	-20%	-23%	-26%	-31%

For a complete analysis see Al-Haj and Yaniv, n. 202 above.

206. Al-Haj and Yaniv, 149.

207. Al-Haj and Yaniv, 154.

208. Al-Haj and Yaniv, 151; citing K. Ammon, "Land Day on Both Sides of the Green Line," *Al HaMishmar* (Apr. 3, 1981).

209. Al-Haj and Yaniv; citing Kalman Benyamini, "Israeli Youth and the Image of the Arab," *Jerusalem Quarterly,* 20 (1981): 87-95; and Elie Rekhess, *The Israeli Arabs Since 1967: The Issue of Identity* (Tel Aviv: The Shiloah Center, Sekirot No. 1, 1976) in Hebrew.

210. Al-Haj and Yaniv, see n. 202 above, 161.

211. Uri Avneri, "Elections, 1981--The Great Draw," *New Outlook* (July-Aug. 1981), 6-7.

212. T.L. Friedman, "Israeli Politicians Court Long-Ignored Arab Voters," *NY Times* (July 9, 1984), 1.

213. Ezer Weizmann's Yahad list drew 6% of the Arab vote, "an indication of the importance of hamula voting in the Little Triangle, where the head of the Kafr Kara local council, Mohammed Massarwa, ran on the Yahad list." Yosef Goell, "Minority Majority," *Jerusalem Post Magazine* (Aug. 10, 1984), 6; and "Shamir and Peres Plan to Meet Today in Israeli Election Deadlock," *NY Times* (Aug. 1, 1984), 4. *Hamula* voting refers to voting based on the extended family, the traditional structure of the village, wherein the *hamula* heads can influence voting either through inducements or coercion. See Al-Haj and Yaniv, n. 202 above, 157, for a further discussion.

214. Goell, "Minority Majority," *Jerusalem Post Magazine,* see n. 213 above.

215. Mark Segal reports that Daher's father was a Knesset member associated with MAPAI in the 1950s. At some point he was dropped by them, and some politicial observers believe Kamel Daher's alliance with Mi'ari and the PLP is "a form of taking vengeance on those who dishonoured his late father." See Segal's article "Focus: Sounding the Alarm," *Jerusalem Post* (Sept. 17, 1985), 5.

216. Segal, "Focus: Sounding the Alarm," *Jerusalem Post,* see n. 215 above. In Sept. 1990, PLP's MK Mohammed Mi'ari left Israel to participate in an international conference involving PLO members. Attorney-General Yosef Harish thereafter initiated a move to strip Mi'ari of his immunity, charging him with violating the Anti-Terror Law banning meetings with the PLO. Mi'ari was already facing charges of having been part of a PLO press conference in Athens with PLO spokesman Bassam Abu Sharif in Feb. 1988 and with supporting an announcement of the PLO's "ship of the return," the dispatch of a shipload of Palestinian deportees to Haifa. Although no vote was taken on the Harish proposal, the Attorney General's move set off a heated debate.

217. The comment was made during the author's telephone conversation (in Israel, Jan. 1985) with Dr. Reches who was then preparing his study on RAKAH.

218. Marda Dunsky "Islamic Bloc makes dramatic gains," *Jerusalem Post International Edition* (Mar. 11, 1989), 3.

219. See Rubenstein, *The Communist Movement,* see n. 1 above, Appendix A, 377-382.

220. Mark Segal, "The Turning Point," *Jerusalem Post* (Aug. 24, 1984), 7.

ROOTS OF THE IDEOLOGICAL—POLITICAL CONTROVERSY
BETWEEN THE RIGHT AND THE LEFT IN ISRAEL

Yaacov Goldstein

In 1977, a political earthquake shook the State of Israel. The Labor party, heir of the Workers' Party of *Eretz Israel,* or *Mapai,* fell from power. For fifty years it had controlled almost every facet of the political system of the Jewish settlement of Palestine, the political system of the world Zionist movement prior to the establishment of the State, and the political systems of all the governments after the establishment of the State. In 1977, the reins of government passed to the *Likud* bloc. The central party of the *Likud* bloc was *Herut,* heir of the Revisionist Party and of *Etzel,* the *Irgun.* Thus, a new chapter opened in the political life of the State, one that has persisted to the present day. The "Right" ascended to govern while the Center-Left and the "Left" went down into opposition.[1]

The two parties that were the focus of the 1977 drama--*Herut,* which is today the *Likud,* and the Labor Party--are the heirs of historical political parties. The two continue the fifty year old political-ideological struggle of their predecessors. In the 1920s, Zeev Jabotinsky, the charismatic leader of the Revisionists, vied with David Ben-Gurion, Berl Katznelson, Yitzhak Tabenkin, Levi Eshkol, and Golda Meir, the leaders of *Mapai.* Finally, Menachem Begin, heir and protege of Jabotinsky, former commander of the *Etzel,* and leader of the Israeli Right, became prime minister.[2]

It must be understood that the deep political-ideological differences of opinion that still exist in Israel's society and policy did not spring up overnight. These disputes have persisted for years, a heritage that has not grown obsolete, but retains significance to this very day. These disputes shape the political arena in Israel. Anyone wishing to understand Israeli politics needs to comprehend the roots of this Right and Center-Left political-ideological controversy.

The Revisionist Party set up by Zeev Jabotinsky in 1925 was rightly identified with its leader. Jabotinsky belonged to the young generation of Zionist leaders who arose after Herzl. He was a contemporary and main rival of Haim Weitzmann. Jabotinsky was a refined man blessed with natural aptitudes; he was a linguist and a brilliant orator imbued with European culture. After World War I, Weitzmann coopted him for the Zionist Board, on which he served until 1923. He resigned because of his differences with Weitzmann over the policy of the Zionist movement.

For two years, Jabotinsky wandered the political wilderness until he founded the Revisionist Party. Its ideology was expressed in its name: a demand to revise Weitzmann's pragmatist policy and the desire to return to the political Zionism of Herzl. Jabotinsky's party staked out a position for itself as the central party of the Zionist Right, and from that vantage point threatened Weitzmann's leadership. It is almost certain that Jabotinsky would have overtaken Weitzmann were it not for the fact that the *Eretz Israel* labor movement came the latter's aid.

In 1930, the two main parties that had comprised this movement established *Mapai,* which became the principal rival of the Revisionists. Being unable to conquer the Zionist organization from within, Jabotinsky and his movement withdrew from the movement in 1935. Two years later there arose in Palestine an underground defense organization, *Etzel,* the Hebrew acronym for National Military Organization, which became known simply as the *"Irgun"* (Organization). *Etzel* accepted Jabotinsky's authority and became a rival of the *Hagana,* the clandestine defense force of the overall *Yishuv,* or Jewish settlement in Palestine. Neither Jabotinsky and his movement nor *Etzel* accepted the authority of the institutions of the Zionist movement or the authority of the Jewish settlement in *Eretz Israel.* As a consequence, they were termed "dissidents," that is, dissenters from national authority. Jabotinsky died in 1940. The Revisionist party, whose strongholds had been in the Jewish communities of Eastern Europe, were effectively wiped out by the Holocaust.

In Palestine, *Etzel,* headed by Menachem Begin, became a central power. After the establishment of the state, *Etzel* was disbanded and the political party, *Herut* was established. *Herut* created a political bloc with the Liberals, a right-of-center civic party. That alliance was finally transformed into the *Likud,* which won the 1977 elections. Menachem Begin, a pupil of Jabotinsky, had arrived after a very long road and innumerable failures. He had attained the goal long awaited by his mentor, Jabotinsky: governance of the Israeli State.[3]

Upon its founding, *Mapai,* a new-old party, encompassed 80% of all (Jewish) workers and their supporters in Palestine. In the political arena, its focus was center-left, meaning a moderate socialist party, becoming the vanguard of the Zionist movement to realize nationalist aims. By 1931, together with its allies throughout the Jewish world, *Mapai* had attained hegemony both in the *Yishuv* and in the Zionist movement. Its ideology and nationalist-social policy earned the broad support of both the labor and middle classes, and it was led by a broad group of talented leaders headed by David

Ben-Gurion. The party won the leadership of the *Yishuv,* the Zionist movement, and the state, though it governed in coalition with the more leftist parties consistently until 1977.

During this long period, *Mapai* achieved momentous successes. The apex of these was the establishment of the State of Israel itself and the absorption of the survivors of the Holocaust and the persecuted of Moslem countries--hundreds of thousands of refugees. The phenomenon of rule by one party for nearly fifty years has no precedent in any democratic society.[4]

The two rival parties were conglomerates; each consisted of a political party, a women's organization, a youth movement, a labor organization, and economic institutions. Our interest here is in the two different political sub-cultures. Each party drew sustenance from a different philosophical-historical source. The Revisionists supped on European Right-Liberal philosophy, especially that from Italy of the second half of the 19th century, and not a little from the special courtly tradition of Poland.[5] *Mapai* drew from the tradition of the revolutionary movements of 19th century-early 20th century Russia and Europe, from the ideas of Mendelsohnian enlightenment, post-Mendelsohn, and pre-Zionism, from the necessity of structural socio-economic change for the Jewish people, from the transition to productivization, and the return to the land. These two blocks-- political Zionism (Revisionists) on one side, and socialist-Zionism (*Mapai*) on the other side, stood at the base of the national philosophy and constituted an integral part of the Zionist movement.

The two were divided in relation to a spectrum of objectives, the nature of national goals, the emphases to be placed on these national objectives, as well as the manner in which to achieve them. These controversies placed the Revisionists and *Mapai* as the premier rivals in the Zionist movement, and later, rivals in the State of Israel.

It is important to stress that in contrast to popular belief, the two parties actually shared much in common. First, each was part of the Zionist movement, and identified with the goals of the national movement of the Jewish people. The two were also popular mass movements. Each was activist, especially in the security domain. Despite these points of similarity, however, that which differentiated and distinguished them substantially surpassed their commonalities, right from the initial appearance of Revisionism in the public-political arena. What follows are the main foci of the dispute, the essence of which has lasted to the present day.[6]

1. The Center-Left embraces a moderate socialist outlook adapted to the Israeli reality.

The essence of the Center-Left outlook argues that social classes exist in every society. Each class has its own socio-economic interests which struggle with the interests of other classes. Hence, the recognition that class conflict is legitimate in any national context, including that of the Jewish people and the State of Israel. The Left furthermore, continues to believe that the interests of the workers, unlike the interests of all the other classes, identify completely with the national interest. The supporting argument is that only the labor class (a definition that encompasses everyone who lives on a salary) aspires to the building of a more equal society, one that is unexploitive to the extent possible, and therefore a qualitatively superior society. The Left continues to believe that only the establishment of such a society in Israel will insure that its citizens will be content and devoted to nationalist goals. Further, only this type of society will attract Jewish immigration from the countries of the free world.

The Right has argued that the national interest is superior to all other interests and the national interest subordinates any other interest to its needs. From this flows the Right's tendency to boast that it is above any class. The Right tends to negate class distinctions and the legitimacy of class differences, to negate the differences in class interests, and to negate the right to a clash and free struggle among these interests.

2. The Left has always favored the simultaneous striving for two goals.

In the opinion of the Left, the socio-economic goal and the national goal are mutually sustaining and non-contradictory. In the past, this two-flag approach was called parallelism (as compared to monism, which is a solely national approach. The Center-Left believes that the struggle for a more just, more equal, and in sum, better society has to be carried on simultaneously with the struggle for the attainment of national aims. The person who lives in a decrepit, discriminatory, oppressive, or exploitive society is unable to identify with national goals or to fight for them. Thus, the struggles must be simultaneous, each strengthening the other.

In contrast, the Right claims priorities; national goals are superior and take precedence over everything else. The Right pushes to the side, temporarily or absolutely, all other interests and goals.

The Right-Left debate was not only theoretical, but actually manifested itself in many incidents of labor strikes. In many cases, the Right took a stand that rejected the strikes. It used the argument that the strikes impaired the budding economy of the evolving state, and handicapped the state itself after its establishment. Thus, strikes were seen to harm the national interest. The Right demanded restrictions on strikes and insisted on the establishment of a compulsory arbitration regime to restrain the too-free striding of the workers' struggle.

3. The Center-Left has always believed that Zionist ideology obligates a revolution in the socio-economic structure of the people, as well as manifesting itself in the territorial concentration of the Jewish people in the Land of Israel.

This means a transition from go-between or brokerage vocations and commerce, to productive sectors of the economy, with the aim of building a healthy, "normal" economy. The Center-Left is very sensitive, not only to the quantitative side, but also to the qualitative side of the society that is being constructed in Israel. This outlook necessitates the return to working the land and agriculture as well as the establishment of industry. The demand resonates with the myth about a people uprooted from their birthplace then returned to their land. Thus, a positive attitude toward agriculture creates the proper demographic dispersal throughout the country, not just concentrations in urban foci. The value concepts of productivity and agriculture--the laborer and the farmer--are of supreme importance for the Center-Left.

By comparison, the Right sees the essence of the matter from the quantitative side; urban development can facilitate the absorption of a Jewish concentration in the State of Israel. Its preference is for the city over the village as a central tool for implementing Zionism. Despite the claim of being above class, the Right relates most positively to the urban middle classes and sees their contribution to the national effort as equal to, if not superior to, the labor and farmer classes. The Right raises the myth of the *Fourth Aliya,* (the unselective immigration wave of the Jewish lower-middle class from the Polish *stetl,* who came to Israel when the gates to the United States closed with the imposition of quotas, 1924-1929), which concentrated principally in the cities. This myth is meant to counteract that of the *Third Aliya,* (1919-1923) which built the agricultural infrastructure.

4. The Center-Left favors the *Histadrut*-Israel General Federation of Labor as an inclusive organization dealing with all spheres of the workers' lives.

The Center-Left hopes to change the people in Israel into a working people (proletariat). To that end, the *Histadrut* does not suffice with being merely a trade union. It is also involved in culture, mutual aid, and even ownership of economic enterprises that are intended to serve both the national goals and the interests of the workers.

The Right rejects the all-encompassing structure of the *Histadrut* and favors its existence only as a trade union. For years, it struggled against the *Histadrut* from without. In the past two decades, it has tried to conquer it from within.

5. In the political sphere, the Labor party operates on the basis of the historic right of the people of Israel to all of the Land of Israel.

The Labor Party hedges its outlook with three qualifications:

1. The concept of the Land of Israel has never been defined territorially. In various periods of history, such as the First and Second Commonwealth, the borders of the Land of Israel changed; ideologically therefore, no one territorial pattern can possibly be obligatory today for the concept of the Land of Israel.

2. A significant Arab population with rights exists within the land of Israel. This fact cannot be avoided. Furthermore, the *Yishuv* in the past, and the State in the present, are surrounded by a significant Arab periphery. Therefore, the pragmatic-political conclusions necessitate moderating Israel's approach to the problem of territory in which a huge Arab population is living.

3. For reasons of defense, for peace, for moral and for practical reasons, the State of Israel has a need to exist. The value of peace is not inferior to the historic rights of the people of Israel to the Land of Israel. Therefore, the Labor Party, heir to *Mapai,* favors in principle and in practice, territorial compromise (in current terminology, "land for peace.") This was *Mapai's* position in 1937 in discussing the recommendations of the Peel Commission, which decided on the division of Palestine. It behaved the same way in 1947, when it agreed, along with a majority of the Zionist movement, to accept the UN partition plan. Its stand has been consistent to the present day.

In contrast, the *Likud* and its ally, the Right, stand for the historic right of the people of Israel to rule over all of the Land of Israel, or what was western Palestine, from the Jordan to the Mediterranean. This belief is the most vital part of the political-ideological outlook of the Right. Although Menachem Begin could concede the Sinai to Anwar Sadat, since that peninsula was never considered part of the historic Land of Israel, Yitzhak Shamir cannot surrender Judaea and Samaria, which were the backbone of the Kingdom of Israel in the past. Their retention as part of the State of Israel is the supreme guiding principle of the world outlook and policy of the Right in Israel.[7]

In summary, both the Center-Left and Left, on one side, and the Right on the other, arose within the Zionist movement during the pre-State period against the background of socio-economic and political reality, which in large part has lasted to the present day. The substantive differences of the past characterize, to a large extent, the roots of the political-ideological controversy between the Center-Left and the Right in present day Israel. Whoever understands the past will find it easier to comprehend the political storms that are passing through Israel today.

Endnotes

1. Shevah Weiss, *The Upheval* (Tel-Aviv, 1979) (Hebrew).

2. David Ben-Gurion, "The Workers' Movement and Revisionism," *World League for Labor Israel* (Tel Aviv, 1933) (Hebrew); Walter Laqueur, *A History of Zionism* (Tel Aviv, 1974), part 2, chaps. 6, 7 (Hebrew).

3. I.B. Schechtman, *Zeev Jabotinsky His Life* (Tel Aviv, 1956).

4. Yaacov Goldstein, *The Israel Workers' Party (Mapai), The Causes of Its Establishment* (Tel Aviv, 1975) (Hebrew); idem, *The Road to Hegemony* (Tel Aviv, 1980) (Hebrew).

5. Yaacov Shavit, *The Mythologies of the Zionist Right Wing* (Tel Aviv, 1986) (Hebrew).

6. Y. Goldstein, *The Israel Workers' Party,* 70-96.

7. Yosef Gorney, *The Arab Question and the Jewish Problem* (Tel Aviv, 1985).

INTEGRATION AND SEGREGATION:
THE DEVELOPMENT OF DIVERSE TRENDS
IN ISRAELI RELIGIOUS POLITICAL PARTIES

Gary S. Schiff

Introduction

To some observers the further fragmentation of Israel's religious parties in recent years is the result of new developments within them and within the overall political system. If left unchecked, it is argued (and in some cases hoped), the result might be the diminution of their overall impact on Israeli political life, as has happened in the case of other small, ideologically-oriented parties as they splintered (such as the Communists and *Mapam* on the left, the Sephardi and Yemenite factions among the original ethnic parties, and the old General Zionists on the right).

In fact, many of the recently articulated divisions between and among the religious parties are deeply rooted in their pluralistic origins as umbrella parties covering the diverse spectrum of views that once was Orthodoxy. The recent spate of hyper-fragmentation may well reflect the resurfacing of internal tensions and factions long inherent in these parties. They were triggered in large measure by the fundamental changes in the Israeli political system initially brought about by the rise of Begin and the *Likud,* rather than to any basic trend towards their dissolution.

As I have argued elsewhere,[1] and continue to believe, the two core religious parties are very different from one another and should not be simplistically lumped together for purposes of analysis. Nevertheless, taken as a whole they do constitute what Elazar refers to as one of the three major "camps" in Israeli politics[2] (the other two being labor and civil). Viewed in this way, the recent splits, mergers, recombinations, and permutations these parties have experienced may well constitute more of a realignment of forces within that "camp," rather than any fundamental breakdown thereof. Indeed, the pattern may more closely resemble the decline and disaffection of the old leftist *Mapam,* for example, from today's more centrist Labor party within the socialist camp rather than the disintegration of the short-lived Democratic Movement for Change.

Despite their fragmentation and relative decline, the religious parties continue to exhibit remarkable resilience and potency. Indeed, as I have suggested previously,[3] given the crystallization of Israeli politics around two major poles--*Likud* and Labor--neither of which is capable of governing on its own, and given the relatively more durable staying power of religion over many other issues as a central concern in the Israeli polity, the religious parties' influence is likely to be enhanced, despite their ostensible divisiveness and erstwhile decline. Thus, while voting for all the religious parties together declined from an all time high of 15.4% and 18 Members of Knesset (M.K.'s) in the Fifth Knesset elections of 1961 to an all time low of 11.3% and 13 M.K.'s in the Eleventh Knesset elections of 1984,[4] the parties remain a potent political force. This resilience was evidenced by their remarkable come back in the Twelfth Knesset elections of 1988, when they garnered 14.6% of the vote and 18 M.K.'s, although the balance by now had clearly shifted to non-Zionist, *Agudist*-type parties.

Origins of the Religious Parties

What were the origins of these parties? And what were the diverse elements and forces that historically divided them into internal factions?[5]

First, it must be stressed that all Israeli parties aspiring to the label "religious," unlike those of Western Europe, claim to represent the same religion, indeed the same "denomination" thereof, Orthodoxy. It is because of this common professed allegiance to Orthodoxy that these parties are often indiscriminately lumped together and are alleged to have similar (usually "conservative," "extremist," "clericalist," or "right wing") political characteristics or behaviors.

There is as yet no party claiming to represent the other two main denominations of Judaism in the world, Conservative and Reform, both relatively new to Israel--and, in the latter instance, to Zionism. However, recent developments, such as the formation of Reform and Conservative parties within the World Zionist Organization, suggest that these groups may be overcoming their previous American-derived inhibitions about mixing religion and politics. The eventual formation of two such parties, or one non-Orthodox religious party, cannot be ruled out. This scenario would be even more likely if the movements are frustrated in their present attempts at achieving their political ends via cooperation with one or the other major secular party,[6] and/or if the prospect for electoral reform fades, both of which are likely.

In fact, the two core religious parties are very different and have clearly distinguishable political social characteristics, as well as often divergent roles in the Israeli political system. Initially, each of the two developed as different reactions to the modernization of Jewish life in Europe in the late 19th and early 20th centuries, and particularly to the challenge of modern political, largely secular Jewish nationalism, or Zionism. At the same time, neither party was monolithic. From the very beginning, each contained divergent internal strains and factions, divisions which have only become more manifest in recent years and in some cases have led to party splits.

Mafdal: The National Religious Party

The oldest and largest of these parties--founded in 1902 as the first officially recognized faction within the World Zionist Organization--is the National Religious Party (NRP), or in its Hebrew acronym, *Mafdal.* With an attitude that affirmed, or at least accommodated, religious tradition to modern life (including modern education and political activity), the party has a long history of active participation in the Zionist movement and later in the State of Israel, where it has traditionally played the role of essential but junior coalition partner to whichever of the two leading parties, Labor or *Likud,* was in power.

As a result of its loyal participation, *Mafdal* was able to achieve many gains within its overall objective of "nationalizing" or institutionalizing religion within the legal and political framework of the State.[7] It became the dominant force in the religious establishment of the State, which includes the Chief Rabbinate, the rabbinical court system that adjudicates all matters of personal status for Jews in Israel, and the religious state education system, as well as the principal proponent of religious legislation.

The party historically has had a broad socioeconomic, geographic and ethnic base to draw upon, and was run by its lay (rather than clerical) leadership, derived in no small measure from its extensive labor organization, *Ha-Po'el Ha-Mizrahi. Mizrahi,* an acronym for *Merkaz Ruhani* or Spiritual Center, was the original name of the party and remained the name of the smaller, non-labor sector until their reunification in 1956 under the umbrella of *Mafdal.* Ostensibly a large (typically garnering nearly 10% of the vote and 12 M.K.'s as recently as 1977), unified party with a well articulated ideology, *Mafdal* has a long and at times bitter history of factional conflict.[8] While some of these factions have been based on personalistic cults of various leaders, the party has always had factions that emphasized one of the three central pillars of its ideology over the other: religion, nationalism or socialism.

Bitter debates as early as that over the Uganda scheme (1903-05) as to whether to accept an alternate, if temporary homeland (nationalists v. religionists); or later in the 1920s, over whether to join the secular socialist *Histadrut* labor organization, or whether to prefer an alliance with other religious elements, including the non-Zionist *Agudat Yisrael* (socialists v. religionists); or in the 30s whether to support the Revisionists as against the established leadership of the World Zionist Organization and the *Yishuv* on the partition of Palestine (nationalist hawks v. religionist or socialist doves); or even whether to declare independence in 1948, punctuated the history of the party. In different periods one or the other view prevailed, but the tensions were never fully resolved.   These ideological divisions within the party were criss-crossed and at times reinforced by interest groups that developed within it, including those of the party's labor, agricultural, women's and rabbinic/educational sectors.

In fact, these three basic issues--the role of religion in the State; the definition of nationalism vis a vis the territories and the Palestinian Arabs; and the transformation of a once predominantly socialist, egalitarian, communitarian economy and society into a post-industrial, technological, individualistic and consumer-oriented one--constitute three of the fundamental cleavages in post-Begin Israeli society.   In many ways the conflicts within *Mafdal* are a microcosm of those in Israeli society at large.

Similarly, the party has not handled the knotty questions of generational change of leadership or of ethnic (read Sephardi) politics much better than most other Israeli parties, despite the fact that Sephardim were involved in the party from very early on and that a majority of its members has long been Sephardi.   As a result of all these internal tensions, when powerful forces of change in the overall Israeli political system swept over *Mafdal*, beginning in the late 60s and early 70s, and reaching epic proportions beginning in 1977, the stitches that had long held party's patchwork quilt together began to give way.

Agudat Yisrael

The other core religious party, *Agudat Yisrael* (Society of Israel, founded in 1912), developed out of the opposite or negative reaction of traditional Orthodox European Jewry to the challenges of modernity, secularism and nationalism embodied in the Zionist movement.   Believing Divine intervention, rather than political self-help, to be the only way to restore the Jewish people to its land, a land to be governed by the laws of the Torah not of man, *Agudat Yisrael* cultivated a separatist mentality vis a vis the rest of the Jewish community in general, and towards Zionism in particular. For the first few decades of its existence, then, it embraced a vigorously non- or anti-Zionist stance.

During and since the Holocaust, which led to the destruction of the wellsprings of its support in Eastern Europe, and the establishment of Israel, *Agudat Yisrael* adopted a more pragmatic view of the State, viewing it as a de facto legitimate secular political authority to be dealt with like other governments in the interests of its adherents. However, in *Agudat Yisrael's* view, that State (like the Zionist movement that gave it birth) has no religious significance per se.

Thus, while the party has always participated in the Knesset, it has tended not to join coalition governments except selectively when the interests of its constituents warranted it. Alternatively it has adopted the practice of supporting the coalition (in exchange for various concessions), but not actually participating in the cabinet. In this way *Agudat Yisrael* has been an effective advocate for the interests of its followers, especially in obtaining funding for its independent network of religious institutions, including a separate school system.

Agudat Yisrael was historically a clerically dominated party, with a limited socioeconomic, geographic and ethnic constituency that was almost entirely confined to certain urban areas. Nevertheless, it, too, was far from monolithic. And while its internal divisions were not ideological in the same sense that *Mafdal's* were--the party's principal platform was religion; as a non-Zionist group it had no use for nationalism, let alone socialism, which it viewed as yet another secular, alien ideology--they were no less profound.

Found under the umbrella of the early *Agudat Yisrael,* for example, were both German Jewish neo-Orthodox intellectuals of the Hirsch school of *"Torah 'im Derekh Eretz"* ("Torah and the Way of the World") who, while opposing Zionism, were advocates of modern education (many of them held doctorates from leading German universities), with all that implied; as well as Hungarian rabbis of the Hatam Sofer school of thought which believed that *"He-Hadash Asur min Ha-Torah"* ("Innovation is Forbidden by the Torah"), which opposed modern education as the opening wedge that would destroy traditional Jewish life. Likewise found under its early banner were the followers of various major Hassidic rabbis, who very often were at odds with one another; as well as the disciples of the great *yeshivot* of Lithuania, whose Mitnagdic interpretation of Orthodoxy was poles apart from, and often in open conflict with that of the Hassidim.

Like *Mizrachi, Agudat Yisrael* also spawned a labor wing, *Po'alei Agudat Yisrael* (PAY). But unlike *Mizrachi,* the labor wing remained smaller than the parent party. Nevertheless, it did at times skirt perilously close enough to certain Zionist, even socialist ideas and practices (like the kibbutz) as to result in the eventual split of the two into separate parties.

Given its clericalist mentality, which tends to venerate age, the party has traditionally had a problem with what Pareto called the "circulation of elites." Over the course of the first thirty years of the State, for example, *Agudat Yisrael* had one of the oldest Knesset delegations.[9] Likewise, because of its heavily East European character and ambience--meetings were often conducted in Yiddish--the party missed the proverbial boat in securing the allegiance of the many Sephardim who were quietly becoming a significant segment of its voters by failing to advance any of Sephardi representatives into key leadership positions.

The Winds of Change--*Mafdal*

For *Mafdal*, the winds of change can be identified as beginning at the 1967 Six Day War, a process that was only intensified by the 1973 Yom Kippur War, and which culminated in major upheavals beginning with the accession of Begin and the *Likud* to power in 1977. Each of the aforementioned long-standing, if dormant conflicts came into play with great intensity during this period.

First, generational conflict erupted with the rapid rise of the *Tze'irim* or Young Guard faction, led by Zevulun Hammer and Yehudah Ben-Meir. Composed largely of Israeli born and/or raised Sabras, products of *Mafdal's* own national religious education system and the army, the more militant *Tze'irim* were impatient to take over the reins of power and patronage long dominated by older European-born leaders like Yosef Burg and Yitzhak Refael. Under the latter the party, in its "historic partnership" with the then *Mapai*, it largely confined itself to religious and educational issues, leaving broader matters of the economy and of foreign and defense policy to *Mapai*. As mostly upwardly mobile urban professionals--Hammer was an educator; American-born and educated Ben-Meir was a Ph.D. psychologist--this new leadership cadre had little interest in the socialist aspects of the party's ideology, especially with the opportunities opening up as a result of the rapid economic growth, foreign investment and urbanization (particularly in Jerusalem) that followed the '67 victory.

But more importantly, the victory in the Six Day War and the newly won control over territories that covered most of historic *Eretz Yisrael* (the Land of Israel) opened up whole new vistas for the party's long-standing, if largely dormant nationalist element. Suffused with a religious messianism long a part of religious Zionism, this new vision spawned a separate populist movement, *Gush Emunim,* devoted to settling the land, which provided common ground and a convenient bridge between *Mafdal* and other nationalist parties, notably the *Herut* (later *Gahal,* later *Likud*) party of Menachem Begin. Indeed, under the influence of the *Tze'irim,* the changing emphasis among the party's historic triad of ideologies towards the dominance of nationalism predisposed *Mafdal* to rethink its historic partnership with Labor and to seriously contemplate joining a *Likud*-based coalition if and when the time came, which it did in 1977.[10]

Two additional factors militated in favor of that new connection. One was Begin's much vaunted personal traditionalism (viewed by some observers somewhat more cynically as the culmination of a process of manipulation of traditionalist symbols and myths in a largely successful attempt to remake Israel's "civic culture" that had begun earlier under the Labor Party.)[11] While not shared by his entire party, this attitude and behavior did mark a radical change from previous, Labor party prime ministers' avowed secularism.

A second and related factor was *Mafdal's* own somewhat belated attempt to give greater recognition and visibility to the Sephardi element in the party. It was precisely the coming of political age of the Sephardim in 1977, and their rejection of previous allegiances to what they now viewed as a patronizing Labor party, that precipitated the *"mahapach"* (revolution) of 1977. Insofar as *Mafdal* was able to ride on the coattails of this phenomenon of ethnic politics, it benefitted from the Sephardi (and *Likud's*) rise to power.

Mafdal's joining of the Likud-led coalition in 1977 symbolized not only the ascension of the nationalist element of its ideology (and the concomitant decline of its socialist one), but also marked the coming to fruition of the long-sought ambition of the *Tze'irim* to break out of the confining mold the party had been placed in under Labor, symbolized by its traditional control over the Ministries of Religion and Interior and the Deputy Ministry of Education that would oversee the religious state education system.

Its aspirations to broader involvement in the general political life of the country were now rewarded by its being awarded the Deputy Ministry for Foreign Affairs, the entire Ministry of Education (not just its religious "ghetto"), and by having its one of its senior ministers chair negotiations with Egypt. As the third largest party, with a restored 12 M.K.'s to its credit, *Mafdal* began to view itself as a broad based, religiously affiliated party with wide national appeal a la the Christian Democratic parties of Europe. *Mafdal* seemed to be riding the crest.

These dreams came crashing down around *Mafdal* in the Tenth Knesset elections of 1981, when the party's parliamentary delegation was halved to six seats. About one quarter of *Mafdal's* votes (three M.K.'s) were siphoned off by a newly created, Sephardi (largely Moroccan) ethnic party, *Tami* (The Tradition of Israel Movement). It was headed by a former *Mafdal* M.K. and Minister of Religions of Moroccan extraction, Aharon Abu-Hatzeira, who had been groomed and touted as an example of how *Mafdal* was being solicitous of the needs of its Sephardi constituents. Apparently it was too little too late. Many of its long-time Sephardi adherents were turning away from *Mafdal*, viewing it as a predominantly Ashkenazi led and dominated party, much as their confreres in the Labor party had done in the previous election. Again, developments in *Mafdal* often mirror those in other, larger parties and in the Israeli political system as a whole.

True to form for ethnic parties in Israel, (though Abu-Hatzeira's run-ins with the law might also have had something to do with it), *Tami* did not survive the long haul. It declined to one M.K. in 1984 and has since been absorbed into *Likud* for the upcoming 1988 elections. Nevertheless, it set a precarious precedent for ethnic (and other) fragmentation in *Mafdal* and in the religious parties as a whole.

Mafdal's turn to the nationalist right also provided the rationale for significant numbers of its other voters to "go all the way" and vote directly for *Likud*, the even more right wing *Tehiya*, or other extreme nationalist parties like Meir Kahane's *Kach*. If, as *Mafdal* seemed to be saying, the basic issues of religious life and law were well in hand by now, thanks to its efforts; and the central concern of Israeli politics revolves around the territories and settlements, then why not vote for right wing parties for whom those issues have always been paramount and which, in any case, evince a generalized sympathy for religion?

The ascendancy of the nationalist right within *Mafdal* was inspired in no small measure by the mystical writings of the late Chief Rabbi of Palestine, Abraham Isaac Kook, and by the more explicitly political teachings of his son, Rabbi Tzvi Yehudah Kook, head of the prestigious Merkaz Ha-Rav yeshiva in Jerusalem. Inevitably, it engendered a reaction from among the party's small, but vocal dovish minority, based among the remnants of the party's old committed socialist/labor/agricultural wing and among some younger academics and intellectuals, mostly of Ashkenazi extraction. Paralleling such movements as *Shalom 'Ahkshav* (Peace Now) in the general community, groups such as *'Oz ve-Shalom* (Power and Peace) and *Netivot Shalom* (Paths of Peace), emphasizing the elements of peace, accommodation and the saving of human life in the Jewish tradition over those of territory, settlements and security, arose from within the ranks of the party. They found their own rabbinic patrons, several of American provenance (as are many of the leaders and members of the party's settlement movement as well).

The long and costly war in Lebanon gave further impetus to the peace movements generally, and to those in *Mafdal* orbit specifically. Whereas previous Israeli wars could be defined in traditional rabbinic terms as *"milkhemet mitzvah,"* defensive, obligatory wars of survival, the Lebanon war was increasingly viewed by some as *"milkhemet r'shut,"* an offensive, optional, political, unnecessary war, and the inevitable outcome of the unrestrained nationalism of the Begin era. Even one-time hawks like Hammer himself began to express reservations, both about the war and of *Mafdal's* ultra-nationalist stance.

It was at this time and out of similar concerns that Abraham Burg, son of *Mafdal's* long-reigning chieftain, Yosef Burg, abandoned the party and joined the Labor party, where he has since been given a secure spot on the list for the upcoming elections in 1988. (The Labor party has always had a small religious wing, *Ha-'Oved Ha-Dati*). Failing to make much headway within *Mafdal,* many other dovish members of the party have since moved over to the Labor camp as well.

With the party's leadership seeming to have second thoughts about its turn to the right, yet another break-away faction--this time to the right--appeared before the 1984 elections. Initially calling itself *Matzad* (The Religious Zionist Party), the new party was led by former *Mafdal* M.K.'s who were more unambiguously identified with the settlers in the territories. When they merged with the remnants of the old PAY, the party was renamed *Morasha* (Heritage). Under this banner it earned two seats in the Knesset, thereby almost directly reducing *Mafdal's* delegation to an all time low of four M.K.'s. Subsequently one of these two returned to *Mafdal* after receiving assurances of *Mafdal's* continued devotion to the nationalist cause under its new leader, Avner Shaki. With only one M.K., *Morasha's* political future as a separate political party is doubtful.

Shaki headed *Mafdal's* Knesset list in 1988. He was one of the few bright younger Sephardim (he is Israeli-born of Yemenite extraction) who was belatedly fast-tracked by *Mafdal* for a leadership position in the very first

Knesset election following the 1967 war (the Seventh Knesset elections of 1969) in an attempt to pacify and secure the loyalty of its Sephardi adherents. A law professor at the party-affiliated Bar-Ilan University, which itself has since become the intellectual home of many of the party's right wing academics, Shaki was rapidly advanced from first-term M.K. to Deputy Minister of Education, a post that traditionally presided over a key *Mafdal* fiefdom, the religious state education system.

However, when he displayed more interest in the overall educational advancement of Sephardi children, irrespective of educational track, than in the party's religious state education system; and when he broke party discipline to vote for an *Agudat Yisrael* sponsored amendment to the Law of Return to limit conversions to those done according to *Halakha* (religious law), Shaki was deposed from his portfolio, declared himself an independent and lost the confidence of the party leadership.[12] He clearly harbors no lost love for the old *Mafdal* elite that once ousted him and whom he is now replacing.

Known for his stridently nationalist views, Shaki's ascension to power in *Mafdal* marks the triumph of both its nationalist and remaining Sephardi elements. Symbolic of this transformation, the party announced the removal of its national headquarters from Tel Aviv to (East) Jerusalem in July of 1988.[13]

The Arab uprising or *intifadah,* beginning in December of 1987, further polarized existing opinions within Israeli society as to what to do vis a vis the ("liberated," "administered," or "occupied") territories in general, and those of the "West Bank" or "Judea and Samaria" in particular, given their religious, strategic, demographic and economic relationship to Israel. Again, the debate in *Mafdal* mirrored that in the larger society.

But now that what remained of *Mafdal* was once again firmly in the nationalist camp, and dominated by Sephardim to boot, some of its veteran members and others, mostly Ashkenazi in their ethnicity, liberal in their Orthodoxy, academic in their education, and moderate in their nationalism, sought a new venue for political expression. Unlike those who had abandoned *Mafdal* for the Labor party for these reasons (or for *Likud,* for that matter, for the opposite ones), they sought the framework of a religious party.

Thus, a new religious party called *Memad* (the Religious Centrist Party) was established in the summer of 1988 in anticipation of the elections. It was headed by Rabbi Yehudah Amital, who heads the Har Etzion yeshiva (itself built beyond the "green line"!)[14] Also highly placed on the new party's

Knesset list is Dr. Naomi Cohen, a university lecturer in Jewish philosophy and wife of the Chief Rabbi of Haifa.[15]

This placement is indicative of an assertive new feminism found among the ranks of left wing Orthodoxy in recent years, which has seen Orthodox women successfully overcoming stiff legal, political and social (though not really *Halakhic*) obstacles to serve in such once all-male preserves as local religious councils and even electoral bodies for city-wide chief rabbis.[16] This trend, too, has its roots in *Mafdal* and its women's organization. *Mafdal* had a woman M.K. as early as 1959. Yet, it is this very trend that underscores *Memad's* (and more broadly, modern Orthodoxy's) profound alienation from most other Orthodox religious groups and parties, be they in *Mafdal* or certainly in *Agudat Yisrael,* where the trend has been in the opposite direction.

While some preliminary public opinion polls predicted as many as four seats, the party would have had to draw substantial votes from the remaining *Mafdal,* as well as win back those who left for Labor, in order to do so. In fact, the party did not garner enough votes to earn a single Knesset seat. Despite the outcome, the very establishment of this new party itself harks back to antecedents in certain moderate factions of *Mafdal* extant in its very origins.

The triumph of the rightist, nationalist elements within *Mafdal* in recent years has not only alienated (and therefore led to the departures) of its veteran leftist, socialist, dovish wing, many of its once numerous Sephardi adherents, and even some if its ultra-nationalists who now prefer "the real thing." It has also offended some of the party's "religionists," who have long evinced a deeper sympathy for other religious groups, like *Agudat Yisrael,* than for ties with either socialists or secular nationalists.

Indeed, *Mafdal* has long had to look over its religious shoulder not to be outflanked by *Agudat Yisrael* and even more extreme groups who have traditionally berated it for its compromises on religious issues, most notably on the question of "Who is a Jew?" for purposes of immigration and citizenship. The capturing of this issue by *Agudat Yisrael*--specifically the demand for an amendment to the Law of Return defining "Jew" in more strictly *Halakhic* terms--has only highlighted the vulnerability of *Mafdal,* historically a moderate, modernist religious party, at a time when Orthodox Judaism in Israel and elsewhere--much like Christianity and Islam--is increasingly dominated by fundamentalists.

Nowhere is the difficulty in walking the tightrope between fundamentalism and modernism more palpable than in the state religious education system, once the pride and joy of *Mafdal* and the prime source of socialization and recruitment of new members and leaders. Rising from 24.5% in 1953-54 to a high of 29% in 1964-65, nationwide enrollment in the primary grades of religious state education declined to a low of 20% in 1984-85. In intermediate schools the decline was even more dramatic (from 37.5% in 1969-70 to 16.3% in 1985-86); while at the secondary school level the decrease was more moderate (from 21.9% in 1969-70 to 19.6% in 1985-86).[17]

Most of these losses have been to the (secular) state school system, which has increased markedly in all categories, indicating a movement away from the party by younger generation parents (many Sephardim). Some of the loss has been to the Independent Education schools dominated by *Agudat Yisrael,* which have maintained fairly constant enrollments (see below), but which have shown remarkable growth at the key secondary level. This pattern reflects a trend among even some of *Mafdal's* own (mostly Ashkenazi) leaders to denigrate the religious and/or educational attainments (and ethnic heterogeneity) of the party's system and to opt for educating their children in the more traditionally Orthodox (and supposedly largely Ashkenazi) schools of *Agudat Yisrael.* However, the same trend towards the right in religious matters has affected Sephardim as well, with increasing numbers of yeshiva students (and their parents) being of Sephardi extraction. The growth of the Sephardi sector in *Agudat Yisrael* is one of the key sources of the upheavals that have wreaked that venerable party in recent years.

The Winds of Change--*Agudat Yisrael*

While profound changes have taken place in the *Agudat Yisrael* camp, too, given the very different nature of the party from *Mafdal,* the changes are of a somewhat different character. As it never was a nationalist, Zionist party per se, and as it (with the exception of PAY) was never involved in land settlement or in military service, it was far less troubled by the whole range of issues engendered by the territories. Indeed, *Agudat Yisrael,* often portrayed as the "extremist" Orthodox party, has been consistently dovish on these questions, (while the supposedly "moderate" *Mafdal* has been counted among the leading hawks!)

Rather *Agudat Yisrael* been far more concerned with social and economic issues of direct import to its constituency (like the expansion of child allowances for larger families, which its members tend to have), as well as with the expansion and funding of its network of educational institutions. While not necessarily always a member of the government coalition, the party exercised considerable influence in these areas via its traditional chairmanship of the powerful Finance Committee of the Knesset. The party's long-time incumbent in that position, Abraham Shapira, nicknamed "the country's director-general," was widely considered one of the most powerful politicians in the country.[18]

The party has always been concerned with religious issues too, of course, but there has been a significant change in its attitude in this area in recent years. Initially the party was most concerned with the creation of the basic conditions that would allow its adherents to maintain their religious life and institutions in an unencumbered fashion. It was in this spirit that *Agudat Yisrael,* it is too often forgotten, served in the government from the establishment of the State until 1952, with its venerable leader, Rabbi Yitzhak Meir Levin, holding the Ministry of Social Welfare portfolio. It was only when two issues which it viewed precisely as fundamentally inimical to such conditions, namely conscription of religious women for military service and the abolition of the separate Orthodox "trends" in education were raised, that the party reverted to an earlier pattern of separatist, isolationist behavior.[19]

Given its traditional separatism and non-affiliation with either the Zionist movement or the official religious establishment long dominated by *Mafdal, Agudat Yisrael* was not initially overly concerned with religious legislation affecting the population at large, beyond the four basic tenets of the "Status Quo" agreed to between Ben-Gurion and both *Agudat Yisrael* and *Mafdal* immediately prior to the founding of the State. These arrangements provided for: kosher food in public facilities, personal status law for Jews adjudicated by rabbinical courts, separate religious education systems, and official observance of the Sabbath and Jewish holidays.

In more recent years, however, *Agudat Yisrael* has extended its purview in the religious sphere to embrace issues that not only affect its members directly, but also impact on the larger society (like the redefinition of the Law of Return to provide for recognition of converts to Judaism as being limited only to those converted according to *Halakha*). There are several reasons for this development.

First is the aforementioned rightist trend in Orthodoxy, both in Israel and among the growing and increasingly assertive Orthodox circles abroad, particularly in the United States, which exert important political and financial pressure on *Agudat Yisrael*. Many of the old accommodations and compromises under the "Status Quo" were simply no longer good enough. It was no longer sufficient to be allowed to practice one's religion within one's own four walls. Rather an aggressive outreach vis a vis the rest of society--whether it welcomed it or not--was now being sought. In American parlance, equal opportunity was now being replaced by demands for affirmative action. *Agudat Yisrael* was under pressure from such elements within the party and to the right of it to produce results, whether in terms of legislation, funding or other entitlements.

Second, as *Mafdal* turned its attentions increasingly to non-religious issues such as defense, foreign policy, the territories, and the economy; as it was increasingly splintered by factional conflict; and later, as it suffered withering electoral losses, making it a less key coalition partner; the field was now wide open for *Agudat Yisrael* to move in and stake its claim to be the upholder of "Torah-true" Judaism. From a senior coalition partner's point of view, *Agudat Yisrael's* assumption of *Mafdal's* old position of limiting itself mainly to religious issues made it a much more attractive junior partner than the new *Mafdal* that was seeking substantive involvement in other areas of national policy.

Furthermore, not only had the parliamentary and coalitional strength of *Mafdal* been reduced, but also many of the once powerful institutions of the religious establishment it built and dominated were clearly in decline, including the Chief Rabbinate and the aforementioned religious state education system. By contrast, the number of (draft exempt) students in mostly *Agudat Yisrael* oriented yeshivot had increased from several hundred in the early 1950s to over 20,000 in the late 1980s! Enrollment in the *Agudat Yisrael* affiliated Independent Education schools had essentially maintained its strength over the decades, declining from a high of 7% in 1953-54 to a low of 5.7% in 1979-80, recovering to 6.2 % in 1985-86; while enrollment in party affiliated secondary schools jumped from 3.7% in 1969-70 to 5% in 1985-86.[20] Among the new students in the party's related schools were significant numbers of Sephardim.

If *Agudat Yisrael* was the principal beneficiary of the rightist trend in Orthodoxy and of high Orthodox birthrates and school enrollments, what accounts for its steep decline in electoral support from 3.7% and four M.K.'s in 1981 (almost unchanged since the 1950s) to 1.7% and only two M.K.'s in 1984?[21]

The sources of this decline lie deep in *Agudat Yisrael's* long history of its own unique brand of factionalism described earlier. Of the original component units, few of the always small, modernist-leaning German-Jewish intellectual and organizational leadership of the party survived the Holocaust.

Of those that did, most were now attracted to the party's labor offshoot, PAY, whose intellectual leader, Yitzhak Breuer (himself a member of the Hirsch family), came closest to capturing the essence of their *weltanschauung.*

The principal groups that remained were the remnants of the large (mostly Polish, some Hungarian) Hassidic communities and their long-time antagonists in Orthodoxy, the Mitnagdim of the (mainly Lithuanian) yeshivot that had been transplanted to Israel after the war. While the Hassidim were well represented in both major centers of party strength, Jerusalem and B'nei B'rak, an almost all Orthodox satellite city of Tel Aviv, the Mitnagdim were concentrated most heavily in the latter, thus adding a geographic--and in some cases, a socioeconomic--factor to the mix.

One additional group, which never existed in Europe, consisted of the descendants of the Old Yishuv, the pre- and largely anti-Zionist, largely pietistic Jewish community of Palestine that was concentrated almost entirely in Jerusalem. As the original core group of *Agudat Yisrael* in mandatory Palestine--which interestingly included some Sephardim--the Old Yishuv element was particularly militant in its anti-Zionism, spawning such even more radical anti-State groups as the *Neturei Karta* early on in its history.

For most of the history of *Agudat Yisrael* in Israel generally and in the Knesset elections specifically, the party's traditional four seats were allocated along these factional lines:[22] two seats for the numerically superior Hassidim (one each to the Polish *Gur* sect, one to the Hungarian *Wischnitz*), one to the Lithuanian yeshiva circles, and one to the Old Yishuv Jerusalemites. Given the limited circulation of the elites in clericalist *Agudat Yisrael* (one *Agudah* M.K. was "ousted" after 33 years in office!), the various factions became quite entrenched. This alliance of factions, however uneasy, held solid for the first twenty years of the State.

But as in *Mafdal,* the ethnic complexion began to change--literally and figuratively--following the 1967 war. In an unprecedented move, one of the factional *Agudat Yisrael* M.K.'s resigned his post during the last year of the Seventh Knesset (1972-73) in favor of a Sephardi rabbi of Yemenite extraction. (The Yemenites, while not strictly speaking Sephardim, i.e., descendants of 15th century Spanish and Portuguese Jewish exiles, are one of the "Eastern communities" often loosely referred to as Sephardim. They have tended to be more religiously observant than some other such groups, and were among the earliest Sephardi adherents of *Agudat Yisrael*). Even more than *Mafdal's* belated attempts at mainlining Sephardim to retain and attract

Sephardi voters, however, this was a blatantly symbolic gesture, as the individual was afforded no real political power.

As demands for real representation by the party's growing (and younger) Sephardi element grew stronger, and as *Tami* appeared on the scene in 1981, as the example of the successful Sephardi break away party from *Mafdal*, pressure grew within the old party elite as to whose seat was to be sacrificed for the newcomers.   Growing personal and factional enmity, especially between leaders of the *Gur* Hassidic and Lithuanian yeshiva factions, led to the latter giving his blessing to a nascent Sephardi break away party that had earlier run a successful list is the Jerusalem municipal elections to go national for the 1984 Knesset elections. Its Hebrew acronym is *Shas* (Association of Sephardi Torah Observers, not "Guardians" as often mistranslated)].

Thus, drawing on the Sephardi element in *Agudat Yisrael,* plus the (largely Askkenazi) yeshiva faction, plus any other observant Sephardim who may have been attracted from *Mafdal,* or *Tami* (both of which further declined that year), or elsewhere, the party achieved a remarkable 3.1% or four M.K. showing, while halving *Agudat Yisrael's* delegation to 1.7% or two M.K.'s.[23] The remaining *Agudat Yisrael* seemed to be an essentially Hassidic party, with some other, smaller elements, such as the Old Yishuv, still in the fold. Nevertheless, spurred by the "Who Is A Jew?" issue and the massive intervention by the Lubavitcher rabbi in New York and his followers in Israel, the 1988 elections saw *Agudat Yisrael* rebound to 4.5% and 5 M.K.'s, despite a youthful break away party, *Degel Ha Torah,* that itself garnered 2 M.K.'s, and despite *Shas'* impressive 4.7% and 6 M.K. showing.

The new *Shas* party emerged from the 1984 elections with the same size parliamentary delegation as the veteran *Mafdal,* and quickly was courted into the coalition with the lures of ministerial portfolios (including the Ministry of Religions, which must have made old *Mafdal*-niks wince) and coalition promises. Subsequent disillusions with some of the latter led to resignations from the former, while the party itself of late is undergoing its own, largely personalistic internal conflicts. In the long run, whether *Shas* will beat the historical odds and survive as Israel's only principally ethnically based party is problematic at best, especially in light of its current legal problems which involve allegations of corruption and misuse of public funds by some of its highest public officials. Nevertheless, as its 1988 results would indicate, it is now still the single largest and most influential religious party.

More importantly, the development of *Shas,* like the rise and fall of *Tami* before it, reflects the as yet incomplete political integration of the Sephardim into the religious parties in particular, and into the Israeli political system as a whole. Nevertheless, if the examples of the larger, secular parties are instructive, the bridging of this ethnic gap appears to be far more feasible over time than is the overcoming the profound and growing political and social chasms that continue to divide religious (read Orthodox) from non-religious Jews in Israel.

Summary

The religious political parties of Israel have experienced major internal, structural--as well as external, behavioral--changes in recent years. Many of these changes stemmed from long-standing internal cleavages within the two core religious parties: *Mafdal* and *Agudat Yisrael.*

These divisions in turn originated in various ideological, religio-ethnic and/or geographic factions that were inherent within these parties from their outset at the turn of the century, but which have been materially exacerbated in the wake of Begin and *Likud's* rise to power. For it was precisely the same ideological issues relating to nationalism (the territories, the Palestinians, etc.); the nature of the society (socialist egalitarian v. free enterprise consumerist); and the relationship between religion and state, that the Begin *"mahapach"* thrust so forcefully onto center stage.

Likewise, it was the confluence of these issues with the rise of the Sephardim to political power that further compounded the problems of the once ethnically heterogeneous religious parties. As a result of these powerful ideological and ethnic cross-currents, the religious parties individually, and the religious "camp" as a whole, has experienced serious fragmentation, which in Israel has almost invariably meant decline in votes and Knesset seats, at least initially.

Thus, in many ways the problems of the religious parties mirror those--albeit on a much smaller scale--of the highly divisive and fragmented political system as a whole. Yet, the religious camp, despite its seeming fragmentation and decline, remains a potent political force in Israeli politics. Their collective influence has, if anything, increased in recent years, as religion continues to play a pivotal role in political discourse in contemporary Israel.

Endnotes

1. Gary S. Schiff, "Israel After Begin: The View From the Religious Parties," in *The Begin Era: Issues in Contemporary Israel,* ed. Steven Heydemann (Boulder and London, 1984), 41-43.

2. Daniel J. Elazar, *Israel: Building a New Society* (Bloomington, 1986), 71-72.

3. Gary S. Schiff, "Israeli Politics: The Renewed Centrality of Religion," in *Israel Faces the Future,* ed. Bernard Reich and Gershon R. Kieval (New York, 1986), 43-48.

4. State of Israel, Ministry of the Interior, *Results of Elections to the Eleventh Knesset, 23-7-1984* (Jerusalem: Central Bureau of Statistics, 1985), 9, 11.

5. For a comprehensive history of the religious parties of Israel see Gary S. Schiff, *Tradition and Politics: The Religious Parties of Israel* (Detroit, 1977), especially Chapter 2, "The Parties of Participation," and Chapter 3, "The Parties of Separatism."

6. Peter Steinfels, "Conservative Judaism Tilts Toward Israeli Left," *The New York Times* (September 11, 1988), 21.

7. Schiff, "Mafdal and the Nationalization of Religion," *Tradition and Politics,* see n. 5 above, chap. 6.

8. Schiff, *Tradition and Politics,* 54-62.

9. Schiff, *Tradition and Politics,* 113-117.

10. Moshe Krone, "Political Zionism in the Political Arena," in *Year Book, Religious Zionism, 1987,* ed. Yitzchak Pessin (Jerusalem, 1987), 32.

11. Charles S. Liebman and Eliezer Don-Yehiya, *Civil Religion in Israel: Traditional Judaism and Political Culture in the Jewish State* (Berkeley, 1983), 181-182; and Charles S. Liebman and Eliezer Don-Yehiya, *Religion and Politics in Israel* (Bloomington, Indiana, 1984), 53.

12. Schiff, *Tradition and Politics,* see n. 5 above, 118-119, 204.

13. Michael Yudelman, "NRP Plans Move to East Jerusalem," *The Jerusalem Post,* 21 (July, 1988): 1.

14. Yakir Tzur, "Rabbi Amital Will Run at the Head of Memad," *Davar* 15 (July, 1988): 1 (Hebrew).

15. Haim Shapiro, "Rabbi's Wife Says Woman's Place Is in House," *The Jerusalem Post* (July 15, 1988), 2.

16. Thomas L. Friedman, "In Israel, A Confluence of State, Temple and Gender Issues," *The New York Times* (October 12, 1986), 7; Hugh Orgel (Jewish Telegraphic Agency), "For the First Time in the History of Israel, Panel Electing Chief Rabbi Includes Women," *The Jewish Exponent* (September 9, 1988), 93.

17. Schiff, *Tradition and Politics,* see n. 5 above, 180, table 7.3; State of Israel, Central Bureau of Statistics, *Statistical Abstract of Israel, 1986* (Jerusalem, 1986), 581, table 22/16.

18. Avi Temkin, "The Country's Director-General," *The Jerusalem Post* (July 22, 1988), 7.

19. Schiff, *Tradition and Politics,* see n. 5 above, 83.

20. Schiff, *Tradition and Politics,* 180, table 7.3; *Statistical Abstract of Israel, 1986,* 581, table 22/16.

21. *Results of Elections to Eleventh Knesset,* 9, 11.

22. Schiff, *Tradition and Politics,* 97-101.

23. *Results of Elections to Eleventh Knesset,* 9-11.

RELIGIOUS-SECULAR ACCOMMODATION IN ISRAELI POLITICS

Alan Dowty

It is rare these days to find a hopeful view of relations between the religious and secular communities in Israel. Both academic and non-academic analysis, whatever their viewpoint, paint a dismal portrait of sharpened conflict, unyielding dogmatism, and impending catastrophe. One observer notes that "far more than the Sephardi/Ashkenazi split, the conflict between the varying demands of religious observance is the most potentially disruptive threat to the unity of Jewish Israel."[1] An academic analyst concludes that the demands of religious parties may be as serious as the Arab threat: "Indeed, the latter groups may be more willing to compromise their demands than the religious parties have ever shown a willingness to do."[2] An Israeli long active in opposing religious demands states that "We are now witnessing the Judgement Day of the State's domestic affairs."[3]

Indeed, religious differences do seem, in some senses, to be less amenable to resolution than other cleavages in Israeli society. The split between Jews of European and Afro-Asian background, though serious and persistent, is regarded by both sides as a temporary phenomenon, the result of historic accident, that will eventually be erased or a least blurred in the forging of a common Israeli identity. The sharp differences between Israelis and Arabs can at least in theory be settled through compromise on a "live and let live" basis. But religious differences seem less susceptible to such compromise; they are deeply rooted in opposed ways of life that deny the legitimacy of coexistence and seek, either actively or defensively, not only to defend ground won, but also to undermine the enemy. Nor are these divisions a transitional phase, as different degrees and definitions of religious observance and competing religious authority appear to have always been part of the Jewish condition.

The social distance between the religious (or Orthodox) and nonreligious publics, reinforced by such factors as residential concentration and educational segregation, has been amply documented. One study of eleventh-graders in 1973 found, for example, that 65 percent of nonreligious respondents were unwilling to have a religious friend, and 81 percent did not want a religious neighbor. Among religious respondents, 68 percent rejected a nonreligious friend, and 65 percent a nonreligious neighbor.[4] Such attitudes reflect not only the inconvenience of conflicting lifestyles in situation of close social proximity, but also the fear that one's own lifestyle might be threatened by changes in the neighborhood (a problem raised, for example, by the expansion of religious neighborhoods in Jerusalem). From the religious side, it seems normal to maintain sharp boundaries protecting the integrity of religious life, since "separation and distinction are characteristic of the *Halakhic* legal system that lies at the heart of the Jewish world view."[5]

Religious-secular relations are of special significance for the political system because of the historic blurring of civil and religious matters in Jewish life and the lack, even today and even among many secular Israelis, of strong support for the principle of separation of religion and state. In Jewish tradition, "religious" and "secular" matters overlapped; in fact, the very distinction would have made little sense to pre-modern generations. The weight of tradition was reinforced, in the Zionist and Israeli experiences, by the practical necessity of compromise on religious demands in order to preserve unity. Ultimately, this developed into ingrained habits of coexistence according to formulas that fit neither side's world view squarely, but also impinged in neither's basic way of life unduly.[6]

The result of all this is, at best, constant struggle and uneasy compromise over the role of religion in politics. But as this is not a novel occurrence in Jewish history, the traditional patterns of accommodation may help to explain how the Israeli system has coped with religious cleavages--and why these cleavages have not torn the system asunder. In fact, religious power in Israel appears to be a classic expression of the bargaining pattern in the Jewish political tradition. Furthermore, this tradition has enabled Israel to deal with religious division much more successfully than most observers would credit--and certainly more successfully than those actively engaged in the conflict would concede.

Jewish Political Traditions and the Role of Religion

Jewish communities throughout history had long experience in maintaining many institutions of a self-contained political system. In Tsarist Russia--where half of the world's Jews lived in the nineteenth century--the Jewish *shtetl* had enjoyed a wide-ranging autonomy (which the Russian government tried to whittle down in the last few decades before the Revolution). These communities regularly elected both secular leaders and rabbis; they also levied taxes (or apportioned the taxes levied on the community as a whole by the state), maintained courts with varying types of sanctions, established extensive welfare systems, passed laws (*takanot*) regulating extensively all aspects of life in the community from commerce to codes of personal dress, and appointed agents (*shtadlanim*) as "diplomats" to represent the community in its relations with external authority. A distinctive and persistent political tradition grew out of the normative institutions of Judaism as shaped by the peculiarities of Diaspora existence that most Jewish communities (non-European as well as European) experienced in common.[7] Certain features of this environment strike a familiar chord to anyone familiar with the political history of the Zionist movement and the state of Israel.[8]

Clearly, the voluntary character of Jewish self-government was of decisive importance. Except in such limited spheres as collection of state taxes (backed by state enforcement), the Jewish community had very limited means of coercion at its disposal. The ultimate sanction available--the *herem* or excommunication--had been of great importance in the pre-Emancipation period when life centered around religion and the community, and was still of some importance thereafter. But in the circumstances of Tsarist Russia, by the late nineteenth century, active participation and cooperation was highly dependent on the good will of community members. In a very real sense, it was government by consent of the governed. In Daniel Elazar's analysis, it was a "convental" relationship whose roots lay in the biblical covenants freely contracted between God and Israel. This also had "democratic" implications, since government based on contractual relationships suggests formal equality and a general right of participation, as reflected by the regular conduct of elections in an age and geographical setting where the right to vote was unknown. Shmuel Eisenstadt refers to "the basic 'democratic' or rather egalitarian premisses of the Jewish tradition, premises of basic equality and of equal participation and access of all Jews to the centers of the sacred realm . . . in contrast to the potentially more oligarchic tendencies of priesthood, the predominant modes of Jewish belief."[9]

Since it was voluntary, Jewish self-government also had to be inclusive. Disgruntled groups and individuals were not at the mercy of the will of the majority; they could opt out of active participation in the community. Given the need for unity against a hostile environment, there was a strong incentive to give all groups in the community a stake in the system. It was understood that benefits must be broadly shared among all members of the community, even where this meant overcoming deep social, ideological, and religious divisions that would ordinarily make cooperation difficult. The principle of proportionality in the distribution of power and benefits was widely understood and applied before the term itself came into use, as the only conceivable approach in a community or movement that lacked governmental powers.

It follows from these two points that Jewish politics were inevitably pluralistic. In the first place, each community chose secular officials as well as a rabbinic leadership, and the lines of authority between the two were often unclear and thus the cause of controversy. As Jacob Katz writes, "there was no clear-cut dichotomy between the lay and rabbinical authorities."[10] This softened the theocratic potential inherent in the selection of a religious hierarchy, and set the precedent of a tension between political and religious authority as well as a blurring of the lines between political and religious issues. Apart from this, there was a proliferation of groups of all types: artisan guilds, mutual aid societies, cultural associations, political parties, educational groups, savings and loan associations, defense organizations, charitable associations, burial societies, and workers' groups. According to one estimate, each Jewish community had on the average some twenty different associations, while the large city of Vilna, in 1916, had a total of 160 associations.[11]

The presence of so many groups, many of them carrying out quasi-governmental functions, served to increase the diffusion of power and to blur yet further the lines of authority within the community. An essential unity was preserved through mutual recognition and accommodation among the groups, and by an underlying understanding that the legitimacy of these divisions rested on the adherence of all to the collective norms and interests shared by the entire community. But the result was that the formal structure of government was often at odds with the informal arrangements by which governmental functions were actually exercised. In such a situation, bargaining and uneasy compromise among the de facto power centers was often of more import than formal decisions. The existence of different centers of power also helped legitimize opposition to decisions that might be reached, by providing institutionalized alternatives. Even rabbinical decisions could be impeached, since there were competing authorities who could be invoked against each other.[12]

It is, therefore, no surprise that the style of politics under such conditions was contentious. The bargaining by which the system operated was noisy and confrontational, since the rules were themselves fluid. Each group sought to influence communal affairs as best it could, and the outcome tended simply to reflect the pressures that they were able to mobilize. Battles between contending factions could even turn violent.

This pattern of politics has much in common with what political scientists refer to as "consociational" or "consensus" democracy. Consociationalism, as opposed to majoritarian democracy, rejects the idea that the untrammelled will of the majority is the essence of self-determination, and instead embraces the idea that all major groups in society should have some influence over decision-making. The diffusion and sharing of power, according to some principle of proportionality, is the ideal to be pursued. Consociational systems are characterized by grand coalitions (making minorities a part of the system), by explicit representation of minorities, by multiparty systems divided along many lines of cleavage (socioeconomic, ethnic, religious, etc.), by proportional representation, by decentralization, and by formal or informal rights of veto by the major groups in society. Such systems are especially characteristic, analysts point out, of deeply-divided societies such as Switzerland and Belgium.[13]

The resemblance of religious-secular politics in Israel to the consociational pattern has been noted by several observers. Sammy Smooha points to the maintenance of separate institutions, the organization of religious Jews to procure a share of the resources and benefits of government, the ability of religious parties to cast a veto on religious issues, and the general pattern of accommodation and negotiation rather than a pattern of confrontation and decisive outcomes.[14] Eliezer Don-Yehiya concludes that the consociational democracy model helps to explain, to a large extent, how "the Israeli political system has managed to resolve religious conflicts by peaceful means, while preserving its stability and democratic character."[15]

The attempt to encompass the religious and the nonreligious together in the Zionist movement goes back to its earliest days. Though religious delegates to the First Zionist Congress in 1897 were a small minority, Theodor Herzl made an important gesture in their direction by attending services (for the first time in years) at a Basel synagogue on the Sabbath before the Congress opened.[16] The Zionist movement, which lacked even the slight aura of governmental authority enjoyed by Jewish community leaders, could attract religious Jews only by offering them a sense of participation and a proportional share of influence and benefits. The logic of the situation was expressed by Max Nordau at the Third Zionist Congress in 1899, when he appealed to religious Jews to join the movement: "Within Zionism everyone is guaranteed full freedom to live according to his religious convictions. . . . For we do not have the possibility of imposing our will on you if it happens to be different from yours!"[17]

By the early years of the century, religious Zionists had organized as the *Mizrahi* movement, and were participating in power-sharing arrangements within the World Zionist Organization. The same patterns carried over into the organized Jewish community in Palestine (*Yishuv*) as Zionist institutions came to dominate there in the post-World War I period. Beginning in the 1930s, the secular leadership of the *yishuv* made explicit arrangements, first with Hapoel Hamizrahi and later with the *Mizrahi* movement itself, on the proportionate division of jobs and other benefits, beginning a forty-year period of partnership between Labor Zionists and religious Zionists.[18] Efforts were also made to bring *Agudat Yisrael,* representing the ultra-Orthodox (*haredi*) non-Zionist or anti-Zionist population of the *"old yishuv,"* within the purview of the new communal institutions.   Chaim Weizmann sought throughout the 1920s to bring *Agudat Yisrael* into the National Council (*Va'ad Leumi*) which had the advantage of controlling most of the funds available.   In the first stage, this led to Zionist funding of *Agudat Yisrael* educational institutions, and later, in 1934, to formal cooperation between *Agudat Yisrael* and the World Zionist Organization.   Finally, following World War II, the *Agudat* leadership supported the establishment of a Jewish state, and in return David Ben Gurion, the Chairman of the Jewish Agency, pledged public adherence to certain basic religious laws.[19]

Ben-Gurion's pledge, formalized in a letter to the leadership of *Agudat Yisrael,* embodied certain concessions that had become customary during the Mandate period.   It also came to be regarded as a "status quo" serving as a point of reference for future bargaining.   This status quo included recognizing the Jewish Sabbath as a day of rest, maintaining Jewish dietary laws (*kashrut*) in governmental institutions, state funding of religious public schools, and leaving jurisdiction over marriage and divorce in the hands of religious authorities as it had been in the Ottoman and Mandatory periods.   On other matters the status quo meant recognition of anomalous situations that had developed; for example, banning public transportation on the Sabbath in the country as a whole, but allowing it to continue in localities where it already existed.

Elements of the Accommodation

Description of the substantive compromise in the status quo does not, however, adequately cover all the elements in the basic patterns of accommodation that have governed Israeli secular-religious relations.   These patterns are much broader, and some of them apply to other cleavages (ethnic and communal) as well as to the religious split.   But it is often on religious issues that they find fullest expression.

There are three major elements to this accommodation, as identified by Eliezer Don-Yehiya.   The principle of *proportionality,* as implemented through "party key" arrangements, is of primary importance.   The "party key" extends the idea of proportional representation beyond the electoral system, and applies it to the division of offices, patronage, public financial support, access to state lands, etc.--in fact, to all the "goods" that the political system has at its disposal.   In this regard the religious parties, as well-organized groups representing a distinct subculture with its own network of institutions, have been particularly successful in getting benefits from the political system.[20]

The religious minority in Israel, more than the Sephardi community or even the Arab minority, has chosen the path of separate party lists to secure its interests. Occasionally there has been debate on this score, within religious circles, from those who argue that making the major (secular) parties compete for an uncommitted religious vote would be more effective in gaining concessions.[21] It is argued that a comparison of the army to the educational system demonstrates the advantages of integration over separatism: in the integrated army, kosher food is served to everyone, while in the divided educational system, the secular schools typically take no account at all of religious sensitivities (scheduling events on the Sabbath, etc.). But the political system seems designed to reward the separatist strategy, and most religious political activists feel (with some justice) that the strategy of forming a religious bloc able to play off the two major parties against each other has proven itself over the years.

The second major element of accommodation is the *autonomy* of religious institutions and culture, which protects the religious subculture from the threat of assimilation by secular society.[22] This is especially marked in education, but extends through a network of institutions designed to preserve the integrity and vitality of religious life. It is, of course, most readily apparent in the *haredi* community, with its own courts, welfare institutions, religious authorities, and private (i.e. not state-run) schools. This autonomy is not only an expression of Jewish traditions and customs, of course, but is also in some ways a continuation of the *millet* system of the Ottoman Empire, which left matters of religious law and other communal affairs in the hands of religio-national minorities themselves. The existence of these networks gives most parties an additional stake in the status quo as it stands, since most of these institutions are state-supported despite their autonomy (even the "independent" schools in the *haredi* community receive government funding).

The third element in the basic secular-religious compromise is the *mutual veto,* the recognition by each side that it cannot push the other past a certain point without disrupting the entire system and endangering its own interests. In this acceptance of informal limits, the status quo serves an almost sacred role as a "constitution" that forbids basic challenges to the existing order.[23] It serves as a basic point of reference that both sides respect in its basic features, though this does not rule out efforts to nudge it slightly in one direction or the other (particularly with new issues not covered clearly in the original understanding).

The veto power of the religious minority does not, contrary to conventional wisdom, rest primarily on its ability to deny a majority to governmental coalitions.   Religious parties (and especially the National Religious Party, or NRP, the successor to *Mizrahi*) have participated in every government since 1948, except for brief interims, but in most cases their participation was not actually necessary to achievement of a majority (the government formed in June, 1990, was one of the exceptions). It is rather the fear of a broad-ranging *Kulturkampf* that has reinforced the respect for boundaries not to be crossed: "The religious minority's veto powers in religious matters are not due to coalition politics but rather to their institutional capability to resort to mass dissent and disruption if necessary."[24]

The reality of these arrangements, then, is that implied or open threats to disrupt the tenor of public life, and charges that the other side is encroaching upon or endangering the status quo, are built into the bargaining process on secular-religious issues. The constant jockeying for position over the status quo generates heated and noisy debate, and even violence--all of which creates the impression that the existing order may be torn apart at any moment. Both sides express dissatisfaction with the status quo, though neither is in a position to challenge it seriously, and the expressed fear of both is that the other side will challenge it. Nor does the status quo express any coherent and logical position on the issues in contention, since it simply registers the point beyond which neither side can push the other, given their relative strengths. (Why, for example, should there be public transportation on the Sabbath in Haifa but not in Tel Aviv?) In such a situation, it may be that the mutual and roughly comparable dissatisfaction on both sides is in fact an index of the success of existing arrangements in balancing opposed worldviews.

Other moderating influences also operate on secular-religious relations. There are cross-cutting affiliations, as religious Jews are integrated fairly well into the economy, governmental service, the army, and the media (this is, of course, offset by separatism in education, culture, political parties, residential patterns, and elsewhere).[25] The politicization of religious issues is itself a moderating factor in some analysis, since it means that these issues are threshed out in bargaining between party leaders, rather than being worked out directly on the popular level.[26] Also the very existence of a vociferous debate on religious issues is interpreted positively by some close observers, since it indicates an underlying sense of commonness and shared destiny; neither side is prepared to write off the other.[27]

The Question of Relative Power

The success of religious parties in the consociational politics of Israel has, however, has given rise to the widespread perception among secular Israelis that these groups enjoy *more-than-proportional* power over Israeli politics and society and that the role of religion in public life is expanding. Although religious parties have never won more than 15 percent of the Knesset seats, they have won concessions in nearly every coalition agreement since the state was established. The power of the rabbinate in matters of personal status, marriage, and divorce impinges on every Israeli, no matter how secular. In everyday life, both the expansion of religious neighborhoods, and the greater assertiveness in religious demands reinforce the perception of a tide of religiosity. One academic analysis concludes that "the religious minority exercises power in religious matters to an extent which far exceeds its actual political representation or its size. . . ."[28] Among the general public, one 1986 poll found that 66 percent felt that *haredi*/religious influence in Israel was increasing, and 67 percent characterized the *haredim* as "unacceptable," against only 48 percent who put Israeli Arabs in that category.[29]

Other polls reflect similarly dismal views. The Continuing Survey of the Louis Gutmann Israel Institute for Applied Social Research has comparable data on public perceptions of secular-religious relations since 1969. The percentage who describe these relations as "good" or "very good" has varied from 19 percent to 49 percent, while averaging between 20 and 30 percent in recent years.[30] In a 1987 poll, 83 percent of those polled said that they had little or no confidence in religious parties or in the rabbinate--a level of respect below that toward nearly any other public institution.[31]

Clearly the low respect for religious figures is partly a function of their involvement in politics. The aura of spiritual leadership is quickly dissipated by the posturing, electioneering, and bargaining inherent to the political process. Even the elections of the chief rabbis themselves have been politicized, presenting an unedifying spectacle of manipulation and protection of special interests.[32] This has led some members of the religious community--Yeshayahu Leibowitz being the most prominent--to attack organized religion as "a kept woman of the secular power" and to call for a separation of religion and politics that would remove the former from the corrupting influence of the pursuit of power.[33]

The discontent about the role of religion in Israeli life is real, but it needs to be seen in perspective. As noted, *both* parties to the debate object in principle to certain aspects of the status quo, which represents no one's preferred solution, but is simply a compromise that most Israelis--despite their specific grievances--accept for want of a better option. Clearly the long-term goals of secularists and Orthodox are incompatible, but in the meantime, the level of mutual dissatisfaction seems to be in reasonable balance.

Despite dissatisfaction, therefore, there is little actual challenge to the basic elements of the status quo, or to the general division of territory between the secular and religious spheres of life. The only religious arrangement that impinges in a major way on the "freedom of conscience" of a secular Israeli is the monopoly of marriage and divorce matters in the hands of an Orthodox rabbinate; most other pieces of "religious legislation" are either matters of minor inconvenience, or are unenforced, or in practice affect only religious Jews. Furthermore, there is widespread support, or at least tolerance, among secular Israelis for many of the symbolic expressions of religion in public life, as will be documented below.

Moreover, a close look at the specific issues that have troubled religious-secular relations in recent years will show that few, if any, of them involved real challenges to the status quo. They represent, rather, either minor issues where the existing guidelines are murky, or efforts to move the line very slightly to one side or the other; they are border skirmishes rather than full-scale warfare. Prominent among them were: opposition to bathing suit ads in Jerusalem bus shelters; the legality of organ transplants in Jewish law; the inclusion of women on local religious councils; the opening of a football stadium in Ramat Gan and a movie theater in Petah Tikva, on the Sabbath; the Sabbath operation of a cable car in Haifa; charges of archeological digs desecrating ancient Jewish cemeteries; and controversy over the right of physicians to conduct autopsies without consent of the family. None of these questions were earthshaking; the only issue with broad significance for religious-secular relations was the question of recognizing non-Orthodox converts as Jews in immigration policy and legal status--the *"Who is a Jew?"* issue. Even here the number of individuals directly affected was small.

On these "border skirmishes," the religious camp was, contrary to secular Israeli belief, seldom victorious. In the area of Sabbath closings, for example, the overwhelming trend in recent years has been toward the opening of more restaurants, theaters, and other places of entertainment. Even in Jerusalem, dozens of establishments now operate openly on Friday night and Saturday. The *haredi* community in Jerusalem lost battles to close a road and a swimming pool in Ramot on the Sabbath, and to prevent the building of a new football stadium in Manahat.[34] From the religious side, in fact, there have been numerous complaints of "regressions from the status quo" over the years, on matters ranging from the increased number of Sabbath work permits issued by the Minister of Labor to the continuing failure to resolve the *"Who is a Jew?"* issue according to Orthodox criteria.[35]

Rather strikingly, therefore, there is not even agreement on which side is gaining. In fact, *both secular and religious Israelis tend to perceive themselves as losing ground to the other side*--which may help account for some of the bitterness and desperation in public rhetoric. For example, in the 1986 poll cited, those (59 percent of the total) opposed to an expansion of *haredi*-religious influence thought, by a 6 to 1 margin, that such expansion was nevertheless taking place, while those (25 percent) who welcomed such expanded influence believed by a 3 to 2 margin that it was *not* taking place.[36] It is difficult to understand such a gap in basic perceptions, except on the basis of deeply-rooted habits of pessimism on all sides. But whose pessimism is more factually correct?

The Reality of Secularization

Modernization has, in most societies, been associated with secularization and the decline of traditional religious practices. If Israel were indeed undergoing a growth of religiosity, it would be exceptional among modernizing states. There is considerable evidence that Israel is not the exception in this regard. A number of studies have documented the changes in leisure and recreation patterns that undercut traditional religious practices, and the growth of Sabbath entertainment reflects this.[37] The difference between this kind of secularization and the classical "secularism" of Labor Zionism is that the latter was more ideological, and is declining along with Labor Zionist ideology generally, while the former is a secularism of "convenience," reflecting new styles of life in modern urban Westernized societies, and seems to be gaining ground.

A closer look at demographic data indicates that religious observance, by Orthodox definition, is at best, holding the line. The best comparable data over time is that of the Gutmann Institute, whose Continuing Survey has been tracking degrees of religious observance for over two decades. Respondents have been asked about the extent to which they observe traditional religious practices. Some of the results are summarized in Table 1:

These figures show remarkable stability, with hardly any change over almost thirty years in the percentage of Israelis who observe traditional religious practices strictly or to a great extent. It would appear that the higher birth rate among religious families, and the higher percentage of observant among new immigrants, must be offset by attrition due to the processes of secularization. Other surveys of religious identity in Israel have typically cut

Table I: Degrees of Religiosity in Israeli Jewish Public

	1962	1989	Range During Interim
Observe strictly	15%	12%	8-17%
Observe to a great extent	15%	17%	11-19%
Observe somewhat	46%	40%	37-48%
Don't observe at all	24%	30%	24-38%

Source: All data from the Gutmann Institute; 1962 figures reprinted in Aaron Antonovsky and Alan Arian, *Hopes and Fears of Israelis: Consensus in a New Society* (Jerusalem, 1972); All other figures supplied directly by the Institute. Similar figures for 1986 and 1987, also from surveys carried out by the Gutmann Institute, are provided by Simon, *op.cit.*

the data in a different way, using the threefold self-categorization of "religious" (*dati*), "traditional" (*masorti*), or "secular" (*hiloni* or *lo dati*) to describe the population. Some of the data along these lines are summarized in Table 2.

It is apparent from a comparison of the two sets of data that some who observe traditional religious practices "to a great extent" prefer to identify themselves as "traditional" rather than religious, and that some who observe religious practices "somewhat," nevertheless tend to identify themselves as "secular." There may also be a slight trend, in recent years, away from "traditional" as a self-description, and toward "secular" (now accounting for half the population). This is probably a reflection of increased secularization among the Sephardi population, who comprise most of the "traditional" category; many observers have noted a strong secularizing trend among the Israeli-born generation of the Sephardi community.[38]

Table II: Religious Self-Identification Among Israeli Jews

	1979	1986	1989
Religious	17%	15%	16.5%
Traditional	41%	38%	32.8%
Secular, Non-religious	42%	47%	50.7%

Sources: 1979 date from Yehuda Ben-Meir and Peri Kedem, "Index of Religiosity of the Jewish Population of Israel," *Megamot* 24 (February, 1979): 353-362; 1986 data from a poll by the Smith Research Center, *Jerusalem Post*, May 15, 1986, and personal interview with Hanoch Smith, (June 11, 1988); 1989 data from Hanoch Smith and Rafi Smith, *Judaism in the Jewish State: A 1989 Survey of Attitudes of Israeli Jews* (New York: American Jewish Committee, Institute of Human Relations, 1989).

Further evidence for a decline in self-identification as religious can be found in surveys carried out among youth. In one poll reported in 1985, only 12.3 percent of the 15-18 year olds described themselves as religious, 27.3 percent as traditional, and fully 59.5 percent as secular.[39]   The same trend was reflected in a 1985 Smith survey, in which 49 percent of the youths surveys reported that they were less religious than their parents, 41 percent that they were just as religious, and only 7 percent that they were more religious than their parents.[40]   Polls among youth cannot be regarded as conclusive, since religiosity may increase with age, but clearly these surveys give more support to the thesis of secularization than to the image of growing religiosity.

More concrete evidence for a decline in religious identification can be found in school enrollments and in voting patterns. Religious schools, including both state religious schools and the independent schools in the *haredi* community, accounted for 34.4 percent in 1969-1970, but only 27.2 percent in 1986-1987; in intermediate schools the decline was from 37.5 percent to 17.3 percent.[41]   In voting patterns, the total vote for all religious parties declined from the 15 percent level (18 seats of the 120 in the Knesset) in the 1959, 1961, and 1969 elections, to barely above the 10 percent level (13 seats of the 120) in the 1981 and 1984 elections.

The 1988 elections seemed to represent a reversal of this trend, as religious parties gained 5 seats, an increase of almost 40 percent. But this increase only returns religious representation to its previous high point at 18 seats, and simply mirrors that proportion of the public (about 15 percent) that identifies itself as religious. Thus, these results do not represent any basic demographic shifts. They are rather, a result of two new factors in Israeli politics. The first of these was an unusually high mobilization of the vote in the *haredi* community, where voting participation had been low in the past. This mobilization was triggered by the formation of new *haredi* parties that competed intensely against each other, and was especially effective because of the high group cohesiveness within this community. The second factor was the success of *haredi* parties in attracting Sephardi votes beyond the *haredi* community; this was particularly true of the Sephardi ultra-orthodox party (*Shas*), but was also achieved by *Agudat Yisrael* (which, for example, secured the support of the popular *Baba Baruch,* scion of an important Moroccan religious dynasty).[42]

Another element in the threat to Orthodoxy, as perceived by the religious public in Israel, is a "softening" toward non-Orthodox (Reform, Reconstructionist, and Conservative) forms of Judaism. In the past the general public attitude toward these movements, even among secular Israelis, was fairly negative, and only a tiny percentage of the public have actually joined or been active in non-Orthodox congregations. This now seems to be changing; a representative survey conducted for the Ministry of Religious Affairs in 1988, (and later leaked to that Ministry's critics), reportedly showed that 12 percent of the respondents identified themselves as Orthodox, 3 percent as Conservative, and a surprising 9 percent (far beyond the movement's actual numbers) as Reform. The self-described Reform even included 19 percent of those who said they observed most of the religious commandments.[43] The 1989 Smith poll for the American Jewish Committee also found that 51 percent of the respondents favored giving Reform and Conservative rabbis the same rights to perform marriage and divorce as Orthodox rabbis, a rise of 6 percent since an earlier survey in 1986; the analysts conclude that "overall, the findings seem quite positive for Reform and Conservative Judaism."[44]

Overall, therefore, the (Orthodox) religious establishment in Israel is justified in feeling threatened from several quarters. But why have these developments not been perceived more clearly by the nonreligious public? The forces of secularization or liberalization have been disguised, it would appear, by a number of factors. Not the least of these is the success of religious political parties in preserving their influence. In fact, with the much closer balance between the two major blocs since 1977, the bargaining leverage of the religious parties has actually increased even when (in 1981 and 1984) the number of seats they controlled declined. This has been reinforced by the greater visibility of religious figures, including some from the *haredi* camp, in positions of responsibility as ministers, chairmen of key committees in the Knesset, heads of government corporations, and other positions where the religious community was under-represented (in part by its own choice) in the past.

A second factor is the increased vitality and assertiveness of the religious subculture, as expressed in the scope of its activities, the proliferation of new institutions and publications, and its higher visibility in public life. The rise of the *haredi* community is important in this regard, as it often appears to the secular public as a more visible and more vocal champion of religious causes viewed as a threat to secular patterns of life.

A third development that contributes to an appearance of greater religiosity is the growth of what has been labelled a new "civil religion" in Israel, in which traditional religious symbols assume an increasing importance in public life.[45] This does not indicate a higher level of religious observance as such, but to the contrary, the appropriation and secularization of religious elements as part of national identity. As Liebman and Don-Yehiya put it, "Whereas religious symbols play an increasingly important role in Israeli public or collective life, Judaism has no great significance to the individual in terms of his spiritual and personal self-definition or his behavior."[46] Holidays once observed mainly in prayer have become national commemorations marked by public ceremonies and events, while holidays that were once only secular, (such as Independence Day), have begun to acquire some religious connotations and symbols.[47] The greater mixture of secular and religious does indeed make religion more visible in public life, but at the cost of diluting its religious content--and it is therefore small comfort to many religious leaders.

The rise of the new civil religion is also made more significant and more visible by the general decline of ideology in Israeli society, which makes the turn to traditional images and customs seem more important. In particular, the decline of Labor Zionist and "statist" ideologies, which in as sense served as competing civil religions, has left a vacuum for the reassertion of symbols rooted more deeply in Jewish history and ritual.[48] Tied to this, and accounting for much of it, has been the growing Sephardi contribution to Israeli culture and politics. Israelis of Afro-Asian background never engaged in the same revolt against tradition that marked much of European Zionism (especially for Labor Zionists), and have thus clung to traditional Jewish symbols and customs even while undergoing a process of secularization.

This reality is reflected in continuing support for Jewish religious expressions in Israeli public life, going well beyond the community that defines itself as religious. In the 1989 Smith survey, the respondents split evenly, 46 percent in favor and 46 percent opposed, on the question of separation of religion and state (remarkably similar to a 1971 Harris poll, in which 47 percent rejected separation of religion and state and 46 percent supported the idea). In the 1989 survey, 63.5 percent of those of Asian-African background, and 58.7 percent of those defining themselves as "traditional" (largely within the same group) opposed separation of religion and state.[49] The widespread support for religious symbolism on the national level was also expressed in a 1987 survey that found that only 47.5 percent of the *non-observant* supported the idea of making civil marriage available and only 41.1 percent of the same group wanted to end the ban on public transportation on the Sabbath.[50]

Again, these data do not demonstrate the rise of Orthodoxy, but rather the broad acceptance of religious symbolism in a "civil religion" mode. They also demonstrate, as do the earlier data on the numbers identifying themselves as "traditional" or as "observing somewhat," that the customary dichotomous division of Israelis into "religious" and "nonreligious" categories is overly simple. There is, in fact, a broad range of religiosity. In an important study published over a decade ago, Yehuda Ben-Meir and Peri Kedem checked the observance of specific religious practices and found a broad range of responses: only 6 percent refrained from travel on the Sabbath, 44 percent separated milk and meat utensils in their homes, 53 percent lit candles on the Sabbath, 79 percent did not eat bread during Passover, and fully 99 percent participated in a Passover Seder. In conclusion: "The results of this study demonstrate that there is no clear-cut dichotomy in Israeli society between religious and non-religious Jews, but that there exists a continuum of religiosity, ranging from the extremely religious through various degrees of religious and traditional behavior, to the completely non-religious."[51]

It is also doubtful that the development of civil religion poses any increased threat to democracy. A recent poll of the Israel-Diaspora Institute, (which surveys public opinion on matters relating to democratic values), found that only 12.6 percent of the respondents would "generally" or "always" give priority to rulings of the Rabbinate over acts of the Knesset.[52] If this is the case, and if the general picture painted here is accurate, what, if anything, is the threat to the status quo?

The Two Threats

The major threats to the stability of secular-religious relations in Israel at the present time are: one, the rise of *haredi* influence within the religious camp; and two, the strong link that has been forged between religious Zionism and uncompromising territorial nationalism.

The strength of *haredi* influence is measured by the fact that they hold more than two-thirds (13 out of 18) of the "religious" seats in the Knesset, while twenty years ago the representatives of religious Zionism (the NRP) commanded two thirds (12 of 18) of the religious camp. Observers speak of "the apparent retreat of modern Orthodoxy" before the *haredi* resurgence, noting that "the distinction between an ultra-Orthodox and a modern religious person is as basic today as it once was in Eastern Europe."[53] The particularism of the *haredi* lifestyle, with its hermetic closure to the outside world, may have enabled it to withstand assimilative pressures better. In any event, the *haredi* community has continued to grow (principally through natural increase and immigration) while the ranks of the modern Orthodox have thinned (apparently, in large part, through the natural processes of secularization rather than by conversion to *haredism*).

The gap in worldview between the *haredi* community and the rest of Israel--secular and "modern Orthodox" alike--is indeed serious and constitutes a challenge to the nation's integrative capacities. From the ultra-Orthodox perspective, there is no validity to a secular Jewish identity; as one of the founders of the Israeli *haredi* community remarked, "If they are Jews--they are not free, and if they are free--they are not Jews."[54] But strangely enough, while the *haredi* community is not committed in principle to the political system, they have nevertheless learned how to use it effectively and are doing so with increasing skill. In fact, this community scores very highly on scales of access to, and participation in, the political system (even before the 1988 election).[55] They use the rules of the game to maximize their own benefits and to influence the entire system more in their direction, if only slightly. In playing this game, they also become more integrated into that system, however conditionally, and run the risk of a two-way flow of influences.

Some observers believe that the *haredim* are dominated, in the end, by pragmatic considerations. One analyst, who approached a study of religious parties ready to take their demands at face value, became convinced that the more fanatic demands of the ultra-Orthodox parties were often theatrics, and that "the issues truly important to *Agudat Israel* are those which it has pushed to actual implementation" (i.e., the practical issues of funds and patronage rather than the broader issues of principle.)[56]   In any event, most of the *haredi* parties have now overcome their earlier refusal to participate as active coalition partners in Israeli governments, and now contend vigorously for ministerships and deputy ministerships. *Shas,* the Sephardi ultra-Orthodox party, now has a representative on the plenum of the Israel Broadcasting Authority--the first *haredi* representative on that body.

The 1988 elections probably indicated the full measure of success that the *haredi* parties can achieve in this way--and they probably also indicate the limits of this success.   When the post-election demands of these parties brought about a backlash in public opinion, Prime Minister-designate Yitzhak Shamir backed away from a coalition based on their votes, and returned to a National Unity Government in which their bargaining leverage was considerably reduced.   And when the National Unity Government finally collapsed in early 1990, and Shamir turned once more to the formation of a narrow right/religious government, the *haredi* and religious parties did not renew their more far-reaching demands.

The second area of concern among "non-religious" Israelis is perhaps more serious.   Many Israelis have felt threatened by Orthodoxy not because of religious issues per se, but because of what they see as a linkage between religious fervor and extreme nationalism.   The highly-charged issues connected with Israeli-Arab relations, including such questions as Jewish settlement in the territories held by Israel since 1967, are widely seen as religious issues since many of the more fervent nationalists are in fact religious.   With the decline in secular ideologies, the crusading commitment of such groups as *Gush Emunim* seems to be filling a spiritual vacuum.   Moreover, many of these nationalists preach a "higher law" on the basis of religious claims, that sanctions civil disobedience and threatens the principles of democracy.   The discovery of a Jewish "underground" some years ago provided testimony to this danger.

It is small comfort to be reminded, in this regard, that not all religious leaders espouse this sacralizing of territory in the name of religion.   The *haredim* in particular, reject the interpretations of tradition that forbid Israel's withdrawal from the occupied territories, arguing that the saving of life (*pikuah nefesh*) takes place over other considerations.[57]   But the dominance of the religious/national view among religious Zionists (in the NRP) has contributed to a fundamental shift in the Israeli political system, the final implications of which are still uncertain.

Endnotes

1. Peter Grose, *A Changing Israel* (New York, 1985), 46.

2. Rita Simon, "The 'Religious Issue' in Israeli Public Life," *Israel Horizons* (Summer, 1989): 29.

3. Uri Huppert, *Back to the Ghetto: Zionism in Retreat* (Buffalo, NY, 1988), 183.

4. Survey by O. Cohen, cited in Sammy Smooha, *Israel: Pluralism and Conflict* (Berkeley, CA, 1978), 196.

5. Charles Liebman and Eliezer Don-Yehiya, *Religion and Politics in Israel* (Bloomington, IN, 1984), 130.

6. See discussion of this point in Asher Arian, *Politics in Israel: The Second Generation,* 2nd ed. (Chatham, NJ, 1989), 238-239; and in Alan Dowty, "Religion and Politics in Israel," *Commonweal* 110 (July 15, 1983): 393-396.

7. The general picture of the Jewish political tradition is based on Mary Zborowski and Elizabeth Herzog, *Life is with People: The Culture of the Shtetl* (New York, 1952); Stuart Cohen and Daniel Elazar, *The Jewish Polity: Jewish Political Organization from Biblical Times to the Present* (Bloomington, IN, 1984); Daniel J. Elazar, ed., *Kinship and Consent: the Jewish Political Tradition and its Contemporary Uses* (Lanham, MD, 1983); Elazar, *Israel: Building a New Society* (Bloomington, IN, 1986); Louis Finkelstein, *Jewish Self-Government in the Middle Ages* (New York, 1972); Jacob Katz, *Exclusiveness and Tolerance: Studies in Jewish-Gentile Relations in Medieval and Modern Times* (Oxford, 1961); Katz, *Tradition and Crisis: Jewish Society at the End of the Middle Ages* (New York, 1971); Katz, *Emancipation and Assimilation: Studies in Modern Jewish History* (Gregg International Publishers Limited, 1972); Katz, *Out of the Ghetto: The Social Background of Jewish Emancipation, 1770-1870* (Cambridge, MA, 1973).

8. For suggestive discussions of this point see Elazar, *Kinship* (1983) see n. 7 above, especially 49-50; and Shlomo Avineri, "Israel as a Democratic State," *Skira Hodshit* (May, 1973): 25-37 (Hebrew). It should be noted that while this analysis focusses on Eastern European political traditions, Jewish experiences everywhere had much in common, and non-European (Sephardi) political traditions were in many respects similar to those of Eastern Europe. In the Ottoman Empire, in particular, the *millet* system gave each religio-national community considerable self-government in religious, legal, social, and economic affairs, though generally in a more oligarchic framework. In addition, Sephardi immigrants to Palestine and Israel were likely to be more fully identified with their traditions than their Ashkenazi counterparts, who were in some senses engaged in a "revolt" against age-old patterns of Jewish life.

9. Eisenstadt, *The Transformation of Israeli Society* (Boulder, CO, 1985), 46.

10. Katz, *Tradition* (1971), see n. 7 above, 126; see also 96, 125.

11. Isaac Levitats, *The Jewish Community in Russia, 1844-1917* (New York, 1981), 70-71; Salo W. Baron, *The Russian Jew under Tsars and Soviets,* 2nd edition (New York, 1976), 100.

12. Zborowski and Herzog, 214; Katz, *Tradition* (1971) see n. 7 above, 93-94, 116-117; on the Jewish opposition to authority see Dan V. Segre, "The Jewish Political Tradition as a Vehicle for Jewish Auto-Emancipation," in Elazar, *Kinship and Consent* (1983), see n. 7 above, 300-301.

13. Arend Lijphart, *Democracy in Plural Societies: A Comparative Exploration* (New Haven, 1977), 25-44; Lijphart, *Democracies: Patterns of Majoritarian and Consensus Government in Twenty-One Countries* (New Haven, 1984) 1-9.

14. Smooha, *Israel,* see n. 4 above, 43-45, 109, 143, 222.

15. Don-Yehiya, "The Resolution of Religious Conflicts in Israel," in *Conflict and Consensus in Jewish Public Life,* ed. Stuart Cohen and Eliezer Don-Yehiya (Ramat Gan: Bar-I, 1986), 203.

16. See the account in Amos Elon, *Herzl* (New York, 1975), 237.

17. *Stenographisches Protokoll der Verhandlung des III Zionisten-Kongresses,* 20-22, quoted by David Vital, *Zionism: The Formative Years* (Oxford, 1982), 206.

18. Ehud Shprinzak, *Every Man Whatsoever Is Right In His Own Eyes--Illegalism in Israeli Society* (Tel Aviv, 1986), 46-47 (Hebrew).

19. Elazar, *New Society* (1986) see n. 7 above, 130, 132.

20. Don-Yehiya, "Resolution," see n. 15 above, 206.

21. See, for example, Shubert Spero, "Who Needs Religious Political Parties?" *Jerusalem Post* (May 26, 1988).

22. Don-Yehiya, "Resolution," see n. 15 above, 207.

23. Don-Yehiya, "Resolution," 208.

24. Smooha, *Israel,* see n. 4 above, 223.

25. Smooha, *Israel,* 220.

26. Smooha, *Israel,* 98-99.

27. This viewpoint is expressed by Eliezer Schweid; see his article "Religious-Secular Relations in the State of Israel," *Skira Hodshit* 33 (May 11, 1986) (Hebrew). It might also be noted that only 27 percent of the Israeli public, in a 1987 survey, regarded *haredi*

or religious groups as a "quite big" or "very big" threat to Israeli democracy (Simon, "The 'Religious Issue'," see n. 2 above, 28).

28. Smooha, *Israel,* 144.

29. Poll carried out by Smith Research Center; *Jerusalem Post* (May 15, 1986).

30. Data supplied by the Gutmann Institute. Wartimes are an exception to this pattern, perceptions of good relations jumped to 74 percent in 1967 and 67 percent in 1973. Ratings of relations between Ashkenazim and Sephardim, for the sake of comparison, were always 20 to 30 percent higher.

31. Simon, "The 'Religious Issue'," see n. 2 above, 27.

32. Liebman and Don-Yehiya, *Religion and Politics* (1984) see n. 5 above,99.

33. See the description of Leibowitz' thinking in Lawrence Meyer, *Israel Now: Portrait of a Troubled Land* (New York, 1982), 369.

34. Abraham Rabinovich, "O Jerusalem, Where is Thy Sabbath Gone?" *Jerusalem Post Magazine* (June 2, 1989): 7.

35. On the Sabbath work permit controversy historically, see Peter Y. Medding, *The Founding of Israeli Democracy 1948-1967* (Oxford, 1990), chapter 5.

36. *Jerusalem Post* (May 15, 1986).

37. See, for example, Elihu Katz and Michael Gurevitch, *The Secularization of Leisure: Culture and Communication in Israel* (Cambridge, MA, 1976).

38. Interview with Hanoch Smith, (June 11, 1988); see the evidence collected by Smooha, *Israel,* see n. 4 above, 113.

39. Charles Liebman, "The Religious Component in Israeli Ultra-Nationalism," The Eighth Annual Rabbi Louis Feinberg Memorial Lecture in Judaic Studies, University of Cincinnati (April 16, 1985).

40. *Jerusalem Post* (May 15, 1990).

41. Israel Central Bureau of Statistics, *Israel Statistical Yearbook* (1987), 590.

42. For a full analysis of the religious factor in the 1988 election, which emphasizes the importance of the Sephardi vote in development towns, see Eliezer Don-Yehiya, "Religion and Ethnicity in Israeli Politics: The Religious Parties and the Elections to the 12th Knesset," *Medina, Mimshal, Vihasim Benleumiyim* 32 (Spring, 1990): 11-54 (Hebrew).

43. Haim Shapiro, "Reform Jews charge ministry kept their strength a secret," *Jerusalem Post* (May 17, 1989); the poll was conducted by the Gutmann Institute.

44. Hanoch Smith and Rafi Smith, *Judaism in the Jewish State: A 1989 Survey of Attitudes of Israeli Jews* (New York, 1989), 5.

45. For a full statement of this thesis, see Charles Liebman and Eliezer Don-Yeyiha, *Civil Religion in Israel: Traditional Judaism and Political Culture in the Jewish State* (Berkeley, CA, 1983).

46. Liebman and Don-Yehiya, *Religion and Politics* (1984) see n. 5 above, 6.

47. Elazar, *New Society* (1986) see n. 7 above, especially 124, 143 provides a fuller description of this process; see also Grose, *A Changing Israel,* see n. 1 above, 42-44.

48. Liebman and Don-Yehiya, *Religion and Politics,* (1984) see n. 5 above, 52-53.

49. Hanoch Smith and Rafi Smith, *Judaism in the Jewish State,* see n. 44 above; the 1971 Harris poll is reported in Smooha, 82-83.

50. Survey carried out by the Gutmann Institute; see Simon, "The 'Religious Issue'," (1989), see n. 2 above.

51. Yehudah Ben-Meir and Peri Kedem, "Index of Religiosity of the Jewish Population of Israel," *Megamot* 24 (February, 1979): 353-362.

52. Yochanan Peres, "Most Israelis are Committed to Democracy," *Israeli Democracy* 1 (February, 1987): 17-18.

53. Liebman and Don-Yehiya (1984), 122; Menachem Friedman, "'If they are free--they are not Jews'," *Israel Democracy* 1 (February, 1987): 22; see also Grose, 44-46.

54. Quoted in Friedman, *loc. cit.*

55. I. Galnoor, *Steering the Polity: Communication and Politics in Israel* (Beverly Hills, CA, 1982), 354-355.

56. Ira Sharkansky, *What Makes Israel Tick: How Domestic Policy-Makers Cope with Constraints* (Chicago, 1985), 59.

57. For the religious arguments against the sacralizing of territory, see Adam Doron, *The State of Israel and the Land of Israel* (Tel Aviv, 1988) (Hebrew).

AMERICAN JEWRY—ONE OR MANY JUDAISMS?

Panel Discussion

Joseph R. Rosenbloom
Rela Geffen Monson
David A. Teutsch
Morris S. Gorelik

Joseph R. Rosenbloom:

One may hold that there is a paradox in the rhetoric relating to Judaism. Ostensibly, there is a single Judaism. From this point of view, it began over 3000 years ago in Canaan and developed as part of an emerging nation-state into a mature religion. This process continued after the canonization of the Bible with work of the rabbis, leading to the Talmud and other literature.

The reality is quite different. There was a developmental process during the fifteen-hundred-year period covered by the Bible. Ideas of divinity changed radically and civil and cultic laws were varied and, occasionally contradictory. Emphases were different, depending on the time, internal and external influences and the interests of various political leaders, priests and prophets. This is particularly clear in the Greek and Roman periods. Many Judaisms were to be found then: Sadducean, the "old-time" religion of the Bible; Pharisaic, the amplification of Biblical law and the precursor of Rabbinic Judaism; apocalyptic, those with an "end-of-days" ideology; the Judaisms of John the Baptizer, Jesus of Nazareth, the Damascus covenanters, the Essenes and the Qumran community. Still later came Karaism, Kabbalism, Mysticism and Messianism, often in combination with one or more of the others. Finally, in the nineteenth century, came Reform and Conservative Judaism, which may be characterized as non- or anti-revelationary. These were truly radical, breaking with the revelation based Rabbinic Judaism and its contemporary counterpart, Orthodoxy.

In the modern period, several cultural and political developments led to a diversity of Judaisms among and within the various denominations. The political emancipation of Jews, first in the United States and France, and then throughout Western Europe, led to Jews being fully integrated into secular culture. The consequences of this cultural freedom led to individuals selecting his level of involvement with his own ethnic and religious groupings.

Individualism, where each person is primarily concerned with self over group, effects a diminution of group loyalties. As like-minded individuals band together to form a Judaism in harmony with their own proclivities, the result has been the loss of in-group solidarity, authority and structure and greater diversity.

Reform Judaism is a clear example of this process. From a study of it, one might conclude that there are in reality Reform *Judaisms*. Congregational styles vary, often within a given community where there is more than one Reform congregation. There remain some "traditional" or "classical" Reform congregations. These are characterized by emphasis on ethics rather than ritual and with cool, formal worship services, generally devoid of overt emotionalism. The "new" Reform has adopted practices which until a few decades ago were found only in Orthodox or Conservative congregations. These include: rabbis and laity wearing *kippot* and *talesim,* observing the second day of holidays, *kashrut,* the use of cantors, daily *minyanim,* day schools, licensing *mohelim* and the greater use of Hebrew in prayers.

Even as Reform is incorporating more traditional forms, it has also taken positions perceived as radical while in conformity with "traditional" Reform's liberality. These include the ordaining and investing of females as rabbis and cantors, and patrilineal descent for children's Jewishness, both contrary to rabbinic law. The position of accepting acknowledged homosexuals as rabbinical students is against Biblical law.

One may characterize these developments in a positive sense as "accommodationist," or in a negative sense as "unprincipled." If the central imperative of Judaism is survival, then Reform has been successful in developing a variety of Judaisms which makes it possible for most Jews to identify as Jews. If, however, the central imperative of Judaism is the maintaining of a series of irreducible sancta, then these Reform Judaisms may be viewed as destructive. Looking into the future is difficult. Historical and sociological analyses may be helpful in understanding the past, but predicting the future is always problematic.

What is certain is that Reform has moved in two diametrically opposed directions during the past fifty years and has been successful at least in an institutional sense. It has grown numerically, often at the expense of other movements. In Boston, for the period 1965-1985, the Orthodox have gone from 14% to 4% of the total Jewish population, Conservatives from 44% to 33%, and Reform from 27% to 42%. Those with no Jewish denominational preference have gone from 5% to 14%. Reform continues to grow in its old strongholds in the Midwest and South.

The movement of Reform toward greater traditionalism was decried by Prof. Jacob R. Marcus, teacher of Reform rabbis for over sixty years. In 1959, he wrote:

> There are too many Reform Jews who have ceased to be liberals. Their Reform, crystallized in a new Orthodoxy, is no longer dynamic . . . We cannot lead our people forward by stumbling backward.

Dr. Marcus was wrong regarding Reform's dynamism. While Reform may be "stumbling backward," it has never been stronger institutionally or larger in numbers of congregations and membership. Others have rationalized Reform's changes as a move toward greater authenticity. Ritual, rather than being denigrated, is seen as shaping and stimulating one's ethical impulses.

Reform seems to be fully in harmony with typical American individualism and pragmatism. Reform Judaism thus enters the last decade of the Twentieth Century transformed from an insecure to a self-assured, growing movement. Its ideology has been revamped and its practices broadened to appeal to a larger constituency, particularly those who had been alienated by the other Judaisms of America: feminist women, mixed married couples, homosexuals and Jews in other denominations who wished a freer exercise of their Jewish commitment. Reform is the most inclusive Jewish religious movement and is seeking to "harvest the demographic trends" of American Jewry. What it has been doing is effective since it is growing more rapidly than the others, often at their expense. The future is never certain, but a Reformed Reform Judaism is now doing very well.

Rela Geffen Monson:

This evening we've been asked to discuss the issue of whether there will be two or more Jewish peoples in the future. In my view, a better question would be "What will the quality of Jewish life in America be in the future?" and "Will American Jews be able to relate to Jews all over the world?" In other words, will American Judaism be too heterogeneous or too unrelated to connect with Judaism in the rest of the world?

Unity does not equal uniformity, nor does it necessarily mean higher quality. Uniformity may reflect the lowest common denominator and may not be desirable at all. In fact, uniformity can be very dangerous.

The Conservative movement has always been attacked from the right and from the left precisely because it embraced Abraham Joshua Heschel and Mordecai Kaplan, Isaac Klein and Harold Schulweis, David Aaronson and Robert Gordis, Simon Greenberg and Saul Lieberman and Joel Roth. Pluralism is often mistaken for fuzziness, while absolute answers to ultimate questions are mistaken for authenticity, and are therefore very attractive in this age of transition and uncertainty.

Today in American Jewry, we do have problems with extreme antinomianism on the left, and messianism on the far right. I think the messianism of the far right is the greater problem today with its sect-like development.

Is there such a thing as normative theory, or normative Judaism? The perspective of the Conservative movement is that of the historical school started by Zechariah Frankel, prescribing loyalty to *Halakhah* along with the idea that change was always, and would continue to be a normative aspect of *Halakhah*. There is no Jew today who would take an adulterous woman and put her up against a wall and stone her! It's quite clear that there have been developments in Jewish law and that the normative condition of Jewish Law is development, not stagnation. It is those who will not change it in any way who are the modern Karaites. Of course, the most serious question is how you change the law and who effects the process.

Rabbi Harold Schulweis, who most Conservative Jews would agree, is one of the leading and most creative Conservative rabbis in the United States, mentions three general rabbinic concepts that are very important for us to consider. The first is *Ahavat Israel,* which means the love of all of those who are members of a covenant-*B'nai Brit.* The second concept, *Tikun Olam,* refers to the repair of the world. Daniel Elazer translates: *Ltakayn olam b'malhut shuddai* as "to create the good commonwealth on earth." The third concept which has been used with reference to relationships between Jews and non-Jews, and today is also being used for relationships between Jews of different denominations, is *Mipnei Darkey Shalom.* For the sake of having more harmony, and for the sake of creating peace and a good society, sometimes we do things that we don't altogether agree with.

There are those who say that vigorous diversity is something bad. They would rule pluralism out of Judaism. Schulweis says that being Jewish is like being part of a family. And then he says:

> What's at stake is the severing of the Jewish organism in the sectarian parts, the fracture of the Jewish family. For years, we had heard the officials from Israel's minister of religion propose a devastatingly simple solution to the problem. Let the Conservatives and the RReformers, and the Reconstructionist group as well, declare themselves to be sects, and they will be accorded the full rank and privileges enjoyed by the Armenian Orthodox, the Greek Orthodox, and miscellaneous other non-Jewish religious minorities. That is, the tragic direction in which America's triumphalist element is now moving. It seeks to transform the largest religious constituencies of our people into Sadducean, Samaritan, and Karaite sects ("Our House Divided," *Moment Magazine* 7, no. 4 [April, 1982]:56-59. Quote used is on 57).

In sum, contrary to those described by Schulweis, I see the resurgence and reemergence of Jewish institutions--especially a variety of religious institutions--as a sign of a healthy, vigorous Jewish community rather than a stagnant one. Judaism can compete in the marketplace of ideas, and alternatives have persisted, and were meant to persist throughout all of Jewish history.

This view is articulated by Neil Gillman from the Jewish Theological Seminary, editor of the Conservative movement's first attempt at a statement of principles *Emet V'Emunah* when he says:

> Finally on the issue of unity and diversity in the contemporary Jewish community, my sense is that it is futile and unrealistic to strive for any sense of unity at the expense of diversity and pluralism. If the *Midrash* can acknowledge that the Divine Voice is heard differently by each of the 600,000 Jews that stood at the foot of Sinai, why should our situation be any different? The issue is not the diversity itself, but the self-righteousness and acrimony that accompanies the debate. That acrimony stems, at least in part, from the fact that we all care passionately about the issues, for which we can only be grateful. And also from the fact that some of us believe that we are in possession of God's absolute and moralistic truth, which is

unfortunate. What we need than is not less diversity, but much more theological humility, sharper recognition of the inherent human limitations of all of our belief structures, and a greater willingness to accept the limitlessly diverse sets of needs that human beings bring to their forms of religious expressions ("On the Frontiers of Religious Diversity," Critical Issues Conference II, *One Jewish People: From Conflict to Cohesion* [New York, 1988], 79-83. Quote used is on 83).

David A. Teutsch:

Many of you may know the tale of the Jew who visited the community on the Shabbat morning in time for the Torah service. Partway through the Torah service, there's a sharp disagreement about the exact *minhag* (custom), and the people got into a terrible argument. The service grinds to a halt, and the visitor says, "Wait! Quiet down!" He turns to the rabbi and says, "What is the custom here, rabbi?" And the rabbi says, "The custom is for both sides to yell until they are exhausted."

It is true that the Jewish community has a history of diversity. Would that it were also true that it had managed to carry on that tradition of divergence with a truly pluralistic attitude. Think about the examples cited for divergence over the years. Some of them--for example, Ashkenazi and Sephardi, the Jews of Europe and the Jews of Spain and later, parts of the East--have different cultures. They acknowledge each other's legitimate divergences as having validity in their own spheres, and there is virtually no dispute about the difference of backgrounds. Then think about the quite awful example of the Karaites and Rabbanites, in which the Rabbanites declared that the Karaites would not be allowed to marry their children. The question is not whether there will be divergence. The question is how we will manage that divergence. We look at Jewish history and find both positive and negative models for dealing with it.

What values will allow us an optimal Jewish community? Perhaps the most fundamental element is *"Kol Yisrael arevim zeh bazeh."* All of Israel are related to each other; we all have obligations to each other. The only way that statement can be vivified is if we each recognize a fundamental authenticity in the other, so that our pluralism grows out of mutual commitment.

To put it differently, the demand for absolute unity can be understood only as an unreachable absolutism, a demand that would result in the breakup of the Jewish people if it were enforced, given the inevitable, ever-changing diversity of world Jewry. What divides us is not only a response to historical change, not only differences in thoughts and generational perceptions, as powerful as they are. The most fundamental differences are in values, beliefs, and commitments that are part of our cultural mosaic.

The Reconstructionist movement was the earliest and the strongest in standing up for a variety of commitments in the areas of egalitarianism, democracy, and equality of groups. The equality for women, with the first bat mitzvah in 1922, and equal admission of gays and lesbians in our seminary are examples. The examples are less important, though, than the fundamental principles. It is not accidental that the Reconstructionist movement took the stance on women that it took, because it has a fundamental commitment to egalitarianism, democracy and full equal access in Jewish life. The commitment to *Halakhah* in the traditional segment of our community is just as deep and committed. The different segments of our community embrace fundamentally different sets of principles and values.

As Reconstructionists, we believe we are right; we believe with the full passion of our hearts that we are right. And we recognize that our Orthodox brothers and sisters believe with an equal passion, with an equal commitment, that they are right. We have to learn somehow to recognize that we cannot make the final determination of who is right. We must learn to accept those differences that stem from fundamental differences in belief and values. That's much more difficult than reconciling difference in style, like *Kipah,* or not *Kipah* or *Talit* or not *Talit.*

The most serious threat to the unity of the Jewish community is on the issue of personal status. What will we do about divorce? What will be do about conversion? "Can our kids marry each other?" That will determine whether there is a unified Jewish community. A portion of the Jewish community is currently turning the question of personal status into a political football, using it as an opportunity to try to dismiss as unauthentic other parts of the Jewish community, by dismissing its leaders as illegitimate and challenging the authenticity of some of their members.

Today the battle is engaged around the way American Jews interact with Israel. It's interesting to note that the American Lubavitch movement provided the money (for the most part) for the attempt to change the Law of Return in Israel, an attempt to deny Conservative, Reform and Reconstructionist converts in America the right to *Aliyah.*

The point at which we deny each other's legitimacy and authenticity in that way is the point at which we have to begin talking about more than one Judaism. Despite this threat, we have many models of cooperation that move us toward unity.

When I was living in New York City, I often was part of *Batei Din* (rabbinic courts) that took place in the Orthodox-controlled and run *mikveh* on the Upper West Side. The Orthodox rabbis involved in the *mikveh* are committed to the notion that, even though they disagree with what some of us liberals do, we should have access to the *mikveh*. Their commitment is to join together to strengthen the American Jewish community. One afternoon, I was at the *mikveh* with a liberal *bet din* (rabbinic court), while several Orthodox colleagues were there as an Orthodox *bet din*. We were all involved with conversion ceremonies. The Orthodox *bet din* had failed to bring the forms needed to generate certificates, and so they came to the liberals and asked for copies of our certificates, which are virtually identical with theirs. That was a wonderful moment for me. Here were the liberals using an Orthodox facility, and the Orthodox benefitted too, saying, "You have something that we need in order to finish what we are doing here." We shared in each other's holy acts. It is true that we each were participating in actions that the other group would not. We were both doing our best to serve the Jewish community, and engaging in what we all recognized as holy acts. That is a model for cooperation.

I believe that if we can develop joint *batei din,* perhaps by using complex models for merging *batei din,* we can circumvent the problem of *ishut* (personal status). That would make a huge difference in our efforts on behalf of unity. this can only happen when we love each other enough, when we trust each other enough, when we respect each other's authenticity enough. Only *then* can we argue toe to toe about what's right or wrong, and still go on working hand in hand.

We need to remember that the largest group to reach isn't Orthodox, Conservative, Reform or Reconstructionist. It is "none of the above." Most Jews in America have not found any of the current streams of Judaism sufficiently compelling to make it a basis for the fundamental rhythms of their lives. Our task is not just to argue among ourselves as to whether Orthodox, Conservative, Reform, Reconstructionist, or secular is better. We must reanimate exciting forms of Jewish life that are at once rich in tradition and true to our values and norms, in order to reach out to those people who haven't found a spiritual direction in their Judaism. We all have failed to reach most of the unaffiliated and uneducated of that group, which includes the vast majority of Jews, who at the least are under-involved.

Being members of a synagogue, or indicating in a survey that people are members of this or that denomination, doesn't mean that they are fully at home in Judaism, that it is compelling for them or providing a fundamental orientation for their way of life. In dialogue with that group of Jews, all of us, from all the different communities of Jewish life, are challenged to change, to open up to their concerns. I believe that the forms of Judaism that we have today are quite different from the forms of Judaism that will exist 40 or 50 years form now. Because Jewish law was enforceable during the rabbinic period, the form and tradition of Jewish law worked. With emancipation, Jewish law has not been enforceable in the same way. Look at what is going on, at the mobility in the Jewish community today. The Jewish neighborhood is gone, and the isolation and ennui of the Jews in American life is greater than ever before. In this situation we will have to come up with new forms of voluntary community, something that we Reconstructionists hold dear, in order to create a sense of bondedness and extended family, a sense of "roots" that will allow people in the Jewish community to reestablish their contacts with their own sources of authenticity. We should acknowledge that reaching these Jews requires recognizing that our Judaism transcends our books and official boundaries.

We are not dealing with rigid boundaries between Orthodox, Conservative, Reform, Reconstructionists, Hasidic or secular Judaism. There are many fragments and degrees in between the Right and the Left in each movement are organized and arguing and sometimes the right wing of one movement crosses the boundaries of the left wing of another movement. I smiled to myself when Rela Geffen Monson made a point of quoting Harold Schulweis as an important Conservative statesman, which he is. He also happens to be a member of the Board of Governors of the Reconstructionist Rabbinical College. We have much more cooperation, much more coordination going on in Jewish life than most people acknowledge today. The leaders of our movements are much more able to talk to each other--and happy to do so behind the scenes--than most people realize.

The question is whether we will reject those people who are specializing in alienation, in rejection and in stirring up dissent and disharmony within the Jewish community. Will we reject them in term of whom we fund? Will we reject them in term of whom we talk about when building new institutions? Intolerance is the one thing that the Jewish community cannot tolerate. Maimonides' books were burned in France by Jews who disagreed with him.

Those Jews' views have largely disappeared, and Rambam has emerged triumphant, despite the fact that much of his viewpoint was anathema to a goodly portion of the Jewish community of his day. Jews who say that they know who will be the authentic inheritor or spokesperson for the Judaism of the next century are trying to read a crystal ball, which is forbidden by the Torah. Book-burning and smear campaigning won't determine the winner. We have to recognize that we cannot possible know what Judaism ultimately will turn out like. What we have to do is trust that if we study together, if we learn together, and argue together and if we love each other, than what will emerge will be a legitimate Judaism. Together we can forge a fresh link in the chain of Jewish tradition.

Morris S. Gorelik:

I don't subscribe to all the interpretations, explanations and theories of the previous speakers. I respect their being so candid. I enjoyed this evening. It is really a wonderful and exhilarating experience to share ideas, and to listen to one another as friends and as brothers as *"Kol Israel Haverim."* What I want to do is *react* to the title of this panel discussion, *"One Judaism or Many Judaisms?"* To me it is a very intriguing challenge.

"One Judaism or Many Judaisms?" actually means pluralism--different models of Judaism. Usually I associate the word "models" with a style, with dress fashions, with fads, and the designers that set the patterns. Who is designing these Judaisms? The people? The theologians? The social conditions or the circumstances? Perhaps God ? What do we mean by "pluralism"? What do we mean by "many Judaisms"? There are different *schuls,*--there's always a *schul* that one doesn't go to. I don't mean temples, but *schuls.*

What do we mean by a "pluralism" that can conceive of the possibility of many Judaisms? Perhaps this pluralism emphasizes individual conscience-- each and every one of us has a free choice to make as far as the moral direction we take. Perhaps it advocates that religious denominations should all renounce claims to superiority and that religious views are relativized, and promotes a series of models like Jacob Peutchowski tried to do some years ago in the journal *Judaism.*

Now I don't say I speak for Orthodoxy. I speak for Gorelik. I subscribe to what I believe is Orthodoxy. It's not quite the question of might or political power. Chaim Teshrnowitz said many years ago, "It's a question as to what moral directive we will take."-- Whether it will be the Jewish one, or the non-Jewish one. The choice has already been made when we begin with *ata bechartane,* in the *Smoneh Esreh* prayer of Yom Tov. We thank God for choosing us from among the nations, and we thank God for sanctifying us with His commandments.

To what kind of Judaism does Orthodoxy subscribe? To a covenantal community? If theological pluralism presupposes the absence of absolute normative truth, the concept of Orthodoxy is a falsehood. Orthodoxy stakes its being on a truth that transcends the relativities of man. Either the Torah is the unmediated word of God or it is not. Either God speaks to us through history, or he does not. Where the issue is truth or falsity, the idea that both sides of the contradiction are true is itself a contradiction. Pluralism and Orthodoxy are each ways of viewing the relationship between the belief and truth. Each excludes the other. Long ago, Mordechai Kaplan said that there are two forms of revelation: there is historical revelation and there is theological revelation. A theological revelation means man's response to what he believes is the divinity of the world. It means that no one has the absolute truth, but in each age the Torah is a way of response, the Talmud is a way of response, the Rambam is a way of response. Even Mordechai Kaplan is a way of responding to the divinity of the world, and the meaningfulness of the world. Historical revelation, he says, means that in a specific moment of history there was revelation with a content of *Mitzwot,* the God-given Torah.

And Maimonidies said, "But what is the definition of *Hasidei Umot Olam,"* the "pious of the world." What is the meaning of "the pious of the world"? Not merely goodness and kindness, but he says he believes that he was commanded by God to do good. It is not coming only from personal desire to do good; there is a divine imperative that is commanding us to do good. Therefore, Orthodoxy insists upon binding *Halakhic* standards. We are bound and committed to the authority of an objective *Halakhah.*

I don't subscribe to a theological pluralism that is equated to theological relativism. I adhere to a different definition of pluralism. I mean a pluralism of fellowship.

In order to exist, pluralism demands tolerance as the minimal requirement, affection for one another as the most preferred condition. Jewish unity rests upon an ethnic relationship, religious ethnicism, not an ecumenical proposition. We are a community. We are a nation, and as we sing in *Simchart Torah: "Am Israel Chai . . . "* That's what we are. There is a distinction between integrity and authenticity. I respect the honesty, the sincerity of a spiritual search from any individual, and the persistence of the individual seeking to sanctify life. I will not negate the value, even if he is only partially observant of what I consider to be a covenantly imperative. But I will not accept his rejection of the doctrines of *Yahadus*--Judaism. I believe very strongly *Israel af al pi schota Israel hu* (a Jew, although he transgresses, is a Jew). Even if he rejects this, even if he is not convinced of what I am convinced of, he is a Jew and I love him, and I respect him. But he is a *chata*. I cannot grant authenticity to any model other than that of my imperative. That's why I object very strongly to the terms, *"Datyim and Hilonyim,"* (both of them are Jews).

What the future holds in store is quite a challenge. I would say that Orthodox Judaism will flourish. It always has. We Orthodox Jews overcame the *Kadesh* (memorial prayer). That was said about us long ago, when everybody wondered if the Orthodox were too strict. It is a challenge--the questions of how far we will go with homosexuality, with patrilinearly, with Shabbat, with women cantors, and with Jewish divorces and so forth. We do have problems. There is attempted reform and the biggest challenge today is not talking to ourselves, but talking to the Jews who are not here--to the non-affiliated from any religious community who are falling prey to assimilation. This challenge is morally mandated, and I am comvinced we have the where-with-all to meet the challenge. Hopefully we have the will and conviction to advance our cause.